Social Evolution

Robert Trivers

University of California
Santa Cruz

The Benjamin/Cummings Publishing Company, Inc.

Menlo Park, California • Reading, Massachusetts
Don Mills, Ontario • Wokingham, U.K. • Amsterdam • Sydney
Singapore • Tokyo • Mexico City • Bogota • Santiago • San Juan

Sponsoring Editor: James W. Behnke
Developmental Editor: Jo Andrews
Production Supervisor: Mimi Hills
Designer: Wendy Calmenson
Artists: Carla Simmons (biological art);
Randy Adden, Unicorn Graphic Design (technical art)

The cover photograph, courtesy of Irven DeVore/Anthro-Photo, shows
a young chimpanzee at Gombe Stream, Tanzania.

Library of Congress Cataloging in Publication Data

Trivers, Robert.
  Social evolution.

  Bibliography: p.
  Includes index.
  1. Social behavior in animals.   2. Behavior
evolution.   3. Social evolution.   I. Title.
QL775.T75   1985   591.5′248   85-1347
ISBN 0-8053-8507-X

EFGHIJ–HA–89

The Benjamin/Cummings Publishing Company, Inc.
2727 Sand Hill Road
Menlo Park, California 94025

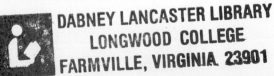

For Lorna

Foreword

OUR ATTEMPT to understand social behavior is an ancient and abiding concern. From the earliest philosophers to the most recent discussions of human sociality, this concern with the nature of society and social evolution predominates. Lacking a satisfying and comprehensive theory, the human social sciences have vacillated between disparate, often contradictory, social theories. Especially troublesome have been attempts to reconcile the pervasive and opposing forces of cooperation and competition, which, because of the lack of a coherent framework, have remained unintegrated and misunderstood features of social life. The revolution in evolutionary theory, over the last two decades, has thus excited many researchers who feel that natural selection is the key which has been missing from every discipline's study of social behavior. This book offers a cogent and lucid treatment of the subject, one that both documents the fundamental processes involved and advances the field to a new level of integration.

While Darwin's original insights continue to inform the subject, the synthesis we now call sociobiology only began to take modern form in the late 1960s through the writings of such theorists as W. D. Hamilton, G. C. Williams, and John Maynard Smith. The exciting rejuvenation of behavioral biology that subsequently occurred in the 1970s is difficult to convey to those too young to have been participants. Armed with a powerful new theoretical framework and notebooks full of hypotheses to be tested, a new generation of ethologists and naturalists turned to field studies. Established journals were soon dominated by the emerging ideas and data of sociobiology, and several new journals appeared that were entirely devoted to the subject. It is therefore not surprising that the great majority of some 750 references in this text are from articles published since 1975. But it is a testament to the vitality of the field, and to the insight of the author, that he is

v

also able to reach back across seven decades to reinterpret data and, for example, pose an intriguingly plausible explanation concerning the nature of deer antlers.

Inevitably such an exuberant outpouring of theory and data has spawned a multitude of subfields. Trivers has judiciously sifted the literature to discuss just those issues and examples that are most useful in promoting an understanding of the present state of the discipline. A particular virtue of the book is the author's single-minded dedication to applying the principles of natural selection to social phenomena. In fact, the book brings together the most data ever gathered on this subject in one place. Another noteworthy accomplishment is that Trivers has enormously broadened the range of data and theory applicable to social evolution. This is apparent throughout the volume, but one of his more remarkable achievements is that, for the first time, the plant world is repeatedly brought into a book largely concerned with social behavior in the animal kingdom. Only a few years ago it would have been considered ludicrous to treat the social behavior of plants and humans in the same volume, and yet Trivers has shown that, with powerful theory, there are good reasons to consider them in the same encompassing framework.

Trivers has done more than introduce the reader to the field of sociobiology; he has advanced theory. His treatment of critical topics, such as kinship, is done in new depth; he leads the reader across an astonishing range of behavioral phenomena, stretching from the intracellular level to the social organization of primates. The breadth of his conception invites one to find new patterns and unity in social evolution. The extension of such principles to human behavior has inevitably been controversial; far from shying away from human applications, Trivers has consciously sought vivid ways to illustrate their operation in human daily life. His discussion of these issues is distinguished from many others by its discernment and responsibility.

One final way in which this book is distinctive is its use of visual materials. Trivers has taken extraordinary pains in his selection of illustrations and tables, and they contribute significantly to the intellectual impact of the book. Indeed, readers can get a flavor of modern ethology from reading the picture captions alone.

Trivers is a pivotal figure in the development of modern evolutionary biology, and brings to his survey of the field a uniquely authoritative voice. He leads the reader through the imposing accumulation of theory and evidence with clarity and precision. His insights and synthetic treatment provide the most outstanding and illuminating introduction to the field that now exists.

Irven DeVore
Professor of Anthropology and Biology
Harvard University

Preface

EVERYBODY HAS a social life. All living creatures reproduce and reproduction is a social event, since at its bare minimum it involves the genetic and material construction of one individual by another. In turn, differences between individuals in the number of their surviving offspring (natural selection) is the driving force behind organic evolution. Life is intrinsically social and it evolves through a process of natural selection which is itself social. For these reasons social evolution refers not only to the evolution of social relationships between individuals but also to deeper themes of biological organization stretching from gene to community.

Having emphasized the generality of social evolution, I hasten to say that we retain a special interest in our own species, which is social in a complex series of overlapping ways. We are, thus, inevitably more interested in some species than in others and in some problems rather than in others. Consider, for example, male parental investment. We are one of a small minority of species wherein the male commonly invests some parental care in his offspring. We, thus, find ourselves interested in details of bird behavior—details that would otherwise escape our notice—because birds also have high male parental investment, along with a host of associated traits. While emphasizing the general themes of social evolution I have chosen throughout the book topics important to our own evolution, from kinship and parent-offspring conflict to deceit and self-deception.

Audience

This book is written for two audiences. It is written for the general reader who wishes an introduction to the subject of social evolution, and it is written for the undergraduate taking an introductory course in sociobiology, animal behavior, evolutionary biology, anthropology, or related disciplines. This book is meant to be self-contained, in the sense that it presupposes no background in biology, and Chapter 5 reviews useful background information on genetics and its relation to behavior and learning.

Organization

There are five introductory chapters. These serve to introduce the reader to Darwin's theory of evolution through natural selection (Chapters 1 and 2), relate natural selection to social traits (Chapter 3), consider the road not taken (Chapter 4), and review genetics and its relation to behavior and learning (Chapter 5). In organizing the material this way, I have purposely taken the reader as quickly as possible to the core of our subject (Chapter 3) and postponed alternate systems of logic and the subject of genetics.

Chapters 6–16 are the heart of the book. They describe an interconnected body of theory and evidence on the principles underlying social evolution. We begin with the central concept of kinship (Chapter 6) and its application to parent-offspring relations (Chapter 7) and reproductive altruism (Chapter 8).

Chapters 9–14 cover sexual selection, the sex ratio, and sex. Finally we close with material which is relevant to social interactions in general: cooperation (Chapter 15) and deceit and self-deception (Chapter 16).

Approach

A wealth of work has appeared in the past ten years on all the major topics of social evolution, including kinship, sex, sex ratio, cooperation, mate choice, and so on. So my first aim in writing this book has been to provide an up-to-date summary of our understanding of social evolution, including especially recent work, both theoretical and empirical.

I have tried throughout the book to emphasize evolutionary logic and to leave out material that would only serve to detract from the general themes of social evolution. These I have conceived to follow from the importance of reproduction itself. Thus I have concentrated on variation in the production of surviving offspring (natural selection), on the genetics of reproduction (kinship), on the parent-offspring relationship, on non-reproduction, on parental investment and on sex, including sexual selection and the sex ratio.

Some of the most exciting and useful material in biology is visual. To give the reader a taste of the rich visual material on social evolution I have made a special effort to collect together photographs, supplemented with excellent drawings by Carla Simmons. Rather than assemble photographs as so many isolated portraits, only loosely related to the text, I have tried to find visual material that is directly connected to the points under discussion and I have linked together series of photographs or drawings on common subjects in order to give a deeper impression.

Quantitative information is illustrated by graphs and tables. Once again I have preferred to link together graphs and tables on common themes, so as to give a deeper treatment. In choosing graphs and tables I have been drawn to those that describe the action of natural selection, or variables closely associated with it.

To make the book easier to read I have removed all references from the text, retaining them only in figure and table captions. At the same time, to give the reader easy access to the rest of the bibliography, I have prepared bibliographic notes—beginning at the end of the text—which are keyed to the page number of text to which they refer. If one is reading page 85 in the text and wishes to see the accompanying references, flip to the bibliographic notes and look for the notes that go with page 85. This arrangement has also permitted me to add references on related topics. In this I have had both the advanced student and teacher in mind as well as undergraduates wishing to write term papers on any topic in the book. Please note that where reference to a subject is given in a figure caption or table and no additional references are offered, I have not bothered to repeat the reference in the bibliographic notes.

For years I have taught the material in this book, accompanying it with weekly problem sets on the major topics of social theory (natural selection, group selection, kinship, sexual selection, the primary sex ratio and so on). These problem sets, along with exam questions, are available from the publisher upon request.

This book seeks to provide an in-depth introduction to the subject of social evolution, a subject which gives us a foundation for a scientific understanding of human behavior.

Robert Trivers
Professor of Biology
University of California, Santa Cruz

Acknowledgments

IT IS a pleasure to acknowledge the help I have received in preparing this book. First and foremost, I would like to thank Hope Hare who for years helped me to assemble the library on which this book is based. Her contribution is evident on every page.

Mrs. Hare's salary was paid by the Harry Frank Guggenheim Foundation which also provided me with money for nine months of research and writing in 1979. I am deeply grateful to the Foundation and its research directors then, Robin Fox and Lionel Tiger, for the encouragement and support they have given me.

I am also grateful to the Smithsonian Institution for providing me in 1980 with a Regents Fellowship to study and write in Panama. For their support and encouragement at the Smithsonian Tropical Research Institute I am grateful to Georgina de Alba, Michael Robinson, and especially Ira Rubinoff.

For encouragement and support at the University of California at Santa Cruz I am grateful to the Faculty Research Council, and to my colleagues on the Biology Board, especially to Eugene Cota-Robles, Charles Daniel, and Robert Sinsheimer.

For reading most of the manuscript at one stage or another and giving me their help and encouragement I am most grateful to John Alcock, Nancy Burley, Eric Charnov, Lisa Rogers, Donald Symons, Randy Thornhill, Aaron Waters, George Williams, and David Sloan Wilson. For helping me with individual chapters I am grateful to George Barlow, Irven DeVore, Frans deWaal, William Drury, William Eberhard, William Hamilton, Robert Hinde, Bert Hölldobler, Sarah Hrdy, Daniel Kriegman, Jeffrey Kurland, James Malcolm, Jon Seger, and Barbara Smuts. Portions of Chapter 16 are taken from a manuscript in preparation on deceit and self-deception (co-author: Huey

Newton). Parts of Chapter 6 are adapted from a manuscript in preparation on natural selection and social theory.

For permitting me to publish their unpublished data I am grateful to Nancy Burley and Judy Stamps.

For sending me their photographs (or drawings) and helping me with the accompanying captions I am grateful to a whole host of people whose names appear with their contributions (and in the index). I am also grateful to Nancy DeVore (Anthro-Photo) for her help in locating pictures.

For help at the office I am grateful to Marie McCullough and Gigi Nabors. For early typing I am grateful to DeLoris Highsmith and Jan Schäfer. For typing the entire book through two drafts I am especially grateful to Judy Burton. For punching the bibliography onto a computer I am very grateful to Claudio Campagna.

I thank Gerard McCauley for his help, especially at the beginning. For help and encouragement throughout, I am grateful to Jim Behnke. For devoting more than a year of her life to improving all parts of the manuscript I am most grateful to Jo Andrews. For their contributions to the production of the book I am also grateful to Mimi Hills, Wendy Calmenson, and Elliot Simon.

I would like to express my appreciation to two of my teachers, William Drury, for setting me on the right road, and William Hamilton, for providing so much illumination along the way.

Finally, for encouragement to publish I am grateful to Sonia Armistad, Robert Bailey, Paul Bartels, Irven and Nancy DeVore, Peter Dow, William Drury, Jay Friedheim, Stella Guerrero, William Hamilton, Charles and Hope Hare, Burney and Joanne Le Boeuf, James Malcolm, Ernst Mayr, Aston McDermoth, Huey Newton, Nola Perez, John Pickering, Jon Seger, Robert Selander, Paul Sherman, Jonathan Trivers, Irma White, Ernest Williams, Edward Wilson, Michelle Winkler, and Richard Wrangham.

Robert Trivers

Contents

A Scientific Theory of Organic Creation

Twenty years ago as an undergraduate in college I was interested in problems of human behavior, especially social behavior. I wanted to know why we do what we do and toward what purpose our lives are organized. I longed for a scientific understanding of human behavior, that is, an understanding based on first principles and, wherever possible, grounded in pre-existing knowledge.

I dabbled in several disciplines, but found myself disappointed in each. History, political science, economics, and psychology all expressed interesting views on human behavior, but none of these views seemed to have a secure foundation in pre-existing knowledge. For example, Western economics usually assumes that individuals are out to maximize personal gain, but where is the scientific justification for this assumption? And what exactly is "personal gain"? Much of psychology at the time assumed that human behavior is built entirely from learning experiences and that a theory of learning is the actual basis for any theory of human behavior. But psychology could give no coherent account of how these learning abilities are organized in us and toward what end we are learning what we are learning.

Then, within months of graduating from college, my life was turned around. I was asked to write children's books on animal behavior, and for the first time I became exposed to facts about the social lives of other animals. I shall never forget the shock and pleasure of learning that the social lives of other creatures are subtle and complex, both similar to ourselves and different. In particular, I was very much struck by pictures of adult male baboons *Papio cynocephalus* disciplining juveniles. Dominant adult males like to watch juveniles play and often keep a close watch on their activities (Figure 1-1). Should one of the youngsters be injured or cry out, one of the adult males may stride over, grab the offending juvenile, and administer a bite to the neck; the

Figure 1-1

Adult interest in juveniles. An adult male baboon watches an infant and a juvenile at play. Should he intervene, he will do so in response to the individual showing distress. (Photo: Irven DeVore, Anthro-Photo)

juvenile howls as if mortally wounded, and the male strides off (Figure 1-2). Partly as a result of the punishment juveniles receive from dominant males, juveniles often show fear in the presence of these males (Figure 1-3).

These pictures of the disciplinary episodes among baboons had a profound effect on me for two reasons, I think. First, baboon discipline seemed at least superficially similar to something I had experienced in my own life, namely, parental discipline. This immediately suggested that there was something common to the two kinds of discipline and that one should search for a deeper explanation of discipline that would apply to both species. Baboon discipline was also striking because it was conducted entirely in silence: the adult baboon made no sound while disciplining the youngster. By contrast, human parental discipline is almost always accompanied by a barrage of words meant to represent to the offspring the reason for the discipline. On the one hand, the moral structure of the universe is described; on the other hand, the offspring's behavior. There is a need to align the two, hence the discipline. But if baboons conduct their discipline without words, it suggests that the verbiage in human discipline may just be so many words. It may be a rationalization on the parent's part, or it may be at the least the way in which the parent represents to itself and others the reasons for its actions, but in no sense does the verbalization

a

b

Figure 1-2

Adult discipline in the baboon. (a) A dominant male baboon in Kenya disciplines a juvenile by grabbing and biting it; another baboon looks on. The bite does not break the juvenile's skin; it may be painful but is not injurious. (b) The male strides off while the juvenile howls in anguish. Although dominant males are the most likely males to be the fathers of the youngsters, whether this male is the father is not known. (Photos: Irven DeVore, Anthro-Photo)

Figure 1-3

Respect for authority. The fear and respect that juveniles show a dominant male is captured here. Juveniles are often disciplined for manhandling or mistreating younger juveniles. (Photo: Irven DeVore, Anthro-Photo)

Figure 1-4

A gull breeding colony.
These gulls are breeding in
Maine. In the foreground
(left to right) are a gull in
its territory, a couple in
theirs, another gull in its
territory, and another
couple. Usually at least one
bird remains in the ter-
ritory. (Photo: William
Drury)

provide an explanation for the phenomenon of parental discipline.
Later we shall see that there are fundamental reasons for conflict between parents and offspring, and that parents may at times be favored
by natural selection to discipline their youngsters even when this is not
in the best interests of the young (see Chapter 7). Verbiage, it may be
noted, is virtually defined by its biological inexpensiveness. The difference in cost between true and false statements must be trivial, at least
as measured by energy expended in speaking (compare "yes" and
"no"), so verbal reality is likely to be a poor guide to social behavior.

   If we ask ourselves what kind of explanation might underlie the
social behavior of a variety of creatures (where would such an explanation come from?) then it seems clear after a little reflection that any
explanation must be based on a theory of how these creatures were
created. Where do baboons and other creatures come from? How were
we all created? How does the process by which we were created shed
light on our behavior now? This is the problem we will take up in this
first chapter. We will begin with a description of purposive organization in an animal. We will then consider the system of logic that Darwin replaced and describe his notion of evolution through natural selection. We shall see that in Darwin's system, living creatures have
been constructed over immense stretches of time by a process going on
around us all the time: the differential survival and reproduction of
individuals. This is natural selection and according to our best understanding of life it is natural selection which has created us.

Figure 1-5

A pair of gulls returns home. As is common in this situation, the bird that has landed gives a "long call." This is a form of territorial assertion: it draws attention to the returning birds and to their territory. It says, in effect, "We're home!" (Photo: Niko Tinbergen)

Organisms Are Designed to Do Something: The Breeding Biology of Herring Gulls

The greatest problem in biology has always been to explain the special characteristics of living creatures. If we compare even the humblest creature, say, a virus, with an inanimate object, such as a rock, the living creature appears organized to *do* something; it acts as if it is trying to achieve some purpose. Let us consider an example: the breeding biology of herring gulls. (Throughout this book we will use the herring gulls—and their close relatives, the other gulls and terns—to illustrate the principles we describe. We choose them partly because they have been unusually well studied, especially by Niko Tinbergen and his students.)

When we watch the intricate breeding pattern of a species such as the herring gull, we see a wonderful series of coincidences by which the gulls are organized so as to reproduce successfully in a particular setting. For example, the view of a gull breeding colony in Figure 1-4 shows that nests are more or less evenly spaced. Experimental work suggests that this pattern may reduce the chance that each nest and its eggs will be discovered by a predator. Boundaries of territories are maintained by aggressive interaction between neighboring pairs (Figures 1-5 to 1-7). The activities of a pair are synchronized so that a male feeds his mate while she is developing the eggs and the couple copulates repeatedly before the eggs are laid (Figures 1-8 and 1-9).

Figure 1-6

The upright threat posture of a herring gull at high intensity. Notice how the wings are held slightly apart from the body, in preparation for a possible strike on the opponent. The neck is held rigid and forward, while the beak is pointed down, all of which prepare the bird for delivering a sharp peck. These intentional movements, which prepare for action, also give away useful information to others. (Photo: Niko Tinbergen)

Figure 1-7

After a charge. The male in front has just been driven off by the other male and is still facing away. Such disputes help establish the boundary between territories. Each bird tends to be dominant in its own territory, presumably because extra space is less valuable to each gull than is protecting its home space. (Photo: Niko Tinbergen)

Both birds regularly alternate sitting on the eggs so that the eggs are rarely left uncovered and each parent has time to feed. A brood patch develops on the underbelly of each gull, and this is placed directly onto the eggs when they are being brooded. The brood patch is devoid of feathers and highly vascularized so that it transfers large quantities of heat to the developing eggs. When an adult settles onto eggs to incubate, there are an up-and-down motion, a rotating motion, and a foot-shuffling motion, all of which help bring the eggs into close contact with the brood patch.

Three eggs are commonly laid, a number from which the gulls are usually capable of raising the most surviving young. (Those laying only two eggs are typically young, inexperienced, or in poor condition.) Gull eggs are speckled and grey in color, matching their background (Figure 1-10). Although they are laid two days apart, the eggs are not brooded until the last one is laid; thus all the young tend to hatch at about the same time. More exact hatching synchrony probably results from the chicks' "peeping" to each other while still in their

Figure 1-8

Courtship feeding in the herring gull. The female (on the left) is begging for food from the male, whose neck swelling indicates he is about to regurgitate food. The behavior of the female is similar to that of a chick begging food from its parent and is, likewise, accompanied by a begging call. It is noteworthy that this begging call is also used by both sexes to invite copulation. An intimate association between food and sex is found in many species, including insects (see p. 252) and humans ("You can't make love on an empty belly"). (Photo: Niko Tinbergen)

Figure 1-9

A couple copulates. The male (on top) presses his cloaca to the female's and transfers sperm. The copulation lasts only a few seconds. (Photo: Niko Tinbergen)

eggs. Parents also make sounds during this time that they will later make to their chicks—warning calls and calls that solicit approach—and a chick deprived of hearing these calls while still in the egg later takes longer to react appropriately. At hatching, parents remove the eggshells, whose inner white surfaces attract the attention of predators.

Gull chicks are born with a pattern of spots on their heads unique to each one (Figure 1-11), and these are thought to make it easier for the parents to recognize their own chicks. In any case, within three days, parents recognize their own young and repel or eat intruding chicks. Once mobile, the chicks learn the boundaries of their parents' territory within a few days and stay within them. The chicks are not left alone by their parents until the chicks are about three weeks old, the age at which they can resist attempts by other gulls to eat them. Since the color of the chicks matches the background in which they live, they are often difficult to spot, even at close distances. Both parents feed the young and each has a red spot on its lower beak at which the chick has an inborn tendency to peck; this in turn induces the parent to regurgitate food, and so on (Figures 1-12 and 1-13).

The behavior, physiology, and morphology of gulls is highly organized in a series of coincidences that tend to promote reproduction. How did this remarkable pattern come about, and what exactly is it that these birds are trying to achieve? Put another way: how is it that

Figure 1-10

A typical gull's nest. The eggs are greyish brown and speckled to blend in with the background. The depression and nesting material give the eggs a protected place where intensive warming by the parents can take place. (Photo: Niko Tinbergen)

Figure 1-11

Individual head markings. Two newly hatched gull chicks show the spots on the head that are thought to aid in parental recognition since they are so distinctive and vary from chick to chick. (Photo: William Drury)

we living creatures display a purpose and what exactly is the purpose
we display?

Darwin's Revolution

In 1859 Charles Darwin established two things. First, he showed
beyond a reasonable doubt that evolution had taken place here on
earth. And second, he discovered the causal agent behind evolutionary
change, something he called *natural selection*. For this reason, natural
selection is the key concept in all of biology. It explains how we got the
traits we have. To appreciate the importance of Darwin's revolution,
let us glance at the system of logic he replaced.

To the problem of how creatures happen to display purposive behavior, Western biologists before 1859 usually answered as follows:
God created all species of living creatures fully formed, and these species have not changed since creation. Because species have not changed
since they were created, it seemed easy to deduce directly the intention
of God by studying living creatures themselves. Thus by studying diverse living creatures and their relationships in nature we are studying
the mind of God. For those who believed in God, this was biology's
finest hour, for it was then an integral part of natural theology. The

Figure 1-12

Stimulating a parent to feed. The gull chick pecks at
the red spot on its parent's beak, stimulating feeding
(next photo). Experiments show that chicks have an
innate tendency to peck at red spots at the end of
long beak-like objects. (Photo: William Drury)

Figure 1-13

Feeding offspring. A parent regurgitates a fish to its
young. The offspring will tear it apart and consume
it. (Photo: William Drury)

entire living world functioned as a giant unchanging machine. Individuals were parts of species that were parts of a larger whole, everything designed to work together in an unchanging way. Some species were expressly created for the use of others, for example domesticated species.

Into this picture there entered some embarrassing evidence. People began to dig up and recognize a great variety of fossils, that is, the remains of creatures clearly organized like ourselves but which no longer existed. How was one to explain fossils? The great majority of biologists responded to the discovery of fossils by embracing the theory of catastrophism, or earlier separate existences of the universe. Instead of imagining that species evolved one from the other, and that fossils were the remains of creatures that had once existed but had died out while evolution swept by them, biologists instead imagined that God had created the world a number of separate times, each time destroying the previous creation. According to this view, evolution on earth did not take place, only the mind of God evolved. As God's mind became more mature and more subtle, God swept aside earlier creations and replaced them with newer, more mature versions. Weak as the theory of catastrophism sounds, it was positively sophisticated when compared with modern-day creationism, which tries to explain the fossil record by reference to a single giant flood that swept nearly all of "lower creation" to its grave, magically depositing the carcasses in the highly ordered pattern we observe in the fossil record. Darwin's work was resisted by some scientists, not because it disproved the existence of God, but because it disproved the particular view of God to which they had become attached: a God who insisted that any creation remains unchanged until it is subject to complete revision.

By "evolution" Darwin meant both modification over time and descent from common ancestors; that is, creatures have changed in shape and behavior over vast periods of time, and, in addition, all lineages traced backwards eventually converge. If we go back about 20 million years, we ourselves are connected to all other apes. Likewise, about 150 million years ago our lineage converges with those of all other mammals. And finally, if we go back a half billion years, all vertebrates are seen to have sprung from a single common ancestor.

In this book we will emphasize Darwin's concept of natural selection, but it is worth nothing that Darwin himself amassed a variety of subtle arguments in favor of evolution. For example, he used findings from zoogeography—that is, the geographic distribution of species— to show that if God created the world unchanged in a single moment, he did so very illogically. Thus, Darwin pointed out, oceanic islands often have freshwater ponds and lakes similar to those found on the mainland, yet containing no frogs or salamanders. Such creatures can clearly survive in these ponds, as accidental introductions by humans have shown several times, so the question naturally arises: Why did

God not place frogs and salamanders in these freshwater ponds and lakes, which he also created?

In an evolutionary view, there is at once an explanation. Oceanic islands are the tops of mountains that were once completely covered by water. (Some, for example, rose above the water about 30 million years ago.) If this is true, then living creatures must have reached the islands from the mainland. The only way frogs can cross from the mainland is by rafting, that is, by clinging to a branch or a tree that has fallen into the ocean and been swept out from the mainland. But frogs breathe through their skin, and their skin needs to stay moist, so they are vulnerable to desiccation and to salt water. They cannot survive even several days in the hot sun, much less the weeks and months required to raft to an oceanic island. By contrast, reptiles can withstand drying out for considerable periods of time. A single pregnant female who happened to raft to an oceanic island could have colonized the island. Thus we might expect to find on oceanic islands those forms that easily colonize across great distances of seawater, and this is precisely what we do find. In addition to lizards we find such small mammals as rats, who are capable of rafting, and bats, who are capable of flying. But we do not find large mammals, which have a much more difficult time rafting great distances. Nor do we find wet-skinned creatures like frogs and salamanders.

To back up this interpretation, Darwin performed a number of experiments. In one, he kept large vats of seawater in his basement and placed in the seawater seeds of plants found on oceanic islands. He removed the seeds at various intervals (such as 110 days) and planted them to see if they would germinate. This evidence was compared with his calculations of how long it would take the prevailing currents to carry a seed from the nearest mainland to the islands. He showed repeatedly that many of the experimental seeds were capable of germinating even after prolonged immersion in seawater, permitting colonization of even the most distant oceanic islands. In the creationist view of zoogeography, God acted capriciously and illogically, failing to place creatures in habitats where they were well suited to survive. By the evolutionary view, the distribution of creatures today follows a logical pattern, since life must come from life, sometimes across the ocean. Creatures on oceanic islands are often similar to creatures on the nearby mainland, but typically they are of different species, sometimes quite different. In other words, these species have evolved since the time they reached the island. Thus, a study of zoogeography alone suggests that creatures have evolved here on earth, and there exists no other good explanation for the distribution of creatures today.

We will say nothing more about the evidence in favor of evolution, but will take it for granted. The evidence is now vast and interconnected and the interested—or skeptical—reader can find it summarized in the books referred to in the bibliographic notes for this chapter.

Natural Selection

In Darwin's view, evolution resulted from two factors: heritable variation and differential reproductive success. By *heritable variation*, Darwin meant that in each living species there is variability, some of which is inherited by the offspring. By *differential reproductive success*, Darwin meant that in each species some individuals leave many surviving offspring, some leave few, and some leave none at all. If these two components are coupled, we are likely to see changes in the heritable constitution of a species. If individuals with some heritable variations—what we would now call *genetic variations*—happen to leave more surviving offspring than individuals with other genetic variations, then these genetic variations have become more numerous. If the same bias is repeated generation after generation, we can expect to see considerable change in the genetic constitution of a species.

What determines differences in reproductive success, that is, differences in the number of offspring individuals produce? For Darwin, the most important factor was high, non-random, *pre-reproductive mortality*; that is, of the creatures who are conceived, most die before reaching reproductive age, and this mortality is non-random, striking some individuals more frequently than others.

Darwin realized that high pre-reproductive mortality was a logical necessity. It followed from a single fact regarding nature, namely, that over long periods of time, the amount of living material on the earth does not increase, or increases very slowly. This means that for a typical species, numbers must remain relatively constant from generation to generation. There might be huge fluctuations in numbers in many species, but taken over long periods of time, it is logically necessary that numbers increase only very slowly, if at all. Otherwise the total biomass of living creatures would increase year after year. Once we assume that numbers remain relatively constant, then it is easy to calculate how many individuals in each generation die before reproduction. For example, in the largest species of Pacific salmon, most individuals reproduce at age five and then die. The adult female produces about 6,000 eggs, and it takes only one male to fertilize the eggs. If numbers stay constant over long periods of time, then we know that for every two breeding salmon adults, roughly two will be alive five years later. In other words, 5,998 out of 6,000 eggs laid will have perished.

Herring gulls produce three eggs a season, and it has been calculated that those who survive to reproductive age can produce about ten clutches of eggs (a total of 30) in a lifetime. Since two adult herring gulls are replaced a generation later by two on an average, then 28 of the 30 eggs (or offspring) must perish before reproducing. Studies in nature show that most of this mortality occurs while the birds are still very young. In some populations about 25% of the eggs laid fail to hatch. Of the chicks that hatch out, another 40% die before fledging, most of them in the first week. Twenty percent of the remainder die by the age of three months (end of September) and another 20% before the end of winter.

On the east coast of the United States and in England, herring gulls were an endangered species 80 years ago, while nowadays they are considered a pest. Beginning in about 1900, for reasons that are not well understood but may be coincident with increasing amounts of the human garbage that the gulls have come to exploit, herring gull numbers have doubled every generation. We know that this increase in population cannot continue indefinitely, but it is interesting to note that even while it has been going on, there has been very high pre-reproductive mortality. Since the gulls double in number every generation, we know that two adult gulls have been replaced a generation later by four. This means that of the 30 eggs typically laid, 26 perish prior to reproductive age.

Human beings probably have, along with elephants, the slowest natural rate of increase of any living creature, and we know that until the discovery of agriculture about 10,000 years ago, human numbers increased very slowly. If a woman who survives through adulthood has about six children, then we know—for numbers to have stayed constant—that four of these six must have perished. We know from studies of contemporary hunter-gatherer cultures that about 20% of the children born perish in the first year of life.

Since the total amount of living material stays roughly constant from generation to generation, high pre-reproductive mortality is a logical necessity, otherwise the numbers of all creatures would increase very rapidly. Darwin saw clearly that the tremendous reproductive potential of all creatures must result in intense competition to survive, a competition, he imagined, that would result in non-random differential mortality. Those creatures who happen to be born with characteristics that make it easier to survive will endure while others will fall by the wayside. Thus, natural selection could be a very powerful process in nature, quickly molding a species to fit the environment in which its members find themselves.

What is the evidence for *non-random* mortality? In the next chapter we shall review a variety of studies showing non-random mortality, but for now let us consider a description of an actual death in nature.

Gustav Rudebeck studied the behavior of sparrow hawks *Accipiter nisus* for many years and kept an account of some of the kills he saw these birds perform.

October 17, 1937
A female sparrow hawk was flying quite low over a sandy stubble field. Suddenly it wheeled around rapidly, alighted, and almost disappeared, although

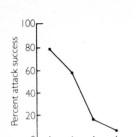

Figure 1-14

Predatory success as a function of size of prey group. The percent of attacks by a goshawk *Accipiter gentilis* that resulted in capture of a wood pigeon *Columba palumbis* is plotted as a function of the size of the wood pigeon groups. The hawk was released at a distance of about 60 meters from the pigeons. Note that the predator's success rate steadily declines with increasing prey group size, apparently as a result of greater vigilance by the prey (see next figure). (*From* Kenward 1978)

the ground was flat and the vegetation very low. Two starlings (*Sturnus vulgaris*) flew up where the hawk alighted. After some minutes, the hawk arose again with a starling in its claws, but settled in a bush surrounded by tall grass. . . . This was a surprise attack from a short distance. The sparrow hawk was flying low but did not otherwise take cover. It apparently discovered the starlings rather late, but before any one of the three birds noticed the danger. The flock of starlings, consisting of only three individuals, was remarkably small. The sparrow hawk appeared probably at a moment when the three starlings happened to be in such a position that they did not observe the danger. Such a coincidence must be practically out of the question for large flocks of starlings.

Rudebeck suggests that group size may be a deterrent to mortality from predators. Any individuals with a genetic tendency to live around other individuals may suffer lower predation and thereby leave more surviving offspring. We have reason to believe that this explanation applies very widely in nature, and it has been suggested that the primary selective force causing creatures to gather in groups is predation pressure. To give but one example: when a goshawk is released at a standard distance from flocks of wood pigeons, its predatory success rate falls steadily as pigeon flock size increases, apparently because the hawk is detected more quickly (Figures 1-14 and 1-15). From each individual pigeon's standpoint the gain in survival is striking: from a one in five chance of surviving when alone to a 99.8% chance when in a group of 50.

Mortality selection is not the only kind of selection. We can live a full life and still never reproduce. More exactly, individuals differ as adults in their capacity to reproduce. For females this usually means differences in fecundity, differences that can be very large: female cod fish differ more than five-fold in their capacity to produce eggs, even when all are the same age (Figure 1-16). Adults can also have their reproductive success limited by access to members of the opposite sex, as the biographies of many male animals show. For example, studies of bullfrogs *Rana catesbeiana* always turn up a sizable proportion of males who appear to achieve no reproductive success. The cause? Female choice. Bullfrog males take to the ponds during the breeding season and spend the evenings croaking in order to attract females, who are, in turn, uninterested in the males until they have a full set of eggs. Stephen Emlen has described the behavior of females who are ready to breed.

When ripe, however, females immigrated into the pond via the small inlet stream, left the cover of the shoreline, and approached the male choruses. These approaches evidently were guided at least in part by the sound of the males' calling, since females could be attracted to a tape recorder by playbacks of chorusing. However, direct observations revealed that females were *not* strongly attracted to males calling from isolated territories; in all observed instances (N = 16) females passed by such males and continued on to the large choruses.

Once a chorus was reached, a female adopted an extremely "low" posture and moved from territory to territory without eliciting any noticeable response from the resident males. After many hours of remaining "low" in first one territory and then another, the female appeared to select a mate, swimming up to him and seemingly making physical contact. Only then would the male respond by immediately seizing her in amplexis.

These observations suggest that an important factor affecting male bullfrog reproductive success is female choice, and that females prefer to swim to large choruses of males because they can then more easily sample the available males in order to make their choice. Thus a male may have characteristics that permit him to survive into adulthood and, indeed, into ripe old age, yet if he lacks characteristics that attract females—or that give success in male-male competition—then from the viewpoint of selection, he may as well have died when young. So important did Darwin consider intrasexual competition and intersexual choice, that he called it by a separate name: *sexual selection*.

In summary then, natural selection refers to differential reproductive success in nature, where reproductive success is the number of surviving offspring produced. This differential reproductive success consists of differences in survival rates and differences in reproductive capacity, including differences in fecundity and (in sexual species) differences in the ability to best members of one's own sex in competition for access to the members of the other sex.

Natural Selection and Herring Gull Breeding Traits

We are now in a position to return to our original questions. How is it that herring gulls are organized to do something, and what exactly are they organized to do? Our answer: Gulls have been subject to natural selection for millennia and, indeed, for eons, and this selection has continually woven together those traits that gave their possessors high reproductive success in the environments in which they found themselves. The result of this selection is individual gulls alive today who are organized to maximize the number of their surviving offspring.

When we see gulls defending territories within which to breed, we must assume that gulls who do not defend territories—or defend ones too small or unnecessarily large—leave few or no surviving offspring. If so, then in competition with gulls such as we see today, their traits would have been eliminated from the population long ago. The "coincidence" of gulls developing traits—such as coloration of eggs and

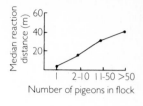

Figure 1-15

Reaction distance as a function of group size. The distance in meters at which wood pigeons took flight in response to an attacking goshawk is plotted as a function of the size of the pigeon flocks being attacked. Rudebeck's hypothesis is confirmed: larger group size means an earlier response to predators. (*From* Kenward 1978)

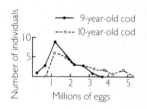

Figure 1-16

Variation in fecundity. Number of females containing a given number of eggs is plotted for a population of 9- and 10-year-old Atlantic cod *Gadus callarias*. Notice the large variation in fecundity in each age class, due largely to differences in size: the most fecund females have more than five times the reproductive success of the least fecund. (*From* May 1967)

Figure 1-17

Camouflage. Notice how well this gull chick blends in with its background, even when viewed from a short distance. This camouflage tends to protect the chick from visually hunting predators such as birds of prey, and presumably resulted from natural selection. (Photo: William Drury)

young—that match the environment in which the gulls nowadays live is explained by natural selection acting in similar contexts in the past. Since the background against which gulls breed often has a particular appearance, selection via visually hunting predators will result in the evolution of gull eggs and chicks that match this background; those that were not thus camouflaged were preyed upon in greater numbers (Figure 1-17).

Natural selection has also produced wonderful coincidences of social organization: males and females cooperating to raise young, or parent and offspring with matched traits that facilitate parental care. These social characteristics evolve because other gulls are part of each individual gull's environment and, like all other parts of the environment, may have selective effects. Parents will be selected for who recognize their own chicks (failure to do so might lower reproductive success by wasting parental care on unrelated young or even by parents eating their own chicks). Since the offspring benefit thereby, they will be selected to make themselves more easily recognized. Thus, spots on the heads of chicks will co-evolve with parental ability to recognize them. A similar argument applies to the offspring's recognition of the parent.

This view of herring gull life as a result of natural selection need not rest alone on plausibility and faith in our evolutionary logic. Because mortality among young birds is high prior to their flying and because mortality can often be measured fairly precisely, we can check to see whether variation in gull traits is associated with variation in reproductive success. We can further check to see whether traits shared by many individuals are those that usually give high reproductive success. In the next chapter we shall see that for gulls there is now a variety of such measures, most of which show powerful selection acting on breeding traits, usually in favor of common characteristics. I hope we shall also see, throughout the book, that the hypothesis of organization to maximize individual reproductive success uniquely explains a whole world of facts concerning the way living creatures act.

Summary

All living creatures are organized to do something. The study of evolution shows us how this came about and what exactly it is that we are organized to do. Prior to Darwin, most biologists believed in a series of unchanging living worlds, all but the most recent creations having been obliterated, leaving only fossils as evidence of their existence. Darwin showed that evolution had taken place, all living creatures today being descendants of but one (or a very few) original species. Evolution, in turn, has taken place because of natural selection.

Natural selection is the differential reproduction in nature of individuals. Some individuals leave many surviving offspring and the genetic traits of those who do become more numerous in succeeding generations. Thus, individuals alive today are expected to be organized to maximize the eventual number of their surviving offspring.

A major component of natural selection is high pre-reproductive mortality. In all species (with the exception of recent human history), more individuals die in each generation than survive to reproductive age. In addition, selection also acts on reproductive output in adulthood. Some of this reproductive output is determined by access to members of the opposite sex, and this is called sexual selection.

Natural Selection

I<small>F</small> <small>DARWIN GAVE US</small> a scientifically valid theory of organic creation (as I believe he did) then it is of value to us to understand the details of this theory. The central concept is that of *natural selection*, because it is natural selection—working on genetic variation—that produces evolutionary change. In that sense, natural selection constructs us, piecing together our various genetic parts through time. In Chapter 5 we will consider exactly what we mean when we say "genetic trait," but for now let us concentrate on the other half of our equation: the differential reproduction of individuals in nature.

After Darwin wrote *The Origin of Species*, many objections were raised to the concept of natural selection. It was claimed that selection was too weak a force to bring about substantial evolutionary change. It was said that life on earth had existed for too short a time for natural selection—acting alone—to produce the wonderful array of complex creatures we see today. And so on. Time has not been kind to these objections. Natural selection has repeatedly been shown to act as a powerful force in nature, capable of producing measurable change even in a single generation. Life, in turn, is now known to have existed on this planet for almost four *billion* years. Alternative schemes for evolutionary change have repeatedly been devised and found wanting; more importantly, we have yet to discover a fact of nature that requires a new theory of evolutionary change. Quite the contrary, we have unearthed a series of facts regarding the social lives of animals which are uniquely explained by our theory (see, for example, Chapters 6 and 11).

In this chapter we will concentrate on the concept of natural selection, primarily by reviewing various examples. We begin by considering the concept itself and emphasize that natural selection is a creative process. We then review its relationship to evolutionary change. We show that selection pressures in nature are often strong and that immense periods of time have been available for selection to act. We show that even differences in apparently trivial traits may be associated with variation in reproductive success, and that no trait is adaptive in all environments. We briefly review the way in which function can be studied. And, finally, we give an overview of the way in which selection acts on one well-studied species.

The Individual That Leaves the Most Surviving Offspring

A shorthand way of describing natural selection is to say that it favors the individual that leaves the most surviving offspring, or favors the traits that permit an individual to leave the most surviving offspring. Let us examine this statement, word by word.

First, natural selection refers to *individuals*, it does not refer to groups or species, and this distinction is vital. It is individuals that are purposively organized, and they are organized to leave surviving offspring. In the pre-Darwinian view, it was common to imagine that some species were created expressly to benefit others: authors sometimes imagined that salmon swam upstream so as to leap into the arms of waiting mammals and birds. This notion is denied in the Darwinian view: the fish do not give themselves up gladly. They attempt to escape their predators, and precisely because of this, predators have to struggle to catch their prey and can only catch some individuals, not all.

The same distinction between groups and individuals applies to interactions within a species. In the old view, individuals could easily be designed to sacrifice for the benefit of the species. They may choose not to reproduce, when they easily could, in order to benefit the species as a whole. In the new view, it is difficult to see how sacrifice of reproductive output could survive in the face of genetic variation and natural selection. Any individual genetically inclined *not* to sacrifice would leave more surviving offspring and the genetic tendency would spread, whether the long-term consequences were good or bad. The alternative view, that life is organized so as to benefit the species or group, has been so widespread and important that we devote an entire chapter to it (Chapter 4).

Second, natural selection favors individuals that *maximize* the number of their surviving offspring. Sometimes, pushing to reproduce too many will result in producing less, but we never expect a pair of herring gulls to say to themselves, so to speak, "Well, we've bred successfully for three or four years, and we've produced 10 surviving offspring; why don't we just retire and live out our days without the quacking of chicks and this constant regurgitating of food?" No, organisms are expected to be maximizing machines. Organisms are expected to attempt to increase their reproductive success over anything they have already achieved.

Third, individuals are selected to maximize the *number* of surviving offspring they produce. This is an important feature of Darwin's theory of creation; at the heart of the theory lies a number. This—more than anything—makes the theory scientific: we can actually measure the creative process and we can devise simple equations in which these measurements appear. In this book we will emphasize measurements of differential survival and reproduction, since these show us directly how natural selection is acting.

Finally, Darwin's theory emphasizes the production of *surviving offspring*. Life is organized around the production of children. This means that we expect behavior to be organized in a clear hierarchy in which activities are biologically meaningful only insofar as they eventually contribute to the production of surviving offspring. Instead of a disorganized list of items that we may care to invest ourselves in, such as children, leisure time, sexual enjoyment, food, friendship, and so on, Darwin's theory says that all of these activities are expected to be organized eventually toward the production of surviving offspring.

Natural Selection as a Creative Process

Because the processes of death and destruction constitute the selection pressures in nature, it has often been claimed that natural selection is not a creative process but a force that merely weeds out the misfits, leaving the fit the same as before. A famous analogy helps us see why this view is erroneous. Imagine that we are trying to create the word "cat" by removing three letters at a time from a bin containing a hundred copies of each letter in the alphabet. The probability of removing all three at once is $6 \times (1/26)^3$, or about one chance in 3,000. Now imagine that after removing three letters from the bin, we discard them before choosing another three letters. In 867 attempts we will have emptied our bin, so most of the time we will fail to form the word "cat" before our supply of letters runs out. This example is analogous to viewing natural selection as a random, destructive process.

Now, instead, imagine that whenever we remove a "c," an "a," or a "t" from the bin we return it again while discarding any other letter. As time proceeds, the bin becomes richer in the three letters we seek. Our chances of forming "cat" improve until we are guaranteed of doing so long before the supply is exhausted. Imagine, further, that whenever we happen to draw two of the right letters, we are permitted to staple them together before returning them to the bin. Now, our chances of drawing the three letters are even greater. This example is

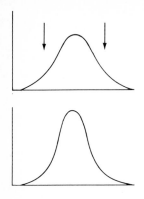

Figure 2-1

Stabilizing selection.
(a) The number of individuals possessing kidneys of a given size is plotted for an imaginary population. Arrows denote individuals suffering greatest mortality. (b) The same population one generation later. There has been no change in the average kidney size and the degree of variability has decreased slightly.

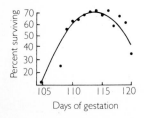

Figure 2-2

Survival of piglets as a function of length of gestation. Percent survival of piglets to six weeks of age is shown as a function of length of gestation, measured in days. Selection is stabilizing, since both extremes are associated with lower survival. (*From* Cox 1965).

analogous to viewing natural selection as a directed, creative process. A very improbable event, the construction of a particular living creature, or a particular adaptation, is made more probable because the various elements tend independently to increase in frequency within the population. Beneficial traits are, thus, knitted together through time.

Through natural selection, species automatically become more fitted to their circumstances. Predators, for example, remove those creatures that are slower, or less alert, or less sociable, and so on, so that over time the prey species improves in its ability to evade predators. At the same time, natural selection acts back on the predators, favoring those that are swifter, more alert, and sometimes more sociable. Thus species cut against each other, and like knives, each is sharpened in turn. Through this process, there is certainly progress toward more complex and subtle adaptations, or in the words of Darwin:

There is grandeur in this view of life with its several powers having originally been breathed into a few forms or into one, and whilst this planet has gone cycling on according to the fixed laws of gravity, from so simple a beginning, endless forms, most beautiful and most wonderful, have been and are being, evolved.

Natural Selection and Evolutionary Change

Natural selection is a simple concept: it refers to differences in reproductive success (abbreviated RS) among individuals in nature. Genetic traits associated with high reproductive success will tend to predominate in future generations. Our attention is focused on variability within a population. We wish to see how variability in the traits of individuals is associated with variability in RS. This represents an important break with pre-Darwinian biology. In the old system, each species was imagined to have been created according to some ideal type. Variation was just so much noise superimposed on the ideal type. After Darwin, the variation itself was seen as real and important, while the notion of an ideal type was recognized as a useless abstraction.

When thinking about the evolution of a trait it is useful to picture variability in the trait and consider how selection affects this variability. Picture the frequency of people with various-sized kidneys. If selection acts against individuals with extreme-sized kidneys, selection is said to be stabilizing, since it keeps the average value of the trait constant (Figure 2-1). This is the most common form of selection, namely, pressure against the extremes. Sometimes stabilizing selection can last for eons. Opossums, for example, have hardly changed in external morphology in 150 million years. This constant state must have been maintained by stabilizing selection, because without some kind of selection, variability in the opossum would have steadily increased.

For another example of stabilizing selection, consider length of gestation in pigs. Among pigs, unlike most mammals, increasing litter size is not associated with shorter gestation time, so the effect of selection on gestation time can be seen directly from its effect on subsequent survival of the piglets. This effect is substantial (Figure 2-2). Optimal gestation time is about 114 days. Larger and smaller values are associated with lowered survival. A gestation time only two days longer or shorter (that is, a 2% change in gestation length) is associated with a five percent decrease in survivorship. With successive increments the effect on survivorship is more severe. Surprising as it sounds, even smaller differences in time spent inside the mother by members of the same litter have even greater effects on survival. This is because first-born pigs grab the best teats on which to suck and suck these teats throughout nursing. Piglets are very aggressive in the first two hours after birth and act as if they know that the teats highest on the mother's belly are the richest in milk (Figures 2-3 and 2-4). The piglets who are born in the second half of the litter suffer about twice the chance of dying before three weeks of age that the first-born suffer (Table 2-1).

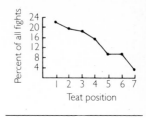

Figure 2-3

Aggressiveness as a function of teat order. The percentage of all fights over teats at a given position is plotted as a function of teat position. Number 1 is the most anterior teat (closest to the mother's head). Notice that piglets fight more often over access to anterior teats, a nice example of aggressiveness adjusted to the value of the prize (see next figure). (*From* Hartsock, Graves, and Baumgardt 1977)

Table 2-1 The Relationship of Birth Order to Birth Weight and Mortality *

Birth Order	Average Birth Weight (kg)	Mortality by 21 Days of Age (%)	Survivors' Average Birth Weight Minus Non-Survivors' Average Birth Weight (kg)
1	1.21	9.1%	.29
2	1.21	9.3	.23
3	1.24	6.8	−.03
4	1.21	15.9	.28
5	1.25	19.0	.16
6	1.11	20.9	.11
7	1.20	20.9	.17
8	1.21	17.1	.08
9	1.20	17.6	.40
10	1.11	30.0	.17
11	1.19	28.6	.09
12	1.19	17.6	.03

Source: Hartsock and Graves 1976.
* Five piglets dying from congenital disorders were excluded.

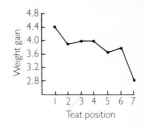

Figure 2-4

Weight gain in pigs as a function of teat order. The weight gain, in kilograms, from birth to three weeks of age is plotted as a function of teat position (see previous figure). In addition to anterior teats being superior in milk, part of the association may be due to the fact that larger piglets grab these teats first. (*From* Hartsock, Graves, and Baumgardt 1977)

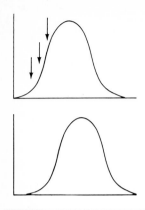

Figure 2-5

Directional selection.
(a) The number of individuals possessing kidneys of a given size (in millimeters) is plotted for an imaginary population. Same as Figure 2-1(a) except mortality (arrows) now works against one extreme only. (b) The population one generation later: the average kidney size has increased due to selection against those with small kidneys.

If selection acts against one extreme of a sample but not the other it is said to be directional because its effect is to move the average value of the trait toward the extreme that has higher reproductive success (see Figure 2-5). Notice that after several generations of selection, the mean value of the trait may have moved outside its original distribution. An example of directional selection is the steady increase in brain size in the human lineage over the past three million years. We must assume that in generation after generation there was a tendency for selection to operate against individuals with relatively smaller brains. Incidentally, brain size apparently has not increased over the past 100,000 years so we assume that the earlier directional selection has given way to stabilizing selection. Studies of the fossil evidence from many animal groups suggest that new lineages often evolve quickly in various directions and then remain stable for long periods.

Selection can also act against the middle, favoring the extremes. In such a case it is said to be disruptive, since its effect is to split the original distribution into two distributions (Figure 2-6). Wherever two forms have evolved from one, disruptive selection has been at work. The two sexes were created, and are maintained, by disruptive selection in which intermediate forms are at a decided disadvantage. (Compare Figures 2-7a and 2-7b.) Many other dimorphisms are maintained in a similar way. In a bird called the ruff, males come in two forms (Figure 2-7(a)). The dark-colored form defends a territory aggressively and courts females. The light-colored form is non-aggressive and does not defend a territory, but instead approaches a dark-colored male, seeking to be permitted to court females from within the dark-colored bird's territory while remaining subordinate to him. This dimorphism must have evolved by selection acting against intermediate forms and favoring the two distinct forms.

The Intensity of Selection

The intensity of selection is a function of the variability in reproductive success. Where variability is high, selection is strong. What evidence we have shows that selection in nature is often surprisingly strong. A variety of studies in plants and animals show selective values of at least 5% and many show values of 50% or higher. Experiments yield similar results. For example, the distance between nests in herring gulls is strongly influenced by egg predators such as crows. When crows are attracted to eggs laid in a pattern, those that are closer together suffer higher mortality. In one trial, when eggs were only 0.5 meters apart, 24 of 27 were found by a crow, while of 27 eggs placed 8 meters apart, only 5 were found. This is a five-fold increase in mortality due to spacing!

In the herring gull (or in closely related species) selection has been shown to act on the size of eggs laid, on the number of eggs laid, on the date eggs are laid, on the order in which eggs are laid, on nest density, on the location of colonies relative to predators and sources of food, on the amount of food fed by a male to a female during courtship, on the tendency of adults to remove egg shells from the vicinity of their nests, and also on the tendency of mates to remain paired in succeeding years. We note that the increase in reproductive success associated with these traits is often 5% or more. *Notice in addition that gulls can cause strong selective effects on each other.* Courtship feeding, breeding density, and rates of cannibalism all affect reproductive success and all are caused by the gulls themselves. Let us consider one of these in a little detail: the cannibalism of young chicks by adults other than their parents.

Gulls are notorious killers during the breeding season and will peck to death or worry to death chicks that wander into their territories (Figure 2-8). In addition, in some colonies a few individuals specialize in preying on chicks as a source of food. As Jasper Parsons showed, mortality from this source can be considerable: at least 23% of over 1400 herring gull chicks marked at hatching were cannibalized before they fledged, yet only one in 500 adults was acting as a cannibal (Table 2-2).

Cannibals are individuals that leave their own nests in search of live chicks from other nests. These chicks are taken from their own nest sites and swallowed in flight or carried back to the cannibal's nest site, where they are eaten (Figure 2-9). Cannibals depend on chicks for their food and take a relatively constant number throughout the breeding season. Since most gulls breed during the middle of the season, the smallest percentage of chicks is eaten at that time (Table 2-3). The effect is substantial: fewer than 8% of chicks hatched at midseason perish to cannibals, but more than 20% of early and late hatchlings are cannibalized. Incidentally, predation is believed to often favor clumped patterns of breeding because individuals breeding alone are, for various reasons, at greater risk. For example, Parsons found that cannibalized nests had fewer close neighbors: cannibalized nests had an average of 2.07 other nests within 3 meters, while a random sample of nests had 2.74 nests within that range ($P < 0.002$). This safety in numbers probably occurs because a cannibal is more easily attacked by several gulls simultaneously when they are breeding close together.

Cannibalism is also selective in other ways. Young chicks are especially at risk since they are easily swallowed: the average time of death was 7 days after hatching. Cannibals also take a higher proportion of

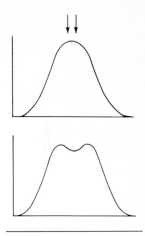

Figure 2-6

Disruptive selection.
(a) The number of individuals possessing kidneys of a given size (in millimeters) is plotted for an imaginary population. Same as Figure 2-1(a) except that mortality acts against the middle, favoring both extremes.
(b) One generation later, the population has begun to separate into two distinct groups, those with large kidneys and those with small kidneys.

a   b

Figure 2-7

Dimorphisms maintained by disruptive selection. (a) *Male dimorphism.*
Male ruffs *Philomachus pugnax* come in two forms: a white non-aggressive
satellite form and a black territorial form. The two black males are pointing
at the ground with their beaks, a typical response to arrival of a satellite.
(Photo: C. S. Doncaster) (b) *Sexual dimorphism.* In contrast to the male ruff,
the female (or reeve) is camouflaged. She alone sits on the eggs and cares for
the young. (For the evolution of sexual dimorphism, see Chapter 9.) (Photo:
J. B. Bottomley and S. Bottomley)

Figure 2-8

Territorial aggression. A well-grown herring gull chick that has wandered
into a neighboring territory is attacked. The adult pecks the chick around
the head and neck. Smaller chicks are often killed in such circumstances.
(Photo: Jasper Parsons)

Table 2-2   Fate of 1,415 Young Herring Gulls Ringed at Hatching on the Isle of May in 1968

	Number of chicks	Percent of total
Known to have fledged	609	43.0%
Eaten by cannibals	329	23.3
Dead, with head scars	47	3.3
Dead, no visible injury	256	18.1
Not accounted for	174	12.3

Source: Parsons 1971.

chicks hatched from the third—and last—egg laid, presumably because these chicks are smaller and weaker (Figure 2-10). As these examples show, mortality does not strike randomly but acts more harshly against some classes of individuals than others. The gulls themselves have strong selective effects on each other.

Although cannibals as a group were no less successful at breeding than were the other gulls, one gull showed that he had a hard time

Figure 2-9

A cannibal in action. An adult herring gull grabs a young chick while the parent challenges ineffectually. The chick will be carried to the intruder's territory and swallowed. (Photo: Jasper Parsons)

Table 2-3   Seasonal Variation in the Numbers of Chicks Eaten by Four Cannibal Herring Gulls at the Isle of May in 1968 *

	Date of Hatching						
	Before 5 June	5–9 June	10–14 June	15–19 June	20–24 June	25–29 June	After 29 June
Number of chicks ringed	99	201	289	443	260	84	22
Number of chicks eaten	22	22	21	34	29	23	7
% eaten	22.2	11.0	7.3	7.7	11.2	27.4	31.8

Source: Parsons 1971.

* The significance of the seasonal variation is $P < 0.001$.

separating the feeding and care of his own offspring from the killing and consumption of others. He ate 40 chicks while he was incubating his own three eggs. When they hatched, he continued to catch chicks and bring them back to his nest but *he failed to kill them,* so that within a week he had eleven chicks at his nest, all of which he fed! Two, including one of his own, died during a rain storm, and the cannibal subsequently ate eight of the nine remaining, including both of his own, so he succeeded in fledging only one chick, someone else's. This observation shows how a trait can cut back on itself, interfering with its own spread.

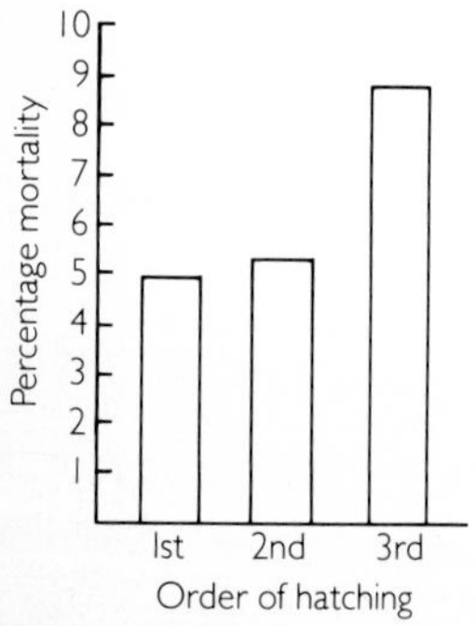

The Time Available for Evolution

The strength of a selection pressure and the time needed for it to produce change are inversely related. The weaker the selection pressure, the greater is the time required to effect a given amount of change, but relatively modest differences in reproductive success translate into rapid evolution. Consider, for example, two females. Female A produces six surviving offspring, as do her descendants, while Female B and her descendants only produce five each. This is a difference in RS of almost 17%. When repeated generation after generation such a difference in reproductive success can bring about striking changes in relative frequencies. In 25 generations, B's frequency will drop to one percent of its original value. If A and B are initially equally frequent, after 25 generations only one in a hundred individuals will be type B. If A and B differ much less in reproductive success, the same change will require many more generations. Thus, a one percent difference in

Figure 2-10

Percentage mortality from cannibalism as a function of hatching order. The difference in mortality between first and third chicks is significant ($P < 0.05$). (*From* Parsons 1971)

Table 2-4   Time and Number of Generations Available for Selection to Act on Various Traits (Approximate)

Trait	Time	Number of Generations
Mental apparatus associated with human language	Uncertain, perhaps 2 million years	50,000
Mental apparatus associated with human technology	5 million years	250,000
Adaptation to living in social groups of the complexity of baboons and macaques	30 million years	3 million
Adaptation to living in small, face-to-face groups of kin, friends, dominants, etc.	At least 50 million years	10 million
Vertebrate physiology, sensory equipment, mental life	½ billion years	200 million
Chemical machinery of the cell, including machinery for reproducing genes and decoding genes	3 billion years	billions

reproductive success requires about 265 generations to effect a change in relative frequency of two orders of magnitude. In humans this means it takes about 10,000 years for a trait with a 1% selective disadvantage to go from 99% of the population to less than one percent.

Yet 10,000 years is but the blink of an eye in evolutionary time. When we consider various human traits we see that enormous numbers of generations must have been available for selection to operate, the more so the more broadly the trait is shared with other living creatures (Table 2-4). Thus, our cellular machinery has evolved during literally billions of generations; our multicellular body, during hundreds of millions of generations; and our social life dominated by relatives and friends, for at least 3 million generations; and so on.

The more uniquely human a trait is, the less time must have been available for selection to act. The best evidence suggests that we are at least 5 million years separated from a common ancestor with the chimpanzees. The traits that differentiate us from chimpanzees have passed through at least 200,000 generations of selection. Most of the rapid increase in brain size took less than 100,000 generations. The development of religion and art has probably experienced about 10,000 generations of selection. Insofar as variation in religion and art affected individual reproductive success, there has been ample time even for weak effects to produce biological evolution in these traits. By contrast, the last 10,000 years have seen enormous changes in human life. Yet this time is too short for any but the strongest pressures to have produced much change. Of course, human warfare stands out as one such pressure. So does selection associated with disease organisms, which were probably spread more easily as urban populations flourished and people undertook long-distance migrations.

Even Trivial Traits Can Be Associated with Reproductive Success

Since selection pressures in nature are often strong, since even weak selection pressures produce substantial change in relatively few generations, and since there is so vast a stretch of time during which natural selection has operated (always as determined by the local environment), we expect that organisms will show numerous elaborate and subtle contrivances to advance life in the circumstances they face. Since we are largely ignorant of the effect living traits have on reproductive success, we must not mistake this ignorance for the face of nature. It is better to begin with the assumption that even apparently trivial traits can affect reproductive success, especially when these traits are widely shared by individuals of a species. Anything less than this bias will tempt us to abandon prematurely the search for an understanding of how living traits function.

Consider one apparently trivial trait, the exact shape of the human head, in particular, the degree to which it is round. The human head as viewed from above can be characterized as relatively round or relatively long. Dividing the width of the skull by its length gives us a "cephalic index," a crude measure of its roundness. For the current human population the index is about 0.83, meaning that the average head is longer than it is wide by about 20%.

One might suppose that minor variation in so minor a trait has no appreciable effect on survival, but this is not so, at least not for Polish army recruits in the late 1920's. A part of the massive Military Anthropological Study of Poland (which covered 120,000 individuals, on each of whom 70 measures were taken) survived the Warsaw Uprising in 1944 to give us a large ($N = 6229$), homogeneous sample of men: most of the recruits were 21−25 years of age, all came from nine counties in the northeastern corner of pre-war Poland (now USSR), and all were farmers. The region was poor, women had high fertility, and mortality in the first year of life hovered around 20%. Besides his cephalic index, we know for each recruit the number of his surviving siblings and the total number of siblings ever born.

As Figure 2-11 shows, the shape of a recruit's head is associated with the number of his surviving siblings. Round-headed soldiers have

more surviving siblings than do long-headed ones, but stabilizing selection must also be acting, since at the extremes individuals do less
well than near the mean. (This, incidentally, is a common feature of
directional selection: it often has a stabilizing component.) Why the
association between shape of head and number of surviving siblings?
We know it does not result from differential fertility. In fact, long-
headed people gave birth to slightly more children, but a higher proportion of these children died (32%, compared to 28% for round-
headed people). Unfortunately, nothing is known about the reason
that shape of head affects survival, but it is worth noting that there
appears to be a long-standing trend toward round-headedness in humans: we are more round-headed than apes and monkeys, and skulls
dug up about 700 years ago in Polynesia, India, and Poland give average cephalic indices of only about 0.73.

In principle, then, it seems like a bad idea to assume that *any* trait
is neutral or lacks association with reproductive success. Of course,
there are exceptions to this rule. For example, "as useless as teats on a
boar" expresses our inability to see any function for nipples on male
mammals. These are apparently maintained in males because of strong
selection on females.

No Trait Is Adaptive in All Environments

The environment determines the action of natural selection. Indeed,
details of the environment determine exactly how selection operates.
We have seen already that the presence of sparrow hawks can select
for sociality in starlings. Keep the environment otherwise constant but
remove this sort of mortality and we may see a tendency for starling
flocks to become smaller. Thus, traits are only adaptive with reference
to a particular environment and few, if any, traits are adaptive in all
contexts.

Consider an example: brain size. Humans stand at the end of a
long line of positive selection for this trait, but such selection is far
from universal. Birds and mammals have experienced 150 million
years of positive selection for brain size, more strongly in some groups,
such as monkeys and whales, than in others; but in fish, amphibians,
and reptiles, there has been no change in brain size (relative to body
size) during the past 300 million years. Indeed, in some specialized circumstances, brains and associated nervous systems have disappeared
entirely. Tapeworms, which live in the human gut, lack a brain but are
descended from free-living forms such as planaria, which have brains
and are capable of simple learning.

Since traits are only defined as useful by reference to a given environment, the concept of natural selection provides no objective support

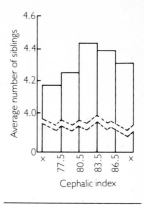

Figure 2-11

*Number of siblings as a
function of shape of head.*
The number of surviving
siblings is given as a function of the cephalic index
(head-width/head-length)
for Polish army recruits in
the 1920s. Note that selection appears to be both stabilizing and directional (in
favor of higher indices).
(*From* Bielicki and Welon
1964)

for terms like "higher" and "lower." Darwin made notes to himself to stop referring to higher and lower animals, but this usage had been built into the taxonomy constructed by Linnaeus a century before, and it has persisted to this day. Schemes for elevating some creatures above others typically do so on the basis of similarity to ourselves, but this is obviously an egocentric approach. Groups of species can be compared according to the number of species within a group, but this leads to the conclusion that some environments favor many species while others do not. There are, for example, 300,000 species of beetles, nearly one-fourth of all animals. J. B. S. Haldane, a famous evolutionist, was once asked by a group of clerics what a lifetime's study of evolution suggested to him about the nature of the Creator, and he responded, "An inordinate fondness for beetles."

The chief effect of using terms like "higher" and "lower" is to underestimate the powers of other creatures; "lower" animals, for example, are often assumed to be too dumb to act in their own self-interest. Unfortunately this assumption—often unconscious—merely blinds us to the true nature of these creatures. I think a better bias is the one William Drury taught me when I was his student: "Never assume the animal you are studying is as dumb as the one studying it."

The Study of Function

Since traits are adaptive with reference to particular environments, the study of function naturally seeks correlations between the environment and the action of natural selection. Consider an example. Between 1942 and 1944, 198 young men died in basic training from heat stroke in the U.S. Army. The Army analyzed the reasons for the deaths. When temperature versus humidity was plotted for the times of these deaths, it was discovered that mortality occurred whenever temperature or humidity was high, both of which variables make it difficult to keep one's body cool. Were the soldiers a representative sample of all soldiers? No. Those who died were typically overweight for their body size (see Figure 2-12). This is not surprising since fat interferes with the body's ability to dissipate heat.

More generally, larger people suffer heat and humidity more intensely than do smaller people, since larger people have smaller surface areas relative to their weight. Thus, we are not surprised to discover that throughout the world there is a clear correlation between mean annual temperature and human body weight, heavier people being more common at lower temperatures. Human body *shape* is also correlated with temperature because different body shapes produce relatively more or less surface area. Thus, in climates where people

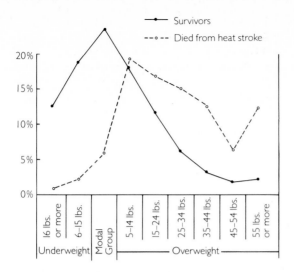

Figure 2-12

Relationship of death from heat stroke to weight for a given size in humans. Plotted is the percentage of 100,000 surviving men and the percentage of 124 who died from heat stroke as a function of the degree to which these men were overweight or underweight. There is a very strong tendency for those who died to be overweight. (*From Schickele 1947*)

need to dissipate a lot of heat, they have long, slender fingers and long limbs relative to trunk size. An Eskimo, by contrast, is short and has a large trunk and short extremities. The deaths from heat stroke in the Army just described were also related to geographic origin. Those raised in warmer climates were less likely to suffer mortality, but whether this was due to acclimatization or a genetic difference in the populations is not known.

Note that we have combined two kinds of information. On the one hand we have correlated mortality data with both environmental and personal variables. On the other hand, we have correlated environmental variation with variation in the distribution of a trait within a species. It is much easier to gather the second kind of information than the first, so most of our understanding of function comes from a study of how biological traits co-vary with the environment and with other traits. The following example illustrates the general methodology.

Most mammals give live birth; most reptiles lay eggs. Why this difference? Among reptiles, a tendency for females to retain eggs within their bodies has evolved repeatedly. The mammalian system of reproduction ultimately resulted from a tendency of certain reptile females to retain their eggs for several days before laying them. What is the functional significance of this trait? We have no data linking reproductive success with variation in egg retention, so we must discover the correlates of a tendency toward live-bearing. It has been estimated that live-bearing has evolved more than 30 times among reptiles. A study of these species compared to 1000 species of egg-layers shows that live-bearing habits are associated with two variables—cold climate

Table 2-5   The Relationship Between Habitat or Presence of
Maternal Care and Frequency of Live-bearing or Egg Retention in
Lizards and Snakes

Habitat	Percent of All Lizard and Snake Species	Percent Live-bearers in Genera with Both Egg-laying and Live-bearing Species	Percent Species with Egg Retention
Cold climate	44%	74%	72%
Wet soil	12	11	13
Arboreal	10	8	8
Maternal Care (at level of genus)	11	24 *	33

Source: Shine and Bull 1979.

Note: Both cold climate and maternal care are associated
with trends toward live-bearing, while wet soil and arboreal habitats are not.

* In egg-laying forms.

and a tendency for females to care for their young after eggs are laid
(Table 2-5).

Studies of the effect of temperature on egg development suggest
that a female benefits by retaining eggs within her because this permits
faster development: females choose warm portions of their habitat,
thus boosting their temperature, while eggs, once laid, are no longer
mobile. Egg retention also protects against lethal temperatures and females that brood eggs gain a further benefit from egg retention: it
shortens their brooding time, partly offsetting the cost of carrying the
eggs. We therefore expect brooding species to be more likely to retain
eggs than non-brooding species. Thus, comparative evidence suggests
that two factors may have operated in early mammalian evolution: if
early mammals lived in colder climates (or were active at night) and if
they already showed parental care, internal development would have
been favored.

Natural Selection Acting on Red Deer

To get an overview of the way in which natural selection acts on a
single species, let us choose a particularly well-studied species, the red
deer *Cervus elaphus* and concentrate on the factors controlling variation in lifetime reproductive success.

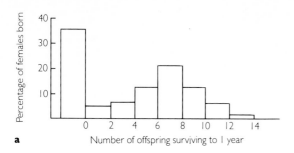

a

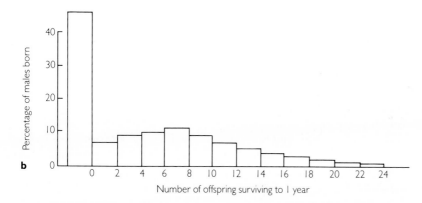

b

Figure 2-13

*Lifetime variation in repro-
ductive success for females
and males in red deer.* The
percentage of (a) females
born or (b) males born
who achieved a given lifetime RS (measured as sur-
viving offspring to a year of
age) is plotted for red deer.
Notice that variation is substantial for each sex but
greater in males. These data
are especially valuable because they give us a clear
overview of the operation of
natural selection on a single
species. (*From* Clutton-
Brock, Guinness, and Al-
bon 1982)

In Figure 2-13 we see that there is substantial lifetime variation in
RS for both males and females, but this is greater for males. For all
females born, about 35% produce no surviving offspring, while some
raise 13 young to one year of age. For all males born, more than 40%
produce no surviving offspring, while some father as many as 24.
Thus, the maximum RS of a male is twice that of a female, and selection is more intense on males.

What controls variation in reproductive success? Although social
factors have effects in both sexes, these are much more pronounced in
males. For females each offspring is costly to rear, as may easily be seen
by noting the superior condition or survival of adult females without
offspring compared to those with dependent young (Figure 2-14). Maternal condition appears to be the key factor controlling survival of a
female's offspring. Mothers in better condition give birth earlier to
heavier offspring, and, in general, both these factors have a positive
effect on survival of offspring (Figure 2-15). In addition, in mother–
offspring pairs shot throughout the year, the size and condition of the
offspring is positively correlated with the condition of its mother. Dominant females outreproduce subordinates (Table 2-6), presumably because dominance gives them greater access to areas with better forage.

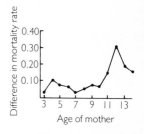

Figure 2-14

*Difference in mortality rate
between red deer mothers
who are nursing and those
who are not.* The annual
mortality rate of nursing
mothers minus that of non-
nursing mothers is plotted
as a function of maternal
age. Non-nursing mothers
either failed to give birth
or lost the calf early in the
season. (*From* Clutton-
Brock 1984)

Figure 2-15

Weight at birth and survival through the summer as a function of maternal age in red deer. Birth weight, in kilograms, (adjusted for sex of calf and year of birth) and survival rate of calves until October is plotted as a function of mother's age in red deer. Note the close, positive relationship between birth weight and survival. (*From Clutton-Brock, Guinness, and Albon 1982*)

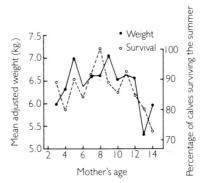

Although females prefer to travel in the company of female kin, the size of such groups is, curiously enough, negatively associated with the survival of their sons—but not their daughters (Figure 2-16).

Social factors have a critical influence on male RS. In the fall mating season, males fight with each other to control mating access to groups of females (Figures 2-17 and 2-18). During this time, the frequency of fighting and the number of injuries sustained is positively associated with the frequency with which females are conceiving. Just like the piglets in Figure 2-3, red deer males appear to adjust their aggressiveness to the value of the prize being fought over. Males virtually stop eating and undergo a precipitous decline in condition (Figure 2-19). Because some males are large, in excellent condition, and good fighters they are able to obtain exclusive mating access to groups of females during the time when these females are conceiving (Figure

Table 2-6   Measures of Breeding Performance in Female Red Deer According to Dominance Rank *

Breeding Performance Measure	Dominance Rank	
	Subordinate	*Dominant*
Median age of first breeding (years)	3.9	3.48
Median weight of calves at birth (lbs)	6.4	6.8
Percent calf mortality in first year	45	28
Mean lifespan (years)	9	11
Median number of calves reared to one year of age	2.3	6.0

Source: Clutton-Brock et al. 1984.

* Females were divided into two equal groups based on rank. All differences are significant except percent calf mortality, which is nearly significant ($P < 0.10$).

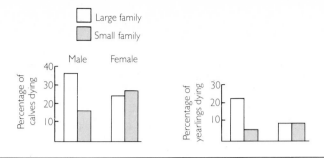

Figure 2-16

Social effects on reproductive success in red deer. The percentage of individuals dying in their first year of life (calves) and in their second (yearlings) is plotted separately for males and females, depending on whether their mothers were part of large family groups or small ones (large groups were those above the median size for their area). Note that large size of kin group has no effect on daughter's survival, but significantly reduces that of sons. Thus, social effects may be strongly sex-specific. The selection pressure shown may favor mothers who give birth to relatively more daughters when they are in large groups. (*From* Clutton-Brock, Guinness, and Albon 1982)

Figure 2-17

Red deer males fighting. The male on the left leaps up and forward in an attempt to dislodge his opponent. Such struggles have a strong influence on male RS since they will help determine access to breeding females (see next figure). (Photo: Timothy Clutton-Brock)

Figure 2-18

A male with his harem. A six-year-old red deer male with a group of breeding adult females. He is roaring, a form of aggressive display intended to intimidate rivals (and possibly attract females). As long as the females stay with him and no other male drives him off, he will enjoy nearly exclusive mating with the females. The number of days in which he holds such groups at the key time and the size of the groups have a strong influence on his lifetime RS (see Figure 2-20). (Photo: Fiona Guinness)

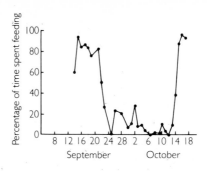

Figure 2-19

A cost of reproduction in male red deer. The percentage of time a nine-year-old male spent feeding during the 1974 rut. Note that for three weeks at the height of the rut he hardly feeds at all, yet this is a time of nearly continual intense activity: fighting other males, roaring, herding females, mating, and so on. Only those males able to feed well the rest of the year and in early life and to minimize the drain of parasites will be able to develop the body size, antler size, and energy reserves that give success in male–male competition. 1974 was a very good year for this male, in terms of number of females held, and presumably mated, at the critical time (see next figure). (*From* Clutton-Brock, Guinness, and Albon 1982)

2-20). This causes a large part of the variation in male RS. Females probably accentuate these effects by gathering in larger groups during the rut and by moving away from less preferred males. Early gains in development have later effects on male RS, since the size of a male's antlers at 16 months predicts mating success five years later. Even though competition to hold large harems is intense, those able to hold them live longer than those holding smaller harems, presumably because the same kinds of traits that aid a male in holding females also aid in survival (see Figure 14-12).

These data show that there is strong selection acting on red deer in nature, that selection is more intense on males than on females (that is, there is greater variation in male RS) and that RS in females is controlled by ability to invest in offspring, while male RS is controlled by ability to inseminate females. We shall see in Chapter 9 that this is a very general—but by no means universal—rule in animals.

Summary

Natural selection refers to differences in reproductive success among individuals in nature. Natural selection is a creative process, since it binds together traits in novel and unlikely combinations. Studies of

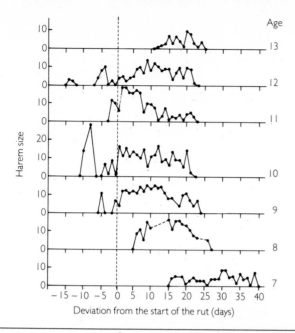

Figure 2-20

A successful male's reproductive life. The number of adult females held each year by one particular male (the same male as in the previous figure) is plotted as a function of deviation from the start of the rut (defined as the time when, throughout the population, females first tend to settle down in one male's area on successive days). Note that in his peak years, this male held as many as ten females for two weeks or more at the time when many were probably conceiving. Note also the day-to-day variation in harem size— females joining and leaving, both in groups and individually. Thus, in spite of intense male–male competition to exclude others, there is enormous scope for female choice (see Chapter 14). (*From* Clutton-Brock, Guinness, and Albon 1982)

natural selection show that selection pressures in nature are often surprisingly strong. The time required for a trait to evolve is a function of the strength of the selection pressure, and there has been abundant time for most traits to show significant selection. For this reason it is a bad idea to assume that any trait is without selective value. The environment determines the action of natural selection, and no trait is adaptive in all environments. The study of function proceeds largely through the search for correlations between the distribution of environmental factors and the distribution of biological traits. An overview of natural selection acting on one species (red deer) shows that variation in reproductive success is greater in males than in females, apparently because RS in males is more tightly tied to social interactions.

Chapter 3

Elementary Social Theory

W E ARE NOW IN A position to apply our theory of creation to social traits, that is, to consider how natural selection affects social traits. These are traits that affect at least one individual other than the possessor of the trait, so the simplest social theory begins with two individuals. We imagine that one individual, the actor, initiates some action that affects a second individual, the recipient. We measure the effects in units of reproductive success; that is, we measure whether the behavior increases the reproductive success of the actor (benefit) or decreases it (cost) and we measure the same thing for the recipient. Neglecting zero effects, we have at once four kinds of social acts: the actor confers a benefit but suffers a cost (altruistic), the actor gains while inflicting a cost (selfish), both parties gain (cooperative), and both parties suffer (spiteful) (see Figure 3-1).

In this chapter we will illustrate the four kinds of social acts and consider the way in which selection acts on each. We will concentrate on altruistic behavior because it is both common and apparently opposed by the action of selection. Three explanations will be reviewed: kinship, return effects, and parasitism. A consideration of the subordinate role in paper wasps serves to illustrate the important concept of inclusive fitness. We close by observing that our social theory applies to creatures very broadly, including plants and parasites.

Altruistic Traits

An altruistic act is one that confers a benefit on someone at a cost to the other. Since cost is measured by a decrease in reproductive success, we know that altruistic acts are opposed by natural selection's working on the actor. They result in the production of *fewer* surviving off-

Actor   Recipient

⊗ ⟶ ○

B	C	Selfish
C	B	Altruistic
B₁	B₂	Cooperative
C₁	C₂	Spiteful

Figure 3-1

The four categories of social traits. The actor causes an effect on the recipient and on self. (*B* is benefit, *C* is cost, both measured in units of surviving offspring.)

spring. Yet altruistic traits are widespread in nature. Examples include honey bee and ant workers foregoing personal reproduction to help the queen reproduce, birds helping a pair raise their young, lionesses nursing cubs that are not their own, ground squirrels warning each other of the approach of enemies, and chimpanzees attempting to raise orphans.

Let us consider an example in more detail. In 1977, Shigeyuki Aoki discovered a previously unknown phenomenon in aphids: in *Colophina clematis* the first larval stage hatching from an egg comes in two forms, one of which never molts but remains in the first stage, where it acts as a soldier protecting the lives of the other form (Figure 3-2). The normal form molts through several stages to reach the adult form, but since the soldier form does not molt, it never reproduces. The aphid soldier is a reproductive altruist, sacrificing its

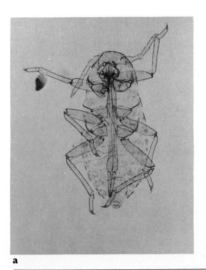
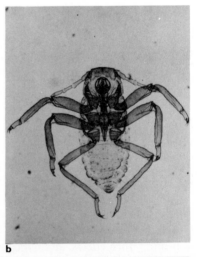

a   b

Figure 3-2

An aphid soldier and her identical twin. Two first-stage larvae of the Japanese aphid *Colophina clematis*. On the left (a) is the normal or primary-type larva, which has thin, uniform legs and long mouth parts (seen running down the center of its body) for sucking the sap of plants. The secondary form (b) acts as a soldier, defending her siblings by attacking predators (such as caterpillars), grabbing tight hold with her enlarged forelegs and midlegs and biting with her shortened mouth parts, usually killing the predator. Only primary-type larvae molt to the next stage and eventually reproduce. Both forms are produced asexually by the same mother; genetically they are like identical twins. (Photo: Shigeyuki Aoki)

entire potential reproduction for the sake of others, yet it has evolved several new features associated with its role: enlarged forelimbs and midlimbs, a tougher outside, and a shorter mouthpiece. Aoki soon discovered other species with similar forms (Figure 3-3).

We also now know that soldier forms have evolved independently in the aphids at least three times. In one species the soldier form itself has split into a larger and a smaller form (Figure 3-4). The soldiers are very effective at attacking and killing predators much larger than themselves; in some species, biting soldiers are produced in great numbers capable of driving off humans. In *Astegopteryx styracicola*, for instance, the aphids live inside partly hollow plant structures (galls), only one of which, the size of an orange may contain 100,000 aphids, of which 55% may be soldiers. These are second-stage larvae, which do not molt again but patrol inside and outside the gall; if the gall is

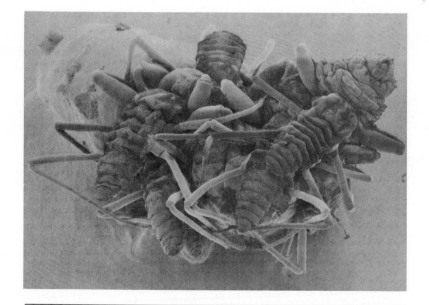

Figure 3-3

Aphid soldiers on the attack. Soldiers of the Taiwanese aphid *Pseudoregma alexanderi* (magnified 20 times) lie embedded on a predatory syrphid fly larva they have killed. They remain clamped to their victim even though both have been preserved in alcohol. Each soldier has two sharp horns on its head, although none is visible here because all have been buried in the victim. In this species, soldiers come in two forms, a large one and a smaller one (see next figure). (Photo: Masahisa Miyazaki)

Figure 3-4

Two soldier forms in one aphid species. In *Pseudoregma alexanderi* the soldiers come in two forms: (a) a large form and (b) a small form. Whether they are specialized to attack different prey is not known. Notice the greatly enlarged forelegs and the heavily sclerotized body (dark coloration). (c) The number of soldier larvae having a head (or thorax) maximum width of a given value. Notice that most individuals fall into one or the other category. (Aphid soldiers drawn from a photo by Shigeyuki Aoki; bar graph from Aoki and Miyazaki 1978)

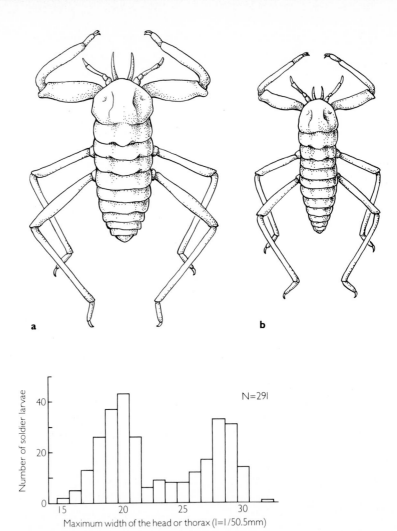

shaken, the larvae readily fall on—and bite—whatever is doing the shaking.

Our first problem, then, is to explain how natural selection might favor the spread of altruistic traits. There are three main ways: through kinship, through reciprocity, and through parasitism. The first two explanations show that apparent sacrifice by the actor may be genetically self-serving, while the third shows that selection on the recipient may induce altruism even when this is costly to the actor.

Kinship

The best way to understand the importance of kinship is to take a gene's eye view of social interactions. Under what conditions will a gene enjoy a net benefit after an interaction between two individuals? Consider an altruistic interaction in which an actor, at a cost of C, confers on a recipient a benefit of B. Imagine, for simplicity, that there is a single gene in an altruist directing the altruistic action. The gene suffers a cost in reduced copies in offspring of magnitude C. If the recipient is unrelated to the altruist, then the altruistic gene only suffers a cost, and decreases in frequency, but if the recipient is related to the actor, then there is some probability that the recipient also has a copy of the altruistic gene, by direct descent from a common ancestor. We call this probability the *degree of relatedness*, and symbolize it by r. For only a fraction of the time, equal to r, is the altruistic gene found in the recipient and enjoying there a benefit (Figure 3-5). The altruistic gene enjoys a *net* benefit when the benefit to the recipient times the degree of relatedness to the recipient is greater than the cost suffered by the altruist, or when

$$Br > C$$

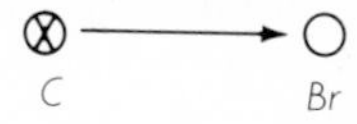

To solve particular cases, we need to be able to calculate degrees of relatedness. This is easy to do in a species such as our own, in which each individual gets roughly half its genes from each parent (who are typically unrelated to each other) and passes on half its genes to each offspring. Thus, r between offspring and parent is ½ and between parent and offspring is ½. With these two r's we can generate the other r's by tracing out the genealogical connections.

Consider your half-sibling, related through your mother but not through your father (Figure 3-6a). The probability is one-half that a gene in yourself will be found in your mother and, if she has the gene, one-half that she passed it to your sibling. Since ½ × ½ = ¼, r between you and your half-sibling is ¼. For natural selection to favor altruism toward your half-sibling, benefit must be greater than four times cost.

What is your degree of relatedness to your full-sibling? Since the two of you are related through both parents, it is necessary to consider both genealogical connections and add the values together (Figure 3-6b). As we have seen, the probability is ¼ that your sibling has any of your genes via your mother. Similarly, the probability is ¼ that your sib has any of your genes via your father. Since ¼ + ¼ = ½, r between full-siblings is ½. For altruism to a sibling to be favored, benefit need only be greater than two times cost.

Finally, consider your degree of relatedness to your cousin—for example, your mother's sister's child (Figure 3-6c). Assuming your

Net effect on actors genes:
$Br-C$

Figure 3-5

Kin-directed altruism. The actor is related to recipient by r. For every altruistic interaction, the actor's genes receive a cost; they also receive a benefit for a proportion of the time, equal to r.

(a) Half-siblings

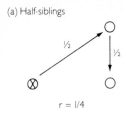

$r = 1/4$

(b) Full-siblings

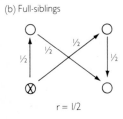

$r = 1/2$

(c) Cousins

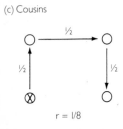

$r = 1/8$

Figure 3-6

Common degrees of relatedness in our own species: (a) half-siblings (related through one parent), (b) full-siblings (related through both parents), (c) cousins. Notice that we always begin with the actor and trace genealogical connections to the recipient.

mother and her sister are full-siblings, we reason as follows: if you have a gene, the probability is ½ that your mother had it; if your mother had it, the probability is ½ that her sister had it, and if her sister had it, the probability is ½ that she passed it on to her child. Since ½ × ½ × ½ = ⅛, *r* between first cousins is ⅛.

The general rule for calculating a degree of relatedness is obvious. As we trace a genealogical connection from one individual to another, we *multiply* the *r*'s that connect the various individuals. If two individuals are related through more than one genealogical connection, we *add* the values together that are obtained for each genealogical connection. Note that it is not necessarily true that one individual's degree of relatedness to another is the same as the other way around (for exceptions, see pp. 129 and 178). Thus, we want to be careful always to specify the *direction* of relatedness (A's relatedness to B) and, in calculating this *r*, to begin with A and end with B.

J. B. S. Haldane, the famous population geneticist, presented the essential features of kinship theory in 1955 in a popular essay on population genetics. To make matters dramatic, Haldane considered a gene that led an individual to try, at the risk of drowning, to save a drowning individual. He argued that you would have to save a cousin more than eight times as often as you drown yourself in the attempt in order for this gene to be positively favored. He then did a very curious thing: having stated the general principle, he at once severely restricted its scope. He said that the two times he himself had jumped into the river to save a drowning individual, he had acted at once without considering the possible degrees of relatedness. Thus he imagined that creatures in general would tend not to discriminate between possible recipients according to the relevant degrees of relatedness, but would instead have to react according to the *average* degree of relatedness they enjoyed to others in the area. If we travel in groups of 50 or more, as humans certainly do, then the average degree of relatedness must usually be fairly low (r << ¹⁄₁₀), so Haldane's restriction rendered kinship relevant only in special circumstances.

It is possible that a trace of egotism kept Haldane from seeing the importance of the general argument he was advancing, so quickly did he push forward his own two cases of altruism, but it seems more likely that he feared the political consequences of arguing, as we would, that selection will rapidly favor the ability to *discriminate* between intended recipients on the basis of degree of relatedness (so that average *r* is only relevant under special circumstances). If this latter possibility is the reason, then it was certainly not the last time someone blinded himself for fear of the consequences of an idea. If Copernicus dethroned us from the center of the universe and Darwin from the center of organic creation, then work on the evolution of altruism has dethroned us once again, making altruism more general than we had ap-

preciated and more deeply self-serving. This has been a painful re-
alization for some, generating minor spasms of resistance to this way
of thinking.

In any case, it fell to William Hamilton, a lowly British graduate
student in the late 1950's and early 1960's, to appreciate the importance of this reasoning. Curiously enough his attempt to make the theory more complete and to show its broad application was barely appreciated at the time. Indeed, he was told in 1963 that his work was
not up to the standards of the University of London and he could not
receive his Ph.D. for it. In order to gain employment, he rushed into
print in 1964 a paper entitled "The genetical evolution of social behavior." This turned out to be the most important advance in evolutionary theory since the work of Charles Darwin and Gregor Mendel.
We will devote Chapters 6–8 to Hamilton's kinship theory and its
applications.

For now it is worth noting that each of the examples of altruism
mentioned above is usually mediated in nature by kinship. Typically,
ant and bee workers help their mothers to raise fertile sisters and
brothers (pp. 169–179), and birds help one or both parents (pp. 184–
192), lionesses nurse cubs of sisters or cousins, ground squirrels warn
sisters, daughters, aunts and other relatives (pp. 110–114), and uncles
and aunts adopt chimpanzee orphans. Regarding aphids, it is worth
noting that they reproduce in two different ways: sexually, generating
degrees of relatedness like those in our own species, and asexually, resulting in offspring genetically identical to the mother and to each
other. It is during the asexual stage that soldiers are produced, and at
that time benefit needs merely to be greater than cost for altruism to
flourish.

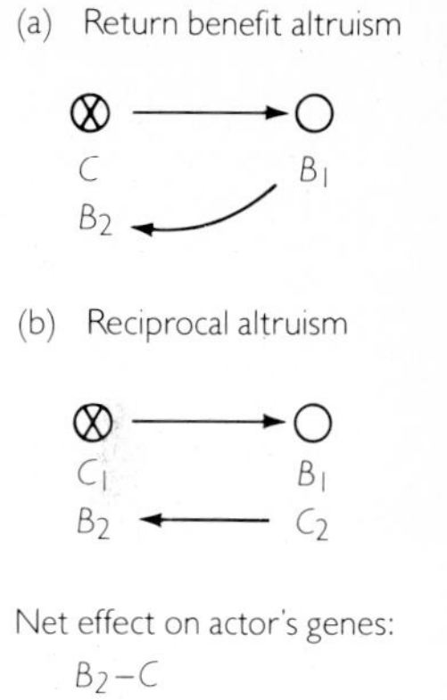

Return Effects and Reciprocity

A second way in which selection may favor an altruistic act occurs
when the act induces a return benefit to the actor larger than the initial
cost (Figure 3-7). In effect, the altruism becomes a form of cooperation. Consider, for example, certain interactions that take place in the
ocean between so-called host fish and their cleaners. Along coral reefs
in the tropics it is common to find species of small fish specialized as
cleaners of other fish. They remove ectoparasites from the skin, gills,
and mouths of various species of host fish. They are strikingly colored
and advertise their profession with a special dance. Their hosts, in
turn, often adopt a trance-like posture while being cleaned.

This interaction is symbiotic: the host loses an ectoparasite, the
cleaner gains a mouthful of food. But hosts also sometimes act altruistically toward their cleaners, warning them of danger. Since host and

(a) Return benefit altruism

(b) Reciprocal altruism

Net effect on actor's genes:

$B_2 - C$

Figure 3-7

Return benefit altruism.
(a) The initial act by the
actor somehow leads to a
return benefit for the actor
(B_2). Where this is larger
than the initial cost (C), selection will favor the initial
altruism. (b) One special
category occurs when the
return benefit comes be-
cause the recipient chooses
to act altruistically in return (reciprocal altruism).

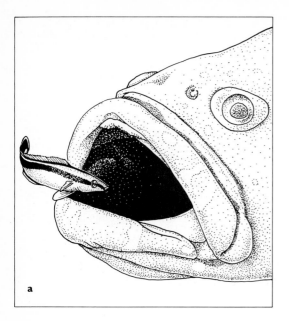 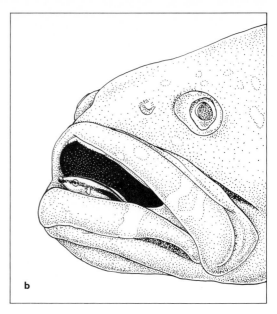

Figure 3-8

Return-benefit altruism: warning a cleaner to depart. (a) The cleaner fish *Labroides dimidiatus* is shown entering the mouth of a host fish to clean it. Should the host need to depart, it may signal the cleaner (b) by partly closing its mouth, upon which signal the cleaner exits. The host may benefit by being cleaned again in the future by the same cleaner.

cleaner are members of different species, kinship cannot be the explanation. Instead, there is good evidence that hosts often return to the same cleaner to be cleaned and, insofar as the host gains from dealing with a particular cleaner (for example, easy to locate), the host may be selected to watch out for its welfare. When a grouper fish has a cleaner in its mouth and is attacked by a predator, it does not swallow the cleaner and flee; it warns the cleaner to exit, the cleaner exits, and then the grouper flees (Figure 3-8). Note the significance of repeated interactions between the pair for this kind of altruism to evolve.

An important kind of return effect occurs when an individual chooses to act altruistically toward another who has already acted altruistically in the past. In effect, two individuals trade altruistic acts. This can be called reciprocity or *reciprocal altruism*. For example, a baboon will sometimes help another baboon in a fight (Figure 3-9). The individual who is helped is more likely in the future to aid the individual who first helped. Thus, baboons appear to trade aid in fights. The key problem is how to discriminate against cheaters, individuals who receive the benefits of altruism without reciprocating. Where individuals frequently interact, the cheater may be spotted and future altruism toward that individual curtailed. If so, the cheater may suffer in lost future altruistic benefits more than it saves in foregoing altruistic acts of its own. We shall see in Chapter 15 that some interactions between birds, between monkeys, between dolphins and whales, and between humans can be explained as cases of reciprocal altruism.

Note one difference between kinship and reciprocity as factors promoting altruism. In the case of return effects, we must remain alive to receive the return effect. There is always some chance that we will not survive to enjoy the return benefit, and this chance of mortality will lead us always to devalue future effects when compared to present effects. Of course there are other factors which may affect the chance of future interactions, such as uncertainty regarding the cheating tendencies of one's partner, and these must also act to devalue possible future effects.

Social Parasitism

A third way in which altruism may be selected is through parasitism. The recipient *induces* altruism that would normally be directed elsewhere or not displayed at all (Figure 3-10). Perhaps the best-known examples are the brood parasites of birds, species whose members are wholly specialized to lay their eggs in the nests of other birds so the hatchlings will be reared to independence by them. Since this is disadvantageous to the host, selection has favored counteradaptations on each side. The host was selected to toss out any odd-looking egg. This has led to the evolution of remarkable egg mimicry by the brood parasites. The host was in turn selected to count its eggs and abandon the nest if it contained too many eggs. This led to the behavior of throwing

Figure 3-9

Cooperative behavior in baboons. Two adult male baboons chase a third, who gives an eyelid threat in return. Such fights are often over sexual access to females near their time of ovulation. The cooperating males are almost certainly not closely related. Evidence of reciprocal benefit in such alliances is reviewed on pp. 372–73. (Photo: Irven DeVore, Anthro-Photo)

Net effect on actor's genes: C

Figure 3-10

Parasitized altruism. The recipient *induces* an altruistic act by the actor. The actor is uncompensated, suffering a cost *C*, and is selected to avoid the altruism. Larger benefit (*B*) to the recipient may lead to more rapid evolution of skilled inducers, which will tend to occur when the parasites are less numerous than their targets, since the cost per target per generation will be low but benefit to parasite per generation high.

out one host egg for each parasite egg laid. The competition continues at hatching. The parasite has been selected to hatch first and to eject the other eggs from the nest so as to monopolize subsequent parental care. When the host eggs hatch first, the hosts may crush the parasite to death against the side of the nest. The inner beaks and throats of the parasites have, like the eggs, evolved striking resemblances to the same parts of the hosts. These are the parts of the chick the parent sees just before feeding. At the very end of the relationship, the parasite may be fed even when it is several times the size of its parents and markedly different in appearance.

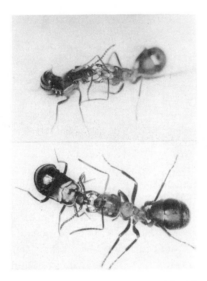

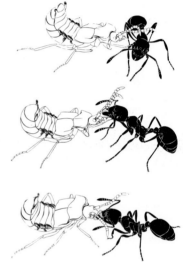

Figure 3-11

Induced altruism. The beetle *Atemeles pubicollis*, on the left, begs food from the ant *Formica polyctena*. At top it can be seen tapping the ant's inner mouth parts with its forelegs. At bottom it is being fed. The beetle is unusual among ant parasites because it lives in *Formica* nests in the summer as larvae and young adults, but lives in *Myrmica* nests in the winter (see next two figures). (Photos: Bert Hölldobler)

Figure 3-12

Social parasitism. The beetle *Atemeles pubicollis*, on the left, begs food from the ant *Myrmica laevinodis*. At top, the beetle gets the attention of the ant by tapping her on her side with its antennae. In the center, the ant turns and the beetle taps her mouth parts with its front legs. At bottom the ant responds by regurgitating food—just as she would when given similar signals by a nest mate. The most vulnerable ant is the one that has just fed and is searching for a nest mate with whom to share the food. (*From* Hölldobler 1970)

Similar parasitisms have evolved repeatedly in connection with the social insects (social bees and wasps, ants, and termites). For example, bumblebee nests are vulnerable to a closely related parasite, *Psithyrus*. In some species, the parasitic female approaches the nest cautiously, avoiding workers, and seeks to reach the underside of the comb, where males often rest. She will then spend a day or two rubbing herself against the nest and the males. Only when she has acquired the smell of the nest will she approach the real queen, whom she quickly stings to death. She then lays eggs of her own, which are cared for by the newly orphaned workers as if they were siblings. For the case of beetles parasitizing species of ants see Figures 3-11 to 3-14.

Although parasitized altruism is really a form of selfish behavior, the actor being the recipient of the altruism, we should note that all systems of altruism are vulnerable to parasitisms in which individuals

Figure 3-13

A beetle larva is fed by an ant. Larvae of the *Atemeles* beetle shown in the previous figure beg for food from worker ants much as do ant larvae, but the beetle larvae beg more vigorously; in mixed groups they are fed in preference to the ant larvae! They also feed on the ant larvae and on each other. (*From* Hölldobler 1967)

Figure 3-14

Ambivalent behavior while being parasitized. This highwayman beetle *Amphotis marginata* has just begged food from an ant *Lasius fuliginosus*. The ant has discovered the parasitism and rears back preparatory to attack, but the beetle will retract its legs and wait for the ant to depart. The highwaymen locate foraging trails of ants by scent and then ambush food-laden workers returning to the nest, begging food by tapping ants on their mouth parts the way nest mates would. (Photo: Bert Hölldobler)

Figure 3-15

Cleaner and mimic. Above is *Labroides dimidiatus*, a cleaner; below is *Aspidontus taeniatus*, a species that mimics the cleaner in appearance and behavior in order to attack host fish. (*From* Wickler 1968)

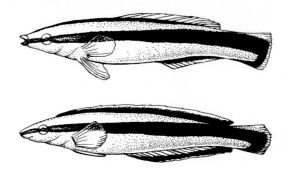

pretend a degree of relatedness they do not possess or a degree of reciprocity they will not express. Even the cleaner–host relationship in the ocean has been invaded by a parasite. One species advertises itself like a common cleaner but instead of cleaning, darts in and seizes a piece of the startled host's flesh (Figure 3-15). These considerations are by no means irrelevant to our own lives. Since there will be selection to misrepresent our actions to others—for example, pretending to be altruistic only to be selfish—it is useful to pay attention to the real effects of our actions as well as to the way in which they are represented. Real effects, of course, are measured in terms of survival and reproduction. While in our own species such effects are often indirect and hard to measure, it will still be useful to conceptualize benefits and costs as ultimately affecting survival and reproduction. When Harvard University paid me a salary for lecturing on reproductive success, which was inadequate to sustain any of my own, I felt myself to be the victim of more than an amusing irony; when the dean told me that low pay was a mark of academic excellence, I thought I was being offered ego-gratification instead of real benefits.

Selfish Traits

A selfish act is one from which the actor gains a benefit while it inflicts a cost on the recipient. Natural selection operating on the actor favors selfish acts, but the potential recipient is selected to avoid receiving the costs. We can speak of a co-evolutionary struggle between the tendency to perform selfish acts and the tendency to avoid being harmed by the selfish acts of others. Note that the relative size of benefit to cost is the relative strength of the selection pressures operating on the two parties. Thus, there is a natural tendency for defenses to be especially well developed towards highly selfish acts. This means that one should always search for counter-strategies when considering selfish acts, the more so, the greater the cost inflicted. For example, male Langur monkeys *Presbytes entellus* often kill infants under the age of six months when they first take over a group of adult females. This behavior inflicts a large cost on the reproductive success of the bereft mothers, and consequently has favored numerous counterstrategies on the part of the females (see pp. 71–77).

The same two factors that favor the spread of altruism, kinship and reciprocity, affect selection as it acts on selfishness. A genetic correlation between actor and recipient means that copies of the genes leading to selfishness located in the recipient will suffer some of the costs of their activities. Thus our rule for the positive selection of altruism through kinship is matched by a similar rule for the negative selection of selfish traits. Natural selection opposes the spread of selfish traits whenever the cost inflicted on the recipient times the actor's degree of relatedness to the recipient is greater than the benefit to the actor; that is, whenever

$$Cr > B$$

Likewise, selfish acts can generate return effects that render their net effect on the actor negative. An important subset is reciprocal selfishness, or (as we shall see later) the withholding of altruistic benefits from selfish individuals.

Being a Subordinate Paper Wasp: The Concept of Inclusive Fitness

Before going on to the other kinds of social traits, let us pause and consider the way in which selfish and altruistic traits may interact in a particular case. We choose the paper wasp *Polistes fuscatus* and concentrate on a decision many females must make: whether to work as a subordinate on someone else's nest or found a nest of her own.

In Michigan, adult female paper wasps, which are inseminated in the fall, overwinter alone but often gather together in small groups in the spring to found nests: in one study about half the wasps joined others in founding nests while the other half nested alone. In the early stages of social nesting the females struggle for dominance (Figure 3-16). This struggle soon produces a linear dominance hierarchy in which each female is dominant to all those beneath her in the hierarchy. One effect of dominance is to reduce the size of the subordinate wasp's ovaries. In Figure 3-17 we see for a related species the ovaries of females from one nest, arranged in order of dominance: the lower an individual is in the hierarchy, the smaller are her ovaries. Experiments show that a subordinate's ovaries will grow if we permit her to rise in

Figure 3-16

Dominance interaction in a paper wasp. The dominant female *Polistes fuscatus* on the left has elevated her body and is biting the leg of the subordinate female who holds herself in a characteristic posture: head, body and antennae low. (Photo: Mary Jane West Eberhard)

dominance, and conversely, if we permit a dominant wasp to be dominated by another, her ovaries will shrink.

Correlated with dominance and ovary size is egg production, as we see for one wasp nest described in Table 3-1: not only did the dominant female lay most of the eggs but she ate four out of the five laid by the second-most dominant, while only two of hers were eaten (Figure 3-18). Dominance is thus a selfish trait that increases the egg production of the most dominant female while lowering that of subordinates. The subordinates, in turn, do the bulk of the work. In Table

Figure 3-17

The association between dominance and ovary size in paper wasps Polistes gallicus. The ovaries of females from one nest are shown in decreasing order of dominance, left to right. (*From* Pardi 1948)

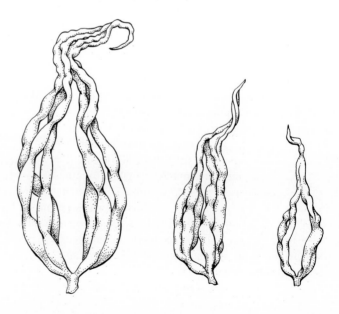

Table 3-1   The Number of Eggs Laid, the Number of Eggs of Others Eaten and the Number of Loads of Food or Paper Brought to the Nest Per Hour in *Polistes Fuscatus* as a Function of Dominance

Dominance Rank of Female	Number of Eggs Laid	Number of Eggs of Others Eaten	Foraging Rate (loads/hour)
1	9	4	.08
2	5	2	.50
3	0	0	1.41
4	0	0	1.56
5	0	0	1.80
6	0	0	1.22
7	0	0	1.50

Source: West Eberhard 1969.

3-1 each subordinate typically brings about a load and a half of food or paper to the nest, while the most dominant female rarely leaves the nest. As a result, subordinates are less likely to survive into the summer and rarely rise to dominant status.

Why does a subordinate wasp bother to help? Why doesn't she leave and found a nest of her own? A careful study by Katherine Noonan sharpens this question for us. In her study, a female nesting alone produced, on average, 18.25 reproductive offspring, while a dominant female produced about 26.7 offspring and a subordinate only 5.2. Comparing reproductive successes, a subordinate makes a considerable sacrifice, compared to nesting alone, and should be selected to desert. But her sacrifice increases the reproductive success of the most dominant female, and if the subordinate is related to her, then we ought to include this effect in our calculation of the subordinate's genetic success.

We now know for several *Polistes* species that adult females arising from the same nest are mostly sisters and preferentially congregate in the spring. For *Polistes fuscatus*, Noonan estimated that at least 75% of the·times a female associates with another, she is associating with her sister, while she associates with non-sisters at least 7% of the time. As expected, the wasps discriminate on the basis of kinship: in experiments sisters were accepted on nests for 15 minutes 67% of the time while non-sisters were accepted only 9% of the time. In nature, individual female wasps with few surviving sisters rarely join others, while females with many sisters often do, suggesting that when sisters are not available, a female chooses to reproduce alone. As we shall see later (pp. 177–179), wasps, along with ants, bees and a few others, are unusual among animals in that males arise from unfertilized eggs and

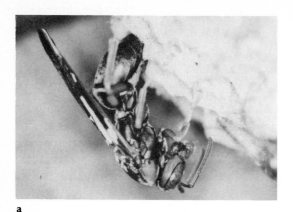

a   b

Figure 3-18

Egg laying and egg guarding. (a) A female *Polistes fuscatus* lays an egg in a cell while holding nest pulp in her mouth. She had just aggressively solicited the pulp from nest mates. Usually she applies the pulp to the nest just before egg laying. (Photo: Mary Jane West Eberhard) (b) Having laid an egg in a cell a female *P. fuscatus* inspects the cell. This inspection may last for 20 minutes and is accompanied by heightened aggressiveness to nest mates. It probably serves to protect the newly laid egg from consumption by a nest mate. Most eggs that are consumed are eaten within 15 minutes of being laid. (Photo: Mary Jane West Eberhard)

carry only one set of genes. All their sperm cells are identical, causing full sisters to be unusually closely related ($r = \frac{3}{4}$). This means that for every increase in reproductive success that a subordinate worker gives to her sister, she places $\frac{3}{4}$ as many genes into the population as if she had produced the additional young herself.

Using Noonan's figures, a subordinate is usually related to a dominant by $r = \frac{3}{4}$ and she has increased the RS of this female by 14.3 offspring. Thus, in addition to producing 5.2 offspring of her own, the subordinate female wasp also added the genetic equivalent of 10.7 more, for a total output of 15.9 (measured in units of her own offspring), which is just short of the 18.25 that females nesting alone achieve. This is exactly what we would expect, since females nesting alone—like dominant females—tend to be larger than subordinates and are therefore expected to do better. But we expect the two strategies to give similar genetic outputs; otherwise, a selection pressure would exist for females to shift toward the more profitable strategy.

Note that we have computed something new. To an individual's reproductive success we have added her effects on the reproductive success of her relatives, after devaluing the effects by her degree of relatedness to these relatives. Hamilton called this quantity an individual's *inclusive fitness*, since it includes not only her own reproductive success (that is, fitness) but also the effects on the reproductive success of relatives. More precisely, we can speak of a gene's effect on an individual's inclusive fitness: the amount by which the gene increases or decreases the reproductive success of the individual, plus the amount by which it increases or decreases the reproductive success of relatives, each amount devalued by the appropriate degree of relatedness. Just as Darwin's concept gave us a single number by which to measure natural selection, so Hamilton's wider concept also gives us a single number. We see from our example that natural selection does not favor the traits of the individual who maximizes her reproductive success but rather the traits of the one who maximizes her inclusive fitness.

Cooperative Traits

Cooperation finds a peaceful home in evolutionary theory, since selection acting on both parties favors the cooperative exchange. But cooperative actions often consist of two individuals subject to a series of costs and benefits over a period of time, so that we are naturally curious as to the extent to which they experience the costs and the benefits equally. For example, the sexual division of labor in lion hunts rather favors the male, since going upwind of herds of wildebeest and frightening them to move downwind is less tiring and less dangerous than waiting downwind and killing a wildebeest out of the thundering herd. Yet when they rejoin the females, males tend to take the "lion's share," so that the costs of the hunt are borne preferentially by the females, while the benefits appear to be preferentially enjoyed by the males. This could be viewed as a selfish interaction within the larger cooperative exchange.

Spiteful Traits

The final category of social interaction appears to have the least to say for itself. Spiteful interactions inflict costs on both parties and should be opposed by selection's acting on both. Repaying with harm someone who has harmed you is a spiteful act, since it costs you something to inflict the harm (compared to doing nothing).

Some people have been tempted to imagine that when $C_2 >> C_1$, spiteful behavior may improve the *relative* fitness of the actor. For example, two people are standing near a 4,000-meter drop, and with a shove costing very little energy, one sends the other over the cliff. Does the actor's relative standing in the species rise sufficiently to offset the cost? The factor of kinship is relevant to this discussion because if the two individuals are related, the action will be inflicting a double cost on the genes of the spiteful individual. The average degree of relatedness to any member of the species ($\bar{r}$) is usually very low, less than $\frac{1}{1000}$, so that you would have to travel very large distances in life to meet people to whom you are less related than you are to the average in the species. Spiteful behavior could only affect positively the spiteful individual's reproductive success if the cost inflicted is exceedingly high and directed preferentially toward those to whom one is very distantly related.

A good example of spiteful behavior comes from mountain sheep *Ovis canadensis*. In the winter, mountain sheep often feed at the top of a hill. Lower down on the hill the forage is better, but the risk of predation is sufficiently greater so that the sheep prefer to forage high on the hill. It sometimes happens that an adult male is injured in the winter; such an individual may choose to feed lower on the hill because he needs extra energy to recover from his injury and is willing to risk the greater chance of predation in order to recover.

When a male leaves the feeding group to feed lower down on the hill, he is sometimes followed by another male lower in the dominance hierarchy. This male does not feed but instead spends his time harassing the injured male. This is spiteful behavior. The subordinate male risks increased predation and expends energy in order to harm another individual. What is the function of this spite?

In the following spring, when the breeding season begins, the male's position in the dominance hierarchy will determine his access to females. By attacking an injured male in the winter, the subordinate male increases the chances that the more dominant individual will succumb to his injuries. Thus the subordinate may rise in the dominance hierarchy and during the breeding season receive a payoff in increased access to females and, hence, increased reproductive success. The spiteful behavior thus appears to be selected for because it is associated with a return benefit. Indeed, one could lump together the initial cost and later benefit, and if the benefit outweighs the cost, term the entire behavior selfish. It seems preferable, however, to classify behavior according to its immediate effect on animals, since the later return is by no means certain, and we are often not in a position to view the return. So, we can classify the behavior as spiteful, and argue that it is ultimately selfish when it is associated with the right kind of return benefit to the actor. For another example, see Figures 3-19 and 3-20.

Some people have imagined that selection may favor garnering more resources than necessary for personal reproductive success, in order the better to limit the reproduction of others. But experimental tests of the hypothesis do not provide support. For example, neither territory size nor rate of territorial defense increases in tree swallows when excess nest boxes (useless for the actor but useful for others) are

a   b

Figure 3-19

Gang murder in the elephant seal. (a) Four adult females gang up and kill a pup less than one week old, repeatedly biting it on the head and rump but especially on the head. One female who hovered nearby but did not take part may have been the mother. The episode lasted about five minutes. The pup was alive two hours later but in very bad shape; it died the following day. (b) From LeBoeuf's field notes: "One female, marked FYS, was more vicious and persistent than the others and she spearheaded the attack. She bit, shook and flung the pup in the air at least six times, always biting it on the head. . . . Whenever the attack started to subside, FYS would renew it with a savage bite. At one point she even bit another female on the nose and shook her." It is not known whether these females gain a return benefit (via reduced competition with their offspring), which if true would mean that this apparently spiteful behavior is actually selfish. Notice other dead pups in the picture. (Photos: Burney LeBoeuf)

Figure 3-20

An orphan is attacked again. An elephant seal pup, about three weeks old and hopelessly separated from its mother, is bitten by an adult female, who stretches over her own pup to do so. Mothers are vulnerable to stolen nursings, especially when asleep, and in elephant seals there is enormous maternal investment in each pup, mostly by way of milk. (Photo: Burney LeBoeuf)

provided. Of course, if there is a return benefit, such spite may be favored. Thus, in several macaque monkey species, adult females go out of the way to harass infant and juvenile daughters of others. This harassment apparently results in lowered female survival, compared to male, and begins when females are still in the womb! Mothers bearing female fetuses are attacked more often than mothers bearing male fetuses, and in laboratory settings they require medical attention more often; mothers requiring such attention are more likely to abort. Only females remain within the monkey troop as adults where they attempt to reproduce and to support the reproduction of female relatives. Since group size is limited by resources, attacking the daughters of others may increase the space available for one's own offspring. For female attacks on females about to copulate, see Figure 3-21.

Social Theory Applies to Plants

When I first became interested in the social lives of other species, I imagined that I was interested only in social *behavior*, meaning animals, particularly those that lived in groups. As time wore on, I came to see that social reality is much deeper than behavior. It can embrace changes in morphology, as we have seen in soldier aphids and in the enlarged or reduced ovaries of paper wasps. Thus, our social theory should also apply to plants. A tree, for example, sucks nutrients and water from the soil while striving for sunlight above ground, all of which tends to make life more difficult for its neighbors. Were a plant closely related to its neighbors, it might be selected to remove less resources from the soil and invest less energy in growth: this should leave more resources, including sunlight, for its neighbors. If their gain were greater than the donor's loss, and the corresponding degrees of relatedness high enough, selection would favor this "act" of altruism, namely, reduced investment in exploiting the environment. Note that this could evolve without the plant's measuring degrees of relatedness. It could be selected to respond instead to its usual r to neighbors, but if there is typically variation in relatedness to neighbors, plants will also be selected for that discriminate: roots may be able to recognize neighboring roots, or leaves may be able to recognize subtle differences in the chemicals emitted by neighboring leaves.

Whether any of these interactions, in fact, occurs is not yet known, but they are made more likely by the recent, remarkable discovery that plants—like animals—in effect "warn" each other of impending dangers to which the plant can take countermeasures. Unlike warning calls in animals, the activity takes place not in seconds but over a period of days, and the danger is not instant destruction by a predator but slow destruction by plant-eating insects. Also, we do not yet know

a

b

c

d

e

Figure 3-21

Return benefit spite? In this remarkable series of pictures of the langur *Presbytes entellus* we see a common monkey behavior exemplified: female harassment of a copulating couple. (a) An adult female solicits a male. (b) He mounts and copulates. (c) A second female approaches. (d) She threatens the copulating couple. (e) In order to chase the second female away, the male must dismount. The harassing female is not necessarily sexually receptive. Is she perhaps harassing in order to delay conception in the female who is copulating? This could conceivably benefit her own offspring by reducing competition. (Photos: Sarah Hrdy, Anthro-Photo)

Figure 3-22

The relationship between quality of leaves and distance of the tree from an infected tree. Plotted are the relative growth rates of caterpillars raised on leaves taken from two trees, compared to growth rates on the distant control trees. Test trees are those loaded with caterpillars on day 0. Near trees are those located 3.3 meters away. Distant control trees are 1.6 kilometers away. By day 11.5 the drop in growth rate of the caterpillars on leaves of the test trees is significant, by 14.5 days the decline for near trees becomes significant. (*From Rhoades 1983*)

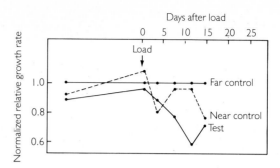

whether an injured plant elaborates a signal to that effect or whether other plants merely respond to the injury itself.

We have known for many years that a plant whose leaves are being eaten by insects may take countermeasures such as reducing the nutrients available in its leaves or increasing the percentage of toxins, which reduces the survival of insects grown on the leaves. We now know that in several species *neighbors* of the infested tree also take countermeasures. For example, among Sitka willow trees *Salix sitchensis*, neighbor trees 3.3 meters away from a tree infested with caterpillars take countermeasures which adversely affect the survival of the caterpillars, and almost as quickly as does the tree itself (14.5 days instead of 11.5: Figure 3-22). Since there are no connections between the roots of these trees and since neighbors as far as 60 meters from the attacked tree may take countermeasures, the warning is apparently communicated by the release and detection of airborne chemicals. Although it seems likely that this has involved selection on both the sender to elaborate a clear signal and on the recipient to detect it, this is not known. If neighboring trees are often related, as seems likely, then selection may favor those trees that warn their neighbors. As we shall see later, many of our theories developed for animals also apply to plants. Plants, for example, express mate choice (see Chapter 14) and may vary the sex ratio among offspring much as do animals (p. 287).

Applications to Parasites

We can illustrate the application of our social theory to parasites by considering parasites that alter the behavior of their host to their own advantage by making it more likely that the host will be eaten by a particular class of predators; this is advantageous to the parasite because its next host is one of these predators. The helminth worm *Ligula intestinalis* infects the gut of various fishes, where it somehow causes these fish to make themselves more vulnerable to fish-eating birds, which are the next host of the worm. Infected fish swim more slowly, more often alone, closer to the surface of the water, and in warmer, shallower water near the shore. The effect on bird predation rate may be substantial: in one species of fish 30% of those eaten by cormorants *Phalacrocorax carbo* were infected by this worm, while only 6% of the fish's overall population was similarly infected.

There is one case of parasitic manipulation in which the individual causing the effect is not the same one gaining the benefit. The parasite is the liver fluke *Dicrocoelium dendriticum*, and it infects ants prior to infecting ungulates such as sheep. An ant picks up the flukes in its food and most of them migrate into the ant's body cavity, where they encyst and await their next host. But one fluke (or occasionally two or three) migrates close to a major nerve controlling the ant's mouth parts. Here the fluke encysts and alters the ant's behavior: instead of returning to its nest in the evening, the ant climbs a blade of grass, bites down, and hangs on until morning. Since sheep feed on grass mostly in the evening and early morning, this must greatly increase the chance that the ant will be eaten by sheep. But the fluke controlling the ant dies with the ant; only the worms encysted in the ant's body cavity are capable of infecting sheep. Since the flukes that infect ants reproduce asexually, all those within an ant *may* be identically related, although this is not known. Ants may sometimes or often ingest flukes from several sources, thereby reducing degrees of relatedness. Our ignorance here only serves to underscore the point we are making. Critical facts are sometimes missing because it is only recently that we have begun to conceptualize the problem of the altruistic plant or parasite in such a way as to require these facts.

One form of cooperation between parasites that may be fairly general is a reduction in immediate exploitation of the host, the better to drain it over the long haul. It is possible, for example, that an individual infected by more than one strain of malarial parasite suffers a more severe attack than someone infected by a single strain, whose members, being asexually reproduced, are genetically identical and may more easily be selected for restraint in exploiting their host. This is consistent with some recent evidence showing that intensity of infection, as measured by number of parasites per red blood cell in a lizard, correlates with an increasing tendency to produce a 1:1 sex ratio of malarial parasites. This is consistent because, as we shall see in Chapter 11, 1:1 sex ratios are associated with outbreeding and reduced r's, while the female-biased sex ratios found in mild infections are, in other creatures, associated with close inbreeding and high degrees of relatedness.

Whatever the facts, we can see from these examples that life is intrinsically social. All creatures must consume something of value in order to live and must consume more in order to grow and reproduce. This consumption is often at the expense of other members of the same species, so that even staying alive may, in effect, be a selfish act. Reproduction, in turn, is intrinsically social—genes and energy are invested in the production of others—and in many species this also requires the cooperation of two individuals (male and female).

Summary

Neglecting zero effects, there are only four categories of social traits: altruistic, selfish, cooperative, and spiteful. These are defined by reference to their effects on actor and recipient. An altruistic trait is one that benefits the recipient at a cost to the actor. While superficially opposed by natural selection, such traits are common in nature, as illustrated by soldier aphids, a special form that does not reproduce but acts to defend its siblings from predators. Altruistic traits may have evolved by three different routes: kinship effects, return effects, or parasitism.

Kinship may favor altruism whenever there is some chance that any gene found in the actor has a copy located in the recipient via direct descent from a common ancestor. This chance is called degree of relatedness (r). Natural selection favors altruism whenever $Br > C$, where B is benefit and C is cost. Degrees of relatedness may easily be calculated by multiplying together r's that connect two individuals genealogically. When individuals are related through more than one individual, r's for the different genealogical connections are summed.

Selection may also favor altruism when it induces a return benefit sufficient to offset the initial cost. An important category is reciprocal effects, in which individuals trade altruistic acts. This kind of altruism will evolve only if altruists are able to interact often enough to discriminate against individuals who do not reciprocate by withholding altruistic benefits from them. Selection may also favor the inducement of altruism, a form of social parasitism.

Selfish traits benefit the actor at a cost to the recipient. When these are related, selection opposes selfish acts whenever $Cr > B$. Selection may also oppose selfish acts because of their return effects. In paper wasps, females dominate others on their nest; this is a selfish act. Subordinate females often choose to remain on the nest, where they primarily help the dominant female reproduce. Although subordinates achieve much lower reproductive success than solitary females, when we add to this their effect on the reproductive success of their sisters, they achieve almost the same genetic representation as solitary females. Natural selection favors not the individual that maximizes her reproductive success but the individual that maximizes her inclusive fitness, where this includes personal reproductive success plus effects on relatives, devalued by the appropriate degrees of relatedness.

Cooperative traits benefit both actor and recipient but may often have selfish components. Purely spiteful behavior is favored only under highly specialized and unlikely conditions, but apparently spiteful behavior can be favored when it, in fact, induces a return benefit.

Social theory applies to all species. Staying alive and reproducing are often selfish acts and their expression in any species may be limited by r's to neighbors or by return effects. Reproduction is a social event and, in addition, often requires the cooperation of two individuals. Social effects in plants and parasites are illustrated by the fact that trees sometimes, in effect, warn each other of impending attack, while some parasites are known to sacrifice their lives for others.

Chapter 4

The Group
Selection Fallacy

AFTER 1859 THERE were three main ways in which people tried to blunt the force of Darwin's argument for evolution and natural selection. The first was to raise doubts about whether evolution had occurred, incidentally distracting attention from the more important concept, natural selection, the force directing evolution. The second was to acknowledge natural selection but to minimize its significance by making it appear to be very weak in its effect. In a long-lived species such as humans, death and reproduction are fairly rare events, so it is easy to imagine that in day-to-day life, most of what we do has very little effect on our survival or reproduction. But as we have already seen in Chapter 2, even apparently trivial traits such as birth order in piglets may be subject to strong selection.

The third approach was to replace the idea that natural selection acts on the individual with the notion that natural selection acts for the benefit of the group or the species. This fallacy has been so widespread and so powerful in its repercussions that it deserves special treatment. Indeed, I remember well the grip it had on my own mind—and the confusion it generated—while I was still an undergraduate. So many disciplines conceptualized the human condition in terms of individual versus society. Sociology and anthropology seemed to claim that the larger unit was the key to understanding the smaller one. Societies, groups, species—all evolved mechanisms by which individuals are merely unconscious tools in their larger designs. In the extreme position, the larger groups were imagined to have the cohesiveness and interconnectedness usually associated with individual organisms. We call this the "group selection fallacy" or "species benefit fallacy," which claims that selection has operated at a higher level than the individual, that is, at the level of the group or species, favoring traits that allow these larger units to survive. In this chapter we review some examples of species-benefit reasoning in biology, and describe their flaws.

Species-Advantage Reasoning Within Biology

Darwin was very clear on the idea that natural selection favors traits that benefit the individual possessing them but that are not necessarily beneficial for larger groups, such as the species itself. Indeed, on several occasions he explicitly rejected species-advantage reasoning. For example, Darwin gathered evidence showing that in many species the two sexes are produced in a roughly 50:50 ratio, yet he could not see how natural selection might affect the sex ratio. He concluded:

> I formerly thought that when a tendency to produce the two sexes in equal numbers was advantageous for the species, it would follow from natural selection, but I now see that the whole problem is so intricate that it is safer to leave its solution for the future.

That is, when Darwin could not solve the problem in terms of natural selection, he held his peace and did not invent a higher-level explanation. Fisher solved the problem in 1930 (see Chapter 11).

Darwin regarded his work as a clear break with past biology, which believed in an instantaneous creation of an unchanging world whose various parts functioned together like so many parts of a clock. In this view it was easy to imagine that individuals could be created to subserve the interest of the species or, indeed, the interest of other species. Darwin's concept required that life be created over long periods of time by a natural process based on *individual* differences in reproductive success.

We might imagine that Darwin's successors clearly grasped his concept and began to apply it systematically to all biological phenomena, but quite the opposite seems to have happened. After a brief period, biologists returned en masse to the species-advantage view, only to cite Darwin as their support! For example, since it was then clear that numerous species had become extinct, it was easy to imagine that natural selection refers not to differential individual success but to differential success of species; that is, natural selection favors traits that permit species to survive. It certainly seems true that extinction is a selective process; that is, species that become extinct are not a random set of species available at the time. But this selection does not explain the traits of the species that do survive. To explain the traits of the species that do survive, we must understand how natural selection acts *within* each species.

Thus, for over 100 years after Darwin, most biologists believed that natural selection favors traits that are good for the species. In retrospect, there seem to be at least three reasons for this curious development. First, the existence of altruistic traits in nature seemed to require the concept of species advantage. As we have already seen, this is an illusion. Most examples of altruism can easily be explained by some benefit to kin or return benefit to the altruist, but these explanations were not well developed until the 1960's and '70's.

The second reason for species-advantage reasoning is that biologists have mostly studied non-social traits and for these traits it matters little whether we imagine they evolve for the benefit of the species or for the benefit of those possessing the traits. For example, the human kneecap locks in place when we are standing upright, thereby saving us energy. Chimpanzees and gorillas lack such a locking device. The device evolved because it benefitted those possessing it, not because it helped the species itself survive, but the latter notion leads to no misunderstanding of how the kneecap operates, since we assume the kneecap benefits the species by benefitting those possessing it. By contrast, social traits immediately pose a problem, because a benefit may be conferred on one individual at a cost to another. Considering the benefit of the species, we may imagine that social traits will evolve as long as the net effect on everyone is positive. But—in the absence of kinship or return effects—selection on the actor favors selfish traits no matter how large the cost that is inflicted and never favors altruistic acts no matter how great the benefit conferred.

Finally, the early application of Darwinian thinking to human social problems frightened people back to thinking on the level of the species. Shortly after Darwin's work, "Social Darwinists" argued in favor of 19th-century capitalism in the following sort of way: The poor are less fit than the rich because they have already lost out in competition for resources (that is, because they are poor). Therefore, the rich should do nothing to ameliorate the condition of the poor since this would interfere with natural selection and, therefore, with nature's plan. Indeed, we can improve on nature's plan by actively selecting against the interests of the poor. Thus, for the good of the species, the poor should suffer their poverty, augmented by a biological prejudice against them!

But, in fact, fitness refers to reproductive success, or the production of surviving offspring. It can only be demonstrated after the fact. In principle, we cannot look at two people and say which is more fit until both are dead and their surviving offspring have been counted. If the poor leave more surviving offspring than do the rich, as is sometimes true, then they are, by evolutionary definition, more fit, and the whole argument can be stood on its head. In reaction to this kind of thinking, I believe, people returned to species-advantage reasoning, partly because it was incapable of saying much about social interactions *within* species, especially social conflict.

Male–Male Aggression and Differential
Female Mortality: Good for the Species?

To get the flavor of species-benefit reasoning we must really study some examples. One comes to us from the Nobel-Prize-winning biologist, Konrad Lorenz, and argues that natural selection favors aggressiveness between males because it is good for the species:

> Darwin had already raised the question of the survival value of fighting, and he has given us an enlightening answer. It is always favorable to the future of the species if the stronger of two rivals takes possession either of the territory or the desired female.

Darwin had indeed argued that natural selection favors fighting, since it is often possible for one individual through force or threat of force to seize a valuable item, whether food, territory, or a contested female, but he did not speculate on whether this was good for the species as a whole. Since males have evolved a musculature and weapons to support fighting, which females of the same species have not, it seems safe to imagine that fighting and associated traits are beneficial to the males possessing them, but not to anyone else. Whether it is advantageous for the species to have the stronger of two males take possession of a desired female may depend upon female choice. Does the female, in fact, prefer the stronger of two males? And if so, why? That is, how does the female's mating with the stronger of two males improve the quality or quantity of her own offspring (see Chapter 14)?

A second example concerns mortality rates in certain female mammals. In most mammals the sexes are produced in a nearly 50:50 ratio. But since males suffer higher mortality, the adult sex ratio usually contains more females than males. This pattern appears to be reversed in several species of the small mammal genus *Reithrodontomys*. Females appear to survive less well than do males, so that the adult sex ratio is biased toward males. Why might this be so? One student of the subject has argued as follows:

> It is usual to assume that fewer males than females are necessary because a few males can inseminate many females, and therefore it is *bio-energetically more efficient* for males to be expendable, while females are at a premium because they bear the young. However, for a small, secretive mammal there may be a *selective advantage* in having many reproductively active males moving about to assure insemination of any female that comes into estrus rather than assume that one male may contact several females. . . . [E]xcess males are *advantageous* in assuring insemination through more frequent contact of male and female. [Italics mine.]

Note that the author explains higher mortality rates in one sex by reference to the entire species. Thus it is bio-energetically more efficient for males to be expendable because they invest very little in raising the young. Likewise, the author uses the concept of selective advantage at the species level. After all, it cannot be advantageous for females to die at a more rapid rate in order to make sure that surviving females will have many active sexual partners. The only way to explain the lower survival rate of one sex is to show that individuals of that sex possess traits that give them some advantage in reproduction, at the cost of lowered survival during the rest of their life. In other words, the cost–benefit analysis must be made at the level of the individuals themselves, not at the level of the entire species (see Chapter 12). Notice how easily the species-benefit theory given above can be changed so as to explain any pattern of mortality.

Infanticide in Langur Monkeys

One example of species-benefit reasoning has been studied in some detail and serves to illustrate some important differences between explanations based on natural selection and those based on group selection. The example is infanticide in langur monkeys *Presbytes entellus*—the deliberate murder of infants by adult males. Reported since the 19th century, langur infanticide is common in several localities although it is not universal (Figure 4-1). Similar behavior has been reported in lions, gorillas, some other species of monkeys and many others.

Langur monkeys travel in groups of about 10–20 adult females and their young, to which is attached a single, dominant adult male. The other males travel in large, all-male groups, dominant members of which occasionally try to displace the adult male attached to a group of adult females. When such displacement is successful, the new male often starts to kill dependent offspring. In particular, he tries to kill infants up to about six months of age or older, but begins by concentrating on the youngest. In addition, he often kills infants that are born during the first months following his takeover, but not thereafter.

In a graphic account Sarah Hrdy has described male behavior in the wake of a takeover:

In the early afternoon of August 12, 1972, the Hillside troop feeds quietly in the trees lining the drive of the Phiroze school. There is an undercurrent of tension, however. Very deliberately, females in the troop avoid Mug. If Mug climbs into a tree where a female is feeding, she immediately moves to another tree. If Mug follows, the female returns to the tree where she was before. At 4:00 p.m., the male, who is grunting softly, climbs to the top of a nearby roof. From his high vantage point, Mug strikes a sentinel's pose and stares off into the distance. Then, abruptly, the stocky gray form descends from his rooftop perch, charges directly at Itch, and grabs at the infant clinging to her belly. Itch whirls to face Mug, plants her front paws as she lunges at him, grimaces, and bares her teeth. Within seconds of this assault, old Sol, the one-armed female

Figure 4-1

Summary of cases of probable infanticide involving two troops of langurs. Under the name of each troop is the male or males associated with the troop. Shifty pursued a double-usurper strategy for several years, that is, he attempted to drive all other males from two troops at the same time. Notice that the repeated disappearance of infants is associated with male take-overs. (From Hrdy 1977)

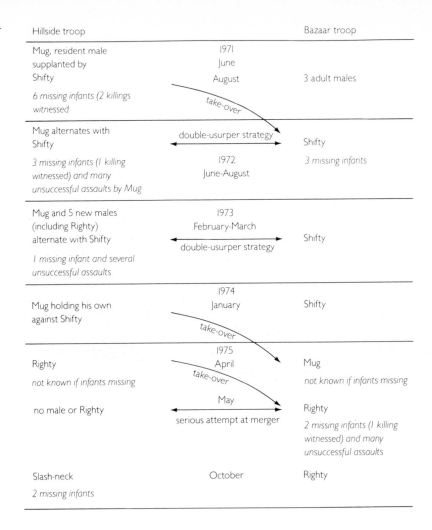

Hillside troop		Bazaar troop
Mug, resident male supplanted by Shifty *6 missing infants (2 killings witnessed*	1971 June August take-over	3 adult males
Mug alternates with Shifty *3 missing infants (1 killing witnessed) and many unsuccessful assaults by Mug*	double-usurper strategy 1972 June-August	Shifty *3 missing infants*
Mug and 5 new males (including Righty) alternate with Shifty *1 missing infant and several unsuccessful assaults*	1973 February-March double-usurper strategy	Shifty
Mug holding his own against Shifty	1974 January take-over	Shifty
Righty *not known if infants missing*	1975 April take-over	Mug *not known if infants missing*
no male or Righty	May serious attempt at merger	Righty *2 missing infants (1 killing witnessed) and many unsuccessful assaults*
Slash-neck *2 missing infants*	October	Righty

Pawless, and a third, unidentified female join in the counterattack. The three defenders interpose themselves between Mug and Itch, lunge at the male, and chase him up a tree. In the wake of this assault, a trembling Itch is left alone to hold her infant Scratch, who is spattered with flecks of blood.

Mug had recently begun associating with the Hillside troop and on August 12 he repeatedly charged Itch and her infant and on each occasion other females intervened. Attacks on this and other infants continued throughout August and into September. Although it is sometimes claimed that infants are injured in attacks on adult females, the following description by Hrdy suggests the reverse is more likely.

Figure 4-2

Two females fight to save an infant. In this famous photo, two langur females, Pawless and Sol, intervene daringly to rescue Scratch, Itch's infant,
from Mug, a male who has spent more than a month trying to kill the infant. The infant is severely wounded (see next photo). Pawless lacks one arm.
She and Sol are older, low-ranking females, without infants, who repeatedly
intervene on behalf of Scratch and other infants. One year later Itch was the
only female to come to the aid of Pawless when her infant was attacked by
another set of male invaders. (Photo: Sarah Hrdy, Anthro-Photo)

Maternal negligence was almost surely at issue in the second attack on Scratch
that I witnessed on September 5, when Itch let Scratch fall out of a jacaranda
tree. Mug was sitting alertly on a wall 50 feet away. When the infant fell, he
raced to it, reaching it just split seconds before Sol and Pawless, who had been
sitting on the wall on either side of him. The mother was the last of these four
individuals to reach her infant. Only by a fierce assault were the females able
to wrest the infant from his attacker. After Itch had retrieved her infant, Sol
persisted in chasing and slapping at Mug.

On September 9 an attack thwarted by two adult females left Scratch
severely injured (Figures 4-2 and 4-3).

Figure 4-3

Victim of an infanticidal attack. Itch sits with her badly injured offspring, Scratch, the morning after the attack shown in the previous photo. Mug's toothmarks are visible on the infant's head and the infant has also suffered a deep wound to its lower abdomen and upper thigh. Scratch subsequently disappeared. (Photo: Sarah Hrdy, Anthro-Photo)

This langur infanticidal behavior has traditionally been explained as a social pathology with no adaptive meaning or as a device for regulating population numbers. In the latter explanation, infanticide is practiced for the good of the species: it tends to ensure that population numbers will be in tune with available resources. This hypothesis predicts an association between the density of monkeys and the frequency of infanticide. In fact, infanticide does occur more frequently in densely populated areas, but apparently because take-overs are then more frequent. No other feature of the behavior can be explained as a device to regulate population size. Why does the population only need regulation when a new male takes over? Some males may be associated with a group of females for as long as five years. Why do males kill only young infants, which are vulnerable to mortality anyway and make a small contribution to future numbers? The best way to regulate a population would be to kill juvenile and sub-adult females. We would also like to know why it is the male who regulates the population. It would be easier if females ceased to breed when numbers were becoming large. Finally, why do females resist the killing impulses of the males?

The facts just cited easily fit an interpretation based on individual advantage. The male did not father the offspring he kills. If he is dis-

Figure 4-4

An infanticidal male copulates. Shortly after his take-over of the Hillside troop in 1971 Shifty copulated with females whose infants had disappeared. Here, one estrous female waits to the left while Shifty copulates in the mist with her troop-mate. Both of these females lost infants shortly after Shifty's take-over. (Photo: Sarah Hrdy, Anthro-Photo)

tantly related to the male he displaces and to the adult females—as seems typically to be the case—then he is only distantly related to the offspring that he kills. So the cost to the male is small, while he enjoys an almost immediate benefit in reproductive success. By killing a suckling infant, the male brings its mother more quickly into reproductive readiness. This is because females who are nursing infants are not ovulating and thus are not ready to produce their next offspring. By killing off their infants, the male saves himself the amount of female effort that would have been expended on unrelated offspring. Females who lose infants come into estrus within weeks, sometimes within days (see Figure 4-4).

When langur infants are about eight months old, they are weaned and no longer inhibit maternal reproduction. They are no threat to the male's reproductive success and he ignores them. The male's preference for killing the very young is also explicable, since these are the ones that will require the greatest investment before their mothers are freed to breed again. Finally, since the gestation period is about seven months in langurs, if a male kills infants born during the six months succeeding his takeover, he will not kill any of his own but will continue to kill those fathered by the previous male.

We expect the langur mothers to resist the male's behavior. Their own reproductive success is directly harmed by the murder of their infants, so we expect natural selection to favor countermeasures. Several of these have now been described. First, females may join the old male in fighting a takeover by a new male. Second, after the takeover, older females, typically related to the mother, may join her in resisting the assault; they are sometimes successful (see Figure 4-2). Third, females with older (but still dependent) young may leave the group with the old male or travel alone on the border of the group until the infant is past the age of vulnerability (see Figures 4-5 and 4-6). They presumably trade a greater risk of predation for a lowered risk of infanticide.

Finally, females may employ deceit so as to fool the new male into accepting their infant. One female came into estrus when the old male was still in the group. He copulated with her many times and a month later she failed to have her period and was judged to be pregnant. Another month later she again failed to have her period and showed changes in coloration that confirmed she was pregnant. At this time, the old male was ousted from the group and a new male took over. Within days this female came into estrus (or pseudoestrus, since she presumably was not ovulating). She copulated numerous times with

Figure 4-5

Female counter-strategy to male infanticide. After the attack on her infant, Pawless and her daughter travelled much of the time apart from the rest of their Hillside troop. Except for one occasion, they returned only when the former male, Shifty, was present and the invading males absent. Pawless later rejoined the troop. (Photo: Sarah Hrdy, Anthro-Photo)

the new male. Five months later she gave birth to an infant who was almost certainly conceived seven months earlier. The new male tolerated the infant as if it was his own.

Because many adult females are associated with a single adult male, there is tremendous pressure from all-male bands to displace the breeding male. This pressure appears to be especially intense where the monkeys are found at high numbers. Such a system, in which only a few males breed who are themselves at constant risk of being displaced by other males anxious to breed, puts a premium on breeding as fast as possible. This is presumably why infanticide is so well developed in langurs. For scenes of infanticide in another monkey, a ground squirrel, and a wasp see Figures 4-7, 4-8, and 4-9.

Consequences of Species-Advantage Reasoning

Species-advantage reasoning has some important consequences. First, it tends to elevate one individual's self-interest to that of the species, thereby tending to justify that individual's behavior. In our example, the adult male's self-interest has been elevated to that of the species: it

Figure 4-6

Another female counter-strategy. Two adult females with offspring temporarily join the males ousted from their troop: the large male in the foreground on the left, grinding his teeth just prior to an encounter with other males, and his eight sons. (Photo: Sarah Hrdy, Anthro-Photo)

Figure 4-7

A different kind of infanticide. In the Belding's ground squirrel *Spermophilus beldingi*, infanticide occurs but is not caused by breeding males. Perpetrators are either yearling males, as in this case, or newly immigrated adult females, who may thereby open up some space for their offspring. Yearling males typically cannibalize their victim, as in this case, consuming the head and thoracic area first. This is perhaps the benefit they gain. The victim shown is the youngest victim recorded; it still has webbed feet and is about five days old. (Photo: Paul Sherman)

Figure 4-8

Victim of foul play. Species: red colobus *Colobus badius. Age*: about five weeks. *Sex*: male. *Cause of death*: repeated bites to the head and body. *Alleged assailant*: "Whitey," sub-adult male, rapidly rising in rank, precocious in development, subsequently attacks or murders all other infants under six months of age, with the exception of his half-sibling. *Evolutionary reason*: Whitey acts to bring mothers of the murdered infants into sexual receptivity. His own mother migrated into the group when he was *in utero*. Thus, he is only distantly related to the infants he attacks. (Photo: Lysa Leland)

is given a new name. What he is concerned with is population regulation, something that is beneficial to all. By contrast, the viewpoint of natural selection should make us suspicious of the notion that one individual's self-interest is the same as that of the species. Instead, we expect individuals to act in their own self-interest. In a verbal species such as our own, we also expect individuals to represent these actions as being in everyone's self-interest.

Secondly, group-selection reasoning distracts our attention from conflict within social groups and from maneuvers that have evolved to mediate such conflict. Hence, unconsciously such reasoning tends to render other individuals powerless. "The male has the power and the power is good for the species." Such reasoning prevents us from predicting female counterstrategies and from seeing the limits to male power. By contrast, an approach based on natural selection demands these counterstrategies. We expect to find them, and we analyze any social interaction from the standpoint of each of the individuals affected by it.

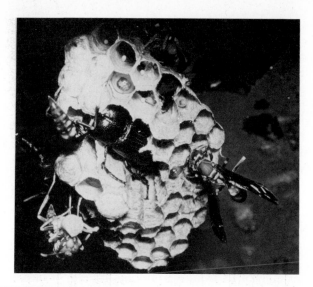

Figure 4-9

Yet another kind of infanticide. While the nest is being consumed by a predatory beetle, one female wasp *Polistes versicolor* has seized a larva and begun
to eat it (lower left). The larva is probably her niece or nephew but may be
her offspring. Since the larva will almost certainly die anyway, its consumption by a close relative may actually increase its inclusive fitness. Whether
this has rendered the experience pleasurable to the larva is another matter.
Note the three eggs in the top cells, capped pupal cells to their left, and the
larva in the cell immediately below the middle egg. (Photo: John Pickering)

The concept of natural selection also has implications for the ease
with which nature can be studied. Little as we know about the causes
of individual mortality, we know much less about the disappearance of
species or large groups within species. Differences in individual reproductive success often show up within a single generation; costs and
benefits may be registered over much shorter periods of time. But extinction of groups or species occurs over many generations. Thus,
species-advantage thinking permits us to argue too easily on any side
of a question. Arguing from natural selection promises to eliminate
some alternatives as logically unsound, and others as contrary to
the facts.

The Group Selection Theory
of V. C. Wynne-Edwards

Species advantage reasoning might have continued right into the 1980's
were it not for V. C. Wynne-Edwards. In 1962, he published a massive,

beautifully written book in which he reviewed hundreds of species and presented the first coherent view of social behavior based on group selection. If his theory was true, almost all of animal behavior could be viewed as the product of group selection. If it was false, then by extension, many other examples of species-advantage and group-selection arguments would be seen as false.

Wynne-Edwards argued that there is a process of group selection going on within each species that is analogous to species selection in that it eliminates some groups within the species while leaving others to survive. Which groups does group selection favor? Wynne-Edwards argued that the primary problem that organisms face is eating themselves out of house and home. Since creatures are capable of reproducing very rapidly, they are capable in times of plenty of increasing so greatly in numbers that they may then be incapable of surviving in times of shortage. The only way to overcome this problem, Wynne-Edwards argued, is to evolve mechanisms within the group that tend to prevent individuals from reproducing in times of plenty in order later not to oversaturate the food supply.

My own contact with Wynne-Edwards' thinking was brief but vivid. In preparing a children's book on caribou, I had come across an exciting new explanation for the function of caribou antlers: antlers are devices by which the caribou species regulates its own numbers within safe limits. Caribou males use their antlers during the rutting season to fight with other males. Antler contact is sexually arousing to these males and, prior to the rut, solitary males will often thrash their antlers in bushes, sometimes achieving an erection. If bushes are scarce, males may not get aroused prior to the rut and may perform poorly during the rut, thus lowering the group's reproductivity. When environmental conditions are unfavorable, bushes are few in number, male caribou will fail to be aroused, and population reproduction will be limited. Antlers function as devices through which the species limits its own numbers in order to decrease its chances of extinction.

I thought this idea was splendid—it provided a larger meaning for the caribou's antlers and his associated reproductive behavior. I was so excited I tried out the idea on my teacher, a biologist overseeing my writing, and I will never forget his reaction. He sat there, the way a priest might if his favorite altar boy had come and relayed heresy to him. He wanted to be friendly, but there was a deeply pained expression on his face. He turned sideways and said to himself, "Sounds like Wynne-Edwards to me."

He began to point out flaws in the argument. Imagine, he said, that there is genetic variability in the tendency of caribou males to be sexually aroused by thrashing in bushes. Imagine that some males do not require the thrashing in order to become aroused. These males will outbreed those that do. Their numbers will begin to increase in the population. At first this will have only a small effect on total population size. Generations must go by before the spread of this "reproductively selfish" type is so far advanced that population numbers may be dangerously high, yet by this time many of these individuals will have dispersed to new areas and populations formerly lacking this selfish type. Once again they will increase in numbers. Given natural selection and dispersal, there is no way the species can retain the tendency to shut off reproduction when bushes are scarce. In addition, he said, there is no evidence that reproduction by female caribou is ever limited by male sexual arousal. There is, in fact, intense male–male competition to fertilize females, and most males are excluded from breeding by the activities of other males, not by failure to become aroused. Thrashing in bushes, he said, is a way of cleaning antlers and practicing their use, and antlers evolved because they are useful weapons for increasing the number of females one can guard from other males.

His arguments left me in a state of confusion. If he was right, then whole worlds of sociology, anthropology, and political science came crashing to the ground. He seemed to be saying that individual reproductive advantage is such a powerful force in nature that benefit to group or species can be neglected as a possible explanation; that group selection is illogical because it requires individuals and their descendants to stay put for long periods of time, even in the face of impending group extinction, which would strongly select for dispersal.

To help me through this crisis, my teacher had me read the work of Wynne-Edwards and his chief opponent, David Lack. I read them for three straight days, one after the other. At first, Wynne-Edwards reconvinced me every time I reread him. But as I continued, his grasp on my thinking began to weaken. Finally, Wynne-Edwards let go completely and slipped off into the surrounding gloom. The evidence was clear: natural selection refers to differences in *individual* reproductive success. When ascribing a function to a trait it only makes sense to see how the trait increases the reproductive success of those bearing the trait, not the reproductive success of the group or the species.

The Evidence Against Wynne-Edwards' Theory

David Lack and other biologists organized several kinds of arguments and evidence against Wynne-Edwards' theory. To give a clearer picture of the possibility of evolution for population regulation, let us review them briefly here. Four points seem especially important.

(1) *There are no natural phenomena that require Wynne-Edwards' explanation.* That is, there are no behaviors that cannot more easily be explained in terms of natural selection. This is important because the

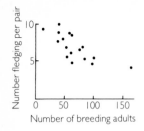

Figure 4-10

The relationship between reproductive success and density. Number of chicks fledged per pair is plotted as a function of number of breeding pairs of great tits in Oxford, England. Notice that as density increases, breeding success declines. (*From* Lack 1966)

existence of unexplained phenomena would necessitate a new or revised theory.

Consider one example. Wynne-Edwards argued that a dominance hierarchy is group selected because in times of food shortage a dominance hierarchy may force individuals at the bottom of the hierarchy to starve to death or die quickly from causes related to lack of food, thus permitting individuals at the top to survive in good condition. A more equitable arrangement might see all the individuals in substandard shape, none of which has a good chance of surviving continued food shortage. This is, in fact, a consequence of a dominance hierarchy, but not necessarily its evolved function.

Dominance hierarchies are maintained in many social species throughout the year, whether food is scarce or abundant. Indeed, stronger hierarchies exist with regard to access to members of the opposite sex than with regard to food. These hierarchies function to give the dominant individual, without fighting, resources it would probably be able to seize if it did fight for them, while the subordinate loses what it would be likely to lose anyway, but saves energy and the risk of injury. The strategy of being subordinate is to accept the lesser of two evils—dispersion or subordinance—in the face of another individual's dominance. Where individuals survive very poorly outside a social group, dispersion may be the more costly alternative.

(2) *There is a natural regulation of animal numbers that operates to prevent the kind of massive extinctions Wynne-Edwards imagined.* This is because of density-dependent factors that operate on mortality and reproduction. That is, when density is low, mortality is likewise low and reproductive rate high, while at high numbers it is more difficult to stay alive and to reproduce, so mortality is high and reproductivity low. Thus, population numbers naturally tend to increase when low and to decrease when high.

Consider, for example, the breeding biology of the great tit *Parus major*. When density of breeding pairs is high, each pair is able to raise only a few offspring (Figure 4-10). So there is a direct relationship between the amount of resources presently available and current reproductivity. Since creatures are attempting to maximize the number of their surviving offspring, they will produce many young when resources are widely available, but will adjust their reproduction downward as resources become more scarce. What we do not expect to find is individuals reproducing at well below the rate they could successfully, all in anticipation of distant, future, population-wide side effects. Thus, in many ways the most important kind of evidence against Wynne-Edwards concerns the actual reproductivity of animals in nature. Could animals easily do better? Wynne-Edwards argues yes; Lack says no.

(3) *Actual data on breeding success suggest that animals are reproducing as rapidly as circumstances permit and without concern*

over the possibility that the species will survive some future resource limitation. Since Wynne-Edwards predicts that creatures with a very low rate of increase are capable of reproducing much more rapidly, it is natural to test his theory on birds that have small clutches. For example, the laysan albatross *Diomedea immutabilis* lays only one egg a year. Could it raise more young if it laid more eggs? To find out, a chick was added to each of 18 nests a few days after hatching. This created 18 nests with two chicks. These nests were compared to 18 nests with only one chick. After three and a half months, only 5 chicks survived from the 36 in the experimental nests, while 12 of the 18 chicks from the one-chick nests survived. Parents were unable to find enough food to feed two chicks, and most of these starved to death. Similar manipulations with other birds produced similar results. Thus, so far as we can measure, the typical clutch size in nature appears to be that which maximizes the number surviving to independence (see Table 4-1).

(4) *Group selection is a weak force and depends on very low migration rates.* Wynne-Edwards' group-selection theory is really a return-effect argument in which the effect takes a very long time to

Table 4-1   Relationship Between Brood Size and Number of Chicks Fledged in the Swift *Apus apus*

Year	Brood Size*	Percent Lost	Number Fledged per Brood
1958	1	28.6%	0.71
	2	4.7	1.95
	3	8.3	2.75
	4	50.0	2.00
1959	1	0	1.00
	2	0	2.00
	3	0	3.00
	4	31.2	2.75
1960	1	0	1.00
	2	5.6	1.89
	3	22.2	2.33
	4	70.0	1.20
1961	1	0	1.00
	2	2.8	1.95
	3	22.2	2.33
	4	65.0	1.40

Source: Perring 1964.

* Broods of 4 were created artifically by adding a newly hatched chick to broods of 3. Broods of 4 occur naturally less than 1% of the time.

return and during which time individuals are free to migrate away from the effect they are producing. If numbers are beginning to reach a level at which extinction would be likely, individuals will be selected to move to less densely settled areas. Thus, at the heart of Wynne-Edwards' theory there is a logical flaw involving animal movements. Wynne-Edwards' theory requires that individuals be restricted to groups, forced to suffer the consequences of each other's over-reproduction, and free only occasionally to colonize areas vacated by extinction of the over-reproductive.

Perhaps because people of my generation first learned what natural selection really meant by reading Wynne-Edwards, we retain a soft spot in our hearts for him. As much as anyone else he "fathered" a whole new line of work in animal behavior. By inadvertently revealing the folly of the alternative, he brought about a renewed appreciation of natural selection: natural selection seems to insist that traits prove themselves at a very local level if they are to become part of life. Typically they must sustain the life of the individual bearing them or increase its reproductivity. Failing this, they must aid closely related individuals, and the less related the recipient, the larger must be the benefit/cost ratio. In addition, some traits do not benefit the organism or its relatives immediately but by somehow inducing a return benefit later. The less certain the return now, the greater must be its later benefit. Evolution is, thus, conservative, tending to build up life-sustaining systems via their local effects, and insisting that the more locally a trait is harmful the more beneficial must be its larger effect if it is to become part of life.

In our desire to see some unity and harmony in life we sometimes wish that natural selection did not act on individuals. How nice it would be, we think, if evolution favored traits that were good for the species, the biosphere, or the universe. Perhaps wisdom lies in trying to see virtues in the way in which life actually evolves. By favoring traits that are locally useful, life is provided a secure foundation for improvement. Attributes negative to themselves are rapidly eliminated, and natural selection gradually weaves together a whole series of individually beneficial traits. Kinship and reciprocity, in turn, provide bases on which selection can mold larger cooperative units.

Summary

Darwin's theory of natural selection refers to differences in individual reproductive success, yet for 100 years after Darwin most biologists imagined that selection favors traits that are good for the group or the species. Examples of such reasoning include the notion that males fight in order to elevate to breeding status genes that are good for the species and the notion that females suffer higher mortality in some species in order to increase the number of available mates for those who do survive.

Infanticide in langurs and some other animals has been interpreted as a group-selected device that regulates population size, but this interpretation fails to explain why males kill only dependent young, and kill only during the months immediately following a group takeover. It also fails to explain female counterstrategies. All these facts, however, are readily explained by the argument that infanticide of unrelated young by males increases the number of young they father and is thus favored by natural selection, while selection of females favors avoiding the murder of their young. Species-benefit reasoning distracts our attention from social conflict and too easily rationalizes the behavior of one actor as being beneficial to all.

The species-advantage tradition in biology came to an end when Wynne-Edwards' massive group-selection theory was shown to be in error. In particular it was shown that birds are reproducing in nature as fast as resources permit, and population numbers are regulated by external checks that act in a density-dependent manner, favoring survival and reproduction when numbers are relatively low. The concept of group selection relies on unrealistic return effects to counteract the spread of traits favored by natural selection. Traits that lower individual reproductive success tend automatically to be eliminated from the population so that later, possible indirect benefits to the species itself are irrelevant to the traits' fate within the species. All traits must begin as rare in a species and can increase in frequency only if they increase the survival and reproductivity of those bearing the traits.

Chapter 5

Genetics, Behavior, and Learning

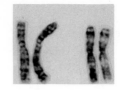

W<small>E CAN NO</small> longer postpone the subject of genetics. Since we know that evolutionary change results from natural selection acting on genetic variability, it will be useful for us to have a concrete image of the gene and some understanding of how genes affect development. To better understand kinship we also need to pay attention to the way in which genes propagate themselves. And because behavior and learning are often assumed to lack genetic components, we need to review a few findings that suggest otherwise.

We begin with a description of the biparental system of inheritance found in humans and many other species. We then describe how genes reproduce themselves and control the ongoing chemical machinery of the cell. We give an example of a simple genetic trait and we review the way in which genes are passed from one individual to another. Regarding behavior, we review studies that show that behavioral traits, like any others, are genetically variable and can evolve. Finally, we close by citing evidence that even the most general kinds of learning abilities in animals have been shaped by the action of natural selection.

The Diploid Genetic System of Human Beings

Humans have what is known as a *diploid* sexual genetic system; that is, the system is bi-parental, with each person having two sets of genes, one from each parent. Two processes are involved: one is the production of sex cells, each of which has only one set of genes, and the second is the union of one sex cell from each parent to form a new individual. Let us begin our account with the union of sex cells.

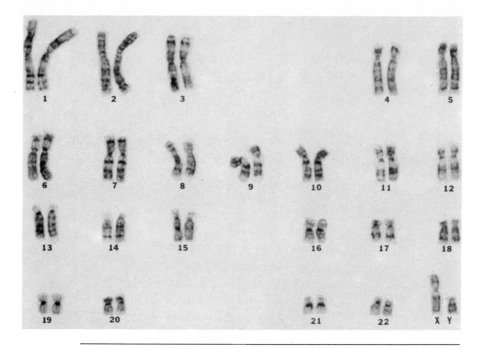

Figure 5-1

A full set (23 pairs) of human chromosomes. Since this individual is XY, he is male. The banding reveals chromosome structure. The vast majority of human genes are located on these 23 pairs of chromosomes, but a few are also found in organelles. (Photo: Beverly S. Emanuel)

Imagine a human sperm cell about to penetrate an egg cell. Each cell contains a nucleus and each nucleus contains one set of 23 chromosomes. A *chromosome* can be thought of as a chemical thread along which is arrayed a series of genes, like beads along string. Along a typical human chromosome there may be 20,000 genes or more. For most of the life of the cell, the chromosomes are dispersed throughout the nucleus, and are not visible.

Surrounding the nucleus is cytoplasm, which is the chemical material in which occur most of the cell's chemical reactions. Although the nucleus is surrounded by a membrane, the membrane is permeable in both directions. Within the cytoplasm are organelles. These provide special functions such as energy (mitochondria) or photosynthesis (chloroplasts). Every cell organelle has some genetic material that helps direct the activities of the organelle. Thus, two kinds of genetic material are united when sperm and egg unite: nuclear and extranuclear. Because there are at least 1000 nuclear genes for each organelle gene, we expect the nucleus to control the development of most traits.

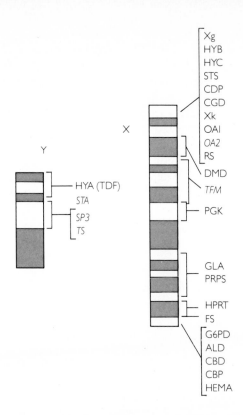

Figure 5-2

Gene maps for the X and Y chromosomes in humans. Depicted are some of the 115 loci found on the X chromosome and their relative locations. Note how comparatively few traits are found on the Y chromosome. This may be because it has been largely shut down by the action of the other chromosomes (see p. 136). *HEMA* refers to the locus controlling hemophilia, *CBD* and *CBP* to the loci controlling color blindness. (Redrawn from map by V. A. McKusick)

When egg and sperm nuclei fuse, 23 pairs of chromosomes are brought together. At certain stages of their life chromosomes condense and can be photographed. These pictures have allowed us to portray the chromosomes in order of decreasing size (Figure 5-1). In every pair of chromosomes, except for the sex chromosomes in the male, each member of a pair is matched to the other, having the same length and the same structure, ultimately ensuring the same structure of genes along its length. Any arbitrary location on a chromosome is called a *locus* (plural: *loci*). There are two genes at each locus, one on each of the paired chromosomes. For a map of genetic loci on the human sex chromosomes (X and Y) see Figure 5-2. We can list all of an individual's genes; we call such a list the individual's *genotype*. The resulting structure, physiology, and behavior we call the individual's *phenotype*.

As we travel down the length of two paired chromosomes, we can compare the genes at each locus. We can ask if they are the same, in which case the individual is said to be *homozygous* at that locus, or different, in which case the individual is *heterozygous*. To the extent that the genes tend to be identical at most loci, the two sets of genes are redundant. At one time it was believed that most of the diploid genotype was redundant. This had the corollary that natural selection

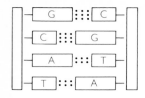

Figure 5-3

The basic structure of DNA. Two backbones run parallel to each other. At regular intervals on each backbone are stuck bases (A, T, C, and G), which form chemical bonds with the complementary base pair stuck on the other backbone. A and T are complementary; so are C and G. The genetic code within an individual refers to the precise sequence of base pairs in its DNA.

was infrequent, locus by locus, and that most of the genetic variation that did occur was deleterious. Once the proper techniques were developed, it was discovered that many loci within each individual are heterozygous. It has been estimated, for example, that within the typical human, 10% of all loci are heterozygous. Consistent with this discovery we believe that natural selection may be active at many of the loci, and that much of the variation may be maintained by frequency-dependent selection that favors genes when they are rare and opposes them when they are common.

We can also compare genes at the same locus in a variety of individuals. For example, we can sample a population to see the degree to which loci are heterozygous in the population. Among humans, about 30% of all loci show some variability within any population of 50–200 individuals.

How Do Genes Replicate Themselves, and How Do They Control Development?

Chromosomes were discovered and photographed in the 19th century; by the early 20th century, chromosomes were known to be the places along which genes were located. But until the 1950's, two problems baffled biologists: how exactly do genes reproduce themselves, and how do they control development? These questions were answered with the discovery of the chemical structure of *deoxyribonucleic acid* (*DNA*), which is the principal material of chromosomes. Far from being a string with a bunch of beads on it, a single strand of DNA is more like railroad tracks held together by a series of ties (Figure 5-3). Each tie consists of two parts, each of which is attached to a track. The parts of the tie come in four different lengths. Thus, DNA consists of two long parallel strands of backbone material connected by what are called base pairs—pairs of chemical bases of complementary length. Each base pair is connected to a backbone, and the two sets of base pairs are joined together by chemical bonds. The backbones are twisted so as to form two parallel helices; hence the nickname for DNA: the double helix.

The chemical structure of DNA is ideally suited to DNA's reproducing itself, for if each of the chemical bonds holding the two strands together were broken, then we would end up with two backbones, each containing a set of bases sticking out from it (see Figure 5-4). Owing to their chemical structure, the bases tend naturally to attract their complementary pairs from the surrounding chemical soup. Once this has happened, enzymes within the nucleus construct a second backbone. Thus, in principle, the reproduction of DNA is simple: enzymes separate the DNA into two parts and each separated half of

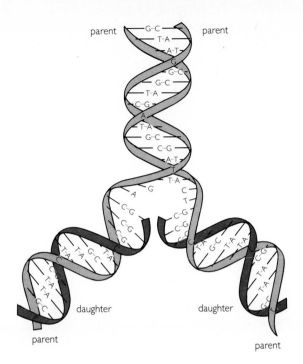

parent   parent

daughter   daughter

parent

parent

Figure 5-4

The replication of DNA.
The two parental strands of
DNA are shown bound to
each other by the chemical
bonds between the bases
sticking out from their
backbones. At a certain
point these strands are
separated—the chemical
bonds between the comple-
mentary bases having been
broken—and each naked
backbone with bases sticking out attracts the complementary bases from the
surrounding chemical soup
and new backbones are
added. The result: the reproduction of one double
helix into two. A, T, G and
C denote the four different
types of bases.

the molecule acts as a template on which the complementary half is
assembled.

An enormous amount of genetic reproduction goes on in the development of each individual organism. Bear in mind that we humans
begin as a single cell and end up with more than 100 billion cells. Each
time two new cells are produced from a single cell, the entire genetic
constitution of the nucleus must be duplicated, and the two halves separated cleanly into two daughter cells. This is achieved by an elaborate
and remarkable mechanism that almost invariably replicates (or reproduces) all the genes faithfully and inserts a full set of genes into
each new cell. Occasionally a tiny section of DNA *mutates*, or under-
goes a spontaneous change in structure. Most mutations appear to result from mistakes in the replication of DNA. In this way, one particular base pair may be replaced by another pair or simply deleted or
added to the genotype (see Figure 5-5). Within a section of DNA large
enough to code for a single protein, this kind of mutation probably
happens once in 100,000 replications. These rare events are the basis
for all evolutionary change.

The ability of DNA to act as a template, which permits the duplication of genes, also provides the basis for genetic control of cellular
processes. Genes exert their effects on the cell in the following manner.

Figure 5-5

Three classes of mutation.
At top is the common, or
"wild-type," gene. Below it
are three kinds of muta-
tions: base pair changed,
base pair added (or de-
leted), set of pairs deleted
(or added). A, T, G, and C
refer to the four kinds of
bases.

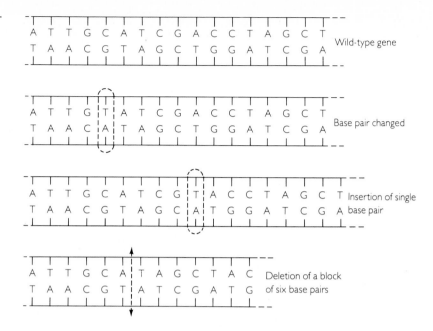

A certain enzyme separates a small section of the DNA helix. Each
separated section then attracts its opposite base pair and another enzyme constructs a backbone along this small section of bases. This
new backbone is made of ribonucleic acid (RNA), a material only
slightly different from DNA. The genetic material then comes back together, that is, the helix strands are again parallel and connected, but a
unit of messenger RNA has been produced that migrates out of the nucleus and connects with other RNA segments at connecting places
called "ribosomes." These segments then act as templates for sections
of RNA that connect to amino acids, the building blocks of proteins.
Thus, proteins are built up by having a linear array of messenger RNA
molecules attract the linear array of amino acids that make up the proteins. Proteins, in turn, run the cellular chemical machinery. Enzymes
are proteins and enzymes control the rate of chemical reactions. The
reactions determine what substances enter and leave the cell, how the
cell is constructed, how it grows and divides, and so on. This great
biochemical discovery is summarized as follows:
DNA → RNA → protein.

Every cell in the body has a full set of genes, yet cells are remarkably different. There are nerve cells, muscle cells, cells that secrete hormones, cells that devour invading organisms, and so on. This cellular
differentiation is brought about by the selective turning on of different
genes in different cells. Part of the genetic machinery consists of the

genes that regulate the process by which other genes are turned on and off. The process by which a single set of genes in one cell controls development into an exceedingly complicated multicellular creature such as the human being is still not a well understood process. But cells are known to differentiate very early in the embryo's development as a result of differences in intracellular environment, and successive differentiation into tissues creates new environments that tend to naturally turn on appropriate genes, leading to further differentiation.

Since DNA → RNA → protein, each gene may be thought of as a portion of DNA that creates a single protein. In this sense a single gene determines a single trait (protein). But since a protein can have many different effects on other parts of the body, each gene typically affects many traits. Likewise, each trait typically requires the action of many different genes. Sometimes a single gene has a major effect on the appearance of the individual bearing it. For example, the gene for blue eyes, when carried in two copies, produces blue eyes instead of brown eyes. But there are always other genes which have at least a minor effect on the same trait. These genes are sometimes called modifier genes, since their effect is to modify a trait. Thus, some individuals have slightly bluer eyes, some have blue-green eyes, some have blue eyes with a little speckling, and so on. These minor variations are caused by differences in the other genes these individuals carry. The importance of modifier genes is that they permit much subtler traits to evolve than if genes had only major effects and one set of genes never modified another.

A Simple Genetic Trait in the Giant Water Bug

Let us consider a simple example of a genetic trait. Normal individuals of the giant water bug *Abedus herberti* are uniformly mottled brown on their backs, but occasionally an individual appears in nature with a bright yellow stripe running down its back (Figure 5-6). When such abnormal individuals are brought into the laboratory and mated with each other and with normal individuals, the yellow stripe is found to be inherited by the offspring and inherited with particular frequencies, suggesting that the trait is controlled by a single dominant gene. Let us symbolize this gene by S and the normal gene by s. S is said to be dominant over s when individuals who are heterozygous (that is, with an Ss gene pair) have the striped trait rather than the normal trait or some intermediate version. When two heterozygous water bugs mate with each other, four kinds of offspring are expected, in equal numbers: SS, sS, Ss, and ss. Since the first three kinds all bear a stripe, offspring of the mating will have the stripe three times as often as they lack it. When an Ss individual mates with a normal ss, offspring will come in

Figure 5-6

Simple genetic trait in the giant water bug. On the left is a larva with a bright yellow stripe running down the center of its back. *On the right* is a normally colored larva, for comparison. Controlled breeding demonstrates that the yellow stripe is under the control of a single dominant gene. (Photos: Robert Smith)

a   b

two equally frequent forms, Ss and ss. These are precisely the ratios Robert Smith obtained when he performed these matings. Were the trait controlled by genes at more than one locus, other ratios would result from these various matings. The study of such trait ratios has permitted biologists to identify a series of genetic traits and to map their locations, relative to each other, on chromosomes. (For an example of such a map in our own species, see Figure 5-2).

The isolation of simple, easily identified genetic traits such as the yellow stripe in giant water bugs is useful to students of social behavior because the traits permit kinship to be measured. For example, if we wish to know whether the first or the second of two males that mate with a female fertilizes the greater number of her eggs, we can use striped and normal males in competition with each other and count the number of striped offspring produced (see pp. 266–267).

The Transmission of Genes:
Meiosis and Recombination

As cells reproduce themselves, they undergo a process called mitosis, in which each of the chromosomes in the nucleus is duplicated and the two full sets of chromosomes separate from each other and migrate to a separate daughter cell (see Figure 5-7 left). There is one exception to this rule in our own species: when sex cells are being formed, only half of the chromosomes go into each sex cell, and one and only one chromosome from each pair enters the sex cell. The process by which the chromosome pairs are separated and placed in the sex cells is called *meiosis* (Figure 5-7 right). Each pair of chromosomes segregates independently, so successive sex cells produced by the same individual differ greatly in their chromosomal makeup. Since there is a 50/50 chance that any given chromosome will be found in a sex cell, and since there are 23 pairs of chromosomes, there are 2^{23} possible combinations of chromosomes that can be found among the sex cells.

The variability of sex cells is further increased by *crossing over*: when two chromosomes are duplicated prior to meiosis, the pairs attach to each other somewhere along their lengths and exchange parts (Figure 5-8). Crossing over has the effect of further increasing the number of possible combinations of genes among offspring. You might think that the effect of crossing over is about the same as having twice as many chromosomes, each half as large. But crossing over can occur anywhere along the length of a chromosome, so almost all combinations of genes will eventually be separated from each other during meiosis. Thus, new combinations can be formed between almost *any* two genes and passed on to offspring.

In summary: Sexual reproduction involves meiosis and recombination. Crossing over further increases recombination, suggesting that the primary function of sex is to generate genetic novelty among the offspring. The production of genetic novelty naturally tends to break up gene combinations that selection in the past had brought together, although this price is presumably repaid by permitting a better evolutionary response to the new conditions facing the next generation. The exact way in which selection favors the production of genetically variable offspring is considered in Chapter 13.

Genetics and Behavior

Regarding inheritance of behavioral traits, it is important to recognize that our nervous system has an enormous effect on our behavior and that every nerve cell has a full set of genes, many of which are turned on in order to regulate the chemistry of the cell. The chemistry of the nerve cell, in turn, affects the transmission of messages across the cell and from one cell to another. Thus, genes can affect the transmission of neural impulses and can, in principle, have minute and specific effects on behavior. We are still largely ignorant of how most of these effects come about, but evidence from breeding experiments in animals leaves no doubt that many behavioral traits have a genetic basis.

Let us consider a typical example of a breeding program affecting a behavioral trait. In the field cricket *Gryllus integer*, males adopt one

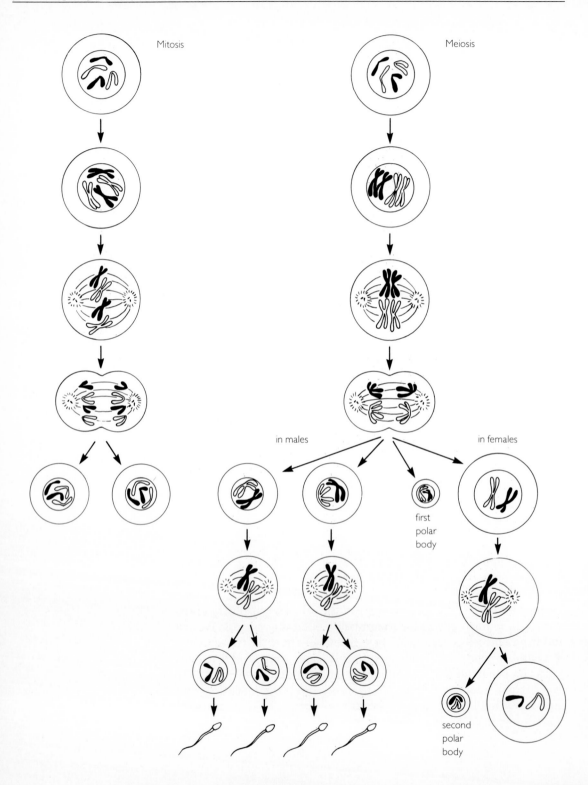

Mitosis

Meiosis

in males

in females

first
polar
body

second
polar
body

Figure 5-7

Mitosis and meiosis. On the left the process of mitosis is summarized; *on the right*, meiosis, which differs in its later stages in males and females. In the first stage, two pairs of chromosomes are shown. These then reproduce themselves and pair. In the next stage, the paired and doubled chromosomes become attached to the spindle apparatus (which is shown radiating out from two points in the cell). The spindle apparatus then pulls one of the doubled chromosomes from each set (two per pair) to the opposite sides of the cell. The cell now splits into two. One parent cell with a full set of chromosomes has given rise to two with full sets of chromosomes. In meiosis in females, the cell's cytoplasm is split very unevenly and the smaller daughter cell degenerates (first polar body). Meiosis continues with one more cell division, one member of each pair of chromosomes being pulled to opposite sides of the cell. Again in females one of the daughter cells degenerates (second polar body). Each final product of meiosis has only one set of chromosomes (here shown as one each from the original two pairs). In females some chromosomes some of the time are able to avoid migration into polar bodies; this favors their spread (pp. 138–139).

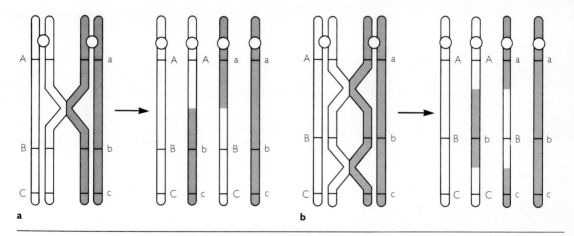

Figure 5-8

Crossing over. (a) Matched pairs of chromosomes exchange parts during meiosis (only one member of each pair exchanges parts). (b) Exchange may occur at more than one location. Crossing over increases enormously the degree of genetic variability generated by meiosis. Rates and locations of crossing over are thought to be under the control of selection. For factors favoring production of increased genetic variability among offspring, see Chapter 13.

of two strategies for mating with females. They either call frequently to attract females or they call infrequently or not at all and intercept females attracted to calling males. It is possible that the strategy adopted by the male depends entirely on circumstances—for example, males in isolation call more frequently than those in groups—but the existence of two strategies implies past selection on genetic variation, and it would be surprising if this variation had been entirely exhausted. William Cade initiated a breeding program that has settled the matter. The average calling time of each male cricket over a series of evenings was measured. In the first generation several males at the low end of calling frequency and several at the high end were mated with females chosen at random. Within one generation the high and low lines differed significantly in average calling time and this difference increased with succeeding generations selected in the same directions (Figure 5-9). In short, the trait of calling time has a true genetic component such that intense, artificial selection produces substantial change in the trait in only four generations. Incidentally, one disadvantage of calling is that it attracts a parasitic fly whose larvae consume the male crickets within seven days, while otherwise they might survive for weeks. Non-calling males are much less vulnerable to the parasite. The frequency of fly parasitism varies year by year, which is interesting because we now believe that fluctuating selection, especially from parasites, may favor the maintenance of large amounts of genetic variability (see pp. 322–324).

A variety of other techniques have also been used to demonstrate the genetic components of behavior. For instance, studies of the offspring of controlled matings like those used with the giant water bug have isolated a series of genes in mice and fruit flies that have behavioral effects. The creation of inbred lines of mice (and dogs) differing genetically from each other reveal behavioral differences even when the environment is held constant. Crosses between closely related bird species that differ in their behavior produce offspring with a mixture of behaviors, suggesting a mixture of genes acting at several loci. The examples go on. Taken together they suggest that behavioral traits are no different from other traits in having genetic components.

Nor is this conclusion different for human beings. The study of the genetics of human behavior has largely concentrated on seeing to what degree the behavior of genetic relatives is more alike than the behavior of otherwise similar people. Of course, genetic relatives are more likely to share similar environments than are two randomly chosen people, so special attention has been directed to the study of twins. Twins come in two genetic kinds, but are otherwise similar. Identical twins result from the duplication of a fertilized cell, so every gene found in one twin is also found in the other. Fraternal twins come from two different egg cells, each of which has been fertilized by a different sperm cell, so they are genetically equivalent to full siblings (same fa-

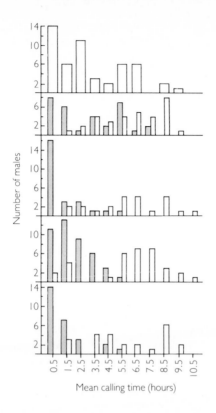

Number of males

Mean calling time (hours)

Figure 5-9

Artificial selection for singing and silent behavior in field crickets. Each graph shows the number of males that sang for a given number of hours per night. The top distribution is before selection. The next graph is after one generation of selection, and so on. Black bars represent offspring of males selected because of reduced calling time; white bars, offspring of males that called for prolonged periods. The black and white distributions are significantly different in every generation. (*From* Cade 1981)

ther). The two kinds of twins are not environmentally identical; for example, fraternal twinning rates vary as a function of mother's age and ethnic group while identical twinning rates do not. Nevertheless, twins' environments are largely similar, and a comparison between the two categories is instructive. When identical twins are compared with fraternal twins on a variety of psychological traits, including IQ, identical twins are found to be especially similar, while fraternal twins often differ as much as do singleton siblings (Table 5-1 and Figure 5-10).

Although these findings are valuable, the study of identical twins often reveals striking similarities in very specific characteristics even when the twins are separated at birth and reared apart (Figure 5-11). Thomas Bouchard has studied such pairs of identical twins intensively. Consider one such pair. Oskar and Jack, who are 47 years old, were separated shortly after birth (Figure 5-12, p. 102). Their mother took Oskar to Germany, where he was raised as a Catholic and a Nazi by his grandmother, while Jack was raised in the Caribbean as a Jew by his father and spent part of his youth in Israel. As might be expected, the men now lead very different lives. Oskar is an industrial supervisor in Germany, married, and a skier, while Jack runs a clothing store in

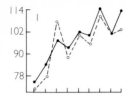

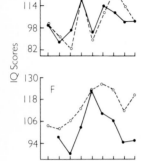

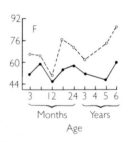

Figure 5-10

IQ scores for identical and fraternal twins. Each graph shows IQ scores as a function of age for a pair of twins. The top two are for identical twins (I), the bottom two for fraternal twins (F). Note the closer correspondence between the identical twins. (*From Wilson 1978*)

Table 5-1   The Average Correlation Between Identical Twins or Fraternal Twins in Various Personality Measures (as Well as Height and Weight)

Trait	Number of Studies	Average Correlation Between Twins *	
		Fraternal	*Identical*
Extraversion	30	.25	.52
Neuroticism	23	.22	.51
Masculinity-Femininity	7	.17	.43
Conformity	5	.20	.41
Flexibility	7	.27	.46
Impulsiveness	6	.29	.48
Height		.50	.93
Weight		.43	.83

Source: Bouchard 1984.

* A score of 1.0 shows perfect correlation; 0 is uncorrelated.

San Diego, is separated from his wife, and enjoys sailing. The following is taken from a recent article describing Bouchard's work.

Their families had never corresponded, yet similarities were evident when they first met at the airport. Both sported mustaches, and two-pocket shirts with epaulets. Each had his wire-rimmed glasses with him. They share abundant idiosyncrasies. The twins like spicy foods and sweet liquors, are absent-minded, fall asleep in front of the television, think it is funny to sneeze in a crowd of strangers, flush the toilet before using it, store rubberbands on their wrists, read magazines from back to front, and dip buttered toast in their coffee.

Another pair of identical twins, Irene and Jeanette, age 35, were separated after birth and brought up in England and Scotland. They turn out to have the same phobias.

Both are claustrophobic and balk when invited into a cubicle for their electroencephalograms. They independently agree to enter the cubicle if the door were left open. Both are timid about ocean bathing; they resolve the problem by backing in slowly. Neither likes escalators. Both are compulsive counters of everything they see, such as the wheels of trucks; both count themselves to sleep.

Some of these similarities are surely coincidental, but it may be doubted whether all are. Identical twins as a genetic category are very unusual because every single gene (except very rare mutations) is iden-

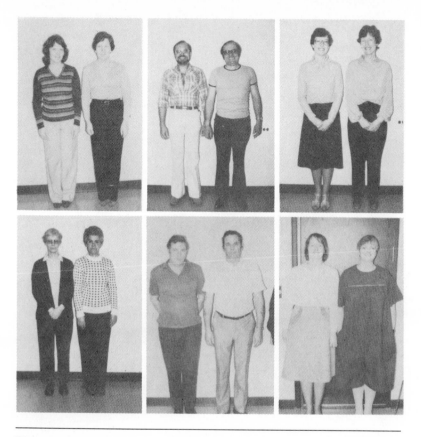

Figure 5-11

Postures of identical and fraternal twins reared apart. The top row shows three sets of identical twins; each individual was separated from its twin shortly after birth and raised separately. Below, for comparison, a set of fraternal twins, similarly reared apart. For their photo, the twins were simply asked to stand with their backs to the wall, yet the identical twins unconsciously assumed similar postures (notice the placement of the hands). (Photos: Thomas Bouchard)

tically shared. Thus, even traits with multiple genetic effects (probably the majority of all traits) have an identical genetic basis in identical twins. By contrast, at each variable locus of a full sibling, there is only a half chance of genetic identity by virtue of relatedness. Thus, traits affected by many loci will be similar between such siblings but rarely *identical*.

Many human traits—the language we speak, the religion we practice, the table manners we display—have a very large environmental

Figure 5-12

Identical twins reared apart. Oskar Stohr, the twin on the left, and Jack Yufe were separated shortly after birth and raised apart, and were not until recently reunited. Striking behavioral similarities in such twins give evidence of genetic components of behavior. (Photo: Robert Burroughs)

component. We speak Chinese because we are raised in a Chinese-speaking family, not because we have Chinese-speaking genes. But strong environmental effects do not mean that genetic effects are completely absent. Perhaps generations of speaking a language with certain sounds has made learning easier where these sounds are concerned. Or there may be genetic variation in the ease with which any language is acquired. And so on. Judging from the enormous variety of animal behavior that has evolved, there has been enormous genetic variation in the past in behavioral traits.

Innate Components of Learning Abilities

According to classical learning theory, animals have a very general ability to learn; yet the more we have studied learning abilities, the more impressed we have become with their specificity. Far from having a single general ability to learn, animals have a variety of more or less specific learning abilities, each tailored by natural selection to a particular task.

Consider the way in which male birds learn to sing, a subject that has been unusually well studied. We now know that learning plays a part in the development of almost all bird song. In order to develop his species-typical song, a male bird must hear other birds singing. He usually has the innate ability to recognize his own species' song and memorizes it in preference to others. In some species the sensitive period for such learning is over long before the male actually begins to sing, so the bird does not learn to sing through simple imitation (itself a sophisticated form of learning). Rather, once the bird starts to sing, he listens to what he sings and tries to match it to the song he has earlier memorized.

When we compare different species we find that even closely related bird species often differ in the details of their song learning. In some species the period of memorization ends before the birds sing, in others it ends in their first season of singing, and in some species males continue to memorize new songs throughout their life. The accuracy of the mimicry also varies—from species in which copying is very exact to ones in which only elements are copied and each individual bird supplies many novel elements. Species also differ in the degree to which individuals copy the song of another species: some do not, some copy only elements, and some copy the song of another species only when they can interact with the individuals producing the song. Still other species perform remarkable feats of copying. For instance, young marsh warblers *Acrocephalus palustris* in their first year of life move south in the autumn from Europe to East Africa, learning the sounds around them as they go, which do not include the calls of adults of their own species. Upon return in the spring each male mimics, on average, the sounds of 76 other species; these are produced in rapid succession, jumbled together in different patterns, almost like a continually varying account of the male's fall and winter travels!

What these and other studies suggest is that learning abilities, like other behavioral traits, have evolved very precise forms in different species. No simple general process can account for vocal learning in any one bird species, much less its variability across several species. We are only now beginning to wonder why selection favors different forms of vocal learning in different birds. One clue comes from considering the intended listener. In some species, male song is primarily a form of territorial assertion, meant to repel other males. In such species, males may be under pressure to develop a species-typical song early in the breeding season, which will select for early, more or less exact copying, sometimes supplemented by later mimicry of territorial neighbors. In other species, song is primarily directed at females and this may select for more variable male repertoires, based partly on mimicry of other species.

The role of the female in molding male song has recently received dramatic confirmation in the cowbird *Molothrus ater*. Adult females prefer the song of their own subspecies, and a male housed during vocal learning with a female tends to develop her preferred song—even when the male is of another subspecies and only hears his own subspecies' song! Males also develop more original songs when housed with cowbird females (instead of members of other species); this presumably reflects female preference. Male cowbirds appear to have evolved to notice the effect of bird song on adult females of their own species and to mimic or retain those elements that females prefer. Once again we see that natural selection has fashioned a very specific form of learning to fit a particular situation.

Natural Selection and Food-related Learning in Rats

Perhaps the most general learning ability is the ability, through trial and error, to modify behavior in response to reward and punishment; yet this general ability still shows biases that may be interpreted in terms of selection. In classical learning theory any stimulus can come to evoke any response, but the response must be reinforced (rewarded or punished) within seconds for learning to occur. These two assumptions provided an attractive image of trial-and-error learning: the animal is completely open-minded and it uses closeness in time as its indicator of causality. We now know that neither assumption is true.

Consider a rat tasting food that differs in flavor (sugared or unsugared) or in size of item (large or small). John Garcia and his co-workers showed that when electrical shock is paired with the size of the food item eaten, the rat quickly learns to avoid the size being punished but does not learn to associate the flavor of the food with electrical shock, even though the rat is shocked immediately after beginning to eat the wrong-flavored food. By contrast, when food is paired with x-ray treatment—which induces illness an hour later—the rat quickly learns to avoid the flavored food but does not learn to associate size of food item eaten with suffering the illness. The experiments showed that both cues were capable of being learned and both forms of punishment were capable of teaching, but learning occurred only for certain combinations of stimulus and punishment (Table 5-2): flavor could easily be associated with sickness, but size of pellet could not; size of pellet could be associated with electrical shock, but flavor

Table 5-2 Design of Garcia's Rat Learning Experiment *

Group	Cue	Reinforcer
1	Size of pellet	X-ray (illness)
2	*Flavor of pellet*	*X-ray (illness)*
3	*Size of pellet*	*Shock (pain)*
4	Flavor of pellet	Shock (pain)

Source: Garcia et al. 1968.

* Combinations that produced learning are italicized.

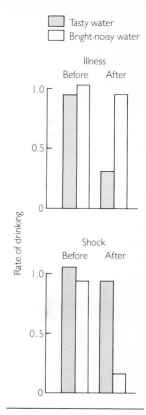

of pellet could not. For the results of parallel experiments using water, see Figure 5-13.

Garcia's findings can be interpreted in terms of natural selection. In nature, an animal can often get sick from eating tainted food, so selection favors an animal predisposed to assume that physical sickness is more likely to result from food it has eaten than from other causes. The taste of food, in turn, provides the most useful information about the food's tendency to cause sickness, while the size of food items does not. By contrast, physical punishment (in Garcia's case, electric shock) may often be associated with cues such as size of items in nature, while rarely being associated with the taste of items. The underlying assumption is that natural selection favors efficient means of learning. If an animal were completely open-minded, that is, considered all possible stimuli as being equally likely to produce a given reinforcement, it would be slow to make some connections, and it would probably be unable to make others. If an animal has appropriate biases, it learns some things very quickly, at a cost of being unable to learn unlikely combinations.

Another important implication of Garcia's findings is that animals are sometimes capable of setting up associations in spite of long delays between stimulus and punishment. Garcia waited as long as 12 hours after feeding the rats before inducing sickness with x-rays and still got conditioning to taste of food items. Indeed, rats can develop an aversion to flavored water when x-rayed an hour later, even if a dry meal has intervened; if two meals have intervened, however, rats tend to avoid the more novel of the two. We can see from these results why it would be a bad idea to design a living creature that responded to immediate reinforcement *only*. In life, some causal connections involve a long time delay, yet they are important for the animal to apprehend. Once we grant that an animal should, in some cases, be able to search further than a few seconds backwards in time for causal connections, then we see that if it were totally open-minded, it would have a very large array of possibilities to consider: everything that had happened

Figure 5-13

Biases in rat learning. The rate at which rats drank either tasty or bright-noisy water before and after each was paired with illness-inducing x-rays (above) or electric shock (below). Tasty water is either salty or saccharine, while bright-noisy water is water that turns on a bright light and a clicking sound whenever it is tasted. Notice that the rats fail to learn that drinking bright-noisy water may cause illness and tasty water may cause shock. (*From* Garcia and Koelling 1966)

to it in the five or ten hours before becoming ill might be the cause of the illness. Given this large array of possibilities, the animal gains from being biased toward those possibilities that are most likely. In Garcia's case, the animal gains from the assumption that bad food or water causes sickness and a whole series of other activities do not.

Other Examples of Biased Learning

Strains of rats have long been known to display what might be called "innate hypotheses." For example, without any reward, some strains of rats tend naturally to turn left on a T-maze more than 50% of the time. Others turn left less than 50% of the time. Some strains of rats learn visual cues more quickly than spatial cues. Others learn spatial cues more quickly. These findings indicate the ease with which selection could affect changes in learning in rats. Although humans undoubtedly possess more sophisticated and complex modes of learning than do rats, such capabilities could only have evolved from past genetic variation and there is no reason to suspect that such variation has now disappeared in our line.

The type of response an animal makes may also affect the form of learning it shows. We have known for many years that dogs can be conditioned to a variety of sounds. We have recently learned that the type of response demanded of the dog will affect the kind of sound to which it most easily responds. For example, we can compare the quality of sound given versus the direction from which it comes. In one study, the quality of sound was varied by using either a buzzer or a metronome, while the direction of sound was varied by having the sound come from in front of the dog or from behind it. When the dog was taught to use its right paw or its left paw to press a bar, it could associate direction of sound with the use of one paw or the other. But it was unable to learn that the quality of sound was associated with which paw it uses so as to give reward under one combination and no effect under the other. By contrast, when it was taught merely to press a bar or not to press a bar, it quickly associated this task with different qualities of sound, but not so well with their direction of origin.

Similar results have been achieved with monkeys, and they can be interpreted in the following way. In nature, sounds coming from different directions may naturally prompt an animal to make different initial movements. The animal may wish to orient toward the sound, and hence to move right or left, depending on the direction from which the sound comes. The quality of sound is much less likely to be associated with a directional bias in the movement of the animal. On the other hand, animals must often learn to habituate to sounds not associated with any danger or special opportunities. Thus, they quickly learn that quality of sound can be associated with responding (pressing bar) or not responding. Usually in nature, a particular sound has a benefit or cost no matter what direction the sound comes from. Since this is not invariably true, animals must be capable of learning not to respond to a particular sound from a particular direction, but they find this learning task a relatively difficult one.

The state of deprivation of an animal also affects the way in which it learns. Compare, for example, the behavior of thirsty versus hungry rats in a T-maze, where the reinforcement is, respectively, water or food. Thirsty animals rewarded with water learn more quickly when the water is always in the same position in the maze (either left-hand side or right-hand side) than do hungry rats responding to food in a constant position. But hungry rats learn more quickly than do thirsty rats when the reward changes position in the T-maze. This difference can be interpreted as follows. In nature, water is more likely to be found in the same place day after day. Standing bodies of water are usually not quickly depleted. By contrast, food usually occurs in smaller quantities, which can be quickly eaten by other animals. Thus, it makes sense to search in the same place for water, but to try alternate locations more often when looking for food.

Finally, regardless of the reinforcer, animals rarely show perfect learning. That is, no matter how long reinforcement has continued, animals rarely achieve 100% correct responses. After continuous reinforcement, animals usually achieve about 95% correct responses, which suggests that they have a built-in tendency to vary their behavior, even in the face of continuous reinforcement. This may be adaptive in nature, even if some rewards continue in a constant pattern, since other rewards may be nearby with even higher positive effects.

Much more could be said about animal learning, but I hope the examples chosen convey the idea that even this most plastic part of our makeup has evolved detailed features through the action of natural selection. For the remainder of the book we will have little more to say about the way in which genes control development of traits, or the effects of learning on behavior, but so far as we can see there is nothing mysterious in these phenomena, nor anything that runs counter to the logic we are developing.

Summary

Each human at conception receives 23 chromosomes from each parent. These chromosomes are the structures along which most of their genes are located. Genes, in turn, control development. Genes consist of stretches of DNA long enough to code for an individual protein. DNA consists of two support strands (backbones) connected by a series of chemical bases located on each strand. DNA reproduces by breaking apart the two strands and allowing each to act as a template on which a new strand is constructed. In a similar fashion, DNA sends small sections of messenger RNA into the surrounding cell, where they help construct the proteins that run the ongoing chemical interactions of the cell.

In a species such as our own, sex cells are produced by the process of meiosis, in which each chromosome of a pair is inserted at random into the sex cells. The resultant variability is further increased by the process of crossing over, in which paired chromosomes exchange segments.

Behavioral traits are no different from any other traits in showing genetic variability. This is most clearly seen in artificial breeding programs, but is also demonstrated by a variety of other evidence. Animals also display subtle and complex learning abilities that vary from species to species and appear to be tailored to the situations in which the animals function. This is shown by a review of song learning in birds and food-related learning in rats.

Chapter 6

Kinship

Kinship refers to genetic relatedness. Every form of reproduction involves the reproduction of genes. One individual copies some fraction of its own genes and inserts them into a new cell, where these copies help direct the construction of a new individual. Thus, an individual is genetically related to each of its offspring. There is some probability that any gene in its own collection will have an exact copy located in the offspring. This probability is called the *degree of relatedness* or *r* (see Chapter 3). Where all the genes in an individual are inherited by an offspring with equal probability, we can speak of a single degree of relatedness between parent and offspring. Likewise, the offspring is related to its parent, since any gene in it may have an identical predecessor copy located in the parent.

But parent and offspring are only two of many kinds of relatives. There are also brothers and sisters, uncles, cousins, and so on. In fact all of us can be considered genetically related, if we are willing to trace our pedigrees far enough back. Just as a degree of relatedness can be calculated between parent and offspring, so can it be calculated between any two individuals, that is, by computing the probability that a typical gene in one individual has an exact copy located in the other, by direct descent from a common ancestor.

Just as natural selection favors traits that increase an individual's production of surviving offspring, because parent and offspring are genetically related, so natural selection favors traits that increase the survival of other categories of relatives, such as siblings and cousins. Since aiding one kind of relative must usually conflict with aiding another, as when investment in nephews and nieces decreases investment in offspring, we expect mechanisms of choice to evolve that reflect differential degrees of relatedness. Each individual will seem to value the reproductive success of others, compared to its own, according to the *r*'s that connect them.

Not only are relations between individuals regulated by kinship, but the individual multicellular creature is itself a product of kinship: cells sacrifice reproduction for genetically identical cells. In this chapter we shall emphasize the fundamental role of kinship in the organization of life. We begin with evidence that kinship has strong effects on altruistic and selfish tendencies in ground squirrels and in monkeys. We then show that kinship reasoning also applies to interactions among sperm cells and egg cells. We review the foundation of kinship theory and show how one calculates degrees of relatedness under conditions of inbreeding. We then review the ways in which animals recognize their relatives. Finally, we show that kinship reasoning helps us to think about levels of organization in life, including selfish genes and the role of somatic mutations in plants.

Warning Calls in Ground Squirrels

Warning calls are dramatic examples of altruism (Figure 6-1). When a predator is about to strike, life itself is at stake; an alarm call may alert others to the danger, but at a real cost to the actor, since the call draws attention to the caller. The importance of this cost is suggested by the evolution in several bird species of alarm calls that have acoustical properties making them difficult to locate. This kind of call presumably evolved because calls without such properties led to increased predation on the caller. Until recently we have only been able to speculate on how this cost was repaid, but an exciting study by Paul Sherman has shown that Belding's ground squirrels *Spermophilus beldingi* call more often when there are more close relatives living nearby. Specifically, adult females—which are often surrounded by relatives—frequently call, while adult males—which are rarely near their relatives—rarely call. More to the point, adult females differ in the number of their close kin living nearby and they adjust their tendency to give an alarm call accordingly.

Among Belding's ground squirrels, warning calls appear to be especially costly. Predators are common and nearly 10% of encounters observed by Sherman resulted in the death of a squirrel. Calls are usually repeated and have acoustic properties that make them *easy* to locate, presumably because squirrels look in the direction of the caller—who often calls from a conspicuous perch while watching the predator—in order to see the direction from which the predator is approaching; but this also makes callers easier targets. Sherman noted that predators stalk and chase callers more often than non-callers, and half of the squirrels killed by predators were giving an alarm call before being attacked. In one case, Sherman was watching a badger who was watching squirrels when a squirrel made an alarm call from behind a

Figure 6-1

Danger! A Belding's ground squirrel mother—who has nursing young—gives an alarm call at the approach of a predatory mammal. Females are more likely to call when they have close relatives alive in the area, whether offspring or others. (Photo: George D. Lepp, Bio-Tec Images)

nearby rock. The badger turned, stalked, and killed the squirrel. With these kinds of interactions, it is not surprising that squirrels are choosy about the circumstances under which they give warning calls.

Among ground squirrels, females disperse as juveniles only short distances (50 meters) from their birthplace; they move little thereafter. As juveniles, males disperse ten times as far as females and continue to move in successive years of breeding (Figure 6-2). As a result, adult males live neither near their parents and siblings nor near their off-spring. After juvenile dispersal, males rarely give calls (Figure 6-3). By contrast, females are surrounded in life by close female kin and frequently give alarm calls (Figure 6-3). However, adult females also differ in the number of their surviving relatives—some have many relatives nearby, others few or none—and Sherman found that this variation is matched by variation in tendency to call: the more close kin nearby, the more likely is an adult female to call (Figure 6-4).

This picture of kin-biased warning calls is nicely supported by data on other behaviors, both selfish and altruistic. Adult females seem

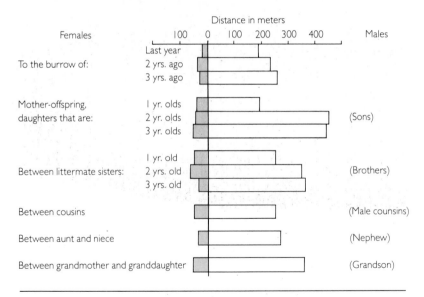

Figure 6-2

Sexual dimorphism in dispersal: Belding's ground squirrels. Mean distances that females and males moved in successive years and that separated them from a given category of relative are shown. For every comparison, males moved significantly more than females ($P < 0.005$). Note that about the same average distance separates a female from any of her relatives. Thus, spatial proximity cannot be used to discriminate between them. (*From* Sherman 1980)

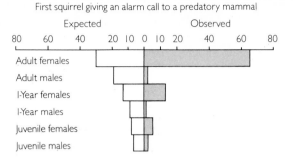

Figure 6-3

Frequency of alarm calls as a function of sex and age of caller. The observed and expected frequencies of calling for various categories of Belding's ground squirrels are shown. Expected frequencies are based on the proportion of time that a given class is available to give a call. Notice that adult females call much more often than expected by chance, while adult males hardly call at all. (*From* Sherman 1977)

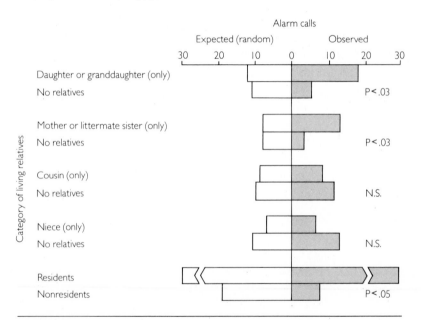

Figure 6-4

Alarm calls as a function of the presence or absence of close relatives. The graph shows the expected number of alarm calls (based on their frequency in the population) and the observed number of calls for adult female Belding's ground squirrels, within a given category of relatives alive or no relatives alive. The final comparison is between resident and newly arrived immigrants. *N.S.* means "not significant." Note that the presence of cousins and nieces has no effect on a female's tendency to call. (*From* Sherman 1980)

to value close relatives in much the same way, whether they are co-defending an area (the more closely related, the larger the area), permitting intrusion into a defended area (less closely related, less often) (see Figures 6-5 and 6-6), fighting to establish a nest burrow (more closely related, less often), or cooperating to protect their young (more closely related, more often). In all of these cases, cousins, nieces, and granddaughters are treated as if unrelated, while sisters, half-sisters, and daughters are favored.

Figure 6-5

A non-relative is chased. A female Belding's ground squirrel chases an unrelated intruder out of her territory. Such territorial defense is probably important in reducing infanticide, which in ground squirrels is done mainly by unrelated adult females, probably to reduce subsequent competition (with their own offspring) for resources. (Photo: George D. Lepp, Bio-Tec Images)

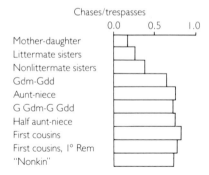

Chases/trespasses

0.0   0.5   1.0

Mother-daughter
Littermate sisters
Nonlittermate sisters
Gdm-Gdd
Aunt-niece
G Gdm-G Gdd
Half aunt-niece
First cousins
First cousins, I° Rem
"Nonkin"

Figure 6-6

Chases per trespass for various categories of female kin. The proportion of times that pregnant or nursing female Belding's ground squirrels chased various categories of relatives from their territory is shown. Only trespasses that occurred when territory owners were present above ground are shown. The proportion for each of the first three categories is significantly different than for each of the others, but all the rest do not differ among themselves. (*From* Sherman 1981)

Figure 6-7

The matrilineal kin universe of one-year-old female Belding's ground squirrels. This graph shows the proportion of one-year-old females with at least one same-age or older female relative alive. The frequency for the first category is significantly higher than for all others, and the frequency of the first three is higher than for the others. (*From* Sherman 1981)

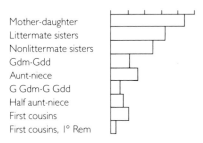

Proportion of 1-year old females
with each sort of (same
age or older) relatives alive

Mother-daughter
Littermate sisters
Nonlittermate sisters
Gdm-Gdd
Aunt-niece
G Gdm-G Gdd
Half aunt-niece
First cousins
First cousins, 1° Rem

Why do the squirrels treat cousins, nieces, and granddaughters as if they were unrelated? One possibility is that the latter relatives are found at greater distances. But, in fact, the average distance to each category in nature is about the same (see Figure 6-2). Instead, Sherman suggests that there is a correspondence between the relative frequency of the different relationships in nature and their degrees of relatedness: sisters and daughters are a relatively frequent part of a female's world while the more distant relationships are infrequently encountered (Figure 6-7). This pattern is brought about by high rates of infant and juvenile mortality, which apparently limit the degree to which selection has fashioned a response to differences in the smaller degrees of relatedness (¼ to ⅛ and less). In addition, as we shall see below, such categories may sometimes have difficulty recognizing each other, due to the disappearance of connecting links.

Sherman's study provides dramatic evidence for the importance of kinship in the social life of a mammal. It implies abilities on the part of the animals to recognize categories of close kin. As we shall see, careful experimentation shows that the squirrels use social cues to discern kinship but are also able to discern kinship where no such cues are available (see Figure 6-31).

Altruistic and Selfish Behavior in Japanese Monkeys

A second test of the importance of kinship in nature comes from the study of monkeys. Most monkey species are organized along kin lines similar to those of ground squirrels: before males reach sexual maturity, they disperse away from the group they were born into, while females stay with their mothers, sisters, and other female relatives. Indeed, within a monkey group, females tend to cluster along matrilines.

Figure 6-8

Matrilines in conflict. Parts of two langur troops, each a separate matriline, come into conflict in a part of their shared home range. Four sub-adults of both sexes (on the right) are attacking two adult females (on the left), while the male associated with the two females looks on (in the background). Defense of the troop's feeding range is very much a female affair. When males take part, most of their action is directed at other males. Through countless such conflicts over months and months, troop boundaries gradually shift in favor of one group or the other. After this particular conflict, both groups simply retreated. (Photo: Sarah Hrdy, Anthro-Photo)

A mother, her daughters, and their offspring will travel in closer proximity than other individuals who are themselves organized in similar matrilines (see Figure 6-8).

Several studies of monkeys have now shown that altruistic acts are preferentially directed to closely related individuals. The most detailed of these is Jeffrey Kurland's study of the Japanese monkey *Macaca fuscata*. Kurland measured proximity within free-ranging troops as a

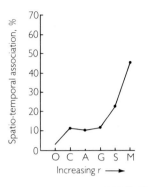

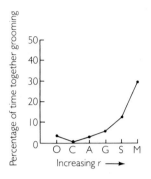

Figure 6-9

Spatial proximity as a function of kinship in Japanese monkeys. The percentage of occasions on which individuals of a particular kinship category were within 10 meters of each other. *Legend*: M (mother–offspring), S (siblings), G (grand-mother–grandoffspring), A (aunts–nephews/nieces), C (cousins), O (members of other matrilines). As *r* increases, individuals spend more time together. Values for G, S, and M are all significantly different from each other, and O is significantly less than all others. (*From* Kurland 1977)

Figure 6-10

Frequency of grooming as a function of r *(corrected for proximity).* The percentage of time in which two individuals were together (within 10 meters of each other) that one was grooming the other. *Legend*: same as previous figure. Differences between C and A, G and S, and S and M are significant. (*From* Kurland 1977)

function of *r* and found, as expected, that as *r* increases, the monkeys spend a greater percentage of time near each other (Figure 6-9). He then showed that when corrections are made for proximity, the monkeys direct altruistic acts preferentially toward closely related individuals—while tending to reserve selfish acts for the more distantly related. Thus, it is not proximity that is causing the kinship effects we observe in nature; on the contrary, kinship causes animals to be near each other, presumably in order to enjoy an increase in altruism and a decrease in selfishness.

As we see in Figure 6-10, Japanese monkeys groom close relatives more often than expected on the basis of proximity alone. Considering only individuals already in close association, we see that monkeys direct most of their grooming toward parents, offspring, and siblings before turning to less-related individuals. (For scenes of grooming in this species see Figures 6-11 and 6-12.) Likewise, defending another indi-

Figure 6-11

A tight grooming cluster of close kin. In contrast to the following pictures, this photo shows the close body contact and nuzzling that is characteristic of grooming between close relatives among Japanese monkeys. The grandmother (lower left) is being groomed by her three children while her grandson (next to the daughter in the middle) rests upon her. (Photo: Jeffrey Kurland)

a

b

Figure 6-12

(a) *A tense grooming interaction in the Japanese monkey.* In this picture a grandmother (on the right) sits near her two grown daughters, one of whom grooms her son in the background while the other sits with her infant son. (b) The most dominant female now arrives and begins to groom the mother (in the foreground), to whom she is unrelated. The mother is noticeably tense and the grandmother has already turned away from the dominant female. (Shortly afterward she departed.) In hundreds of hours of observation this was the only time the dominant female groomed this female; an exception that may have occurred because the female at this time had an infant. The dominant female is the mother of Pyon (see Figure 6-14 and text). (Photos: Jeffrey Kurland)

vidual from attack is an altruistic act, and the monkeys preferentially defend individuals to whom they are more closely related. Although defense occurs in only 7% of all fights, 81% of this defense comes from a member of the monkey's own matriline.

Aggressive acts are selfish, so we expect kinship to be inversely associated with its frequency. This is especially true of violent, aggressive encounters in which the cost inflicted may be considerable. Kurland observed 19 such cases in which five individuals were severely wounded. In every one of these violent attacks, the aggressor and the attacked animals were at best distantly related. The attacked animals were typically members of low-ranking matrilines and did not fight back. One encounter shows the kind of kinship dynamics at work:

Faza-71-f [see Figure 6-13] jumps onto Ponko and Fork (presumably to join in the play). Ponko turns and lunges at Faza-71-f. Faza-71-f and Fork run from Ponko. Ponko chases Faza-71-f up a tree. Ponko's sister Peka, brother Pyon [Figure 6-14], and niece Nira run over and join in the chase. Dark (an adult male), attracted by the noise, runs to the group. Dark climbs up to Faza-71-f and cuffs her. She falls about 10 meters to the ground, runs off, chased by her attackers, and plunges into the icy Kaminyu river. Although Dark, Ponko, Pyon, Peka, and Nira do not follow her into the river, they prevent her from coming back up on the river bank. Meanwhile, her family flees across the concrete dam over the river and into the sugi forest opposite the feeding area. In the face of aggression from members of the dominant matriline and Dark (the alpha adult male), her family appears to be powerless to help her. Faza-71-f swims towards the dam looking for dry land. She finds a small pile of sand under an icy waterfall on the opposite river bank beside the dam. She sits there, still threatened by Dark et al., bleeding and apparently in shock, since she does not immediately attempt to climb the dam wall and join her family. Cyno (an adult male who often consorts with Faza's-71-f matriline) climbs out on a branch of a sugi tree and ho's at her attackers. Finally, the attackers disperse, perhaps because of Cyno's threats. Faza-71-f turns around and runs up a log connecting her sandy haven to the river bank. She rejoins her family and Cyno on the top of a sugi tree. For the following eight days, Faza-71-f and her entire matriline avoid the provisioning area.

Notice that because Faza-71-f joined an interaction between Ponko and Fork, Ponko's sister, brother Pyon, and niece immediately jump in on Ponko's side. The adult male Dark is associated with Ponko's matriline and may be the father of several of the youngsters in the matriline. Likewise, Cyno, the other adult male, is associated with Faza's matriline and may have fathered offspring in it (Figure 6-15). Even months after the attack Faza's matriline avoids the more dominant matrilines, at a cost of less frequent access to preferred feeding areas (Figure 6-16).

Kurland's analysis combined threats, submissive gestures, and mild attacks into a single category of mild aggression. Mild aggression is much more frequently directed toward unrelated individuals than toward relatives, but when the aggression is directed toward relatives, higher degree of relatedness does not reduce frequency of threat or attack. Quite the contrary, there is a steady, though non-significant, increase in mild aggression with increasing degrees of relatedness. This suggests the importance of competition for resources, aggravated by close proximity. That is, close association permits more altruism but also throws individuals into closer competition, thus engendering more opportunities for selfishness. A classic example is sibling conflict for parental investment.

Once we accept kinship reasoning, then it aids us in deciding whether behavior is altruistic or selfish. Consider, for example, alloparenting, that is, taking care of someone else's offspring. Is this act altruistic—saving the mother work and time—or is it selfish? For example, does the alloparent practice to become a mother at a cost to the

Figure 6-13

Victim of an attack. This is Faza-71-f, whose apparently innocent effort to join in the play of her sister Fork precipitated an attack from the dominant matriline (see text). Even before the attack, Faza-71-f was noticeably more cautious when playing with juveniles from the dominant matriline. (Photo: Jeffrey Kurland)

Figure 6-14

A fellow with a nasty disposition. This photo shows Pyon, Point's "spoiled" son, who often gave Faza-71-f a bad time and who joined in the group attack on her (see text). On several occasions, Pyon attacked low-ranking members of the group for no apparent reason. (Photo: Jeffrey Kurland)

Figure 6-15

Before the attack. During the fall breeding season Faza grooms Cyno while her daughter Faza-72-f plays with an unrelated juvenile. Faza copulated with Cyno during the breeding season but failed to conceive. Nonetheless, Cyno later provided critical support for Faza's matriline during the attack on Faza-71-f. (Photo: Jeffrey Kurland)

a   b

Figure 6-16

Aftermath of the attack. (a) Cyno with Faza and Mitis (believed to be Faza's sister) and their children. Both females preferentially associate with Cyno and with each other. Even though this photo was taken months after the attack on Faza-71-f, this subgroup still avoids the dominant matrilines and is seen here away from the primary feeding area of the troop. (b) This picture was taken later the same day and shows that when Faza's subgroup does use the primary feeding area—after other animals have left—they feed quickly and furtively. *Left to right*: Faza-70-m, Faza, Faza-72-f, Mitis (head down). (Photos: Jeffrey Kurland)

offspring? Kurland began his work assuming that alloparenting was altruistic. He expected it to be directed preferentially toward close relatives. Sometimes it is, as when older siblings babysit younger siblings (see Figure 6-17), but in general, Kurland found, alloparenting was common by females who had not yet given birth, and in 122 of 140 cases was directed at *unrelated* individuals. He also found that mothers were more likely to retrieve their infant and show aggression toward the alloparent when its degree of relatedness to the offspring was low. Thus, by taking kinship theory as true, we are able to infer that in Japanese macaques, alloparenting is usually a selfish act that prepares the young female to be a better mother when her chance comes.

If monkey groups are organized along lines of female kin, then growing lineages must regularly split, a fission we expect to go along kin lines. The best evidence for this comes from the rhesus monkey *Macaca mulatta*. A study of 64 matrilines involved in group fissioning showed that the entire matriline typically moved to one of the two products of the group split, although in 13 cases the matriline split. These 13 matrilines were unusual in having a low average degree of relatedness between their members and in being intermediate or sub-

a   b

Figure 6-17

Babysitter. A three-year-old female takes care of her three-month-old brother. On the left, she is taking a motherly role, allowing him to hold her for comfort; on the right, she is showing more typical sibling camaraderie. This infant is a member of the least dominant matriline and its members were especially protective of him, presumably because of his vulnerability to attack by other monkeys. He was, in fact, once severely attacked by Pyon. (Photos: Jeffrey Kurland)

ordinate in rank. Dominant matrilines may stay together to enjoy a good thing; sons of such matrilines, for example, disperse later than do sons of lower-ranking matrilines. These, in turn, split along kin lines in such a way as to raise the average degrees of relatedness of the resulting groups.

Cooperation and Altruism among Sperm Cells (and Egg Cells)

If close degrees of relatedness predispose individuals to altruism, why not search for such examples in sex cells, specifically sperm? Sperm cells are products of meiosis, and under outbreeding, those from a single male are related to each other by $r = \frac{1}{2}$. Sperm from a single male are in competition with each other and, more strongly, with the sperm of other males. In this competition, cooperation or altruism by sperm may gain an advantage.

A striking example of sperm cooperation seems to occur in the opossum *Didelphys marsupialis*. After ejaculation, 80% of the sperm are found joined together in pairs by special headpieces designed to lock together (Figure 6-18). All sperm have these headpieces. Even when violently activated in a saline solution, conjugate spermatozoa remain paired and swim very powerfully in a straight line, in striking contrast to the circular movement of single cells. Conjugate sperm have also been described in a water beetle and a mollusc.

When sperm cells cooperate, each sperm cell retains the ability to fertilize an egg; but there are also many known cases of sperm altruism, in which each male produces two kinds of sperm cells, only one of which can fertilize an egg, the other somehow helping the first (Figure 6-19). In some species, such as butterflies and moths, the helper sperm is anucleate; that is, it lacks a nucleus and nuclear genes. In other cases, such as some pentatomid bugs, the helper sperm has several sets of genes. Either way, we must imagine that in the early evolutionary stages of these sperm cells, genes were favored that led to the elimination of a reproductive role in the cells in order to benefit cell lines that did reproduce. In pentatomid bugs, specialized lobes of the testes, called harlequin lobes (Figure 6-20), produce at the end of meiosis not the usual four sperm cells, each with one set of genes, but giant sperm cells containing four sets of genes (excluding, curiously, the sex chromosomes). Thus each giant should be worth more than four of its fertilizing siblings.

Figure 6-18

Cooperative sperm. In the opossum, most sperm cells join together with others from the same father, connecting with each other at the head, and swimming together. (Drawn from a photo in Biggers and Creed 1962)

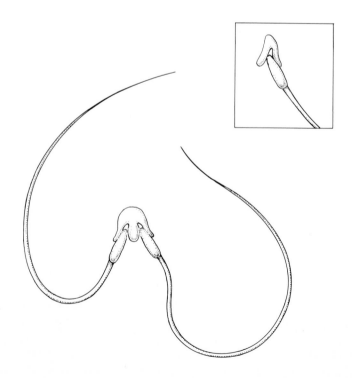

Three general functions have been suggested for helper sperm: (a) they help the other sperm to reach the eggs, (b) they contribute their own nutrients to the female or her eggs, and (c) they interfere with the success of competing sperm. There is no question that helper sperm sometimes serve a transport function. In some molluscs hundreds of tiny fertilizing sperm attach themselves to the tails of giant helper sperm, which swim up the female tract to the ovaries, liberating the tiny sperm along the way (see Figure 6-19). That helper sperm also sometimes make a nutritional contribution seems likely. In many insects, fertilization requires the penetration of the egg by many sperm, only one of which contributes genes while the others are a source of chemicals for the egg. It is possible that the giant sperm cells of the pentatomid bugs are merely more efficient ways of contributing resources to the egg, although this is not known. Nor do we know why species with harlequin lobes are almost always tropical.

Our ignorance of function is well illustrated by the case of the anucleate sperm of butterflies and moths. Although these sperm were

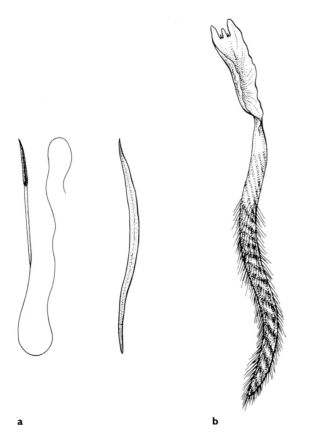

a   b

Figure 6-19

Altruistic sperm. (a) In many prosobranch molluscs, two kinds of sperm are produced, an ordinary fertilizing sperm with a long tail (on the left) and a short, worm-like form. The latter kind may well serve a nutritive function, since they are digested in the female. (b) In some species a very large helper sperm is produced, called a spermatozeugma, to which are attached hundreds of the tiny fertilizing sperm. (From Hyman 1967, and Fretter 1953)

Figure 6-20

Specialization in the testes to produce altruistic sperm. The external view (left) and sectional view (right) of the testes of the pentatomid bug *Alitocoris schraderi.* In the sectional view the five lobes are visible. The fifth lobe is the harlequin lobe, which produces the helper sperm. The harlequin lobe is large relative to the other lobes and its growth has given the testes a coiled shape. (*From* Schrader 1960)

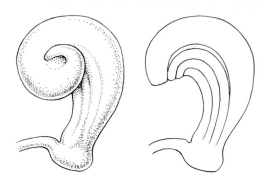

long thought to be a degenerate form that never left the testes, they show a series of traits that suggest strong selection for some function. The morphology of these sperm is characteristic and precise and differs from that of the fertilizing sperm. Thus, like aphid soldiers, anucleate sperm have evolved even though they produce no direct descendants. Also, like aphid soldiers, they may be produced in great numbers (in the moth *Manduia sexta,* two million sperm cells are ejaculated, of which 96% are anucleate). If anything, anucleate sperm are more active than the normal variety and undergo a long migration within the female reproductive system, ultimately arriving at a sperm storage sac, which in some species is divided into two halves, one for each of the two kinds of sperm. The fertilizing sperm later leave their pouch to fertilize the eggs; the anucleate sperm do not, but are apparently digested.

In three species of butterflies it is known that males contribute investment to their offspring via their ejaculations, since marked isotopes fed to males show up in the female and her eggs soon after mating. But in these animals, sperm is enclosed in a protein-rich package that is digested by the female, with sperm making up only about 20% of the package, by weight. Why have butterflies and moths evolved two different ways of investing resources during copulation? And if the anucleate sperm are a form of investment, why are they simpler in structure than the normal sperm instead of more elaborate?

Anucleate sperm seem not to provide help in transport. In some species they are activated earlier than the other sperm and arrive first at the female storage organ. Do they ever interfere with the normal sperm present from an earlier mating? At present we can only speculate on the meaning of these remarkable sperm! It is worth noting that comparable examples of egg altruism are extremely rare (Figures 6-21 to 6-23). Sperm altruism is probably more common because the cost of each sperm cell is so low that many more can be produced than are needed to fertilize eggs, predisposing some to a helper role.

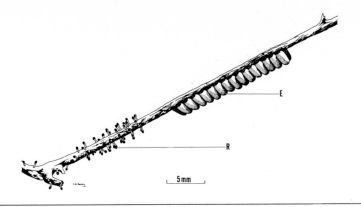

Figure 6-21

Egg altruism. The rapagula (R) of the insect *Ululodes mexicana* are shown where they have been deposited near fertile eggs (E) laid by the same female. The rapagula are modified eggs that for weeks repel egg and larvae predators such as ants. Upon touching the rapagula, an ant immediately and violently withdraws, sometimes falling to the ground. An intense bout of antennal grooming by the ant always follows. (*From* Henry 1972)

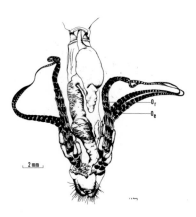

Figure 6-22

Specialization to produce egg altruists. A mature female *Ululodes mexicana* has been dissected to reveal the ovarioles that produce the rapagula (O_r) and the normal eggs (O_e). As many rapagula may be produced as eggs. Whether these are fertilized by sperm or, indeed, whether meiosis is normal in rapagula is not known. (*From* Henry 1972)

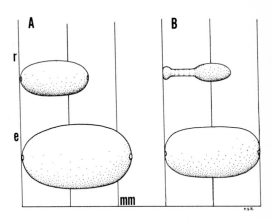

Figure 6-23

The evolution of egg altruism. Comparison of the rapagula (r) and eggs (e) of (A) *Ascaloptynx furciger* and (B) *Ululodes mexicana*. The rapagula of *Ascaloptynx* have no protective function and look like miniature eggs. They serve as a source of food for newly hatched siblings. This is probably their original function, and only later did they evolve a protective role in *Ululodes*. (*From* Henry 1972)

Foundations of Kinship Theory

Given the importance of our kinship theory, it will be worth our while to look more closely at the logic we have been developing. Is it really valid to use the simple kind of genetical reasoning we have employed? To answer this question we will consider some of the objections commonly raised against kinship theory.

One objection runs as follows. Degree of relatedness is not the right measure of genetic overlap in self-interest, since it fails to fully capture the degree of genetic similarity between two individuals. By virtue of being members of the same species, these individuals already share most of their genes in common. If at least 90% of the genome is shared in common by any two individuals in, say, our own species (a conservative estimate), then degree of genetic similarity is already 0.9 before kinship intervenes; kinship merely increases the likelihood of identity in the remaining 10% of the genome. According to this view, Hamilton's approach greatly overemphasizes the importance of kinship in nature, while underestimating the possibilities for altruism. Not only should an individual be altruistic to any conspecific whenever $B > {}^{10}\!/\!_9\, C$ but it should be almost equally altruistic to members of closely related species. Indeed, our altruism ought to be organized in a hierarchy that reflects evolutionary history. That is, each vertebrate ought to value all other vertebrates more than it values any invertebrate, and so on.

The mistake lies, first, in directing our attention to *all* loci, instead of to those coding for altruistic traits. The degree of similarity other loci have attained is no guide to how selection will work on a locus coding for altruism. When a new mutant appears at such a locus, it will (after several generations) be found in a relative with a chance of r and in all others with the negligible probability of the mutation rate (perhaps 1 in 100,000). Such a gene will only begin to spread if it directs altruism to a relative when $Br > C$ and neglects all others. Whether identity at other loci is high or low is irrelevant to its spread.

But having said this, we appear to have created a new difficulty, for as an altruistic gene begins to spread, individuals become more similar to each other *at the altruistic locus*: at a frequency of 0.5, the altruistic gene will be found in an *unrelated* individual half of the time. Shouldn't the spread of an altruistic gene inflate degrees of relatedness, so that a gene that made altruism more likely as it became more frequent would outcompete all others? One of Hamilton's achievements was to show that the answer to this question is "no": the frequency of an altruistic allele has no effect on the conditions under which it will spread.

This fact is easiest to see when we separate the recipient's genotype into two sections, a part which is correlated with the actor's

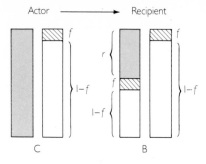

Figure 6-24

A locus controlling altruism. An imaginary locus controlling altruism is shown in an actor and a recipient. The average frequency for two genes in each individual is indicated by shading (altruistic gene) and no shading (alternate gene). The darkly shaded area indicates the *correlated* portion of each individual's genotype: the actor is known to have at least one gene for altruism, while the recipient has an identical copy, r proportion of the time. The remainder of the genotype is *uncorrelated*: the altruistic gene is found at its overall frequency of f (lightly shaded area) and the alternate gene with frequency $1-f$ (unshaded area). Effects on the uncorrelated portion of the genotype do not affect the direction of selection; the two genes are merely benefitted or harmed at random.

genotype because of relatedness and an uncorrelated part in which genes are found at the frequency they have attained in the population at large. Hamilton says that only the effects reaching the correlated part of the genome affect the direction of selection. The effects reaching the uncorrelated part strike the various genes in exact proportion to their frequencies in the general population and hence *do not change* these frequencies. Imagine that an altruistic gene is found at a frequency of 0.9 and its alternative at a frequency of 0.1: 90% of the time the altruistic gene will receive a benefit, but since its overall frequency is 0.9, the *benefit per gene* will be the same as the benefit per gene for the alternative. The same argument applies to the uncorrelated portion of the actor's genome (Figure 6-24). Thus, effects on the uncorrelated part of the genome do not change the relative frequency of the genes. By contrast, effects on the correlated part of the genome only strike the altruistic allele in the actor and, with frequency r, in the recipient. If the net effect is positive, the gene increases in frequency; if the net effect is negative, it decreases in frequency.

Some people object to kinship theory on the grounds that it has isolated an abstraction, "gene for altruism," and based the entire theory on this notion. Altruistic acts probably require many genes located at many different loci. After all, an altruist must have some means of measuring cost and benefit, some means of apprehending degrees of relatedness, and then be able to confer the benefit in question. How can this complicated phenomenon possibly be modelled by imagining a single gene for altruism and considering the conditions under which it will spread?

The simplest way to teach the concept of inclusive fitness is to imagine a single gene at a single locus affecting altruistic interactions and to imagine how such a gene will be affected by selection. But it is easy to show that the same analysis that applies to a single gene at a single locus also applies to genes located at many different loci. As long as these genes are all located on the same kinds of chromosomes (for example, autosomes), they will be inherited according to the same probability, or degree of relatedness. Each of the genes at each of the loci will be found in the recipient with the same probability r; thus if $Br > C$, all the genes at the various loci will receive a net benefit, and all the genes will be positively selected. That complicated behaviors can evolve in such situations is known already from the evolution of parental behavior.

Degrees of Relatedness Under Inbreeding

Inbreeding inflates degrees of relatedness between actor and recipient, because it increases the pathways through which the recipient may have a copy of a gene located in the actor. However, when the actor is a *product* of inbreeding, this also increases the number of genes that are identical by descent *within* the actor. Consider two full-siblings that mate and produce a son. To each parent, the boy is both son ($r = \frac{1}{2}$) and nephew ($r = \frac{1}{4}$), thus r between parent and son equals ¾. Now consider the child's degree of relatedness to his parents. There is a 50% chance that any gene in the boy will have a predecessor copy located in his mother, but if the boy's copy came from his father (with probability of ½) there is still a 50% chance that his mother has the gene, since she and dad are full-sibs. Thus, there is a 75% chance that his mother has the gene, and the same is true of his father.

But we must also consider the boy himself. How many copies of the gene does he have? Since he is a product of inbreeding, any gene in him may have a second copy by direct descent from a common ancestor; that is, the two halves of his genome are correlated (Figure 6-25). We compute this degree of correlation in the usual way. Any gene will have come from one or the other parent. If we assume it came from the mother, then there is a 50% chance that the father also had the gene, and a 50% chance that he passed a copy to the offspring. Thus, ¼ of the time, the boy will have two copies; on average he has 5/4 copies. This means that were he to save his mother's life but lose his

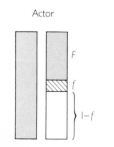

Figure 6-25

An altruistic locus in a product of inbreeding. Same as in previous figure except that the actor is assumed to be a product of inbreeding: there is a chance (of F) that the altruistic gene has a second copy by direct descent from a common ancestor. Thus, inbreeding increases the *correlated* portion of the actor's genotype.

own, 3/4 altruism genes would be saved while 5/4 would be lost. Dividing 3/4 by 5/4 tells us that the child will value his mother's life only 3/5 as much as himself. Call this his degree of relatedness to her.

In our example, the parent's relatedness to the child is 3/4, the child's relatedness to parent is 3/5. We see, then, that under inbreeding, degrees of relatedness can be asymmetrical. An individual that is the product of *out*breeding values itself as 1, but a product of *in*breeding values itself *more* than 1 because the two halves of its genome are correlated. Degree of relatedness is no longer simply the probability that another individual has a copy of a gene in the actor; instead this probability divided by the expected number of copies in the actor. The chance that a second copy of a gene will be found within the same individual by direct descent is called F. Thus, a more general expression for r_{AB}, A's r to B, is

$$r_{AB} = \frac{\text{prob}_{AB}}{1 + F}$$

where prob_{AB} is the chance that the gene will be found in B.

I know of no evidence relevant to the possibility that products of inbreeding value themselves relatively more in interactions with close kin than the kin will in interactions with them. We should, in any case, be cautious in our expectations, because products of inbreeding may devalue themselves—compared to outbred relatives—owing to the deleterious effects of inbreeding. If there were no such effects, inbreeding would be much more common in nature. This is because in the first generation a female could raise her relatedness to her offspring from 1/2 to 3/4 by permitting her brother to mate with her. That females of many species oppose such matings suggests that costs of inbreeding often cancel the 50% gain in relatedness.

Mechanisms of Kin Recognition

Kinship reasoning suggests that animals will evolve the ability to recognize categories of relatives, in effect, to measure degrees of relatedness. Until Hamilton's work, little was known about kin recognition in animals beyond the parent–offspring unit, but recently we have discovered a whole world of kin recognition abilities in animals. The most intriguing of these suggests that many animals, including perhaps ourselves, may literally be able to *smell* kinship, that is, to detect it directly by measuring some feature of the other creature and comparing this to a standard that has been learned.

We now know that animals can sometimes detect very subtle differences in relatedness. In sweat bees *Lasioglossum zephyrum*, females nest in tunnels in the ground, the entrance to which is usually guarded

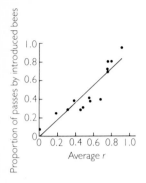

Figure 6-26

Admittance to the nest as a function of degree of relatedness. The proportion of times in which a sweat bee was admitted to a nest is shown as a function of the guard bee's average r to the intruder. Each point represents dozens of experiments. Note that even small differences in relatedness appear to be detected. (*From* Greenberg 1979)

by a bee that permits nest mates to enter and excludes others. In laboratory experiments a breeding program was imposed that included some inbreeding so as to produce a broad range of degrees of relatedness among the bees. When guard bees were tested, it was discovered that each guard admitted other bees as a close function of the guard bee's degree of relatedness to the other bee (Figure 6-26). More distantly related bees were admitted less often. Even slight differences in relatedness induced by inbreeding affected the rate of admittance, yet the bees were raised under uniform laboratory conditions. Each bee was removed from her cell before she had had any contact with other bees and was placed with a group of sisters for several days before being tested. Thus, discrimination implies some ability to discern kinship without any obvious cues except genetic differences. Subsequent experiments showed that recognition was achieved by a form of phenotypic matching, in which the appearance of each bee was compared to some learned standard of appearance (in this case, sisters).

The simplest way to discern kinship is through cues associated with reproduction. Thus, parent and offspring are usually in a position to know each other (Figure 6-27). Association with mothers may permit an individual to learn of other relatives that the mother recognizes. Thus, infant monkeys may learn to recognize their older siblings because these have preferential access to the mother. The absence of the connecting link may make recognition difficult or impossible. In Belding's ground squirrels a mother occasionally perishes just before her young first emerge above ground and consequently there is no chance for the older sisters to meet their new sisters in the presence of their mother. Such females later treat their younger sisters more selfishly

Figure 6-27

Mother and young. A female Belding's ground squirrel greets her pups on their first day above ground. The pups are about three and a half weeks old. Mother and offspring do not learn to recognize each other until about the time the young emerge above ground (only then will there normally be any chance for confusion). (Photo: George D. Lepp, Bio-Tec Images)

Table 6-1   Behavior Between 2-year-old Females and Their
1-year-old Non-littermate Sisters, Depending on Whether or
Not Their Mothers Were Alive During the First Contacts
Between the Non-littermates

Behavior	Mother Present	Mother Not Present	Significance
Fights/hour/day (gestation period)	0.10	0.17	$P < .05$
Percent times chased from defended area (nursing period)	36%	68%	$P < .05$

Source: Sherman 1980.

than do females whose mother was alive when the young first emerged
from their burrow (Table 6-1).

Sibling associations are even more common than the parent–
offspring unit. For example, when frogs hatch, their parents may be
long gone, but nearby hatching frogs are usually siblings. Experimental work demonstrates that early spatial proximity is often taken
as a cue to kinship by sibling groups. When Belding's ground squirrels
are cross-fostered in nature, that is, raised by a foster family, they treat
the new family as if it were their own—as long as the cross-fostering
occurs before the squirrels are weaned and emerge above ground (Figures 6-28 and 6-29). In addition, a juvenile on its first day above
ground occasionally returns in the evening to another burrow, where it

Figure 6-28

Ground squirrel adoptions.
These 5- or 6-day-old pups
have been placed by the
photographer at the en-
trance to the nest burrow
of an unrelated female,
who is nursing her own
young. When the female
emerges she will typically
carry the infants into her
nest; in other words, she
will adopt them. Her own
offspring later treat these
foster siblings much the
same as they treat each
other. (Photo: Paul
Sherman)

Figure 6-29

Results of cross-fostering as a function of time of cross-fostering. The average number of chases per trespass by yearling female Belding's ground squirrels is shown for individuals cross-fostered in nature at different ages. For comparison, the graph also shows rates of chasing for littermate sisters and unrelated squirrels. The sharp rise in aggression for females cross-fostered after the time of emergence is significant ($P < 0.01$). (*From* Holmes and Sherman 1982)

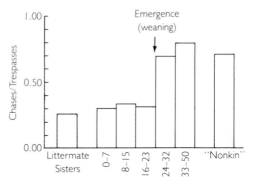

remains. Such females later treat their foster sisters more kindly than their genetic sisters (Table 6-2). But underlying this effect of early association is also a genetic effect. Among pups reared apart, sister–sister pairs are less aggressive when tested together than are unrelated pairs.

Cues of association provide easy ways for animals to know degrees of relatedness, but no matter how reliable such predictors are, much variation in degree of relatedness is not being addressed. Female genealogies in ground squirrels and monkeys usually tell us nothing about the male contribution to kinship. In Belding's ground squirrel, most litters are fathered by more than one male, so that litter mates are either half-siblings or full-siblings, a difference in r of $\frac{1}{4}$ (Figure 6-30).

Table 6-2   Behavior of 1-year-old Females Toward Genetic Sisters with Whom They Were Reared but Whose Company They Left on Their First Day Above Ground, and Toward (Unrelated) "Foster" Sisters into Whose Nest They Were Naturally Displaced and with Whom They Had Lengthy Post-emergence Associations

Behavior	"Foster" Sisters	Genetic Sisters	Significance
Number of fights per hour per day (gestation period)	0.08	0.14	$P < .05$
Percent times chased (nursing period)	27%	58%	$P < .01$
Sequential chases	50%	50%	
Cooperative chases	29%	15%	$P < .05$
Misdirected chases	13%	25%	

Source: Sherman 1980.

Figure 6-30

Siblings. Here we see a litter of Belding's ground squirrel pups at the entrance to their natal burrow. The pups have been above ground about a week so they are about a month old. In the majority of such litters some pups are full-siblings, others are half-siblings. (Photo: George D. Lepp, Bio-Tec Images)

It is difficult to see how cues of association will permit discrimination between the two, yet careful observations in nature show that female squirrels act more altruistically toward full-siblings than toward half-siblings (same litter) (Figure 6-31). This suggests an ability to measure one's own phenotype and compare others to it, a process we call *phenotypic matching.*

Experimental work with monkeys suggests that they are capable of phenotypic matching in which the self is used as the model. In the laboratory, juvenile pigtail macaques *Macaca nemistrina* reared apart from all other kin looked longer at and approached unfamiliar half-siblings (related only through the father) more often than they did to unfamiliar, unrelated individuals, matched for age, size, and sex (but recent work has failed to confirm a kinship effect). Another example of phenotypic matching occurs in tadpoles of American toads *Bufo americanus* and Cascade frogs *Rana cascadae.* In both species, eggs were separated before hatching and tadpoles were raised in social isolation. When permitted to swim freely with others, these tadpoles preferred to swim with siblings rather than non-siblings. When tested for discrimination between half-sibs and full-sibs, *B. americanus* discriminated only paternal half-sibs from full-sibs, suggesting that some factor obtained from the mother (perhaps a chemical in the jelly surrounding the eggs) was used as the standard of comparison.

Phenotypic matching requires some familiarity with one's own phenotype or that of a close relative. From time to time people have imagined that there might exist genes that directly recognize themselves in other individuals and cause some beneficial effect to be transferred. On the surface, this would appear to be an improvement over

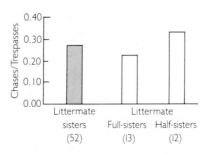

Figure 6-31

Discrimination between full- and half-sisters from the same litter. The average proportion of chases per trespass are shown for yearling female Belding's ground squirrels, depending on whether these were littermate sisters (precise *r* unknown), littermate full-sisters ($r = \frac{1}{2}$) or littermate half-sisters ($r = \frac{1}{4}$) (number of pairs in parentheses). Determination of full- and half-sisters was based on paternity exclusion analysis, using alternate genes at various loci. The difference in chases per trespass between full- and half-sisters is significant ($P < 0.05$). Similar discrimination was also found with other measures of altruistic and selfish tendencies. (*From* Holmes and Sherman 1982)

kin-directed altruism, since altruism would be directed towards others not according to the *average* probability that a gene is located in the recipient but on the exact chance that it was located in the recipient (zero or one). But such a gene would suffer one very serious handicap: should it spread, it would induce very strong selection at all other loci to shut down the gene. This is because the presence or absence of this gene in another person is not associated with the chance that genes at other, independent loci are also found in the recipient. We can conclude that genes do not recognize themselves directly in other creatures, but rather, in many animal species, individuals are able to measure relatedness by learning some standard of comparison, such as the self, by which others are then discriminated.

Recognition of kin may also be important at the time of mating. Individuals may wish to avoid inbreeding and may, at the same time, be selected to avoid excessive outbreeding, where this breaks up sets of genes coadapted to local circumstances. For this reason Patrick Bateson suggests that birds often *learn* while still young what a prospective mate should look like. An innate system of recognition would not as easily permit the subtle discrimination required, but a learned system permits an offspring when young to imprint on the appearance of its parents or siblings, using this as a standard by which to judge a prospective mate. As expected, birds prefer to mate with those who are similar but not identical to those on whom they have imprinted. More recently, Bateson has shown that Japanese quail reared with their siblings later prefer to spend time near first cousins—compared to more or less related individuals—and this correlates positively with courtship (Figure 6-32).

Levels of Organization

A major problem in understanding life has always been to understand the many different levels on which it is organized. Genes, cells, tissues, individuals, families, groups, populations, and species—life seems to be organized in a complex hierarchy of ever more encompassing units. How do we think these different units, and how are the sub-units organized within the units? It is tempting to draw analogies between activities on different levels, but how valid are such analogies? For example, political science has for many years spoken of the "body politic," drawing an analogy between the social group and the individual organism. Just as the different parts of an individual—its kidneys, heart, and lungs—work together toward a common end, so, it might be imagined, human social groups are differentiated into parts working together toward a common, all-encompassing end.

Kinship is critical to distinguishing the various levels of organization. For example, the key fact regarding cells in our body is that all are identically related. Thus, in the early evolution of multicellular organisms, a cell was selected to forego reproduction whenever it transferred a benefit to the reproducing cells greater than the cost suffered. All efficient interactions were favored, and there rapidly developed a set of somatic cells that did not reproduce, but that helped sustain the germinal cells that did reproduce. Since the interests of all cells are identical, specialization evolves without conflict. The kidney and the liver are not in conflict with each other over how many nutrients to remove from the bloodstream; both have been selected to remove the amount of nutrients that maximizes the reproductive interests of the larger unit.

By contrast, most animals live in groups of imperfectly related individuals. Indeed, for large political groups like the United States of America, degrees of relatedness between virtually all members are nearly zero. Thus, many efficient exchanges are not favored; altruism is only favored when a compensating return benefit arrives, and individuals are expected to show conflict over the division of resources. Nevertheless, there is a kinship structure in every social group, and this kinship structure selects for biased exchanges in which individuals tend naturally to favor those to whom they are related by higher degrees of relatedness. Thus there is a fundamental change as we pass the level of the individual and go on to higher levels of organization: degrees of relatedness fall below 1 and social conflict is expected.

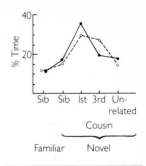

Figure 6-32

A preference for first cousins. The average percentage of time spent by adult Japanese quail near members of the opposite sex is shown plotted as a function of the genetic relationship to this quail (sibling, first and third cousins, or unrelated). Open circles = males; closed circles = females. Two categories of siblings are shown, those with which the tested bird was reared and unfamiliar siblings. Time spent near a member of the opposite sex is closely related to frequency of courtship. (*From Bateson 1982*)

Before biologists developed kinship reasoning there were two opposing views regarding organization above the level of the individual. On the one hand, some people stressed that selection acted at the level of the individual and they therefore emphasized competitive interactions among individuals. On the other hand, the vast majority clung to a species-advantage view of selection in which they failed to see that a problem arises when levels larger than the individual organism are being considered. Kinship reasoning suggests a position between the two extremes. Individuals in a social group are not identically related, and their interests are therefore not identical. But individuals within a social group are not unrelated either. Thus there is always some overlap in self-interest due to degree of relatedness.

The concept of relatedness also permits us to see sources of conflict within the individual. For example, as we have seen, the genes within a single individual are not all inherited according to the same pattern. Ninety-five percent of our genes are located on autosomes and are inherited according to the same pattern. Almost 5% are located on the X chromosome, and the X is inherited in a sex-biased fashion. The Y chromosome has very few genes and is inherited asexually, father to son. Finally, less than one-tenth of 1% of all genes are located in organelles, and these are usually inherited asexually, mother to offspring.

In Table 6-3 we have summarized degrees of relatedness between full-siblings, as a function of sex and portion of genome being considered. Although the dominant degree of relatedness is $\frac{1}{2}$, we see that values vary from 0 to 1. This variation sets up conflict of the following sort. Imagine a mutant appears on a Y chromosome that favors altruistic exchanges among brothers wherever $B > C$. Such a mutant will initially spread, since at this locus $r = 1$ between brothers, but genes at most other loci will be harmed by the spread of such a mutant. This will set up a selection pressure for new genes on these other chromosomes that have the effect of shutting down the selfish mutant on the Y chromosome. Perhaps the new mutant will produce a protein that binds to the mutation on the Y chromosome, preventing it from being expressed. Indeed, Y chromosomal genes are known in several insect species that result in the production of only Y-bearing sperm. These mutations spread at first, but soon their spread strongly favors genes on other chromosomes that shut down the effects of this Y mutation. Hamilton has argued that the Y chromosome is small and inert over most of its structure precisely because of conflict with other genes in the past, so that selection on other chromosomes resulted in the shutting down of more and more of the Y chromosome until it reached its present state, where it controls very few traits beyond maleness (see Figure 5-2).

We can stress the importance of kinship theory for biological organization by considering two topics in more detail. One is the spread

Table 6-3   Degrees of Relatedness Between Full-siblings in a Diploid Outbreeding Species (Male XY, Female XX)

Location of Gene	M → M	M → F	F → F	F → M
Autosome	½	½	½	½
X chromosome	½	½	¾	¼
Y chromosome	1	0	—	—
Extranuclear	1	1	1	1

M = male; F = female.

of truly selfish genes, genes that lower the success of other genes in the individual but are selected because they increase their representation among offspring. The second is selection for higher rates of somatic mutation in plants than in animals because in plants there is a form of reproductive competition that is usually absent in animals.

Selfish Genes

So far we have generated degrees of relatedness by considering the chance that a gene in the parent will be found in an offspring. In a species like our own, meiosis will give a 50% chance, but genes are known that can improve on these chances and thereby gain an advantage; in effect they increase their own r to offspring. For example, instead of r to offspring being determined by a fair assortment of the parental genes, some genes are able to subvert the process of meiosis in their own favor, giving $r > ½$. These genes may be thought of as selfish or parasitic, since they usually have a negative effect on the reproductive success or inclusive fitness of the individual. Thus, these genes confer the narrowest kind of self-interest, one that is not even shared by the other genes of the same individual. To the extent that these selfish genes do lower reproductive success, they set up selection pressures on the rest of the genome to modify or extinguish their effects; this is presumably why such genes are not more common.

Selfish genes gain their benefits in several different ways. Some bias meiosis in their own favor so as to be passed on more frequently than if segregation were truly random. Sometimes whole chromosomes act in this manner, and sometimes genes derived from the mother may suppress the reproduction of the entire set of genes derived from the father. Other genes insert additional copies of themselves in the genome, thereby increasing in frequency. Finally, some genes in organelles bias organelle reproduction so as to exclude paternally derived genes. Let us briefly consider these various ways in which parasitic genes may flourish, for the existence of these parasitic genes gives further support to the genetical view of social life we have been describing: selection at the level of individuals cannot explain the spread of selfish genes, but selection at the level of competing genes can.

Meiotic Drive. Some genes bias the process of meiosis in their own favor. For example, a Y mutant in the mosquito *Aedes aegypti* results in the production of sperm that mostly carry the Y chromosome, because of breakage of the X chromosome during meiosis. When these sperm fertilize eggs, the Y chromosome has doubled in frequency in the resulting offspring, at the expense of the X. Eight categories of X chromosomes have been identified, from highly sensitive to fully resistant. As expected, in Africa and Central America, where the Y mutant is common, the X's tend to be resistant. Although several such examples have been discovered, perhaps the most striking is the degree to which most loci appear truly to assort themselves at random.

Parasitic Chromosomes. Several species of animals are known in which entire chromosomes appear to maintain themselves at sizeable frequencies in nature solely because these chromosomes propagate themselves during meiosis more frequently than expected by chance. They are always supernumerary, that is, the extra chromosomes are not a regular part of the genome. In both sexes these chromosomes lower the ability of the individual to survive and reproduce, yet they are apparently maintained because they parasitize the process of meiosis in their own favor (Table 6-4). Supernumerary chromosomes have been found in numerous species of plants and animals, but they have a sporadic distribution. Thus, they are widespread in grasshoppers and completely absent in closely related mantids. Mostly they are chemically inert, and at least sometimes they are lost from the somatic (nongerminal) cells of fully grown animals. This is precisely what we would expect if such chromosomes are truly parasitic (or if their function is entirely genetic) because their presence in the somatic cells is deleterious, both to the other chromosomes and to themselves.

Parasitic chromosomes gain their advantage in several different ways, depending on the species. Usually, they do one of two things: they bias meiosis in their own favor or they affect mitosis in gonadal tissue so as to increase in number. Often the latter mechanism involves the nondisjunction of chromosomes, so that a cell with one supernumerary gives rise to daughter cells containing either zero or two. The cells with two may then outreproduce those with zero.

It is by no means certain that parasitic chromosomes are entirely parasitic. In some instances, they appear to increase the rate of recombination throughout the genome, and a population with supernumeraries may show greater variance in several biometrical characters than a population without them. When there is geographical variation, factors associated with asexuality in other species (for example, high lati-

Table 6-4   The Maintenance of a Parasitic B Chromosome in the
Grasshopper *Melanoplus femur-rubrum*

	Males	Females
Percent of individuals with one B chromosome		
1971	13.3	10.7
1972	15.7	14.0
1973	12.7	13.6
Percent survival of individuals with one B chromosome (compared to individuals without)	86.0	86.0
Transmission rate of the B chromosome	0.5	0.75

Source: Nur 1977.

Note: The number of individuals with one B chromosome
has remained relatively constant in spite of the lower survival in both sexes but presumably because of the high
transmission rate in females.

tude and altitude) tend to be those associated with fewer supernumeraries (but with exceptions). This is suggestive, because sexuality and
recombination have similar effects (see Chapter 13).

Maternal Suppression of Paternal Chromosomes. In a few groups
of insects, one-half of the genome seems to seize control of an individual's development, suppressing the activity and, finally, the reproduction of the other half (for example, gall midges and some scale insects).
The dominant half in all these cases is the genes that come from the
mother, and their effect is to eliminate the paternal genes from reproduction. This genetic takeover always occurs in males only, so that in
their pattern of inheritance these species are exactly like conventional
haplodiploid species (see pp. 177–178).

Although chromosomes are eliminated by different pathways in
different species, it is always *paternal* chromosomes that are eliminated. The process starts very early in development, typically with the
inactivation of these genes. Why always paternal? Maternal genes
should have an initial advantage because the mother can bias the
intracellular environment in her own favor. Also, if maternal genes
were eliminated from sons, females would no longer be selected to
produce them, so that such tendencies would be replaced by asexual
reproduction.

Jumping Genes. In the last few years it has been discovered that
there are, in the genomes of most species, genes that move around
within the genome. These *jumping genes* are much like the genomes of
viruses in structure and behavior, and they may even have evolved

from ancestors that were once ordinary viruses. But unlike viruses, which are acquired by infection during an individual's lifetime, most jumping genes are present in the chromosomes from conception. When they transpose from one chromosomal location to another they sometimes cause mutations, with significant effects on cellular function. Whether they perform any useful functions within the cell is not yet known. Many of them may be parasites of the genetic system, as are the viruses to which they appear to be related.

Organelle Genes. Genes located in organelles are replicated when the organelle divides to form two new ones. Since male and female gametes both commonly carry organelles, cytoplasmic inheritance ought to be traced through both parents. In fact, the common bias is for cytoplasmic genes to be inherited only through the mother. There seems to be a simple reason for this: the greater investment of the mother in the fertilized eggs. Selection to reduce the size of the male gamete has given numerical superiority to organelles arriving from the mother, while the remainder of the zygote's cytoplasm also comes from the mother and should be biased to help its own organelles. Thus, maternally derived organelles are in a position to assert themselves, and they apparently do so in a variety of ways. For example, in newly fertilized eggs of the sea urchin, the single large sperm mitochondrion is quickly surrounded by several egg mitochondria (Figure 6-33). The membranes appose, and possibly fuse, after which the paternal mitochondrion slowly disintegrates. Usually the paternal organelle is eliminated, as in some species of algae and rodents, but in *Chlamydomonas* only the DNA in the paternal chloroplast is eliminated, leaving the remainder intact. This intracellular equivalent of castration reveals the same acute sense of self-interest, since the potential labor of an entity is, in either case, preserved while the genetic threat is removed.

Somatic Mutations in Plants

Plants and animals differ in the distribution of their reproductive tissue. In most animals, paired gonads issue forth in one section of the body and all sex cells are only several cell divisions removed from a single ancestral germinal cell. Mutations occurring in this line will be incorporated into the sex cells, while mutations occurring in all the other tissues (somatic mutations), will not be found in the sex cells. Somatic mutations are an evolutionary dead end in most animals, never being passed on to offspring, and natural selection should act to lower their rate.

A very different picture is true of most plants. Consider flowering plants. Flowers contain the gonads and flowers are found throughout

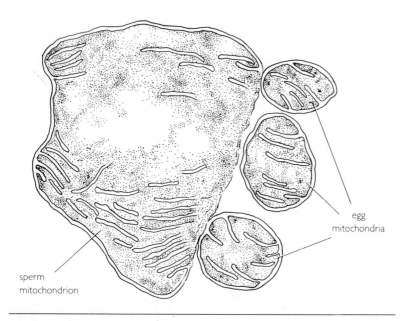

sperm
mitochondrion

egg
mitochondria

Figure 6-33

Sperm mitochondrion under attack? Ten minutes after the first cell division
of a newly fertilized egg of a sea urchin (*Paracentrotus lividus*), a large
mitochondrion from the sperm cell is seen beginning to come apart (notice
empty space in the middle). Three mitochondria from the egg cell are seen
close to the sperm mitochondrion and two are actually connected to its surface. It seems likely that the breakdown of the sperm mitochondrion is caused
by actions of the egg mitochondria. Magnification: ×70,000. (Drawn from a
photo in Anderson 1968)

the plant, at the ends of dozens, perhaps thousands (in large trees) of
different cell lines, separated by hundreds of cell divisions and descended from each other in a branching pattern that is preserved in the
structure of the plant. Virtually all somatic mutations are present in
the sex cells. In many species, roots reproduce new individuals by vege-
tative reproduction so that all somatic mutations potentially are represented as germinal cells. Unlike animals, there will be opportunity for
different successive somatic mutations to accumulate in different parts
of the plant, each combination being expressed in the sex cells (see Figure 6-34). Furthermore, parts of a plant are often in direct competition
with each other for resources such as light. Any slight inherent superiority (for example, in resistance to herbivores) may eventually result in

Figure 6-34

Genetic variation within individual plants. Here are two individuals of the evergreen shrub *Euonymus japonica.* Different parts of leaves, entire leaves, and small and large branches differ in chlorophyll production, appearing either green or yellow. Note that the coloration pattern is completely different in the two plants. Unlike for animals, this genetic variation throughout the individual plant may be passed on to offspring. (Photo: Thomas Whitham)

large differential growth. Consider the possible effects for selection. Not only is a much larger array of mutations and combinations offered to selection by each organism, but those genetic combinations that are inefficient in plant function should suffer the cost of producing relatively fewer sex cells. In species with insect pollinators, the pollinators may intensify the effect by preferring the richer flowers produced by cell lines with more efficient arrays of somatic mutations, leading to greater fertility of superior sex cells. A corresponding difference in quality of fruit may, likewise, lead to better dispersal.

It is very difficult to estimate somatic mutation rates, but what evidence there is suggests that such rates in plants may be higher than germinal mutation rates in animals. This is consistent with the view that somatic mutations confer special benefits on plants. Somatic mutations may be important in enabling long-lived plants to survive attacks by herbivores with short generation times. Not only does the individual plant offer a genetically heterogeneous world to its attackers, but the individual plant *evolves* in response to its attackers. As herbivores damage some portions of the plant, other portions grow faster to make up for the damage. Somatic mutations permit this process to be genetically selective, so that over the years, the plant should evolve so as to express more frequently in its body and in its reproductive tissue advantageous mutations. In this context, it is interesting to note that adventitious buds, that is, buds that grow out laterally in response to damage above, develop from a different embryological layer than the tissue above. This increases the chance that the new buds will differ genetically from the injured tissue that induced their growth.

In summary, plants may benefit from somatic mutations in two ways. The individual plant evolves its genetic constitution, changing through time in an adaptive way, so that beneficial somatic mutations become relatively more numerous throughout its body. This should continually improve the individuals' chances of surviving. At the same time, most of these beneficial somatic mutations will also appear in the sex cells. The offspring benefit from the somatic experience of their parents.

Summary

Kinship refers to genetic relatedness, and evidence from ground squirrels and Japanese monkeys shows that these animals are more likely to act altruistically toward closely related individuals and more likely to act selfishly toward distantly related ones. Benefits to related sperm cells apparently explain the repeated evolution of altruistic sperm, themselves unable to fertilize eggs but somehow assisting those that do. Less frequent evolution of egg altruism probably reflects the greater cost of each egg.

Degree of relatedness is not the same as degree of genetic identity and the latter is irrelevant to the conditions under which altruistic genes will spread. Likewise, the frequency that an altruistic gene has attained in a species does not affect the conditions under which it will spread further. This can be seen by realizing that in the uncorrelated portion of the actor's and recipient's genome, genes receive effects according to their overall frequencies in the population, so that the effects per gene are the same for all of the genes. Thus, only effects that reach the correlated portion of the genome affect the direction of selection. The notion of a "gene for altruism" is seen as a convenient way to conceptualize kinship effects that may, in fact, be mediated by dozens of genes.

Inbreeding increases degrees of relatedness by increasing the genealogical connections among individuals. In addition, products of inbreeding will find that the two halves of their genome are partly correlated. This will lead products of inbreeding to value themselves relatively more, except insofar as the inbreeding has resulted in reduced reproductive potential for them.

Animals have evolved a variety of means by which to recognize their relatives. Although animals may often use cues of association to infer kinship, they are also able to measure relatedness by comparing the phenotype of another to some common standard. Sweat bee females, for example, make very precise discriminations in r by comparing the odor of others to the odor of their sisters. In a variety of species, animals are able to discriminate between full- and half-siblings, based on a similar process of phenotypic matching.

Kinship is useful in thinking about the levels on which life is organized. The multicellular creature is based on kinship; so is the family, including such tightly organized groups as beehives. Some conflict within an individual's genotype is possible when genes in different locations assort themselves to offspring according to different degrees of relatedness. Conflict within the genotype also includes conflict over which genes will be represented in the offspring. There is good evidence for several classes of selfish genes: genes that lower the number of surviving offspring left by an individual but spread by increasing their percentage within these offspring.

In plants, potentially all mutations appearing throughout the body may end up in the sex cells and since the growing parts of a plant are often in competition for resources, superior mutations may increase in number during the lifetime of an individual and be passed on to offspring. Consistent with this view is the apparently high rate of somatic mutations among plants.

Chapter 7

Parent–Offspring Conflict

M<small>Y</small> <small>INTEREST IN</small> the biological approach to parent–offspring relations began years ago, when I noticed in several different species that parents and their offspring were sometimes in sharp conflict. For example, for two years I watched free-living pigeons in Cambridge, Massachusetts. I saw that at the beginning of a chick's life it is treated very solicitously by both parents. Indeed, upon feeding one chick, the parent may stroke the neck of the second chick with its bill in order to arouse it to feed. This early period of parental solicitude gradually gives way to a more ambivalent relationship and, finally, to a time when the parent seeks to avoid the chick. Chicks who are nearly fully fledged often attack their parents when the parents return to the roost, crowding them into corners and begging for food. Parents sometimes then feed the chicks but often fly away, escaping onto a nearby ledge. Indeed, in order to avoid being besieged, they often fly right to the nearby ledge, avoiding their own nest altogether. Likewise, in other city-dwelling species, parent–offspring conflict is easy to observe. It is common to see full-grown starling youngsters quivering their wings near their parents and uttering a series of begging calls. Most of this goes on without any parental response, except continuous attempts to evade the young. Among herring gulls, the nearly fully grown young must adopt a "humble" posture in order to remain near their parents and continue to be fed (Figure 7-1).

In 1972 I traveled to India and East Africa to observe monkey behavior, and I saw some dramatic cases of parent–offspring conflict. Among langur monkeys and baboons, conflict over weaning can last for several weeks. The infant utters a series of piercing cries in its efforts to beg milk from mother and may retaliate fiercely when rebuffed (Figure 7-2). Conflict may also break out when the infant is denied a ride on its mother's back. Baboons are typically silent in most of

Figure 7-1

Submissive posture of herring gull chicks near their parent. Although fully grown, these chicks of two months are still dependent on their parents for food; their parents are now ambivalent about feeding them and tolerating them nearby. As a result of this conflict, the chicks have adopted a very submissive posture (the very opposite of attack): head withdrawn into the body, wings relaxed, body small. Similar postures at this stage are found in other gull species. (Photo: Niko Tinbergen)

their social interactions, yet it is curious that one way to find a baboon troop in the morning is to go to the kind of trees baboons like to sleep in and listen for the sound of weaning conflict. From these observations, it seems likely that weaning conflict among monkeys is a costly process for the infant, its mother, and possibly for other troop members. Certainly the daily harassment of mother is costly in energy to infant and mother. The calls themselves may bring on predators and threaten the entire group. Why, then, do we witness such intense parent–offspring conflict in nature?

Explanations for similar phenomena in humans seem to lack a firm evolutionary foundation. For example, Freudian theory claims that there are fundamental sexual conflicts in the human family. It is alleged that girls wish they had penises and boys are afraid fathers might castrate them because of their sexual interest in their mothers. On the surface, these kinds of conflicts make no obvious evolutionary sense. Selection against close inbreeding is usually powerful in nature, and it seems surprising that so dire a consequence as castration would need to be threatened in order to avoid mother–son incest. It seems more likely that Freud came upon sexual overtones in parent–

a

b

Figure 7-2

Fierce retaliation by an infant langur. (a) High in a tree, having been rebuffed by its mother, the infant first screeches at her. (b) It then leaps across the intervening space and slaps its mother! (Photos: Sarah Hrdy, Anthro-Photo)

offspring conflict and, lacking an evolutionary view of the relationship, misinterpreted the overtones for the real thing.

Another popular view holds that there is a fundamental conflict between biology and culture. The baby is viewed as innately selfish and greedy and in need of socialization in order to become a full culture-bearing creature. This theory sees conflict as arising from the innate barbarity of the child.

A consideration of kinship theory suggests another alternative. In sexually reproducing species, parent and offspring are not identically related. Indeed, under outbreeding they are related by only one-half.

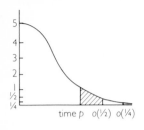

Figure 7-3

Weaning conflict. The benefit/cost ratio *(B/C)* of a parental act (such as nursing) toward an offspring is plotted as a function of time for an imaginary species. *Benefit* is the gain in survival of the offspring receiving the investment, while *cost* is the decrease in the parent's production of additional surviving offspring. Thus, selection ought to oppose parental investment when *C > B* or *(B/C) < 1*. This occurs at time *p*. The offspring is selected to receive investment until *(B/C) = ½*, which occurs at time *o(r = ½)*. The shaded area represents the time of conflict between parent and offspring over whether investment should continue. If future sibs were half-sibs, conflict would continue until (B/C) = ¼ or time *o(r = ¼)*. (*From* Trivers 1974)

Thus there is an overlap in self-interest between parent and offspring, but not an identity of self-interest. In this chapter we will pursue the implications of this partial overlap in self-interest. We begin with the reasons for expecting conflict between parent and offspring over parental investment and we review evidence from mammals and birds that suggests a general pattern to this conflict. We describe ways in which the offspring may manipulate its parent and we review evidence that monkey infants respond to separation from their mother in a way that suggests natural selection for psychological sophistication in the infant. Finally, we show that conflict also extends to the behavioral tendencies of the offspring, and we review some of the implications of this view for understanding human psychological development.

Parent–Offspring Conflict Over the Termination of Parental Investment

Let us begin by considering parental investment from the standpoint of the parent. The parent has been selected to invest in its offspring in such a way as to maximize the number eventually surviving. From the parent's standpoint we can dissolve parental investment into associated benefit and cost. The benefit is the degree to which the investment increases the survival of the offspring at hand, while the cost is the degree to which the investment decreases the parent's ability to invest in other offspring (including those still unborn). Put this way, the parent is naturally selected to maximize the difference between the benefit and the cost. In particular, it is selected to avoid any investment in the offspring for which the cost is greater than the benefit, since such investment would decrease the total number of its offspring surviving.

By contrast, the offspring is selected to devalue the cost it inflicts compared to the benefit it receives. This is because the offspring is identically related to itself but only partly related to its siblings. If we assume, for example, that an offspring's siblings will be full-siblings, then *r = ½*. The offspring will be selected to maximize the difference between *B* and *½C*. In particular, the offspring will be favored to stop asking for investment whenever the cost of the investment is more than twice the benefit it receives.

Because the offspring is selected to devalue the cost of parental investment, it will always tend to favor a longer period of parental investment than the parent is selected to give. This argument can be pictured by drawing the benefit/cost ratio of parental investment as a function of time (Figure 7-3). Initially, parental investment gives a large benefit to the offspring at a small cost to the parent (measured as production of additional offspring). But as the period of investment continues and the offspring becomes increasingly independent, the benefit the offspring receives tends to decrease, while the cost to the parent increases, for example, because the parent becomes increasingly depleted of resources. In any case, the benefit/cost ratio falls. When this ratio equals 1, the parent is selected to terminate investment, because after this point, the cost of further investment will be greater than the benefit, and the parent will suffer a decrease in reproductive success. But the offspring is selected to continue to request investment until $B/C = r$. After this point, the offspring is no longer selected to receive further investment, since if it does, it will inflict such a large cost on its mother's future reproductive success that its own genes will decrease in numbers.

Notice several key features of this argument. First, at the end of the period of parental investment we expect a bounded period of conflict over how long investment should continue, a period which should begin when the parent is no longer selected to invest and end when the offspring is no longer selected to receive investment. Second, conflict results from an underlying difference in the way in which each party maximizes its inclusive fitness. It is not a result of habit (for example, milk tastes good). Nor does conflict occur because transitions in nature are assumed always to be rough (milk tastes good, and it is difficult to develop a taste for solid foods). And finally, conflict does not occur because of the innate selfishness of the offspring. Indeed, it would be just as accurate to say that conflict occurs because of the innate selfishness of the parent.

Finally, we note that degree of relatedness to future siblings is a variable that affects the length of parent–offspring conflict over the continuation of parental investment. This variable suggests the way in which a kinship interpretation of parent–offspring conflict differs from other interpretations. Contrast two species of monkeys. In one, a single breeding male dominates reproduction for five or six years, fathering several of a female's offspring in succession. In such a species, r between siblings will often be ½, and the period of parent–offspring conflict will be relatively short. By contrast, in a species in which breeding males are replaced every year or two, most siblings will be half-siblings, and conflict is expected to last longer. Whether langur parent–offspring conflict is more intense because of frequent male take-overs followed by infanticide (see pp. 71–77) is not known but it is certainly what we would expect.

Conflict During the Period of Parental Investment

The previous argument was concerned with parent–offspring conflict at the end of the period of parental investment. It is easy to show that

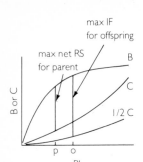

Figure 7-4

Conflict during the period of investment over the amount of investment. The benefit (*B*) or the cost (*C*) of investment at a given moment is plotted as a function of the amount of parental investment (such as amount of milk). The parent is selected to maximize the difference between the two functions (*B* and *C*); that is, to invest *p*. The offspring maximizes (*B* − *rC*) (here, *r* = ½); that is, it is selected to receive investment *o*. (RS = reproductive success; IF = inclusive fitness.) (*From* Trivers 1974)

this is only one case of parent–offspring conflict—specifically, conflict over whether the offspring should receive *any* investment. Parent and offspring are also expected to show conflict over *how much* investment is given. Consider an arbitrary day during the nursing period of a mammal. We can graph the benefit the offspring receives as a function of increasing amounts of milk on that day, and likewise the cost to the mother of dispensing the milk (Figure 7-4). As before, the mother is selected to invest the amount of milk that maximizes the difference between *B* and *C*, but the offspring is selected to maximize the difference between *B* and *rC*. This will always result in the offspring's preferring more investment than the parent is selected to give.

Note that this argument applies to any moment during the period of parental investment. In principle, it refers also to events that occur before birth in mammals. The offspring is capable of producing hormones and other chemicals that pass across the placenta to the mother's system, and these chemicals may induce additional investment. The offspring is also capable of some behavior *in utero*, and this may likewise affect the mother, as was suggested to me forcibly once by a woman who was expecting her second child. Late in the pregnancy the baby would kick her whenever she leaned forward in her seat. It was comfortable for her to lean forward, but this apparently put additional pressure on the baby, and the baby's response was to kick her until she assumed an upright posture.

In order to say whether conflict is expected to increase or decrease during the period of parental investment, we would, in principle, need to make comparisons such as those shown in Figure 7-4 for different times in the period of parental investment. But, in fact, there are three factors that tend to lead to an increase in conflict during the period of investment. First, the offspring increases in size and, therefore, in demands. Secondly, maternal resources are decreasing as a function of prior investment, so that each succeeding unit of investment is differentially costly to the mother. Finally, as we reach the end of the period of parental investment, there is a decreasing chance of self-inflicted cost. To understand what this means, imagine that halfway through the period of parental investment the offspring garners more milk than the mother is selected to give. The mother can respond to this by decreasing milk on subsequent days below what she otherwise would have given. As we reach the end of the period of parental investment, there is less and less opportunity to correct the imbalance in this manner. Thus the offspring can demand additional investment with little or no possibility that this investment will later be subtracted.

Another factor that may affect conflict is parental age. In general, the older a parent is, the less will be its future reproductive success and the lower will be the cost of current investment, measured in terms of future offspring. This should select for a longer period of parental in-

vestment and reduced conflict with its offspring. In red deer, for instance, older mothers appear to invest more in their offspring; the condition of the offspring in their first winter, relative to their mothers',
improves with maternal age (Figure 7-5). In California gulls, rates of
nest attendance, territorial defense, and feeding the chicks all increase
with parental age (Figure 7-6). In baboons, older mothers start rejecting their offspring later than do younger mothers and reduced rejection rate is associated with longer time until the mother reproduces
again (Figure 7-7).

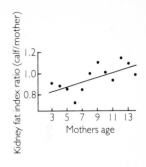

Studies of Parent–Offspring Conflict in Mammals and Birds

In a variety of mammals, conflict increases during the period of parental investment. In dogs and cats, postnatal maternal care can be divided into three periods according to increasing age of the offspring.
During the first period, the mother approaches the infant to initiate
parental investment. No avoidance behavior or aggression is shown by
the mother. In the second, the offspring and the mother approach each
other about equally, and the mother shows some avoidance behavior
and some aggression in response to the infant's demands. The third
period can be characterized as the period of weaning: most contacts
are initiated by the offspring, and open avoidance and aggression characterize the mother.

Detailed evidence from rhesus monkeys shows that the behavior
of both mother and offspring changes during the period of parental

Figure 7-5

*Calf condition relative to
mother's condition as a
function of mother's age
in red deer.* The aver-
age kidney-fat index of a
calf divided by that of its
mother is plotted as a function of maternal age. The
kidney-fat index measures
the degree of fat on the
kidney, a measure of bodily
condition. Notice that
older mothers produce
calves in better condition,
relative to their own condition. (*From* Clutton-Brock
1984)

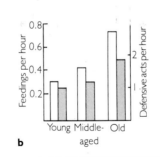

Figure 7-6

*Parental investment as a function of age in the California gull Larus califor-
nicus.* (a) The average minutes per hour in which neither parent attended the
nest (unshaded bars) or foraged (shaded bars) as a function of age. Young are
3–5 years old, middle-aged are 7–9, and old are 12–18. (b) The average
number of times per hour in which parents fed chicks (unshaded bars) or
engaged in territorial defense (shaded bars). All four measures show increasing parental investment with increasing parental age. (*From* Pugesek 1981)

investment, so as to result in increasing conflict. During the first few weeks after she has given birth, the rhesus mother initiates most nipple contacts, but her initiative soon declines rapidly. (See Figure 7-8 for the early mother–infant relationship in baboons.) Concurrently, she begins to reject some of the infant's advances; after her own initiatives toward nipple contact have ceased, she rejects her infant's advances with steadily increasing frequency until at the end of investment all of the offspring's advances are rejected. The infant, in turn, becomes increasingly independent of the mother, as measured by time off of her, but at the same time the infant becomes increasingly responsible for maintaining proximity. Shortly after birth the infant leaves the mother more often than it approaches her; that is, the mother retrieves the in-

Figure 7-7

Extreme dependence. This baboon youngster is now more than a year old but it is still being carried by its mother; its age mates travel on their own. The mother (Kink) is an old and very low-ranking female. Such mothers seem especially protective of their offspring (compare Figure 6-17). For an example of the treatment Kink had to suffer, see Figure 15-6). (Photo: Irven DeVore, Anthro-Photo)

Figure 7-8

Mother and new-born. A baboon mother with her infant who is about a week old. She is picking through its fur for any dirt or parasites. A baboon mother is extremely protective at this stage, reluctant to allow other baboons, who are strongly attracted to infants, to touch or hold her infant. The infant will retain its black coat—which nicely sets off its pink skin—for several months. (Photo: Irven DeVore, Anthro-Photo)

fant. But as time passes the mother begins to reject the infant and the initiative in maintaining proximity shifts to the offspring, so that the infant spends more time away from the mother but is typically the first one to close the distance between them (see Figure 7-9).

In sheep, a mother produces more milk than her lamb can drink during the first weeks of the lamb's life, and the lamb's appetite determines how much milk is consumed. But after the fourth week, the mother begins to produce less than the lamb can drink, and from that time on she is the limiting factor in determining how much milk is consumed. The mother initially permits her lamb(s) free access, but after a couple of weeks begins to prevent some suckling attempts. Mothers in poor condition become the limiting factor in nursing earlier than do mothers in good condition, so that offspring must fight harder to gain the same amount of investment. Mothers who produce twins permit either twin to suckle on demand during the first three weeks after birth, but afterwards permit one twin to suckle only if the other twin is also ready.

That the parent may be selected to hurry its offspring to independence is nicely illustrated by a study of the transition to independence in the spotted flycatcher (*Muscicapa striata*). As in most birds, the major category of parental investment is the feeding of the young, and

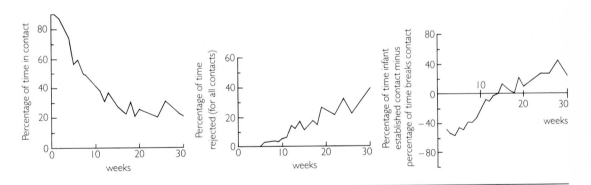

Figure 7-9

Changes in the mother–offspring relationship in captive rhesus monkeys. Left: percentage of total time the offspring is in bodily contact with its mother as a function of offspring age (in weeks). *Center*: relative frequency of maternal rejection; that is, the percentage of the number of contacts in which the offspring was rejected by its mother in its attempts to establish contact. *Right*: infant's role in maintaining contact; that is, the percentage of total contacts established that the infant made minus the percentage of total contacts broken that the infant broke. Negative values mean that the mother is responsible for maintaining contact; positive values, the offspring. (*From* Hinde 1977)

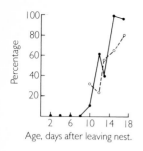

Figure 7-10

Offspring effort and success rate at inducing parental feedings in the spotted flycatcher. The percentage of parental feedings in which the offspring chases the parent (solid circles) and the percentage of such chases in which the offspring receives no food (open circles) as a function of offspring age (in days since leaving the nest) in the spotted flycatcher. (*From* Davies 1976)

offspring are independent when they can provide all their food for themselves. As Nick Davies has shown, in the spotted flycatcher this transition occurs over a period of several days, during which the parent steadily decreases the benefits of parental feeding.

For the first nine days that the spotted flycatcher chick is out of the nest, most parental feeding occurs when the chick is silent (instead of calling); but after ten days the parent brings food only when the offspring calls. At the same time there is a sharp increase in the rate at which chicks chase after their parents. Between the 10th and the 16th day the parents tend more and more to feed their chicks only after being chased by them and, at the same time, an increasing percentage of chases fail to result in food transfer (Figure 7-10). There is even a decrease in the size of the food items transferred.

The joint effect of these actions is a very sharp reduction in the amount of food transferred by the parent per unit time; by the 14th day the spotted flycatcher offspring does better by capturing prey itself than by begging food from its parents. This is exactly the time when it shifts from getting most of its food from its parents to getting the bulk by itself. In effect, the parent forces more and more of the burden of feeding onto the offspring. The offspring is forced first to call, then to chase, then to chase for longer and longer periods, all the while it is being provided with food, time, and—increasingly—the motivation to perfect its own prey-capture techniques. Most of the improvement in these techniques comes while the parent is still providing most of the food, so although the parent hurries the offspring to independence, it still seems to provide a cushion of safety for the offspring to develop its skills.

Recently Judy Stamps and her colleagues have made a remarkable discovery concerning parent–offspring conflict in an Australian bird called the budgerigar *Melopsittacus undulatus*: offspring are unable to manipulate their mothers but easily manipulate their fathers! The key is the offspring's begging rate. In the early stages the chick does not beg frequently and is often fed without begging; when it does beg it is fed. In later stages, it begs more frequently, although this has no effect on the mother's feeding rate. Instead, mother distributes food to the young according to age and size, favoring the youngest and the smallest (Figure 7-11). This bias results in later-hatching chicks actually reaching heavier weights than early hatchlings.

The male budgerigar usually feeds his mate. When he does feed the chicks, he feeds those that beg most intensively most often. Begging rates in such families increase dramatically (see Figure 7-12). Chicks survive no more often as a result of this begging but they do fledge at slightly heavier weights. The female's discriminatory strategy is costly in time—she feeds chicks at about half the rate the male does. Thus, the countering of offspring selfishness is biologically expensive, as expected. Why should the male be so vulnerable to offspring manipulation? Perhaps his lesser evolutionary experience feeding the chicks is responsible. Or perhaps in nature he only feeds the chicks himself when food is short, and discriminating against smaller, weaker chicks may be adaptive at such a time since some may have to starve anyway. What we know is that parent–offspring conflict has evolved a counterstrategy in the mother that is effective but costly, while no counterstrategy is apparent in the father!

Psychological Manipulation by the Offspring

How is the offspring to compete effectively with its parent? An offspring cannot fling its mother to the ground and nurse at will. It cannot even steal the resource at issue (Figure 7-13). The offspring is smaller and less experienced than its parent, and its parent controls the resources at issue. Given this competitive disadvantage, the offspring is expected to employ psychological tactics. It should attempt to *induce* more investment than the parent is selected to give.

Since an offspring will often have better knowledge of its real needs than will its parent, selection should favor parental attentiveness to signals from offspring that signal the offspring's condition. In short, the offspring cries when hungry or in danger, and the parent responds appropriately. Conversely, the offspring smiles or wags its tail when its needs have been well met. Both parent and offspring benefit from this system of communication, but once such a system has evolved, the offspring can begin to employ it out of context. The offspring can cry not only when famished, but also when it merely wants more food than the parent is selected to give. Likewise, it can withhold its smile until it has gotten its way. Selection will, of course, favor parental ability to discriminate the two uses of the signals, but still subtler mimicry and deception are always possible.

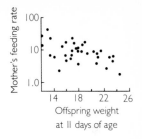

Figure 7-11

Mother's feeding rate as a function of weight of offspring in the budgerigar. All offspring are 11 days of age. Plotted is the mother's feeding rate (rate of regurgitation) to offspring per hour. The log plot means that there is an almost 100-fold increase in feeding rate with decreasing size of offspring. (*From* Stamps et al in press)

Figure 7-12

Begging rate of budgerigar offspring as affected by whether fathers feed young or not. These graphs show the average begging rate of offspring during the final nestling stage in the budgerigar for four female-fed families (A, B, C and D) and four families in which the male also fed (E, F, G and H). (*From* Stamps et al in press)

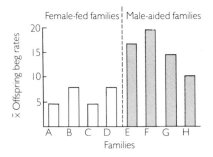

Figure 7-13

A stolen nursing. A year-old male Japanese monkey, involved in weaning conflict with his mother, sneaks up to her and starts nursing while she lies apparently asleep, enjoying a grooming from her three-year-old daughter. Shortly after this picture was taken, the mother slapped her son and he ran off. (Photo: Jeffrey Kurland)

The offspring is typically more helpless and vulnerable the younger it is, so parents will have been more strongly selected to respond positively to signals emitted by the offspring the younger the offspring is. This suggests that at any stage of development at which the offspring is in conflict with its parent, it may be selected to revert to the gestures and actions of an earlier stage of development in order to induce the investment that would have then been forthcoming. In short, it may be selected to *regress* when under stress (Figure 7-14).

Temper tantrums are an interesting behavior by youngsters, since in many circumstances infants have not had an opportunity to learn such behavior through studying others, and since the behavior seems to threaten the parent by suggesting that the offspring may actually harm itself. For example, among pelicans, chicks sometimes indulge in convulsions (Figure 7-15). In George Schaller's words:

Young, ten or more days old, often begged vigorously for their food. Usually a young pelican sat very upright in front of its parent, with neck stretched high and wings beating, until it was admitted to the pouch. Sometimes, however, a young bird ran to an adult, threw itself on the ground, and beat its wings wildly, all the while swinging its head from side to side. Occasionally the young lay on its side, beat one wing, suddenly jumped up, ran at and pecked several young in the vicinity, driving them away, only to continue begging. It also grabbed, shook, and bit its own wing with the bill as it turned its body

Figure 7-14

Regressive behavior in a baboon. This figure shows two mothers with their offspring. The youngster on the right is only about three months old but he rides in mature jockey style. The youngster on the left is at least twice as old but rides with the posture of a clinging infant because it has just been rebuffed by its mother from gaining nipple contact. (Drawn from a photo by Irven DeVore, Anthro-Photo)

around and around, growling all the time. In the words of Chapman (1908, 102) the young "acts like a bird demented." Such begging often continued for one minute, with the young usually facing the adult. Young frequently continued to beg after they were fed and occasionally were fed a second time.

When the young were unsure on their feet, adults could elude their begging by rapidly walking away. However, large young often ran after the adults for 40 or more feet and even pursued them in the water.

The pelican is crazy like a fox. By chasing away its siblings, it makes sure there will be no competitors for the food it is attempting to elicit. By going into convulsions it may convince the parent that withholding food will have dire consequences for the health of the chick.

Temper tantrums in chimpanzees are remarkably similar to human temper tantrums. As Jane Goodall van Lawick has written:

Temper tantrums are a characteristic performance of the infant and young juvenile chimpanzee. The animal screaming loudly either leaps into the air with

Figure 7-15

Convulsion in a pelican.
This portrays a pink-
backed pelican *Pelecanus
rufescens* in convulsions,
biting its own wing. Is this
behavior analogous to a
chimpanzee's banging its
head on the ground, in
effect threatening damage
to a vital part of its own
body? (*From* Burke and
Brown 1970)

its arms above its head or hurls itself to the ground, writhing about and often
hitting itself against surrounding objects. The first temper tantrum observed in
one infant occurred when he was 11 months old. He looked around and was
unable to see his mother. With a loud scream he flung himself to the ground
and beat at it with his hands, and his mother at once rushed to gather him up.
Two infants showed tantrums in connection with weaning and this has been
recorded also in infant baboons and langurs. . . . Yerkes (1943), when describing tantrums, comments that he often saw a youngster "in the midst of a
tantrum glance furtively at its mother or the caretaker as if to discover whether
its action was attracting attention." In captivity, individuals are less prone to
indulge in temper tantrums as they grow older, and this was also true of wild
chimpanzees.

Strangely enough the habit is, under certain conditions, carried over
into adulthood (Figure 7-16).

The normal course of parent–offspring relations must be subject
to considerable unpredictable variation in the condition of both the
parent and the offspring. Both partners are selected to be sensitive to
such variation. Low investment coming from a parent in poor condition has a different meaning than low investment coming from a parent in good condition. This suggests that from an early age the offspring is expected to be a psychologically sophisticated creature. The
offspring should be able to evaluate the cost of parental actions and
their benefits. When the offspring's interests diverge from those of its
parent, the offspring is selected to employ a series of psychological ma-

Figure 7-16

Temper tantrum in an adult chimpanzee. An adult male chimpanzee (named Yeroen) is throwing a temper tantrum and being comforted by a juvenile. Yeroen is distressed because his leadership role is under challenge (see pp. 376–381). (Drawn from a photo in de Waal 1982)

neuvers such as we have already mentioned. Although it is expected to learn useful information (such as whether its psychological maneuvers were having the desired effect), the offspring cannot rely on its parents for disinterested guidance. One expects the offspring to be pre-programmed to resist some parental manipulation while being open to other forms. When the parent imposes an arbitrary system of reinforcement (punishment and reward) in order to manipulate the offspring into acting against its own best interests, selection will favor offspring who resist such schedules of reinforcement. They may comply initially, but at the same time search for alternative ways of expressing their self-interest. Thus, from the offspring's standpoint, an important distinction ought to be made between reinforcement schedules that are imposed by a disinterested environment and ones that are imposed by another organism, which may be attempting to manipulate it against its own best interests.

Maternal Rejection and the Effects of Separation

An individual may be selected to respond to early signals that predict later events in a relationship. If early lack of love predicts later deficient investment, the offspring will be selected to be sensitive to such lack of love so that it can attempt to increase later investment. Since parent and offspring are in conflict, offspring monitoring of the parent will be required if the offspring is to protect its own interests.

The best evidence for the appropriate psychological insight in young mammals comes from the work of Robert Hinde and co-workers on rhesus monkeys. They maintained semi-natural groups of monkeys in large outdoor cages and conducted two main kinds of separation experiments. In one, the mother of a six-month-old infant was removed from its offspring for one week and then returned. The offspring spent the entire time in the familiar group cage with other group members. In the second experiment, infants six months of age were removed from their mothers for one week, kept in a small cage away from the group and then returned. The mothers spent the entire time in the group cage. Hinde and his co-workers then measured the effects on the infant and on the mother–offspring relationship of these separations. In advance, one would expect the second separation to be the more traumatic, since the infant is not only separated from its mother, but also separated from its usual environment and from other group members. In fact, however, the first experiment has a much greater effect on the infant's behavior. The results of their experiments can be summarized as follows.

(1) *The separation of mother from offspring affects their relationship upon reunion.* The offspring spends more time on the mother after separation than it did before. This is caused by the offspring and occurs despite an increase in maternal rejection. These effects on the offspring's behavior last for at least five weeks and often considerably longer. The infant acts as if maternal disappearance is an event whose recurrence it can prevent by devoting more time and energy to staying near the mother.

(2) *The mother–offspring relationship prior to separation affects the offspring's behavior upon reunion.* Upon reunion, all offspring show distress. They show a series of contact cries and relative immobility. The greater the frequency of rejection these infants experience from their mother prior to separation, the greater is their distress upon reunion. In turn, the greater their distress, the greater are their efforts to stay near their mothers. The infant appears to act on the logical assumption that a *rejecting* mother who temporarily disappears needs more offspring surveillance than does a *non-rejecting* mother who temporarily disappears.

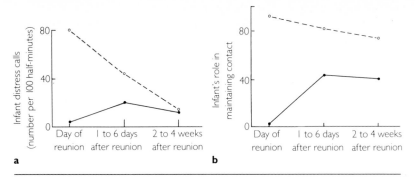

Figure 7-17

An offspring whose mother was separated from it acts differently upon re-union than an offspring that was separated from its mother. (a) The number of distress calls by an infant rhesus monkey (per 100 half-minutes) is plotted as a function of time since reunion after a 13-day separation, depending on whether the mother was separated from the infant (open circles) or the infant was separated from the mother (closed circles). (b) The infant's role in maintaining proximity is plotted as a function of time since reunion for infants whose mother was removed (open circles) or for infants that were removed from their mother (closed circles). The infant's role in maintaining proximity is defined as in Figure 7-9. (From Hinde and McGinnis 1977)

(3) *By contrast, when the offspring is removed from its mother, it shows less distress upon reunion and less effort to maintain proximity than if the mother were removed from it* (see Figure 7-17). This suggests that the offspring responds to the meaning of events affecting it. The offspring differentiates between separations caused by the mother (mother removed from group) and separations caused by itself (infant removed from group).

It is sometimes doubted whether factors like rate of maternal rejection can affect a mother's subsequent reproductive success, but recent work on the same colony of monkeys shows that a mother that rejects her offspring more often in the first ten weeks of its life is more likely to conceive in the next mating season (Figure 7-18). Mothers appear to adjust themselves to their offspring, since mothers of sons and of more active offspring are more likely to conceive in the next mating season. Rate of rejection and activity level of the infant are, in turn, positively correlated, so that mothers may be choosing to hurry along those infants that are more advanced in development. Alternately, maternal rejection may itself hasten infant development. In baboons living in nature, weaning precedes by several months the resumption of the mother's sexual cycles, yet the rate at which weaning occurs has clear effects: mothers that permit their infants more nipple contact between 9 and 32 weeks of age take longer to start their sexual

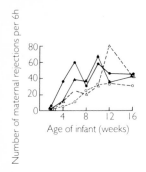

Number of maternal rejections per 6h

Age of infant (weeks)

Figure 7-18

Frequency of maternal re-jection for mothers who are quick to reproduce again and those who are slow. The number of maternal rejections per six hours is plotted as a function of the offspring's age (in weeks) for daughters (closed cir-cles) and sons (closed tri-angles) of mothers who will conceive again before the offspring is a year of age and also for daughters (open circles) and sons (open triangles) of mothers who will not conceive again in the offspring's first year. A rejection included the mother biting, hitting, or pushing the infant; pre-venting nipple or body con-tact; or breaking contact immediately after the in-fant sought contact. The quick mothers are more re-jecting than the slow moth-ers for the first ten weeks of the infant's life. (*From* Simpson et al. 1981)

cycles and longer to give birth to the next infant. It seems likely that rate of rejection also has effects on the offspring's reproductive suc-cess; such effects remain to be discovered.

Conflict Over the Behavior of the Offspring

Conflict may also extend to the behavioral tendencies of the offspring. At the beginning of this book we saw that dominant male baboons will discipline juveniles, presumably in order to alter their behavior (see Figures 1-1 to 1-3). Although we do not know whether the baboons are related to the juveniles they punish, human parents certainly use reward and punishment to mold the behavior of their offspring. We will now show that conflict regarding this activity should obey a simple rule: parents are selected to socialize their children to act more al-truistically and less selfishly than the offspring are selected to act on their own.

Consider parents with two offspring. Imagine that the first off-spring is considering an altruistic act toward the second. It is only se-lected to act altruistically whenever $B > 2C$. The parents are equally related to the two offspring and would therefore enjoy a gain in re-productive success whenever one offspring acted altruistically toward the other at $B > C$. There must exist situations in nature when $C < B < 2C$. In such situations parents are selected to socialize their off-spring to act altruistically, while offspring are selected to resist the socialization.

A similar argument applies to selfish behavior. The offspring is se-lected to act selfishly toward a second offspring whenever $C < 2B$. But parents are selected to discourage all selfish acts in which $C > B$. Since there must exist situations in which $B < C < 2B$, we expect to see conflict between parent and offspring over the selfish tendencies of the offspring. The parent is selected to discourage selfishness more often than the offspring is selected to refrain on its own.

This conflict is expected over offspring behavior directed toward other relatives as well. For example, the offspring is only selected to act altruistically toward a cousin (related through the mother) when $B > 8C$. But the offspring's mother is related to her own nephews and nieces by ¼ and to her offspring by ½, so she is selected to encourage altruism of her offspring toward her own nephews and nieces when-ever $B > 2C$. A similar argument applies to selfish acts. In fact, par-ents are selected to encourage altruism in their offspring and discour-age selfishness as long as these actions have some effect, no matter how remote and indirect, on other kin. For example, an altruistic act by the offspring toward an unrelated individual may induce return al-truism, not only toward the offspring but toward other kin. In this case, the parents will value the return benefit to other kin relatively more than will the offspring.

In the example just given, note that there appears to be greater conflict between parent and offspring over altruism toward kin outside the immediate family than toward altruism among the offspring. This is because other kin are typically related through only one of the parents. Thus the other parent (in the above example, the father) is unrelated to these kin and would be selected to encourage an even less altruistic posture than the offspring is selected to engage in on its own.

Parent–offspring conflict over the behavioral tendencies of the offspring has a series of implications as follows.

(1) *Conflict concerns future behavior of the offspring, not just present behavior.* An offspring who is socialized to act altruistically according to the schedule that benefits the parent's reproductive success will continue to increase its parent's reproductive success if it acts this way throughout its life, even if the parent is no longer alive. Thus conflict concerns not only immediate actions of the offspring (for example, stealing food from another sibling), but also actions that may occur in the distant future. For example, parent–offspring conflict extends to the adult reproductive role of the offspring: whether the offspring reproduces or not, with whom it pairs, and the degree of personal reproduction it achieves if it does reproduce. This is because each of these characteristics may affect the altruistic and selfish acts that the offspring directs at other relatives.

(2) *The personality and conscience of the child is formed in an arena of conflict.* Since the personality and conscience of a child is expected to affect the child's altruism and selfishness, these characteristics may be a matter of disagreement between parent and offspring (Figure 7-19). So far as we know, personality and conscience are formed early in socialization, probably during the first five years of a child's life. We expect the child to develop during this time internal representations of its parents' viewpoints as well as its own. These may be in conflict, requiring mediation by some third entity. This suggests a similarity to Freud's system of the id, the superego, and the ego. The *id* represents internal, innate, egoistic impulses in the Freudian system. We might say it represents the offspring's own self-interest. The *superego* represents the internalized demands of the parents and is developed in interactions with them. The *ego*, in turn, acts as a referee, reconciling the demands of the id and the superego.

(3) *This view of parent–offspring conflict has important implications for the social sciences.* Anthropology, for example, emphasizes cultural factors, which are typically passed primarily from parent to offspring. Cultural factors can, in turn, affect altruistic and selfish behavior. Such virtues as honesty, generosity, and trustworthiness will affect relations with a variety of individuals. Thus we expect offspring to

Figure 7-19

A cartoonist's view of parent–offspring conflict. Copyright, 1974, Jules Feiffer. Reprinted with permission of Universal Press Syndicate. All rights reserved.

be discriminating regarding the cultural elements they are exposed to. Many cultural elements will be directly advantageous to their own self-interest, such as the acquisition of language, but some will benefit the parent while lowering the offspring's inclusive fitness. Although learning psychology emphasizes the ability of reinforcement schedules to mold the behavior of offspring, we must make a distinction in nature between reinforcement schedules passively produced by the environment (such as availability of water and food) and schedules actively produced by parents in order to induce altruistic and selfish impulses that benefit their own self-interest. Regarding the latter, offspring may submit on the surface (for example, to avoid further punishment), but may seek some novel counterstrategy or remember the unfortunate reinforcement schedule and react to it when in a better position.

We expect adolescence to be a time of identity reorganization. Since adolescence signals impending offspring independence, the offspring no longer has to submit to parental demands; were it to continue to act out parental wishes that were not in harmony with its own self-interest, it would continue to lower its own inclusive fitness. Thus, we expect individuals at this time to reorganize their personalities in such a way as to reflect their own self-interest more exactly.

(4) *We are led to a view of the life cycle in which individuals natu- rally tend to repeat the actions of their parents even though they re- sisted these actions when they were young, because the change in role changes an individual's self-interest.* When the individual is young it is selected to resist those parental manipulations not in its own self- interest. When the same individual reaches parenthood it then has the self-interest of a parent toward its own offspring and is thus expected to socialize in a manner similar to the way in which it was socialized. It would be very interesting to know to what degree the precise form of parent–offspring conflict affects the offspring's tendency to act like its parent when it reaches that stage. For example, in extreme forms of child-rearing in which the self-interest of the child is entirely sup- pressed, the reward for such suppression may be seen in the offspring's eyes as its chance to similarly suppress its offsprings' behavior when an adult. By contrast, individuals raised according to a standard of fair- ness in which conflicts are resolved by splitting the difference between the self-interest of the two parties, may be inclined to imagine that they have a responsibility to continue the same standard of fairness when they are in a position of greater power.

(5) *Tendencies toward deceit and self-deception may be especially important in family interactions.* A parent will minimize resistance in its offspring if it can convince the offspring that it is acting in the off- spring's best interest when, in fact, it is merely expressing its own self- interest. Any strategy of parental manipulation that is unfair must, in turn, be represented as fair even if the parent admits that it is not act- ing with only the offspring's self-interest in mind. Thus, deception seems a natural ally of parental domination (see Figure 7-20). The off- spring is in an awkward position in such situations. On the one hand it is selected to resist parental domination; on the other hand such resis- tance may merely engender harsher parental maneuvers. Thus, the child may be selected to acquiesce in parental domination and to ex- press toward the parent the affection and good spirit that the parent desires. This conflict may most easily be handled by rendering negative feelings toward the parent unconscious. Thus, we also expect *self- deception* in these interactions, rendering some facts unconscious on both sides the better to deceive others. We shall return to this topic in Chapter 16.

Summary

In sexually reproducing species, parent and offspring are expected to be in conflict over the amount of parental investment the offspring re- ceives. Offspring are selected to attempt to garner more resources than

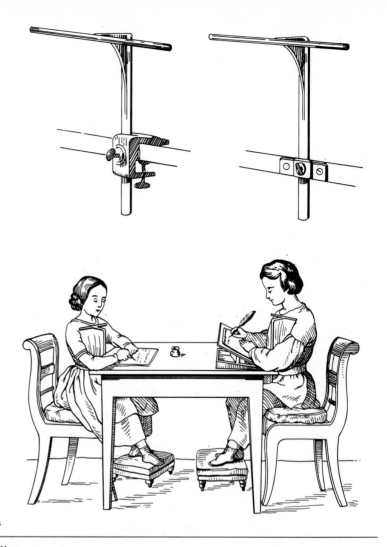

a

Figure 7-20

A system of parental domination. We see here some devices invented by a
noted 19th-century German educator, Dr. Schreber, ostensibly to improve
offspring posture. (a) The *Geradhalter* encouraged children not to slump forward during their studies because to do so with this device in place would
create sharp pains in the chest. A portable version was available for the child
away from home. (b) A device for preventing a child from moving around
during sleep. Dr. Schreber claimed that parents had a God-given responsibility to mold their children toward high cultural attainment. This system
emphasized the importance of absolute obedience. He used his devices on his
own children, one of whom was mentally deranged for most of his adult life
and whose writings were subjected to analysis by Sigmund Freud. (Redrawn
from Schatzman 1973)

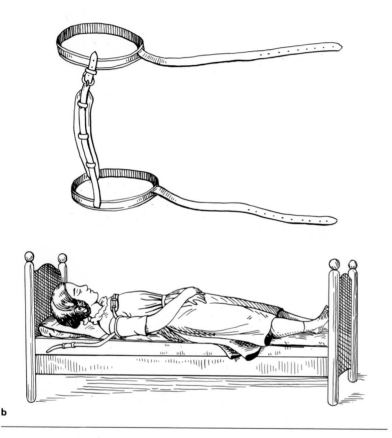

b

parents are selected to give. Conflict over investment is expected to increase during the period of parental investment and older parents are
expected to show less conflict with their offspring than younger parents. Weaning conflict in mammals and fledging conflict in birds are
both explained by this argument. The period of parental investment is
characterized by a shift from the parent to the offspring in who initiates parental care: the offspring must expend increasing amounts of
time and energy to garner investment.

The offspring is selected to use psychological manipulation in
order to induce greater investment. Temper tantrums in chimpanzees

and convulsions in pelican chicks may be examples of such tactics. Among rhesus monkeys, infants act to maintain proximity to their mothers. Infants appear to react to separations from mother in a logical way, increasing proximity when the mother appears to cause the separation or when the mother is more rejecting prior to separation.

Parent and offspring may also be in conflict over the behavioral tendencies of the offspring. Parents are selected to mold their offspring to be more altruistic toward relatives than the offspring would naturally act on their own. Thus, the human conscience and personality may develop in an arena of conflict.

Chapter 8

Reproductive Altruism

Reproductive altruism occurs when an individual foregoes personal reproduction—for one or more years or in many cases entirely—in order to aid the reproduction of others. It must be distinguished from non-reproduction, which occurs when an individual fails to reproduce, whether helping others or not. We expect reproductive altruism, especially when permanent, to be associated with benefits to relatives. When indulged in for only part of an individual's adult life, the trait will be more easily selected for when beneficiaries are relatives, but it may also evolve if it gives the helper a return benefit: a territory within which to breed or a set of individuals to act as helpers when it does breed.

In this chapter we will review the outstanding cases of reproductive altruism, beginning with the ants and termites and concluding with mammals and birds. Although kinship is critical to each of these, we shall see that it can have very different effects in different groups. Finally, we shall explore the extent to which homosexuality in gulls may have been favored by natural selection.

Division of Labor in Ants

Ants, bees and wasps provide—along with termites—the outstanding examples of reproductive altruism in the animal world. Complex colonies are invariably based on a reproductive division of labor in which non-reproductives do the bulk of the work (for *Polistes* wasps, see pp. 53–57). Consider the 10,000 species of ants. In most of these, a single queen produces a large number of wingless ants, the workers, who care for their mother and periodically raise winged reproductives, both males and females. The workers swarm over the surrounding landscape, often following odor trails laid down by nest mates and usually preying on other insects. Such is their dominance that it has been estimated that at least one in every 1000 insects alive today is an ant, and in most areas of the world the weight and energy consumption of all the ants exceeds that of all land vertebrates combined. This is especially true in the tropics, so that ants have been referred to as

a

Figure 8-1

Communal nest-weaving in ants. (a) To make a nest out of living leaves and larval silk, worker ants of the Australian *Oecophylla smaragdina* first choose a pliable leaf, then form a row and pull in unison until they force two leaves to touch or one leaf to curl up on itself. (b) If a single ant cannot bridge the gap between two leaves, workers arrange themselves in chains and pull together to close the gap. (c) Several parallel chains are shown in more detail. Each ant holds another by its waist. The genus *Oecophylla* has existed for at least 30 million years and colonies from 15 million years ago are indistinguishable from those of today. (Photos: Bert Hölldobler)

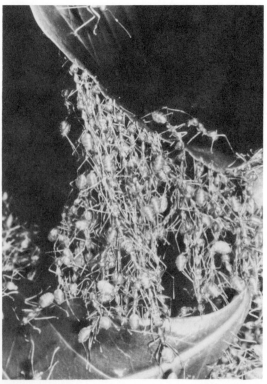

b

c

"the actual owners of the Amazon Valley." It is difficult to escape the impression that this dominance has been achieved through the evolution of complex cooperative societies with such internal cohesion and division of labor that they resemble single organisms. In effect, they are superorganisms (see Figures 8-1 to 8-3).

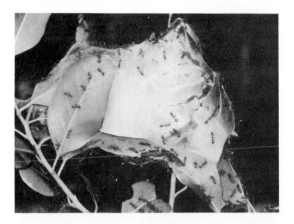

Figure 8-2

A completed nest of Oecophylla longinoda. The nest is formed of living leaves and stems bound together with larval silk. Some of the walls and internal galleries are constructed entirely of silk. A nest of *O. smaragdina* would look the same. One colony usually builds hundreds of such leaf nests, which are distributed over several trees and concentrated in the peripheral canopy. The silk nests permit these arboreal ants to form large colonies of up to a half million members. *Oecophylla* ants are among the most abundant and successful social insects of the tropics. (Photo: Bert Hölldobler)

a

b

Figure 8-3

(a) *An intermediate stage in the evolution of silk weaving.* In this Australian species of *Polyrhachis* an adult worker holds a relatively large larva near its front end and allows it to perform weaving motions, principally figure-eight motions with its head. These are similar to and derived from cocoon-spinning motions in other ants. In this species, larvae no longer spin cocoons for themselves, producing all their silk for colony use. (b) *An advanced silk weaver.* In *Oecophylla smaragdina* the larva has become a passive shuttle and the weaving motions are performed by the adult holding the larva. In this species the larva produces silk early in its last stage before pupation and is small relative to the worker who holds it. The worker first approaches the edge of a leaf with a larva in its mandibles. For a split second its antennae play along the surface like a blind man feeling the edge of a table. Then the larva's head is touched to the surface and stroked several times rapidly by the worker, and the larva shortly produces silk that attaches to the leaf. The larva is then lifted and carried directly to the edge of a second leaf where the procedure is repeated. This back and forth motion soon attaches scores of silk threads to the two leaves. (Photos: Bert Hölldobler)

Figure 8-4

Specialization by size, in ants. A young colony of *Atta sexdens* on its fungus garden. The huge queen is surrounded by the many small workers who tend the fungus garden and care for the eggs and larvae. Notice the large soldier above the queen's head. Experimental work shows that the relative numbers of the different-sized workers are carefully regulated by the colony so as to maximize colony output (eventually measured as the number of reproductives released by the colony). (Photo: Neal Weber)

Although worker ants typically do not reproduce, they have undergone considerable evolution, often splitting into two or more forms (Figure 8-4). A minority of workers, for example, may be large, with especially well-developed mandibles. These large worker ants function as soldiers, defending nest mates and large food items. In extreme cases worker castes have been molded for very specific purposes; ants have evolved, more than once, as living doors (Figure 8-5) and as living storage organs (Figure 8-6).

In some cases ants are capable of a complex series of interconnected activities that parallel human achievements. Both animal husbandry and agriculture were being practiced by ants long before we did so. Many species of ants maintain herds of aphids and other honey-dew–producing insects, which they protect from predators and whose sugary excretions they eat. Fungus-growing ants engage in agriculture (Figure 8-4). Workers cut leaves, carry these into the nest, prepare them as a medium for growing fungus, plant fungus on them, fertilize the fungus with their own droppings, weed out competitive species by hauling them away, and, finally, harvest a special part of the fungus on which they feed. Meanwhile, other workers construct the nest, care for the queen, feed and protect the larvae, and so on. A single colony may live for years, containing more than a million workers and occupying a gigantic nest that may have required the excavation of more than 20 tons of dirt and that contains thousands of

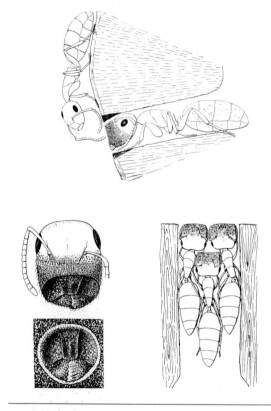

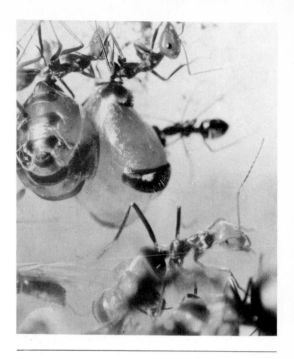

Figure 8-6

Specialization as a living honey pot. Specialized to store food for the colony is the honeypot caste of *Myrmecocystus mimicus*, two members of which are seen hanging from the ceiling of the nest interior. A third, partly full member is below, while the wings and abdomen of a female reproductive can be seen at lower left. The abdomens of the honeypot caste expand to almost the size of a cherry. These ants live in the dry lands of Arizona and utilize food sources that are very unstable. The honeypot caste allows abundant food to be stored for times of scarcity. Their flexible territory system, based on mass display, permits contests over temporarily abundant food to be settled with minimum waste, though badly outnumbered colonies are enslaved (Figures 8-8 and 8-9). (Photo: Bert Hölldobler)

Figure 8-5

Specialization as a living door. These drawings show nest-guarding behavior by soldiers of the European ant *Camponotus truncatus*. (top) A minor worker approaches a soldier that is blocking a nest entrance with its head. The soldier will step backwards, allowing the worker passage. Notice that the nest entrance has been cut and packed so as to match the head, which itself has a flat, door-like structure (lower left). Larger entrances may be blocked by several workers (lower right). (*From Wilson 1971*)

chambers, hundreds of them being employed as fungus gardens. So voracious are these ants that human agriculture is usually sharply curtailed where they are abundant.

Studies of the division of labor in fungus-growing ants show that a particular activity has a characteristic size of worker associated with it. Between the cutting of leaves and the tending of the fungus garden there is an assembly line of ever smaller ants. Studies of particular-sized castes suggest that these have been shaped by criteria of efficiency that apply to the colony as a whole. The particular-sized ant that cuts leaves, for example, is the size that gives the colony the greatest return per unit energy expended on it (Figure 8-7).

Of the many parallels between ants and ourselves, perhaps none is more bizarre than the fact that there are 35 species of ants known to enslave other ant species. Workers of the slave-making species do none of the usual work, such as care for the brood, but instead are specialized to raid the nests of closely related species, stealing worker pupae, which they carry back to their own nest. When these enslaved workers emerge as adults, they go to work as if they were back at home, nest building, caring for the brood, and so on. In effect, their altruistic tendencies have been parasitized by the slave-makers.

A slave raid begins when scouts go out to discover the existence of enslavable nests nearby. The scout returns and recruits individuals, in some species singly, in others en masse. In the latter case the scout then returns to the enslavable nest followed by a long file of slave-makers. Together they may march more than a hundred meters, armed with stings or sabre-like mandibles that can pierce their opponents' heads.

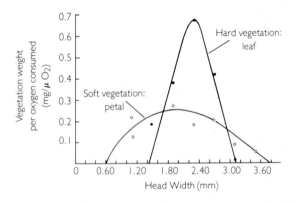

Figure 8-7

Output-per-unit cost as a function of size of worker for two kinds of activities. The energetic efficiency of workers is estimated by measuring the dry weight of vegetation cut per milligram dry weight of worker per unit time divided by the oxygen consumed per milligram dry weight of resting worker (in milliliters per unit time at 30°C). Two activities are shown: cutting soft vegetation and cutting hard vegetation. Notice that the optimal size for cutting hard vegetation is slightly larger than that for soft vegetation. In fact, in nature actual sizes of the workers seen cutting the two kinds of vegetation matches closely these optimal values, workers cutting hard vegetation being slightly longer. The species is *Atta sexdens*. (*From* Wilson 1980)

Some species attack the nest directly. Others merely produce a chemical warning signal that induces panic and flight in the targets. Still other species besiege the nest: lone outdoor workers are attacked and single slave-makers repeatedly advance into the nest entrance for a few seconds, irritating some of the workers inside to come out, where they are overwhelmed. Later, the nest itself is attacked.

All species carry worker pupae back to the nest. These require no additional work. Sometimes large or medium-sized larvae are also carried back. Slave-makers skillfully sort through the potential slaves, discarding small larvae, eggs, and sexual pupae. Slave-making workers only recruit new slaves. They are usually successful at this and their nests contain 10 or more slaves for each slave-maker. Perhaps the chief difference between ants and ourselves is that we enslave members of our own species, while ants rarely do so (but see Figures 8-8 and 8-9).

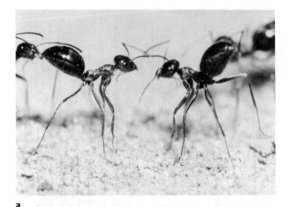

a

b

Figure 8-8

Territorial display in an ant. Two ants *Myrmecocystus mimicus* from neighboring colonies meet in a territorial encounter. In the top photo, the two ants turn to confront each other head-on. Each ant is stilt-walking with head and abdomen raised. In the lower left photo each ant raises her abdomen higher and turns it toward the opponent. Simultaneously (lower right photo) each one drums intensively on the abdomen of the other. After 10 to 30 seconds, one ant usually yields and the encounter ends. The ants quickly meet other opponents and the sequence is repeated (see next figure). (Photos: Bert Hölldobler)

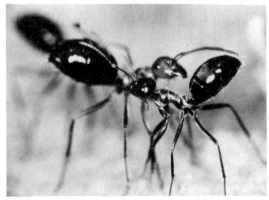

c

Figure 8-9

Territorial tournament. Worker ants from neighboring colonies confront each other en masse, a ritualized display that may last for hours or even days. When an ant encounters a conspecific from another nest it often recruits a hundred or more nest mates to the area of the encounter. All of them stilt-walk and search for opponents with which to perform a lateral display. More and more workers are recruited. When one colony is much larger than the other, the tournament ends quickly and the weaker colony is then raided, its queen killed, and larvae, pupae and honey pots carried back to become part of the victor's nest. Ritualized tournaments are believed to have evolved in *Myrmecocystus mimicus* because the ants have strong mandibles but a thin cuticle (skin). They are, thus, especially vulnerable to injury. (Photo: Bert Hölldobler)

In all of these activities the worker ants are invariably female. Male ants are always reproductives and have wings. Although often the object of care by the workers, they rarely contribute anything in the way of work to their colony (Figure 8-10). Even when the males are in a position to contribute, selection seems not to have molded an altruistic role. For example, in many ants male and female larvae spin cocoons in which to pupate. This habit has been seized upon by adult weaver ants, which take silk from their larvae for nest construction. This has led to remarkable feats of silk production (Figures 8-2 and 8-3), yet despite the fact that male and worker larvae are otherwise

Figure 8-10

Carrying your brother. In *Camponotus sereceus* a worker ant carries her brother, who is a winged reproductive. Notice the small size of his head (since he lacks large mandibles with which to feed himself or work). Male ants are rarely seen to contribute any work to the colony but are cared for entirely by the workers. (Photo: Michael Möglich and Bert Hölldobler)

virtually indistinguishable, they differ dramatically in their silk production: the silk glands of the females are much larger and groups of worker larvae produce about ten times as much silk as similar groups of male larvae. Thus, even where opportunity appears to be equal, selection has more strongly molded an altruistic act in females than in males. (Unfortunately, we have no data on the silk production of queen-destined larvae, since the male's reluctance to contribute may in some way reflect his later reproductive role.)

Haplodiploidy and the Evolution of the Social Insects

One of William Hamilton's great achievements was the discovery of an underlying genetic reason for the complex, female-based societies of the Hymenoptera (ants, bees, and wasps). The Hymenoptera are haplodiploid. That is, females have two sets of chromosomes, one from each parent, and are diploid, while males arise from *unfertilized* eggs and have only one set of chromosomes (they are haploid). This leads to a series of unusual degrees of relatedness (Table 8-1). For one thing, all of a male's sperm cells have the same set of genes that he has; hence, a male's relatedness to his daughters is 1. Likewise, his daughters are unusually closely related to each other, since half of their genes are already identical (by having the same father) and half of the remaining half are identical (through their mother); thus, r between full sisters is ¾. This is balanced by an r of ¼ between a female and her brothers,

Table 8-1   Degrees of Relatedness in Haplodiploid Species (under outbreeding)

	Daughter	Son	Mother	Father	Sister	Brother	Nephew/Niece
Female	½	½	½	½	¾	¼	⅜
Male	1	0	1	0	½	½	¼

since any gene in a female could only be found in her brother through their common mother, with a ¼ chance. On the other hand, a male is related to his siblings by ½, because any gene in him must have come from his mother and been passed on by her with a chance of ½.

We see that haplodiploidy gives females, but not males, a new opportunity for altruism that is not found in diploid species; females are more related to their sisters than they are to their own offspring. If they can add more sisters to the world, at a cost of offspring, they can trade in an r of ½ for an r of ¾. But since they are *less* related to their brothers than to their offspring, they need to raise relatively more sisters than brothers. Alternatively, a female would be selected to remain in her mother's nest if she could raise sisters and sons or sisters and nephews, instead of sisters and brothers, because she is more related to these than to her brothers. Since males are produced from unfertilized eggs, a female need not be inseminated in order to produce sons.

We have evidence that both requirements may be met. As we shall see later (Figure 11-7), there is good evidence that ants often invest more energy in the production of females than males. And in a few ants—but more commonly in bees and wasps—workers are known to compete with their mother over male production.

Notice that the male's average degree of relatedness to his offspring (½) is the same as his r to his siblings, so there are no special opportunities for male altruism. Indeed, if female altruism does evolve (because of the special r's available to the females), a disincentive for male altruism at once appears. For example, if females bias production toward female reproductives, the expected reproductive success of a male *rises*, because there are more females available to inseminate (see Chapter 11). This will decrease the attractiveness of helping as an alternative strategy. If female workers raise sons and sisters, the expected RS of a male also rises, because he now fathers in each generation not only daughters but also grandsons. Once again, helping becomes relatively less attractive to him.

In a nutshell, we can summarize the argument as follows: haplodiploidy gives females unique opportunities for investing in sisters instead of daughters and if females seize on these opportunities by either of the two available routes, then helping in males is at once disfavored.

Thus, kinship not only explains the prevalence of reproductive altruism in the Hymenoptera but also its universal sex bias.

Another consequence of kinship theory is that conflict between mother and offspring is expected over male production. As we have noted, there are frequent instances of such conflict in the Hymenoptera. In addition, in many ant species workers produce "trophic" eggs; these do not result in males but are fed to the queen or the larvae. It is plausible to imagine that the production of trophic eggs followed an earlier stage in which these eggs were destined to become males but were so frequently eaten by the queen that they came to perform a new, nutritional function.

It is interesting that the queen so often seems to dominate male production in ants, even though her offspring are much more numerous and together might be able to impose their will on her. Their failure is partly due to the fact that they no longer act "together" as regards male production (each worker preferring to produce the male eggs herself); but part of the failure probably stems from the unique reproductive role of the queen: only she can give them the sisters to whom they are highly related and in many species only she is inseminated and can produce worker eggs. Thus, a daughter ant in a contest with her mother over male production would have much more reason for restraint than her mother, for killing her mother would deprive herself of full sisters and might abort the life of the colony, while her own death would have a negligible effect. Thus, workers should be careful not to injure their mother in any way and should easily be dominated by her. It is a curious fact that in the highly social meliponine bees—in which mother–daughter conflict is known to occur over male production—workers have evolved an elaborate ritual in which they flee the presence of the queen—almost in mock terror—moments before she inspects a cell and lays an egg in it.

There are other haplodiploid insects besides the Hymenoptera, and there are many haplodiploid mites. Have any of these evolved reproductive altruism? The best candidate is a haplodiploid scale insect that lives in a bizarre symbiosis with a fungus. The fungus interpenetrates some of the scale insects and feeds from their living bodies (Figure 8-11). These insects do not reproduce, but by sustaining a thicker fungal mat, they provide protection for those that do (from such enemies as parasitic wasps). Only females are interpenetrated. That these females may be aiding sisters more often than brothers is suggested by the fact that males come in two forms, winged and wingless (Figure 8-12); in other insect species wingless males are often associated with mating between siblings (since you can find them without flying) and sib mating selects for the production of female-biased sex ratios (see pp. 277–278). Thus, the spectacle of non-reproductive female scale insects laboring to support a fungus may be explained by the same underlying degrees of relatedness that characterize ants, bees, and wasps.

Figure 8-11

Symbiosis between a fungus and a haplodiploid scale insect. A cross-sectional drawing of the fungus *Septobasidium burtii* on top of and interpenetrating a scale insect *Aspidiotus osborni* (center), which is feeding through the bark of a tree (notice the long feeding apparatus). The coils inside the scale insect are parts of the fungus. The scale insect does not reproduce but creates a thicker fungal mat, protecting those that do reproduce. (*From* Couch 1938)

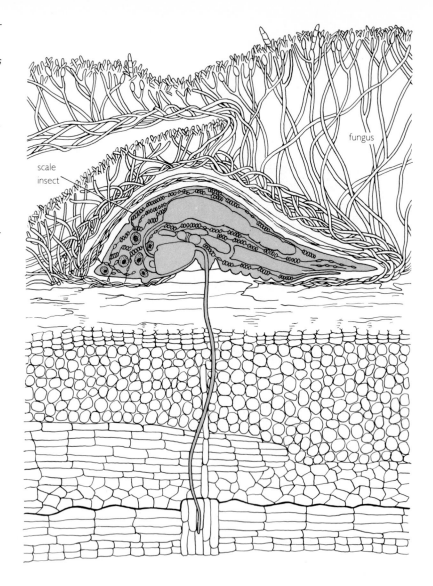

Cycles of Inbreeding in Termites

In the picture we have painted so far, termites stand out as a glaring exception: they are the only diploid insect with a complex, ant-like society. All termites have a non-reproductive caste, which has often evolved into more than one form, usually by the addition of a soldier caste (Figure 8-13). Termites are similar to ants in many other ways

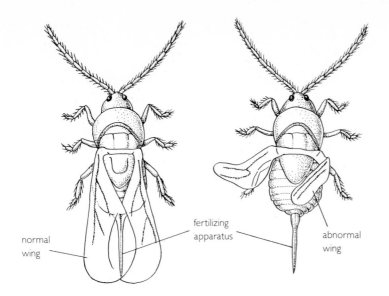

normal
wing

fertilizing
apparatus

abnormal
wing

Figure 8-12

Male dimorphism in a haplodiploid scale insect with altruistic females. Males of the scale insect *Aspidiotus osborni* come in two forms, one with normal wings and one with abnormal wings. Both forms have a long fertilizing apparatus. Flightless males mate where they emerge, often with siblings. (*From* Conch 1938)

(including the evolution of fungus-growing termites) but there are some important differences: termite workers are both male and female, no trophic eggs are produced, and in many termites secondary reproductives are produced, offspring of the founding couple, which mate within the nest and contribute to egg production (Figure 8-14). That male workers occur in a diploid species is gratifying, since degrees of relatedness in such species show no biases by sex (excluding the sex chromosomes). Likewise, the absence of trophic eggs is not surprising—if they really arose in ants because of maternal domination of male production. The key question is why there is so little reproductive conflict in the termites. Why have workers so completely abandoned personal reproduction and what exactly is the significance of secondary reproductives?

Among wood-eating insects, termites are uniquely dependent on symbiotic protozoa to digest the wood. Since these protozoa are passed from mother to offspring through anal feeding, they necessitate some overlap between mother and offspring. But once the offspring has acquired the symbionts, why does it stay and help the mother? One possibility is that the termite is being manipulated by its symbiont, whose aggregate weight may be a significant fraction of the colony's. Since the protozoa probably reproduce asexually, they would be selected to manipulate the termites into acting like they are identically related; but even this argument fails to yield a *bias* toward raising siblings instead of offspring.

A novel solution to the problem of termite altruism has recently been suggested by Stephen Bartz. He showed that under certain condi-

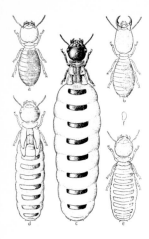

Figure 8-13

Castes in termites. The five castes that make up the colonies of *Amitermes hastatus* are shown here, all drawn to the same scale: (a) worker; (b) soldier; (c) primary queen, about five years old, with greatly swollen abdomen; (d) secondary queen; (e) tertiary queen; (f) egg. The worker is about 5 mm long. The secondary and tertiary queens may develop in galleries distant from the queen. Both the worker and the soldier are non-reproductive and may be either male or female. (*From* Wilson 1971)

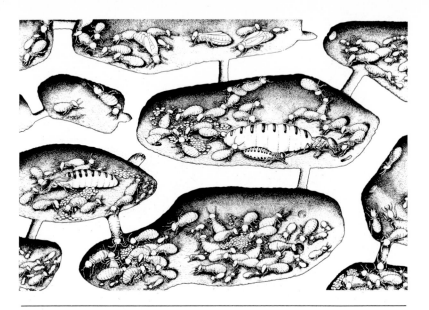

Figure 8-14

Reproductive specialization in a termite. Here is the interior of a typical nest of *Amitermes hastatus* of South Africa. In the middle cell sits the primary queen being fed regurgitated food by workers. Other workers care for her eggs and the male sits alongside her. Her grossly distended abdomen permits rapid egg production, but her output is not sufficient for the colony's needs and we see a secondary queen in the lower left cell. Notice the soldier in the lower right cell and young reproductives (with developing wings) in the top center cell. (Drawing by Sarah Landry, *from* Wilson 1971)

tions of *inbreeding* in diploid species, individuals become more related to their siblings than to their own offspring. This is easiest to see in the pattern of inbreeding that produces the greatest effect. Imagine that the king and the queen are unrelated to each other but that each is the product of intense inbreeding. That is, the two halves of the genotype of each individual are identical ($F = 1$; see p. 129). Since king and queen are unrelated, r between parent and offspring is still ½, but siblings are genetically identical, since each one gets one of the two identical genes at each parental locus. If this offspring outbreeds, then it will tend to value siblings twice as much as offspring! This is the greatest bias toward reproductive altruism known in any genetic system—it is even greater than the bias under outbreeding in haplodiploid species.

Although Bartz has shown that this bias toward siblings exists for a variety of other F's and r's between king and queen, the key require-

Table 8-2   The Number of Winged Reproductives Produced and
Total Colony Size for Colonies of Two Species of Termites, Divided
According to Whether Secondary Reproductives Were Present or Not

Termite Species	Number of Winged Reproductives	Total Colony Size
Marginitermes hubbardi		
secondary reproductives present	110	312
	75	450
	1477	3119
secondary reproductives absent	0	122
	0	2045
	0	2267
Neotermes larseni		
secondary reproductives present	385	1052
secondary reproductives absent	0	10
	0	12
	0	16
	0	33
	16	167
	0	210
	0	566
	0	614
	0	760
	0	813
	0	1828
	0	2911

Source: Bartz 1979.

ment is that the founders of colonies must tend to be unrelated while
the reproductives must be produced through a pattern of inbreeding.
This will occur precisely when winged reproductives are often produced by secondary reproductives, since secondary reproductives
mate incestuously within the nest. That termites go through cycles
of inbreeding within nests followed by outbreeding between nests,
is plausible for many species. Secondary reproductives are found
throughout the termites, including the species most similar to the ancestral forms. Furthermore, there is evidence that winged reproductives in several species tend to be produced only when secondary reproductives are common (Table 8-2). Winged reproductives, in turn,
mate outside the nest after a flight that is often synchronized widely
with the flights of other nests; thus, they presumably outbreed most of
the time. Although some termite species lack secondary reproductives
and although details of Bartz' theory still need to be confirmed, his

theory illustrates the way in which easily overlooked details of the breeding system may have far-ranging effects on social evolution.

Incidentally, conflict is expected between secondary reproductives, since they are typically more related to their own offspring than to a sibling's offspring. In at least one termite such forms are known to fight until only a single pair remains; but in many species several such pairs coexist peacefully within the same nest. At present we do not know why this is so or whether coexistence is always as peaceful as it seems.

Helpers at the Nest in Birds

Over the past 20 years we have discovered a growing number of bird species in which a breeding pair may be accompanied by helpers at the nest, that is, individuals that help them raise their young, usually by feeding the young, protecting them from predators, and defending the territory from intruders. More than 1% of all bird species are known to have helpers, and this number should grow, especially since we barely know the social lives of most tropical birds. Unlike helping among social insects, helping in birds is never obligatory. An individual bird may help in one or more years and may die in that role, but so far as we know, it always remains alert for breeding possibilities of its own; and helper birds are not known to be morphologically distinct from non-helper birds.

Bird species with helpers share several traits in common:

(1) The species are almost always tropical, subtropical, or Australian.

(2) In most cases, the helper is at least a year old and is physiologically capable of breeding.

(3) In contrast to the social insects, in the majority of cases, though not always, the helper is a male.

(4) As in most monogamous birds, the sex ratio for the entire adult population is biased in favor of males: males may be at least 50% more common than females.

(5) Helpers often feed nestlings and may help defend the territory, but they are usually excluded from incubating and from nest-building by the aggression of one or both of the parents.

(6) When measures have been taken, helpers typically are found to increase the number of offspring that survive from the nest they help.

(7) The helper is almost always a helper at his parents' nest or his siblings'. Thus the helper usually is raising close relatives: full-siblings ($r = \frac{1}{2}$), half-siblings, or nephews and nieces ($r = \frac{1}{4}$).

Table 8-3 The Reproductive Success of a Pair, with and without Helpers, for Seven Species of Birds

Species		Reproductive Success of Pair		Measure of Reproductive Success
		Without Helpers	*With Helpers*	
1. Harris' hawk	*Parabuteo unicinctus*	1.3	2.0	Advanced nestlings/nest
2. Tasmanian native hen	*Tribonyx mortierii*			
Inexperienced breeders		1.1	3.1	Independent young/group
Experienced breeders		5.5	6.5	Independent young/group
3. Kookaburra	*Dacelo gigas*	1.2	2.3	Fledglings/nest
4. Red-throated bee-eater	*Merops bulicki*	2.3	2.7	Fledglings/nest
5. White-fronted bee-eater	*Merops bulockoides*			
1973		1.0	1.2	Fledglings/nest
1975		0.27	0.38	Fledglings/nest
1977		1.31	1.94	Fledglings/nest
6. Superb blue wren	*Malurus cyaenus*	1.5	2.8	Independent young/year
7. Brown and yellow marshbird	*Pseudoleistes virescens*	1.3	2.0	Fledglings/nest

Source: Emlen 1978.

The sixth point is critical. Some people have doubted that helpers actually do increase the reproductive success of those they appear to be helping. If generally true this would be surprising; but it appears to be false. Data from several species show that helpers always have at least a slight positive effect on the reproductive success of those they are helping and they typically raise parental reproductive success by between 30% and 100% (Table 8-3). This gives us a crude estimate of the benefit of helping, but computation of the cost is much more difficult. A first estimate is to assign a helper the reproductive success that a pair would achieve without helpers. If this were the true cost, helping would have to increase the parents' reproductive success by at least 100% (assuming that the individuals added to the population are full-siblings); but it is unlikely that the helper would have the same reproductive success as a pair. The biased sex ratio means that young adult males will have a difficult time finding mates. In *Malurus* wrens the percentage of adults accompanied by helpers rises as the local adult sex ratio becomes more male-biased (Figure 8-15). Likewise, in acorn woodpeckers *Melanerpes formicivorous* an increasing percentage of yearlings remains as helpers as the rate at which new territories open up declines (Figure 8-16).

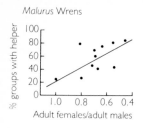

Figure 8-15

Helping as a function of adult sex ratio. The percentage of groups of *Malurus cyaneus* and *M. splendens* with helpers is plotted as a function of the number of adult females per adult male. The frequency of helping increases as the relative number of adult females decreases. (*From Emlen and Vehrencamp 1983*)

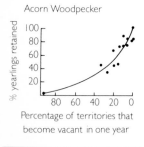

Figure 8-16

Helping as a function of availability of a breeding territory. The percentage of year-old acorn woodpeckers who remain in their natal group is plotted as a function of the percentage of territories that become vacant in a year. (*From Emlen and Vehrencamp 1983*)

The frequency with which breeding pairs are accompanied by helpers is also sensitive to the environmental conditions prevailing at the time of breeding. In Figure 8-17 we see that poor availability of food is associated with a higher percentage of helpers. This is probably because the benefit of helping is greater at these times and also because the reproductive success a pair would achieve on its own is so small that helping is not associated with much of a cost.

The biased adult sex ratio in birds helps to explain why females are rarely helpers, since they will have a much easier time finding a mate than will males. In addition, in many monogamous birds, young adult males that occupy territories occupy smaller ones than do older adult males, although young females often pair with older males and gain the benefit of their superior territories.

There is an alternate explanation for the frequency of male helpers in birds, one that parallels the explanation for altruism in Hymenoptera. Birds are among the few species in which male sex chromosomes are XX and female sex chromosomes are XY. Thus, across their X, males are related to their brothers by ¾. The X chromosome is a large chromosome, and perhaps 5% of the total genes are located on it. Helping genes may be located on the male's X chromosome, since this would facilitate their spread, but selection on the other chromosomes would oppose the preference for brothers that selection on the X chromosome induces. Incidentally, although in one species there is evidence of a male-biased sex ratio by the time of fledging, this probably reflects the return investment of a son, not a bias toward brothers induced by the sex chromosomes.

Tropical and sub-tropical environments are associated with greater adult survivorship, which facilitates helping. High adult survivorship means that opportunities for young birds will be less frequent, which leads to deferred breeding, and so the cost of helping is small. It also means that couples will tend to remain together for long periods of time, so helpers will be raising full-siblings instead of half-siblings. Many of the habitats of helping species appear to be saturated with family territories that are passed on from one generation to the next, in some cases probably for centuries.

Incidentally, one species with helpers, the Australian Bell Miner *Manorina melanophrys*, provides a nice test of kinship theory. Individuals live in clans that may contain two or more related breeding pairs, each of which can be helped. When we compare the rate at which individuals feed nestlings at two nests, we see that even though the young are usually not being fed at the same time, the greater the degree of relatedness to the nestlings, the greater is the feeding rate (Table 8-4).

Although helpers are found in a growing number of bird species, we should not overlook the fact that kinship interactions in birds are otherwise conspicuous for their absence. There is no bird analogy to

Table 8-4 Helping as a Function of Relatedness (r) in the Australian Bell Miner. Comparison of Mean Adjusted Feeding Rates (Visits per Hour) at Which an Attendant Fed Juveniles of Two Different Nests. The Relationship and Degree of Relatedness of the Attendant to the Recipient is Given

Attendant	Relationship	r	Average Number of Feeding Visits per Hour
1	Parent	½	6.85
	Grandparent	¼	3.33
2	Parent	½	10.41
	Half-sibling	¼	4.82
3	Full-sibling	½	3.23
	Half-niece/nephew	⅛	0.22
4	Full-sibling	½	1.98
	Half-niece/nephew	⅛	2.08
5	Full-sibling	½	3.40
	Half-uncle/aunt	⅛	0.73

Source: Clarke 1984.

Note: The nests were fed several days apart. We see in all cases except no. 4 that the attendants feed juveniles more frequently when r is higher.

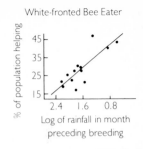

White-fronted Bee Eater

% of population helping

Log of rainfall in month preceding breeding

Figure 8-17

Helping as a function of harshness of the environment. The percentage of the population that is helping is plotted as a function of the log of rainfall in the month preceding breeding in white-fronted bee-eaters *Merops bullockoides.* Greater rainfall is closely associated with greater insect abundance, the primary food of bee-eaters. (*From* Emlen and Vehrencamp 1983)

the overlapping home ranges of related female mammals (e.g., ground squirrels, p. 113), and the common pattern may be that of great tits *Parus major*, in which individuals show no gain in reproductive success by nesting next to relatives.

Family Dynamics in the Florida Scrub Jay

In some species with helpers at the nest, we know enough to describe in some detail the social dynamics within families. One such species is the Florida scrub jay *Aphelocoma coerulescens*, which has been studied with unusual care for a number of years by Glen Woolfenden and his associates (Figure 8-18). Scrub jays pair for life on permanent 10–30-acre territories whose boundaries are rigidly defended throughout the year. Couples raise one brood per year and the fledglings invariably remain in the parental territory for a full year. The offspring usually help in territorial defense, mobbing predators (sometimes more intensely than the breeding pair), and feeding the young, but are apparently excluded from constructing the nest and incubating the eggs,

Figure 8-18

A helper at the nest. A breeding pair of Florida scrub jays is shown with their helper son. The breeding female is on the nest in the foreground; partly on the nest behind her is her mate. Their son is on the right. All three birds are in a stiff posture with chest feathers ruffled as a defense of the nest against the photographers. (Photo: John Fitzpatrick and Glen Woolfenden)

perhaps because these activities too directly threaten the breeding pair's RS. A scrub jay usually breeds for the first time by dispersing to another territory in which a breeder of the same sex has disappeared. All females breed in this fashion, and they do so more quickly than males, so that older helpers are predominantly males. Some of these older helper males breed not by dispersing but by carving off a piece of the parental territory or by inheriting it directly on the death of the breeding male. Some males help for more than five years.

What is the effect of helping on the reproductive success of the breeding pair? As we see from Table 8-5, pairs with helpers have higher RS than pairs without. However, this comparison is biased by the fact that individuals that have been successful in the past tend to have helpers and therefore tend to have low reproductive success. Woolfenden has corrected for these biases by considering, in years with helpers and without, only pairs that have already fledged young and are breeding on the same territory (Table 8-5). The correction hardly changes the calculation, and the presence of helpers appears to raise parental RS by about 65%. Helpers also appear to decrease the chance that the breeders will die that year (Table 8-5).

Who are the helpers genetically? From Table 8-6 we see that where degree of relatedness is known, helpers are nearly 70% of the time raising full-siblings ($r = \frac{1}{2}$), while about one-fourth of the time they are raising individuals to whom they are related by $r = \frac{1}{4}$ and average relatedness ($\bar{r}$) is 0.41. In only 3% of the cases are they raising unrelated individuals. We are reminded of the gull that had a hard time killing other chicks and raising its own (p. 28). Perhaps it is difficult to evolve a concern for the young of relatives without occasionally di-

Table 8-5   The Reproductive Success (Fledglings per Pair) and Annual Mortality Rate (Percentage Dying) of Breeding Florida Scrub Jays Depending on Whether They Have Helpers or Not

	Without Helpers	With Helpers
Fledglings per pair		
All pairs	1.5	2.3
Experienced pairs on the same territories	1.5	2.5
Percentage dying per year	20	13

Source: Woolfenden 1981.

Note: All comparisons based on helping are significant.

recting help to the unrelated. Or there may be return benefits to helping. One male helped his mother for two years (his father having died); when she died, he remained in the territory and helped his stepfather and his stepfather's new mate. This may have increased the chance that he succeeded to the parental territory.

Notice another interesting feature of Table 8-6: it appears that each sex is more likely to help a relative of the same sex. When both parents are alive, each sex is equally likely to help, but when one parent is gone, females are twice as likely to help their mother as their father, while the reverse is true for males. Males are also much more likely to help another male relative than are females. Woolfenden has noted that birds returning to the parental territory after an absence (usually because of an attempt to breed elsewhere) are more likely to return if the same-sex parent is present. Presumably conflict with a same-sex breeder who is *not* related inhibits the return of the potential helper. Conflict between breeders and their stepchildren is often intense but is especially so when the stepchildren have been absent. In one case an injured mother was replaced by a new female who was highly aggressive to her stepdaughter when the latter tried to help. Since the helper had at first remained with her injured mother, away from the new pair, the stepmother may have taken her sudden reappearance as an invitation to her mate. The only time Woolfenden saw a female dominate her mate was when this same female had just driven off her stepdaughter.

Dominance relations between the scrub jays reveal clearly the tensions over breeding status. A dominance hierarchy exists within each family: males dominate females and, within each sex, older birds dominate younger ones. When two males from the same clutch serve as helpers, one invariably dominates the other. The breeding male dominates all other males, but the breeding female is dominated by the male helpers. More dominant helpers tend to breed earlier, either by dispersing to another territory and pairing with a female or by succeeding to breeding status within the family plot.

The importance of dominance for breeding is suggested by the fact that male scrub jay breeders are especially likely to dominate their male helpers (their chief reproductive threat) and are most likely to do so at the time when eggs are being laid. The death of the mother is expected to be a tense time for the father because a helper son would then have a new incentive to succeed his father: he will then be only half as related to his father's future reproduction as when his mother was still alive. Indeed, male breeders are especially aggressive toward their helpers after the death of the mother, and so great is the dominance of fathers over sons that three cases are known in which the father succeeded in pairing with a female whom one of his helper sons had been courting for months!

What is the relationship between dominance and helping? On the *Polistes* model we would expect the least dominant to do the most work, dominant helpers conserving energy for their own reproduction. In fact, in scrub jays more dominant individuals (which are older)

Table 8-6   Whom do Florida Scrub Jay Helpers Help? The Number of Male and Female Helpers Seen to Aid Various Categories of Breeders for a Season, Their Relatedness (*r*) to the Offspring They are Helping to Rear, and the Percentage of the Total That Are Raising Offspring of a Given *r* *

Breeders		Number of Helpers		*r* to Offspring	Percent of Total
Male	*Female*	*Male*	*Female*		
Father	Mother	60	65	½	67
Grandfather	Mother	1	0	5/16	1
First Cousin	Mother	1	1	5/16	
Father	—*	14	8	¼	
Brother	—	8	1	¼	27
—	Mother	5	12	¼	
Uncle	Grandmother	1	0	¼	
Half-brother	—	3	1	⅛	2
—	—	1	4	0	3
	TOTAL	94	92	*r̄* = 0.41	100

Source: Woolfenden 1981.

Note: Each season a helper helped is included, as are four cases in which relationships were probable but not certain.

* — indicates unrelated.

give greater help. One reason that a dominant male helper may be especially helpful is that this will increase group size, which increases territory size, which probably improves his chances of budding off a portion of the parental territory for his own.

Males invariably dominate their mothers, and fathers frequently intervene on behalf of the mother in disputes with grown sons. Mother and son are especially likely to come into conflict if father disappears, because they cannot breed with each other and only one can usually breed in the family plot. Yet in spite of the son's dominance, it is the mother who usually remains, pairing quickly with a new male arriving from elsewhere, who then dominates his stepsons. Remember that the adult sex ratio is biased in favor of excess males. These exist as helpers in other territories, waiting for the opportunity to occupy a territory of their own. Females will be courted during this period and will presumably have expressed a preference for the more dominant helpers in other families. One of these will quickly pair with her and usually will be able to dominate his mate's most dominant helper (often her eldest son).

Although there is evidence of dominance interactions between females, these are much more relaxed and infrequent than those between males. Since a female cannot dominate her brother (males are the larger sex), she will almost never inherit the family plot. Thus, the death of her father gives her no new opportunities. Nor does dominating her sister give her the benefit in future breeding that such behavior gives a male.

Some of Woolfenden's most intriguing findings come from his case histories of families breeding over several years. One such example is summarized as follows. In the first year, a helper begins to pair at the periphery of the family territory, then he disappears. At the beginning of the next season the parents die, and a one-year-old helper who dominates his brothers takes over the territory. He pairs with a female who immigrates from afar. His brother replaces a lost breeder in an adjacent territory. His brother's mate dies, and his brother returns to the family territory, where he resumes his hierarchical position between his brothers. Another male helper departs during the following winter, pairs, breeds, fails, and then returns home with his new mate. He feeds his brothers' fledglings, but his mate is forced to remain at the periphery of the groups' activities within the territory, presumably because she constitutes a threat to the reproductive success of the family. In the following year the female leaves her mate and returns to the general area where she had bred before. She pairs with a previously unmated male. Her former mate remains in the family territory but is now prevented by his brother and his brother's mate from feeding their nestlings! Having returned to their territory with a female, he was permitted to feed nestlings, but now that his mate has left him, he is considered a threat. Is this because feeding the nestlings might lead to a sexual relationship with his brother's mate? One male helper that managed to feed the breeding female at one brood was severely attacked by the male breeder at the beginning of the next brood.

Helpers in Mammals

Although kinship interactions are important in mammals, reproductive altruism among mammals seems relatively infrequent, being confined mostly to members of the dog family. (For the one conspicuous exception, see Figure 8-19.) Since the hunt is cooperative and food can be carried to the pups, non-reproductives can easily aid in the reproduction of relatives. Wolf and jackal packs may retain offspring from

Figure 8-19

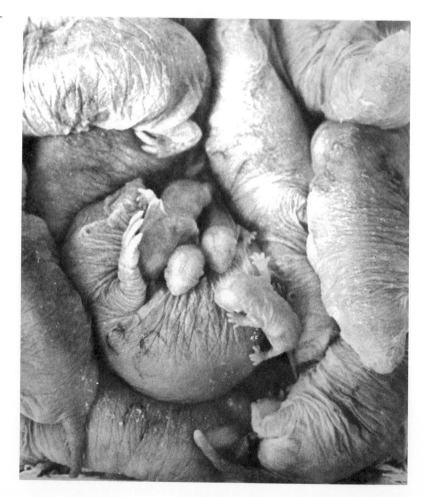

Division of reproductive labor in naked mole rats. Shown is a laboratory colony of *Heterocephalus glaber*. The breeding female is in the center with her pups. She is on top of and surrounded by other colony members, who huddle together for warmth. Most are adult and all except the breeding male (who is unknown) are non-reproductive. The animals have been marked for identification. The smaller animals do the bulk of nest building and foraging for food. Medium-sized mole rats perform the same tasks, but less than half as frequently, while the few large individuals rarely do either task but do assist in the care of the young. Only one adult female breeds per colony. Colonies are probably extended families, but whether naked mole rats, like the termites they resemble, practice cycles of inbreeding is unknown. (Photo: Richard Alexander)

previous litters as helpers in the next. In silver-backed jackals *Canus mesomelas* these helpers are associated with an increase in the number of offspring that survive (Figure 8-20). Pairs are typically monogamous, so that helpers raise full-siblings. A quarter of all surviving pups stay with their parents to help, and most jackal packs have helpers (Figure 8-21). The pack hunts cooperatively and members groom each other and share food (Figure 8-22). As the number of adults in a pack increases, the rate at which pups are fed increases, and the percentage of time when at least one adult is at the den increases quickly to 100% of the time. Both factors are important in increasing the survival of pups. Males and females are equally likely to be helpers.

The most interesting dog species with helpers is the hunting dog *Lycaeon pictus*. Packs consist of a set of male relatives, which are paired with one or more adult female relatives to whom the males are

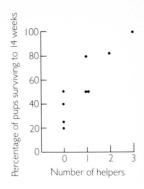

Figure 8-20

Pup survival as a function of the number of adult helpers in silver-backed jackals. The percentage of pups that survived from 3 to 14 weeks of age is plotted as a function of the number of adults found in the pack minus the breeding pair. The number of helpers has a positive effect on pup survival ($P < 0.01$). The number of pups alive at 3 weeks of age is also positively associated with the number of helpers. (*From* Moehlman 1983)

Figure 8-21

A helper and his younger sibling. A one-year-old male plays with his younger sibling. The male was the lone surviving pup from a litter of five in 1976. The following year he remained with his parents and helped them raise three surviving pups, one of whom is shown here. (Photo: Patricia Moehlman)

Figure 8-22

Father, mother, and son. A mated pair of silver-backed jackals groom their one-year-old son, who, along with another offspring, is acting as a helper at their parents' den, permitting them in 1977 to raise three surviving pups. (Photo: Patricia Moehlman)

Figure 8-23

Three brothers. Three two-year-old hunting dog brothers converge to check on the pups, one of which is shown. They may lick the genital area of the pups to stimulate defecation and urination. The male on the left is the alpha male and the father of the pups. Notice the striking similarity between the coat patterns of these three brothers. (Photo: James Malcolm, Anthro-Photo)

unrelated (Figures 8-23 and 8-24). Typically, only one pair breeds, all other adults acting as helpers. Helpers may help for years and many males die in this role, but helpers are in no way morphologically special. In hunting dogs the usual mammalian pattern of dispersal is reversed: males stay in the packs where they were born, while females emigrate to new packs. After a group of adult sisters joins a group of male relatives, only one of the females will usually be permitted to

Figure 8-24

Greeting. A three-year-old female on the left greets a two-year-old male prior to a hunt. Both are subordinate non-breeders in a group containing three adult brothers. The female's greeting is more intense, witness her flattened ears, retracted muzzle, and waving tail. This probably reflects her greater eagerness for the hunt, perhaps because she is hungrier. Notice the contrast in coat color between these unrelated individuals. (Photo: James Malcolm, Anthro-Photo)

Figure 8-25.

Conflict between two sisters over their pups. The three adult hunting dogs shown are three-year-old sisters. The female holding the pup is the beta female. She is trying to bring the pups back to her den. She is being challenged by the alpha female behind her, who is less aroused (ears forward, muzzle unretracted, tail lower). The pups belong to both females; the beta's (born first) are slightly larger (compare second and third pup from right). Both females tried to carry all the pups back to their own dens. Later some of the beta's pups disappeared, with evidence of infanticide. The gamma female on the left is showing subordinance and avoiding the dominant female. (Photo: James Malcolm, Anthro-Photo)

breed (Figure 8-25), and the other females typically disperse again to join a new group of male relatives or attempt to breed with a single male from the original troop; the latter is rarely successful.

Detailed studies of packs show that male helpers typically contribute as much food to the pups as does the father, sometimes more (Figure 8-26). All males contribute to the hunt, and individual differences in hunting ability probably account for most of the difference in effort

Figure 8-26

Feeding his nephews and nieces. A two-year-old male hunting dog prepares to regurgitate to his nephews and nieces. The pups are about 8 to 10 weeks old and came from two females (see preceding picture). (Photo: James Malcolm, Anthro-Photo)

expended during the hunt, except that the more dominant individuals are more likely to take the risky step of downing the prey (Figure 8-27). Many breeding efforts are a complete failure, and these are more frequent when packs are small; when dogs do raise some pups successfully, they raise more when the number of adults in the pack is greater.

Dominance relations in hunting dogs are so subtle that for many years it was believed that hunting dogs lacked a dominance hierarchy; in fact, the dogs are arrayed in a clear hierarchy. Only the dominant pair of individuals breeds, all others help. The most intense conflict between males occurs at or shortly before the time of mating. The most intense conflict of all occurs between females, and the pups of the subordinate female may be killed by her dominant relative. This is partly because litter size has increased in hunting dogs, presumably in response to the addition of helpers, so packs can at best raise the offspring of only one female. At almost all other times, the dogs appear to live together in a peaceable, non-aggressive manner. Individuals arouse each other before the hunt by a series of gestures that seem to express enthusiasm for the cooperative effort about to be undertaken, and the dogs usually exchange these gestures in a reciprocal fashion (see Figure 8-24). Dominance is established very early in life, within the first year, probably within the first four months. Reversals occur among adults, but not often.

It is interesting to note that the alpha-male may be happy to see his brothers regurgitate food to his pups but may exclude one or more of them from playing with the pups. This suggests that helpers may

Figure 8-27

(a) *Cooperative hunt*. Four hunting dogs have a kongoni *Alcelaphus busela-phus* surrounded. The alpha male is directly behind the kongoni; he is about to bring it to the ground by biting its achilles tendon. The adult female is directly in front of the kongoni, having only joined the hunt after the kongoni was cornered. (b) After the kongoni was dropped, the beta male grabbed the muzzle. Data from many hunts by this pack showed that the alpha and beta males typically took the initiative in the hunt but that all the males regurgitated equal amounts of food to the pups. (Photos: James Malcolm, Anthro-Photo)

sometimes form friendships with the pups in such a way that the pups come later to prefer the helper to their father. This may make it more likely that the helper will become the dominant individual in the pack, or be able to split off from the pack aided by some of the individuals whom he helped when they were young. Such reciprocity has been documented among helpers in birds.

More hunting dog males than females are born, and females suffer higher mortality than do males in their first year of life. Thus about 60 males are raised to one year of age for every 40 females. Since a male and a female are about the same size, each probably costs the pack about the same amount to rear. Thus, hunting dogs appear to expend more total effort raising males than females. The most likely explanation for this is that males are less expensive to the pack in the long run than are females, since males are more likely to stay and help raise future offspring, while females emigrate (see pp. 276–277).

Lesbian Gulls

With the advent of kinship theory it was natural to wonder whether such anomalous activities as human homosexual behavior might, in reality, be a device promoting kin-directed altruism. If there had been no such kin effects in the past, it is difficult to see how four billion years of selection could produce such a high frequency of human beings (more than 2%) whose sexual choice largely precludes personal reproduction. But on the surface, the sexual and romantic side of homosexual relations would seem to interfere with kin-directed altruism: insofar as one is sexually attracted to another individual, one will naturally be inclined to invest some resources in intrasexual competition to gain this individual's favors. Should the relationship blossom into a love relationship, it will be natural to devote some of the same resources and energy that would go into a loving heterosexual relationship. So sexuality is a threat to the altruistic role that may associate non-reproduction with benefit to kin. Presumably this is why parents may be pleased when an offspring joins a celibate priesthood, a position with some power to benefit kin, while they will be less pleased to learn that an offspring is living in an exclusively homosexual relationship in some distant city. That parents in our society often consciously fear the expression of a homosexual orientation in their children suggests that homosexuality is not normally a means for aiding the reproduction of kin; otherwise, they should be delighted, since they are more closely related to the recipients of this altruism than is the offspring (see pp. 162–163).

Having said this, we must emphasize that homosexual behavior is turning up in a variety of creatures besides ourselves. I have observed occasional homosexual copulations between marked adult male green lizards *Anolis garmani* in Jamaica (for a normal copulation in this species see Figure 9-22). Much more striking is the discovery of long-term lesbian relationships in monogamous birds. In five species of gulls we have now discovered populations in which frequencies of lesbian couples exceed estimates for our own society. The couples—like heterosexual pairs—often stay paired in successive seasons. They defend a territory, court each other, build a nest, and alternate sitting on the eggs (Figure 8-28). In some couples, one female shows such normally male behaviors as courtship feeding, mounting, and attempted copulation, although the courtship feeding is never as intense as in heterosexual couples, which may explain why lesbians commonly lay smaller eggs than do heterosexual females.

Since both females lay, lesbian couples are hampered by the fact that they commonly produce five- or six-egg clutches (Figure 8-29). At least 10% of these eggs and sometimes as many as 20% are fertile, which means that the lesbian couples are sometimes copulating with males. Although fertility is reduced, as is chick survival, in some species lesbian couples do achieve measurable reproductive success (Figure 8-30). Clearly such pairs are being selected against—relative to heterosexual couples—but the lesbian is doing better than not reproducing at all (unless there is a large cost to reproducing) and it may be that when the adult sex ratio is biased in favor of excess females, as often seems to be the case in these gulls, lesbian relationships permit some females to achieve reproductive success they otherwise would not.

Figure 8-28

A presumed lesbian couple. A pair of Western gulls *Larus occidentalis* is shown at the nest. One is attempting to relieve the other from sitting on the eggs. As in heterosexual couples, the incubating bird is reluctant to leave the nest. The couple is presumed to be lesbian because it is attending a supernormal clutch (five or six eggs). (Photo: George Hunt)

Figure 8-29

A supernormal clutch. This nest of the Western gull contains five eggs and was almost certainly laid by two females. Notice that the eggs have been marked for identification. This marking confirms that the eggs were laid too quickly to have been laid by a single female. (Photo: George Hunt)

Summary

Reproductive altruism occurs when an adult foregoes reproduction in one or more seasons in order to aid the reproduction of others. The outstanding examples occur in the social insects: ants, bees, wasps, and termites. In ants, most individuals are non-reproductive workers aiding the reproduction of the queen, their mother. Workers are invariably female and in many species have evolved into several complementary forms. Through reproductive altruism, ants have evolved complex, interconnected activities such as silk-weaving, animal husbandry, agriculture, and slave-making.

All ants, bees, and wasps are haplodiploid: females have two sets of chromosomes but males, which originate from unfertilized eggs, have only one. This results in unusual degrees of relatedness. Females are more closely related to their full sisters ($r = \frac{3}{4}$) than to their own offspring ($r = \frac{1}{2}$). If they tend to produce more sisters than brothers ($r = \frac{1}{2}$) or raise sisters and sons, instead of sisters and brothers, selection will favor reproductive altruism. This system also generates a bias against male helping. Conflict is expected between mother and offspring over male production. In ants the queen seems to have won this conflict, perhaps because she alone can provide workers with full-sisters.

Termites are diploid and yet have evolved complex, ant-like societies based on a reproductive division of labor. Both males and females act as workers, and secondary reproductives are a common feature of many nests. If the winged reproductives that leave the nest are often produced by secondary reproductives (which mate incestuously within the nest), then cycles of inbreeding within nests are followed by outbreeding between nests. This pattern of breeding raises the relatedness of individuals to their full-siblings above their relatedness to offspring, thus favoring reproductive altruism.

Helpers at the nest are now known from more than 100 species of birds. These individuals help a breeding pair raise offspring. They are usually offspring of the pair they are helping and their willingness to help is sensitive to parameters that affect the cost/benefit ratio of helping; fewer available territories in which to breed or mates with whom to pair are associated with higher frequencies of helping, as is lower availability of food. In one species individuals may help more than one pair in the same season and they do so more frequently the higher is their degree of relatedness to nestlings. In a territorial bird without helpers, there is no evidence that kin benefit from occupying adjacent territories.

In Florida scrub jays all yearlings remain in the parental territory to help and some males help for five years or more. Carefully gathered evidence shows that helpers increase the reproductive success of the pair they are helping, an effect that diminishes with increasing numbers of helpers. Helpers mostly raise full-siblings, but about one-fourth of the time they aid individuals to whom they are related by $r = \frac{1}{4}$. Males dominate females and, within sex, older birds dominate younger. Dominance determines access to breeding: the breeding male enforces dominance over his male helpers, and dominant helpers breed earlier than subordinates. Male helpers come into conflict with their mother on the death of her mate, but she usually wins by pairing quickly with an outsider. Dominant individuals provide more help for the young than do subordinates, and this may hasten the day when they inherit a portion of the family territory.

In mammals, reproductive altruism is known from naked mole rats and the dog family. Jackal helpers appear to increase the reproductive success of close relatives. In the hunting dog, males are more likely to help than females and groups consist of adult male relatives, one of whom is paired to an unrelated female, who sometimes is helped by a female relative. Hunting dogs appear to invest more energy in the production of sons than daughters, probably because sons are more likely to give a return benefit to their parents in the form of future aid.

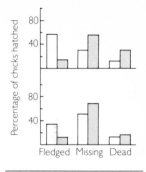

Figure 8-30

Fledging success and mortality as a function of heterosexual or homosexual pairings in gulls. The percentage of chicks hatched that fledged, were missing, or were known dead is plotted separately for normal clutches (unshaded bars) and superclutches (shaded bars) in ring-billed gulls *Larus delawarensis*. The latter were laid primarily by lesbian couples. Hatching success was also lower in lesbian couples (34% in 1979 and 30% in 1980 compared to 77% and 61% for normal clutches). (*From* Kovacs and Ryder 1983)

Homosexuality in humans may be associated with benefits to kin, but the attitude of parents toward homosexuality in their offspring suggests that at least in our society this is not usually the case. In five species of gulls, lesbian couples are found at frequencies as high as 10% of breeding pairs. Although lesbian couples achieve lower reproductive success than heterosexual pairs, in some species they achieve measurable reproductive success, which may be preferable to not breeding at all.

Chapter 9

Parental Investment and Sexual Selection

IN THE MID-1960's I was studying free-living pigeons in Massachusetts. Pigeons are strongly monogamous and every night I watched three couples who regularly roosted outside my window. What soon became apparent was that the males seemed much more sexually insecure and aggressive than their mates. If a new couple arrived, the male was attacked more frequently by other males than the female was by other females. If a male arrived alone, he was attacked much more strongly than if he arrived with a mate. When settling near each other, males preferred to see their mates sitting on the outside, so that each male was between his mate and any other male. Prior to egg-laying, males were especially attentive to their mates, following them around closely and giving way in disputes over where to sit.

Why should male pigeons be more sexually insecure than females? Why should the sight of another male close to "his" female be harder for the male to bear than a similar sight for a female? Males act as if they are concerned their mates will mate with other males. Imagine that this occurs. A male risks having his offspring fathered by another male. If he works to raise unrelated young, he will suffer a large cost in reproductive success. By contrast, a female need have no such concern. No matter who her mate copulates with, a female's eggs are her own and any subsequent investment benefits her own genes. Of course, we do not expect the female to be indifferent to her mate's "extramarital" activities. They may divert time and energy and, more importantly, may lead to his desertion, but both sexes risk desertion: only the male risks being cuckolded.

Concern over cuckoldry suggests that monogamous males may be interested in sexual relationships outside the pair. This was easy enough to confirm. Each of the monogamous, sexually insecure males I observed courted females at a nearby park when his mate was at home on the eggs. Thus, males acted out a double standard, seeking for themselves what they acted to deny their mates.

The parallel to our own behavior is obvious. In most human cultures restrictions are placed on female sexuality that are not placed on males. In the past females were expected to be virgins at marriage, or even risked being put to death if found in adultery. Chastity belts were imposed during separations and kings' harems were guarded by eunuchs. Women's feet may be bound to limit mobility and women may have their clitorises removed to decrease sexual interest, and so on.

The underlying difference between the sexes is one of investment. In both pigeons and humans a sexual act that is inexpensive for a male triggers a large, costly investment by the female. Even when a male helps his mate raise young, copulations with other females may give a big increase in reproductive success, while copulations of his mate with other males will tend to have the reverse effect. If lack of male investment can have this effect in a species in which males commonly care for their young, then it should have an even greater effect where males make no parental contribution at all, for in such species a male will be able in theory to fertilize many, many females, so that competition between males for access to females should be intense. The general rule in animals is that female investment leads to female choosiness and male lack of investment leads to male–male competition. In this chapter we review the reason for this rule. We begin with the classic experiments of A. J. Bateman on *Drosophila*. We then review the distribution of sex differences in animals and test the theory of relative parental investment by reviewing sex-reversed species. We briefly review sperm competition. We review examples of male dimorphisms generated by sexual selection and we close by describing the way in which male–male competition may explain sexual dimorphism in species lacking male parental investment.

The Effect of Relative Parental Investment

Darwin was the first to appreciate that a special kind of selection he called *sexual selection* occurred at the time of breeding. Individuals who do not differ in ability to survive may differ greatly in their breeding success. This, in turn, depends on two factors: (1) competition within one sex for access to members of the opposite sex and (2) choice by individuals of one sex for particular members of the opposite sex. Darwin realized that in nature it was often the males who competed with each other for access to females and females who were discriminating in choice of sex partners. This, he appreciated, could result in more extreme selection in males, that is, in greater variation in male reproductive success than female reproductive success. To this intense selection Darwin attributed such male characters as antlers, tusks and fangs, bright and extravagant plumage, courtship song and dance, wings when one sex is wingless, and so on; but Darwin could not figure out why it was so often male–male competition and female choice and not vice versa. This key advance was made by A. J. Bateman in 1948 when he published an account of experiments on the factors associated with reproductive success in the two sexes of the fruit fly *Drosophila melanogaster*.

Bateman used flies with different genetic markers so that offspring could be assigned to their parents based on the presence of these markers. In a typical experiment he introduced five virgin females to five virgin males (or three of each) in a bottle and allowed them to spend several days together, mating and laying eggs. When offspring emerged, he classified them according to the genes of their parents. By noting which markers appeared together he was able to estimate the number of effective inseminations in which each fly participated. From these observations, he discovered two important differences between the sexes:

(1) *Males show greater variation in reproductive success than do females.* In all of the experiments only 4% of the females produced no surviving offspring, while 21% of the males failed to leave any surviving offspring. This implies that some males were very successful. In fact, in every single experiment, *variance* in reproductive success (a measure of variation) was greater in males than in females.

(2) *Frequency of copulation had no effect on female reproductive success (beyond the first copulation), but the more copulations a male had, the higher was his reproductive success.* Most females mated only once or twice. When Bateman studied the relationship between the number of copulations and the number of surviving offspring, he discovered that, providing females mated at least one time, additional matings had no effect on their reproductive success (Figure 9-1). By contrast, with each new mating, a male typically elevated his reproductive success. Since most females mated only once, each new mating by a male typically gave him a new batch of eggs to fertilize.

Bateman explained his results by reference to the difference in cost between sperm cells and egg cells. Each egg is expensive, and this cost limits the number that can be made. Most of the variation in female reproductive success is a function of variation in female condition. Those females capable of producing many eggs are presumably those that have more food reserves stored in their bodies. By contrast, sperm are so inexpensive that each could, on this basis alone, fertilize the eggs of dozens of females; but if one male fertilizes dozens of females, then dozens of males will be left with no one to fertilize. Thus the inexpensiveness of male parental investment naturally induces strong competition between them for access to females. At the same time it leads

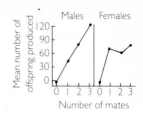

Figure 9-1

The fertility of males and females as a function of the number of their mates, in fruitflies. The reproductive success of a male and a female is plotted as a function of the number of mates in outbred *Drosophila melanogaster*. The data demonstrate a reason why males may attempt numerous copulations but not a reason for females. (*From Bateman 1948*)

Figure 9-2

Variation in lifetime reproductive success of elephant seals. The percentage of males born or females born who produce a given number of offspring surviving to the age of weaning. Notice the enormous variability in male RS. (From LeBoeuf and Reiter *in press*)

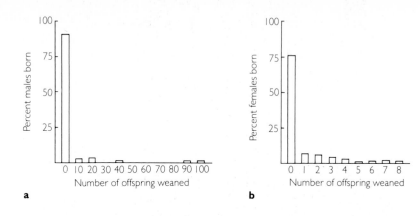

males to be relatively undiscriminating in their choice of sex partners. To take an extreme, if they make a mistake and mate with a female of the wrong species, males will only lose a single batch of sperm. By contrast, a female may lose her entire set of eggs.

Bateman's interpretation should apply very widely in nature, for in most species of animals, parental care ends with the production of the fertilized egg. In these species, male parental investment is invariably very small compared to female PI, and we expect to find higher variation in male reproductive success than female. Likewise, we expect to see male–male competition for access to females, and female choice in favor of particular males. Finally, we expect to find males interested in copulating many times with a variety of females, while females may often be interested in copulating only a few times or once. Greater variation in male RS has now been confirmed for a variety of species in nature. As we have seen already (pp. 35–38), lifetime RS varies more widely in male red deer than in female and male RS is controlled by access to breeding females, while female RS is controlled by ability to invest in offspring. Similar evidence has been gathered for the elephant seal *Mirounga angustirostris* (see Figure 9-2).

It is important to emphasize that Bateman's argument only applies to species with negligible male parental investment. Whenever in a species a male typically invests the same amount per offspring as does the female, the sexes are expected to show equal variation in reproductive success, to be equally discriminating in choice of sexual partners, and to be equally limited in reproductive success by access to members of the opposite sex. For evidence on variation in reproductive success in a bird with high male parental investment see Figure 9-3.

The Major Sex Differences

The two sexes differ in a wide range of characters and these can be organized as follows. The sexes differ in: (1) relative parental invest-

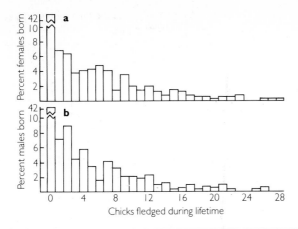

Figure 9-3

Variation in lifetime reproductive success of male and female kittiwake gulls.
Shown are the percentage of female or male gulls *Rissa tridactyla* hatched
who achieved a given lifetime reproductive success as measured by the number
of chicks they fledged. Notice the similarity between sexes, but note also the
enormous variability within each sex, suggesting the possible importance
of mate choice in monogamous species (see Chapter 10). (From Clutton-
Brock 1983)

ment, (2) degree of intrasexual competition for access to the opposite
sex, (3) degree of choosiness in mating, and (4) life history parameters.

(1) *Relative parental investment.* The single most important difference between the sexes is the difference in their investment in offspring. The general rule is this: females do all the investing, males do
none of it. Parental investment can be defined as anything done for the
offspring that increases its chance of survival while decreasing the parents' ability to produce additional offspring. As such, it includes the
cost of producing the sex cell, but also includes any other time or
effort expended on behalf of the offspring. Difference in investment is
especially obvious in mammals. Females suffer the cost of pregnancy,
the cost of nursing, and the additional responsibility of protecting the
young and showing them a place in the world. The male's contribution
to this entire enterprise is the sperm cell, weighing on the average one
10-trillionth of a gram.

One example serves to illustrate the difference for mammals. A female elephant seal weighing 650 kg gives birth to an offspring that
weighs 50 kg. In the following five weeks the offspring may gain 100
kg, entirely from mother's milk (see Figures 9-4 to 9-6). Studies show
that females lose 2 kg for every 1 kg the offspring gains. Thus females
may lose as many as 200 kg. By contrast, the male who fathered the
offspring weighed 2700 kg and contributed a few hours' production of
sperm cells to ensure fertilization. Although mammals are dramatic

Figure 9-4

Mother and offspring. In this photo we see an adult elephant seal and her offspring. The mother herself does not feed while nursing. Age and dominance have a strong positive effect on a female's ability to rear pups to independence. (Photo: Burney LeBoeuf)

Figure 9-5

An orphan next to a nursing pup. The orphaned elephant seal pup on the left, about the same age (three weeks) as the other pup but considerably smaller through failure to nurse, is scarred over its back through attempts to nurse from females other than its mother (see also Figure 3-20). By contrast, the largest pup ever weighed (almost 300 kilograms) was a male who nursed from two mothers simultaneously. (Photo: Burney LeBoeuf)

Figure 9-6

Super-mother. A flock of elephant seal orphans (note scars) has discovered one of the few adult females willing to nurse each of them. Such a surrogate mother is usually a young adult, breeding for the first time, who has lost her own pup. Some of her investment may well benefit her in increasing her reproductive performance the following year. Since the orphans are dividing one mother between them, none is very large. (Photo: Burney LeBoeuf)

examples, in fact the same general sex difference is also found in creatures who lay eggs, which are invariably many orders of magnitude larger and more costly than the sperm cell with which they unite. Consider, for example, the eggs of birds, turtles, snakes, fish, and insects (see Figure 9-7).

There are exceptions to the general rule that relative parental investment (PI of male/PI of female) = o. These exceptions are especially important because, as we have seen, relative parental investment controls the evolution of the other sex differences, so that the species that are exceptional in relative parental investment are also exceptional in other regards. Birds are the most prominent exception. In about 95% of the 8000 bird species, male parental investment is common. Other exceptions are the carnivorous mammals, some species of fish and frogs, and many species of insects. Species with male parental investment are reviewed in Chapter 10.

(2) *Degree of intrasexual competition.* The general rule regarding intrasexual competition is that males compete with each other for access to females, while females rarely compete with each other for access to males. Male competition, in turn, takes at least three forms: (a) aggressive interactions to limit the access of other males to a set of females, (b) competition to disperse and find sexually receptive females, and (c) competition in courtship to be chosen by females. Each

Figure 9-7

Maternal investment in a beetle. Like so many fledgling birds, the larvae of the burying beetle *Necrophorus vespillo* are fed by their mother, who is seen regurgitating food to one larva while another reaches to feed. The larvae rest in a depression excavated by their mother in a ball of rotting carcass provided by both parents. The larvae also feed from the ball. In some related species the male regurgitates food to the larvae but less so than the female. (Drawing by Sarah Landry, from Wilson, 1971).

Figure 9-8

Two elephant seal males fight. These two dominant elephant seal males are squaring off in a fight. Each will attempt to push its rival around and to wound the other on its heavily padded neck or more vulnerable flanks. These contests concern sexual access to the highly aggregated breeding females, seen here with their pups. By delaying the implantation of the early embryo in their uterus for several months, females are able to prolong development in their young so that the females can mate right after they have finished nursing their current offspring—instead of three months later. (Photo: Burney LeBoeuf)

of these differences in behavior has in turn generated a series of structures and physiological adaptations to support the behaviors.

Where there is a sex difference in aggressiveness, males are typically the more aggressive sex. This is especially pronounced at the time of breeding. Females rarely fight each other over access to males, yet males may fight for hours, wounding each other and on occasion killing (Figure 9-8). A series of structures has evolved to support this fighting. For example, males are usually the sex that is ornamented with weapons, such as the enlarged canine teeth of primates, antlers of deer, larger horn size in antelopes, tusks in pigs and elephants, horns on staghorn beetles, enlarged jaws (relative to body size) in lizards, and so on (see Figure 9-9). Naturally, males have the musculature to use these weapons, and this increases the cost of the weapons.

In most species of animals, males disperse more widely than do females. That is, if individuals of the two sexes are marked and recaptured sometime later, the male will have moved a greater distance. In plants it is the male sex cell that is mobile, while the female sex cell is stationary until pollination. Studies of movements in salamanders, snakes, turtles, lizards, and mammals show a consistent pattern of greater male dispersal. This is often especially pronounced during the mating season. In some species the sex difference appears at an early age. For example, male deer fawns at six months of age wander greater

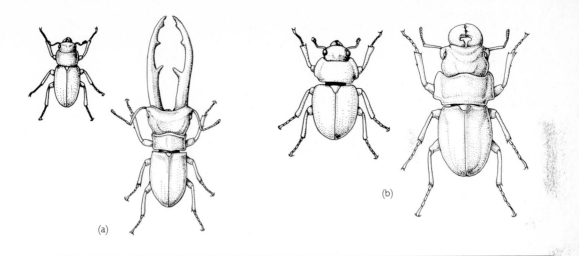

Figure 9-9

Sexual dimorphism in beetles. (a) Male and female of *Cyclommatus imperator*, the male having huge forceps-like mandibles, which in other species are used to lift another male off a surface such as the trunk of a tree. (b) Male and female of *Odontolabis lowei*, with the male showing well-developed pincher-like mandibles, probably useful for crushing. In both species the male's head is much enlarged in order to hold the muscles that move the mandibles. Notice also the enlarged body size. Such extreme examples of sexual dimorphism are usually found in the species with the greatest body size within a group (*From* Otte and Stayman 1979)

distances from their mother than do females. When one species of insect lacks wings, it is usually the female. As with the other rules, there are exceptions. Birds, which are exceptional in so many other ways, are the only large group of animals in which females regularly disperse greater distances than do males.

Males typically court females rather than vice versa. Males are often very active in courtship and display parts of themselves. They also are almost always the more conspicuous of the two sexes. Virtually all sounds that are produced during the breeding season are produced by males. Males are the more brightly colored of the two sexes, and in birds colorful parts of the plumage are often displayed to the female during courtship. For scenes of the rut in red deer, see Figure 9-10.

Underlying these differences may be a widespread tendency for the metabolic rates of males to be higher than the metabolic rates of females. For example, in the human species a boy's resting metabolic rate is about 5% higher than a girl's, and this sex difference persists

Figure 9-10

Male activities toward females during the rut in red deer. (a) Males frequently approach lying females and lick the back of their heads and necks, gradually working toward the front of their eyes, as shown here. This may be followed by an attempt to sniff and lick around the base of the tail. Bouts of sniffing and licking may last for several minutes and are usually terminated by the female moving away. (b) In addition to herding females attempting to leave his territory, a male often chases a female over short distances within the harem, his neck outstretched, sometimes with tongue extended. Such chases are terminated by the male and are often followed by a bout of roaring. (c) A male prepares to mount. The female has signaled her acceptance by spreading her hind legs, while the male licks her rump. (d) At the moment of ejaculation, the male may leap clear of the ground, as in this picture. Mating sequences between two individuals involve several mountings spread over an hour or more. (Photos: a, c Timothy Clutton-Brock; b, d Fiona Guiness)

a

b

c

d

into adulthood (when corrections are made for differences in adult body weight).

(3) *Females are discriminating, males are not.* In most species females are highly discriminating in their choice of sex partners, while males are much less discriminating. A female is typically courted by many males and refuses access to all but one or a few. This choice is by no means random. Wherever female preference has been studied in nature, females have been shown to choose in very particular ways. Most females in a species choose in a similar way, so that the result of female choice is to give some males many copulations and many other males none (see Chapter 14).

By contrast, males court many females and will copulate with most or all if accepted. In addition, males will court inappropriate objects. For example, males have been observed courting other males, females of the wrong species, stuffed females, portions of stuffed females, and inanimate objects. Sometimes they are seen courting a combination of the above. In many frog species, courtship of males by other males is so common that males have evolved a special release call given to another male who has clasped him, which says, in effect, "Release me, I'm a male."

The fact that males will court stuffed females is useful for field biologists, since it means that stuffed females can be introduced to males in order to test their reactions under experimental conditions (see pp. 349–352). Biologists studying turkeys decided to see how much can be removed from a stuffed female and still produce a full male sexual response. It turns out that a head suspended 15 inches above the ground is capable of eliciting complete courtship behavior from some males. These males circle the head, display themselves, and behind the head jump into the air so as to land where the female's back would normally be. A wooden model of a female's head is less arousing than a stuffed head, but is still successful with some males. Indeed, some will even respond when the eyes, the eye sockets, and the beak have been removed.

It is not accurate to characterize the male as active during courtship and the female as passive. The process of choice is an active process. Often females move from male to male, eliciting courtship and responding in various ways to the courtship in order to make their choice. It was often claimed in the past that females of many species were unwilling to participate in sex and had to be courted by numerous males before being aroused to the point where they would indulge in sex. What appears to be true is that females are uninterested in sex with most of the available males and require courtship by many different males in order to make their choice. Thus males appear to be indiscriminately eager for sex, while females are choosy.

(4) *Sex differences in life history parameters.* In most species males suffer higher mortality than do females, and this is often true throughout their lives (see Chapter 12). Males may also mature at a different age than females.

Sex-role-reversed Species

To test Bateman's theory of parental investment and sexual selection, it would be ideal to find species in which males invest more in the production of offspring than do females. In such species we expect to find that female reproductive success varies more than that of males, we expect to see females limited in RS by their access to males, and we expect males to be more careful in choice of mating partner than are females. But relative parental investment is difficult to measure in nature, and it has proved easier to find examples of sex role reversal, which on inspection turn out to be associated with unusually high male parental investment. Since George Williams first drew our attention to sex-role-reversed fish and birds, a growing number of examples have come to light. These convergent examples give support to the view that relative parental investment is the underlying variable controlling the evolution of sex differences.

Insects. A couple of cases have now come to light of high male parental investment correlating with sex-role reversal. In the Mormon cricket, male investment in the form of a spermatophore may be considerable (Figures 9-11 and 9-12). In high-density areas—where food is relatively scarce—these large spermatophores are especially valuable yet difficult to produce. The result is female–female aggression for access to males, inflated female size (relative to male), and males that are discriminating. About half the copulations are terminated by the male before he transfers his spermatophore: females who are accepted are, on average, larger than those that are rejected and contain 60% more eggs. The result of sexual selection on females in high-density areas is an increase in the degree of variation in the number of their mates: some females, especially large ones, have their naturally high fertility augmented by many male spermatophores. In low-density areas—where the crickets are 1000 times less numerous—food is relatively abundant and many males are able to produce spermatophores. Even though male investment is relatively greater (as measured by percentage of body weight committed to each copulation), there is no female–female aggression, nor are males choosy!

Seahorses. In fish, the pipefish-seahorse family (Syngnathidae) has several species that appear to be sex-reversed. In each of these species a male invests in young by receiving the eggs of a female in his pouch

Figure 9-11

Sex-role-reversed cricket. The female Mormon cricket *Anabrus simplex* starts to mount the male prior to copulating. The male has already arched his abdomen in anticipation. The long structure at the female's rear is her ovipositor; through it she will lay her eggs. At copulation the male transfers a spermatophore, which may amount to 30% of his weight (see next photo). When he has a spermatophore ready, a male calls to attract a female. (Photo: Darryl Gwynne)

Figure 9-12

Consuming male parental investment. After mating, a female Mormon cricket turns and begins eating the large, protein-rich spermatophore that the male has just transferred along with his sperm. In a related species, heavier males are known to produce larger spermatophores, and females given a choice between two singing males that differ in weight prefer to mate with the heavier male. In the decorated cricket *Gryllodes supplicans* the spermatophore is consumed in two portions, the second of which contains the remaining sperm. The first portion is, on average, just large enough to ensure that all sperm are transferred before the second portion is eaten. (Photo: Darryl Gwynne)

and caring for the eggs in the pouch almost like a kangaroo. Several species have been studied in the laboratory. Courtship is mutual in these species but more active on the part of females. Females are more brightly colored than males and develop their coloration at the time of courtship. Coloration correlates with motivation to breed: the brightest females court with the greatest intensity. Males court by pumping water into their brood pouch so that it expands like a balloon; thus they appear to advertise their capacity to carry eggs. In turn, two field studies show that females typically contain more eggs than males carry within their brood pouches. In both sexes, larger size correlates with a greater number of eggs carried, but for the same size, females contain more eggs than do males. This is suggestive evidence that females may be limited in reproductive success by access to male brood pouches. Unfortunately, we lack information on how long males carry eggs compared to the time it takes females to produce a batch of eggs. In summary, in the Syngnathidae, male parental investment is unusually high and may be higher than female parental investment. In turn, females compete with each other for access to males, are more vigorous in courtship, and are more brightly colored.

The poison-arrow frog. In one frog, the Panamanian poison-arrow frog *Dendrobates auratus*, females are more vigorous in courtship than are males and have been seen chasing them. Females lay a clutch of eggs every 5–10 days, while males care for each clutch for 10–13 days until hatching and carry tadpoles to standing water. Males are also capable of caring for two clutches of eggs at the same time, and both sexes show aggression toward members of the same sex.

Sex-reversed birds. Sex-reversed birds are a mixed assemblage, including phalaropes, various shorebirds—such as the dotterel, various so-called primitive birds—such as the emu and tinanou, and the lily-trotting jacanas. These species are characterized by the following:

(1) Females invest nothing in the young after the eggs are laid. Males brood the eggs until chicks emerge and care for the chicks for several weeks.

(2) The young are precocious; that is, they are able to move about on their own shortly after hatching and are capable of feeding themselves.

(3) Some females are polyandrous; that is, they breed with more than one male per season, depositing a clutch of eggs with each male. Males always breed only once per season.

(4) Females usually outnumber males. This alone generates female–female competition to pair with males.

(5) Females are larger than males, more brightly colored, more aggressive, more active in courtship, and arrive first on the breeding grounds.

Female competition for males has been described as follows in the Wilson's Phalarope *Steganopus tricolor*:

Immediately after arrival, courtship behavior increases gradually in intensity for a week or two, reaching a peak about mid-May. At this time it is common to see solitary males swimming nervously along the edges of grassy ponds pursued by several females. Often one female seems to be dominant or to have already formed a pair bond with a male. This female usually follows the male more closely and manages to stay between him and the other females. Occasionally, if another female approaches too closely, the dominant female attacks and drives her away. . . . The male usually watches attentively from several feet away or swims about aimlessly and nervously nearby.

Phalarope males are often happy to engage in an extra copulation; these, after all, cost a male very little, so that he is easily aroused to copulate with a female even if he is already encumbered with eggs or young. But at the time when eggs hatch, males drive away females and do not permit them near their young. Females sometimes court a male at this time, so it at first seems curious that males should respond so aggressively to female courtship. Yet a female could destroy a male's young (much as does a langur male) in order to be able to deposit her own eggs with the male. Indeed, this appears to happen in another sex-reversed species, the jacana: a female take-over of another's territory was associated within a day with the disappearance of a male's clutch in the territory, suggesting female infanticide. The male repeatedly tried to distract the female's attention from his nest. Likewise, in the sex-reversed little button quail, females have been seen killing chicks in an enclosure in circumstances that suggest they might practice infanticide in nature. Incidentally, the sex-reversed button quail is the only bird known in which the female feeds the male during courtship, while the reverse is widespread.

The phalarope system and other examples of polyandry in arctic shorebirds are believed to have arisen through the habit of double-clutching. Where nest predation is high, females are selected to lay replacement clutches. At the same time, to reduce visibility, only one parent is selected to remain with the eggs. Since the young are precocious, only one parent is required after the chicks hatch. Thus, as females concentrated on laying replacement clutches, males became saddled with incubation and post-hatching care. This forced males into greater investment than females, in particular, requiring them to stay in the breeding habitat long after food resources were optimal, while females migrated to better feeding grounds. Greater investment led to greater mortality (see Chapter 12), which intensified female–female conflict for males. A second clutch could also be placed with a male who had no clutch, either through loss or failure to pair. This occasional polyandry further intensified female–female conflict.

Recently, Marion Petrie has conducted a remarkable study of the sex-reversed moorhen *Gallinula chloropus* that shows that large size in females is favored by female–female competition, while small size in males is maintained by the energy efficiency of high parental investment. Males perform 72% of the incubation, which is energy-expensive: they lose almost 10% of their body weight during the breeding season. Males in better condition at the beginning of the season spend more days incubating throughout the season and initiate more new clutches, while female condition has no effect on the number of clutches initiated. Instead, females fight with each other for access to males (more than vice versa) and court males (more than vice versa). Occasionally females are polyandrous but they seem primarily to compete for access to high quality males. Heavier females win fights more often and pair more often with males in good condition, as expected (Figure 9-13), but male condition is inversely correlated with male size, so that large females preferentially mate with small, fat males! We see that large variation in male quality—rather than the number of mates a female may acquire—can induce female–female competition.

Sperm Competition

In one sense all male–male competition is just so much sperm competition (pollen in plants): sperm are so inexpensive that far more are produced than the eggs they fertilize, and in the absence of additional male investment in the young, males compete with each other in order to give their sperm differential reproductive success. Even when there is high male investment, there may be sperm conflict in the form of cuckoldry (see pp. 260–267). The differentiation into small, mobile male sex cells (sperm or pollen) presumably followed from the fact that more of them could be produced for the same cost without a commensurate decrease in fertilizing efficiency. Presumably, in sperm cells as well as in adult males, dispersal and mobility select against large size.

In insects, sperm competition is a major factor affecting male reproductive success. When two males copulate with the same female, the general rule is that the sperm of the second male takes precedence: last one in is first one out. Sometimes this competition is very aggressive. In the damselfly *Calopteryx maculata* the male's penis is designed both to deposit sperm and to remove any that has already been deposited (Figure 9-14). In other species the penis appears designed to enter the female's sperm storage organ and compress any existing

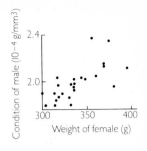

Figure 9-13

Relationship between male condition and female weight in mated pairs of moorhens. A male's condition (weight in grams × 10^{-4} divided by the cube of the length of part of his leg—tarsus plus metatarsus—in cubic millimeters) is plotted as a function of his mate's weight (in grams). Weights were either measured at the beginning of the breeding season or standardized to reflect values at that time. Note that heavier females are paired with males in better condition. (*From* Petrie 1983)

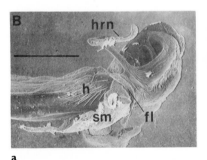
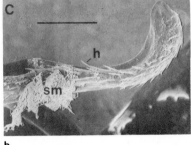

a   b

Figure 9-14

The penis of a damselfly: designed to remove sperm already deposited.
(a) The penis of the male damselfly *Calopteryx maculata* showing the backward-projecting horn (hrn) and the hairs (h) that catch masses of sperm (sm). (b) A close-up of the horn. (Photos: Jonathan Waage)

Figure 9-15

A penis for compressing rival sperm to a corner. The penis of the male dragonfly *Sympetrum rubicundilum* is shown inserted into the female's vagina. Note the two inflatable lobes extending into the female's sperm storage sac. They probably compress rival sperm to the far corner, from where they are unlikely to fertilize eggs. (*From* Waage *in press*)

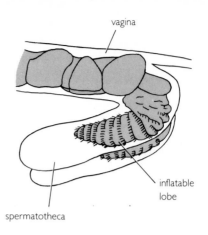

vagina

inflatable lobe

spermatotheca

sperm to a corner (Figure 9-15). In an acanthocephalan worm sperm competition takes the form of homosexual rape: after copulating, males use the same cement gland with which they usually seal off the female to seal off the genital region of male competitors!

Since the rule regarding insect sperm is last-in first-out, there is a premium to copulating just before oviposition. Often a male will choose to guard his mate for a period of time after sperm is transferred so as to increase the chance that oviposition will occur before remating. As expected, the frequency of this guarding is greater—and lasts for a longer period—when the adult sex ratio is more biased toward males. This makes sense since extra males will decrease the matings available elsewhere to each male, while increasing the chance that another male will mate with the female he is about to release.

Duration of copulation itself may be lengthened in order to guard the sperm being deposited. In caged populations of the stink bug *Nezara virigidula* duration of copulation is more than doubled when there are two males for each female instead of vice versa (Figure 9-16). Note that copulation in this species may last for seven days! The record in insects for duration of copulation is 79 days and is held by a walking stick. In species of these insects, copulation is longer when the male is relatively smaller. This makes sense, because when the male is relatively small, he will mature at an early age; other things being equal, this should increase the adult sex ratio and, therefore, the degree of competition from other males.

This brief glimpse of sperm competition in a well-studied group with internal fertilization has not permitted us to review such well-developed phenomena as the production of mating plugs by males—physical barriers to further copulation, which may include part of the

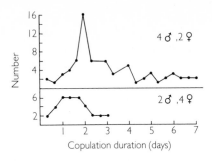

Figure 9-16

Relationship between adult sex ratio and length of copulation in an insect.
The number of copulations is plotted as a function of their length, for a sex
ratio of 4 males and 2 females (top) and 2 males and 4 females (bottom).
Relatively more males result in longer copulations. (*From* McLain 1980)

male's body, as in honey bees *Apis mellifera* (which still does not prevent the female from copulating with as many as a dozen males!). Nor
have we reviewed the evolution of traumatic insemination in bedbugs
and others in which the male seems to short-circuit the normal means
of sperm transport by piercing some portion of the female's body and
injecting sperm directly. In some species, sperm is injected also into
other males, where they migrate to join the sperm of the penetrated
male! In this intense competition between sperm that are partly related
and partly unrelated, selection has more often generated dimorphisms
than between related eggs, though we must admit that we still know
little regarding the way in which altruistic sperm confer their benefit
(see pp. 121–124). Even the size of a male's testicles may partly reflect
sperm competition: in monkeys and apes, testicles are larger (relative
to body size) in species in which several males may mate with a single
female during her fertile period, compared to species in which only
one male typically copulates with a female (see Figure 9-17). Altogether, the world of sperm competition reinforces our impression that
for most species male–male competition results from the low cost of
individual sperm and the consequent competition between males to
fertilize eggs with these sperm.

Alternative Mating Strategies and
Male Dimorphisms

One of the curious facts of biology is that two very different forces
have tended to produce dimorphism in nature. On the one hand, selection associated with reproductive altruism has generated complemen-

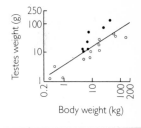

Figure 9-17

*Weight of testes as a func-
tion of body size in mon-
keys and apes.* The average
weight of the testes (in
grams) for males of various
genera is plotted as a function of their body weight
(in kilograms). Closed
circles represent species
with multi-male groups;
open circles, monogamous
species or single-male
groups. Genera with multi-
male troops have larger
testes. (*From* Harcourt
et al. 1981)

tary forms, such as soldier and reproductive aphids, worker and re-productive ants, altruistic and fertilizing sperm, and so on. On the other hand, male–male competition in species lacking male parental investment has also generated dimorphisms. We have already encountered the white and black morph of the ruff (p. 26); likewise, we have seen that there is a calling and non-calling strategy in crickets (p. 98). We now pause to review alternative mating strategies more fully because they serve to illustrate the way in which male RS depends on interactions with other males.

Male dimorphisms are believed to be generated by selection for alternate mating strategies. (For an example of a male dimorphism, see Figure 9-18). Alternative mating strategies occur because there is a strong interaction between the reproductive success of males such that each alternative does relatively well when it is infrequent. In many spe-

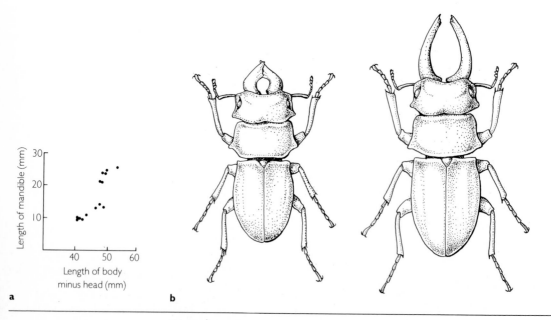

a   b

Figure 9-18

Male dimorphism in a beetle. (a) Mandible length (in millimeters) is plotted for males of the stag beetle *Odontolabis siva* as a function of length of body minus the head (in millimeters). Notice that the points form two clusters. (b) A small male and a large male are drawn, showing the change from a pincher-type mandible to a forceps-type. These are probably associated with different behavioral strategies. (*From* Otte and Stayman 1979)

cies males establish territories within which females will breed or around places from which adult females will emerge. When such territories are few in number, each new male establishing a territory can expect a gain in RS through greater exposure to breeding females; but when many such territories are held, most of the reproductive success available through this means is already being taken, and so an alternative strategy may do better. Instead of patrolling sites at which females will emerge, a male may do better to hover at nearby sites that females are likely to visit. Another alternative strategy is to remain within another male's territory, intercepting some of the RS associated with that place or male. In a chorus of calling crickets or frogs, a male frog may remain silent and mate with some of the females attracted to calling males. One advantage of the alternative strategy is that it may be less expensive to maintain. Non-calling crickets are parasitized less frequently by one fly than are calling males, and defense of a territory may be energy-expensive.

We expect satellite males to be more often associated with high quality territory-holding males and to be more frequent where variation in territory quality is high. We also expect satellites to be more frequent where arrival of females is more synchronized, since each male will then have more difficulty monopolizing all the females. These predictions are supported in dragonflies. In one species, *Plathemis lydia*, males that defend the best sites for opposition are associated with up to four satellite males, while those on poorer areas have none. Female arrival is synchronized at the better sites but not at the poorer ones. With increasing number of female arrivals, copulation rates of territorial males fail to keep pace, presumably creating opportunities for satellites. Satellites are not found on ponds that appear to have little variation in quality of site.

The non-territorial strategy may involve deception. The male may need to remain inconspicuous or he may actually mimic a female, the better to gain access to his "mate's" reproductive success. Deceivers will do well when rare, as will territory holders. This kind of selection has actually generated complementary male morphs in a fish, one of which is considerably smaller than a territorial male and mimics a breeding adult female (see pp. 407–408).

The effect of size on alternative strategies is nicely illustrated by the digger bee *Centris pallida*. Males fight for control of sites from which females emerge from their pupae; the size of the male has an important effect on success in aggressive encounters. The very largest males achieve disproportionate reproductive success (Figure 9-19). Most smaller males do not take part in this competition but instead hover at nearby sites from which they have a good vantage point to dart after unmated flying females. In this species, offspring grow to maturity on provisions supplied by the mother. An advantage to the

Figure 9-19

Size and its effect on alternate mating strategies and mating success in bees. The percentage of male bees *Centris pallida* of a given head width (in millimeters) that hovered, patrolled, or copulated. Sample sizes are indicated. (*From* Alcock 1979)

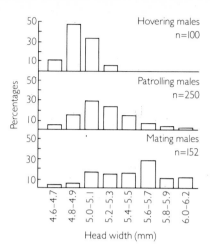

mother of smaller sons is that more of them can be produced for the same cost. In frogs the male adopting the alternate strategy is, on average, smaller than the territorial form (Table 9-1).

The most extreme male dimorphisms are found in fig wasps, in which a flightless form may coexist with a winged, dispersing form. The flightless form is often armed with huge mandibles—attached to an enlarged head—and will attack and kill other males. (For a parallel in bees, see Figure 9-20.) To understand this dimorphism we need to know a few facts about fig wasps. Each species of fig wasp lives in an obligate symbiosis with a species of fig tree: the fig provides the nutrients and home for the developing wasps and the latter pollinate the fig trees. Although males of these wasps are flightless and compete among themselves for matings within a fig, they are never heavily armed, nor are they seen to fight. The reason for this can be found in their breeding system: each female crawls into one fig and lays all her eggs there; although more than one female sometimes lays in a single fig, the offspring preferentially mate with their siblings. The result is high degrees of relatedness between the wasps, a fact that is confirmed by the strongly female-biased sex ratios produced by these wasps. (Such sex ratios are known to correlate in other species with mating between sibs: pp. 277–278.) High relatedness within each fig means that a male will value another male's reproductive success almost as much as his own and will place a similar value on his sister's RS. Both effects should inhibit lethal aggression: each male will not wish to see his sister unmated and may even value her occasional outbreeding (for the benefits it will bring her in genetic novelty and variability among her offspring).

A series of wasp species has parasitized the fig wasp–fig symbiosis, so that a single fig often houses several species simultaneously. In these

Table 9-1   Average Sizes of Males Adopting Alternative
Strategies in Frogs

| | Mean size of males (mm) * | |
Species	Strategy 1	Strategy 2
Bufo bufo	Fight 65.8	Search 61.9
Rana temporaria	Fight 67.9	Search 62.9
B. calamita	Caller 69.6	Satellite 63.4
Hyla cinerea	Caller 53.1	Satellite 47.2
H. crucifer	Caller 45.1	Satellite 43.0
H. regilla	Caller 44.2	Satellite 43.9
H. versicolor	Caller 46.5	Satellite 46.2
R. catesbeiana	Territorial 139.9	Satellite 112.8

Source: Arak 1983.

* All differences are significant except that for *Hyla cinerea*.

Figure 9-20

Male dimorphism in a bee. In this Australian species of *Lasioglossum*, males
come in two forms: a large form, with huge head and mandibles, and incapable of flight, and a smaller, dispersing form. Presumably the armed form
fights for access to females emerging from the communal nest from which he
emerged. (*From* Houston 1970)

species each female stays outside the fig and lays a few of her eggs in the fig by piercing it with a long ovipositor. Because several females commonly lay in each fig, the resulting males will often be competing with unrelated males for access to unrelated females. An enclosed space with large numbers of females waiting to be fertilized is conducive to a very severe form of male combat: a single male can monopolize many females not merely by chasing off other males (which is impossible) but by murdering them. In one species, in which all males are wingless and well armed, male mortality within each fig is high but uneven: large males are most likely to survive and medium-sized males may do the worst of all, suggesting selection for two morphs. The mixture of attack and caution that characterizes these males has been captured by William Hamilton as follows:

A male's fighting movements could be summarized thus: touch, freeze, approach slowly, strike, and recoil. Their fighting looks at once vicious and cautious—cowardly would be the word except that, on reflection, this seems unfair in a situation that can only be likened in human terms to a darkened room full of jostling people among whom, or else lurking in cupboards and recesses which open on all sides, are a dozen or so maniacal homicides armed with knives. One bite is easily lethal. One large *Idarnes* male is capable of biting another in half, but usually a lethal bite is quite a small puncture in the body. Paralysis follows a small injury so regularly and quickly as to suggest use of venom. . . . If no serious injury results from the first or second reciprocal attempts to bite, one of the males, injured perhaps by loss of a tarsus or in some way sensing himself outmatched, retreats and tries to hide. Usually he finds an empty gall into which he plunges, turns, and comes to rest with mandibles agape at the gall's opening. From this position he can bite at the legs of the victor or another passing male with much less danger. Such an inactive male only ventures out again when long undisturbed and then very cautiously.

More surprising than the evolution of wingless males, which may or may not fight, is their coexistence in some species with winged males. These winged males avoid females within their fig but disperse to breed in other figs. As long as some figs—through chance—contain no males, there will always be opportunities for mating outside one's fig, and so the dispersing form should flourish when rare. Likewise—as long as females within one's fig can be mated as they first emerge—the wingless form will do well when uncommon. We thus expect the two forms to coexist in nature at some intermediate frequency. Since the winged form does not mate in its home fig and probably mates with very few females in figs containing at least one wingless male, the expected reproductive success of winged males should be in direct proportion to the proportion of females that develop in figs without any wingless males. By measuring this proportion in ten species of Brazilian fig wasps, William Hamilton showed that the fraction of males that are winged is about the same as the fraction of females that are not exposed to wingless males (Figure 9-21). This correspondence suggests that the alternative forms are giving about equal average payoffs, as required for long-term stability. Incidentally, this kind of explanation—in which the relative frequency of two forms of males is predicted by the relative frequency of the two kinds of females with whom they mate—will reappear when we come to explain the relative frequency with which the two sexes are produced (see Chapter 11). In the case of the fig wasps the underlying variable seems to be the number of young that habitually emerge within a fig. Where this number is low, males are winged; where it is high, males are wingless. Both forms occur at intermediate densities, winged forms being more common at lower densities (where more figs will contain females without wingless males).

Incidentally, competitive dimorphisms are by no means absent in females. In some species, female fig wasps can be divided into separate categories based on the length of their ovipositors, and different females within a single butterfly species may mimic in appearance members of several very different species. Circumstantial evidence suggests that the evolution of similar mimetic polymorphisms in males has often been countered by female choice for the ancestral form. More important than these polymorphisms is a dimorphism in female reproductive mode. In some species, sexual and asexual females coexist in the population; in others, females are sexual or asexual depending on conditions. But as we shall see, the payoffs from these two options are very different, so that their stable coexistence has generated something like a crisis for evolutionary theory (Chapter 13).

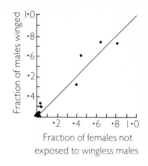

Figure 9-21

Fraction of males that are winged as a function of fraction of females that are not exposed to wingless males. Values are plotted for ten species of Brazilian fig wasps. Note the nearly 1 to 1 correspondence. (*From* Hamilton 1979)

Sexual Dimorphism in Size and Male Fighting in Species Lacking Male Parental Investment

In species lacking male parental investment, there is tremendous variation in sexual dimorphism. Let us consider only closely related animals. In seals, sexual dimorphism in size ranges from species such as the northern elephant seal, in which adult males are at least three to seven times as heavy as adult females (depending on whether the latter are weighed just prior to giving birth or after weaning) to species such as Weddell's seal *Leptonychotes weddelli*, in which adult females are larger than males. Similar variation in male size and in armature is found in deer, although there is no underlying variation in relative parental investment. In both groups (seals and deer), male parental investment is negligible, consisting only of sperm cells. Similarly, in closely related groups of birds, such as the grouse family, sexual dimorphism in plumage may vary from negligible to considerable, while most of the species show little or no male parental investment. How do we explain sexual dimorphism in species lacking male parental investment?

Two factors suggest themselves as important in explaining sexual dimorphism in species lacking male parental investment: first is the degree of variation in male RS and second is the particular set of conditions with which this variation is associated. Where variation in male RS is large, we expect male characters to be accentuated. Where this variation is associated with a particular trait, we expect this trait to be accentuated. Two critical factors affecting male reproductive success will be male–male competition and female choice. For male–male competition, we wish to know the distribution in space and time of breeding females; for female choice we wish to know to what degree females do choose and what they prefer (Chapter 14). In this section we will take one variable—sexual dimorphism in size—and see to what degree we can explain its distribution as a function of patterns of male–male competition. We shall assume for the moment that females are so many passive observers in this game and that their distribution in space and time is the key factor determining the form of male–male competition.

We know that in many—though not all—animal species, larger size gives an advantage in aggressive encounters. Thus, we expect to find an association between male–male aggression and enlarged male size. In snake species, males are usually the smaller sex, but in species in which males are known to fight with each other over access to females, the males are more likely to be larger. Where males fight over many females, instead of few, we expect larger male size to be associated with disproportionate gains in reproductive success: male size, relative to female, should be accentuated. Evidence from three different groups of mammals—seals, ungulates, and primates—has now been reviewed, and in all of these there is a strong, positive relationship between the number of females observed in male harems (that is, groups of breeding females defended exclusively by a male) and sexual dimorphism in body size (Figure 9-22).

The importance of female distribution in space at the time of breeding is suggested by the seals. Where females breed on land, they often form dense aggregations, probably for mutual protection, thus greatly accentuating male–male combat; males are especially large. When females breed on ice, they often do so alone or in small groups, and thus male combat will concern a dispersed resource and should be substantially reduced; size dimorphism may even be reversed. In addition, females tend to be more highly synchronized when breeding on ice, making male monopoly even more difficult.

There are other factors operating besides degree of harem polygyny. In the primates (monkeys, apes, and their relatives), degree of harem polygyny predicts some of the variation in size dimorphism, but

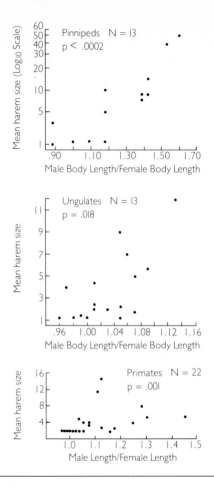

Figure 9-22

Harem size as a function of sexual dimorphism in body size in various groups of mammals. Top: pinnipeds (seals). Middle: ungulates (deer and antelope). Bottom: primates (monkeys and apes). Each point represents a species. For seals and primates harem size refers to the average number of breeding females per breeding male. For ungulates and the elephant seal the mean number of copulations per breeding male was used as the estimate of harem size. (*From* Alexander et al. 1981)

two other factors have strong effects: terrestrial species are more dimorphic than arboreal species and large ones are more dimorphic than small species. Neither of these effects is well understood. For example, male–male aggression may be more dangerous in trees than on the ground, or large size may make feeding in trees more difficult (reduced access to terminal buds). The association with body size has attracted a swarm of explanations, but none is very satisfactory.

Whatever the explanation for the association between body weight and sexual dimorphism, we know it is very general; for instance, smaller species of fig wasps and of stag beetles show reduced dimorphism. Notice in Figure 9-23 the enormous variation in sexual dimorphism in stag beetles, a result almost entirely of variation in the males. Presumably, sexual selection is acting with different intensity and in different directions in different species, but of the underlying causes we know little. Chief among our deficiencies is our ignorance of the factors controlling variation in *female* reproductive success.

Evidence from frogs suggests that the *time* distribution of breeding females may affect sexual dimorphism in size. This is because length of breeding season is associated with size dimorphism. Only frogs with a growing season of intermediate length show males larger than females—short seasons and especially long seasons are associated with larger females. This is explained by two opposing selection pressures: in explosive breeders too many females are simultaneously available for large males to mate disproportionately, while in species with long growing seasons the energetic costs of male–male competition are so severe that small size is preferable. Male frogs are known to feed less in the breeding season than females, to have smaller fat re-

Figure 9-23

Sexual dimorphism in stag beetles. The length of an individual's mandible (in millimeters) is plotted as a function of length of body (in millimeters) minus the head for males and females of almost 400 species of stag beetles. Note that in males mandible length increases disproportionately with body size. Notice also the tremendous variability across males of different species, as compared to females. (*From* Otte and Stayman 1979)

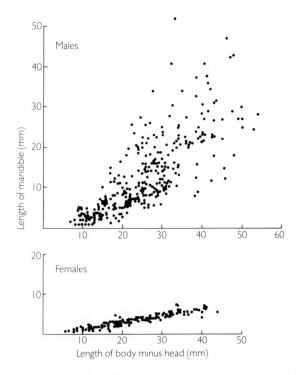

serves, and, in one species, to lose as much as 30% of body weight during the breeding season. In *Physalaemus pustulosis*, calling males have significantly higher oxygen consumption than non-calling males. But note: this explanation fails to describe the way in which selection acts on *female* size and, we do not know how variation in female reproductive success is associated with variation in male characteristics.

A model for the way in which sexual selection acts differently on male and female size is provided by the Jamaican green lizard *Anolis garmani*. Adult male weight is 2.25 times as much as adult female weight, and the males achieve their greater size through faster growth rates (Figures 9-24 and 25). Large size increases survival in both sexes about equally, but in males size has a large positive effect on the number of copulations achieved per unit time, while in females it has a weak positive effect on the number of eggs laid per unit time (Figure 9-26). This effect on males apparently occurs because females distribute themselves in territories within trees and large males are able to

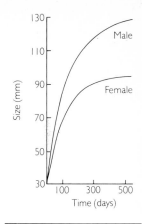

Figure 9-24

Sexual dimorphism in growth rate. Male *Anolis garmani* grow faster than females, at all sizes. Both sexes reach maturity at about the same age. (*From* Trivers 1976)

Figure 9-25

A conspicuous copulation in a dimorphic lizard. Male and female *Anolis garmani* copulate face down on the trunk of a tree, about a meter from the ground. The lizards are bright green—a color difficult to see in the foliage but easy to spot against the trunk. This male is probably about four times as heavy as the female with whom he is copulating. Copulations may last for 25 minutes. (Photo: Joseph Long)

defend a large territory (a tree or several trees) containing many adult females. There is no evidence that females prefer the larger of two males (interlopers that succeed in copulating are about the same size as territory holders), although females choose conspicuous perches on which to advertise sexual readiness and this presumably reflects a preference for the male able to copulate uninterrupted in public. In any case, sexual selection puts an enormous premium on high growth rates in males. These, in turn, show consistent differences: males who grow fast when small are likely to grow fast when large (Figure 9-27). In short, selection on males seems strongly to favor genes associated with rapid and efficient accrual of resources.

If aggressive male conflict is generating large male size in *Anolis garmani*, then we expect a reduction in the importance of male–male

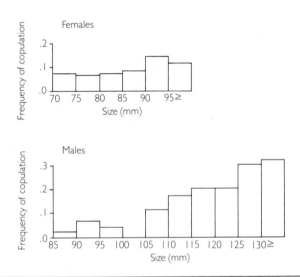

Figure 9-26

Effect of size on reproductive success of females and males, in a lizard. This graph shows the frequency with which females (top) or males (bottom) of *Anolis garmani* were seen to copulate as a function of body length (in millimeters) excluding the tail. Females are believed to copulate once per egg laid, so that frequency of copulation measures reproductive success in both sexes. The positive relationship between male size and reproductive success is significantly stronger than that relationship in females. Notice that intermediate-sized males (100–104 mm) copulate significantly less often than expected for their size, apparently because they are then being forced out of the territories of large males. Thus, we can see selection for a size-dependent change in male strategy. Small adult males may even accept an occasional homosexual copulation to remain in a large male's territory; two such copulations were observed. (*From* Trivers 1976)

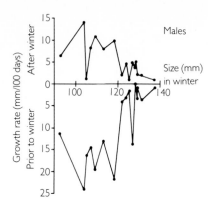

Figure 9-27

Growth rates are positively correlated throughout a male lizard's life. Shown are the growth rates (millimeters per 100 days) before and after winter of male *Anolis garmani* plotted as a function of size in winter (body length in millimeters minus tail). Note that the two lines look like mirror images: high growth rates prior to winter correlate with high growth rates afterwards. (*From* Trivers 1976)

combat to be associated with a reduction in size dimorphism. An instructive case is the closely related white-croaking lizard *Anolis valencienni*, among which adult males are only 1.8 times as heavy as adult females, probably because male reproductive success is less strongly influenced by size than in *garmani* (Figures 9-28 and 9-29). This may result from an underlying difference in the way in which females distribute themselves in the two species. In *garmani*, females are found in more or less non-overlapping feeding territories—maintained by aggression—while in *valencienni*, female home ranges overlap widely and females show no hostility toward each other. Two components of sexual selection change. Female choice probably becomes more important, and the ability of males to gain exclusive access to many breeding females is diminished. In fact, female *valencienni* often mate with dif-

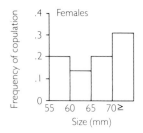

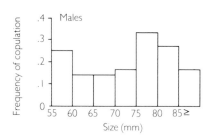

Figure 9-28

Frequency of copulation as a function of body size, in a lizard. The frequency with which adult males and adult females copulated is plotted as a function of body size in the lizard *Anolis valencienni*. Females may copulate several times per egg laid, so copulation frequency may not measure reproductive success in females. (*From* Hicks and Trivers 1983)

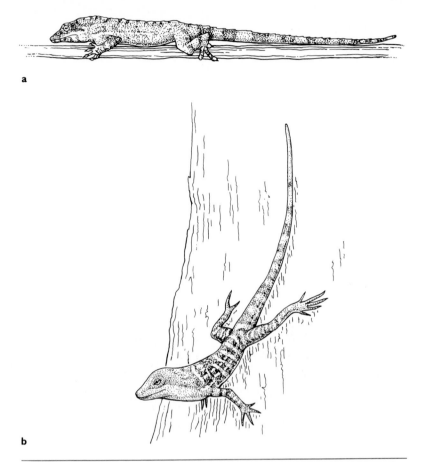

a

b

Figure 9-29

A percher and a searcher. (a) A large adult male *Anolis valencienni* is seen motionless, hugging the side of a stick. This species is unusually well camouflaged and less dimorphic in body size than either *lineatopus* or *garmani*. Members must be constantly on the move in search of cryptic, diurnally inactive insects and are, thus, more vulnerable to visually hunting predators and more strongly selected for camouflage. Perhaps the camouflage makes it harder for the lizards to spot each other, giving small males an advantage. (b) A large adult male of the Jamaican common lizard *Anolis lineatopus* perches high in his territory. From this place he will occasionally dash to catch active prey, mostly insects. He also displays at other territorial males and courts females within his territory. Unlike females, he defends a territory much larger than optimal for his feeding needs. Female home-range size is small in this species and sexual dimorphism in size relatively great (adult males weigh about 2.5 times what adult females do). (Drawn from author's photos)

ferent males on the same or successive days. Thus, lack of aggressiveness among females appears to have reduced the selection pressure for male combat.

Robin Andrews has discovered an entirely different factor underlying sexual dimorphism in body size in *Anolis* lizards. She concentrated on the difference between mainland species and island species. Individuals in mainland species (Central America) have little difficulty finding food: they feed infrequently and on large food items, and grow rapidly in nature at rates that are not increased in captivity by adding food. These species show little dimorphism in size (Figure 9-30). On islands (West Indies), *Anolis* species tend to be food limited: individuals in nature grow slowly, feed frequently on small food items, and grow faster in captivity when additional food is supplied. Yet sexual dimorphism in size is pronounced (Figure 9-31); that is, where food is difficult to find, males are especially large! This is a striking and unexpected discovery. We might think that male–male competition would tend to inflate male size in both settings, but be restrained more sharply when amount of food is limited. Instead, the reverse is found.

Figure 9-30

A relatively non-dimorphic mainland species. Male and female *Anolis limifrons* copulate on a branch in Panama. In this species females do not appear to be food-limited. (Photo: Robin Andrews)

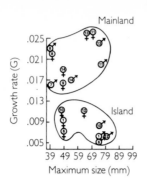

Figure 9-31

Growth rates of juvenile males and females in mainland and island species of Anolis *lizards.* Shown are the growth rate constants (G) which have been fitted to growth rate data for juvenile lizards. A higher G indicates a higher growth rate. These are plotted as a function of maximum body length (minus the tail) in millimeters. Each number refers to a particular species of *Anolis* lizard. Note that mainland species have higher juvenile growth rates but *less* sexual dimorphism in body size. (*From* Andrews 1976)

Andrews' discovery has an interesting feature when viewed from the female's standpoint. As we shall see in Chapter 13, it is useful to ask whether sexual selection elevates to breeding status genes in males that also benefit their daughters. For *Anolis* this appears to be the case. That is, where female RS is apparently strongly limited by ability to grow quickly, males grow especially fast and mate frequently at large sizes; thus their genes should give their daughters increased growth rates. Where female growth rate has a small effect on female RS, male size is not inflated. A similar argument can be applied to the difference between *A. garmani* and *A. valencienni.* Females are aggressive in the former and pacific in the latter. Other things being equal, we expect fast growth rates in female *garmani* to be more advantageous; and it is in this species that males attain especially large sizes, compared to females (see also pp. 353–358).

The correlation Andrews discovered is easily explained by reference to male–male competition. Food availability is closely associated with the density of lizards. On the mainland, lizard species are numerous, but individuals within each species are few in number: female home-range size is large and the ability of a male to sequester several females is correspondingly low. On islands the lizards are abundant, female home-range size is small, and one male may more easily mo-

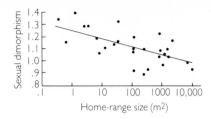

Figure 9-32

Sexual dimorphism as a function of female home range size in territorial species of lizards. Sexual dimorphism (adult male body length, minus tail, divided by adult female body length, minus tail) is plotted as a function of adult female home range size (in squared meters). A line has been fitted to the points. There is a highly significant negative correlation. (*From* Stamps 1983)

nopolize several females. In turn, in territorial lizards sexual dimorphism in body size is inversely related to density (Figure 9-32). Note that this larger correlation for lizards in general retains the relationship between variation in female reproductive success and sexual dimorphism that was observed in *Anolis*. More densely crowded species will tend more often to be food limited, and aggressive interactions between females will be more frequent. Thus, where fast growth rate in females is especially favored, males attain especially large sizes.

The pattern we have described in *Anolis* could have resulted from female choice—females when food limited or aggressive preferring large males, yet there is no evidence in *Anolis* that females prefer larger males, and in one dimorphic species females appear to be nearly indifferent to male size. It would be very interesting if male–male competition—without the intervention of female choice—tended to elevate to breeding status in males genes beneficial for females. Unfortunately we are usually unable to test for this possibility because while we may often know how male aggression (and thus size) relates to reproductive success, we know little or nothing about the factors controlling female RS.

Summary

The underlying variable controlling the action of sexual selection is the relative investment of the sexes in their offspring, where this is the relative amount of work or energy or risk they invest in raising offspring. The sex that invests less is expected to show greater variation in reproductive success, to compete within itself for access to members of the opposite sex, and to be subjected to more discriminating choice by the opposite sex than it itself expresses in mating. Evidence from *Drosophila* and red deer is consistent with this view.

In general, males invest little or nothing parentally in their offspring, but instead compete among themselves for access to females. This competition takes the form of aggressive combat to exclude others from breeding and searching for and courting females. Females tend to be more discriminating in choice of sexual partners, and males often suffer differential mortality.

In insects such as crickets and vertebrates such as seahorses and polyandrous birds, the normal sex roles are reversed: females are aggressive and fight with each other for access to males, females initiate courtship, and males are relatively choosy. All such species are characterized by very high male parental investment. In the sex-reversed moorhen, large aggressive females succeed in pairing with males high in ability to invest, which tend to be short and fat.

Male–male competition generates alternate strategies. Thus, territorial male dragonflies and frogs attract non-territorial satellite males and fighting beetles may come in a large form and a small one. Deception is a common feature of alternate male strategies, and in a fish has generated a female-mimic that is radically smaller in size than territory-holding males. The most extreme male dimorphisms occur in fig wasps: a winged, dispersing form coexists with a nondispersing form that is often heavily armed to fight. The relative frequencies of winged and non-winged forms closely match the relative number of females available to males through the alternate routes.

Relative parental investment does little to explain variation in sexual dimorphism in species lacking male parental investment. Even within closely related groups this variation may be considerable; witness body size in seals and relative mandible length in stag beetles. In various mammals, greater numbers of females per male harem are associated with greater size dimorphism. Other correlates are less easily understood; thus, larger primate species and terrestrial ones are more dimorphic. In many other groups, such as stag beetles, there is a similar tendency for degree of dimorphism in size and in armature to increase with increasing body size. In frogs, distribution in time seems to affect sexual dimorphism, males being larger only in species with a breeding season of intermediate length. In *Anolis* lizards larger size in males seems to be a direct consequence of the greater effect of size on male reproductive success than female reproductive success. Where females are densely distributed, male size is relatively large. At the same time, sexual selection seems to generate large size in males where large size is especially important for female reproductive success.

Chapter 10

Species with Male Parental Investment

Mᴇɴ ɪɴ ᴏᴜʀ own species commonly invest time and energy in the care of their offspring or, less commonly, in the offspring of their kin (such as sisters). In many ways this is a surprising feature of human life, something we share with male sea spiders, butterflies, birds, and wolves but not something we share with our closest living relatives, the great apes, nor the monkeys closest to them. To be sure the primate heritage is not entirely lacking male parental investment. For instance, South American monkeys commonly show male parental investment and in baboons and probably chimpanzees males form special relationships with adult females, trading, in effect, grooming and protection from others for increased sexual access. Still, there is nothing like the male provision of food and protection for offspring found in humans. Thus, human male parental investment is an example of convergent evolution. In this chapter we will concentrate on certain aspects of the biology of species with male parental investment. We begin by describing the forms of male parental investment and the species in which these forms have appeared. We then discuss the factors associated with male parental investment, as revealed by the comparative method. We concentrate on one of these, mate choice, reviewing studies from various species that show how mates choose for ability to invest. We show in the monogamous zebra finch that relative attractiveness (a signal of genetic quality) is traded for parental investment, the more attractive of a couple reducing its workload. We shall explore some of the consequences of low initial male investment—attempts to cuckold others and to avoid being cuckolded—and we shall briefly consider another form of mate choice, desertion.

The Evolution of Male Parental Investment

Male parental investment is practically unknown in invertebrates outside of the insects. In several polychaete worms, males are known to incubate the eggs in a mucoid tube. In *Neanthes arenaceodentata* the male broods the eggs of one female at a time. He often devours the female after mating; if not, she dies in a few days after fighting any female who approaches her mate. Males also fight males. In one crustacean, the monogamous desert wood louse *Hemilepistus reaumuri*, male and female together occupy and defend a burrow and divide up the other activities, including care of young. In this species, male investment seems secondary to monogamous defense of the burrow, and it illustrates the fact that though monogamy often co-occurs with male parental investment, it need not do so.

The only other examples of male investment by invertebrates I know of outside the insects are found in the pycnogonids—sea spiders—an unusual group allied to the crustacea (Figure 10-1). In seven of the eight families, males carry eggs attached to specialized legs. In most species males can carry the egg masses of more than one female. However, in one exceptional species, *Pycnogonum littorale*, a male cares for the entire egg production of a single female. Such a mating pair may remain attached for up to five weeks, and the male may carry the eggs for up to ten weeks.

In five arctic species of *Nymphon*, degree of male polygyny is reduced when male investment is high. Eggs appear to be carried by the male until yolk reserves are exhausted. Where eggs are small (and numerous) they are carried for a few days; at any one time, each male carries the eggs of about 2.4 females. Where eggs are large (and few in number) they may be carried for months, until sub-adult development has been achieved; males, on average, carry only 1.3 egg masses.

In a wide variety of insects the male makes a nutritional contribution to the female before, during, or after copulation. Males may secrete nourishing material from dorsal glands or salivary glands. The sperm may be packaged in a highly proteinaceous material (the spermatophore), which the female digests, and the female may digest mating plugs. Spermatophores are quite widespread in the insects and are characteristic of entire groups, such as the butterfly-moths and the grasshopper-crickets (see Figure 10-1). In some insects, males capture prey and bring it to the female in courtship, males not being accepted who are bearing prey less than a certain size (described in the later section "Female Choice for Male Investment"). In some insects the male is devoured by the female during or after copulation, which may be a form of paternal investment. In water striders, males carry eggs on their backs (see Figures 10-2 and 10-3). For an example of monogamous division of labor in an insect, see Figure 10-4, p. 244.

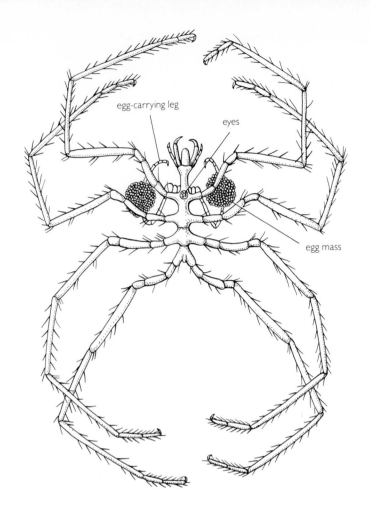

egg-carrying leg

eyes

egg mass

Figure 10-1

A male sea spider carrying eggs. The species is *Nymphon rubrum.* The eggs have been formed into a spherical, adhesive mass by the male with the help of cement glands located on his legs. The eggs are carried on specialized front legs which are reduced or absent in females. (*From* Barnes 1963)

Among the vertebrates, male parental investment has evolved repeatedly in some groups, although not in others. Paternal investment is nearly universal in birds, and has evolved several times in mammals—especially rodents, primates, and carnivores—but relative to female care it has evolved more commonly in fish and frogs.

Of the fish families whose mode of reproduction is known, about one-third have some kind of parental care after eggs are produced, and about half these cases show care by the male alone. In the great majority of these cases the male remains with the eggs and cares for them. Typically he protects them from predators, but he may also build a nest to receive them, aerate them, remove parasitized eggs, and protect the hatchlings. In many other species, males brood the eggs in their

Figure 10-2

The beginning of male parental care in the giant water bug Abedus herberti. A female on top lays eggs on the back of a male, which will require about three weeks of his care to hatch. Eggs detached from the backs of males fail to develop for a variety of reasons: they may be parasitized by a fungus, they may suffer insufficient gas exchange, they may dry out, and so on. (Photo: Robert Smith)

mouths, and in some species they brood the eggs elsewhere, chiefly the Syngnathidae, in their kangaroo-like pouches (see pp. 215–217).

A typical example of male parental investment occurs in the three-spined stickleback *Gasterosteus aculeatus*. The male builds a nest and defends a territory around it. In courtship he displays the nest and other examples of his care-giving behavior, such as aerating the eggs. He may spawn in the nest with several females. (Females prefer to spawn in a nest which already contains eggs.) He may repeat this cycle up to three times in a season.

In many of the species of fish in which males remain with eggs, males are known to be territorial, although the life history of the other species is often poorly known, so many of these may also be territorial. It is also true of many of these species in which males remain with eggs that males are able to care for the eggs of several females simultaneously. Both factors may be important in favoring male parental investment. A male who has just mated with one female is fully capable of breeding with another female in the same spot, and if females prefer investing males—as they often do (see next section)—then sexual selection favors male parental investment.

All frogs have external fertilization and eggs are laid in water or require moisture for development. Parental care by one sex or the

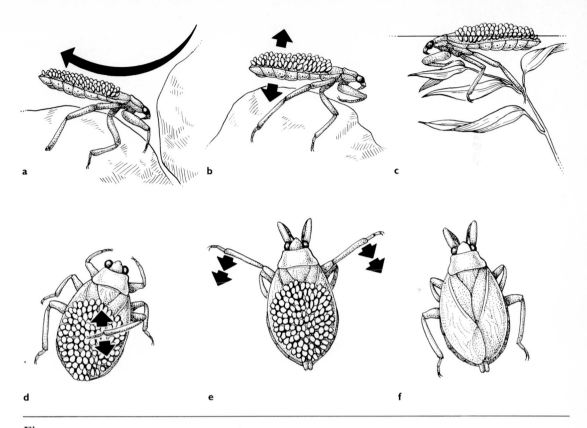

Figure 10-3

Male parental care in the giant water bug Abedus herberti. (a) Male with immature eggs seeks out turbulent water. (b) Male with mature eggs rocks back and forth, increasing the water flow over the eggs. (c) Male with mature eggs aerates them at water's surface. (d) Male feels eggs with his hind leg to confirm that he is still carrying them. (e) A male with eggs must expend considerable energy to remain at the surface to breathe, in contrast to (f) a male without eggs doing the same. (*From* Smith 1976)

other is found in about ten percent of all species. Although there are scattered cases of care in aquatic breeders, care occurs most frequently in terrestrial breeders of the humid tropics, probably to avoid egg predation in water. When care occurs, eggs are protected from predators and from conspecifics; they are sometimes aerated and sometimes kept moist. In some species, eggs are carried, usually by the female. In some species tadpoles are carried to water. Male care occurs in seven families of frogs. Males typically defend a territory within which one or

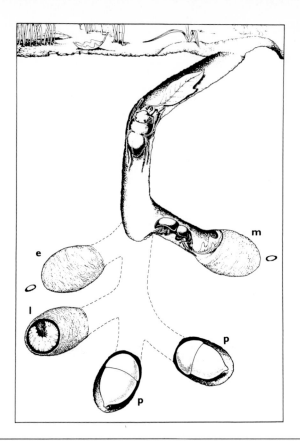

Figure 10-4

Division of labor in a monogamous beetle. A pair of *Lethrus opterus* are shown provisioning their nest. *Legend*: (m) leaf masses; (e) eggs; (l) larvae; (p) pupae, which are enclosed in acorn-shaped cocoons. The male is pulling a freshly cut leaf backward through the entrance gallery, while the female packs another leaf into the brood cell currently being provisioned. These are sex-specific tasks. Both sexes excavate the tunnel and pack soil into the galleries leading to provisioned cells (see dashed lines). The male alone sweeps clean the courtyard outside the nest entrance, using two long tusks that have apparently evolved for this purpose. One tusk is shown here, projecting below the male's right mandible. (Drawing by Sarah Landry, from Wilson 1971)

more females deposit eggs. Male care also occurs in salamanders, but only in the families with external fertilization.

Male care is unknown in reptiles, and female care after egg deposition is rare (e.g., egg brooding in pythons). Lizards and snakes have seen the repeated evolution of a tendency for the female to retain eggs in her body for further development, the mammalian tendency (see pp. 33–34). Male investment is very common in birds. In the great majority of species there is care by both sexes, but in a few the male alone cares for the eggs and young and these species are often sex-reversed (see pp. 215–219). In birds, males are almost invariably territorial during the breeding season.

In all species of mammals, females nurse, so there is always post-natal female care. Male care has evolved sporadically in such groups as the rodents and the primates and seems to be universal in the dog family, where males commonly feed pups, in addition to protecting them (see pp. 192–198). In some South American monkeys, in gibbons, and in humans, male parental investment has co-evolved with a tendency to monogamy. In other primates, the male may carry the young and protect them and their mothers; but only humans add the carnivorous habit of feeding the young. Territoriality is widespread in mammals.

Factors Associated with the Evolution of Male Parental Investment

Several factors seem to be associated with the evolution of male parental investment. Chief among these are the mode of fertilization, male territoriality, and the extent to which male parental investment is costly.

Mode of fertilization. In Table 10-1 we review the different kinds of parental care found in fish families. The clearest association is between mode of fertilization and sex of parent giving the care. Fertilization is external or believed to be external in 48 out of 49 cases of male care only, as well as in the 10 cases of biparental care. Yet in 22 of the 28 cases in which there is female care, fertilization is internal! In fish this correlation even holds within single families. In sculpins, for example, most species have external fertilization and male care. Those with internal fertilization show no care by either sex.

Salamanders continue this trend exactly. Male care is found in the two families with external fertilization. In the rest of the salamanders, fertilization is internal, and with few exceptions, care, if it occurs, is by the female. In frogs, fertilization is external, and slightly more families have female care than male care; biparental care is unknown. Altogether, the amphibians show the same association between internal fertilization and female care as do fish (Table 10-2). Reptiles, birds, and mammals all have internal fertilization. Care is rare in reptiles, and when it occurs it is by the female. In birds the great majority of species have biparental care, and when one parent alone cares it is usually the female. The great majority of mammals show care by the female only; care is biparental otherwise.

Table 10-1. Numbers of fish families with different types of parental care and mating systems*

Male Care	
Fertilization external or unknown	
Male site attached	29
Male stays with eggs	12
Male carries eggs	6
Female territorial	1
Fertilization in male	1
Female Care	
Fertilization external or unknown	6
Fertilization in female	
Female viviparous or oral-brooding	22
Biparental Care	
Fertilization external or unknown	10
No Parental Care	
Fertilization external	100
Fertilization in female	10

Source: Ridley 1978; "No Parental Care" data from Gross and Shine 1981.

* Families may be counted more than once if they exhibit different systems of care or mating. "No parental care" only occurs when parental care is unknown in the family.

Thus, among the vertebrates, internal fertilization is associated with female care or biparental care and external fertilization is associated with male care. (Only in insects is this pattern reversed. Insects are small enough that their ejaculates can have a nutritional benefit, and internal fertilization facilitates this investment.) To explain the association in vertebrates, three factors have been proposed: decreased confidence of paternity, order in which egg and sperm are released, and delay in production of eggs.

One effect of internal fertilization is to make cuckoldry easier and probably more frequent. A higher rate of cuckoldry suggests that more male resources that might have gone into investment will go into promiscuous activities. Note that a hypothetical male contemplating whether to invest in a batch of offspring or seek copulation elsewhere will devalue each set of offspring by his decreased confidence of paternity. Thus, lowered confidence of paternity in a mating system does not automatically select against male parental investment. But higher rates of cuckoldry do mean that there will be more copulations available outside the bond, which should divert male resources in this direction, roughly in proportion to the higher availability. Once a new equilibrium is reached, selection may favor mechanisms that increase a male's relatedness to the offspring. Altogether, then, frequency of

Table 10-2.   Numbers of families of amphibia with male parental care, female parental care, or no care *

	Male Parental Care	Female Parental Care	No Care
External fertilization	14	8	10
Internal fertilization	2	11	0

Source: Gross and Shine 1981.

* A family may appear in more than one column. "No care" means that parental care is completely unknown in the family.

cuckoldry should have an effect on total male investment roughly proportional to its magnitude. It seems unlikely that this effect alone could generate a strong association between mode of fertilization and form of parental care.

Note that external fertilization does not guarantee paternity. Sneakers and other cuckolds are common in some fish with external fertilization and male care (pp. 406–408). Also, species with internal fertilization often show evidence of male energy diverted into promiscuous activities co-existing with strong male investment (see below). But it seems likely that in species with male care, greater care is associated with higher confidence of paternity. For example, in ducks, rape attempts are much more frequent in species with modest male investment. Selection for greater male investment reduces selection for promiscuous activities and probably makes it easier for an investing male to guard his paternity.

In species with external fertilization the eggs are usually released first and quickly fertilized with sperm. In species with internal fertilization, sperm are ejaculated first, then eggs are laid. It has been argued that in species in which only one parent is required to attend the young, such as fish, male and female tendencies to assume this role may be so delicately balanced that the last one to discharge the sex products will most easily be stuck with the labor of care. This argument suggests a race between male and female to desert their young and seems unlikely to be an important factor. Although it correctly predicts that internal fertilization will be associated with female care and external fertilization with male care, it fails on more detailed tests. For example, where gametes are released simultaneously, each sex has equal opportunity to desert, so parental care should show no bias by sex. In fact, 36 of 46 of these species with care by one sex have male care. Most frogs with male care remain in amplexus until spawning is finished, so that female chances to desert seem no greater than male chances.

The independence of male parental investment from those details of sex relevant to desertion is suggested by a few fish species in which a male first releases sperm that a female takes into her mouth and then uses to fertilize eggs held in her fins. She later places these fertilized eggs in a froth nest built by the male. Despite numerous opportunities to desert, he cares for the young.

A related trait is probably the most important. Internal fertilization is almost always associated with a delay before eggs are deposited. Sometimes this is a matter of minutes but often it is a matter of hours or days and even months (e.g., many mammals). This is because internal fertilization is often associated with additional female investment. Thus, a reptile female deposits a hard outer shell on her egg, permitting it to be laid away from water but requiring internal fertilization. Once internal fertilization has evolved, selection can easily favor egg retention for additional investment. Each successive female investment lengthens the time between ejaculation and egg deposition and makes male investment less likely. In fact, the mammalian pattern of internal fertilization, live birth and postnatal fraternal care has appeared repeatedly in fish and amphibians.

Male territoriality. Male defense of good sites for oviposition will predispose him to parental investment as long as his territory has room for more than one clutch. If so, then he may be selected to remain in his territory, making incidental investment in the offspring, while the female is selected to desert. There are 39 families of fish in which the male is territorial and invests in his young, but there are 20 families in which the male is not site attached and yet shows care. In most of these latter species, he carries the eggs. In 14 closely related species of darters (Percidae) there is a positive correlation between tendency by the male to defend his territory and tendency to guard eggs. (Likewise, there is increasing size dimorphism, males being larger.)

In amphibians, territoriality is more common in species with male parental care than in the average species. Considering only species with external fertilization, 6% are known to be territorial (as demonstrated by male combat), while in species which also show male care, 31% are known to be territorial. This suggests an association but does not tell us cause and effect. The suspicion of a link between male territoriality and male investment is strengthened when we turn to birds and mammals. In birds, males that contribute care almost universally defend nesting places and often defend territories in which to feed the young. Likewise, territoriality is widespread among mammals with paternal care.

Inexpensiveness of male care. In fish the chief form of parental care is defense of the eggs, which are numerous and small in comparison to the adults, so that the latter can often defend the eggs from many of their predators. A male can usually defend several batches as easily, or almost as easily, as one. This means that male care evolves hand in hand with male–male competition. Females will usually be exhausted from egg production so that where they spawn more than once in a season, males are expected to be the caretakers. This is nicely confirmed in blennioid fish, a large marine group. Tropical and subtropical species have a long growing season in which each female produces several clutches. Care is by the male alone, who often cares for the eggs of several females. In temperate and subarctic species the growing season is short and females produce only one clutch, breed synchronously, and usually care for the eggs alone.

By contrast, in birds the major components of parental investment are incubation and feeding of the young. Since two can usually do the job better than one, biparental care is the rule, while in species with care by either one parent or the other, the young typically feed on their own.

Note that in all of the known cases of paternal investment, the female is in a position to exercise choice in favor of greater male investment. In the pycnogonids, legs adapted for carrying eggs have a special structure. In fish and amphibia the female can directly judge the quality of the male's territory, including any improvements such as nests, the number of eggs already being cared for, male defense of territory, and related variables, such as male size. In insects, females can certainly measure size of a male spermatophore once deposited. Courtship feeding in insects and birds can be evaluated directly. And so on. To the evidence for such choice we turn next.

Female Choice for Male Investment

Let us consider one factor that may predispose a species to male investment, female choice: females may prefer to mate with males who will invest strongly in their offspring. Most of the major kinds of male parental investment have been shown to affect female choice or may easily do so. At one time this would have been a controversial statement, but it is now well established, as the following studies suggest.

Insects. In insects, both nuptial feeding and size of spermatophore may affect female choice. In the scorpion fly *Hylobittacus apicalis* males gather prey items that are, on average, larger than those gathered by females (Figure 10-5). This is presumably because males present food items to females in order to mate and because females refuse to mate with males carrying food smaller than a certain size. At intermediate prey sizes, females may consume the prey and terminate the copulation before all of a male's sperm has been transferred. Up to about 20 minutes, length of copulation correlates with amount of sperm transferred; and males typically catch insects that will give them

Figure 10-5

Sexual dimorphism in prey capture in a scorpionfly. The percent of males and females found carrying prey of a given size (measured as length × width, in square millimeters). A prey item of 20 mm^2 will give a male a full copulation. The species is *Hylobittacus apicalus*. (*From* Thornhill 1976)

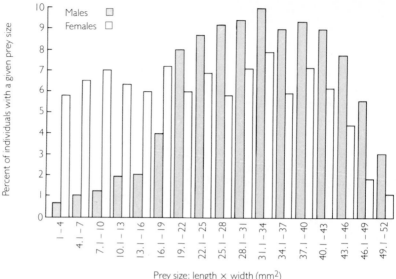

at least 20 minutes of copulation (see Figure 10-6). Males, incidentally, suffer higher mortality in spider webs than do females and this is believed to be related to their search for larger prey.

In the katydid *Conocephalus migropleurum*, small males produce spermatophores about half as large as those of large males. When given a choice between calling males who differ in weight, females invariably choose the larger male, sometimes moving directly to him after a short pause and sometimes making physical contact with the smaller male before rejecting him in favor of the larger. Larger males emit more intense sounds. In a related species, larger males are known to sing louder songs and to attract more females.

Fish and frogs. In fish and frogs with male investment, both males and females often prefer to mate with larger individuals. In monogamous species this leads to large individuals of each sex pairing with one another. Typically, female fecundity increases with body size; but for one species only—the biparental cichlid fish *Cichlasoma maculicauda*—do we have evidence for the effect of size on male parental abilities. Males defend territories containing spawning sites. Larger males are more likely to defend deeper nests, which are less affected by wave action and give higher survival of eggs (Table 10-3). Both sexes fan the eggs and embryos, the female more so, and both sexes protect eggs and young from predators. Both sexes lead the young from food patch to food patch and, in competition for such sites, small males and their families give way to large males and theirs. In turn, growth rate of young correlates with male size. Young of large males grow about

Figure 10-6

Eating while she copulates.
On the right, a female scorpionfly *Hylobittacus api-*
calis feeds on a fly provided
by her mate while she and
her mate copulate. The
length of time it takes the
female to consume the fly
will determine the length of
copulation (up to 20 min-
utes). The male retains a
loose hold on the prey, and
if some prey remains at the
end of the copulation both
may struggle over who will
retain it. (Photo: Randy
Thornhill)

30% faster than young of small males (Figure 10-7), which permits
the parents to breed again more quickly and also shortens the time the
young spend at small, vulnerable sizes. Of course, the correlation between male size and offspring growth rate may be partly genetic, large
males having genes good for fast growth.

Altogether, the relation between male size and survival of young is
very strong, stronger than the relation between female size and fecundity. Males, in turn, are larger than females. Assortative mating by size
weds the high fecundity of large females to the high offspring survival
of large males. In mottled sculpins, females prefer to mate with larger
males and male size is positively related to ability to defend the egg
mass and the chances that it will survive to produce young.

Table 10-3.   Percent survival of broods to swimming interval as a
function of size of male parent and depth of nest in *Cichlasoma*
maculicauda

Depth of nest (m)	Size of Male (cm)			
	≤ 17	18	≥ 19	*mean*
< 1.0	2.0	0	0	1.2
1.0–1.2	6.3	3.5	5.6	5.1
> 1.2	3.8	24.8	30.9	22.0
mean	4.3	11.1	18.2	

Source: Perrone 1978.

Figure 10-7

Growth rate of offspring as a function of father's length. This graph shows the growth rate (milligrams per day) of young *Cichlasoma maculicauda* as a function of their father's length (centimeters) during the period of parental care. (*From* Perrone 1978)

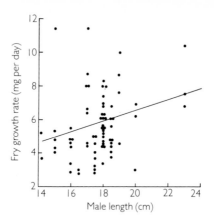

In the highly aggressive gladiator frog *Hyla rosenbergi*, males excavate nests and defend eggs until hatching (about three days). Larger males do not win more fights and do not mate more often than smaller males, but there is evidence that male attachment to his site is important to female choice. In 65% of courtships the stationary male is tested by a deliberate bump from the female: the female moves deliberately and quickly to the male and strikes him with enough force to make him rock back and forth. In four cases where the male bolted from the nest upon being bumped, the female quickly withdrew and did not return; only one female rejected a male who did not move when bumped. Bumping may help a female decide which male is more likely to defend her clutch aggressively. In all five cases in which clutches were destroyed by intruders, the male parent was not defending the eggs. Females also sometimes incite male aggression by splashing and by jumping into nests, thus advertising their presence.

Birds. There is a wealth of circumstantial evidence for female choice of male parental investment in birds. For example, in species in which males build nests and then attempt to attract females, such as weaver birds, the female usually inspects various nests closely, both inside and out, pulling and tugging at the pieces. The male displays a nest by hanging from the nest, upside down, flapping his wings and forcing the nest to bob up and down (Figure 10-8). This presumably tests the strength of the nest and its attachment. Nests repeatedly rejected by females are torn down by the males and replaced by new ones.

Two examples will show that females at the time of pairing may be able to choose males who will later strongly invest. In courtship feeding, which is widespread in birds, the male feeds the female during pair formation and, more intensively, during egg formation. Evidence from common terns *Sterna hirundo* suggests that this feeding is itself an important part of male investment and that it may also be used by

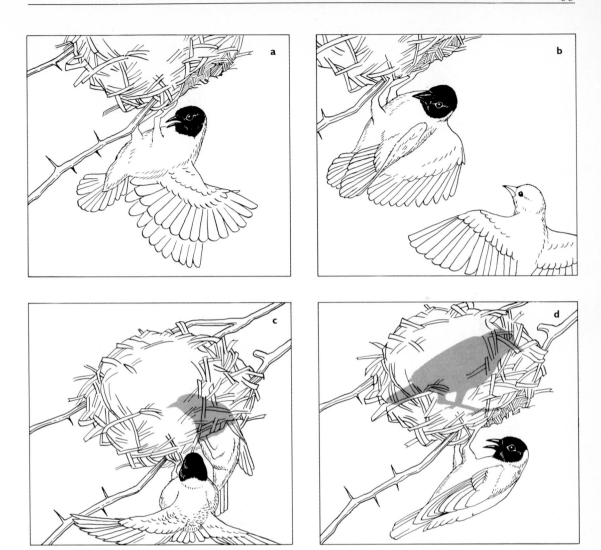

Figure 10-8

Nest invitation and nest inspection in the African village weaverbird.
(a) When a female *Ploceus cucullatus* arrives in the vicinity, the male displays the most recent nest he has built by hanging upside down from the bottom of the nest and beating his wings vigorously. This forces the nest to bounce about and, because of various yellow feathers on the male, creates an impression like a flashing yellow light. (b) As the female approaches the nest, the male stops flapping his wings but continues to rotate his body in a horizontal plane. (c) The female enters quickly and (d) sits inside. Once inside, she inspects the nest while the male sings to her from underneath the nest or nearby. She may poke and pull at the nest materials for as long as ten minutes and may inspect a nest several times before accepting it, which she usually signals by adding some nest lining herself. (*From* Collias and Collias 1970)

females during pair formation as an indication of the male's potential to invest. Courtship feeding takes place in three phases. In the first, males carry fish around the colony and display with them to prospective mates. A male with a fish tries to lead a female to his territory (within which they will later nest). At first the male is reluctant to give up his fish, but as the pair-bond becomes established he starts to feed his mate. The first copulations take place late in this phase, usually immediately following a feeding.

In the second phase of courtship feeding the pair spends most of the day on the feeding grounds. The female is frequently fed by the male and she rarely feeds on her own. Feeding rates are most intense during this phase, by the end of which females have amassed most of the extra weight that goes into eggs. In the third phase the female stays at the nest and is fed until she has laid her eggs. Where rates of feeding are higher in the second phase, due to superior habitat, females lay earlier and larger clutches. Where rates are higher in the third phase, due to male quality, the total weight of the clutch is higher, as is the survival of the last, and most vulnerable, chick. We know that the rate of courtship feeding in the third phase correlates with the rate at which young chicks are later fed at the nest, which is associated with chick survival. It seems likely that rates of courtship feeding are positively correlated throughout the breeding period. Thus, females in the first phase may be able directly to measure later ability of males to invest.

In stonechats *Saxiola torquata* there is wide variation in song production prior to breeding. Unpaired males sing more than paired males do. Males who sing more in courtship tend later to bring more food to the young and to defend the brood more in the face of a predator (by giving warning calls and performing distraction displays). Thus, song rate in stonechats can be used to discriminate degree of later investment by males.

Female choice for genes. Even when females choose according to ability to invest, they may also choose according to genetic criteria. For example, females of the scorpionfly *Harpobittacus nigriceps* lay more eggs in the first hours after mating when given a large prey instead of a small one (see Table 10-4 and Figure 10-9). But females likewise lay more eggs when their mate is large instead of small—independent of the size of his nuptial gift. Large size is known to increase adult survivorship in both sexes—as well as mating success in males and fecundity in females—so it is likely that mating with a large male gives a female better genes for her offspring than mating with a small male.

Pigeons prefer to mate with older birds (to age seven) and more experienced birds (in birds both these variables correlate positively with ability to invest). At the same time, however, pigeons also prefer certain colors and patterns in plumage. These traits are genetic, but their effect on survival is unknown.

Table 10-4.   Female choice for large nuptial gifts and large males in *Harpobittacus nigriceps**

	Number of Eggs Laid Within 10 Hours of Mating
Male Has:	
small prey	5.5
large prey	9.1
Male Is:	
small	6.3
large	13.2

Source: Thornhill 1983.

* Each of the two comparisons is significantly different. For the first, male size was kept constant; for the second, size of nuptial gift was held constant.

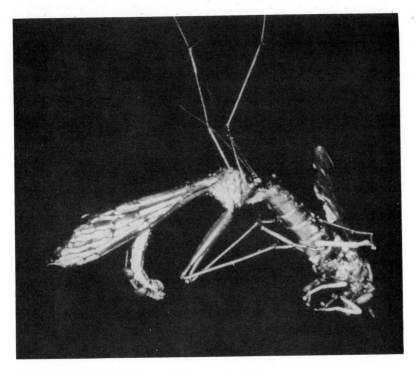

Figure 10-9

Advertising for a mate. A male scorpionfly *Harpobittacus nigriceps*, on the left, holds onto a large fly he has captured and everts paired scent glands on his abdomen that give off a pheromone attractive to females. This particular male would have conflicting effects on a female. Because he has a large prey item, his mate would tend to lay more eggs during the first ten hours after mating, but because he is smaller than average, she would tend to lay fewer eggs (see Table 10-4). (Photo: Nancy Thornhill)

Male choice. Male investment implies male choice. There is evidence for this in several species. As we have just seen, male frogs may prefer large females, where fecundity is positively related to size. In pierid butterflies, males contribute resources with their sperm that may amount to 7% of the male's body weight. When given a choice,

Pieris protodice males spend more time courting young females and large females. Both kinds of females show high fecundity. In pigeons, males invest substantially, but less than females do. Consistent with this, males discriminate on the same bases as do females, but are always less discriminating.

The Importance of Relative Attractiveness

In the ordinary course of events we would have little to say about the effect of relative attractiveness on relations between the sexes in monogamous species. We know from pigeons *Columba livia* that individuals are variable in plumage and that this variation affects attractiveness: some plumage types are attractive to the opposite sex, others are not. Experiments show that those who are relatively unattractive to others are less discriminating in choice of partners. They act as if they know that their low value to others means they will have to settle for what they can get. We also know from our own species that in early childhood we are sensitive to physical attractiveness and that it plays an important role in relations between individuals from then on.

Until recently we could say little about the way relative attractiveness affects the reproductive success of individuals or their relationships after pairing. Then Nancy Burley made a surprising discovery: in the monogamous zebra finch, colored bands on the legs affect attractiveness (much as does plumage in pigeons). Burley made her discovery when she:

. . . purchased 40 zebra finches *Poephila guttata* for a study on parental behavior. Upon receipt, birds were color-banded with unique combinations of seven colors and then released into an aviary. Birds were monitored for reproductive activity and within five months it became apparent that most birds wearing red or pink leg bands were breeding (10 of 14) whereas those wearing light green bands were not (6 of 9). This trend was complicated by the fact that some birds were wearing combinations of red, pink, and two tones of green bands. Three of the 5 green-banded males still not breeding after 7 to 13 months in the aviary were rebanded with a red band on each leg. Within 11 weeks of this manipulation all three rebanded birds were reproducing, whereas neither of the two remaining males (those still banded green) changed reproductive status during this time.

Subsequent experiments showed that males banded red and females banded black were more attractive (than unbanded) to the opposite sex while males and females banded green or blue were less attractive. With this discovery Burley had hit upon the perfect tool for studying the effects of attractiveness. Had she used the plumage types of pigeons, she would not have known whether any effects observed were due to attractiveness or traits associated with it, such as health or vigor. By contrast, with her zebra finches she could match adults as closely as possible for other characteristics and allow only their leg bands—thus, attractiveness—to vary. The result was as striking as Burley's initial discovery: within couples, adult zebra finches trade attractiveness for parental investment, attractive individuals doing less work while their mates do more!

In one experiment only males were banded and reproductive success was monitored for 22 months in a laboratory colony. Even though food was superabundant, variation in RS was striking: the RS of red-banded males was twice that of orange-banded (neutral) or green-banded (unattractive) males (see Table 10-5). This was partly due to a difference in survival but was more directly related to a tendency for red-banded males to become polygynous: by cutting back on his work with his mate, some males were able to acquire more than one mate. In turn, the RS of each of the polygynous males was higher than those of any of the monogamous ones.

In a parallel experiment females were banded and males unbanded and reproductive success was monitored for ten months. Then, bands were removed from the females and RS monitored for another five months. Once again attractive individuals had higher RS (Table 10-6). Most of this was probably due to the higher survival of attractive females. Attractive females did not become polyandrous, although they invested less in the rearing of offspring while their mates compensated,

Table 10-5. Reproductive success of male zebra finches as a function of their attractiveness (as determined by color bands)

	Attractiveness of Male* (color of leg band)		
	Attractive (red)	*Neutral (orange)*	*Unattractive (green)*
Average reproductive success of all males**	32	16	15
Number surviving	7 of 8	6 of 9	4 of 10
Average reproductive success of males surviving**	40	23	19
Average number of mates	2.6	1.9	1.7

Source: Burley unpublished data.

  * All differences between red-banded and orange-banded
    or green-banded males are significant, except for the
    difference in number of mates.
 ** Reproductive success is measured by the number of off-
    spring raised to two weeks post fledging (when they are
    independent from their parents and removed from the
    colony).

Table 10-6.   Reproductive success of female zebra finches as a
function of attractiveness as determined by leg bands*

	Attractiveness of Female (color of leg band)		
	---	---	---
	Attractive (black)	Neutral (orange)	Unattractive (blue)
Average reproductive success of all females	18.0	12.8	8.1
Number surviving	9 of 10	7 of 11	5 of 14
Average reproductive success of females surviving	17.8	15.8	14.0
Average number of mates	1.5	1.4	1.3

Source: Burley unpublished data.

* Trends for the first two rows are significant. Females
were banded for ten months, then unbanded for five
more. Reproductive success is measured by the number
of offspring surviving until two weeks post fledging
(when they are independent of their parents and removed
from the colony).

so total investment remained the same (Table 10-7). Lower investment
probably caused increased survival. In short, it appears that females
trade attractiveness for parental investment and thus survival, much as
do males.

There are two reasons why attractive females might be expected to
have superior reproductive success: (1) their attractiveness will allow
them to pair with superior males and (2) it will lead their mates to
do relatively more of the parental work. The first possibility is supported by the fact that mates of attractive females appear to have
higher RS than other males, suggesting that they are, indeed, superior
(Table 10-8). On the other hand, there is no relationship between a
male's *survival* and his mate's attractiveness, suggesting that both factors are operating: males paired to attractive females should be superior and survive better, but since they do more of the parental work,
they should survive less well. Incidentally, a female paired to an attractive male has higher RS—at least when her mate is monogamous—
and there is a tendency for mates of attractive males to survive better,
though this is not significant (see Table 10-9). Thus, there is evidence
for both sexes that individuals differ markedly in their reproductive
abilities and that physically attractive individuals are able to pair with
superior individuals, who also take a greater share of the common parental investment.

Note the important role that physical attractiveness plays in the
life of zebra finches. Why should individuals prefer to pair with attrac-

Table 10-7.   Parental investment as a function of attractiveness: total time invested in care of offspring and percentage of this care given by the male as a function of his mate's attractiveness, in zebra finches *

Attractiveness of Female (color of band)	Total Time	Percent Care by Male
Attractive (black)	1537	49.6%
Neutral (orange)	1466	40
Unattractive (blue)	1418	33.3

Source: Burley unpublished data.

* The trend in percent care is nearly significant ($p < 0.10$).
  The trend in total time (seconds at nest for both birds) is
  not significant.

tive mates? Our best guess is that physical attractiveness usually correlates in nature with superior genes. Just how this is true in any given case is usually a mystery. As we shall see later, across species of monogamous birds, high parasite load is associated with bright plumage, suggesting that where parasite pressure is important, individuals have preferred as mates those with bright plumage (see pp. 358–359). Presumably it is difficult to develop bright colors when heavily infested with parasites, so this form of mate choice favors genes good at avoiding parasites. In any case, Burley's work suggests that mate choice for genes is important in monogamous species and that genetic quality may be traded for male investment. This suggests that male parental investment may be common in nature in those situations in which mate choice for genes has a relatively modest effect on reproductive success, for example, where parasite pressure is low (the arctic, deserts, mountain tops). We shall return to this possibility after we have described the way in which selection acts on sexual reproduction itself.

Table 10-8.   The reproductive success of male zebra finches as a function of their mate's attractiveness *

	Male's Mate Is: (color band)		
	Attractive (black)	*Neutral (orange)*	*Unattractive (blue)*
Reproductive success*	19.9	13.4	7.9

Source: Burley unpublished data.

* The trend is almost significant.

Table 10-9.   Reproductive success of female zebra finches mated to males whose color bands vary in attractiveness*

	Female's Mate Is: (color band)			
	Attractive (red)		Neutral (orange)	Unattractive (green)
	Monogamous	Polygynous		
Reproductive success	34.3	22.2	14.2	14.3
Number surviving	8 of 11		2 of 5	1 of 4

Source: Burley unpublished data.

* Males are divided into those that are monogamously paired and polygynously paired. Female reproductive success is significantly higher for females monogamously paired to red-banded males. The trend in survival is not significant.

Why should an individual be willing to increase the level of its parental investment when its mate is attractive? If attractiveness indicates genetic quality, then each individual will want to match higher investment to higher genetic quality. Both sexes can be polygamous over their lifetimes by outsurviving their mates and pairing anew. Being paired now to an attractive mate means that offspring produced now will be of high genetic quality and that they should be given heavier weight than the average expected at repairing.

Why red legs in males? Zebra finch legs are orange (Figure 10-10). Burley believes there is a transference from the red beak. Females prefer males with the brightest red beaks. Evidence suggests these reveal superior condition. A red leg band enhances the effect. Males prefer female beak colors that are intermediate—more orange-red than bright red; thus, they prefer orange legs unadorned with red. A black band, on the other hand, provides a nice contrast to set off the orange legs. That colors may be preferred in one place because they augment a visual effect elsewhere is suggested by some experiments Burley performed involving hats. She designed a little hat with a feather sticking up and glued it on zebra finches (Figure 10-11). To her surprise, males with white hats were preferred and all others were disfavored. It turns out that the white feather enhances white stripes already found on the bird's face.

Cuckoldry

In species with strong male parental investment, it is still true that males invest very little at the time of copulation. Because copulations for males are so inexpensive, males are selected to pursue a mixed

Figure 10-10

Sexual dimorphism in zebra finches. The female is on the left, the male is on the right. Both sexes are grey above and white below and have orange legs. Both sexes have vertical black and white eyestripes and horizontal tail stripes. Males only have golden brown cheek patches, reddish brown flank feathers laced with white spots. Both cheek and flank feathers are erected during courtship. Males also have narrow black and white stripes on throat and a black breast band of variable size. Beak color varies from slightly yellow-orange to bright red. Male beaks tend to be darker and redder than those of females.

strategy. That is, males are selected to try to pair with a single female whose offspring they will help raise, while at the same time attempting to copulate with other females, whose young they will not raise. Insofar as males are sometimes successful at gaining such copulations outside the pair-bond, these copulations imply a danger to paired males of being cuckolded, that is, of investing in young that are not their own. Being cuckolded has a much stronger negative effect on a male's reproductive success than failing to breed, since in cuckoldry a male invests considerable energy in addition to failing to breed.

The success of cuckoldry attempts will almost certainly depend on the female. In particular, it will depend on the degree to which female choice for good genes is at variance with female choice for investment (since a female need not get her genes and her investment from the same source). It may also depend upon the degree to which genetic variability in her offspring is favored by selection, since offspring fathered by more than one male are genetically more variable, though only slightly more so. The evidence for selection in favor of genetic variability is reviewed in Chapter 13. The evidence for female choice in favor of good genes (in species lacking male investment) is reviewed

Figure 10-11

An especially attractive fellow! A male zebra finch with a white hat glued in place is more attractive to females than a hatless male; but this is the only color hat that enhances a male's attractiveness. (Photo: Nancy Burley)

in Chapter 14. At present we know little about female choice for good genes in monogamous species, but we know that females choose on criteria other than investment and that the two sets of criteria may be complementary (pp. 254–255).

Judging from the literature on birds, females in many monogamous species at least occasionally indulge in copulations outside the pair-bond. Unfortunately, our only measurement of the incidence of such copulations in birds comes from a polygynous species. In the red-winged blackbird *Agelaius phoeniceus* males defend territories in which several females may nest. Though males defend nests from predators, their rate of nest defense appears to be unrelated to the rate of nest predation. Males also sometimes feed nestlings, but at a rate far below that of females. By vasectomizing some males and looking for fertile clutches within their territories, it was possible to show that about 50% of females mate outside their territory, and do so more often when there are other territorial males close by. There are similar findings for a harem-forming tropical bat. It is worth noting that even a small incidence of cuckoldry may generate strong adaptations in male behavior; we review some of these here.

Close-following in male bank swallows. Bank swallows are highly monogamous birds. The two sexes are identical in appearance and in much of their behavior, as well. Both sexes participate in nest-building, incubation, and feeding of the young. But bank swallows nest in large colonies containing hundreds and sometimes thousands of birds, which should exacerbate tendencies toward cuckoldry in males. There is sufficient variation in breeding time of these birds that a monogamous male at any point in his breeding cycle may encounter females ready to lay eggs. The result is an extraordinary pattern of male behavior. For approximately a week prior to egg-laying, the male follows his mate on every one of her flights from the burrow—sometimes as many as 100 in one day—usually remaining within one meter of her, even as she engages in acrobatic flight. By the time her last egg is deposited, the male no longer follows his mate at all, while he starts following other females on their flights, preferring those who will soon lay eggs, probably detecting them by their heavier, slower flight. These females are usually accompanied by their mates, who may impede and attack other followers. In short, when their mates are fertile, males follow them slavishly. When their mates are not fertile, males follow the fertile females of others. These flights continue, despite the fact that they only infrequently give rise to copulation attempts, much less actual copulations. Whether success in closely following one's mate affects subsequent mate choice is unknown. For examples of male sexual harassment in gulls, see Figures 10-12 to 10-14.

Separation anxiety in zebra finches. Concern for cuckoldry suggests that separation from mate may be more threatening to a male

Figure 10-12

Extramarital courtship. A male lesser black-backed gull *Larus fuscus* in England courts an incubating female by head-tossing while other gulls watch. The female is paired to a male (absent) and she reacts to the extramarital advance by snapping at the intruder. Unlike courtship that leads to copulation between a mated pair, extramarital courtship is always initiated by the male, who leaves his own territory to court a neighboring female, almost always when his own mate is present (so that his own nest is attended) but his target's mate is absent. (Photo: Michael MacRoberts)

Figure 10-13

Unwanted advance. Even when a female has reacted negatively to a male's extramarital advance, 40% of the time the male will make a half-flying jump onto her back, as shown here. This female is incubating eggs and turns to peck at him. Females are mounted more after they have begun laying eggs than before, presumably because they are easier targets then and their mates more often absent. (Photo: Michael MacRoberts)

Figure 10-14

Preventing sexual access. A female lesser black-backed gull pecks violently into a male's breast and keeps her tail lowered, thus preventing cloacal contact. This is invariably her response when a male attempts to establish cloacal contact: of 74 mountings observed in nature not one resulted in sperm transfer. The population studied had recently increased from 18,000 breeding pairs to 45,000 and extramarital courtship or mounting was rarely observed at the lower densities. Just as in humans, frequency of sexual harassment may be affected by population density and other social factors. (Photo: Michael MacRoberts)

than to a female. Behavior at separation was studied experimentally in the zebra finch, a monogamous bird in which females invest more than males. When a pair is separated but members keep in sight of each other, both male and female issue contact calls. Males call more often than do females and move about more actively. In nature, contact calls serve to inform pair members of each individual's location, while increased activity makes it easier to find the other member of the pair. When separated but outside of visual contact, males—not females—become much more active. Both sexes stop giving contact calls and instead emit very loud calls. Again, activity and calling are positively associated within each sex, and males call much more often than do females. This suggests that separation is more threatening to a male than to a female, so that he is more strongly selected to re-establish contact. This makes obvious sense, since separation from his mate, even for a short period of time, risks (in theory) her insemination by another male, while a female suffers no similar danger.

When members of a pair are kept out of sight of each other, both sexes eat more, defecate more, and lose weight compared to those kept in sight of their mates. This inefficient syndrome is taken as a sign of anxiety and increased emotionality. It suggests some of the costs of breaking the pairbond. When reunited, a pair typically indulge in sexual activity. The longer the separation (up to 6 hours) the greater the frequency of sexual activity on reunion and the greater the length of time until sexual activity ceases (up to 50 minutes). This seems especially interesting from the standpoint of male psychology. The longer the separation from his mate, the greater the sexual threat. Sexual anxiety then produces greater sexual activity. This increased sexual activity probably has two effects. First, it tends to counter directly the threat that the female may have engaged in sexual activity during the separation. By engaging in sex at once, the male tends to displace any sperm already deposited, while of course depositing competing sperm of his own. Second, the male's sexual activity probably affects the behavior of his mate during future separations. In effect, the female is given a sexual reward to compensate for possible sexual abstinence during the separation. The same argument may apply to females. Their increased sexuality may counter any tendency to desert. But the male may be more vulnerable to desertion (see the later section on "Desertion").

That males are especially sensitive to seeing their mates in compromising situations is nicely shown by experiments in which males were trained to turn on a light for ten seconds in an adjoining room into which they could see, thus allowing a measure of the male's interest in viewing who was in the next room. This room was occupied by either the male's mate, another mated female, another mated male, or combinations thereof. The experiments revealed that a male was more interested in seeing his own mate than another female, and that he had an intermediate interest in seeing the two females together. He was least interested in watching the other male alone and only slightly more interested in watching the other male and his mate. He was most interested in watching what was happening in the next room when his mate was there alone with another male!

Incidentally, there were no comparable data for females, because—when separated from their mates—females were not terribly active and thus never discovered they could turn on a light in the next room by the pattern of their movements.

Male response to quick female sexual arousal in ring doves Streptopelia risoria. If a female responds too quickly to male courtship it may imply that she has already been sexually aroused before meeting the male or that, once paired, she may too easily respond to the courtship of others. Thus, we expect some ambivalence in males toward easily aroused females. We have evidence from the highly monogamous ring doves that in early stages of pair formation males respond aggressively to quick female sexual response, the latter being induced in females by giving them prior exposure to other males.

In ring doves, ovarian activity, which culminates in ovulation and egg-laying, is stimulated by male courtship. The female usually exhibits little courtship behavior when first paired with a male, but the secretion of ovarian hormones induced by male courtship soon stimulates her to engage in the nest-soliciting display with increasing frequency. This display, coupled with the female's attachment to the nest site, seems to signal her readiness to build a nest and lay eggs. In several experiments, a male was paired with one of two kinds of females, either a female who had been exposed to an active male for six 15-minute periods spread over several days, or to a female who had not been exposed to any other male before being paired with the test male. Unexposed females elicited much more nest-soliciting activity from the males than did the pre-exposed females. By contrast, pre-exposed females provoked male aggression: they were more frequently chased and pecked than were the unexposed females. Typically, the nest-soliciting displays of the male in the presence of a pre-exposed female occurred prior to any nest-soliciting performance by her. When she did display, the male usually stopped nest-soliciting and attacked the female. These results suggest that males prefer females whose ovaries have not been primed through exposure to other males.

Male aggression may be more effective if it protects the male's genetic paternity without driving the female away. In ring doves, females can be fertilized for up to six days after sperm have been deposited. When female doves are paired with males exhibiting highly aggressive courtship, they require about eight days to lay their first egg. On the other hand, females paired with much less aggressive males require only about five days to lay their first egg. Thus, aggressive actions by males in response to previously aroused females may drive such females away from the males or may postpone their egg-laying until any sperm previously deposited are no longer capable of fertilization.

Repeated copulations among water bugs. In the giant water bug sub-family Belostomatinae, males invest time and energy caring for the eggs, which are deposited on their backs by females. In one such species, *Abedus herberti*, adults may live for more than a year. Unlike birds, bugs are adapted to store sperm in a pouch especially evolved for this purpose, and in *A. herberti* sperm remain motile within this pouch for at least five months. When a vasectomized male was paired with a female who had mated one month before, 11 of the 75 eggs deposited on his back were fertile (see Figure 10-15). Thus, males cannot guarantee paternity by sequestering their mates for six days as can ring doves. Instead, males must guard against cuckoldry by ensuring that their sperm take precedence, which they do by copulating many times for each set of eggs they carry. Three eggs are the most that a female can deposit before the male insists on another copulation. In one extreme case, a pair copulated over 100 times in 36 hours during the transfer of 144 eggs.

In most insects, sperm from the last male to mate predominate in fertilizing the eggs, but *A. herberti* seems extreme in this regard. Smith varied the interval between first and second matings from three weeks to six weeks and discovered that more than 99% of the eggs laid were fertilized by the second male. This is the highest level of sperm precedence ever reported for an insect. More surprising still, these bugs show almost complete precedence when the second copulation takes place shortly after the first. For example, Smith permitted 8 females to pair with one male and to lay 5 eggs on his back. Then the female was immediately paired with a second male and allowed to lay the rest of her eggs on his back. Smith used the mutant striped form (see pp. 93–94) to differentiate offspring of the two males. All of the second males in this experiment succeeded in fertilizing all of the viable eggs ($N = 584$) they received. In an even more intensely competitive arrangement, Smith alternated a female between two different males, permitting her to lay three eggs on the back of one male before being transferred to the second, and so on until the female had laid all of her eggs. This experiment was conducted three times, and only 2% of the eggs that developed on either male's back was fathered by the other male. Thus, male sexual behavior, possibly combined with special sperm characteristics, ensures male paternity for the eggs he raises, even when a female copulates frequently with other males.

In general, males appear to have two different ways of guarding against the disadvantage of being cuckolded. One is to guard their females, keeping them in sight at all times and responding to any sign of earlier sexual access by aggressiveness so they can sequester the female

Figure 10-15
Cuckoldry in the giant water bug. A vasectomized male carrying 11 large white eggs fertilized by a striped male who had mated with the female one month earlier. Sixty-three other eggs failed to develop, presumably because they were unfertilized. (Photo: Robert Smith)

for a sufficient period of time to guard against earlier insemination. Second, males copulate repeatedly with their mates in order to counteract the effects of any earlier copulations with other males. This is especially obvious in water bugs, but appears also to happen in birds. Studies of forced copulations in ducks show that males who see their mate being raped by another male respond even to attempted forced copulations by forcing a copulation on their own mate. If the forced attempt of the predecessor is successful, males are especially likely to copulate immediately with their own mate. There is some suggestion that a similar psychology may operate in humans. It is known that males often respond sexually to their mates when other males appear interested. Some males even seek out the sight of another male copulating with their mate in order to achieve sexual arousal. Though this latter syndrome may have homosexual components, it seems from descriptions of participants that the sight of his mate responding sexually to another male arouses very strong sexual impulses in the observer.

Desertion

In species with strong male parental investment, couples often cooperate for a period of time in raising young. In birds, couples may cooperate for two or three months in the production of a single brood, during which time each partner is, in principle, vulnerable to desertion. The mate may find better opportunities for breeding elsewhere or may desert in order to stick the partner with the remaining work, assuming this is associated with increased mortality. Unfortunately our information concerning desertion is still rather scanty.

Desertion after copulation. Females are especially vulnerable to being deserted right after copulation, since the copulation will cost the male very little and may give him paternity of her eggs. Females are expected to reserve sex until such time as they have tested a male's affections. In species in which males maintain a territory, a female can wait until she has been accepted as the male's mate before copulating. In some species, however, this is not possible. For example, in the red-necked phalarope *Phalaropus lobatus* the male alone incubates the eggs and cares for the young after hatching, and females are sometimes desperate to lay their clutch of eggs with a male. Since the male's initial investment is nil, the female is vulnerable to being deserted right after courtship. Niko Tinbergen once observed a female vigorously courting a male and then flying away as soon as the male responded by attempting to copulate. This coy performance was repeated numerous times for several days and may have been a test of the male's willingness to brood the female's eggs. The male was, in fact, already brooding eggs and was courted when he left the eggs to feed on a nearby pond. In order to view a complete egg-laying sequence, Tinbergen destroyed the clutch the male was brooding. Within a half day the female permitted him sexual access, and he subsequently brooded her eggs. The important point is that the female could apparently tell the difference between a free male and an encumbered male, and thus withhold sex from the latter. Courtship alternating with flight may be a test that reveals the male's true attachments. It can show, for example, whether he is free to follow the female.

Desertion during the breeding season. It is very difficult to get data on desertion during the breeding season in monogamous species, but some long-term studies of birds have given us a few findings. For example, Margaret Nice saw 12 cases of desertion in her study of song-sparrows. In 11 cases, the female deserted the male. In only one case did the male desert the female. The one male deserted to a new territory after being trapped, and one of the females did likewise. One female had paired to a male with a broken leg, whom she later deserted. Another female stayed with a victor in a territorial dispute, where the first male was pushed to an adjoining territory. Five desertions appeared early in courtship, and Nice could not see any reason for them.

I once thought that the sex investing more would be less likely to desert, since it had more to lose in the event of failure. Actually, past investment should be irrelevant in determining desertion; only future opportunities should be considered. The song-sparrow provides a nice test. Females invest more than males yet they desert more frequently. Opportunities for breeding are probably greater for females because

the adult sex ratio gives an excess of males. This, in turn, probably results from lower male investment (see pp. 311–313) and is general
in monogamous birds. Also, a male is attached to his territory; to
switch mates he would have to drive his first mate off—which is more
difficult than simply deserting.

Males show bigamous tendencies in the song-sparrow. For example, the male pounces on neighboring females when the mates of
the latter are at the other end of their territories. These are usually
much more severe attacks than those on his own mate, and they elicit a
violently antagonistic response in the female, who fights back while
uttering loud threat notes. Usually her mate comes rushing to the
rescue and fights the interloper, while the mate of the interloper hurries near, gives a sexual call note, and postures. As in some other species, males stop singing during the time of courtship and egg-laying.
The male spends much time with his mate, mounting bushes as if to
guard her while she searches for food. Occasionally the female deserts
at this stage, and Nice has wondered whether anxiety over mate desertion may have something to do with the inhibition of song. Once a
female is established with a set of eggs in a nest, males renew their
singing. The males' habit of pouncing on neighboring females led to
several cases of bigamy when the female had lost her mate during the
incubation stage. Nice also noted instances in which females had lost
their mate during the time when they had young chicks in the nest.
Such females became hypersexual and they solicited sexual advances
from neighboring, paired males. Nice says that the most sexually
aroused females she ever observed were females who had recently lost
their mate and had chicks still to care for. Females are not ovulating at
this time.

Separation after failure to breed. In some long-lived birds, such as
the kittiwake gull, pairs achieve higher reproductive success in successive years as long as they remain together. When they split up they
lose this advantage (see Table 10-10). Nevertheless, some pairs separate after one breeding season. Failure to hatch eggs is especially likely
to lead to separation. Of those couples who succeeded in hatching
eggs, only 17% separated in the following season, while 52% of those
couples failing to hatch eggs separated. Similar results have been obtained in red-billed gulls *Larus novaehollandiae* and the manx shear-
water *Puffinus puffinus*. In the red-billed gull, those who separated
fledged 44% of their chicks, while those who did not fledged 65% of
their chicks.

Summary

Cases of male parental investment are reviewed. In the insects, males
sometimes invest by transferring protein-rich material with their

Table 10-10.   A comparison of the productivity of old, established pairs and newly formed pairs

	Fledglings per Pair		
Bird	*New*	*Established*	Difference
Blue-faced booby *Sula dactylatra*	0.48	0.74	43
Arctic skua *Stercorarius parasiticus*	1.10	1.51	27
Kittiwake *Rissa tridactyla*	1.19	1.59	26
Red-billed gull *Larus novaehollandiae*	0.81	0.92	12

Source: Rowley 1983.

sperm. In a few species the male feeds the female. In fish, males often care for eggs and male care is more common than female care. In frogs and salamanders, males sometimes care for eggs. Male care is absent in reptiles, and in birds it usually co-occurs with female care. In some mammals, males join females in caring for the young. In vertebrates there is a very strong association between external fertilization and male care, the most likely explanation being that such eggs more often require care (for example, compared to reptiles) and that there is no delay between ejaculation and egg availability. Territoriality and the extent to which male investment can be shared are two important factors affecting the frequency of male parental investment.

Relative attractiveness affects the sexes at courtship and during parental investment. Attractive individuals of both sexes have higher RS and show a tendency to survive better, probably because they are able to attract superior mates and because their mates do more of the work. In addition, attractive males are able to pair with more than one female. Even when investment is identical between the sexes, males have opportunities for and dangers from cuckoldry not found in females. Male adaptations include close-following of the mate, anxious behavior at separation, hostility toward quick early sexual arousal in the female, and repeated copulations to ensure paternity. It seems unlikely that paternity uncertainty induced by cuckoldry has been a strong factor in the evolution of male parental investment.

Females may be able to guard against desertion immediately following copulation. Desertions are found to be more frequent by females than by males, and in some long-lived species separations may be caused by breeding failure.

Chapter 11

The Primary Sex Ratio

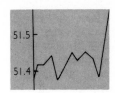

THE PRIMARY SEX ratio is the sex ratio with which each generation begins. Ideally it is the sex ratio among fertilized eggs, but in many species, particularly those with parental care, the sex ratio of fertilized eggs is difficult to measure, and the primary sex ratio in this book may refer to the sex ratio when eggs hatch or when babies are born. Darwin collected evidence showing that in a wide range of species the primary sex ratio is about 1:1 (male:female), but he was unable to explain how natural selection acts on the sex ratio. As far as Darwin could see, an individual leaving ten surviving offspring had the same reproductive success whether these ten were all males, all females, or five of each. Mathematician Ronald Fisher solved the problem in one stroke in 1930 by showing that the sex ratio of one generation affects the reproductive success of these individuals in the following generation.

In this chapter we present Ronald Fisher's reasoning regarding the primary sex ratio, plus a wide range of connected notions that allow us to explain deviations from 1:1 sex ratios and also allow us to describe how individuals may adjust the sex ratios they produce to fit particular conditions. But this chapter is not only about the sex ratio. There are now many facts supporting Fisher's theory and virtually none opposing it, so that the theory can be taken as confirmed and the sex ratio can be used to test some of our other theories. As we shall see, the sex ratio provides direct and valuable evidence concerning the underlying assumptions of our thinking in regard to kinship and sexual selection. More than that, our ability to explain the facts concerning the primary sex ratio in dozens of contexts and hundreds of species is one of the great achievements of modern evolutionary biology and one that gives strong support to a whole host of assumptions.

Fisher's Sex Ratio Theory

The easiest way to appreciate why 1:1 sex ratios are so common in nature is to consider the alternative. Imagine, for example, a species in which the two sexes are produced in a ratio of 1:3 (male:female). Knowing nothing else about the species, we still know that a male can expect, on average, three times as much reproductive success as a female. If, for example, all females are inseminated, a male will, on average, inseminate three. If a male costs the same as a female, then for each daughter, a mother could as easily make a son, thereby tripling the number of grandchildren expected from that offspring. Of course, as genes for investing more heavily in sons begin to spread, the overall sex ratio becomes less female-biased, reducing the advantage of concentrating on males. But as long as the sex ratio is female-biased, however slightly, there remains a selection pressure for females to concentrate more effort on rearing sons. At a 1:1 sex ratio, the return per unit work is equal for the two sexes, and selection for altering the primary sex ratio dies away. The sex ratio is now said to be in equilibrium; it is no longer expected to change.

The same argument applies in reverse if the primary sex ratio is male-biased. If the primary sex ratio is 3:1 (male:female) and all females are inseminated, each male can expect, on average, to inseminate only one-third of a female. Thus, daughters are three times as valuable as sons, and mothers are selected to concentrate on the underrepresented sex. As selection continues, the primary sex ratio tends toward 1:1.

Fisher's theory is based on two steps. First, the sex ratios we expect to find in nature are those at which the return per unit work on a male equals the return per unit work on a female. Consider an individual, typically a female, who is investing in offspring of the two sexes. She will be selected to produce the sex ratio that maximizes her eventual genetic return. Fisher argues that this will occur when the genetic return per unit work on a female equals that on a male, where genetic return is measured as number of surviving grandchildren. If the return per unit work is higher for one sex, there automatically exists a selection pressure on parents to invest more in that sex, and the sex ratio will change so as to reestablish equivalency between the sexes.

Second, Fisher realized that the expected reproductive success of a male relative to that of a female is itself a function of the primary sex ratio. High sex ratios (many males per female) mean that each male has only a small chance of fertilizing a female and hence has low expected reproductive success compared to a female. Low sex ratios mean that each male has high expected RS, since he will fertilize, on average, more than one female. In short, individuals of the underrepresented sex enjoy higher RS than the others, and their numbers are expected to increase accordingly. Only at a 1:1 sex ratio does a male's expected RS equal that of a female.

Note that we expect the primary sex ratio to reflect the relative cost of producing a male compared to a female. Consider a species in which it costs twice as much to produce a son as a daughter. Since a male is twice as costly as a female, we know that he must achieve twice the RS of a female in order to be worth producing. A male will achieve twice the RS of a female when the primary sex ratio is 1:2. Males are twice as costly as females but only half as many are produced, so *total work on the two sexes is equal.* Fisher saw that this made intuitive sense, since in a sexual species all offspring have both a father and a mother. Therefore we know that the total reproductive success of males must equal the total reproductive success of females. Hence, parents will be selected to invest the same total effort in the production of males as they do in the production of females. The ratio of investment in the two sexes will be 1:1. When a male costs the same as a female, the sexes will be produced in equal numbers; when a male is more expensive, fewer males than females will be produced, and vice versa. Cost and numbers will be adjusted so that total effort is equal. Or, in symbols, the cost of a male (Cm) times the number of males (M) equals the cost of a female (Cf) times the number of females (F):

$$Cm \cdot M = Cf \cdot F$$

Several features of Fisher's theory are worth stressing. First, the primary sex ratio is independent of the type of breeding system. In our earlier example of a 1:3 sex ratio, males were assumed to be polygynous and capable of fertilizing three females. If we impose the restriction of monogamy, all males will mate once, but only one-third of the females will mate. Thus, the expected RS of a male is three times that of a female, exactly as it is under polygyny.

The primary sex ratio is also independent of differential mortality by sex acting after the end of parental investment. At first glance it would appear that differential mortality by sex ought to affect the primary sex ratio. If males die more quickly than females, then females seem like a better bet; yet the males that do survive will exactly make up in increased RS what they have lost in decreased chances of survival. For example, if all females survive to breed from an initial sex ratio of 1:1 while only one-tenth of the males survive to breed, then those males that do survive will have ten times the RS of each female surviving to breed, since the sex ratio then will show 10 females for every one male. Put another way, if the sex ratio at the end of the period of parental investment is 1:1, then a male can expect in his lifetime, on average, to fertilize a single female. Differential mortality by sex after this moment, and the form of the breeding system, only affect

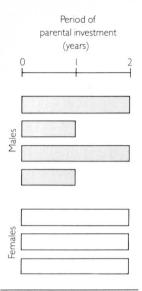

Period of
parental investment
(years)

0   1   2

Males

Females

Figure 11-1

Differential male mortality during the period of parental investment affects the primary sex ratio. In this hypothetical species, parental investment is assumed to last two years and to be equally costly each year for both sexes. Females suffer no mortality during parental investment, but half the males die at age 1. Total investment in each sex is equal (six years). Note that the sex ratio is male-biased at conception (4:3) and female-biased at the end of the period of parental investment (2:3).

the distribution of RS within each sex; they do not affect the average expected return for investing in a male compared to a female.

Differential mortality by sex operating *during* the period of parental investment affects the relative cost of a male and a female and thereby affects sex ratios. Consider the sex ratio at conception in a species with a period of parental investment. Imagine that more males die during this period than do females. Knowing nothing else, we know that average expenditure on each male conceived will be less than on each female, since a higher proportion of males will die before investment is complete. By contrast, each male reared is on average more costly than each female reared, since the average cost of an individual reared must include the cost of those in whom investment was begun but never completed, and since this is more frequent in males (see Figure 11-1). In short, our principle of equal total investment in the two sexes requires that the sex ratio at conception be biased toward the sex suffering greater mortality during investment, while the sex ratio at the end of the period of parental investment should be biased in the opposite direction.

The Evidence Regarding Fisher's Theory

In most animals the cost of a male equals the cost of a female and the sexes are produced in a 1:1 ratio. This appears to be true for those species in which parental care ends with the production of eggs, in virtually all of which an egg that produces a son is the same size as an egg that produces a daughter, so the cost of producing a male and a female is equal. Likewise, in most species with additional investment, such as birds and mammals, the investment is commonly shared more or less equally between sons and daughters. In turn, in most species of insects, fish, frogs, lizards, birds, and mammals, the primary sex ratio is about 1:1.

This general rule is true for all breeding systems (monogamy, polygyny, polyandry, and promiscuity) and for all patterns of differential mortality by sex occurring after the offspring are produced. In most mammals, males die faster than females, yet the primary sex ratio is roughly 1:1. In most birds, females die faster than males, yet the sex ratio among young is also about 1:1. All the breeding systems are found in mammals and birds, yet none affects the primary sex ratio.

But sex ratios also deviate from 1:1. One such deviation occurs when members of one sex are more expensive to produce than members of the other. Some wasps nest in holes in wood and build a succession of cells into each of which a single egg is placed, along with the provisions needed to support development to adulthood (Figure 11-2).

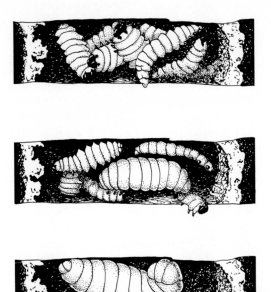

Figure 11-2

The study of trap-nested wasps. Three views of the same cell in a trap nest. Notice the mud partitions at both ends of the cell. Top: a female wasp *Symmorphus canadensis* has stuffed the cell with paralyzed beetle larvae *Chalepis dorsalis* and has laid an egg in it. The egg is not visible. Middle: three days later a half-grown wasp larva is visible. Bottom: two days later the full-grown wasp larva is consuming the last beetle larva. The volume of the cell is a rough measure of maternal investment in the offspring. (From Krombein 1967)

Since each cell is typically packed with food, the volume of the cell gives us a measure of the amount of food provided for the offspring. Wasps can be attracted to artificial nests (holes bored in pieces of wood), which can be opened at any time so as to measure the volume of the cells and the sex of the associated wasps. In a sample of 15 species studied in this manner, the relative cost of a male and a female varied by a factor of about three. But relative cost was inversely correlated with the sex ratio produced, so that ratios of investment for all species were about 1:1 (Figure 11-3). In ants the relative cost of a male reproductive (compared to a female) varies by a factor of ten, but the

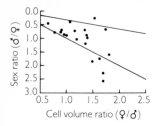

Figure 11-3

Ratios of investment in trap-nested wasps. The sex ratio (male/female) is plotted as a function of the cell volume ratio (female/male) for various species attracted to trap-nests. Note that sex ratio and relative cost of the two sexes are inversely related. (*From* Trivers and Hare 1976)

associated sex ratios are, again, inversely related: as females become more expensive, relative to males, fewer of them are produced (see later Figures 11-6 and 11-7, pp. 279–80).

Differential male mortality during the period of parental investment affects the relative cost of a male and a female: we expect to find that the sex that dies more quickly is initially produced in relatively greater numbers. In mammals, males usually die faster than females, apparently throughout life, including the time *in utero*. In cattle, sheep, and several species of whales, in addition to ourselves, males die faster than females *in utero* and are conceived in greater numbers. In general, there appears to be a tendency for especially high rates of differential mortality *in utero* to be associated with especially high fetal sex ratios (see Table 11-1). Unfortunately, for none of these species, except humans, do we know the sex ratio at the end of the period of parental investment.

Mammals show that 1:1 sex ratios at birth in a diploid species are not a simple consequence, during meiosis, of splitting XY chromosomes equally between the two kinds of sperm. Indeed, by some unknown mechanism Y-bearing sperm appear to be more frequent at the time of conception, and the degree of this bias varies among species. As we shall see below, it also varies among individuals within a species.

Investment in male and female may change in a complex way with age of offspring. In many mammals the sex ratio is slightly male-biased at birth, and in some, such as red deer, it remains male-biased at the time of weaning. Since male red deer are larger at birth and are permitted to suckle more often during nursing, the overall ratio of investment appears to be male-biased. But females remain as adults near

Table 11-1.   The degree of differential male mortality in utero and the average fetal sex ratio in whales

Species of Whale	Degree of Differential Male Mortality *	Average Fetal Sex Ratio
Humpback	.04	.531
Blue	.02	.513
Sei	.01	.498
Minke	.005	.510
Fin	.005	.506

Source: Seger et al., in preparation.

* The degree of differential male mortality is the rate at which the sex ratio changes per month during the fetal period (all values are negative). The last three rates are too similar to be distinguished.

their mothers, while males emigrate, and there is evidence that this close settling imposes a cost. Thus, sons are more costly early in life, whereas daughters are more costly later (Figure 11-4). This pattern may be fairly common in mammals. It is also possible for members of one sex to return a benefit to their parents, as when they remain as helpers at the nest, and this should result in relatively more of the helping sex being produced (see p. 198).

In summary, Fisher's theory explains the prevalence of 1:1 sex ratios in nature; it explains the inverse relationship between the relative cost of a male and the relative number of males produced; and it explains the association between differential male mortality *in utero* and the sex ratio bias at conception in mammals.

The Sex Ratio Under Sib Mating

Fisher's theory assumes populationwide competition for mates: each male competes with all others for access to all females. If we assume, instead, that males compete much more locally with their male relatives for access to females, then parents may be selected to produce less males. Consider the extreme case, a species in which males compete only with their brothers for access to sisters. Were parents to produce a 1:1 sex ratio, many of their sons would be redundant, since only a few males are needed to fertilize a large number of females. Thus, parents are selected to economize on the production of males: we expect each clutch of eggs to contain some males, but only enough to guarantee that all their sisters will be fertilized. With some sib mating and some outbreeding, individuals are selected to produce intermediate ratios of investment, still female-biased but not extremely so.

Most of the extreme examples of sib mating come from mites and insects. In some cases, siblings actually mate with each other inside their mother (Figure 11-5). More typically a batch of eggs is laid together on or in a host, and larvae develop together. Males emerge into adulthood first and can mate many times, although they usually do so with their sisters in the host or directly outside it. Indeed, males are often wingless. Primary sex ratios in such species are strongly female-biased, usually at least 1:5 and sometimes surpassing 1:20, yet typically each batch of offspring contains at least one male. Females store sperm so that a single insemination is sufficient to fertilize all her eggs. It is noteworthy that such species are almost always haplodiploid, since this permits precise control of the sex ratio; the mother can make a male by a simple contraction of a muscle that prevents sperm from leaving her spermatotheca.

Only one mammal is known in which the primary sex ratio seems regularly to be female-biased. This is the wood lemming *Myopus*

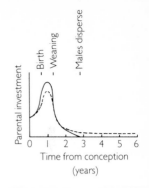

Figure 11-4

The pattern of parental investment in sons and daughters of red deer (hypothetical). The cost per unit time of investing in sons and daughters in red deer is plotted as a function of time. Although the curve is hypothetical, differences between males and females are based on actual field data. Males are slightly larger at birth and are permitted to suckle for longer periods during nursing, but they emigrate out of the group when young, terminating investment in them; daughters remain and are permitted to settle near their mothers. This pattern of investment in sex of offspring may be fairly general in mammals and may help to explain a common tendency for sex ratios at birth to be slightly male-biased. (*From* Clutton-Brock 1982)

Figure 11-5

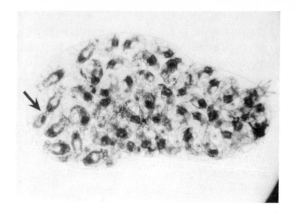

Local mate competition. A brother mates with his sister (see arrow) inside their mother. The species is a *Pygmephorus* mite. Broods typically consist of two to four males among 16 to 160 females. Most will mate with each other before their mother bursts. When she does, her daughters scurry away but her wingless sons continue to patrol the remaining pile of eggs. (Photo: William Hamilton)

schisticolor, which produces a sex ratio of about 1:4. Lacking the special mechanism of haplodiploidy, wood lemmings achieve this sex ratio in an unusual way. Sex chromosomes in males are XY, as in our own species, but there are two kinds of females, normal XX and X*Y. The X* chromosome is a normal X containing special genes that, in development, suppress the action of the Y chromosome, so that such females develop just as normal XX females do. At the time of meiosis, the special genes on the X* chromosome also prevent the formation of Y-bearing eggs. Thus, X*Y females produce only daughters. When the two kinds of chromosomes are about equally frequent, only one-fourth of the individuals produced are XY, while the remainder are females.

Why wood lemmings? Lemmings have extreme population cycles and wood lemmings are extreme among lemmings. In good years, populations increase by a factor of 1000 or more. There is extensive migration and probably high outbreeding. But in bad years, lemmings are found in small, widely scattered pockets, and it is likely that within pockets sibling and parent—offspring matings are common. If so, female-biased sex ratios will be favored, since sons are somewhat redundant. The wood lemming case is instructive because the X* chromosome can also be viewed as a selfish chromosome that, by preventing the formation of Y-bearing eggs, doubles its frequency when it appears in males. But we must still explain why selection on other chromosomes has not shut down the X* chromosome, since under outbreeding, deviations from 1:1 are selected against. This, of course, is exactly the point: inbreeding relaxes this selection, permitting the spread of an otherwise selfish chromosome. This suggests a renewed caution we should feel about other cases of selfish genes (see pp. 137—141).

a   b

Figure 11-6

Variation in sexual dimorphism in size, in ants. (a) The female on the right, with a large head and large mandibles, copulates with a male. He has degenerate mandibles and a pinhead but his abdomen is full of sperm. The species is *Formica polyctena* and the female is only slightly heavier than the male. Dry weight of each is taken as a rough measure of their cost to the colony in being produced. (b) In the ant *Xenomyrmex floridanis* the reproductive female is many times larger than the male. As shown here, the pair copulate while the workers—sisters of the female—watch. Although sexual dimorphism in size differs among ant species by a factor of 10 or more, ratios of investment are often close to 1:3 (see Figure 11-7). (Photos: Bert Hölldobler)

The 1:3 Ratio of Investment in Ants

One of my most enjoyable experiences in science was the discovery with Hope Hare of a previously unknown fact about ants: despite enormous variation in the relative size of male and female reproductives, the total invested in females is about three times as great as that invested in males (see Figures 11-6 and 11-7). Why should this be so? In a typical ant species the reproductives are produced not only by their mother, the queen, who lays the eggs, but also by their sisters, the workers, who provide them all their food and care until they reach adulthood. The workers are more closely related to their sisters ($r = \frac{3}{4}$) than to their brothers ($r = \frac{1}{4}$) and should prefer to raise sisters. If the workers are able to control the ratio of investment it will equilibrate at 1:3, since then the greater relatedness of the workers to their sisters is exactly cancelled out by the greater reproductive success of their brothers.

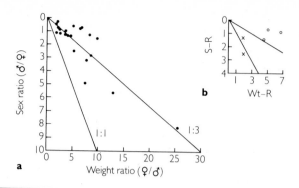

Figure 11-7

The ratio of investment, in ants. (a) The sex ratio (male:female) is plotted as a function of the dry weight ratio (female:male) for 21 species of monogynous ants (one queen per colony). Note that sex ratio and relative cost of the two sexes are inversely related and that the points cluster around the 1:3 line instead of the 1:1. (b) Same thing for two slave-making species (X) and three closely related non-slavemakers (taken from a). (*From* Trivers and Hare 1976)

At first we expected ratios of investment in ants to fall between 1:1 and 1:3, since selection on the mother would produce a 1:1 ratio, and we were biased toward seeing compromises between parent and offspring. However, the first few species we inspected soon convinced us that 1:3 sex ratios were common in ants. Apparently the vastly greater biomass of the workers compared to their mother—and the fact that they do most of the investing—gave them the effective power. If this were true, then an interesting exception should occur in the case of slave-making ants, for in these species the young are raised by members of other species, stolen from their nests as pupae (see p. 175). These slaves have no stake in the ratio of investment they produce and are not expected to evolve counterresponses to any new ploys the queen introduces. That is, the slaves may still attempt to produce a 1:3 ratio of investment, but selection acting on the slave-making queen favors some new ploy for increasing investment in males and the slaves fail to evolve a counterploy. Thus, the ratio of investment should evolve back to 1:1. Fortunately, excellent data exist for two slave-making species, which produce ratios of investment of almost exactly 1:1 (Figure 11-7b).

Taken together, the evidence from ants supports our kinship theory. It suggests that we are calculating degrees of relatedness correctly and it supports our assumption that offspring are able to evolve their own strategies in the face of parental resistance (Chapter 7). This latter assumption was still controversial at the time (1976). Since Richard Alexander had championed the view that parents in all species, including the social insects, must inevitably win in any disagreement with their offspring, it was perhaps not surprising that he and Paul Sherman soon published a sharp critique of our work on ratios of investment. On the one hand, they raised doubts about the assumptions underlying a 1:3 ratio and the validity of our evidence. On the other hand, they argued that female-biased ratios were already expected on quite different grounds, namely, local mate competition between male relatives.

Known cases of local mate competition leading to female-biased ratios of investment invariably involve sib mating or close inbreeding, but we can be fairly certain that 1:3 ratios of investment in the ants do not result from sib mating. Fully one-half of all matings would have to be between siblings in order to produce a 1:3 ratio, yet we have strong evidence that ants commonly outbreed. For one thing, males do not mate in the nest but require a flight before they will mate. In turn, flights in some species are widely synchronized, producing huge mating swarms. It seems unlikely that ants avoid inbreeding and local mate competition where it would be easy (in the nest) only to practice it in large numbers where it would be difficult (in the sky). So strong is the tendency to outbreed that in one species wingless females advertise their sexual readiness from perches near their nest while their brothers walk by without responding and fly off to seek copulations elsewhere. Incidentally, the sex ratio data themselves argue against inbreeding, for within each species, sex ratios of nests tend to show greater than random variance. For example, all-male nests and all-female nests are surprisingly common. This is exactly what we would *not* expect if sib mating were common. How, for example, do males from all-male nests find sisters with whom to mate? Yet this kind of variation in the sex ratio is expected if there is ongoing conflict between the generations: in some nests, the queen prevails (all male nests), but in more nests her daughters do (strongly female-biased nests). Overall result of the conflict: a ratio often near 1:3.

The other main possibility is that the data we used were unreliable. The evidence on sex ratios came from dozens of independent sources and so is unlikely to be biased. However, we sometimes sent for specimens to weigh, and although we asked for specimens typical in size for their sex, Alexander and Sherman imagine that people sent us relatively large females and relatively small males, since females are typically the larger sex. If this ever occurred, it does not seem to have happened very often, since ratios of investment are the same whether specimens were sent to us, were chosen ourselves, or were limited in number so no choice was exercised. Since Alexander and Sherman's work, additional species have been studied by others, and ratios of investment are usually strongly female-biased, often surprisingly close to 1:3.

The human mind is a wonderful organ. Alexander and Sherman's critique was extremely distasteful to me at the time it was published (1977). It seemed vicious and unprincipled, full of innuendo and slander. On rereading the paper I see that their wording is much gentler than I remember, that some of their doubts have merit, and that some others are at least reasonable. While it is still not my favorite piece of science, it is less biased than I remember. The ability of the mind to misperceive and to misremember is part of a larger system of biases we call "self-deception." These biases have evolved, in Alexander's opinion and my own, because natural selection favors ever subtler ways of deceiving others (see pp. 415–420). If this is true, then there is a nice irony in seeing that selection may have given us the capacity to discover 1:3 ratios in nature, as well as the capacity not to see them when they are actually there. Or, as Richard Alexander might prefer to put it, not only has selection given us the capacity to create illusory 1:3 ratios, it has given us the ability to see through them!

Variation in the Primary Sex Ratio

When the primary sex ratio in a population is in equilibrium, all sex ratios are equally adaptive as long as they continue to cancel out to give the equilibrium sex ratio. The 1:1 sex ratio is said to be an evolutionarily stable strategy; that is, under outbreeding, a population producing this ratio cannot be invaded by genes producing a different sex ratio. But evolution never stops, and selection continues to favor ever subtler strategies. In this setting, selection favors any parents who can adjust the sex ratio they produce to factors associated with variation in the relative success of a son and a daughter.

That we need some such explanation is suggested by evidence on naturally occurring variation in the primary sex ratio. For example, in three species of seals, females who give birth early in the pupping season produce an excess of males, but as the pupping season progresses, the sex ratio drops until females giving birth late in the season produce a corresponding excess of females (Table 11-2). Altogether, the primary sex ratio is about 1:1, but the variation associated with time of birth suggests that males born early in the season may outreproduce females born then, while the reverse may be true late in the season.

Three general factors have been proposed which may control sex ratios within species adaptively: (1) parents may adjust the sex ratio to the level of inbreeding that they expect their children to practice; (2) parents may respond to fluctuations in the local population's sex ratio by producing the sex that is in short supply; and (3) parents may

Table 11-2.   The sex ratio produced in different quarters of the pupping season by three seal species

	Seal Species		
Quarter	Grey[a]	Weddell[b]	So. Australian Fur[b]
First	139	122	117
Second	111	104	100
Third	100	81	85
Fourth	74	79	69

[a] Coulson & Hickling 1961. Quarters consisted of 13-day intervals.
[b] Stirling, 1971. Quarters consisted of one-fourth of the animals. Data for fur seal are not significant.

adjust the sex ratio to factors operating early in the offspring's development that later affect reproductive success in the two sexes differently. Let us consider each of these factors.

Variation in Inbreeding

As we have seen above, sib mating is expected to be associated with the production of more daughters. A species with sib mating may show variation in the degree of sib mating, and parents able to respond to this variation may gain an advantage. Consider a parasitoid wasp that lays her eggs in a host. The young that emerge will mate among themselves before the females disperse. If only one female lays her eggs in a host, the offspring will mate entirely with siblings. If two females lay on a host, the offspring will engage in a mixture of sib mating and outbreeding. In many such parasitoid wasps, females commonly lay their eggs in a single host on which other females will not lay eggs, although two females sometimes lay eggs in the same host. The first female to lay in a host may have a hard time predicting whether a second female will also lay in the same host, but a second female who detects that a host has already been parasitized is expected to decrease the number of eggs she lays (since a single host can only support the development of a limited number of parasitoids) and to increase the percentage of sons in these eggs (since her offspring will not be entirely sib mated). Indeed, if she lays only a few eggs, most of her offspring will probably mate with the offspring of the first female and should be sons in order to take advantage of the female-biased sex ratio produced by the first female.

These possibilities have been investigated in several parasitoid wasps and mites; the best evidence comes from the wasp, *Nasonia*

Figure 11-8

The average number of off-spring emerging and the sex ratio among these as a function of the order in which females lay their eggs. Eggs are laid on the same host by the parasitic wasp *Nasonia vitripennis.* Note that later females lay fewer eggs, which results in a higher proportion of males. (*From* Holmes 1972)

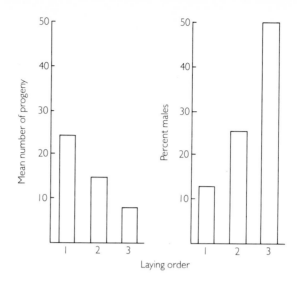

vitripennis. One experiment used genetically marked females in competition with each other. Each female contained a unique marker that showed up in her offspring, so it was easy to determine the number of eggs laid by each female and the percentage of males among the resulting young. In Figure 11-8 we see that the second female to lay on a host lays fewer eggs and increases the percentage of males among them. Likewise, when a third female lays eggs on a host previously parasitized by two others, she lays still fewer eggs and further increases the percentage of males among these offspring.

Females detect whether a host has been parasitized, or is likely to have been, by a variety of means. If, for example, a female encounters other females while laying eggs, she increases the percentage of males she produces. More importantly, females can determine directly whether a host has already been attacked. Female *Nasonia* can detect whether a blowfly larva has already been pierced. This was shown experimentally by permitting wasps to bore a single hole in various larvae, but removing the wasps before any eggs were laid. When *Nasonia* females are offered pierced versus unpierced larvae, they lay relatively more sons on the pierced ones.

More remarkable still, a female wasp is capable of measuring the number of eggs already laid in a host. This permits her to adjust the sex ratio she produces to the relative number of eggs she will add to the host. In *Nasonia*, the great majority of hosts are only attacked once, so the first female is expected to produce near the sex ratio expected under inbreeding. The second female is then in a position to match the sex ratio she produces to the relative number of eggs she

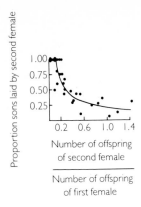

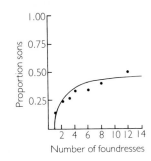

Figure 11-9

Sex ratio as a function of relative number of eggs laid, in a parasitic wasp. The proportion of sons produced by the second female *Nasonia vitripennis* laying eggs on a host is plotted as a function of the number of eggs laid by the second female divided by the number laid by the first (under laboratory conditions). The line shows values that maximize the second female's inclusive fitness. Notice the close fit of observed sex ratios to this line. (*From* Werren 1980)

Figure 11-10

The primary sex ratio as a function of the number of females contributing offspring (foundresses), in a parasitic wasp. The average proportion of sons emerging is plotted as a function of the number of foundresses in laboratory experiments with *Nasonia vitripennis*. The dotted line shows the value that maximizes inclusive fitness, assuming foundresses contribute equal numbers of offspring. (*From* Werren 1983)

adds. The equation is easy to solve as long as we know the relative number of eggs added by the second female. Under experimental conditions, *Nasonia* females appear to solve the equation exactly: when the second female produces relatively few eggs, most of these are males; as the relative number increases, the sex ratio among them drops so as to match closely the predicted values (see Figure 11-9).

Local mate competition may also occur in *Nasonia* when hosts are aggregated together. In laboratory experiments, John Werren has shown that the sex ratio changes as a function of the number of foundresses laying eggs on an aggregated batch of hosts exactly as predicted by Hamilton for cases of partial sib mating (Figure 11-10). Werren was also able to test sex ratio theory by collecting fly pupae from nature in such sites as birds' nests and rotting carcasses. Since offspring number will be positively correlated with foundress number, it will be inversely correlated with degree of sib mating, and the sex ratio should increase with offspring number until it reaches 1:1, exactly the pattern shown (Figure 11-11).

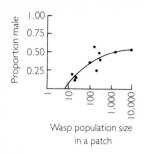

Figure 11-11

The sex ratio among off-spring as a function of off-spring population size, in a parasitic wasp. The proportion of males emerging in patches of hosts collected in nature is plotted as a function of the total number of wasps emerging for *Nasonia vitripennis.* (Two small patches of super-parasitized hosts have been eliminated). Numbers of offspring presumably reflect numbers of females contributing offspring to the population (foundresses). (*From* Werren 1983)

Variation in the Population Sex-Ratio

In nature the sex ratio of a population fluctuates around some average value. We may imagine that these fluctuations sometimes give advantages to the sex temporarily in short supply. What is required is that the temporary deviation fail to correct itself in one generation: then, selection will favor individuals who produce the sex that is in short supply.

These expectations were tested in a woodchuck population by removing females of all ages from a 333-acre study site during two successive years. Results were compared with control areas, which were similar in other respects but suffered no experimental manipulation. One year after each intervention the sex ratio in the experimental population remained biased toward females (Table 11-3). In turn, the sex ratio among the young was strongly female-biased compared to the sex ratio produced in the control area. By killing a sample of pregnant females in the two years, it was discovered that in the experimental area the sex ratio among fetuses showed a strong bias in favor of females. The woodchucks seem to be responding to the unusual decimation of females by producing more of them.

Similar evidence has been gathered from guppies and various copepods (Crustacea), since in these species the primary sex ratio is inversely correlated with the sex ratio of the larger population. In addition, a wide variety of other species probably show a similar effect, as first pointed out by John Werren and Eric Charnov, since females deprived of males in these species—when finally given a mating—produce an excess of males. Delayed fertilization leads to male-biased sex ratios in one species each of frog, trout, fruit fly, and butterfly, and in several species of mealy bugs and copepods. Likewise, in rabbits the more time that elapses between ovulation and fertilization, the greater is the proportion of sons born. In various species, the longer the female is deprived of fertilization, the more male-biased are her eventual progeny: in the mealy bug, mating 0, 6, 8 and 10 weeks after emergence results in sex ratios respectively of 102, 181, 327, and 991 males per 100 females. Presumably, the longer the female must wait for a

Table 11-3. Effects of removing female woodchucks on sex ratio one year later (number of males per 100 females)

Sex Ratio Among:	Control Site	Experimental Site
Yearlings and adults	95.6	126
Young of the year	103.4	45
Fetuses	123.0	55

Source: Snyder 1960.

male, the rarer the males are, making investment in sons a better bet. For data relating delay in fertilization to sex ratio in white-tailed deer see Table 11-4.

There is evidence that plants may also adjust their sex ratios to the local sex ratio. When pollen fall is excessive, males are presumably very common locally, so that a tendency then to produce daughters may increase parental reproductive success. In two species of plants the sex ratio of seedlings varies inversely with the density of pollen reaching the stigma. For example, in *Rumex*, sparse pollen fall produces a sex ratio of nearly 1:1 (58:70), while excessive pollen fall produces a strongly female-biased sex ratio (40:206). It is noteworthy that high pollen fall always produces female-biased sex ratios, but sparse pollen fall does not produce male-biased sex ratios. Perhaps this is because both sex ratio and density of plants affect the amount of pollen reaching a stigma. Sparse pollen suggests that individuals of both sexes may be infrequent, which may make inbreeding more likely; and hence, the two pressures tend to balance out. Indeed, the inbreeding effect may be more powerful, since under sparse pollen fall, sex ratios are still slightly female-biased.

The effect of fluctuations in the population sex ratio has been studied in the shrimp *Pandalus jordani*, in which individuals can determine their own sex and tend to change from male to female as they grow. Because of large year-to-year variation in survival of immature shrimp, the fraction of the adult population that is made up of first breeders (small shrimp) varies greatly. Where old breeders are common, there will be many females and first breeders should prefer to be male. Where first breeders are common, some will wish to be female. These expectations are confirmed exactly in natural populations (Figure 11-12a). Furthermore, where first breeders are relatively uncommon, more older breeders will prefer to remain male; this also is confirmed (Figure 11-12b).

Table 11-4. The sex ratio (percentage males) produced by female white-tailed deer *Odocoileus virginianus* in captivity as a function of the number of hours delay between the onset of estrus and insemination

	Number of Hours in Estrus			
	13–24	*25–36*	*37–48*	*49–96*
Percent males among offspring*	14.3	38.7	62.5	80.8

Source: Verme and Ozoga 1981.

* The trend is highly significant. Total number of fawns was 125.

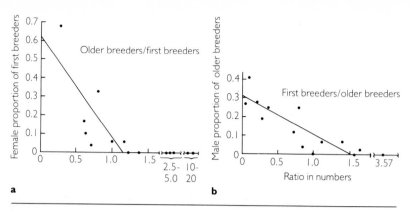

Figure 11-12

The sex ratio of first and older breeders as a function of their relative numbers, in a shrimp. (a) This graph plots the proportion of first breeders that are female as a function of the ratio of older breeders to first breeders, in *Pandalus jordani*. (b) This is a plot of the proportion of older breeders that are male as a function of the ratio of first breeders to older breeders. (*From* Charnov et al. 1978)

There is even a human sex ratio effect that fits the general pattern. After both World War I and World War II there was a small rise in the sex ratio at birth in countries involved in the conflict and a less consistent but similar trend in other countries (Table 11-5 and Figure 11-13). Warfare tends to decimate males—perhaps raising the expected reproductive success of sons; but if so it is perhaps surprising that the sex ratio effect is of such short duration. It has been hypothesized that the effect is due to a high frequency of copulation after couples are reunited and there is some evidence that high frequencies of copulation in humans may be associated with a greater number of male births.

Variation in Early Conditions: Environmental Sex Determination

We are used to thinking that sex is determined by genes or chromosomes (XY in the human male, XX in the female), but in a variety of species sex is determined by the environmental conditions the organism experiences when it is young. In various lizards, turtles, and crocodilians, for example, sex is determined during early development by the incubation temperature the embryos experience. Eggs are laid in the ground or in nests and most nest temperatures produce only males or only females, with a narrow range of temperatures produc-

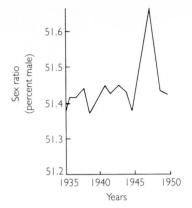

Figure 11-13

The sex ratio at birth among white people in five selected states in the United States from 1935 to 1949. Notice the sharp rise in the sex ratio after World War II. (From MacMahon and Pugh *1954)*

Table 11-5.   The sex ratio (number of males per 100 females) at birth during World War I, immediately thereafter, and shortly thereafter in countries engaged in the conflict and in neutral countries

	1915–1918	1919–1920	1921–1923
Countries Engaged in Conflict			
Germany	106.4	107.5	107.0
Austria	105.3	107.0	106.1
Belgium	105.0	106.2	105.3
Bulgaria	106.9	107.6	106.2
France	105.2	106.1	105.0
United Kingdom	104.7	105.5	104.8
Italy	105.4	105.9	105.2
Mean for 12 countries	105.8	106.9	105.8
Neutral Countries			
Denmark	105.3	105.4	105.9
Spain	109.8	109.8	109.4
Finland	106.0	106.7	106.1
Norway	105.3	106.9	105.0
Switzerland	105.2	105.5	105.2
Mean for 7 countries	106.1	106.7	106.2

Source: Russell 1936.

ing both sexes. In lizards and alligators, warm temperatures result in males, while cool temperatures give females. The reverse is true in most turtles: for example, in nature, map turtle *Graptemys* nests in shaded locations produce males, whereas nests in the open sun produce females.

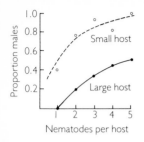

Figure 11-14

Sex determination in a nematode worm as a function of size of host (mosquito larva) and number of worms per host. Plotted here are the sex ratio in the worm *Romanomermis culicivorax* on large host (solid circles) and the sex ratio on small host (open circles) as a function of the number of nematodes per host. (*From* Bull 1983)

The adaptive interpretation of environmentally determined sex ratios assumes that some early environmental variable, such as temperature, affects later reproductive success differently for the two sexes, so that it will pay off to produce each sex under the conditions that most benefit it. If we also assume that the mother laying these eggs is unable to predict the circumstances the young will face or is unable to adjust the sex ratio of her offspring, then an adaptive adjustment can only come about if the sex of offspring is determined by the appropriate environmental conditions. For example, since the 1920's we have known that in the mermithid family of nematode worms, nourishment available to the young determines sex. Mermithid worms are free living as adults, while as larvae they parasitize insects. When the insect host is small or when there are several worm larvae per host, food available per larva decreases, resulting in smaller adults and, separately, in an increasing percentage of males (Figure 11-14). It seems reasonable to imagine that the nematodes would have difficulty predicting in advance the nutrition available per larva. In turn, size increases female fecundity and is believed to have smaller effects on male reproductive success, since male mermithids show no antagonism toward each other and since males are almost universally the smaller sex in nematodes.

A similar relationship has been found in the silverside fish *Menidia*. Large adult size increases survival in both sexes, increases fecundity in females, and probably has weaker effects on male reproductive success. Large size even seems to handicap a male's endurance over the breeding season and there is no evidence of a strong positive effect of male size on breeding success. In any case, the sex ratio effect is clear: cooler waters at 50 days after hatching produce females, while warmer waters produce males. Spawning occurs from May to July and water temperatures increase during this period. Thus, eggs laid early tend to become females, and these females have a long growing season and reach a larger adult size than the males, which hatch from later-laid eggs. Incidentally, it is not clear why sex ratios are environmentally determined in this species, since in other animals with genetic control of sex (such as seals: Table 11-2), sex ratio may also be adjusted to the time of breeding. But environmentally determined sex ratios are more extreme and this is probably their advantage. Genetic adaptations in diploid species must constantly run counter to the 50:50 mechanism of meiosis and have difficulty achieving strongly biased ratios.

Environmental sex ratio effects in reptiles are especially intriguing because they are so common and so variable (Figure 11-15). In alligators, temperature has effects on size and sex similar to those found in silversides: incubation in cool temperatures produces both femaleness and greater adult size. In many turtles, as we have noted, males are produced at cooler temperatures. Is this because male reproductive

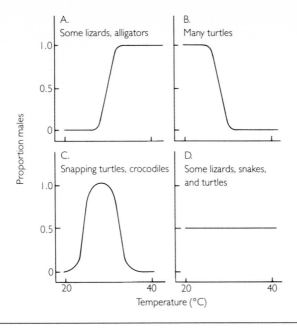

Figure 11-15

The effect of incubation temperature of eggs on the sex ratio of hatchlings in reptiles. The proportion of males is plotted as a function of incubation temperature (in Centigrade). (a) In some lizards and alligators low temperatures give females, high temperatures males. (b) In many turtles the reverse pattern is found. (c) In snapping turtles and crocodiles females are produced at low and high temperatures, males at intermediate ones. (d) Finally, in some lizards, snakes and turtles incubation temperature has no effect on the sex ratio. (From Bull 1983)

success is more benefitted by large size in these turtles? If so, we want to know why. Furthermore, in some turtles, females are produced at both low and high temperatures, while males are produced at intermediate ones. Why is this so? Finally, in some lizards, snakes, and turtles, hatchling sex ratio is not at all affected by temperature. Is this because temperature has no effect on adult size or because the two sexes are affected similarly by changes in adult size, so that there is nothing to be gained were sex associated with temperature?

The evidence on environmentally determined sex ratios opens up a world of new possibilities concerning the evolution of sex differences in reptiles. The particular way in which temperature is associated with sex in different groups implies differences among these groups in the role that adult size plays in the life of the two sexes. As in the case of ant ratios of investment, we see the potential value in linking one body of theory with another.

Variation in Early Conditions:
Parental Investment

In mammals and birds, early development takes place during the period of parental investment. Because of sexual selection, investment may differentially affect the success of males and females: males in better than average condition as adults may enjoy larger gains than females in better than average condition, while the reverse may be true when condition is poor. Since condition in adulthood is affected by investment when young, parents may prefer to raise males when there is relatively more investment available per offspring and females when there is less. At one time I thought that there was strong evidence supporting this principle in mammals, but careful scrutiny of some of the evidence fails to reveal clear trends. Nevertheless, there are now enough examples of biased sex ratios in birds and mammals to suggest that this principle sometimes operates in nature.

The best evidence for such an effect comes from red deer. Dominant females outreproduce subordinate ones by a variety of measures, including mean weight of offspring at birth (see Table 2-7). Sons of dominant females, in turn, outreproduce their sisters, while daughters of subordinate females outreproduce their brothers (Figure 11-16). As expected, maternal dominance has a positive effect on sex ratio at birth (Table 11-6).

In mammals it seems likely that differential male mortality during the period of parental investment permits more daughters to be raised in conditions of low investment. For example, female wood rats *Neotoma floridana* fed substandard diets appear progressively to kill male offspring by refusing them milk until finally they are nursing only daughters. Although males normally reach a slightly larger size by weaning than females, under food deprivation males grow less quickly than females.

Female mammals in better condition are more likely to produce larger litters, but for mammals with small litters, increasing litter size decreases the amount of investment per offspring. For example, in mule deer, females fed on a deficient diet usually produce singletons, while females fed on a good diet typically produce twins, yet the weight of each twin at birth is lower than the weight of each singleton. As expected, the sex ratio is biased appropriately: singletons are male-biased, twins are female-biased. In some other mammals (such as sheep and humans) the sex ratio decreases as litter size increases. In mammals with large litters there is usually no regular association between sex ratio and litter size, but in laboratory mice larger litters contain relatively more sons. The reason for this association is unknown.

In birds the female is XY and may be able to control sex of her offspring directly. Recent work suggests that the order in which eggs

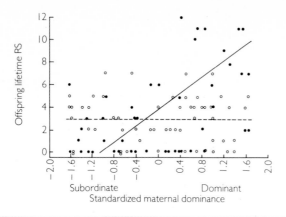

Figure 11-16

The effect of maternal dominance on a son's and a daughter's lifetime re-productive success in red deer. The offspring's lifetime reproductive success (number of grand-offspring surviving to one year of age) is plotted separately for males (closed circles) and females (open circles) as a function of their mothers' standardized dominance rank. The latter is based on the number of hinds a female dominates, divided by the number who dominate her, calculated for each segment of the population and then combined on a standardized scale. A straight line has been fitted to the male points, a dashed line to the female. (From Clutton-Brock et al. 1984)

Table 11-6.   The effect of maternal dominance rank on the sex ratio of offspring at birth (percentage males) in red deer *

	Dominance Rank		
	Low	*Medium*	*High*
Percent males born	46.9	53.9	60.6

Source: Clutton-Brock et al. 1984.

* Based on 543 births to 98 mothers separated into three
  roughly equal divisions based on rank.

are laid is associated with sex of the offspring. In the ring-billed gull *Larus delawarensis* first-laid eggs are often male, while the second is female and the third may be either sex. In gulls the adult male is slightly larger than the adult female, and the first egg is likely to be slightly heavier than the second. The third egg is markedly smaller than either and its chick may best survive when one or both siblings fail. In the lesser snow goose *Chen caerulescens* the first two eggs tend to give males, the second two, females (Table 11-7). Once again, males

Table 11-7. The number of lesser snow goose goslings, by sex, from sequential eggs in 4-egg clutches *

Sex	Order in Which Egg Is Laid				Total Number
	1st	*2nd*	*3rd*	*4th*	
Male	17	16	7	5	45
Female	10	9	17	14	50

Source: Ankney 1982.

* The trend is significant ($P < 0.01$).

are larger as adults and the first two eggs are about 5% heavier than the second two.

A more extraordinary sex ratio adjustment in birds has been discovered by Nancy Burley. Here the birds adjust the sex ratio they produce, not to the degree of parental investment but to the relative attractiveness of the couple. Attractiveness in her experiment is determined by the leg bands the birds (zebra finches) wear (see p. 256). When a male is attractive relative to his mate, more sons are produced; when he is unattractive, more daughters. This result has now been confirmed in experiments in which only one sex was banded. Attractive males (red-banded) produce more sons, attractive females (black-banded) produce more daughters, findings that make sense if we assume that attractiveness is partly sex-limited, so that the sons of an attractive male are more likely to be attractive than are his daughters. That sons of attractive males *are* more attractive—even in the absence of leg bands—has been beautifully confirmed by Burley. She showed that sons of red-banded males (who themselves remain unbanded) are preferred by females who have never seen them or their fathers! Why are these males more attractive? Do they pick up an attractive self-image from their fathers, are they more attractive because their mothers are superior, or do they receive more investment when young? Burley is planning new experiments to discriminate among these possibilities.

Sex Ratio Adjustment at Conception

If at the time of conception a female could predict the amount of investment her offspring would receive, then it would be adaptive for her to adjust the sex ratio then. Several lines of evidence suggest that this may occur. Over several years of the life of a captive rat colony, the sex ratio being produced varied inversely with the weight of the adrenal glands of the adults. The adrenals are known to respond to the stress of crowding by increasing in size. These findings suggest that when crowding is intense and resources per individual few, relatively more daughters are produced. To test this possibility, ACTH—a hormone produced by the adrenal glands—was injected into female rats during their period of sexual receptivity. A control group was mated in a similar fashion but received no injections of ACTH. In those females given ACTH, the sex ratio produced was significantly biased toward daughters. Since the average litter size of the injected females was about the same as that of the non-injected ones, the sex ratio adjustment to ACTH was probably achieved around the time of conception.

It is not known how sex ratio adjustment at conception takes place, but we suspect that the sex ratio may be affected by the amount of time elapsing between ovulation and fertilization. In rabbits, ovulation is closely associated with the onset of estrus, typically occurring about 12 hours after. The later a male is mated to a female during her estrus cycle, the higher is the percentage of sons born. In species of whales the sex ratio near conception may change as a function of time of year in which breeding takes place. For example, in humpback whales, females who conceive early in the season conceive nearly three times as many males as females, while females conceiving late in the season conceive only 25% more sons than daughters. By contrast, in the blue whale the sex ratio near conception is unchanged by time of breeding.

Variation in the Human Sex Ratio

Humans are potentially one large, interbreeding population. But in fact, the chance that two people from opposite ends of the earth will pair with each other is vanishingly small. Thus, populations from around the world can be treated as separate breeding units, each one of which is expected to satisfy Fisher's rule.

There exist good data from many different societies around the world on the sex ratio at birth. As we see in Table 11-8, the sex ratio is almost always male-biased at birth, although the degree of male bias varies considerably. In eastern Europe the sex ratio at birth approaches 110:100, while the lowest sex ratios, approaching 1:1, are found among West African peoples and their descendants in the New World (compare non-white and white people in the United States). In India until recently, male-biased sex ratios at birth were compounded by infanticide preferentially directed against daughters. Sex ratios among children in some sections of India reach values exceeding 2:1. Likewise in Taiwan, male-biased sex ratios at birth become relatively more male-biased by the end of the period of parental investment.

What can explain this variation in the human sex ratio at birth? Residency patterns affect the degree to which children may later make a

Table 11-8. The Sex Ratio at Birth (Number of Males per 100 Females) in Various Countries *

St. Lucia	98.5
Grenada	100.0
Barbados	101.6
U.S. (nonwhites)	102.2
Jamaica	102.8
Chile	103
Panama	103.9
Puerto Rico	104.4
El Salvador	104.5
France	104.9
Spain	105.3
Italy	105.5
Japan	105.5
U.S. (whites)	105.7
Mexico	106.5
Portugal	106.7
Poland	107
Hungary	107.2
Hong Kong	109.1

Source: Visaria 1967.

* Data are taken from countries with relatively complete
  registration of births.

return investment to their parents. For example, in strongly patrilocal, patrilineal societies adult males live close to their parents and other male relatives. They may, indeed, live as adults in their parents' home. In such societies, males may contribute resources to their parents that their sisters do not, since the females disperse from their kin group to marry outsiders. This return investment decreases the net cost of the male to his parents. Patrilineal, patrilocal residency patterns are common in many parts of India and may explain male-biased sex ratios as well as female-biased infanticide. Female infanticide is also known among the Eskimos, where virtually all of the food comes from hunting, an exclusively male enterprise. By contrast, matrilineal, matrilocal societies are more common in West Africa, where sex ratios at birth are often close to 1:1. Although these associations are suggestive, so far as I know, no one has attempted to demonstrate carefully a correlation between residency patterns and the primary sex ratio in human populations. This would be valuable to do.

In considering whether the overall ratio of investment is 1:1 in human populations, we must remember that males are individually more expensive than females. Male resting metabolic rate is 5% to 10%

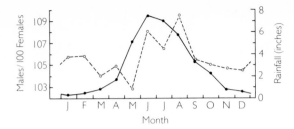

Figure 11-17

The relationship between rainfall at conception and sex ratio at birth in humans. Shown are the number of males born per 100 females, plotted at the time of conception (broken line), and the number of inches of rainfall (solid line) as a function of month of year in Perth, Australia. (Lyster and Bishop 1965)

Table 11-9.   The sex ratio at birth (number of males per 100 females) in good and bad harvest years in rural Portugal from 1671–1720*

Harvest Years Were:	Average Number of Male Births per 100 Female Births
Bad (14)	90.7
Good (35)	112.10

Source: Cowgill and Johnson 1971.

* The difference is significant. Good years are those in which the price of grain was low; bad years are those in which the price of grain was high.

higher than that of females, and males are larger after puberty. Yet in some populations, as we noted, the sex ratio remains biased toward males throughout the period of investment. In others, it does not drop as low as needed to guarantee equivalency. Perhaps this is because in many societies males return to their parents some of the investment they receive. This return could come via work performed while still under parental care or while adult.

Within a population the sex ratio produced varies according to circumstances. There seems to be a general rule for more favorable circumstances to be associated with the production of males. For example, in Australia, rainfall at the time of conception and in Portugal, good harvest at the time of birth are both associated with greater production of sons (Figure 11-17 and Table 11-9). An important variable affecting sex ratio in several human populations is socioeconomic status. In Table 11-10 we see that in the United States, people high in socioeconomic status tend to produce sons: they have about an 8% higher chance of producing a son than people at the bottom of the scale. Similar effects have been noted in England and in India. Income, in turn, has a very strong effect on the chance that a man will marry: in

Table 11-10.   Sex ratio at birth as a function of socioeconomic status, United States *

Socioeconomic Status	Sex Ratio
0–1.9	95.6
2–3.9	100.0
4–5.9	104.9
≥ 6	103.9

Source: Teitelbaum and Mantel 1971.

* The trend is significant. The sample has been corrected
  for effects of race and parity. Socioeconomic status is
  a hybrid of earnings, years of education, and status of
  occupation.

1960, men at the bottom of the scale remained single more than 30% of the time, while men at the top of the scale were single less than 5% of the time. Income has a much smaller effect on chance of marrying in women, and the effect goes partly in the opposite direction, so we expect women at the low end of the socioeconomic scale to have a higher chance of marrying and bearing children than men at the same end of the same scale. Some tendency for females to marry up the socioeconomic scale is a natural consequence of the sex ratio bias we have described, and vice versa.

The sex ratio in human twins is about 3% lower than the sex ratio of singletons. If this variation is adaptive, then we expect that the reproductive success of a male twin will be lower than the reproductive success of a female twin. The only evidence comes from the genealogical records of the Mormons: a twin of either sex achieves lower reproductive success than a singleton, but the decline is stronger among males (Table 11-11).

A similar association is found for schizophrenia. Women who have suffered or are suffering from schizophrenia tend to produce relatively more daughters (324 sons for every 417 daughters). Since schizophrenia is a trait that children to some degree inherit, we can study the reproductive success of male and female schizophrenics to see whether the sex ratio adjustment is in the right direction. Male schizophrenics have a more difficult time marrying than do female schizophrenics, and as a result their reproductive success is lower (Table 11-12). But schizophrenia occurs in only about 1% of the population, and such individuals have low reproductive success whether male or female, so it may be doubted whether natural selection has fashioned an adaptive sex ratio response to schizophrenia. Apparently, however, schizophrenia, like many other adverse conditions, affects males more severely than females, and natural selection has fashioned a general, adaptive response to negative conditions.

Table 11-11.   The effect of being a twin on various measures of reproductive success in humans *

	Effect of Being a Twin (percent change)	
	Male	*Female*
Number of children born	−7.4	−3.6
Percent childless	+8.3	−12.2
Reproductive span	−8.4	−5.2
Number of children born to those with at least one child	−7.7	−6.6
Lifespan	−2.1	+0.3

Sources: Wyshak and White 1969; Wyshak 1978.

* Data are from 18th-century and 19th-century Mormons in the United States, based on 6049 twins and 8929 siblings. The decrease in number of children born is significant for both sexes. The decrease in lifespan for males is significant. For all measures, twins are compared to their singleton siblings. Reproductive span is the number of years between the births of the first child and the last child.

Table 11-12.   Reproductive success of men and women hospitalized with schizophrenia *

	1934–1936		1954–1956	
	Men	*Women*	*Men*	*Women*
Children per patient	0.6	1.1	0.8	1.2
Children per marriage	1.8	1.9	1.7	1.9
Percent ever married	32.7	58.8	48.4	63.8

Source: Erlenmeyer-Kimling et al. 1969.

* Reproductive success measured in 1941 for those hospitalized in 1934–1936 and in 1961 for the others. Total sample is about 18,000 patients in the United States.

Summary

The primary sex ratio is controlled by natural selection. The sex ratio we expect to find under outbreeding in nature is that at which return per unit work on a son equals that on a daughter. This will occur when total investment in the two sexes is equal. This theory explains why 1:1 sex ratios are so common in nature, and it also explains deviations from 1:1. In particular it explains the inverse association in ants and wasps between the relative cost of a male and the number of males produced, and it explains the association in mammals between male-biased sex ratios at or near conception and differential male mortality *in utero*.

Female-biased ratios of investment in certain mites and insects are explained by the prevalence in these species of sib mating: where siblings commonly mate, parents are selected to economize on sons. In ants 1:3 ratios of investment apparently result from the closer relatedness of workers to their sisters (¾) than to their brothers (¼).

Wherever possible, individuals are expected to adjust the sex ratios they produce to any variable that predicts differences between the sexes in their expected reproductive success. There is good evidence that parasitoid wasps adjust the sex ratio they produce to the chance that their offspring will practice sib mating. Evidence from a variety of species, including plants, show that individuals tend to respond to fluctuations in the population sex ratio by producing the underrepresented sex. In some species, sex itself is determined early in development, apparently in order to permit development of each sex in conditions better suited for it. In birds and mammals, parents may sometimes adjust the sex ratio to available parental investment, usually reserving females for conditions of lower investment. In mammals and birds sex ratio adjustment may sometimes occur at conception.

In humans the sex ratio at birth varies across populations, which may be associated with patrilocal residence patterns. There is evidence that total investment in males is greater than that in females, possibly because males return more of the investment in work for the parents. People low on the socioeconomic scale have an almost 10% higher chance of producing a daughter. This is probably adaptive, since males at the low end of the scale are outreproduced by their sisters.

Altogether, the evidence on the sex ratio gives strong support to our underlying system of cost-benefit analysis, to kinship theory and the way in which we compute degrees of relatedness, and to our understanding of sexual selection.

Chapter 12

Differential Mortality
by Sex, Especially
in Humans

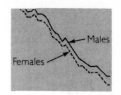

SOME PEOPLE ARE reluctant to admit to biological differences between the human sexes. They grant that menstruation, gestation, and lactation belong to women and ejaculation to men, but beyond this they believe the sexes are essentially identical. Some of this view is undoubtedly a response to centuries of claims that women were biologically inferior and that men were created or selected at the level of the species to perform wonderful, higher-level functions denied to women. The approach taken in this book gives no support for the notion of biological inferiority. Each sex, far from having evolved traits at the level of the species, is governed by individual reproductive advantage, sometimes in conflict with that of the other, and sex differences have evolved because of an underlying difference in the work each invests— or fails to invest—in the raising of offspring. If anything, male traits now threaten human species survival, since the potentially high reproductive success of males more easily tempts them into policies of aggression and aggrandizement.

If we find no support in our thinking for the notion of biological inferiority, we may feel more free to consider the possibility of biological differences. One difference between the sexes that is often overlooked and implies a wealth of other differences is the tendency throughout life for men to suffer higher mortality rates than women. In this chapter we review the facts concerning differential mortality by sex in humans. We then consider a societal explanation for this difference and a non-functional biological explanation. We review the facts concerning two other species in nature and we conclude with an explanation derived from our theory of parental investment and sexual selection. In organizing the material this way, we will take the opposite approach to the one we have taken so far. That is, instead of deriving a general principle and illustrating it with a variety of species, we will begin with a phenomenon in one species and consider alternative explanations. These possible explanations will inevitably draw us into evidence from other animals, which, in turn, will suggest an explanation we might have derived in the first place. In this manner, we gain a partial test of our thinking, seeing to what degree we can begin with a phenomenon and end with an explanation.

In Humans, Differential Male Mortality Is Nearly Universal and Has a Common Pattern

In the United States today, males die faster than females, at all ages and for all segments of the population and regardless of the level of mortality. This is true of most populations in the rest of the world, again regardless of the level of mortality. In particular, it is true of those hunter-gatherers for which we have evidence. Exceptions occur in India, Pakistan, and Sri Lanka and appear to result from a very pronounced preferential treatment of males in those countries. Differential male mortality is true of past populations, as well: data from 19th-century England, Sweden, and the United States show differential male mortality, and in the United States Clark observed in 1786 that "human life in males is more brittle than in females" (see Figure 12-1).

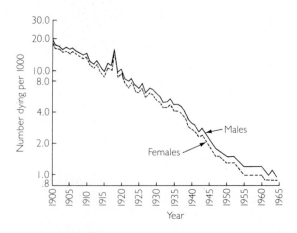

Figure 12-1

Annual mortality rates for males and females aged 1–4 years for different years of the 20th century. Rates are for the United States, per 1000 individuals. Note that despite a continuing reduction in level of mortality, the sex difference is maintained. (*From* Shapiro et al. 1968)

In Figure 12-2 we see plotted the percentage of excess male mortality as a function of age. We note that males suffer approximately 50% higher mortality throughout childhood, that the greatest differences between the sexes' mortality rates occur during adulthood (ages 20–50), and that males suffer higher mortality rates than females throughout the senescent period. In addition, there is abundant evidence that males suffer higher mortality *in utero* than do females; the sex ratio at three months after conception is at least 120:100, falling to about 106:100 at birth. This pattern of differential male mortality as a function of age appears to characterize many human populations. In the exceptional populations in which male mortality is reduced compared to that of females, a similar pattern is observed, but female mortality is increased overall. Finally, the senescent decline, which begins for both sexes in the late twenties, appears to accelerate more rapidly for males than females. In Figure 12-2 the increased rate of differential male mortality after age 40 reflects an increase in senescence-related illnesses.

Nearly All Causes of Mortality Show a Sex Difference

Causes of mortality can be organized into three categories: disease, stress and trauma, and murder and suicide.

Disease. Males carry more infections than do females. For most kinds of disease, males are more often infected than females, and the

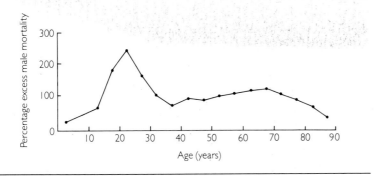

Figure 12-2

Excess male mortality in humans as a function of age. The percentage excess male mortality as a function of age (in years) for Canadians in 1976. The peak in early adulthood is mainly due to sex differences in mortality from accidents and homicide. (From Daly and Wilson 1983)

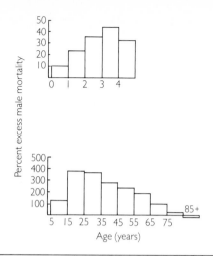

Figure 12-3

Percent excess male mortality from all accidents, as a function of age (in years). Based on data from the United States, 1959–1961. (*From* Iskrant and Joliet 1968)

infections are more severe. This sex difference begins at birth. Male mortality from disease is higher than female for most kinds of disease.

Stress and Trauma. Males die more frequently from accidents and wounds. In Figure 12-3 we see the percentage of excess male mortality as a function of age. For every age up to 85 years, males suffer higher mortality from accidents. Even in the first four years of life males suffer about 30% higher mortality from accidents. By adulthood they suffer 400% excess mortality compared to females. Only after age 85 is female mortality from accidents higher than male, due to accidental falls.

This sex difference in mortality from accidents is true for nearly every category of accident, including falls, accidental poisoning, drowning, firearm accidents, automobile accidents (whether the victim is a pedestrian or a driver), and fires and explosions. Males suffer higher mortality from these causes throughout life with the exception that fires and explosions claim the two sexes equally often between the ages of 3 and 14, and elderly women suffer differentially from falls. As pedestrians, boys suffer between 50% and 100% higher mortality from car accidents for every year between birth and age 4. Even inside automobiles males suffer 10% to 20% higher mortality for all ages between 1 and 4, although there is no such difference between birth and age 1. Data from rats show that the same trauma produces higher mortality in males than in females. In humans the ratio of injuries to

Table 12-1.   Annual death rate per 100,000 from homicide, by age and sex: United States, 1959–1961

Age (years)	Males	Females
All ages	7.0	2.4
Under 1	4.6	4.2
1	1.3	1.2
2	0.9	1.0
3	0.7	0.7
4	0.7	0.4
5–14	0.6	0.5
15–24	8.9	2.7
25–34	14.3	4.7
35–44	12.2	4.1
45–54	9.6	2.8
55–64	6.6	1.7
65–74	4.7	1.3
75–84	3.9	1.6
85 +	3.8	1.8

Source: Iskrant and Joliet 1968.

deaths (from accidents) is lower in males than in females; that is, males more often die of their injuries than do females (Figure 12-4), probably partly because they withstand injuries less well but also because the injuries they sustain are more severe.

Human males die more quickly from starvation than do females, a difference that is also found in rats, pigs, and chickens. For example, in a study in which pigs were fed inadequate diets, 87% of the females were alive a year later, while only 22% of the males survived. Nutritional stress increases risk of infection, but male sex hormones result in greater utilization of proteins, thereby making males more vulnerable.

Murder and Suicide. Males suffer differentially from murder and suicide. They are more often murdered than females, and this sex difference even holds for infants and children, though the difference is slight during these years (see Table 12-1). Surprisingly enough, there is a strong sex difference in the tendency to be murdered over age 85. Males die more frequently in warfare and from daring behavior such as wild driving. And males have higher rates of suicide.

There are three general explanations for why males die faster than females: (1) Society exposes males to greater stress than females; (2) the unguarded X chromosome of the male predisposes him to greater mortality; and (3) sexual selection acting on males predisposes them to higher mortality. We consider each of these explanations in turn.

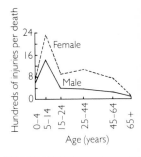

Figure 12-4

Ratio of injuries to deaths for all accidents, as a function of age and sex. Males die more frequently from injuries than do females. (*From* Iskrant and Joliet 1968)

Societal Stress

It is often argued that society reserves different roles for men and women and subjects men to considerably more stress. Males are encouraged from an early age to be more aggressive and competitive than females, and this behavior subjects them to higher mortality. Although this explanation has some surface plausibility, all the available evidence argues against this factor playing much of a role in generating differential male mortality.

Males die faster than females *in utero*, a time when society has not yet had an opportunity to shape the sexes differently. Males die faster than females in infancy, likewise before sex-role differentiation is very pronounced, and causes of mortality in infancy are similar to those that act throughout life. Indeed, in some human populations the smallest difference between the sexes in mortality rates occurs when sex-role differentiation is the greatest, that is, in early adulthood.

It is difficult to subject this explanation to a direct test, since we would need to raise the two sexes in identical environments from birth. But a partial test has been achieved by Francis Madigan, who studied the survival of men and women who were members of a religious order from the age of about 20 years. The daily work regime in the order was very similar for the two sexes. Diet, housing, and medical care were very similar, and many temptations were absent. For example, Madigan states, "While in the general public, single men are more given to dissipation than single women, a life of dissipation is equally out of the question for both sexes in religious communities." Some differences remained. For example, until recently Brothers—but not Sisters—were permitted to smoke. This is potentially a serious bias, but the rate of smoking in males was probably low.

When mortality rates for the Brothers and Sisters were compared to the population at large, it was discovered that the Brothers and Sisters lived longer than their counterparts on the outside but that the sex difference in mortality found in the general population was exactly maintained. Thus life expectancy at age 15 in the general population in 1950 was 54.5 years for men and 57 for women. For the Brothers and Sisters it was 60 years and 63, respectively. Thus each sex in the religious community showed a 10% gain in expectation of life. The sex difference was maintained over a period of years (see Figure 12-5).

Finally, data from other animals suggest a general cause for differential male mortality. Considering only mammals, it appears to be generally true that males suffer higher mortality than females. In well-studied species, the pattern of differential mortality appears similar to that for humans. For example, in cattle, sheep, and several species of whales, there is differential male mortality *in utero*. In various species, males likewise show differential rates of senescence. It is difficult to be-

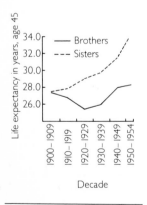

Figure 12-5

Life expectancy, in years, at age 45 for various decades of the 20th century. Subjects were members of Roman Catholic religious orders in the United States. (*From* Madigan 1957)

lieve that a theory of societal stress, which fails to explain the human data, could ever explain the parallel animal evidence.

The Unguarded X Chromosome of the Male

If social factors appear not to explain differential male mortality in humans, it is natural to consider a biological cause. Many people have argued that it is the chromosomal difference between the sexes that causes higher male mortality. A female's sex chromosomes are XX, a male's are XY. The X and the Y in the male are unpaired, thus every gene located on the male's X chromosome is found only one time in the male's genome. This means that negative traits on the X chromosome will at once be expressed in males, but since these traits are usually recessive, they will often be unexpressed in females. This is because at the same locus on her paired chromosome, the alternate gene will usually be present. For example, hemophilia is an almost exclusively male trait. It is found on the X chromosome and in females is usually guarded by a gene that brings about normal clotting of the blood. A female heterozygous at the hemophilia locus will produce sons, half of whom will inherit the hemophilia gene, and lacking any compensating gene, will express the trait and bleed to death before reproducing. Likewise, color blindness is a trait located on the X chromosome and is about ten times as frequent in men as in women, since only females double-recessive for the trait are color-blind. In this fashion, the unguarded X chromosome of the male may predispose him to higher mortality (as for hemophilia). But the evidence suggests that this cannot be a general explanation. There are three lines of evidence.

First, differential mortality by sex cannot be predicted from a knowledge of the distribution of sex-determining mechanisms in animals. In mammals and reptiles, males are usually XY and females XX, and males suffer higher mortality than do females. In fish, however, both sexes are usually XX and yet males suffer higher mortality. In birds, females are XY and males XX, yet males still suffer higher mortality rates in those species of birds that lack male parental investment. Thus differential male mortality seems to occur without regard to the system of sex determination. In birds it is better predicted by a social variable: the degree of male parental investment.

The second reason we cannot accept the unguarded X chromosome of the male as a general explanation for higher male mortality is that it is possible to increase the rate of mutations on the X chromosome—for example, by irradiation, but such treatments do not result in an increase in differential male mortality. Indeed, the predicted effect from X-linked mutations is far too small to account for the pervasive pattern of differential male mortality (see also Figure 12-6).

Male   Female

Accidents	35.1
Influenza & Pneumonia	15.7
Congenital Malformations	12.3
Malignant Diseases	11.7
Gastroenteritis	3.8

Accidents	26.3
Influenza & Pneumonia	14.0
Congenital Malformations	12.4
Malignant Diseases	9.5
Gastroenteritis	2.8

Figure 12-6

The five leading causes of death in children aged 1–4 years: United States, 1959–1961. Rates are per 100,000 per year. Notice that the only category with a strong expectation of an X-chromosome effect—"congenital malformations"—shows no sex difference. (*From* Shapiro et al. 1968)

Finally, studies of castrated male mammals show that it is the sex hormones and not the chromosomal constitution that cause differential male mortality. For example, since domestic cats are often subjected to gonadectomy, we can compare the lifespan of intact animals with the lifespan of those who have lost their gonads. In one group of gonadectomized cats, the median age of gonadectomy was six months, and 85% of the gonadectomized cats had the operation before one year of age. Gonadectomy increased the lifespan of females only slightly, from 7.7 years to 8.2 years, whereas it had a strong effect on the lifespan of males, increasing it from 5.3 years to 8.1 years. In other words, among those who had lost their gonads, males had the same lifespan as females, even though they remained XY. In short, the shorter lifespan of intact males versus intact females was due to the presence of the male's testes and not to his XY chromosomes. The earlier the castration, the greater the increase in lifespan, and intact males tended to suffer more infections and greater trauma than did gonadectomized males.

Similar data exist from human beings. In the early 20th century in Kansas, mentally retarded men were often castrated; thus it is possible to compare the lifespan of castrated men with that of intact men, both groups living in institutions for the mentally retarded. As in cats, the earlier the castration, the greater the increase in lifespan. Likewise, intact males suffered more infections and more trauma than did castrated males. Castration had a marked effect on lifespan. Castrated males survived on average to age 69, while intact males survived only to age 56. The chief difference that distinguished intact males from either eunuchs or intact females was the high incidence of death in intact males from infections. There was a tendency for castrated males to die more frequently from cancer (also true of cats), and a tendency to die less frequently from trauma.

These studies show that it is not the chromosomal constitution of males that causes their higher mortality, but sexual differentiation dependent on the gonads. This is just as well, because if unguarded chromosomes caused large mortality, we would then need to explain why they were not eliminated long ago. The chromosomal hypothesis is, in fact, a typical example of a non-functional explanation: an important phenomenon is explained away as a by-product of something else whose benefit is never specified.

Differential Male Mortality in Belding's Ground Squirrels and in Red Deer

If differential male mortality is not a function of the sex chromosomes but of sexual differentiation, then we expect there to exist associated benefits, measured in terms of reproductive success, that outweigh the costs of greater mortality. The only time for these to be registered is during the breeding season. We expect that the traits that cause increased mortality in males will be the same traits that give high reproductive success when the males do survive. Let us consider these possibilities by reviewing the evidence on differential mortality by sex in two well-studied species in nature: the Belding's ground squirrel and the red deer. Evidence from the two species is complementary and suggests that male–male competition for access to females has selected for traits in males that lower their survival relative to females.

In most mammals, males disperse more widely than females, resulting in a higher disappearance rate of marked males, independent of differential mortality by sex. To correct for this bias in the Belding's ground squirrel, a large area around the study area was systematically trapped so as to capture about 80% of those present, which permitted most migrant individuals to be included in the sample. Extensive capture-recapture data spanning more than ten years demonstrates a clear pattern of differential male mortality, which is small in the first two years but large and significant for subsequent years (Figure 12-7). Males that survive their first winter typically remain in the population only 1.1 years; females remain 1.6 years. The result is an overall sex ratio biased toward females (2:3), with older age classes consisting increasingly of females (Figure 12-8).

Breaking down mortality by time of year reveals that differential male mortality occurs at the time of reproduction. Although mortality over the winter is high, claiming nearly 70% of all juveniles and nearly 50% of all adults, the sex differences are small and statistically insignificant (Table 12-2). By contrast, mortality throughout the active season is strongly biased against males and appears to peak at the time of male conflict for access to females. This is most intense from the 10th day of emergence to the 30th; between the 20th and the 30th days

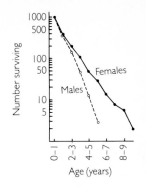

Figure 12-7

Sex difference in survivorship in Belding's ground squirrels. This graph shows the number of males and females surviving out of an initial 1000, as a function of age. (*From* Sherman and Morton 1984)

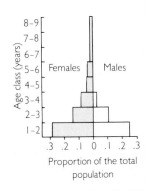

Figure 12-8

Proportion of the total population consisting of various age-sex classes, in Belding's ground squirrels. Age is measured in years. Notice that because of differential male mortality, males are increasingly rare among older animals. (*From* Sherman and Morton 1984)

Table 12-2. Percent disappeared (and presumed dead) of males and females for various periods during the breeding season (above ground) in Belding's ground squirrels *

Breeding Season Period	Percent Disappeared	
	Males	Females
First 30 days	26.5%	16.3%
Second 30 days	22.7	11.4
First 10 days	24.1	—
Second 10 days	25.9	—
Third 10 days	50.0	—

Source: Sherman and Morton 1984.

* Male and female values are significantly different and males disappear significantly more often in the third 10-day period compared to the earlier two 10-day periods.

50% of all males disappear, significantly more than before or after. Clashes between males are common during the mating season and, especially in the presence of females, may result in injury, so that more males show signs of injury than do females (Table 12-3). Indeed, three males were seen to be killed outright by other males, in each case because an artery in the neck was severed. Males were also run over by cars about twice as often as females, almost certainly a consequence of their greater dispersal. In summary, differential male mortality in Belding's ground squirrels seems to be the direct and indirect consequence of male–male competition for access to females.

In red deer, males appear to suffer differential mortality when young and later when adult. In the careful study of Clutton-Brock and his colleagues, sample sizes were too small for differences within age classes to be significant, but males suffered higher mortality at all ages except 3 to 6, when mortality among breeding females is high and males are not yet breeding. As population numbers increased, a drop in the survival of adult males—but not in the survival of adult females—was noted. These findings are consistent with evidence from other deer, which shows higher mortality among yearling and two-year-old males and higher adult male mortality when numbers are high or food is short.

Differential male mortality when red deer are young may result from the importance of large size for them as adults. As we have noted elsewhere (p. 36), larger males are more successful in the rut and leave more surviving offspring, which has apparently selected for faster growth rates in young males. To achieve these rates, however, males must sacrifice part of their fat reserves, which act as a buffer

Table 12-3.   Percent of adult males and females with particular kinds of injuries, in Belding's ground squirrels

Injury	Percent of Animals Sustaining Injury	
	Males	*Females*
Torn ear	17%	8%
Torn throat	22	0
Pulled-out toenail	33	13
Pulled-out eyeball	6	0
Broken toe	28	4
Broken tooth	11	4
Broken neck	6	0
Broken shoulder	6	0
Infected foot	22	8
Infected neck	28	0
Infected eye	11	0

Source: Sherman and Morton 1984.

against lean times, especially the winter. Smaller fat reserves, in fact, characterize many male mammals. Consistent with this trend, male red deer also reduce their growth rates less in winter than do females. Poor survival of adult males is believed to be a direct result of high energy expenditure during the rut, which leaves males in poor condition to face the winter. Their larger size only makes matters worse.

In summary, in both species—Belding's ground squirrels and red deer—sexual selection seems to have favored traits in males that reduce their survival but aid them in aggressive male–male competition for females. In each case, breeding females are a sufficiently clumped resource that some males can achieve high reproductive success by aggressively excluding others from females. This immediately suggests that high variation in reproductive success is important in generating differential mortality by sex. How might this be?

The Importance of Relative Parental Investment

Why would we expect males to be predisposed to higher mortality? For species with negligible male parental investment the key predisposing factor is the high potential reproductive success of a male. Imagine that an animal is trading mortality rate prior to adulthood for an increase in its reproductive success at adulthood, assuming survival. Such an animal will be selected to suffer a one-half reduction in survival if this is associated with more than double the reproductive success in adulthood. Likewise, it will be selected to suffer a 75% reduction in survival if this is associated with a more than quadrupled reproductive success. To specify to what extent we expect one sex to be selected to incur higher mortality rates, we must know the possibilities for increasing reproductive success. Because of a male's trivial parental investment, he typically has a high potential reproductive success, much higher than that of a conspecific female, and this should predispose him to higher mortality. In effect males pursue a high-risk–high-gain strategy, and the high potential gain selects for any traits that give the gain, even at a cost of higher mortality, as long as this mortality is not so great that it cancels the gain. Other things being equal, we also expect the traits that cause the higher mortality to be precisely those that confer advantages to males in the breeding season through success in male conflict or in being chosen by a female. That female choice can cause differential male mortality is supported by observations of differential male mortality in *Drosophila* and in bower birds and birds of paradise, all species in which male–male interference has been strongly reduced, male reproductive success depending mostly on female choice.

Note that differential male mortality is, to some degree, self-correcting. That is, as the degree of differential mortality increases the adult sex ratio shifts more toward females. This should reduce variance in RS among the surviving males, thus reducing selection for further differential mortality. Perhaps this helps explain why we fail to see more extreme patterns of differential mortality by sex.

An ideal test of these ideas would be to compare species lacking male parental investment that differ in variation in male RS. We expect that the greater the variation, the greater will be the degree of differential male mortality. Unfortunately, I know of no data of this sort. The nearest is evidence from lizards. We know that in lizards, adult sex ratios closely reflect patterns of differential mortality by sex. We also know that in territorial species, sexual dimorphism in body size is closely related to the ratio of the home range size of a male to a female (see also pp. 336–337). The latter, in turn, gives us a rough measure of the degree of variation in male RS. As expected, in territorial lizards there is a negative correlation between the adult sex ratio and sexual dimorphism in body size. This strongly suggests that where variation in male RS is large, there is strong differential male mortality. Similar evidence comes from the grouse family: the adult sex ratio is more female-biased in species with greater sexual dimorphism in body weight (males being larger) (Figure 12-9).

Monogamous species give us another test of these ideas, since variation in reproductive success is similar for the two sexes and thus mortality rates are expected to be similar. In most monogamous birds,

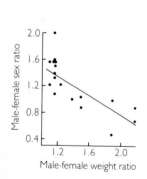

Figure 12-9

Adult sex ratio as a function of the ratio of a male's weight to a female's weight, in various species of grouse. Many of the species with low weight ratios are monogamous. Adult sex ratio is measured in the autumn and is assumed to reflect differential mortality. Thus, where males are especially large—relative to females—they are especially vulnerable to mortality. (*From Wittenberger 1978*)

however, females suffer higher mortality than males do. One possible explanation goes as follows. If males invest more than half of what females do in each offspring but less than what females invest, then male–male competition may be small, since each male invests so much that he can usually only pair with a single female. But if each male invests less than each female, then males will suffer less mortality because of their lower investment. This interpretation hinges on a sharp reduction in male–male competition due to high male parental investment, so that mortality rates primarily reflect differences in degree of parental investment. This idea would be supported if higher rates of differential female mortality correlated with lower degrees of male investment.

Why do humans fail to fit the monogamous bird pattern? Certainly the evolution of monogamy is far more recent in humans than in birds, being a matter of hundreds of thousands of years in our case and tens of millions in the case of birds. Although monogamous birds show a sharp reduction in male–male competition, our own reduction occurs only within the group. We appear to have built on a chimpanzee proclivity for organized intertroop conflict and murder to produce a sexual selection extravaganza, in the form of full-scale war: the death of many or all male combatants, the capture of concubines or rape of the defeated women, the plunder of wealth, and the enslaving of peoples. Perhaps the recency of human monogamy and the continuation of male conflict, especially at the group level, explain the human conformity to the general mammalian pattern.

I do not believe that there is any one male trait that causes differential mortality across species. Indeed, the human evidence suggests that almost every male trait is associated with increased mortality. Perhaps the most we can say is that males usually lead a more expensive life. For example, greater adult size in red deer males appears to be achieved at a cost of lower fat reserves and lowered survival in winter among young males. Male–male competition is itself expensive in energy. Red deer males do not feed during the rut and this is a common pattern in many breeding male animals: sharp reduction in food intake. In addition, female choice may favor expensive traits in males precisely because these reveal ability to accrue resources (see pp. 354–355).

Summary

In most human societies males suffer higher mortality rates than do females, and this throughout their life, including the time *in utero*. The exceptional cases are often associated with a marked, society-wide bias against women. In the United States almost all causes of mortality act more harshly against males of all ages, including murder, accidents, and infectious diseases.

It is easy to show that differential male mortality in humans does not result from a difference in the way in which the two sexes are treated by the larger society. It is likewise clear that the difference in sex chromosomes between the two sexes cannot account for the pattern of differential male mortality. Instead it seems likely that males suffer higher mortality than do females because in the past they have enjoyed higher potential reproductive success, and this has selected for traits that are positively associated with high reproductive success but at a cost of decreased survival. Evidence from Belding's ground squirrels and red deer suggests that males suffer differential mortality as a direct or indirect consequence of male–male competition for females. In red deer the same factor known to be associated with male reproductive success—large size—appears to cause increased mortality among young males.

In monogamous birds, males suffer lower mortality than do females, probably because they commonly invest less in the young than do females but invest enough so that male–male competition is sharply reduced. Despite their monogamy, humans probably conform to the general mammalian pattern because the monogamy is evolutionarily recent and male–male conflict has been retained, especially in intergroup relations.

In general, we seem to have had some success in beginning with a phenomenon and ending with an explanation based on natural selection. Alternative, non-functional explanations from sociology and biology have been shown to be clearly inadequate. While we are able to explain differential male mortality in species lacking male parental investment and differential female mortality in monogamous birds, the comparative evidence on rate of differential mortality by sex is not yet developed enough to give us a definitive test of our theory. The best we can say is that in territorial lizards there is evidence that greater variation in male reproductive success may be associated with stronger differential male mortality.

Throughout this chapter we have seen the value of considering our own species in a wider context: to arrive at an explanation of an important human phenomenon we are inevitably drawn into evidence from other creatures. In the future, evidence from this source will probably be decisive in our interpretation of the human phenomenon.

Chapter 13

The Evolution of Sex

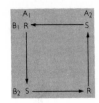

Perhaps the deepest mystery in all of biology concerns the meaning of sexual reproduction. Why is sex the rule throughout the living world? Until recently biologists were hardly aware there was a problem. The belief was that sex speeded up the rate of evolution, so that over long periods of time sexual species replaced asexual by virtue of their more rapid evolutionary response to environmental change. Then in the 1970's it came to be seen that, from the standpoint of parental investment, sex is a very inefficient form of reproduction. In a sexual species half of all investment is being spent on males, who in most species do not make any parental investment in the young, while in asexual clones all offspring are daughters and all of these grow up to invest. Not only should asexual species more rapidly occupy ecological space shared with sexual species, but an asexual mutant appearing in a sexual species should begin to double in frequency, and within a few generations the entire species should have become asexual. Given such a huge defect, how is it that sex has not only survived in evolution but has become the dominant, and even exclusive, form of reproduction in group after group?

The most obvious effect of sex is the production of genetically variable offspring. Asexual reproduction usually results in offspring that are genetically identical copies of their mothers, but sex, through meiosis and recombination, gives rise to a wide array of genetically unique offspring. There must be some positive value associated with the production of genetic variability, but what exactly is it?

In this chapter we shall try to understand the advantages of producing genetically variable young. We will begin with a review of the older theories and then turn to the crisis that was precipitated in biology when biologists appreciated the disadvantages of sex to the individual. We will review some of the attempts made to explain the advantages of sex, and concentrate on the most promising, which argues that sex is an adaptation to interspecific competition, especially pressure from parasites. We review the factors associated with the occurrence of asexuality in nature and conclude with some implications of the new view for understanding breeding adaptations in sexual species.

The Rate of Evolution

Until the 1960's biologists believed that sex was advantageous because it allowed beneficial mutations appearing in different individuals to be rapidly combined into a single individual. In an asexual clone, advantageous mutations must appear successively in a genealogical line, since single individuals with more than one advantageous mutant will be vanishingly rare. In a sexual population, however, advantageous mutations that appear simultaneously in different individuals may nonetheless be incorporated into a single individual whenever those with different advantageous mutations mate with each other. In short, sex allows genetic recombination, which speeds up the appearance of individuals with more than one favorable mutation (see Figure 13-1). This should lead to more rapid evolution in sexual lines; in competition with asexual clones, this should result in lower rates of extinction.

In recent years we have come to see that this advantage of sex is restricted in scope. In small populations, sex gives no advantage because favorable mutations may appear so infrequently that each new one tends to become fixed before another new one appears. In large populations with even moderately strong selection, favorable mutations are rapidly incorporated in both sexual and asexual lines, so that the benefits of simultaneous incorporation are small. In very large populations, sexual reproduction may actually retard the spread of favorable mutations that are "cooperative," that is, those favorable mutations that are even more beneficial in combination than the sum of their effects when appearing singly. Recombination will continually break up such combinations, while they will spread unimpeded in asexual lines. In sum, the advantages of sex will mostly fall to large populations, with weak selection acting on many independent loci. The most recent calculations show that in large populations ($N > 10^6$) sexual species will evolve more rapidly than asexual by a factor of L, where L is the number of loci at which favorable mutations are experiencing weak selection.

A related advantage of sex is the elimination of deleterious mutations. Inevitably in an asexual clone that is positively selected for, some genes with negative effects will also be present. These can be eliminated only by mutation; yet for each elimination, new, negative mutations will have appeared. By contrast, in a sexual line, recombination will continually produce some individuals largely free of negative

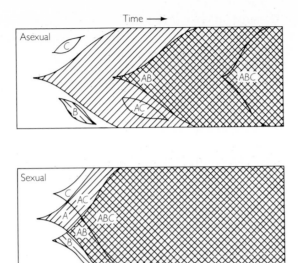

Figure 13-1

The effect of recombination on the speed of evolution. The relative number of individuals having favored genes at three different loci is plotted as a function of time for an asexual species and a sexual species. In the asexual species, genes A, B, and C initially appear at about the same time in different individuals. Although C and B increase in number they never combine with each other and eventually die out in competition with A. Not until time t_2 do we see AB together (because of a new mutation), and we must wait until t_3 to see ABC. In the sexual species, A, B and C appear at the same time as in the asexual. All three begin to increase and soon recombine to form AC and AB and shortly thereafter ABC. No new mutations have been required and t_2 and t_3 occur earlier than in the asexual species. The drawing corresponds to a large population, with a high rate of favorable mutations, compared to the rate at which these mutations spread. (*From* Maynard Smith 1978, after Muller 1932)

mutations (while producing others who are loaded with them). Thus, sexual reproduction acts like a good broom, sweeping the species clean of deleterious mutations.

If asexual species suffer higher rates of extinction, we would expect many asexual species to be of recent origin. We would not expect higher taxonomic units, such as orders or classes, to be entirely or mostly asexual. Nor would we expect to find asexual species that are taxonomically distant from any sexual form. This is exactly the pattern we find. Although existing asexual species of animals probably represent thousands of independent origins, only one (the bdelloid rotifers) has given rise to a major taxon (subfamily or above) that is predominantly asexual. We also find no taxonomically isolated asexual species, and the same general pattern is found in plants.

The advantages of sex we have been describing so far accrue to the whole population and require generations before they are realized. But during this time, asexual reproduction should have a strong, immediate advantage for the females practicing it because it conserves parental investment. To this, the cost of sex, we turn next.

The Two-fold Cost of Sex

Sex is a very inefficient arrangement. In the great majority of species the female invests resources in each offspring, while the male contributes nothing beyond his genes. This lack of male parental investment means that a female switching to asexual reproduction would enjoy an immediate doubling in her reproductive success.

Consider an asexual mutant in a sexual species that lacks male parental investment. Assume that the species is outbred, so that the sexual individuals produce the two sexes in a 1 : 1 ratio. The asexual mutant produces only daughters, the survivors of which will all invest in the production of additional daughters. The sexual female produces the same number of offspring, half of whom are males. These offspring will produce half as many offspring per individual as the asexual mutant, because half of the individuals are non-investing males (see Figure 13-2). In other words, compared to asexual forms, reproductive output in sexual forms is halved every generation. Other things being

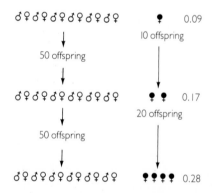

Figure 13-2

The spread of an asexual mutation in a species lacking male parental investment. The species is assumed to be outbred and producing a 1:1 sex ratio. The asexual female (♀) and the sexual female produce 10 offspring each, of which two survive to breed. Both numbers of offspring and adult numbers have been permitted to rise, but the same comparison would hold if total population size were held constant. The frequency of the asexual female in each generation is shown at the right.

equal, an asexual mutant appearing for the first time in a sexual species should roughly double its number in the first generation. In very few generations the sexual forms should be completely eliminated, other things being equal.

One might suppose that it would be easier to simply note that an asexual female is related to her offspring by $r = 1$, while the sexual female is related (under outbreeding) to her offspring by $r = \frac{1}{2}$ so that she is half as effective at propagating her genes. But this way of putting the argument is misleading, since *at the locus for sexual reproduction* the sexual female is as related to her offspring as the asexual. This is because she mates with a male who is necessarily the offspring of sexual females. The sexual female gives up half her genes for sexuality but receives them back from the male (Figure 13-3).

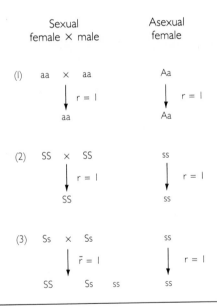

Figure 13-3

Degrees of relatedness at a locus controlling sexuality, under various assumptions. (1) The asexuality gene is dominant (A) and uncommon. Most asexuals are, therefore, heterozygotes, as shown. The male is assumed to be aa because his mother was aa, likewise his paternal grandmother, and so forth. (2) The sexuality gene is assumed to be dominant (S) and common. Most sexuals are, therefore, homozygous. As in (1) the fact that a male is the offspring of a series of sexual females implies that he is typically SS. (3) Same as (2) except s is assumed to be common. Most sexuals are heterozygous, as shown. These produce three kinds of offspring—SS, Ss, and ss—in frequencies of 1:4, 1:2, 1:4; average r to offspring is 1.

Given the high cost of sex, we might be tempted to imagine that sex is actually disadvantageous and is maintained only because the appropriate mutations are rare when compared to the frequency with which asexual clones go extinct. But in two kinds of species, sex is maintained at a regular frequency even when the asexual form is readily available. In some plants (and an occasional animal), females simultaneously produce both sexual and asexual eggs, yet the asexual fail to displace the sexual. In cyclically asexual species, there is a regular alternation between asexual and sexual generations. Examples include some sponges and bryozoans, many rotifers, and some insects, such as gall wasps and aphids (see Figure 13-4). In a few of these species some asexual females are known to forego sexual reproduction entirely, yet the sexual generation is retained. Since these two kinds of species—in which asexuality coexists with sexuality—are widely scattered throughout the living world, sex may be paying its way wherever it is found.

Is Sex an Adaptation to Sibling Competition?

One way out of the dilemma is to imagine that distribution of reproductive success is highly skewed and that the production of genetically variable offspring increases the individual's chances of producing some offspring with very high reproductive success. This implies strong selection. Imagine, for example, that offspring settle in large numbers in patches, each of which will eventually support only one individual. Imagine that several offspring from each parent settle in a given patch. If eventual success depends on the genotypes of those settling, and not on initial numbers, then asexual reproduction introduces into each patch redundant chances of success, while each offspring of a sexual parent represents a unique chance. In George Williams' analogy, the asexual parent is like someone with several tickets to a lottery, all of them having the same number, while the sexual parent has a different number on each ticket (but, due to the cost of sex, has fewer tickets). Where siblings are commonly thrown into competition and where selection is intense, sex will gain a net advantage. Although this explanation may apply to such diverse creatures as oysters, aphids, and elm trees, it cannot be a universal explanation for sex, because long-lived species with low fecundity do not experience sufficiently intense selection to generate by this means a benefit greater than the cost of sex, even though sex is almost universal in such species. Most of these animals possess powers of dispersal that should permit siblings to avoid each other when competition is intense.

A related argument emphasizes that genetic variability may allow more individuals eventually to inhabit the same patches. Sex may be

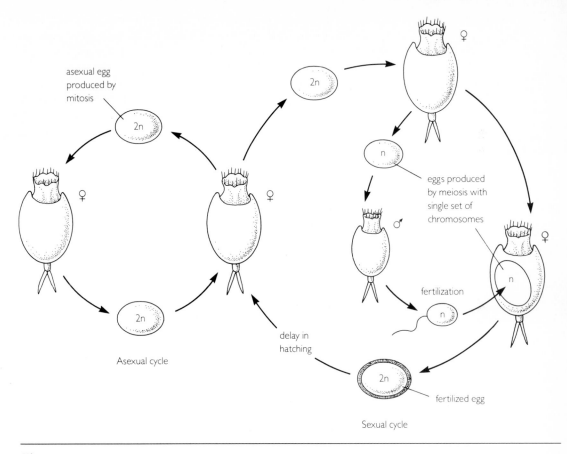

Figure 13-4

Asexual and sexual reproduction in a single life cycle. Shown is the life cycle of a rotifer *Euchlanis dilatata.* On the left is the asexual cycle, which, by mitosis, produces eggs containing two sets of chromosomes (2n). On the right is the sexual cycle. Males are produced by meiosis and contain only one set of chromosomes. Their sperm join with eggs also produced by meiosis, giving fertilized eggs with a full double set. Somehow the sexual stages must be making up for the cost of sex; otherwise the species would be expected to become entirely asexual. (*From* Pearse and Buchsbaum *in press,* after King 1967)

favored because it increases the number of niches which can simultaneously be occupied. Identical individuals have identical requirements and their numbers will be limited by the availability of these requirements. Sexual offspring have different requirements and can occupy a broader space. An analogy can be drawn from human industrial manufacturing. Under what conditions will a company prefer to produce a

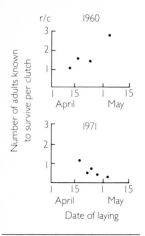

Figure 13-5

Fluctuating selection for date of laying in the great tit. The number of individuals per clutch known to have survived into adulthood is plotted as a function of the date on which laying of the clutch began, for two different years in the same area. Assuming that dispersal is not affected by date of laying, we see that the direction of selection has reversed between the two years, later clutches being favored in 1960 and earlier ones in 1971. Similar data for 16 consecutive years suggest that the direction of selection on date of laying shows a significant reversal every three years or so (generation time is about two years). Earlier laying correlates with higher early spring temperatures and food availability prior to laying. (*From* van Noordwijk et al. 1980)

variety of buttons instead of only one kind? When there are only a few buttons available all will be bought regardless of kind, so the company will produce only one kind, thereby saving the cost that goes into producing variability. On the other hand, as the market becomes saturated, new buttons can be sold only if they are novel and the company produces several kinds. Similarly, at low numbers, animals may be selected to reproduce asexually (saving themselves the cost of sex), while at high numbers they may reproduce sexually so as to occupy new space. This explanation has even less chance of being universal than the previous one, for it leads only to the coexistence of the two kinds of reproduction. When asexual individuals are common, sexual offspring will occupy more habitats and will survive in greater numbers; but when sexual individuals are common, this advantage dies away because all habitats are being exploited, and asexual females should enjoy an advantage. Since both forms should, thus, coexist at some intermediate frequency, at best this explanation applies only to species that alternate sexuality with asexuality. It is noteworthy that in such species, sexual offspring are often produced when population numbers are high. However, as we shall see below, the precise facts better fit another explanation, which we shall now consider.

A Biotic World that is "Contrary"

Another approach to understanding the advantages of sex has been to explore the possibility that a temporally variable and unpredictable environment might favor sexual reproduction. Several models suggest that environmental variation only favors sex when successive environmental states are negatively correlated in time. Environmental variation may also favor sex when the immediate correlation between successive states is positive but the environments nevertheless reverse within a few generations (see Figure 13-5). When the states are randomly distributed, sex confers no advantage. When they are positively correlated for long periods, sex is disadvantageous because it tends to break apart successful combinations of genes.

The requirement that over a short span of generations environments should be negatively correlated is sufficiently unusual that we can draw attention to it by saying that the environment must be "contrary": just when a species has evolved a response to a changed environment, the environment changes back in the general direction from which the species came. At first, the requirement that the environment be contrary seemed difficult to satisfy. Successive states of the physical environment are believed usually to be either uncorrelated or positively correlated over fairly long periods (e.g., climatic cycles), but it was soon realized that the living environment is in one respect different: antagonistic pairs of species, such as predator and prey, or parasite and host, react to each other's ongoing evolution by evolving counterploys. They are contrary. Just when a species evolves a response to a common trait, a new one becomes common.

The key to visualizing this effect is to imagine variability in each of the antagonistic species matched to the other. Imagine that the predator has two forms, A and B, which are specialized on two prey forms, a and b. When A is numerous, a will be heavily predated, and b will increase in numbers, which will favor B. When B is numerous, b will be heavily predated and a will increase in frequency, and so on. The two kinds of predators will cycle in numbers and—out of phase—the two kinds of prey will do likewise. As long as no single predator can be specialized on both kinds of prey, predators will act like a contrary environment, causing the genes that are favored in the prey to continually reverse. In turn, the prey will be a contrary environment for the predator, continually favoring one kind and then the other. The same kind of model applies to host–parasite relations (Figure 13-6).

This model of genes matched in predator and prey or in parasite and host is by no means unrealistic. In the classic work on flax *Linum usitissimum* and its parasite, the flax rust *Melampsora lini*, evolution has produced complementary genetic arrangement in the two species such that for each gene conditioning rust reaction in the host, there is a specific gene conditioning pathogenicity in the parasite. Similar systems have now been described in other plants and in animals. That parasites may maintain genetic polymorphisms in their host is known from malaria, which maintains several polymorphisms in humans. If all major diseases maintain a similar number of polymorphisms, much of genetic variability may be maintained by parasite selection.

The key to this cyclical effect is, first, that fitness is frequency dependent. That is, when a genotype is common in one species it evokes a genetic response in the second species such that its own fitness is reduced. Second, this frequency dependence has a time lag. That is, the genetic response in the co-evolved species takes some time to develop. With these two features, cycles of selection will naturally develop, thus reversing the direction of selection. The more quickly the cycle completes itself, the more often the direction of selection is reversed, and the greater and more immediate is the benefit of sexual reproduction. Sex is advantageous because it increases the frequency of uncommon genetic combinations, and these are being favored by frequency-dependent selection caused by other species. Sex also decreases the frequency of genetic combinations when selection has made them common. But compared to what a mixture of genotypes reproducing asexually could achieve, the net effect is positive. Sex reduces the variance in genotype numbers through time, and since population expansion depends on the *geometric* average of achievements over a representative series of generations, steadier numbers mean faster growth rates. An equivalent genotype that reproduces asexually varies its

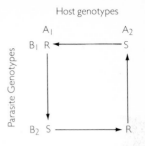

Figure 13-6

A hypothesis concerning cyclical relations between host and parasite. Species of host and parasite are assumed (for simplicity) to be haploid. At a locus in the host, one of two genes can appear, A_1 or A_2. These are matched to two genes in the parasite (B_1 or B_2) such that A_1 is resistant (R) to B_1 but susceptible (S) to B_2, while A_2 is susceptible to B_1 but resistant to B_2. Arrows show the directions in which the frequencies of genes are expected to move. Many such systems are expected to cycle indefinitely, continually moving around the loop. (*From Clarke 1976*)

numbers more widely and this leads to a disadvantage that can more than cancel its advantage in not having to mate and produce males.

The best I can do at giving an intuitive understanding of these ideas is to say that sex will obviously be good at putting together certain combinations of genes at different loci, then breaking these up and putting together another combination, then a third or back to the first, and so on. If this is what the environment is, in fact, demanding, then sex will do well against asexuality, any gene in an asexual individual being stuck in an unchangeable alliance. In this view, sex is not an adaptation permitting more rapid directional evolution, but an adaptation permitting individuals, over long periods of time, to stay in the same place with greater equanimity of numbers. By analogy, sex permits individuals to tread water over evolutionary time more efficiently.

The most likely interactions to generate the required rapid cycles are those between parasite and host. Remember that a species may be preyed upon by only a few species, but invariably it will be parasitized by hundreds of viruses, bacteria, protozoa, and so on. These parasitic species may evolve for hundreds of generations during the lifetime of a single host, so it is to be expected that they will rapidly become good at exploiting the commonest host genotypes! This, of course, is especially true of large, long-lived species, such as many vertebrates. If this view is correct then sexual species may be seen, in William Hamilton's memorable phrase, "as guilds of genotypes committed to free fair exchange of biochemical technology for parasite exclusion."

Although I think these ideas concerning the evolution of sex are the most promising that have appeared, I do not want to leave the impression that the problem has been resolved. The models that have so far proved successful in generating an advantage for sex even in low fecundity species employ huge changes in reproductive success for genotypes over a few generations: reproductive success changes by a factor of 20 or more. Not only have such changes *not* been observed in nature, but they seem especially unlikely for species with very low fecundity. It may be that more realistic models (employing, for example, more than two loci) will not require such huge changes in genotypic fitness, but at present we cannot say if this is true.

That pressure from co-evolving species is in some way the key to the evolution of sex is strongly suggested by a review of the evidence concerning the factors associated in nature with sexuality. These factors can be reviewed under three headings: distribution of asexual species in nature, the factors associated with sexuality in species showing intermittent sexuality, and dormant and dispersive stages in species with intermittent sexuality. In doing so, we follow Graham Bell, who was the first to gather together in one place the facts concerning sexual and asexual reproduction in animals.

The Distribution of Asexual Species in Nature

Asexual species are not distributed at random in nature. They are found in some kinds of habitats and some kinds of species more often than in others. For example, asexual reproduction is more frequent in fresh water than in the ocean, at high latitudes instead of the tropics, and among the smallest multicellular creatures rather than the largest (Table 13.1). These three facts and many others are aspects of a single, general rule: asexual reproduction tends to predominate in all sorts of novel or disturbed habitats or habitats that suffer wide fluctuations in physical conditions. As a corollary, these habitats are low in species diversity and in the intensity of interspecific interactions.

Consider the marine environment versus fresh water. The marine environment shows less variation in physical features than do all but the largest lakes. In 17 out of 18 major taxa that have forms in both habitats, asexuality is associated with fresh water and sex with the ocean. Small bodies of fresh water show even greater fluctuations than do large bodies and they show greater frequencies of asexual reproduction. In ostracods, for example, asexual species are frequent in small, temporary ponds and streams, while sexual species predominate in larger, more permanent bodies of water. The most ephemeral habitats are small rock pools and water film found on lichen and moss. Consistent with the general trend, this habitat is occupied almost exclusively by asexual species.

In the ocean, habitats become less stable and more disturbed as we approach the shoreline. For sessile marine invertebrates such as sponges, asexual forms are found more frequently as we approach the shoreline more closely. Where other kinds of environments can be classified in a similar way, we find the same pattern. For example, asexual

Table 13-1.   Characteristics of species that tend to be sexual or asexual

Sexual Species	Asexual Species
Marine	Fresh water
Large bodies of fresh water	Small bodies of fresh water
More distant from shore in the ocean	Closer to shore in the ocean
Large organisms	Small organisms
Low latitudes	High latitudes
Low altitudes	High altitudes
Wet	Dry
Undisturbed	Disturbed
Productive	Unproductive
Parasitic	Free-living

Source: Bell 1982.

oligochaete worms occur in the upper, more disturbed soil layers, while the sexual species are found in the deeper soil.

As we move from the tropics to the poles, the physical features of the environment fluctuate more widely and asexuality becomes more common. This is clearest for the insects, but with few exceptions the pattern is true of other creatures, such as mites, isopods, and monogonont rotifers. When we consider a single group, asexuality is associated with ephemeral, physically variable habitats. In insects, asexual reproduction occurs at high latitudes, high elevations, in more exposed, dry habitats, in recently glaciated areas, and among recently introduced forms that are successful at colonizing new habitats.

The same trends are found in plants. Weedy and colonizing species are often asexual or self-fertilizing hermaphrodites. The frequency of self-fertilization is highest in marginal populations, and asexuality and self-fertilization are rare in the tropics.

Taken together the evidence strongly argues against the notion that sex could be an adaptation to varying and unpredictable *physical* conditions. Instead, sex is associated with more intense and frequent *biotic* interactions, both within species and between species. The importance of interactions between species is suggested by two additional comparisons. First, parasites live within individuals of other species and biotic interactions are expected to be especially intense. As predicted, asexuality is rare in parasites and appears to be more common in closely related, free-living forms. Second, species that feed on dead organisms or detritus lack a major source of biotic interaction. Their food, being dead, does not evolve counterstrategies. As expected, asexual reproduction is relatively common in such species. Incidentally, detritus feeders noticeably lack the feeding specializations so common to other insects, suggesting that co-evolving food prey may also maintain alternate feeding specializations *within* species. Changing frequencies of these specializations is expected to impose selection on the prey species that frequently changes in direction (contrary).

It should be noted that fluctuating environments not only reduce interactions between species but decrease interactions within species. Habitats are frequently opening up, and early exploitation of the habitat may depend more on reproductive rate than on superior genotype. If so, then such environments naturally favor the economic efficiency of asexual reproduction.

Factors Associated with Sexuality in Species with Intermittent Sexuality

The conventional interpretation is that in species with intermittent sexuality, asexual reproduction occurs during the growing season, capped off by the production of sexual, dormant eggs. However, this only fits aphids, cladocerans, and monogonont rotifers, and fails as a general rule. Sponges and bryozoans, for example, have a sexual period during the growing season and are asexual at the end.

Sex may, in fact, occur at any time of the year and is tied more closely to periods of maximum population size than periods of maximum environmental predictability. The sexual periods of rotifers and cladocerans occur at *or shortly after* the population maxima (see Table 13-2). Species with two maxima in the growing season often have a sexual period associated with each. If such a species has only one sexual period, the period is generally associated with the larger of the two. Finally, the intensity of the sexual period may vary with the height of the population maximum: larger maxima are associated with higher proportions of males and sexual females (compared to asexual females). In the laboratory, the chief factors eliciting sexuality in a variety of species are crowding and starvation.

At first glance the association between high numbers and sexuality suggests the importance of intraspecific competition to occupy a variety of niches, since such competition will be most intense when numbers

Table 13-2.   Time of maximum population numbers and sexual reproduction, in various genera of Cladocerans

Genus of Cladoceran	Population Numbers	Sexual Reproduction
Diaphanosoma	Does not become abundant until July–August; maximum in late August–early September, disappears in October	September, sometimes into October
Sida	Common through summer, with maximum in August–September	September–November
Bosmina	Spring maximum in May–June; fall maximum in September–November	June–July; October–November
Acantholeberis	Maximum usually in fall	Shortly after fall maximum
Drepanothrix	Maximum in August–October	October–November
Lathonura	Maximum in September	October–December
Leptodora	Maximum usually during August–October	October; after peak of maximum

Source: Bell 1982.

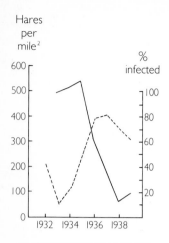

Figure 13-7

Density of snowshoe hares (solid line) and percentage infected with three species of intestinal nematode worms, as a function of time. Note that maximum rates of infection occur shortly after peak densities. The snowshoe hare is *Lepus americanus*; the worms are trichostrongylids. (*From Erickson 1944*)

are high. But according to this view, one would expect sex to occur *prior* to maximum numbers so that sexual offspring could be produced to *face* conditions of maximum density. The evidence suggests, instead, that sex occurs at the *end* of the maximum. In monogonont rotifers, for example, the sexual period commonly occurs at the end of the maximum, just before return to much lower densities. This is consistent with the explanation of selection through parasites, since the latter presumably attack most fiercely at or shortly after high densities (Figures 13-7 and 13-8). That migration often co-occurs with sex is consistent with escape from parasites.

Dormant and Dispersive Stages

A dormant stage will almost always be associated with dispersal in space and time, but many organisms also produce dispersive stages that develop directly without a dormant period. Although dormant propagules are produced sexually in a variety of organisms, they are produced asexually in as many others. By contrast, in sedentary and colonial animals, purely dispersive propagules are produced by sexual reproduction. The association between sexuality and dispersal is consistent with our theory of biotic interactions if dispersal permits escape from such interactions. This is especially likely in the case of parasites, whose numbers are expected to be high when their hosts are very numerous.

Implications for Understanding Sexual Species

The theory and evidence we have been reviewing do not apply only to explaining the existence of sexuality but also apply to phenomena within sexual species. This is most obvious for traits such as rates of recombination (e.g., rates of crossing over and chromosome number), which increase genetic diversity just as sexuality does; but it is also true of characteristics of the breeding system. In the words of William Hamilton:

. . . to understand social behavior at a deeper level evolutionary biologists may soon need to pay closer attention to transgenerational patterns in the major forces of selection on their organisms: in such patterns eventually may be found reasons why one species tolerates or prefers incest, why one has lower fecundity, more parental care, and why one has males that are more showy, less industrious, and yet more preferred.

In other words, if we are to understand things as diverse as inbreeding, fecundity and male parental investment, we must pay attention to the way in which major selection pressures change from generation to generation.

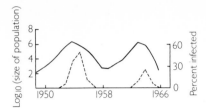

Figure 13-8

Host population size and frequency of parasitism, in a moth. This graph shows the logarithm of population size of the larch budmoth *Zeiraphera diniana* and the percent infected by a granulosis virus (dashed line) as a function of time. Notice that rate of infection is especially high right after maximum population sizes. (*From* May 1983)

In species lacking male investment, inbreeding increases a female's relatedness to her offspring while decreasing genetic variability within her brood. Thus, inbreeding is expected to be common in the same kinds of conditions that favor asexuality. Changes in fecundity may affect the intensity of selection, a variable in our models of selection that favor sexuality. And mate choice may produce benefits that are both economic and genetic. Insofar as choice for genes is important, selection may oppose male investment.

Slow cycles of co-adaptation may increase mate choice for genes because these cycles will result in positive correlations between parent and offspring in such characters as resistance to parasites. Consistent with this expectation, parasite frequency in birds predicts both male color and song (see pp. 358–359). Whether decreased pressure from slow-evolving parasites increases the frequency of male investment, as might be expected, is not known, but one's impression is that species of birds lacking male parental investment are more frequent in the tropics, where parasite pressure is high.

Dispersal is another trait that may be selected for in a similar manner as sex. We have already noted that the two are associated in nature and may be common adaptations to parasite escape. Dispersal in males may also be accentuated by female choice if males bring with them genes valuable for combatting parasites that in the immediate locality are not yet abundant but soon may be.

Conclusion

Twenty years ago biologists hardly knew there was a problem where sex was concerned. Since then a whole new world has opened up. On the theoretical side, it seems that when the environment tends to change over a few generations in such a way that what was favored is now disfavored, and vice versa, there may be an advantage to sexual reproduction sufficient to offset the loss in male parental investment. Only interactions with hostile, co-evolving species are likely to provide this effect, and a review of factors associated with sexual reproduction shows that sex is especially frequent when interacting species are many and when conspecifics are at peak densities. Both of these facts are congenial with the notion that interactions with parasites are especially likely to favor sex, since selection pressures are often strong and cycles of co-adaptation short.

Although we have made considerable progress, much work remains to be done. We need more realistic models of the way in which hostile, co-evolving species may favor sex. We may still be in for some surprises concerning the real meaning of sex.

Summary

Sexual reproduction is very common in nature, even though asexual reproduction should enjoy an immediate two-fold advantage in species lacking male investment. Under certain conditions sex may speed the rate of evolution and reduce the frequency of deleterious mutations; but neither effect is strong enough to overcome the cost of sex. Although sex may gain a net advantage when sibling competition is frequent, this explanation will not work for the large numbers of low-fecundity species, very few of which are ever asexual. Although sex may allow greater niche utilization when sexual individuals are rare, this factor will not give a benefit when sexual individuals are common.

Environmental unpredictability is in itself unable to give an advantage to sex. Instead, successive environments must be negatively correlated. This suggests that biotic interactions may be important in maintaining sex. A species' predators, prey, and parasites evolve responses to its evolution, so that what is favored in one generation may be disfavored in another. Parasites seem an especially important factor because they typically enjoy many generations of evolution for each one of the host. This should result in rapid cycles of co-adaptation by host and parasite, with selection favoring sex and recombination, since these increase survival through time by reducing variance in numbers from one generation to the next.

In nature, asexual reproduction predominates in all sorts of habitats that suffer wide fluctuations in physical conditions. These are precisely the conditions in which biotic interactions are relatively weak. Thus, species diversity is greatest in the tropics and asexual reproduction correspondingly rare. In species with intermittent sexuality sex is associated in nature with population maxima and in the lab with crowding. Parasite pressure is presumably most intense at these times. Dispersal is also associated with sex and may be another form of parasite escape.

Theories of sex have important implications for how we view reproductive traits in sexual species. Degree of inbreeding, fecundity, and mate choice may each be affected by the same kinds of generational patterns of selection that favor sex itself.

Chapter 14

Female Choice

THE LOGIC BY which animals choose their mates is one of the most intriguing problems in biology. It is also one of the more controversial. Where males invest parental care, both sexes choose partly according to the ability of the other to invest in the offspring, and evidence for this seems to be widely accepted (see Chapter 10). We are certainly aware of this factor in our own species. In the United States those males who marry in a given year earn nearly 50% more money than males of the same age who fail to marry, and part of this correlation is probably due to female preference. Male interest in female secondary sexual characteristics such as breasts and hips may be due in part to his interest in female fecundity, and a similar interest by females in the male body may partly reflect concern over ability to hunt and such matters; yet we also pay attention to minor features of the face and it is difficult to see how these relate to ability to invest. Certainly, physical beauty has a partly genetic basis, but what exactly does physical beauty say about the rest of the genotype, if anything?

The problem is much more acute when we turn to species lacking male parental investment entirely, for females are no less discriminating in these species—indeed, they may be more so. Yet beyond such minor matters as getting the species right and choosing a sexually competent male, female choice can only concern the genes of the available males: which male offers the better genes (where "better" refers to the degree to which these genes increase the survival and reproduction of her offspring)? In this chapter we shall review some of the evidence regarding female choice for genes. We shall see that choice is not just a matter of permitting sex, and that the opportunities to express choice may sometimes be limited. We shall review evidence of mate choice in plants, and we shall review some of the common objections made to female choice. We shall see that females may prefer particular males because they are likely to produce superior sons, daughters, or both, though female choice to benefit daughters will more quickly spread. Finally, we shall review evidence that mate choice for resistance to parasites may have been an important factor selecting for bright plumage and complex song in birds. We begin with Darwin's view of female choice.

Figure 14-1

Male display. We see here a male Emperor bird of paradise *Paradisaea guilielini* in his initial display to a choosing female. Males invest nothing beyond their sperm cells and they do not display together. Thus, the exaggerated and bright plumage has presumably evolved via female preference. (Photo: Michael Renner/Bruce Coleman, Inc.)

Darwin and Female Choice

Darwin was the first to recognize the importance of female choice in nature. He inferred its power and importance from a study of male morphology and courtship, primarily in birds such as birds of paradise, bower birds, and lek-breeding birds. In birds of paradise, males have beautiful plumage, which is useless outside of the breeding season, but which is displayed to females during courtship (Figure 14-1). From this, Darwin inferred that females have a sense of beauty. The peacock is another good example. The male has a large set of tail feathers, normally not displayed. In the presence of a female, however, the tail feathers are fanned apart to produce a beautiful array of eye

a

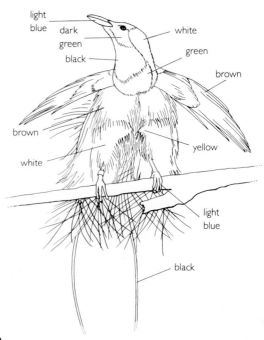

b

spots. In the absence of any other function, it appears, the peacock's tail plumage has evolved solely through a female preference that is partly guided by a sense of beauty. Only recently has it been shown that in a bird, females prefer males with artificially enlarged tails and discriminate against those with cropped tails (Figure 14-2).

In bower birds, males spend countless hours and days building huge structures out of wood—so-called "bowers," which serve only as a place near which copulation occurs. In some species, males decorate these bowers by gathering brightly colored eggshells and other objects (Figure 14-3). Indeed, in some species males paint their bowers, mixing together various berries in order to produce particular colors. In these species, the more pronounced the bower is, the duller is the male's plumage. Thus, female choice appears to have switched from the male's morphology to his bower, females preferring ever larger and more striking bowers. In lek-breeding birds, many males gather together at a single spot and compete with each other to display in front of arriving females. The females inspect a variety of males before choosing one. Different females choose in similar ways, so preferred males may inseminate dozens of females.

Although his views are strongly supported today, Darwin was ridiculed for his notion of female choice. Gradually his emphasis on female choice gave way to a more conservative approach, which dominated the study of animal behavior until the 1960's. In this view females were concerned only to choose the right species and the right sex. Females were slow to arouse, and once aroused, would accept anyone. Courtship existed not to permit females to discriminate between different males, but to overcome female reluctance to mate. For example, one theory argued that females are naturally afraid to be touched, since when touched by a predator they are shortly thereafter dead; thus, males indulge in elaborate courtship displays in order to quiet the fears of sexually hesitant females. As a reaction against this view, a study of female choice in dogs in 1965 showed that females were highly discriminating:

Females exhibited clear-cut preferences for particular males as sexual partners. Feminine rejection behavior ranged from simple avoidance to active attack. Some females were more selective than others, but all showed discriminatory responses. Some males were rarely rejected by any bitch, whereas others were generally unpopular. It is suggested that any concept of sexual receptivity as an endogenously controlled condition leading to indiscriminated acceptance of all conspecific masculine partners must be evaluated separately for each species.

If the concept of female choice was controversial in Darwin's day, it certainly remains so today. With the reality of choice itself more widely accepted, the argument has shifted to the question of whether

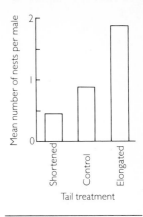

Figure 14-2

Male tail length affects female nesting behavior in the long-tailed widowbird. The mean number of new active nests in a male's territory in *Euplectes progne* is shown for three categories of males: those with artificially shortened tails, those with artificially elongated ones, and a control group (tail feathers cut and then glued back together). In this species the male's tail averages one-half meter in length, and displaying males can be seen from a distance of one kilometer. Shortened males had tails cut back to about 14 centimeters length, while elongated males had tails of about 75 centimeters length. (*From* Andersson 1982)

Figure 14-3

Decorating his bower. A male great bowerbird *Chlamydera nuchalis* deco-
rates his bower with a red hibiscus flower. Note the shells and other objects
he has already brought. In some species, males crush berries and paint their
bowers. The bower is the place at which copulations occur. Across species of
bowerbirds, the more elaborate the bower, the less colorful the male, female
choice having switched from the male himself to his bower. If bright coloration in males correlates with resistance to parasites (p. 358), then it is difficult to believe that the same is true of bright coloration in bowers. Why
females should attach such significance to bowers is not known. (Photo:
Hans and Judy Beste/Animals Animals)

mate choice for genes *can* operate in nature, and if so, does it operate,
and in favor of what? Opinions are sometimes extreme: on the one
hand are those who imagine that females get nothing out of mate
choice in improved genes for their offspring; on the other hand are
those who believe that females get large genetic benefits from their
choice. The latter are said by the former to have a supermarket men-
tality in which females are imagined to act like so many shoppers striving to bring home the best genes for their families! I must admit I fall
in this latter camp—I have a hard time believing that the variety and
subtlety of female choice in nature has evolved for no other purpose
than to favor males that others already favor. But notice that I stated

Table 14-1.   Average wing length of mating males (compared to non-mating) and the variance for two samples of the California Oak Moth *

	Average Male Wing Length (mm)	Variance	Variance of Restricted Sample
Females Mostly Able to Choose:			
mating males	77.7	8.97	6.79
non-mating males	75.2	21.58	
Females Mostly Unable to Choose:			
mating males	77.1	14.01	15.19
non-mating males	77.6	19.91	

Source: Mason 1969.

* Differences between males when females were able to choose are significant; differences are not significant when females were unable to choose. The restricted sample eliminates a few discrepant females in each sample and the difference between the variances of the restricted samples is significant.

the matter in terms of *belief*, not logic or fact. The field is now wide open and many opinions are possible. Indeed, it remains to be seen whether female choice is an arbitrary and amusing evolutionary side-show or a powerful force directing male evolution for female benefit. Let us turn now to some of the evidence.

Evidence of Female Choice

Female choice is difficult to study in nature, since it is confounded with the effects of male–male competition. This was solved for the California oak moth by comparing the characters of males who mated when females were able to exert a choice to the characters of males who mated when females were unable to resist unwanted advances. In the California oak moth, couples copulate for about an hour, so it is easy to get a large sample of copulating couples to compare with non-copulating individuals. Females are capable of choosing males a few hours after emergence from their pupae, since they are then capable of swinging their abdomens from side to side, thus preventing a male from copulating. When the size distribution of males copulating with such females is compared with the sizes of all males in the population, we see that males who mate are larger than average, but do not contain the very largest individuals (Table 14-1). Thus, female choice exerts both directional and stabilizing selection. Females discriminate against both extremes (low variance), but prefer males who are larger than average. Females who have emerged within the previous few hours cannot swing their abdomens to reject approaching males. The males copulating with them are no different in size from the general population.

How is female choice made? That is, what characteristics do females use to discriminate males? Michael Ryan studied this problem in the neo-tropical frog *Physalaemus pustulosus*. Breeding takes place in ponds. Females come to the pond only once to mate and deposit eggs, and there are many males available per female. The mean size of mating males is greater than that of non-mating males. Indeed, for each night of the breeding season, males larger than average mate more frequently. The main advertisement of males is their call, which consists of a whine followed by a chuck (Figure 14-4). Experiments have shown that the "chuck" is especially important in female choice, and frequency variation in the chuck correlates inversely with male size. That is, larger males have lower voices. This suggests that females may be able to choose larger males on the basis of their calls.

To test this possibility Ryan set up an experiment in which females could choose to move towards one of two loudspeakers, each playing the call of a different male. Such experiments reveal that females almost invariably move toward the speaker playing the deeper call.

Size and age are intercorrelated, so it may be that females prefer larger males because they are older, or because larger males have

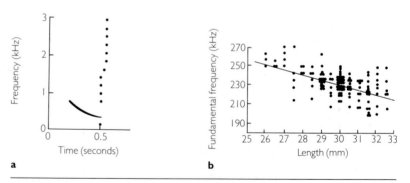

a   **b**

Figure 14-4

The chuck component of male song in a frog contains information about male size. (a) The advertisement call of a male *Physalaemus pustulosus* typically consists of a whine followed by several chucks. Shown here is the frequency, in kilohertz, of a whine followed by a chuck, as a function of time. (b) The fundamental frequency of the chuck sound as a function of male body length (minus the tail), in millimeters. Despite large variation there is a negative correlation. (*From* Ryan 1980)

thereby shown their ability to accrue resources relevant to female reproduction. At present we have no clear understanding of why females
in so many species appear to prefer the larger of two males.

Male advertisement in *Physalaemus* is, incidentally, a dangerous
operation. Frog-eating bats cue on the chuck call of males, and the
males have been selected to be sensitive to the presence of bats: within
seconds of a bat's appearance over a pond, males cease calling and
lower themselves in the water. In this response they discriminate between frog-eating bats and other bats, reserving their silence for the
species dangerous to them.

In some species, very simple decisions, such as direction of flight,
may produce preferential mating. For example, in many species of
flies, males display in mating swarms. These are clouds of males that
fly back and forth over a small area, typically above some prominent
landmark, such as a bush or the branch of a large tree. Studies have
shown that these swarms possess a vertical organization. Perhaps because wind velocity higher up tends to be greater, strong-flying males
tend to be found at the top of vertical columns of displaying males. In
some species, males fly against the wind for short distances and then
let the wind carry them backwards. Thus, they seem to perform a constant zig-zag dance. Females enter these swarms from above, and are
typically seized and mated by the males at the top of the swarm. Thus,
without making any active discrimination, a female can mate with
better-flying males merely by entering the top of swarms. In many such
species, males, in turn, have evolved specialized, enlarged facets of their
eyes on the tops of their heads. These facets permit males to detect
movement more quickly, and their orientation allows them to spot females arriving from above. In some species the vertical organization is
reversed: larger males hover closer to the ground around emergence
sites of adult females and achieve higher rates of copulation (Table 14-2).

Perhaps the most subtle example of female choice has been shown
experimentally, primarily in *Drosophila*, but also in some other insects. This kind of choice is called rare-male advantage. It was discovered independently by Claudet Petit in France in the 1950's and Lee
Ehrman in the U.S. in the 1960's. The experimental procedure is to
expose a female to two different kinds of males of the same species.
Call them type A and type B. When the two kinds of males are made
available to females in different frequencies, females respond to the
relative frequency of the two kinds, always preferring the kind that is
in a minority (see Table 14-3). Their preference for the rare male
is stronger the less frequent he is in the sample. This is true when the
two kinds of males come from different geographical areas, when they
are chromosomally different, when they have developed under different conditions, or even when they merely smell different through the
addition of a scent. While the preference for the rare male operates

Table 14-2.   Non-random mating and male location in the lovebug *Plecia nearctica* as a function of male size*

| | Male Size | |
Swarm	Hovering	Copulating
A	64	76
B	65	73
C, 1.2–1.7 m above ground	53	—
D, 0.7–1.2 m above ground	64	—
E, 0.0–0.5 m above ground	73	—

Source: Thornhill 1980.

* Male size is the length of the thorax in ocular units (1 mm = 35 ocular units). Differences between hovering and copulating males are significant. Differences between males at various distances above ground (in meters) are significant.

regardless of whether the female is type A or type B, in nature she will usually be of the majority type, so that preference for the minority male results in her mating with a male unlike herself.

What is the significance of this form of female choice? By preferring a male typically different from herself, the female tends to produce offspring who are more heterozygous and genetically variable. Since we have seen that there are powerful selective forces favoring the production of genetic variability, as well as heterozygocity among offspring, this female bias is consistent with our view of the importance of sexual reproduction. Our best guess is that rare-male advantage is a means of producing greater genetic variability, both within individuals and between them.

Only one study has attempted to measure the effect of female choice on offspring survival. Linda Partridge maintained fruitflies *Drosophila melanogaster* in the laboratory under conditions of larval competition for food. Some females were allowed to choose their mates, while others had their mates assigned at random. The offspring of females permitted to choose showed survival rates 4% higher than the offspring of females prevented from choosing. The laboratory is an impoverished environment compared to nature, and it is tempting to imagine that female choice may confer greater benefits in nature. That differential male mating success has a strong influence on gene frequencies in nature is suggested by evidence from *Drosophila pseudoobscura*: gene frequencies were different at one-third of all loci in a random sample of adult males, compared to a sample of larvae grown

Table 14-3. Rare Male Mating Advantage in the Guppy *Poecilia reticulata*

Common Strain (9 males)	Rare Strain (1 male)	Strain from Which Females Were Taken	Number of Broods Sired by Rare Males*	Number of Broods Sired by Common Males
Armatus	Maculatus	Armatus	3	0
Armatus	Maculatus	Pauper	0	1
Maculatus	Pauper	Maculatus	3	4
Pauper	Maculatus	Maculatus	0	2
Pauper	Maculatus	Armatus	1	0
Armatus	Pauper	Pauper	1	2
Pauper	Armatus	Pauper	1	3
		Total	9	12

Source: Farr 1977.

* Regardless of the strain of the female, the rare male tends to be preferred.

from females collected at the same time as the males. These changes in gene frequencies may be due to female choice or to some other aspect of male mating success, though male–male competition in *Drosophila* seems a relatively unimportant factor compared to female choice.

Choice Is Not Just a Matter of Permitting Sex

Female choice does not end at the moment at which a female permits a male to copulate. In some species, choice continues during and after the act of sex. As we have seen in scorpionflies, females may vary the number of eggs they lay in response to such male characteristics as size and size of nuptial gift (Table 10-4). Choice may also be involved in the timing of a copulation. For example, in primates, females ovulate at the height of estrus, yet they often copulate for several days prior to ovulation. Are females more discriminating in choice of sexual partners at the height of estrus, tending at such time to prefer the more dominant males? The dominant males certainly prefer to copulate with a female when she is near the time of ovulation. In human females, ovulation occurs typically between 12 and 14 days after the onset of menstruation, and this is the time at which women are most sexually receptive. Human females enjoy sex most and engage in it most frequently at the time they are ovulating (Figure 14-5).

Female choice may also occur when a female helps or hinders sperm transport after copulation. It has been suggested, for a variety of

Figure 14-5

Fluctuations in sexual activity of women as a function of day in the monthly estrous cycle. The mean number of autosexual activities (masturbation) per day and the mean number of female-initiated heterosexual activities are shown as a function of the day in the monthly menstrual cycle, either counting forward from menstruation or counting backward from the next menstruation. Sample is white women in the United States with intrauterine devices or whose husbands had been vasectomized. Time of ovulation is shaded. Note the peak in sexual activity at this time. (*From* Adams et al. 1978)

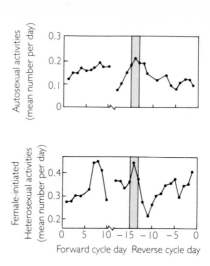

domestic mammals, that female orgasm may actively transport sperm nearer to the eggs that the sperm fertilize; but until recently, it was not certain that females outside of humans experienced orgasms. Indeed, some people have claimed, without any evidence, that only human females experience orgasms. With the publication of Masters and Johnson's work on human sexual functioning, we were given criteria by which to judge orgasm in humans, independent of a woman's assertion that she had experienced orgasm. When these same criteria have been applied to rhesus monkeys and cats, females were found to experience physiological events that in humans correlate with orgasm. Although the evidence is not very strong, it seems likely that female orgasm may play an active role in increasing the chance of fertilization through differential transport of sperm. If so, it acts as a mechanism of choice. Of course, insofar as orgasm makes it more likely that the female will mate again with the same male, female orgasm also affects choice in the future.

Even when a female's eggs have been fertilized, she still has the choice of whether to implant and rear the fertilized eggs. In rats, it has been shown that the number of intromissions a female receives prior to ejaculation affects the female's chance of becoming pregnant. By giving some males partial copulations with other females first, it was possible to vary the number of intromissions a female received. When females receive three or fewer intromissions before ejaculation, fewer females become pregnant than when they receive more than three. By contrast, vaginal stimulation *after* ejaculation reduces transport of sperm within the female and her subsequent reproduction (see Table 14-4). Female mice are also known to spontaneously abort their young when exposed to the smell of a strange male within two or three days of insemination

Table 14-4.   Effect of vaginal stimulation before and after ejaculation on a female's reproduction in the rat *Rattus norvegicus* *

	Females		
	Percentage Pregnant	*Average Number of Sperm in Uterus × 10⁵*	*Average Number of Fetuses Implanted*
Number of Intromissions			
***Before* Ejaculation**			
Few ($\leq$ 3)	22%		
Many (average = 8.4)	90		
Amount of Vaginal Stimulation			
***After* Ejaculation**			
None		446	13.5
Manual stimulation within 15 minutes of ejaculation		99	2.4

Sources: Wilson et al. 1965; Adler and Zoloth 1970.

* Each comparison based on degree of stimulation is significant.

by the regular male. The smell of a strange male in nature would probably signal a take-over of the area by the new male, and he may respond to young born to the previous male by killing them. If so, spontaneous abortion is a means of preventing the wastage of male infanticide.

Altogether, the evidence from mammals suggests that there exist means by which females exercise choice after accepting a male for copulation. The male's sexual performance may affect a female's chance of achieving orgasm, which in turn may affect the chance that her eggs are fertilized. Likewise, a male's sexual performance affects the chance that a female will implant and invest in the fertilized eggs.

Can Females Always Choose?

Females are not always free to exercise choice. As we have seen in the California oak moth, shortly after emergence, adult females are incapable of resisting the advances of males with whom they would not ordinarily mate. Forced copulations have been described in several other species, including ducks and flies. Nevertheless, forced copulations seem relatively infrequent in nature.

A stronger bar to female choice may come from the effects of male competition. In many species of mammals, males are capable of sequestering a group of females from other males. This should reduce the chance of the sequestered females choosing a different male. For

Figure 14-6

No! A female elephant seal loudly protests attempts by an adult male to mount her. She will also whip her hindquarters from side to side and may try to escape. In a partial protest she will do these things at first but will then stop resisting. (Photo: Burney LeBoeuf)

example, in elephant seals a single dominant male may prevent subordinant males from approaching a group of 20 or 30 females. But even in this species, with tremendous sexual dimorphism and intense male–male competition, mechanisms of female choice have been discovered. Females can resist the courtship of less dominant males by crying out (Figure 14-6). These cries invariably bring a more dominant male to the scene. Field observations show that females resist copulations more intensely the less dominant is the male attempting copulation (Table 14-5).

In deer species, a male may keep all other males away from groups of females; but data from nature show that female groups continually change in composition. Females continually leave some groups and join others, thereby expressing choice (see Figure 2-21). In highly territorial lizards, such as the Jamaican green lizard, female choice is again limited by male–male aggression. But females can always change the territory in which they reside. Likewise, they can advertise within their territory that they are sexually receptive. Females do, in fact, choose very prominent places on which to signal their sexual readi-

Table 14-5. Percentage of mounts not interrupted by another male that were protested, partially protested, or not protested by the female, in elephant seals

Dominance Status of Mounting Male*	Percent of Mounts Totally Protested	Percent of Mounts Partially Protested	Percent of Mounts Not Protested
Alpha	37%	43%	20%
Adult	49	34	17
Sub-adult 4	78	22	0
Sub-adult 3	100	0	0

Source: Cox and LeBoeuf 1977.

* Alphas were dominant over a segment of the beach.
  Adults were 8–14+ years old, subadult 4's were 7–8
  years old and subadult 3's were 6–7 years old.

ness, and this presumably increases the incentive of other males to invade the territory for copulation. Indeed, slightly more than 5% of a female's copulations take place with an invading male instead of the territory holder.

In summary, in some species, males are able to force copulations; in others, male–male competition puts constraints on female choice; but nowhere are these constraints absolute. A more important effect of male–male competition may be to force females to choose large or dominant males in order to gain protection from other males. A growing number of cases have been found in insects and vertebrates in which male–male competition has negative consequences for females—who may even be killed in the frenzied grasping. Infanticide is but another example. Often a female can protect herself from harassment by associating with dominant, victorious males. In one insect, females are known to oviposit more frequently when guarded by a male than when alone. At present we must confess we are ignorant of how widespread this factor may be in female preference.

Mate Choice in Plants

Not much is known yet about choice in plants, but what we do know suggests that most plants have ample means by which to choose; in some species, they clearly exercise choice in response to the genotype of the pollen or its producer. Furthermore, some of this choice can be shown to increase the reproductive success of the resulting offspring. Like animals, plants can affect which males (or male parts of other plants)—and how many—contribute pollen. For example, a large floral display probably attracts pollinators from greater distances; it certainly can attract more visitors. Plants can also affect which pollen preferentially fertilize eggs and which of the fertilized eggs are allowed to develop (by aborting some seeds and fruits). This latter form of choice discriminates on the basis of the genotype of the *offspring* and is thus, strictly speaking, not an example of "mate" choice; yet its effects are so closely related to the other forms of choice and in plants so difficult to separate that we can easily treat it here as an example of mate choice. It is a widespread feature of plants.

A clear example of mate choice has been shown for the trumpet creeper *Campsis radicans* by Robert Bertin. He hand pollinated plants, using pollen from different plants to pollinate the flowers of one plant. Each flower was pollinated by only one donor, eliminating pollen competition within flowers. Nevertheless, each plant showed a strong tendency to set fruit in response to some male donors and not others (Table 14-6). No particular male was favored by all plants, but some were more favored than others. Tendency to set fruit was, in turn, positively associated with other measures of reproductive output, such as seed number, seed size, and percent seed germination. If plant A favored the pollen of plant B, then there was a strong tendency for the reverse also to occur.

Choice probably occurred largely after fertilization; certainly many fruits were aborted. It is interesting that plants were more selective later in the season rather than earlier (Table 14-7). This makes sense for a species such as the trumpet creeper, which in nature is not always adequately pollinated: lowered selectivity early increases the chance that some fruit will be set, while greater selectivity later can be practiced with little or no loss in total output.

Bertin's study did not show that choice increased the reproductive success of the plant. A similar study of another species showed that

Table 14-6. Female choice in plants: numbers of fruit resulting from pollinations using different donors, in the trumpet creeper *

Recipient Number (female)	Donor Number (male)								
	2	3	4	5	7	8	9	11	12
3	3	—	9	14	10	12	12	1	1
4	15	15	—	3	5	15	2	4	13
5	16	13	4	—	0	5	3	3	11

Source: Bertin 1982.

* Each of the three distributions of fruit set is highly significantly different from random.

seeds grown from preferred pollen donors produced plants that were heavier after one month, but this could also have resulted from the fact that the seeds were heavier. In the case of inbreeding, however, we can have no doubt that plants exercise choice—almost always in favor of outcrossing—and that this is clearly to their advantage. Choice against inbreeding seems to involve all the possible mechanisms. Many flowers are designed to make self-pollination difficult or impossible. In addition, many species have self-incompatibility systems by which self-pollen is rejected. These systems probably also regulate breeding with close relatives. Even in self-compatible species, equal amounts of foreign pollen and self-pollen usually result in greater foreign fertilization, although the reverse is common in highly inbred lines. Post-fertilization choice also commonly acts against self-fertilization: seed abortion and fruit abortion are both increased. In turn, we have known from Darwin's time that self-fertilization is usually associated with decreased survival and reproduction of the resulting offspring.

It seems likely that pollen competition to fertilize eggs is a more important avenue of mate choice in plants than sperm competition is in animals. Once pollen arrives it still must grow a tube in order to reach the egg. A variety of studies have now shown that more intense

Table 14-7. Degree of selectivity shown by individual trumpet creepers in the first half of their fruit production compared to the second half

Recipient Plant Number	Percent Contribution by Disfavored Donors *	
	1st Half of Fruit Production	*2nd Half of Fruit Production*
2	0%	0%
3	16	3
4	17	21
5	42	14
7	24	15
8	4	3
9	40	10
11	36	30
12	0	0
Mean Percent	20	11

Source: Bertin 1982.

* Disfavored donors were those donors that for a given plant contributed less than the median amount of fruit production. Distributions for the two halves are significantly different.

pollen tube competition is positively associated with the ability of the resulting seeds to germinate, grow, and survive. Competition is increased either by increasing the amount of pollen deposited or by increasing the distance the pollen tubes must grow before they reach their goal. Both treatments produce more vigorous seedlings. It is interesting that plants are also known to abort fruits less frequently when pollination is more abundant. A general tendency to abort fruits with fewer seeds probably has a similar effect, since lower rates of seed production are associated with smaller pollen fall.

Altogether, the evidence suggests that mate choice—in the enlarged sense—may play an important role in the life of plants in increasing the genetic quality of offspring. Most striking is the ability of the plant to vary its selectivity in response to such variables as time during the breeding season and, possibly, the relative attractiveness of its own pollen (as shown for the trumpet creeper).

Objections to Female Choice

For some reason, the notion of female choice for genes has attracted a swarm of objections. Recently it has been claimed that selection has long ago exhausted any genetic variation in males affecting reproductive success, so that there is no point in choosing. Alternatively, it is said, selection in each generation is intense, but there is no correlation between what is useful in one generation and the next. Once again, there is no point in choosing. It is also said that because female choice has a runaway effect, rational decision-making will be swamped by arbitrary effects. Group selection objections have also been advanced: because mate choice for genes will not necessarily raise the mean reproductive success of the *population*, we should not expect such choice to evolve. It has even been held against female choice that it cannot increase the number of eggs a female lays—only their later survival or reproduction—as if this made for a weaker kind of selection! Before we proceed to outline a theory of female choice for genes, let us briefly consider the more serious of these objections.

It is sometimes claimed that selection will have exhausted all genetic variation affecting reproductive success. Traits distantly associated with RS—like bristle number on a fly's abdomen—will have high genetic variation, while traits close to RS—such as egg production—will have low genetic variation. Evidence in support of this is cited from various species, using estimates of heritability: estimates of the degree to which phenotypic variation in a trait is due to genetic variation (as opposed to environmental variation). These estimates show the predicted association, but I believe this association is, in any case, expected on other grounds. Of course, selection will have worked more strongly on traits closely associated with reproductive success. This will produce numerous adaptive associations—based on environmental cues—and these will inflate environmental effects, even when genetic variation is held constant.

We should bear in mind that in many species large amounts of genetic variation are maintained (p. 90) and we have reason to believe that strong, ongoing selection is associated with the maintenance of this variability (p. 315). These two facts suggest that there is ample genetic variability available each generation, which affects reproductive success. Furthermore, we know for sure that evolution is a continuing process; this means that even when genetic variability is low, females must in principle prefer males with one or more genes undergoing positive selection, or with the minimum undergoing negative. What is required is some mechanism by which these males can be identified. This is less of a problem than it appears.

Imagine that high growth rate is valuable in females and that only the very fastest-growing males mate often (as found in green lizards: p. 232). Can anyone deny that the males achieving high reproductive success must, on average, have genes promoting high growth? It does not matter if selection has favored such growth rates for eons—and if the average growth rate has changed little or not at all. Selection must still be continually weaving together genes that in ever-new circumstances give high growth rate. The key is that the environment is continually co-evolving. In the case of growth rates, parasites, prey species, and predators all play a role. The fact that in co-evolving systems the species may chase each other through evolutionary space, with little or no average gains through time, does not mean that selection is not occurring—quite the contrary (p. 324). The alternate view is that large amounts of genetic variability are maintained by static selection in favor of heterozygotes. But besides the lack of evidence in favor of this view, it is implausible, since asexual reproduction would seem to be doubly favored; economically efficient, it can maintain heterozygocity indefinitely.

But the strength of selection for sex suggests another objection to female choice: perhaps environmental conditions are so variable that what is achieved in one generation is no guide to the next. However, such a chaotic structure to the environment hardly seems to permit adaptive evolutionary change of any kind. A more plausible line of argument can be based on the biotic theory of sex.

Since the environment must be "contrary" in order to maintain sex, successive environmental states will be *negatively* correlated. But, note that this will not eradicate choice—it will lead to inverted preference: where co-evolving parasites reverse the sign of selection in one generation, females will do best who choose the sickliest males, not forego choice entirely! Much more likely than these instantaneous cycles are slower ones in which several generations of positive environmental correlation are followed by a reversal. Tighter cycles will favor sex and slightly looser ones, mate choice: as William Hamilton and Marlene Zuk have shown, cycles congenial to mate choice may produce a parent–offspring correlation in reproductive success as high as 0.5. Remarkable evidence consistent with this view will be reviewed below.

A less interesting argument has been the claim that the self-reinforcing or runaway aspect of female choice will result in large, random effects that swamp those of choice for genes. As an example of this, one recent author has claimed to find possible situations in nature in which a mutant gene that decreases survival sweeps through the population to fixation in spite of the fact that females, in general, have a stronger preference for the more viable alternate gene! This is a remarkable discovery, indeed, since such a gene would seem to proceed rapidly in the face of *two* obstacles, something we would all like to be able to do. It turns out that these situations occur when females preferring the less viable male are allowed to reach arbitrarily high frequencies in the population without the introduction of any of the males they prefer! Naturally, when we introduce the less viable male into this specially created heaven he enjoys enormous reproductive success! By this kind of reasoning one could evolve almost anything, since it allows one to create artificial worlds ideally suited to the spread of otherwise disadvantageous traits. These traits cannot even spread in the face of genetic variability in what they prefer, much less the existence of alternate genes that through skillful choice increase their own survival and reproduction among offspring.

The Logic of Female Choice for Genes

How is a female to know which male has the best genes to give her offspring? Offspring come in two kinds—male and female—and the task of choosing good genes differs for the two kinds. Males are selected for who maximize the probability of survival times the number of females inseminated, assuming the males survive. That is, a male is selected for who survives to adulthood and maximizes his success in sexual competition. A female is selected for who maximizes survival times fecundity. This means she must survive to adulthood and maximize the resources available for conversion into offspring.

Biologists have concentrated almost entirely on female choice for sons. Male–male competition will naturally tend to elevate to breeding status males whose sons will likewise do well in male–male competition. Thus, a female who prefers a male good at dominating other males will tend to have sons similarly talented. Likewise, by directly observing the choice of other females, a female can learn which males are likely to be attractive to the daughters of other females. Thus, female choice for quality of sons would seem relatively easy to evolve. Once such choice gets underway, it would tend to feed back upon itself, thereby gaining evolutionary momentum. This is because males being chosen by females will tend to have a disproportionate number of genes for such female choice.

Consider an example: the lek-breeding black grouse. Males gather on traditional display grounds in the early morning and spend a good part of each day on breeding territories within which they do not feed but attempt to attract females for purposes of mating (see Figures 14-7–14-9). Females are attracted to concentrations of males, which facilitates their choice. They are attracted to males who are fighting and to the victors of fights. Finally, they are attracted to males who have already attracted other females. Each female spends several days on the lek grounds, copulates once, and leaves to lay her eggs. Most females tend to choose the same male, so there is high variation in male reproductive success. The presence of a female nearby tends to excite male–male aggression, and males will attempt to interrupt the courtship of their neighbors. A highly dominant male is one who is able to interrupt the courtship of his neighbors while avoiding interruption during his own courtship.

Courtship tactics play an important part in male success. Those who have a subtle courtship seem to do well in attracting females, and this is especially true when courting presumptive virgins. The oldest males are at the center of the lek and are most dominant. If the courtship tactics of males are influenced by experience, then a skillful courter is likely to have had considerable reproductive success in the past and a good chance of more in the future. What constitutes skillful courtship among black grouse? At least four elements have been identified.

(1) It is important to direct courtship to a specific spot on the male's territory. Older males do this more often and are more successful at courting females. Males use past copulations as a guide to choosing the spot. By using stuffed females, it is possible to offer an inexperienced male a copulation at a particular spot. He then directs future courtship of females to that spot. Inexperienced males court females without inviting them to a particular place. By offering a male successive copulations at different spots, it has been shown that the most recent copulation usually determines the spot toward which future courtship will be directed.

(2) A male does well when he heads off a female leaving his territory. This is done by circling between her and the closest boundary, and is ideally done as far from the female as space permits. Circling

Figure 14-7

A female's-eye view of male courtship. While flying toward the lek grounds, a female black grouse can expect to see males *flutter-jumping*—flying up to a height of one or two meters, over a distance of 10 to 15 meters, while making a crowing sound. This energy-demanding behavior serves to draw attention to the male and could permit females to evaluate males on the basis of flying strength and agility. Males flutter-jump in response to flying black grouse—male or female—departing and arriving. Flutter-jumping may also occur as a prelude to a fight with a neighbor who is about to intrude. (*From* Kruijt and Hogan 1967)

tends to prevent a female from leaving the territory. One male circled 17 females who had begun to leave his territory. In response, 13 stayed. A second male allowed 15 females to depart without circling them, and only one stayed.

(3) Halfway through the courtship it is valuable to reject the female. This is done by the male's turning his back on the female and walking away from her. This maneuver occurs especially when a female has spent some time in a territory and still appears hesitant and undecided. The male suggests that time is limited and, in effect, turns the initiative to the female.

Figure 14-8

A light-and-sound show. Once a female black grouse lands on the lek grounds and looks at a male, she may expect to see a male bowing toward her and making a rookooing sound. When seen from the front, white wing-bow patches are alternately hidden and exposed as a result of inflation and deflation of air sacs during rookooing. Thus, sound and light effects are co-ordinated. Are males who put on a good light-and-sound show superior in other respects (for example, relatively free of parasites)? Or has an innate female interest in sounds and flashing lights (selected in other contexts) favored males who put on a good show? (*From* Kruijt and Hogan 1967)

(4) It is important to approach the female closely when the time seems right. Males begin by circling the female at some distance and gradually tightening the circle. While the male does not rush the female, it appears important for the male to shorten the distance. Some males appear to hesitate at the key moment, and females often shortly lose interest.

These findings suggest that female choice in black grouse is not an all-or-nothing process but, in fact, a series of choices, each one permitting greater intimacy. A male must allow the female to be in control at all times, including shifting the initiative to her when she seems undecided. Overeagerness is a threat to female control, and insofar as it is a measure of the male's desperation, it may indicate the time that has elapsed since he last copulated. All of the tactics in successful courtship benefit from experience. A male probably does not learn much from his failures. A variety of mistakes could be responsible, but his successes need merely reinforce all actions that immediately precede them and his courtship will improve. Do inexperienced males fear rejection, thus vacillating between overeagerness and timidity? A preference for the self-confident is probably a preference for the previously successful.

Figure 14-9

The final moments. (a) As a female black grouse approaches a male's territory he will often rookoo while squatting with legs bent and wings touching the ground. (b) Once the female is in his territory, a male will often circle her, taking small rapid steps, touching the ground with his wings, and rookooing. (c) Only if a female crouches will a male mount; forced mating attempts have not been observed. (d) The average copulation lasts only two seconds. The male usually holds the female's head feathers, tramples on her back, releases his hold, and flaps his wings vigorously while attempting to make cloacal contact. (e) The female then withdraws quickly while the male often tramples his feet and assumes the copulatory position. He then typically circles the same or another female. Squatting or fighting with a neighbor may also occur. A male may copulate again—usually with a different female—within 15 seconds. (*From* Kruijt and Hogan 1967)

In summary, the lek-breeding system of the black grouse allows females to choose males whose sons are expected to be successful at attracting the daughters of other females. Females can easily choose in this manner by (1) watching male–male interactions, (2) watching male–female interactions, and (3) watching the skill of each male's courtship.

Selecting Good Genes for Daughters

Imagine a gene in a female leading her to choose a male whose genes improve her daughters' chance of surviving by 10%, while decreasing her sons' survival by a similar amount. At first glance, genes for this kind of female preference appear to be neutral in their evolutionary effects: what is gained in daughters is lost in sons. But since the genes for this kind of female choice will have increased in one generation among females, more females will choose in this way, giving a benefit to the males they prefer. These males will tend to contain a disproportionate number of the very same female choice genes, since these males will—more often than randomly—be the sons of males preferred by such females one generation previously. Thus, the net effect of such genes is positive: they enjoy an increase in survival in females, a comparable decrease in survival in males, but an offsetting increase—however small—in reproduction among males due to the increased number of females who prefer males likely to have these genes.

Notice also that genes in males that increase survival in sons make life slightly more difficult for these sons (fewer females per male), while genes in males that increase survival in daughters make life slightly easier for males carrying these genes (more females per male). Thus, female choice genes for sons inhibit their own spread, while choice genes for daughters do not.

If these arguments are valid, it suggests that genes in males that reveal quality of the remaining genes *for daughters* will more rapidly be selected for by female choice than similar genes that merely reveal quality in sons. Of course, beneficial genes need not be as sex-antagonistic as we have described. The genes most favorably selected for through choice will be those that improve survival in both sons and daughters, although it must inevitably be true that males will be selected for in ways that are not advantageous to females. Our theory of female-biased female choice suggests that genes in females for protecting themselves from this will easily gain a toehold. They are self-reinforcing within one generation. Male–male competition, in turn, may begin to adjust itself appropriately. In the hamadryas baboon, lower-ranking males are more likely to attack a dominant in consort with a female if she lacks a special relationship with him, presumably because their payoff—via choice—is higher.

There is another reason for expecting that this neglected form of female choice may be important in nature. We have reasons to believe that the type of female choice in a species may affect its chances of survival. Consider two species: one chooses to benefit daughters in every generation, the other benefits sons. Imagine that these two species are in close competition. Since only females invest in young, their numbers control the rate of increase. Increased survival of sons will temporarily increase population size but will result in no increase in the number of offspring produced. Thus, the species that improves daughters should have a competitive advantage. It has the capacity to increase its numbers in each generation compared to the second species. Thus, species with female choice for daughters will tend to increase at the expense of other species.

Of course, female choice for daughters should lead to the evolution of male–male competition to display traits valuable for daughters. Insofar as female reproductive success is strongly dependent on ability to accrue additional resources for reproduction, males will be selected who demonstrate that they are good at accruing such resources. In this context, it may be useful to think in terms of "handicap genes." Originally this term was introduced by Amotz Zahavi to describe a gene in a male that lowered the male's survival, but which demonstrated, with his survival, the superiority of his *other* genes. If the handicap genes are only expressed in males, then daughters will gain the beneficial genes without the handicap, while males will gain both the handicap and the offsetting genes. Computer simulations have shown that even with this assumption, it is difficult to get handicap genes favorably selected. They always induce a cost in males, and the offsetting genes among the males who do survive are unlikely to give daughters a *greater* increase in survival than the decrease in survival suffered by handicapped sons.

A more realistic possibility is that of a handicap gene that leads a male to demonstrate to females that he possesses the kinds of genes that allow him to survive and accrue the resources a female would need in her reproduction. Such a gene would allow females to discriminate, not between the living and the dead, but between those males who do survive, revealing which one has better accrued the kind of resources females need.

Regardless of how females actually choose males in nature, we can ask, "To what degree do the males who mate have genes that benefit females?" Consider, for example, lek-breeding birds such as the black grouse. Males are larger than females, they arrive earlier on the breeding grounds and spend most of each day in energy-costly display and aggression, with very little time for feeding. Thus, only males who have fed well in the past and are capable of quickly replenishing lost energy will be able to court females effectively. Older males who have been successful at this for a period of several years are the most likely to breed. Males bear additional plumage that is energy costly, and some of this is brightly colored, which may entail additional costs, both in energy to produce the colors and in energy necessary to avoid any associated increase in risk of predation. Thus, a cursory view of black grouse suggests that those males who breed contribute genes that are beneficial for both their sons and their daughters.

Consider another example. Although we know little or nothing about female choice for antlers in deer, we may ask to what degree antler development in males may signal valuable genes for daughters as well as sons. Antlers are energy-expensive organs grown only when other needs have been met. Their annual growth cycle roughly corresponds to the annual cycle of female investment: maximum antler growth occurs at roughly the time females are nursing their young (but a test of this correspondence across species of deer has not been performed). Antlers certainly reveal ability to form bone and we have reason to believe that bone formation is more important to female reproductive success in large species than in small. As body size increases, a relatively greater proportion of the body consists of bone; likewise at weaning, litter size is reduced and offspring are relatively large, further increasing a female's need for resources that go into bones. Thus, the fact that antlers among species of deer are *relatively* larger as body size increases is consistent with female needs. It would be interesting to know whether other sources of variation in female need for bone growth were matched by similar variation in antler development.

Antlers also reveal more detailed information about a male than the amount of extra resources he has available for bone growth. Injury to a male's skeleton might be expected to affect antler growth in the year of the injury, since antler growth will compete with skeletal repair. But injury to the skeleton produces not merely stunted antlers but antlers that are malformed. Furthermore, these malformations persist for several years after the injury was sustained. In addition, such malformations show at least one other regularity: Injury to a forelimb produces malformation to either antler, but injury to a hindlimb seems invariably to malform the antler on the opposite side of the body (Figure 14-10). Antlers grown in successive years by a male resemble each other, but if grown too far apart or too close together, antlers from successive years more closely resemble some ideal form. Malformations also usually decrease in successive racks. Perhaps the most remarkable feature of antlers is their ability to communicate back to the organism forming them in such a way as to affect the growth of later antlers. If we make an incision in the skin surrounding a growing antler, we can cause a malformation. The antler is then cast, leaving no evidence of our manipulation, yet a year later or later still a new set of antlers will show a malformation in precisely the spot where our incision induced the first malformation (Figure 14-11).

Taken together, these lines of evidence suggest that antlers may reveal very detailed information about a male's skeletal health and development. Subtle differences in skeletal configuration affecting repro-

Figure 14-10

Leg injury and antler deformity in white-tailed deer Odocoileus virginianus. (a) Five years after he cracked part of his left rear heel bone (the tuber calcis) this male still shows a deformed right antler. (b) This right antler deformity occurred in the same year as amputation of the left rear leg. (*From* Marburger et al. 1972)

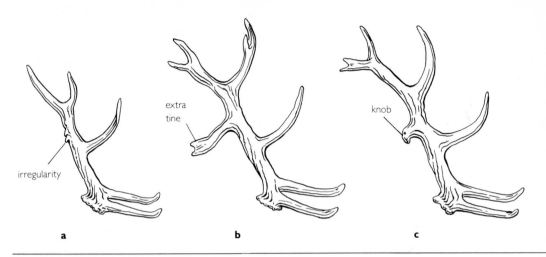

Figure 14-11

Experimental manipulation of an early set of antlers affects later sets in the Siberian red deer. (a) When this antler was 40% of its final length a small portion of the growing tissue was removed, leaving the little irregularity visible at the arrow. (b) In the following year an extra tine grew out at the place of the original injury. (c) One year later this tine was reduced to a knob. (*From* Bubenik and Pavlansky 1965)

ductive success are perhaps reflected in antler shape. Certainly the left-right symmetry of antlers and their branched form make them highly revealing of a male's ability to grow bone.

But all these facts may as easily be explained by arguing that antlers have evolved solely as weapons in male–male competition. Perhaps crippled males fight better with an abnormal antler and a male gains better purchase on his opponent if with a rear leg injury the antler on the opposite side (instead of the same side) is deformed. That antlers are used in combat is certain, but this is expected whether or not they have also been formed by female choice. Thus, like other cases of sexual dimorphism, our evidence regarding the role of female choice is suggestive but hardly decisive (see also pp. 335–337). The field is still wide open to newcomers!

One final fact regarding deer. Holding large harems of females for a couple of weeks at the peak of breeding must be an exceedingly demanding experience. Feeding stops and intense courtship and sexual activities are continually being interrupted by challenges from other males. One might suppose that success in one year is poorly correlated with success in another, but the opposite appears to be true (see, for

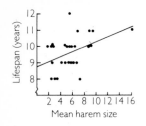

Figure 14-12

Lifespan as a function of harem size in male red deer. The age at death is plotted against the mean size of harems held by males during the years when they held harems in the rut. The positive relationship means that males that survive best as adults do most of the breeding. (*From* Clutton-Brock 1983)

example, Figure 2-20). Likewise, within a season larger harems are held for longer periods of time. Is the price paid perhaps in survival? Again, the very opposite seems to be true: males survive better the larger their harems (Figure 14-12)! This suggests that sexual selection is, indeed, improving the quality of genes being passed by males; those that do well are those that also survive well.

Parasites and Female Choice

William Hamilton and Marlene Zuk have recently suggested that there is one source of variation in reproductive success, affecting both sexes, that is especially likely to generate powers for its detection: variation in parasite load, that is, variation in mortality and fecundity due to parasites. As we saw in the previous chapter, parasite-host interactions are especially likely to generate the cycles of co-adaptation that may favor the evolution of sexual reproduction, even when accompanied by paternal neglect. If continual selection by parasites (and on them by hosts) can overcome this large cost, it suggests that there is high variation in female RS from this cause. To the degree that these differences are genetic, females would be favored who could discriminate among males according to parasite load or parasite damage. This, in turn, would favor the evolution of male characters that would make it easier to discriminate between them on the basis of parasite damage. Expensive structures and behavior come to mind as one possibility. Another is sexually dimorphic characters such as the combs and wattles of fowl or male song. In the words of Marlene Zuk:

Poultry breeders can detect the presence of several diseases in their fowl by the condition of the comb, wattles, and bare skin around the head. Bluish comb and wattles can indicate avian tuberculosis, while a scaly, shrunken comb means hepatitis or perhaps fowl typhoid. Swollen wattles suggest either fowl colera or infectious coryza, and a swollen purplish snood (the pendulous skin over the beak of a turkey) is diagnostic of erysipelas. Female turkeys are probably not as intelligent as turkey breeders, but they have a great deal more at stake in diagnosis and might therefore be expected to perceive signs of ill health at least as well as their human keepers. . . .

Singing complicated series of notes may well be particularly taxing, and females could use song as another clue to the health of the courting male. An ill mockingbird, for example, might have a difficult time imitating a grackle, switching to a gull cry, switching to a frog call, and continuing to mimic several different sounds for much of the day.

Reasoning in this way, Hamilton and Zuk were led to discover a previously unknown and unsuspected relationship between parasite load and brightness of plumage in birds and complexity of male song.

Surveys already existed for the frequency of blood parasites in 109 species of passerine birds. Each species was scored separately for brightness of female plumage, brightness of male plumage, and variety and complexity of male song. Measured across all species, each of these characters correlated positively with frequency of blood parasites. Those species most frequently parasitized tended to have brighter plumage in both sexes (more strongly so in males) and more varied and complex male song. Since these species are mostly monogamous, mate choice is exercised by both sexes and both sexes are selected to be showy when parasite frequency is high.

It is possible that this explanation applies to other correlates of plumage brightness in birds. For example, brightness declines on islands, as does degree of parasitism. More recent work by Hamilton on ducks shows that brightly colored species have parasites that are more specific to their hosts. This is interesting because specific parasites are most likely to cause the co-evolutionary cycles congenial to sex and mate choice!

Summary

Female choice is well developed in species lacking male parental investment. This can be inferred from the evolution of male plumage and other characters used in display in species lacking strong aggressive interactions between males. In addition, evidence from the field and the laboratory shows that females are often highly discriminating in choice of mates. In California oak moths, females prefer larger than average males but discriminate against the very largest. In a frog *Physalaemus pustulosus*, females prefer large males and apparently use the male's call as a partial estimate of his size. And in many species, females appear to prefer the least common male in a sample. Only in fruit flies do we have direct evidence that female choice improves the genetic quality of offspring.

Choice may also occur after sex. Females may degrade sperm or preferentially utilize it. In rodents there is evidence that increased sexual stimulation of the female prior to male ejaculation increases the rate at which offspring are raised. It is not always possible for females to choose, but even when strongly limited by male–male competition some choice is usually exercised.

Plants are discriminating in their use of pollen, preferring some donors to others. Plants may be more discriminating in choice of pollen after some fruit has been set. In many species, plants discriminate against close inbreeding. In some species, increasing the degree of pollen competition increases the viability and vigor of the resulting seedlings.

Female choice for genes is easy to imagine where females attempt to improve the quality of their sons' genes. In the black grouse, females typically mate with males that are preferred by others and male display is geared to previous success. But there are reasons for supposing that female choice for genes benefitting daughters may more quickly spread than similar choice benefitting sons. Choice genes for benefitting daughters become self-reinforcing after one generation.

There is strong evidence in birds that where parasite pressure is high, both sexes are more brightly colored and male song is more complex. These associations make sense if we assume that bright plumage and complex song reveal more clearly an individual's freedom from parasites.

Chapter 15

The Evolution of Cooperation

ONE FORM OF cooperation possible between individuals is *reciprocal altruism*: the trading of altruistic acts in which benefit is larger than cost so that over a period of time both enjoy a net gain. The problem with this system is that an individual is always tempted to cheat—to fail to reciprocate altruism—the better to maximize gains. Where individuals interact infrequently, this narrow strategy is expected to predominate, but where interactions are frequent, a cheater will suffer lost future altruism if altruists respond to non-reciprocation by withholding future aid. This they are selected to do in order to protect themselves from cheaters.

In this chapter we shall review the implications of repeated interactions between individuals for the evolution of cooperation. We begin with the importance of the degree of association, as illustrated by the live-and-let-live system that developed in the trenches of World War I. We then describe a careful study of reciprocity in vampire bats and evidence that neighboring birds discriminate against cheaters. We describe coalitional behavior in baboons and chimpanzees, and we consider whether dolphins and whales are reciprocal altruists. Finally, we describe the emotional system underlying human reciprocal altruism and the success—in games of reciprocal altruism—of a strategy called "tit-for-tat."

The Importance of Association: Mutual Restraint in Trench Warfare

In kin-directed altruism, the main problem for the altruist is to ensure that the degree of relatedness to the recipient times the cost/benefit ratio of the act is larger than 1.0. In studying such altruism, we look for positive associations in nature between degree of relatedness and frequency of altruism. In reciprocal altruism, the main problem for the altruist is making sure it receives the return benefit. This will tend to occur when frequency of interaction is high, because early in the relationship the altruist can respond to non-reciprocation by cutting off future acts of aid. This will keep the costs of altruism low. At the same time, the non-reciprocator will lose the benefit of future aid, which—because interactions are frequent—is likely to be large.

In searching for evidence of reciprocal altruism in nature, we look for evidence that (1) degree of association is positively correlated with degree of altruism, and that (2) individuals tend to direct altruism toward those that direct altruism toward them, and to discriminate against non-reciprocators by failing to extend to them additional altruism. The frequency of interaction between individuals is critical, because when this is low, individuals that extend altruism will have insufficient opportunities to direct this beneficence only to others who tend to reciprocate, so that losses from non-reciprocators may outweigh the occasional gains.

Several factors are expected to increase the chances that two individuals will repeatedly interact in such a way as to be able to share the benefits of reciprocal altruism. For example, both a long lifespan and a low dispersal rate will tend to maximize the chances that two individuals will interact repeatedly. The same is true for the degree of mutual dependence. Interdependence of members of a species (to avoid predators, for example) will tend to keep individuals near each other and increase the chance that they will encounter altruistic situations together. Parental care and more general kin-directed altruism are relationships that tend to bind individuals together so as to encourage reciprocity between them, but any predictable association—as, for example, between neighbors—should give opportunities for reciprocal altruism. Of course, any asymmetries among the individuals in their ability to affect each other will decrease the possibilities for altruistic exchanges. A strong dominance hierarchy usually means that those on the upper end are able to seize benefits from those lower down without any need to reciprocate. But even in such species, individuals low in the hierarchy may be able to trade many small altruistic acts for occasional large return benefits. Thus, a subordinate may groom a more dominant individual and gain some protection in return.

The importance of association in generating reciprocal altruism can be illustrated by the emergence in World War I of a live-and-let-live system of accommodation between the opposing forces. Although appalling battles were fought over a few meters of space and the war itself was unprecedented in its carnage, across the trenches troops often displayed considerable restraint: enemies within rifle range were left to be; rifles when fired were often aimed to miss; dangerous weapons were used infrequently; certain times of day were reserved for a complete cessation in hostilities; and so on. This cooperation flourished in spite of considerable efforts by senior officers to stop it. Soldiers were even court-martialed and entire batallions punished. With this pressure, the soldiers often had to appear to fight while actually avoiding contact, yet most of the time they were prevented by officers from arranging verbal truces with their opposites. In this situation, regularity of individual behavior became useful to the adversary and, through reciprocal action, to self. Thus, artillery was used in a highly predictable manner. As one German described the evening round fired by the British: "At seven it came—so regularly that you could set your watch by it. . . . It always had the same objective, its range was accurate, it never varied laterally or went beyond or fell short of the mark." In turn, German artillery was so predictable that British soldiers could appear to take risks while, in fact, being safe, for example, by moving toward places where artillery was about to stop landing. This wonderful image of ritualized combat in humans makes us wonder if similar considerations do not lead to ritualized combat in other animals. Regularity and predictability are reassuring in an adversary. At the same time, they suggest what might be effected in the absence of restraint. Thus, they serve as deterrents.

The key to the live-and-let-live system was the frequency with which the same individual opponents interacted. The same small army units faced each other in immobile positions for long periods of time. This sustained interaction permitted a stable system of mutual restraint to develop, based on reciprocity. If the opposition killed five, five or more would be killed in retaliation, but if the opposition restricted their fire to noisy and harmless displays, they would receive noisy and harmless displays in return. Once started, strategies of restraint based on reciprocity can spread in a variety of ways. A restraint undertaken in certain hours is extended to others. One particular kind of restraint suggests another kind. Progress achieved by one unit can be imitated by another. And so on. So popular was this system that at one time as many as one-third of the British troops had adopted a live-and-let-live policy.

The live-and-let-live system was destroyed by the introduction of raids, carefully prepared attacks on enemy trenches by ten to 200 men ordered to kill the enemy in their trenches or take them prisoner. There was no way to pretend that raids had been undertaken when they had not. Nor was there possibility for reciprocal restraint during the raid, and raids at once generated counter-raids. The system of restraint broke down.

Reciprocal Food Sharing in Vampire Bats

Vampire bats practice reciprocal altruism. This is the conclusion of a careful study by Gerald Wilkinson that showed that vampire bats

Desmodus rotundus regularly regurgitate meals of blood to each other to compensate for failed feedings and that they do so in a reciprocal fashion such that each partner enjoys a net benefit from the exchange. In showing this Wilkinson was able to demonstrate nearly every feature of reciprocal altruism: that individuals associate for long periods of time, that degree of association predicts degree of altruism independently of kinship (which also has an effect), that benefits are greater than costs, that roles of donor and recipient frequently reverse, and that individuals are more likely to aid those that have recently aided themselves.

Vampire bats live in groups of 8 to 12 adult females. One-year-old males, recently independent of their mothers, disperse from their natal group, but females remain. Thus, groups of adult females consist partly of kin, but not entirely so: on average one unrelated female joins a group every other year, so that average r in each group is about 0.1 or less. These females associate closely over long periods of time, often for more than two years and sometimes for more than eleven. Wilkinson was able to show that the degree of association between two bats—the percentage of total sightings in which they are seen together—predicts the degree to which one bat will regurgitate blood to another (Figure 15-1). This effect is in addition to an independent kinship effect of about the same magnitude. No individuals regurgitate to others unless they are seen together at least 60% of the time.

The bats fly at night to suck blood—mainly from cattle and horses—and a striking number of these return to their daytime roosts without having fed: 33% of those under two years of age fail to feed, while 7% of older animals also fail. Failure results from the wariness of the large mammals under attack, which frequently brush off the feeding bats, and young bats must apparently learn to feed unobtrusively. Wilkinson could find no other variable that correlated with failure to feed, so it seems likely that all individuals fail at some time or another. This satisfies a key requirement of reciprocal altruism: roles of donor and recipient frequently reverse. In turn, the benefit of the altruism can scarcely be questioned, for bats that are prevented from feeding starve to death within three days. If failure to feed strikes bats randomly, then fully 10% of those under two years of age and about 0.5% of older bats will fail to feed on two successive nights. Given these figures, it is difficult to see how vampire bats could survive *without* a system of food sharing!

By capturing bats and preventing them from feeding for a night, Wilkinson showed that most of these were fed by their roost mates soon after being returned to them, while well-fed bats that were returned to their roost mates were never fed. Since bats being starved lose weight more slowly as their weight decreases, transfer of a meal from a well-fed bat to one that is starving gives the recipient more time

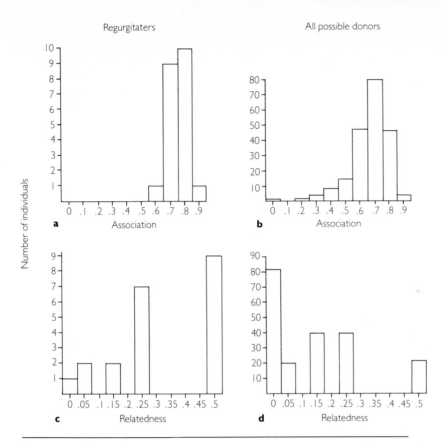

Figure 15-1

The effects of degree of association and degree of relatedness on regurgitating blood meals in vampire bats. The number of individuals seen receiving blood meals is plotted as a function of the recipient's degree of association and degree of relatedness to the donor (a and c). This can be compared with the recipient's degree of association and degree of relatedness to all potential donors within the roost (b and d). Mothers feeding nursing young are excluded. Degree of association is the fraction of times in which two individuals were seen together at the roost, compared to all sightings at the roost. Note that regurgitation is only seen between individuals who are associated at least 60% of the time. Degree of relatedness has an independent effect. Frequency of regurgitation is independent of age in either sex and reproductive condition of females, but females receive more regurgitations than males. (*From* Wilkinson 1984)

until starvation than the donor loses (Figure 15-2). This ensures that benefit will be greater than cost.

By depriving individual bats of food on different evenings in a captive colony, Wilkinson showed that regurgitation was directed prefer-

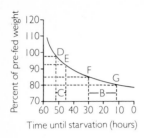

Figure 15-2

The benefit and cost of transferring blood in vampire bats. The weight of a non-feeding bat is plotted as a function of time (measured as hours remaining until starvation). Each bat was captured in the evening, weighed, permitted to feed once, and then recaptured two or more hours after the feeding; thus, weights are given as a percentage of pre-fed weights. We imagine that one individual at 95% of pre-fed weight (D) regurgitates blood equal to 5% of its pre-fed weight, which moves the individual to point E, for a cost of C, measured as a reduction in time available before death by starvation. This blood is transferred to a second individual, who is at 80% pre-fed weight and who moves to point F for a gain of B hours to starvation. As long as better-fed bats regurgitate to worse-fed ones, benefit will be larger than cost. (*From* Wilkinson 1984)

entially at individuals in dire need (only 13 hours from death by starvation) by individuals in average condition (almost two days from starvation). Furthermore, starved bats that received blood later reciprocated the donation significantly more often than expected by chance. In short, vampire bats are reciprocal altruists.

Discrimination Against Cheaters in Neighboring Birds

About the only thing Wilkinson did not show about vampire bats is that they get angry when associates fail to reciprocate meals. This, in fact, is the most difficult thing to show in a system of reciprocity—that there is discrimination against the cheater or non-reciprocator. But evidence from birds suggests that a system of mutual restraint between neighbors is regulated by a renewal of aggression when the rules of the restraint are violated.

Any relationship with a neighbor is usually a partly hostile, partly cooperative interaction. Imagine two neighboring birds setting up breeding experiments in the spring. They share a common boundary and initially they display and fight over exactly where the boundary should be. They could fight for months over the exact location of the boundary, at the end of which period the boundary would probably be located about where it is located after one week of conflict, yet both would have wasted time and energy in constant bickering and would probably have made themselves more available to predators and more vulnerable to incursions from other males. Thus, there should often exist a selection pressure in nature to say, in effect, of one's neighbor, "This is my neighbor. As long as he stays in his territory, he is fine with me. I will not waste energy in foolish strife."

That male birds learn to recognize the songs of their neighbors and respond to them less aggressively than to the songs of strangers is now well known for several species, but the key is the *location* from which the songs are heard. In the white-throated sparrow *Zonotrichia albicollis* individuals respond much less aggressively to tape recordings of their neighbor's songs than to those of strangers when these are played back from the neighbor's boundary, differences that disappear when the recordings are played from elsewhere within the tested individual's territory (Figure 15-3). More precisely, the territory owner still shows less aggression toward his neighbor than toward a stranger when both are calling from the center of his territory—though the response to the neighbor is then more intense than when he is calling from their boundary—but differences between stranger and neighbor disappear entirely when their calls are coming from the side of the

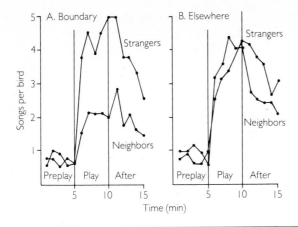

Figure 15-3

The location from which a neighbor sings determines a male's response, in white-throated sparrows. The average number of songs per minute by male *Zonotrichia albicollis* given in response to playback of songs of neighbors and strangers when the speaker is located on the regular boundary (left) or elsewhere in the territory (right). "Songs per minute" is taken as a measure of territorial assertiveness or aggressiveness. Notice the relatively relaxed response rate of a male to his neighbor calling from their common border, and how this disappears when the neighbor calls from within the territory. The most aggressive response to a neighbor occurs when he is calling from the opposite side to his territory. (*From* Falls and Brooks 1975)

male's territory *opposite* to that of his neighbor. In other words, the male birds treat their neighbors with more restraint than they treat strangers, but this restraint progressively disappears as the neighbor shows greater evidence that he is violating their implicit agreement not to contest the other's territory. The male bird acts as if he is discriminating against a cheater in the system. Similar results have been shown for the response of groups of vervet monkeys *Circopithecus aethiops* to the tape-recorded calls of neighboring groups.

Relations between neighbors might be expected to become more peaceful the longer the neighbors associate. In Belding's ground squirrels, unrelated females that share a common border show a reduction in aggressiveness compared to those that do not, but the reduction is small and is not shared by related individuals (Table 15-1). Similarly, length of association is inversely related to aggressiveness in unrelated ground squirrels ($P \cong 0.07$) but shows no consistent relationship for related individuals. These kinds of measurements are badly needed for other species if we are to build up a general understanding of relations between neighbors.

Table 15-1.   Percentage of encounters in which a fight occurred, in Belding's ground squirrels, depending on whether the squirrels occupy contiguous or non-contiguous territories *

	Percentage of Encounters in Which a Fight Occurred	
	Contiguous	Non-contiguous
Mother-daughter (1 year apart in age)	6%	6%
One-year-old sisters	8	8
Non-littermate sisters (1 year apart in age)	13	16
Two-year-old non-kin	22	27

Source: Sherman 1981.

* The last two comparisons are significant.

Coalitions in Baboons

Twenty years ago in Kenya, Irven DeVore discovered that there were two kinds of dominance hierarchies in baboon troops. First, there was the usual linear dominance hierarchy in which each individual dominated all individuals below it in the hierarchy. This could be observed by arranging one-on-one confrontations over food. Second, there was also a central hierarchy in which individuals banded together so as to dominate all others. The most dominant individual was not necessarily a member of the central hierarchy and if not he could be excluded by the actions of the others from mating with females close to ovulation. For example, in one troop DeVore watched, Kula was the single most dominant individual, whereas in contests for sexual access to females, Dano, Pua, and Kovu acted together to exclude Kula. One such interaction is shown in Figure 15-4.

In 1972 I was able to watch baboons with DeVore. In troop after troop we saw a central hierarchy of dominant males who gave support to each other in conflict with others. At Gilgil in Kenya we observed a set of males arrayed in decreasing order of dominance as follows: Arthur, Carl, Sumner, Rad, and Big Sam. However, Carl formed a central hierarchy with Sumner, Rad, and Big Sam and this permitted Carl to dominate Arthur in conflict over access to females, in particular, to Anne, who at the time of our visit was at the height of her sexual receptivity.

We arrived one morning to find Carl feeding close to Anne, and Arthur feeding nearby. Arthur seemed to be pretending disinterest because he avoided looking at Anne or Carl but always moved in the same direction they did. DeVore soon noticed that Anne seemed to be

a

b

c

Figure 15-4

A baboon harassing sequence reaches its climax.
In this sequence of photos, a harassment sequence—which may have lasted for as long as an hour—reaches its climax. (a) After pacing in display and grinding his teeth while continually narrowing the distance, Mdomo finally directs a full canine display at Pua, the male who sits near the estrus female, Notch. Kovu, on the left, who is the key to the subsequent interaction, appears not to notice, although, in fact, he is paying close attention to the interaction. (b) The canine display precipitates a joint reaction from Kovu and Pua. While Pua first slaps the ground and then takes a step toward Mdomo, Kovu looks at Mdomo, possibly giving eyelid threats. Mdomo is already starting to break and run. (c) Now Kovu and Pua chase Mdomo from the scene. Pua will return to grooming Notch, and Kovu may remain in the vicinity or wander off. Mdomo will certainly be back to harass again. The entire interaction concerns sexual access to Notch, who is near the peak of her estrus and thus is close to the time of ovulation. Kovu will not gain any greater sexual access to Notch for his support of Pua, but he may get Pua's support in the future in a fight of his own. (Photos: Irven DeVore, Anthro-Photo)

playing her own game in this relationship; namely, she was leading Carl away from other troop members, perhaps because she wanted to separate Carl from his supporters (in order to see a one-on-one confrontation between the two). In any case, the three baboons wandered through much of the troop that day, and we saw three separate occasions in which a member of the central hierarchy (different in each case) intervened to try to prevent Arthur from interrupting one of Carl's copulations. Carl would mount Anne and start thrusting, at which point Arthur would rush in to try to break up the copulation, and one of the other males—whichever happened to be closer—would respond by interposing himself between Carl and the onrushing Arthur. If this was successful, then Carl would be able to bring his copulation to completion, and the two males would join together and chase Arthur off.

Arthur had joined the troop several months earlier. He was not only not related to any of these males (so far as we knew), but he also had not had much time to establish friendly relationships with them. By contrast, Carl and the other central males had been in the same troop for some time. Studies of many baboon troops show that males do not stay in the troops in which they are born but disperse as young adults to new troops. And they appear to disperse independently of each other, so that two brothers growing up in the same troop are unlikely to end up as adults in the same troop. This alone suggests that these coalitions are based on mutual support more than on kinship.

Late in the same day we saw Arthur send a surprising double message to Rad, suggesting that Arthur might be trying to form a central hierarchy of his own. After Rad had interposed himself between copulating Carl and onrushing Arthur, Carl and Rad first chased Arthur, then Carl settled down to groom Anne while Arthur turned his attention to Rad, threatening him from close quarters: Arthur circled Rad and flashed his eyepatches at him, crouched and flashed again, then rose and displayed his canines. The double message was this: while displaying his canines at Rad, Arthur also turned his rear end toward Rad. In baboons, presenting the rear end is usually a gesture of subordinance (although a subordinate will sometimes clasp the rear of an animal he is supporting (see Figure 15-5)), whereas threatening with the canines is decidedly hostile. The threat seemed to say, "You do this again, and I am going to eat you alive," while the affiliative gesture seemed to say, "There is potential for a new central hierarchy in the Gilgil troop, and if you play your cards right, there could be a special place in it for you." By his behavior, Arthur seemed to be giving Rad an either-or choice, which could not have been more obvious to us if it had been expressed in English.

Incidentally, while Arthur threatened Rad, Carl repeatedly positioned himself so his back was to the interaction. Only occasionally

Figure 15-5

Gesture of support in baboons. Mdomo (center) presents his rear end to be grasped by Kovu. Mdomo is the more dominant of the two and is soliciting this sign of support from Kovu. In other contexts, the more dominant individual grasps the hind quarters of the subordinate; thus, this mode of solicitation suggests the reversal in roles that reciprocity requires. Note that Kovu will sometimes support another male in the central hierarchy against Mdomo (Figure 15-4). (Photo: Irven DeVore, Anthro-Photo)

did he leave Anne to chase Arthur. The importance of eye contact in reciprocal relations was also suggested to us by observation of another troop at a garbage pit. The most dominant male chased all the other baboons out of the pit, but one female with a very young infant (possibly his own offspring) joined the male and was permitted to feed near him. This enraged the second most dominant, who threatened the female from the edge of the pit. She turned so as not to see the male. He ran all the way around the pit, but she had moved again, and so on. Apparently as long as eye contact was not made, the female could pretend the threat had not been seen and thus required no response.

I cannot tell you the excitement that went through me watching all this. From our observations it was clear that support from others was critical to a male's reproductive success and that one baboon will engage in psychological warfare with another over its support for a third party. Suddenly I could see that portions of our psyche that I had imagined to be dependent on language had probably been molded by selection in our own lineage long before the advent of language. There was another reason for my excitement and this was an unconscious identification with Arthur. Arthur was a superb young male in his prime. Carl was a middle-aged male who had seen better times but who now had the right connections. Unconsciously this mimicked my relationship with Irven DeVore, my friend and teacher. Rashly I predicted that in a matter of days this thing would be wrapped up: Carl's body would be found somewhere, cast aside in the undergrowth, and Arthur would be treated with the respect that was his due. But DeVore was saying, "You don't understand social change. You don't understand the power of the establishment. No dramatic change is going to take place. The system is stronger than you think."

DeVore was right. No dramatic change did occur. Anne did manage to separate Carl and Arthur from the others and they had a one-on-one confrontation in the evening, viewed by the rest of the troop from nearby cliffs. Arthur won, and spent the night with Anne, but early next morning the central hierarchy reasserted itself, Arthur was driven off, and Carl renewed his consortship with Anne. There were other females who came into estrus during the next several months, but Anne was not one of them, and the competition between the males seemed less intense. Then one day Arthur was shot to death for raiding someone's fruit trees, so we never did find out if he was able to establish a new central hierarchy with the help of Rad.

In the examples so far we have seen evidence of support but none of reciprocity. Craig Packer studied support between males in three troops over a long enough period of time to see many opportunities for reciprocation. Packer saw 140 solicitations for help, of which 97 resulted in support. A baboon solicits help primarily by repeatedly and rapidly turning its head from the solicited individual toward the third individual (the opponent) while continually threatening the third. Twenty of these solicitations involved conflict over a female in estrus in which the attacker solicited aid from another male, and these solicitations were supported significantly more frequently than were solicitations over other matters. In six of the 20 cases, the female was lost by the defender to the two attackers, but in all of these cases, the female then went into consort with the male who solicited the help. Thus, the helper does not receive an immediate benefit for his help, but instead receives support later, when the shoe is on the other foot. This is not always true: more recent work shows that the solicitee sometimes ends up with the female. In fact, there is a strong correlation between a male's overall tendency to take part in coalitions and his getting the female.

Packer found 13 different pairs of males who reciprocated in joining coalitions at each other's request. In six of these pairs, each pair member enlisted the other against the same opponent. Individual males who most frequently gave aid were those who most frequently received aid. Likewise, each male tended to request aid from an individual who, in turn, requested aid from him. Ten males solicited other males on four or more occasions. For nine of these ten, the partner that was solicited most often, in turn, solicited the other male more often than he solicited a typical adult male in the troop.

These correlations could result entirely from effects of kinship. An individual may act more altruistically toward another because of kinship and vice versa, which will give the appearance of reciprocation when, in fact, each may merely be increasing its inclusive fitness by aiding a relative. Fortunately, we can rule out kinship for some of these baboons. For example, for four of the 13 reciprocating pairs, both individuals of the pair were first seen as young adults in different troops, before they had dispersed: they did not end up residing in the same troop until at least five years had passed. This suggests that kinship is not mediating these four relationships and, by extension, does not have much to do with central hierarchies in baboon troops.

One other fact from Packer's study. Adult males were sometimes solicited by adult females and by juveniles of both sexes, but they responded to such solicitations less frequently than to those of other adult males. This also suggests reciprocity in interactions between adult males, because adult females and juveniles cannot, in fact, return the favor very effectively. Their support is of little value in a fight with another adult male and is unnecessary in other disputes. In fact, adult males only solicit each other.

The situation regarding female coalitions in baboons is less clear. Certainly, females support each other in conflicts (see Figure 15-6), but females are often related, and we have no study separating the effects of kinship from those of reciprocity. In the gelada baboon *Theropithecus gelada*, female support is more likely when frequency of association is high and when return support is frequent (Figure 15-7), yet both of these effects, which suggest reciprocal alliances, could result from kinship.

Recently Robert Seyfarth and Dorothy Cheney conducted novel field experiments with female vervet monkeys *Circopithecus aethiops* that showed that grooming an unrelated individual increases the likelihood of support, while grooming a relative has no such effect. Seyfarth and Cheney tape recorded various females giving the call with which they solicit support. Each female's call was played back to a second female about an hour after the first had groomed the second or after two hours in which no grooming had occurred. As we see in Figure 15-8, prior grooming between unrelated individuals makes it more likely that the recipient will look around in response to the solicitation call, while prior grooming between relatives has no effect!

One final point. In Figure 15-6 we saw a male baboon intervening on behalf of a female under attack. Studies of male intervention show that this is frequently the case—the male intervenes on behalf of the underdog. But males usually intervene only when they have a special relationship with the female, a relationship that makes it more likely

a

b

c

Figure 15-6

Two female baboons oppress a third. (a) Titi (on the right) holds up Kink's face preparatory to biting it again while Nama, who initiated the attack, looks on. From DeVore's field notes: "Suddenly, for no reason I could see, Nama rushed at Kink, knocked her down and began biting her. Titi joined her almost immediately. . . . They would crouch, eyebrow threaten, and then start biting, pulling a hand out and biting it or biting Kink's sexual skin." Nama is the most dominant female in the troop and Titi the second-most dominant. Nama is extremely aggressive, constantly attacking subordinates. Titi is just past the peak of estrus while Kink, who is much lower in the hierarchy, is just coming into estrus. We do not know whether Titi and Nama are related, but they frequently support each other in fights. (b) Shortly after the attack the centrally most dominant male, Dano, rushes up. Although he has been copulating with Titi for several days, he now intervenes on behalf of Kink, trying to pull the other two females off of her. His attention is repeatedly diverted by the presence of Mark, who has been copulating with Kink and who also rushes up when the attack breaks out. Dano alternates between chasing Mark back to the troop and pulling the females off of Kink. DeVore: "When the two females paused in their mauling, Kink would get up and run weakly, staggering on three legs for about 20 yards, where she would be caught and the mauling would continue." The attack lasted for ten minutes. Kink never made a sound, nor did the other two females. Only Dano's grunting could be heard. (c) Finally, Kink ran 300 meters from the troop and the two females gave up the chase. DeVore: "Though Kink's wounds must have been superficial, she looked more dead than alive: both front feet bleeding, limping on right rear foot, sexual skin torn and bleeding and her face, especially the muzzle, a mass of blood, running down onto her chest." As she continues away from the troop, Dano follows her. He approaches her and immediately begins grooming her and does so for ten minutes, but only her back, not her wounds. Within an hour Dano is back with Titi, grooming her. However, on the next morning he is seen with Kink, who looks much better. (Photos: Irven DeVore, Anthro-Photo)

that the male will father her offspring. In disputes between adult female gelada baboons, males show a nearly significant tendency to support lower-ranking females in their unit the most, probably because they are the most vulnerable. As we shall see in the next section, there is good evidence that the alpha (or most dominant) chimpanzee male intervenes as peacemaker and upholder of the downtrodden.

Chimpanzee Politics

From the study of chimpanzees *Pan troglodytes* in the wild we know that alliances between males are important in determining dominance status within groups and that groups of males will, in turn, act in concert to hunt and kill outsiders. Chimpanzees are also similar to ourselves in that males usually do not disperse out of their natal group but remain there to breed as adults, while female kin disperse elsewhere.

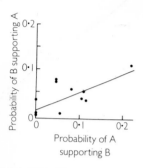

Figure 15-7

Reciprocal support among female gelada baboons. The probability of B supporting A is plotted as a function of the probability of A supporting B, where A is the more aggressive of the two females. A line has been fitted to the points. Its slope is positive but less than unity; in other words, the more aggressive individual is more likely to support the other than vice versa, but there is evidence of reciprocal support. The degree to which this association is due to kinship is not known. (*From* Dunbar 1980)

Thus, male chimpanzee alliances partly express kinship, but only partly, for each chimpanzee is likely to be engaged in a complex series of shifting alliances: A and B may be in league against C and D while A, B, C, and D may join together to murder E. Many of these interactions will involve males only distantly related.

Recently our knowledge of chimpanzee alliances has been greatly expanded by study of a captive colony housed during most days of the year in an outdoor enclosure large enough to give the animals some freedom of movement but small enough to permit intensive observations. Study of this captive colony reveals that alliances are critical in determining which male becomes the alpha male, that males regularly try to isolate their opponents from others, thus decreasing their support, and that males rapidly shift alliances in order to further their aims. In addition, the alpha male usually has a reciprocal relationship with the adult females: they support him in his status and he acts as peacemaker among them and defender of those under attack. Finally, chimps show a tremendous need for reconciliation with their opponents; this, too, probably reflects the importance of alliances, since each individual is both friend and foe, depending on context.

These conclusions have been beautifully summarized in a provocative book by Frans de Waal, entitled *Chimpanzee Politics*. The observations span several years and revolve around three males competing for dominant status in a group that contained nine adult females and their offspring. Two dramatic power take-overs occurred, which nicely show the forces at work. In the beginning Yeroen was the alpha male. He received more than three-fourths of all the submissive greetings given in the group (in these a chimp approaches the more dominant animal, giving a rapid series of panting grunts and lowering itself so as to look *up* into the eyes of the dominant). Luit was second in dominance; he was greeted much less frequently than Yeroen and two dominant females did not greet him at all. Nikkie was just becoming fully adult and none of the adult females greeted him.

When Luit began to challenge Yeroen with a series of intimidating displays, Yeroen sought out the company of the adult females, doubling the time he spent in their presence. When Luit first struck Yeroen, the latter burst out screaming, ran to a group of females, embraced each, and, followed by them, drove Luit to a far corner of the enclosure. Although he was supported by most of the adult females, Yeroen was not supported by all: twice he begged one female to join him and twice she turned her back. Others began to show ambivalence toward Yeroen, and just prior to the attack on him, Nikkie and an adolescent male passed Yeroen without greeting him, highly unusual for them. Meanwhile, Luit was far from indifferent to the support Yeroen was receiving from the females. Luit leaped on the back of a female who had been sitting near Yeroen and jumped up and down, causing the female and her clinging son to scream.

Note that just as support given to an opponent may trigger re-taliation, so failure to provide protection from this retaliation may provoke fierce attacks (the chimpanzee discriminates against the non-reciprocator). In a later encounter, a large adult female Puist sup-ported Luit in chasing Nikkie. When Nikkie later displayed at Puist she held out her hand to Luit, soliciting his support, but Luit did nothing. Puist at once turned on Luit, barking furiously, chased him across the enclosure and hit him. This is more than withholding future aid from non-reciprocators: this is moralistic aggression, designed to influence others directly into mending their ways.

Yet in spite of their intense conflict on that day, the day did not end before the two males were reconciled: they looked each other in the eye, embraced, and Luit presented his backside to Yeroen and was groomed (see Figures 15-9 to 15-11). So great is the need for recon-ciliation that one chimp may punish another by refusing to allow a reconciliation. Thus, later when Mama supported Yeroen against Nikkie, Nikkie punished her for her support but shortly afterwards sought a reconciliation with her. Only after several attempts did Mama permit a reconciliation. The frequency of reconciliations suggests the

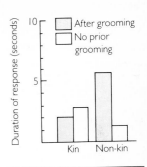

Figure 15-8

The effect of previous grooming on tendency to respond to solicitations for help, in vervet monkeys. The duration of attentive response (in seconds) of an individual to playback of the recruitment call of kin or non-kin in the presence or absence of prior groom-ing by the caller. Attentive response = looking toward the speaker. Duration of looking was measured from a film of the interaction. The difference for non-kin—after grooming or with no prior grooming—is significant. Other com-parisons are not. (*From* Seyfarth and Cheney 1984)

Figure 15-9

Requesting a reconciliation. Yeroen holds out his hand to his rival, Luit, invit-ing him out of the tree into which he had chased him. This attempt at recon-ciliation is watched by other group members, including the adolescent male next to Yeroen and an adult female. (Photo: Frans de Waal)

a   b

Figure 15-10

Intense reconciliation. Two male chimpanzees (Nikkie and Luit) groom each other after a conflict. (a) At first each avoids the other's face and grooms his rear end instead. (b) Later they adopt a more relaxed posture. (*From* Frans de Waal 1982)

importance to the chimps of maintaining larger alliances. Although Yeroen and Luit were in strong conflict for alpha status, in the wild they still had many opportunities to act together in the face of other groups.

In the two months that followed this first dramatic encounter, Luit waged a relentless campaign of separating interventions at Yeroen. Whenever Yeroen sat near a female, Luit would become restless and would soon punish the female for sitting near him and Yeroen would be unable to prevent this (Figure 15-12). Soon Luit only had to *display* at the sitting couple and they would separate (for the reverse case, which happened later, see Figure 15-13). From spending 60% of his time in the company of adult females, as he had just prior to Luit's first overt moves against him, Yeroen's time steadily fell until he was spending less time with them than he had back when Luit was still openly subservient (30%).

Luit's negative behavior toward the females only occurred when they sat near Yeroen. At other times he was very friendly, sitting with them, grooming them, and playing with their children. Indeed, these friendly contacts sometimes occurred at moments of tactical importance. On the same day he first struck Yeroen, after being chased by the adult females and reconciling with Yeroen, Luit soon began a new series of intimidation displays at his rival—but not before first groom-

Figure 15-11

Kissing as a form of reassurance. A dominant female (Mama), with clinging infant, kisses an adult male (Yeroen) to reassure him during an aggressive interaction among the adult males, including Yeroen. Mama frequently attempted to calm males in aggressive situations even when she was not otherwise involved. Kisses are also especially likely to occur during reconciliations. (Photo: Frans de Waal)

ing several females in rapid succession, as if bargaining for their subsequent neutrality!

None of this might have worked were it not for the indirect aid Luit received from the actions of Nikkie. Nikkie was just beginning to assert his dominance over the adult females, and he found it useful to mimic Luit's treatment of females: if Luit slapped a female, Nikkie slapped her as well. When females intervened on Yeroen's side against Luit, Nikkie attacked one or more of the females. In turn, Luit sometimes helped Nikkie in his conflict with the females. In de Waal's terminology, they formed an "*open* coalition." Their interests were not in conflict, but ran in parallel: as Luit became alpha male, Nikki advanced above all the females and soon dominated Yeroen as well.

Now Nikkie's interests and Luit's were no longer in parallel, for Nikkie was in a position to challenge Luit. The key to this was Yeroen, who now supported Nikkie in a closed coalition: when Nikkie threatened Luit, Yeroen would back him up, literally standing behind him and placing his hands on Nikkie's back, often hooting along with him (for comparable scenes from the wild see Figures 15-14 and 15-15). Although Luit was, at first, supported by the females, the new male coalition was too strong for Luit, and Nikkie rose to alpha status. This coalition of a deposed leader with another male to oust the deposer has also been observed in the wild.

The relationship between the alpha male and the group's females is a reciprocal one: they support him in his conflicts with other males while he acts as a peacemaker and defender of the downtrodden. As a

Figure 15-12

Punishing a rival's sup- porter. Luit leaps on Tepel's back, bouncing and pum- meling her while she screams. He is punishing her for recently having made contact with his rival, Yeroen, who stands just off camera unable to intervene. (Photo: Frans de Waal)

peacemaker he attempts to break up fights without intervening on the side of anyone:

For example, on one occasion a quarrel between Mama and Spin got out of hand and ended in biting and fighting. Numerous apes rushed up to the two warring females and joined in the fray. A huge knot of fighting, screaming apes rolled on the sand until Luit leapt in and literally beat them apart. He did not choose sides in the conflict, like the others; instead, anyone who continued to fight received a blow from him.

As a supporter of the downtrodden, the alpha male intervenes in fights on the side of the individual who would otherwise lose. This policy is nicely shown by Luit, who prior to his take-over supported the loser only 35% of the time but immediately afterwards supported the loser 65% of the time.

De Waal has made the important suggestion that female support for the alpha male may be contingent on his playing a control function in their lives. This is suggested by the female's relationship with Nikkie. After Nikkie, with the help of Yeroen, displaced Luit, he failed to exer- cise a control function and the females failed to support him. They were slow to greet him, and long after the take-over continued to greet Yeroen more than Nikkie. Yeroen, in turn, acted as peacemaker,

and later prevented Nikkie from playing the same role! Further evidence comes from the fact that Luit supported the loser most intensively (87%) a year after his take-over, when dominance relations were unsettled, as if he was then making a special bid for the support of the females as a group.

In captivity, female chimpanzees also form coalitions: they frequently intervene in fights between adult females and, as we have seen, between adult males. Also, chimpanzee females often intervene in disputes between juveniles, while males rarely do so. But the great difference between female and male coalitions is that female coalitions are not aimed strategically toward obtaining high rank. This is presumably because a male chimp who achieves alpha status gains increased access to breeding females, while a dominant female gains no comparable payoff. As a result, female alliances are much more stable over long periods of time, and females are more likely than males to support those with whom they spend a lot of time in close proximity. In short, female alliances seem to run along affectional lines of kinship and friendship, while male alliances change in response to new opportunities, especially those provided by the maturation of newly adult males (such as Nikkie) and those provided by the assumption of the control function.

Figure 15-13

A separating intervention. Yeroen, with his hair on end, approaches Tepel (with infant) and Luit. This approach is a form of intimidation designed to force the two adults to break off their contact and separate. (Photo: Frans de Waal)

a   b

Figure 15-14

Intense reassurance behavior. Two fully adult male chimpanzees in the wild at the edge of their ranging area respond upon hearing a neighboring group. (a) One male mounts the other. More than likely both males have erections but there is no penetration. (b) The male on top has removed the partly eaten fruit and is showing a scream-face. The calls were very distant, so the chimps listened intently and for about eight minutes showed other reassurance behavior, such as holding hands. (Photos: Richard Wrangham)

Altogether, de Waal's work gives us a glimpse of a fascinating world of strategic interaction in chimpanzees in which shifting alliances play a critical role in determining the alpha status.

Are Dolphins and Whales Reciprocal Altruists?

Before turning to reciprocity in ourselves, let us consider a possibly parallel case. From the time of antiquity, dolphins and whales have been known for their altruism and for the ease with which they extend this altruism beyond the boundaries of their own species. Ancient Greek coins depict dolphins rescuing humans, and an entire book of the Bible tells the story of a man, Jonah, who spends three days in the belly of a whale but is eventually cast ashore. Stories of human rescue also come from the present time. Whether or not these stories are authentic, it is clear from a recent review by Richard Conner and Kenneth Norris that dolphins and whales often direct similar forms of altruism to members of other species. Likewise, the behavior of dol-

Figure 15-15

Reassurance behavior. One adult male reaches over and feels another's erect penis after hearing a twig snap. The males are at the edge of their ranging area and are easily frightened. An adult female sits unconcerned nearby. The males continue to listen, hear nothing more, and resume eating. Why grasping another male's penis is reassuring and exactly who is reassured is not clear, but in monkeys and in apes in general, it seems that grasping the genitals of another male is often associated with alliance formation. (Photo: Richard Wrangham)

phins and whales shows a subtlety and sophistication that suggests they could easily appreciate the dilemma of drowning human beings and come to their rescue.

Carrying individuals to safety is easily derived from a common dolphin-whale habit, which is to give physical support to the sick, injured, or very young. This help comes in three forms: standing by, assisting, and, supporting. *Standing by* occurs when an animal stays with another animal in distress, but does not offer obvious aid. Often an individual will remain in a dangerous situation far longer than if there were no one in distress. *Assisting* includes approaching an injured comrade and swimming between the captor and its prey, biting or attacking capture vessels, and pushing an injured individual away from a would-be captor. Most of these examples come from descriptions of capture attempts. *Supporting* occurs when one or more animals maintain a distressed animal at the surface of the water. A supporting animal usually does not feed, stations itself below the sick animal—either right-side-up or upside-down—and presses upward, leaving this position only long enough to breathe, but keeping the stricken animal at the surface. The behavior stops when the sick animal dies or recovers enough to swim by itself.

A striking feature of this help is that it is often extended to dolphins and whales of other species. Standing by even has been observed at sea between members of widely different genera. For example, Kenneth Norris reports that during the capture of a young-adult female Pacific pilot whale *Globicephala macrorhynchus*, a group of Pacific striped dolphins *Lagenorhynchus obliquidens* stood by the struggling whale during capture and stayed while the whale was being brought aboard the vessel. There is no doubt that whales and dolphins understand when another cetacean is being captured. They will often bite restraining lines of harpooned animals during capture, propel injured animals away from captors, and even attack the captors. Again an interesting example was observed by Norris. An adult pilot whale was shot and killed instantly. It drifted toward the capture vessel. When it was a few meters from the vessel's rail, two other pilot whales rose on either side of the animal and, pressing their snouts on top of its head, took it down and away from the vessel so that it was never seen again. Notice that the dead whale was not supported in the usual fashion, but was spirited away from the would-be captors in exactly the opposite manner usually seen during support. For another example of support see Figure 15-16.

How are we to explain these unusual examples of altruistic behavior in dolphins and whales? Our first assumption might be that altruistic behavior has been favored through effects on kin. But this explanation fails to account for the fact that altruism often is directed very widely, even to members of other species, and that in some dolphins, group structure is very fluid, yet altruism is common. The frequent examples of interspecific altruism observed in captivity might be supposed to result from an unnatural association, but, in fact, interspecific associations in nature are very frequent. In some cases species travel together regularly: groups are sometimes intimately mixed, and one species may imitate the behavior patterns of the other. Helping behavior has been reported between species that associate regularly as well as those that do not.

The second factor that argues against kinship is dispersion. In some species, animals travel in separate groups (called *pods*) and these may remain distinct for many years; but in many species of dolphins there is good evidence that herds are composed of subgroups that may vary continually in composition. For example, a herd of a hundred bottlenose dolphins *Tursiops truncatus* living along a 40-km stretch of Florida coast did not intermix with adjacent herds, but within the herd, traveling groups varied on a daily basis, though some association patterns were frequently seen. Another herd of the same species contained some subgroups that remained stable for months and then

Figure 15-16

Mass aid to a dying whale. Twenty-nine adult false killer whales *Pseudorca crassidens* surround a large male (near the center), who has rolled over on his side and is bleeding from the right ear, heavily infested with parasitic worms. The whale is normally an open-water species, but the adults remained with this stricken male for three days until he died. Prior to his death, the whales resisted being pushed out to sea, but after his death many left on their own and the others no longer resisted being pushed out to sea. Before departing, the whales even pushed a snorkelling human (the photographer) to shore repeatedly, perhaps mistaking his labored breathing for signs of drowning. (Photo: James Porter)

changed, while other subgroups were continually breaking up and being formed.

This degree of fluidity in group structure, combined with high altruism toward group members, is not what we would expect on the basis of kinship. By contrast, the ability to recognize a large number of other animals and strong benefits to reciprocal interactions would both permit and encourage this kind of fluidity. It seems likely that it is predation that has selected for this pattern. Dolphins and whales are vulnerable to sharks and probably travel in groups in order to minimize shark attacks. Individuals warn each other of the approach of a predator, they aid each other in escaping the predator and come to the aid of an individual injured during predation. If predation pressure molded dolphin group formation and early altruism, then it must often have favored distantly related individuals traveling together for mutual defense. Dolphins and whales are long-lived, slowly-reproducing animals, so that increase in group size via reproduction would be a very slow process. For this reason members of different species probably often travel together as opportunity arises for mutual protection. In these circumstances fluidity of social structure maximizes the possible number of altruistic relationships.

Reciprocal Altruism in Human Evolution

It seems likely that during our recent evolutionary history (at least the last 5 million years) there has been strong selection on our ancestors to develop a variety of reciprocal interactions. I base this conclusion in part on the strong emotional system that underlies our relationships with friends, colleagues, acquaintances, and so on. Humans routinely help each other in times of danger (for example, accidents, predation, and attacks from other human beings). We routinely share food, we help the sick, the wounded, and the very young. We routinely share our tools, and we share our knowledge in a very complex way. Often these forms of behavior meet the criterion of small cost to the giver and great benefit to the recipient. Although kinship often mediates many of these acts, it never appears to be a prerequisite. Such aid is often extended in full knowledge that the recipient is only distantly related.

During the Pleistocene, and probably before, a homonid species would have met the preconditions for the evolution of reciprocal altruism: for example, long lifespan, low dispersal rate, life in small, mutually dependent and stable social groups, and a long period of parental care leading to extensive contacts with close relatives over many years. Likewise, it seems likely that dominance relations were very complicated, with many opportunities for reversal, depending on aid from others and preferential access to weapons. Aid in intraspecific combat, particularly by kin, almost certainly reduced the linearity of the dominance order in early humans. Studies of fights in living hunter-gatherers, such as the San of the Kalahari Desert, show that in almost all fights that are initially between two individuals, others soon join in. Mortality, for example, often strikes the secondaries rather than the principals. Tool use has also probably had an equalizing effect on human dominance relations, and the San have a saying that nicely illustrates this. As a dispute reaches the stage where deadly weapons may be employed, an individual will often declare: "We are none of us big and others small; we are all men and we can fight; I am going to get my arrows."

Before turning to the emotional system underlying human reciprocal altruism, it is useful to distinguish between two kinds of cheating. In *gross* cheating the cheater fails to reciprocate at all and the altruist suffers the cost of whatever altruism has been dispensed without compensating benefits. More broadly, gross cheating may be defined as reciprocating so little, if at all, that the altruist receives less benefit from the gross cheater than the cost of the altruist's acts of altruism to the cheater. Clearly, selection will strongly favor prompt discrimination against the gross cheater. *Subtle* cheating, by contrast, involves reciprocating but always attempting to give less than one was given, or more precisely, to give less than the partner would give if the situation were reversed. In this situation, the altruist still benefits from the relationship but not as much as if the relationship were completely equitable, while the subtle cheater benefits more than if the relationship were equitable. Because human altruism may span long periods of time, and because thousands of exchanges may take place that involve many different goods and many different cost/benefit ratios, the problem of computing the relevant totals, detecting imbalances, and deciding whether they are due to chance or to small-scale cheating is a difficult one. Even then, the altruist is in an awkward position, captured by the folk saying "Half a loaf is better than none," for if attempts to make the relationship equitable lead to the rupture of the relationship, the altruist may suffer the loss of the substandard altruism of the subtle cheater.

The importance of this last idea depends upon the degree to which relationships are mutually exclusive. To some degree, they inevitably are, since altruistic acts exchanged between two individuals could be directed elsewhere. An individual who feels that another individual is subtly cheating on their relationship has the option of attempting to restore the relationship to equity or attempting to pair with another individual, thereby decreasing the possible exchanges between the altruist and the subtle cheater and replacing these with exchanges between reciprocal individuals. In short, he or she can switch friends.

The human altruistic system is a sensitive, unstable one. Often it will pay to cheat, namely, when the partner will not find out, when the partner will not discontinue his or her altruism even if he or she does find out, or when the partner is unlikely to survive long enough to reciprocate adequately. And the perception of subtle cheating may be very difficult. Given the unstable character of the system, where a degree of cheating is adaptive, natural selection will rapidly favor a complex psychological system in which individuals regulate both their own altruistic and cheating tendencies and their responses to these tendencies in others. The system that results should allow individuals to reap the benefits of altruistic exchanges, protect themselves from gross and subtle forms of cheating, and practice those forms of cheating that local conditions make adaptive. Individuals will differ not in being altruists or cheaters but in the degree of altruism they show and in the conditions under which they will cheat. This kind of selection should lead to the following sort of emotional system.

Friendship. The tendencies to like other individuals (not necessarily closely related), to form friendships, and to act altruistically toward friends and toward those one likes, provide the immediate emotional rewards to motivate altruistic behavior and the formation of altruistic partnerships. We know from the work of social psychology that the relationship between altruism and liking is a two-way street: one is more altruistic toward those one likes and one tends to like those who are most altruistic.

Moralistic Aggression. Once strong positive emotions have evolved to motivate altruistic behavior, the altruist is in a vulnerable position, because cheaters will be selected for that take advantage of these positive emotions. This, in turn, sets up a selection pressure for a protective mechanism. I believe that a sense of fairness has evolved in human beings as the standard against which to measure the behavior of other people, so as to guard against cheating in reciprocal relationships. In turn, this sense of fairness is coupled with moralistic aggressiveness when cheating tendencies are discovered in a friend. A common feature of this aggression is that it often seems out of proportion to the offense that is committed. Friends are even killed over apparently trivial disputes. But since small inequities repeated many times over a lifetime may exact a heavy toll in inclusive fitness, selection may favor a strong show of aggression when the cheating tendency is discovered.

Gratitude and Sympathy. If the cost/benefit ratio is an important factor in determining the adaptiveness of altruistic behavior, then humans should be selected to be sensitive to the cost and benefit of an altruistic act, both in deciding whether to perform one and in deciding how much to reciprocate. I think the emotion of gratitude has been selected to regulate human responses to altruistic acts, and that the emotion is sensitive to the cost/benefit ratio of such acts. I believe the emotion of sympathy has been selected to motivate altruistic behavior as a function of the plight of the recipient of the behavior. Crudely put, the greater the potential benefit to the recipient, the greater the sympathy and the more likely the altruistic gesture, even to strange or disliked individuals. Of course, this feature of sympathy applies to kin-directed altruism as well as reciprocal altruism, but gratitude only seems to apply to reciprocal relationships. Psychologists have shown that human beings reciprocate more when the original act was expensive for the benefactor, even though the benefit given is the same.

Guilt and Reparative Altruism. If an individual has cheated on a reciprocal relationship, and this fact has been found out, or may shortly be found out, and if the partner responds by cutting off all future acts of aid, then the cheater will have paid dearly for the misdeed. It will be to his or her advantage to avoid this, and it may be to the partner's benefit to avoid this, since in cutting off future acts of aid, the partner sacrifices the benefits of future reciprocal help. If so, the cheater should be selected to make up for the misdeed and to show convincing evidence that future cheating is not planned; in short, a reparative gesture is called for. It seems plausible that the emotion of guilt has been selected for in humans partly in order to motivate the cheater to compensate for misdeeds and to behave reciprocally in the future, thus preventing the rupture of reciprocal relationships. The key is that one's cheating tendencies have been discovered. Social psychologists have produced a variety of evidence that publicly harming another individual leads to reparative altruistic behavior, but only when this harm is known to others.

Sense of Justice. As we have already noted, in complex systems of reciprocal altruism, individuals need a standard against which to judge the behavior of others. This will be especially true in species such as our own in which a system of multi-party altruism may operate so that an individual does not necessarily receive reciprocal benefits from the individual aided but may receive the return from third parties. This sense of justice involves two components: individuals share a common standard or sense of fairness, and infractions of this standard are associated with strong emotional reactions and aggressive impulses. Moral philosophers contend that a social arrangement is judged as fair when an individual endorses it without knowledge of which position in the arrangement the individual will occupy. In other words, a fair social arrangement must appear fair equally for each individual involved in the arrangement.

The Prisoner's Dilemma and Tit-for-Tat

Game theorists have likened reciprocal altruism to the problem of "the prisoner's dilemma." The prisoner's dilemma refers to the imaginary

Player B

Player A   Cooperation   Defection

Cooperation

	Cooperation	Defection
Cooperation	R=3 Reward for mutual cooperation	S=0 Sucker's payoff
Defection	T=5 Temptation to defect	P=l Punishment for mutual defection

Figure 15-17

The game of prisoner's dilemma. This is the pay-off matrix used in the tournament run by Robert Axelrod. A game consisted of 200 match-ups between two strategies. The game is defined by $T > R > P > S$ and $R > (S + T)/2$. (*From* Axelrod and Hamilton 1981)

situation in which two individuals are imprisoned and accused of having cooperated to perform some crime. The two prisoners are held separately, and attempts are made to induce each one to implicate the other. If neither one does, both are set free. This is the cooperative strategy. In order to tempt one or both to defect, each is told that a confession implicating the other will result in his or her release and, in addition, a small reward. If both confess, each one is imprisoned. But if one individual implicates the other, and not vice versa, then the implicated partner receives a harsher sentence than if each had implicated the other. We can symbolize the payoffs as follows: T is the temptation to implicate the other; R is the reward each one gets if neither one defects; P is the punishment each one gets if both defect; and S is the sucker's payoff, the penalty one suffers if implicated by the partner. Thus, $T > R > P > S$ (see Figure 15-17).

The dilemma is: If each one thinks rationally, then each one will decide that the best course is to implicate the other, thus making both worse off than if each had decided to trust the other. Consider the first individual's problem: If his partner fails to implicate him, then he himself ought to implicate his partner in order to gain T instead of R; and if his partner implicates him, then it will be better for him to implicate his partner, since he will then suffer P instead of S.

The prisoner's dilemma mimics reciprocal altruism in the following way. Each individual stands to gain R from reciprocal altruism. But each is tempted to enjoy the altruism without reciprocating, thereby gaining T. But if neither reciprocates, then each only gains P, while the altruist who is not reciprocated does worst of all and ends up with only *S*. In single encounters there is no solution to the prisoner's dilemma except to cheat, and both individuals end up relatively badly off. But if the prisoner's dilemma is repeated a number of times, then it may be advantageous to cooperate on the early moves and cheat only toward the end of the game. It is possible to play repeated games of prisoner's dilemma in which each individual must decide which option to take without knowing what the other is simultaneously choosing, and each learns the results only after both have chosen. A new game then presents itself. When people know the total number of games to be played, they do, indeed, cheat more often in the final games.

The relationship between reciprocal altruism and the prisoner's dilemma is significant because the mathematics of the prisoner's dilemma is fairly well worked out. By conceptualizing reciprocal altruism as a series of prisoner's dilemmas, it is possible to derive some very interesting results. Recently, Robert Axelrod and William Hamilton have been able to prove that one tactic is superior to all others in playing repeated games of prisoner's dilemma. This tactic is called *tit-for-tat*.

Axelrod discovered the superiority of the tit-for-tat strategy in an unusual way. He conducted a computer tournament. People were asked to submit strategies for playing 200 games of prisoner's dilemma. Fourteen game theorists in disciplines such as economics and mathematics submitted entries. These 14, and a totally random strategy, were paired with each other in a round-robin tournament. Some of these strategies were highly intricate. For example, one strategy modelled the opponent's behavior and then used certain rules of mathematical inference to select what seemed to be the appropriate counterstrategy. But the result of the tournament was that the highest average score was attained by the simplest of all strategies submitted, tit-for-tat. Tit-for-tat had only two rules. On the first move, cooperate. On each succeeding move, do what your opponent did in the previous move. Thus, tit-for-tat may be characterized as a strategy of cooperation based on reciprocity.

Alexrod saw the computer tournament as an analogy to the evolutionary process. Imagine that a species finds itself in a situation in which individuals have about 200 opportunities to exchange altruistic acts with each other. We may imagine that mutation and recombination provide a series of possible strategies, including an entirely random one. These strategies then interact and we see which one ends up gaining the greatest average benefit. Many people have pointed out that there is a similarity between genetic mutation and human mental innovation, but so far as I know, Axelrod is the first person to use this similarity to gain deeper insight into the evolutionary process.

To intensify the competition between tit-for-tat and other strategies, Axelrod circulated the results of the first round-robin and solicited entries for a second round. (In the second round, the *average* length of each game was 200 moves, with a probability slightly less than 1.0 that a given move would not be the last.) This time there were 62 entries from six countries. Most of the contestants were computer hobbyists, but also present were professors of evolutionary biology, physics, and computer science, as well as the disciplines represented earlier. Tit-for-tat was again submitted, and once again it won.

Each tournament may be considered a single generation of natural selection. So as to mimic the evolutionary process more exactly, Axelrod constituted the next generation by selecting entries according to their success in the previous interaction. The strategies were then played against each other in their new frequencies, and successive generations of selection were generated in the same way. The results showed that, as the less successful rules were displaced, tit-for-tat continued to do well. In the long run, it displaced all the other rules. This provides further evidence that the simple strategy of what we might call *contingent reciprocity* is highly successful in competition with a variety of counterstrategies at various frequencies.

An analysis of the 3 million choices made in the second round identified three features of the tit-for-tat strategy as important in its success: (1) *Never be the first to defect.* That is, tit-for-tatter begins by cooperating and defects only after the partner has defected. (2) *Retaliate only after the partner has defected.* The tit-for-tatter is a very cautious individual who immediately responds to non-reciprocation by cutting off additional altruism. (3) *Be forgiving after just one act of retaliation.* The tit-for-tatter is ever optimistic, taking any altruistic act by the partner as an invitation to reciprocity.

With the computer results to spur them on, Axelrod and Hamilton were able to prove that as long as the chance of future interaction is sufficiently great, tit-for-tat is the best strategy. No competing strategy can oust it once it has become established. The only other strategy that is nearly this stable is that of constant defection, but this strategy will be replaced by tit-for-tat whenever tit-for-tatters can interact preferentially with each other.

It remains to be seen what strategies will prove stable in more complex games in which there is opportunity for punishment, as well as mere non-reciprocation, and in which benefits and costs are allowed to vary from interaction to interaction. But the unexpected success of this simple strategy suggests that reciprocal altruism may be quite widespread in nature. Even bacteria are capable of contingent responses to their immediate environment, which responses could take the form of a tit-for-tat strategy: first do unto others as you wish them to do unto you, but then do unto them as they have just done unto you.

Summary

Reciprocal altruism is expected to evolve when two individuals associate long enough to exchange roles frequently as potential altruist and recipient. The key is the ability to discriminate against non-reciprocators by withholding future aid. The importance of association is illustrated by the widespread, spontaneous break-out of a live-and-let-live system of mutual restraint across the trenches of World War I. Because combatants interacted in stable positions for long periods of time, restraint on one side could be matched by restraint on the other.

Vampire bats in nature feed other bats that have failed to feed. Degree of association and kinship each have independent effects on food sharing, and evidence from an experimental colony demonstrates that an individual is more likely to feed another that earlier fed it. Bats respond to others on the basis of need in such a way that benefit transferred is greater than the cost suffered.

Birds respond less aggressively to a familiar neighbor calling from their common territorial boundary than to a stranger calling from the same place, but this difference disappears when they call from the opposite side of the territory. This suggests that birds discriminate against individuals that violate an implicit agreement not to invade each other's territory.

Baboons frequently support each other in fights with third parties. Within a troop, a central hierarchy of males may give its members mating success they could not gain acting alone. Males that aid others are more likely to be aided in return. In vervet monkeys, prior grooming by an unrelated individual increases the likelihood of gaining support, but such grooming has no effect on support by relatives.

Studies of a captive colony of chimpanzees show that alliances are critical for a male attaining alpha status, that males isolate opponents from other group members, and that males shift alliances frequently and strategically. The alpha male typically has a reciprocal relationship with the adult females such that they support him in his status and he acts as peacemaker and protector of the weak. Chimpanzees have a strong need for reconciliation, probably because opponents are also allies in larger conflicts.

Evidence from dolphins and whales suggests that they may be reciprocal altruists. At least it is clear that they display several forms of altruistic behavior to each other, that altruism may easily be extended to members of other species, and that altruism is common within some species with very fluid group membership.

There can hardly be any doubt that reciprocal altruism has been a potent force in human evolution. The emotions of friendship, moralistic aggression, gratitude, and sympathy, as well as our sense of fairness, probably arose primarily as mechanisms to regulate reciprocal altruism. Study of tournaments of iterated games of prisoner's dilemma—which mimics systems of reciprocal altruism—demonstrate the superiority of one very simple strategy, tit-for-tat: on the first move cooperate; on all subsequent moves do what your partner did on the preceding move.

Chapter 16

Deceit and Self-Deception

O NE OF THE most important things to realize about systems of animal communication is that they are not systems for the dissemination of the truth. An animal selected to signal to another animal may be selected to convey correct information, misinformation, or both. Consider a species in which males court females by offering them food. A female wishing to be courted may be selected to show that she is a conspecific, receptive female. At the same time, a *male* may attempt to convey the fact that he is a receptive female, since this may induce courtship by a male and permit him to steal the male's food. As we shall see below, exactly this deception is practiced by male scorpionflies. The female conveys correct information, the male incorrect, and a courting male must decide which is which.

In this example there is some priority to the communication of correct information, since deceit consists of mimicking the truth. This is probably always the case, namely, that deception is a parasitism of the pre-existing system for communicating correct information. Whatever the case, there is induced a co-evolutionary struggle between deceiver and deceived that is frequency-dependent: as deception increases in frequency, it intensifies selection for detection, and as detection spreads, it intensifies selection on deceit. In our example, a male scorpionfly is selected to tell the difference between females and pseudofemales, and this selects for more plausible pseudofemales, which in turn selects for more discriminating males. When pseudofemales are rare, they easily escape detection; as they become more frequent, life becomes more difficult. With powers to deceive and to spot deception being improved by natural selection, a new kind of deception may be favored: self-deception. Self-deception renders the deception being practiced unconscious to the practitioner, thereby hiding from other individuals the subtle signs of self-knowledge that may give away the deception being practiced.

Partly because it has been so neglected, we devote this chapter to a study of deception and its offspring, self-deception. We begin by reviewing camouflage and mimicry in interspecific relations. We then describe some deceptions practiced by plants. Within species we review examples of sexual mimicry and deception in aggressive encounters. In our own species we describe the way in which self-deception may serve deceit. We show that self-deception can be demonstrated experimentally in humans, and we describe some of the mechanisms of self-deception.

Camouflage and Mimicry

Deceit has long been recognized in relations between members of different species. Predator and prey often benefit from remaining concealed from each other, and this advantage has led to the evolution of many remarkable instances of camouflage and mimicry. In *camouflage* the creature seeks to remain invisible against its background (Figure 16-1). This involves a variety of mechanisms. The color and pattern of

Figure 16-1

A famous find-the-bug puzzle. Upper left we see a specimen of the weevil *Lithinus nigrocristatus,* which is conspicuous against a white background. The rest of the picture shows how two additional specimens can literally disappear from sight when mounted against an appropriate background, lichen-covered bark. (*From* Cott 1940)

the background are imitated. The creature is often countershaded; that is, the portion of the animal normally in shadow is more lightly colored so as to cancel out the shadow. Conspicuous features such as eyes may be hidden by larger markings. And the outline of the animal may be broken up by conspicuous markings that tend to distract the eye.

Some insects have had their entire shapes remolded so as more perfectly to resemble parts of plants such as sticks or leaves (Figure 16-2). These deceptions sometimes induce further deception. Consider a Panamanian stick insect that so closely resembles a stick it requires precious seconds to unfurl its wings and fly away. Its hind wings have evolved a bright red color. When detected, the stick insect rapidly displays its hind wings, thus startling the predator so that the insect may escape before the enemy recovers.

The value to the individual of having more than one deceptive ploy is suggested by the adaptations of tropical moths. These rest on exposed trunks and limbs during the daytime, when they are hunted by visually oriented predators such as birds. The moth's first line of defense is camouflage: it is colored so as to blend in naturally with the surface on which it rests. But in many tropical species, frightening im-

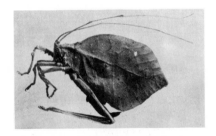

Figure 16-2

Leaf mimics. Here are three examples of insects that bear a strong resemblance to leaves. Notice that not only is the shape, size, and color of a leaf mimicked but also its veins and fungus spots. This implies that insects lacking such subtleties were more often spotted as fakes. Antennae may be long and twig-like or short and flattened. *Upper left*: species of *Cycloptera. Lower left*: *Cycloptera elegans. Right*: *Chitoniscus feedjeanus. (From* Cott 1940)

ages are cryptically hidden in the background coloration, images that resemble creatures that prey on birds, such as cats and monkeys. These images are subtle and become detectable at about the distance at which a bird might recognize the moth as distinct from its background (see Figure 16-3).

Specific behaviors often accompany the effort to be cryptic, as was

a   b

Figure 16-3

Sinister images in moths. Each of these moths found in Panama is camouflaged and difficult to spot when resting against an appropriate background. But in addition to the camouflage, each appears to be protected by an image frightening to creatures that feed on it, such as birds. Moth (a), for example, resembles a well-camouflaged catlike predator. Notice the eyes sunk into large, shadowed sockets. Legs are held sideways and highlighted with white markings (only one is visible—above, on the left—the others having broken off). When all the legs are present, they resemble a cat's whiskers. Notice the antennae are slung sideways so as to heighten this effect. (b) This moth resembles a bat or a cross between a bird and a mammal. The hairs on its thorax are shaped so as to give the impression of ears and eyes. Its arms have been given mammal-like hairs. The birdlike wings are a very threatening feature, suggesting that this predatory creature could quickly traverse the intervening space. I believe these kinds of sinister images in moths often deter predators from taking a closer look and, thus, give protection. (Photos: Nicholas Smythe)

nicely shown for the pronghorn *Antilocapra americana* by John Byers and Karen Byers. After nursing her fawn, the mother leaves it in hiding and goes some distance away to feed and rest (Figure 16-4). Coyote predation on fawns is frequent and the mother quickly moves to a distance of about 70 meters. At this distance a coyote hunting the fawn and using the mother as the starting point would better spend its time

a

b

Figure 16-4

A pronghorn mother takes leave of her fawn. (a) Now that her week-old fawn is fed and has urinated and defecated, the mother ceases all activity toward the fawn and stands silently in one place. This apparently acts as a signal for the fawn to seek out a hiding place, as begins in this picture. (b) When the fawn is several meters away or has settled down, the mother may start her departure. Intense bouts of maternal care followed by long separations are part of a strategy for protecting young fawns from predators through camouflage. (Photos: Peter Bromley)

hunting ground squirrels. The mother stays away an average of 225 minutes, so that a coyote waiting for the mother to return to its fawn would again better spend its time hunting ground squirrels. Maternal activities such as standing, feeding, and reclining are distributed evenly across time away from the fawn, so that a coyote cannot infer an imminent movement to the calf from the pattern of the mother's activities. There is one cue, however, that gives away valuable information: the mother orients her body or her head more frequently toward the fawn than away. A coyote using either cue to demarcate a 90° search area, instead of 360°, starting from the mother's head or front of body, would do better hunting pronghorn fawns than ground squirrels. Whether coyotes use such information is not known, but the behavior of the pronghorn mother suggests that they may. Mothers who have just left their fawns tend to orient *away* from the fawn. As time passes, their orientation shifts to parallel to and, finally, facing the fawn. It is as if an increasing need to contact the fawn results in increasing orientation to it. The fawn is probably most vulnerable when just deserted and it is at this time that mothers are openly deceptive by orienting away from the fawn.

In mimicry an organism seeks to resemble something specific. This may be something cryptic, as in the moth mimicry described above, but it is usually very conspicuous. Poisonous snakes are brightly colored to facilitate recognition and avoidance by potential predators. This system has spawned a series of mimics, species that are neither poisonous nor closely related but that are often remarkably similar in appearance to the poisonous species (Figure 16-5). They gain protection by being mistaken for the poisonous species (the model). Where mimics are infrequent compared to their models, they will gain a greater advantage than where they are relatively common. Sometimes a mimetic species may come in as many as five distinct forms, each of which mimics a different model species (Figure 16-6). This remarkable mimicry has presumably evolved because each new mutant mimic initially enjoys the benefit of being rare. The importance of relative frequency of model and mimic is suggested by two observations from butterflies. In a species that mimics several models, the frequency of the mimetic forms correlates in nature with the frequency of the models (Figure 16-7). In two species, the frequency of imperfect mimics increases when mimics are relatively common (Figure 16-8); that is, the mimic begins to evolve *away* from its model, the imperfect mimics probably being less conspicuous than the more perfect mimics.

Sexual Mimicry in Plants

Plants are known to deceive insects in a variety of ways. Some passion-flower vines (*Passiflora*) have evolved leaves that resemble those of

Figure 16-5

Mimicry. The pupa of a butterfly *Dynastor darius* found in Panama bears a striking resemblance to the head of a snake. Notice the fake scales, the snakelike eyes, and the constriction behind the fake head. The snakelike pattern of colors is made up of brown, beige, and white. Detected at close distances, this mimic will give humans a bad scare. When disturbed, the pupa waves violently back and forth. The pupal stage lasts about two weeks. (Photos: Annette Aiello)

other plants in order to make it more difficult for *Heliconius* butterflies to find them and deposit their eggs. Eggs give rise to caterpillars, which consume the leaves, along with any eggs. Some species have evolved egglike structures that give the appearance that butterfly eggs have already been laid (Figure 16-9). This usually deters egg-laying by the butterflies, since they are selected to avoid laying eggs where eggs have already been laid.

Perhaps the most striking examples of deception by plants involve sexual mimicry. In order to maximize pollination, many species of plants employ insects as pollen carriers. This is a strictly symbiotic relationship, in which each party benefits. The plant typically offers nectar, or sometimes pollen, as food in order to induce insects to visit its flowers and carry pollen from one plant to another. Orchids of the genus *Ophrys* provide neither nectar nor pollen but instead offer male wasps, bees, and flies—depending on the species of *Ophrys*—the illusion of sexual contact with a female of their own species.

Consider the "looking glass Ophrys" *Ophrys speculum*, which is found in Algeria and southern Europe (see Figure 16-10) and whose flowers are small and without nectar, yet striking in color. As described in 1870, the brilliant polished surface of the center of the flower shines like a blue-steel looking glass, edged with gold and set in a velvety maroon background. These colors are rare in the plant kingdom but are

Models: species of *Bematistes*   Mimics: *Pseudacreae eurytus*

alcinoe, females   females only

epaea, females   females only

vestalis, male or female   either sex

macaria, males   males only

epaea, males   both sexes

Figure 16-6

Multiple mimics within a single species. On the left are the models, species of *Bematistes*; on the right the mimics, all of which are members of a single species, *Pseudacreae eurytus*. Both the models and the mimics were collected in a single locality in Sierra Leone. (*From* Owen 1971)

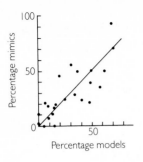

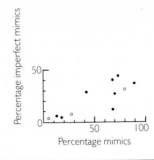

Figure 16-7

The frequency of mimics and their models among butterflies. The percent frequency of each of five mimetic patterns of *Pseudacreae eurytus* is plotted against the percent frequency of each of the five model species (of *Bematistes*). The close correspondence suggests that the relative frequency of the models controls the relative frequency of the mimics. A 1:1 line has been drawn for comparison. (*From* Shepard 1959)

Figure 16-8

The frequency of imperfect mimics as a function of the relative frequency of the mimics, in two butterfly species. The percentage of individuals deemed imperfect mimics (variants that deviate from the mimetic form) is plotted against the percentage of mimics in samples of models and mimics for two species (closed circles *Pseudacreae eurytus*; open circles *Papilio dardanus*). (*From* Shepard 1959)

common in the kinds of wasps, bees, and flies that are attracted to *Ophrys*. In fact, the plant achieves a remarkable likeness to the appearance of female wasps of the species *Scolia ciliata*, the primary pollinator of *Ophrys speculum*. The violet-blue center of the flower resembles the reflections from the halfway-crossed wings of a resting female. A thick set of long, red hairs imitates the hair found on the insect's abdomen. The antennae of the female wasp are beautifully reproduced by the upper petals of the orchid which are dark and threadlike.

Male *Scolia* wasps are strongly attracted to these flowers and land on them as they would land on a female's back. The result is a pseudo-copulation: the male presses himself down on the labellum or lip of the orchid, moves about rapidly, and probes the hairy structures with his copulatory structure, apparently searching for the complementary female structure. In some species, during the male's movements he thrusts his head against the base of the pollen-bearing structures, which become attached to the male's head. In others, the male turns

Figure 16-9

Egg mimicry by a plant.
The passion flower vine
Passiflora candollei
produces yellow egglike
structures on its leaves,
which actually are modified
nectar glands. Although
nectar glands in closely related species are usually located in a regular pattern,
in this species they are randomly distributed, much
like the butterfly eggs they
mimic. Experiments with
egg-mimics of other species
of *Passiflora* show that the
removal of the egg-mimics
increases the rate at which
butterfly eggs are de-
posited. (*From* Gilbert
1982)

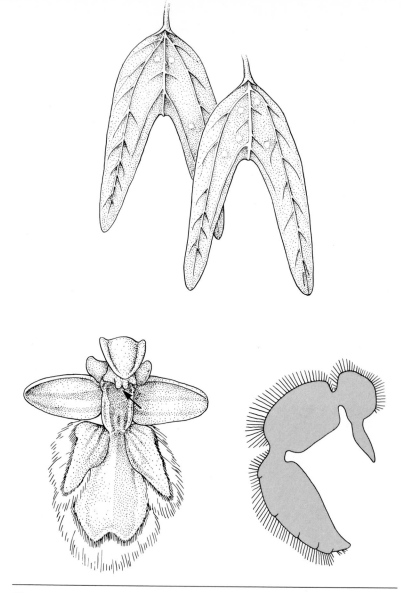

Figure 16-10

A flower that mimics a female wasp. On the left is the flower of the orchid
Ophrys speculum. On the right is a cross-section of what the flower mimics,
a female wasp *Scolia ciliata.* Notice that the hairs on the two are about the
same length. The arrow points to where the pollen is located and becomes
attached to the wasp's head. Hidden beneath the pollen-bearing structures is
the place where pollen is deposited. (*From* Kullenberg 1961)

around and the pollen structures become attached to his abdomen. In either case, the male's search for the "female" he has spotted leads him to carry pollen from one flower to another.

The orchid's attraction of insect males is a three-step affair. In the first and most critical step the orchid produces a strong scent that mimics the sexual pheromones of various insects. This attracts and arouses the males. The following steps merely orient them more exactly. The flower itself resembles the female of the pollinating species, not closely to our eyes, but similar enough to act as a screen, eliminating inappropriate insects and guiding the appropriate male into grasping the flower as he would a female. At this point, the third factor, tactile stimulation, becomes important: the upper surface of the flower (the lip or labellum) has evolved a series of rigid hairs that mimic the hairy abdomen of the female insect and that males use to orient themselves during copulation. The male's movements are coordinated by the precise topography of the hairs. When the male tires of one pseudofemale, he moves on to another, thus eventually cross-pollinating the plant.

The labellum of the flower appears to be the main source of the sexual smell. In scratching the surface of the labellum, or in biting it (in apparent frustration), the visiting male releases further pheromones, which increases his excitement. (It is also during biting that he sometimes transfers the pollen.) Yet no one has seen a male ejaculate. Instead, he seems to be caught in a world of hyperarousal that lacks the specific stimuli for provoking ejaculation. These stimuli must include tactile stimulation—showing that his copulatory apparatus has become attached to the female insect's apparatus—and this the plant fails to provide. Thus, the male's interest is not diminished. Sexually intoxicated by the strong scent, the male moves about energetically in search of consummation and is unconsciously steered by the plant's hairs to pick up pollen for transfer to another flower. Failing to copulate, he flies in search of another female.

In many insect species adult males emerge before adult females. The orchid species typically bloom before the emergence of the female insects, so that most visits to the flowers occur before males have seen what their own females look like. Yet such is the quality and quantity of the sexual perfumes released by the flowers that when females and female-mimicking flowers are both present, males usually alight on the flowers!

A plant is typically many, many times the size of its pollinating insect, so that the cost of producing sexual odors should, other things being equal, be lower to the plant. This, combined with the fact that most pollination is achieved before the females emerge, gives an evolutionary advantage to the plant. That is, selection more quickly molds more exact mimicry in the plant than it molds defensive elements in the pollinating insect. Indeed, it seems likely that the sexual attraction the plant exudes makes use of the millions of years of selection for insect enjoyment of plant smells (as a guide to finding food). Thus, the insect is presented with a superoptimal stimulus—copious sexual smells intermingled with food smells.

Sexual Mimicry Within Animal Species

In the ten-spined stickleback fish *Pygosteus pungitius*, males build nests shaped like small pipes into which females swim to lay their eggs. A typical nest can hold the eggs of as many as seven females, and females prefer to deposit their eggs in nests that already contain eggs. A male defends a territory containing his nest and cares for the eggs entrusted to this nest (by aerating them, for example). He courts a female arriving at the edge of his territory by performing a zig-zag dance that invites the female to inspect his nest and his parental actions. If she accepts him, she deposits her eggs and he swims into the nest and fertilizes them.

It sometimes happens that while one female is spawning in his nest, another one appears at the edge of his territory. Thinking (so to speak) to double his reproductive success, the male swims to her and invites her in. After courtship, she swims into his nest and deposits her own clutch of eggs. The male then swims in and fertilizes both clutches—or so he supposes. The second female is, in fact, a male; far from laying a clutch of eggs, "she" actually fertilizes the first clutch! The male has been cuckolded; his eagerness for reproductive gain has betrayed him.

How is the deception achieved? In many fish, coloration can be controlled by the individual. For example, in response to fright, the bright breeding coloration of a male can be rapidly altered so as to take on the cryptic non-breeding coloration shared by females. Thus, the cuckold approaches in the drab coloration of an adult female, timing his arrival to coincide with the courtship of a female. His behavior mimics that of a female. Even when fertilizing the eggs, the male holds himself in the posture of a female depositing her eggs.

Although this behavior was initially imagined to be an unusual effect of crowding in aquaria and was misinterpreted as homosexuality, the behavior is known to be common in several species of fish in their natural habitats, where it is termed *creeping*. Creeper males do not hold territories, but creep around under cover near the edges of territories, searching for opportunities to pass themselves off as females. Creeping is self-limiting. When creepers are infrequent they may be very successful; when they are frequent each creeper has a difficult time finding naive males with territories. Thus, the success of deceit is frequency dependent.

The most striking example in fish of this kind of sexual mimicry occurs in the bluegill sunfish *Lepomis macrochirus*. Territorial males are often courted by pseudofemales—who later return when a real female is present (Figures 16-11 and 16-12). Here there can be no question of one male pursuing both kinds of strategies. As Wallace Dominey has carefully shown, pseudofemales are about the same age as territorial males (five or six years) but are considerably smaller and are packed with sperm, unlike younger, similar-sized males destined to become territory-holders (Figures 16-13 and 16-14). Whether this male polymorphism is genetic or based on a very early developmental specialization—slow-growing individuals opting for a deceitful life—is, at present, unknown. What is clear is that opportunities for deception have been so long-continued and predictable in this species that they

Figure 16-11

Courting a transvestite. The large nesting bluegill sunfish male on the left courts a male, who has the size and coloration of a breeding female: dark background, dark eyes, and pronounced vertical bars. The female-mimic will turn along with the nesting male, but he will not lie sideways and release eggs. By approaching a nesting male and permitting himself to be courted, the transvestite apparently gets the other male used to his presence so that he can join the male again when the male is courting a real female (see next photo). In some colonies more than half the couples seen courting are, in fact, male–male pairs! (Photo: Wallace Dominey)

Figure 16-12

A fish foursome. Three male bluegill sunfish are attracted to the same female, who has turned on her side to spawn. Directly to her right is a female-mimic, who, as usual, is smaller than she is. In the center is the large nesting male, who has turned his body to display at another large male, who has intruded. This latter male is marked for identification with a white tag near his tail. The female-mimic has gained the preferred spot next to the breeding female. (Photo: Wallace Dominey)

have given rise to an obligate deceit-specialist. It would be interesting to know whether females spot pseudofemales as such and, under certain conditions, prefer to mate with them!

A parallel case of transvestitism has evolved in scorpionflies. Males mimic females in order to steal food with which to court females. In *Hylobittacus apicalis*, males court females by presenting them with nuptial gifts of food (see p. 249). A male who spots another male advertising for a female with his nuptial gift may approach the male and lower his wings as would a female. In two-thirds of the cases he is offered the nuptial gift. Otherwise he is rejected. Since females are always given the food, the deception is only partly effective. The male presenting the nuptial gift attempts to couple his genitalia with those of the female-mimic, but the latter keeps his abdominal tip out of reach. Within a couple of minutes the first owner attempts to retrieve his food and a wrestling match ensues. The transvestite male is able to keep his food about a third of the time. Thus, the overall success rate for appropriating food is 22% of encounters. Males with food are encountered sufficiently often that a transvestite male can save time and effort by approaching other males instead of hunting on his own.

Figure 16-13

Three kinds of males. The female bluegill sunfish is shown at the bottom. Directly above her is a territorial, nesting male. Above him on the right is a female-mimic and on the left, a sneak male. A sneak male hovers on the edge of a nesting male's territory and darts in to release sperm at exactly the moment when a female spawns. His arrival and departure are so rapid he can barely be seen on film. (Photo: Wallace Dominey)

Figure 16-14

Males and their testes. At bottom left we see a sneak male and on the right a female-mimic bluegill sunfish. In front of each are the testes of a same-sized male of the same category. We see that the testes are relatively large: a slight pressure on the abdomen of a female-mimic releases copious quantities of sperm. At top we see similar-sized males destined to become large, nesting males: each has small, immature testes and each is two or three years younger than the comparable fish at bottom. (Photo: Wallace Dominey)

Deception Related to Aggression

In aggressive encounters it will often be useful to appear larger, more capable, more motivated, and more confident than one actually is. We know many examples of animals inflating their apparent size in display (Figure 16-15), but demonstrating that an animal is bluffing its motivation or status is more difficult. Yet recent studies leave no doubt that deception is a very general feature of aggressive relations.

Vulnerability and bluff. A unique opportunity for studying deception has been discovered by Rick Steger and Roy Caldwell in the mantis shrimp *Gonodactylus bredini*. Normally the mantis shrimp is hard-shelled and possesses enlarged claws with which it attacks opponents and crushes hard-shelled prey. The mantis shrimp defends a cavity, usually attacking individuals and chasing them away but sometimes displaying its claw (Figure 16-16). This display tends to be followed by attack and to inhibit attack in the opponent. In short, it acts as a threat.

A mantis shrimp that has just molted is soft-shelled; it can neither attack nor defend itself and, when cornered, is easily killed. But it *can*

Figure 16-15

Intimidation display. The adult male chimpanzee on the left (Nikkie) looks much larger than the one he is trying to intimidate (Luit). In reality they are about the same size. The dominant male characteristically keeps his hair partly erected. (Photo: Frans de Waal)

Figure 16-16

The claw display of a mantis shrimp. An individual *Gonodactylus bredini* raises its head and displays its large clawlike appendages. At high-intensity threat, it will open and shut the claws. (From photographs by Roy Caldwell)

threaten and this is exactly what it does: it responds to an intruder by greatly increasing the frequency of its claw display, sometimes combining this with a lunge at the opponent (Figure 16-17). About half of the time this bluff is successful and the intruder retreats, but the other half of the time the intruder keeps coming, at which point the cavity-holder invariably departs. Not a single soft-shelled bluffer persists when its bluff is called!

The mantis shrimp only molts once every two months, so most of the claw displays are made by individuals with hard shells. Most of these displays probably honestly indicate probability of attack. Indeed, it is possible that the shrimp is especially likely to display honestly when hard-shelled in order to train its neighbors into believing the display, thus increasing the display's value when the shrimp is vulnerable. Recently Caldwell has discovered striking evidence in support of this possibility. Not only are mantis shrimp especially aggressive just prior to molting but they are especially likely to *combine* claw displays with attacks on the opponent, as if building up a reputation that threats will be backed up by aggressive actions just before the time when they will not be.

Continual bluff? A case of nearly continual bluff may occur in the fathead minnow *Pimephales promelas*. Males defend territories around oviposition sites and guard eggs for several weeks. Solitary males lose weight throughout this period but males breeding near other males do not. The reason may be bluff. Both males lose the same amount of dry weight, but the social males retain increasing amounts of water so as to maintain the same robust appearance. Less robust males (lighter for a given length) are attacked more often. (Bluff is not the only interpretation, since water retention may, in some way, aid an individual in fights.) The importance of appearing robust is also suggested by the coloration of territorial males. Like humans wishing to appear most robust, this fish alternates lateral stripes of white and black. Solitary males are more lightly colored but quickly show the black and white stripes when placed with other males.

Hiding ambivalent motivation. Often, aggressive motivation will be mixed with non-aggressive tendencies. A tendency to fight may be balanced with a tendency to flee; otherwise the animal would be over-aggressive and subject to severe injury when outclassed. Although individuals may be selected to hide their ambivalent motivation, this is made more difficult by the need to prepare for alternate action, such as fleeing (Figure 16-18). Sometimes conflicting tendencies result in yet another kind of action being expressed apparently irrelevant to the situation at hand. Such displacement activities may, in fact, serve to distract attention from salient features of the interaction (Figure 16-19). That animals in aggressive situations are selected to hide ambivalent motivation is beautifully illustrated by the behavior of adult male chimpanzees in tense situations of display. As observed by Frans de Waal:

After Luit and Nikkie had displayed in each other's proximity for over ten minutes a conflict broke out between them in which Luit was supported by Mama and Puist. Nikkie was driven into a tree, but a little later he began to hoot at the leader again while he was still perched in the tree. Luit was sitting at the bottom of the tree with his back to his challenger. When he heard the renewed sounds of provocation he bared his teeth [a sign of fear] but immediately put his hand to his mouth and pressed his lips together. I could not believe my eyes and quickly focused my binoculars on him. I saw the nervous grin appear on his face again and once more he used his fingers to press his lips together. The third time Luit finally succeeded in wiping the grin off his face; only then did he turn round. A little later he displayed at Nikkie as if nothing had happened and with Mama's help he chased him back into the tree. Nikkie watched his opponents walk away. All of a sudden he turned his back and, when the others could not see him, a grin appeared on his face and he began to yelp very softly. I could hear Nikkie because I was not very far away, but the sound was so suppressed that Luit probably did not notice that his opponent was also having trouble concealing his emotions.

For an example of a chimpanzee hiding its focus of interest, see Figure 16-20.

Experiments in deception. In some species, variability in physical appearance correlates with variability in dominance status. For example, in the Harris sparrow *Zonotrichia querula* the degree of dark plumage on the neck and chest correlates closely with dominance, darker birds being more dominant (Figure 16-21). This system of signalling dominance has evolved in species living within flocks and is especially common where these flocks are fluid in composition. At first

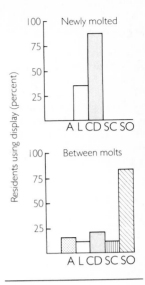

Figure 16-17

Bluff by a vulnerable mantis shrimp. The percentage of individuals engaging in various activities in response to the arrival of an intruder is plotted for newly molted mantis shrimp *Gonodactylus bredini* and for those which are in between molts. *Appear* (A): the resident stations itself at the entrance to its cavity. *Lunge* (L): the resident makes a rapid head-first move toward the opponent but does not strike nor leave its cavity entirely. *Claw display* (CD): the resident displays its claws (see previous figure). *Strike cavity* (SC): the resident strikes the inside of its own cavity to produce an audible click sound. A mantis shrimp is especially likely to strike its cavity when an opponent is fleeing. *Strike opponent* (SO): the resident attacks using its claws. (*From* Caldwell 1983)

Figure 16-18

Ambivalent motivation in a gull. Both birds are in the upright threat posture at the edge of their territories, but the bird on the left has its neck partly withdrawn (compare with Figure 1-6). Its motivation to attack is partly counteracted by a tendency to withdraw. Notice that its neck appears much thinner than the opponent's. (Photo: Niko Tinbergen)

Figure 16-19

Why is this male looking at his feet? The female gull on the right has just tossed her head in courtship to the male. He is apparently caught between conflicting impulses—to respond in kind or not to respond; instead, he looks at his feet. This may or may not distract the female's attention from his dilemma. (From a photo by William Drury)

Figure 16-20

A sudden interest in his fingernails. An adult male chimpanzee (Luit), on the right, has been driven away from the female in estrus, on the left, by another adult male (Nikkie). Now sitting nearby, Luit appears to have developed a deep interest in his fingernails. It is sometimes difficult to figure out who is actually fooled by this behavior, unless it is Luit himself! (*From* de Waal 1982)

glance, this system poses something of a problem, since it is unclear why subordinate individuals do not simply develop darker plumage and thereby gain in status. Put another way, why bother to wear a badge of your own inferiority—why not fake it?

To see what was preventing light-colored individuals from appearing darker and thereby enjoying higher status, Sievert Rohwer dyed some birds darker. To his surprise these individuals immediately suffered a large cost: they were persecuted by the naturally dark birds, repeatedly attacked, and in some cases, driven to feeding alone or on the periphery of their group (Figure 16-21). Only one individual appeared to gain by the operation; before being dyed he had often dominated darker individuals, so dying may actually have improved the accuracy of his status signalling. All others suffered immediate costs imposed by the actions of other sparrows. This remarkable discovery suggests that, when detected, deceivers are normally held in check by strong aggression. It also suggests that deception poses a real threat to the status of darker birds, for not only might the darker birds have to give way when they otherwise need not, but other birds may learn— through experience with the deceivers—to disrespect their own badge of authority.

Rohwer also bleached several individuals and discovered that bleached birds sharply increased their aggressiveness, nearly quadrupling the rate at which they actively chased other birds. Since others treated them as the low-status birds they appeared to be, they were, in effect, living in a society of disrespectful birds, in which they had to

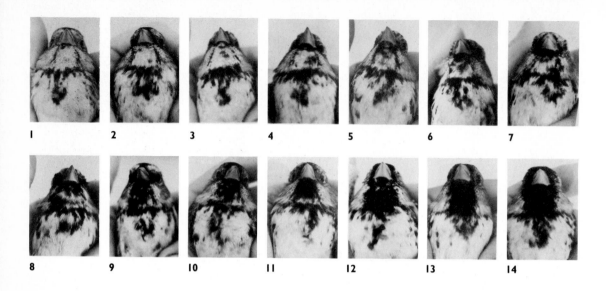

Figure 16-21

Variability in plumage that signals dominance, in Harris sparrows. Shown are the 14 categories of increasingly dark neck and chest feathers that Sievert Rohwer used to rank birds. Dark birds outrank lighter ones. Color of neck and chest feathers is a better predictor of dominance than is size, sex, or age, though older birds tend to be darker, as do males. (Photos: Sievert Rohwer)

fight for what was formerly allotted to them through their appearance. One bleached bird became so aggressive that he regularly arrived at a feeding patch by whirling about and displacing nearly every bird in his path! Violent fights were sometimes precipitated in which the bleached bird was forced to dominate a disbelieving foe of nearly equal pre-bleaching rank. These experiments suggest that a bird reacts aggressively to those that would cheat on the system by disrespecting that bird's legitimate status.

In later experiments Rohwer supplemented birds' natural testosterone levels with implants that effectively mimicked an individual with maximum levels. Since in other creatures testosterone is associated with aggressiveness, it was expected that individuals given this hormone treatment would act like the most dominant individuals (category 14 in Figure 16-20). For one set of individuals, Rohwer also dyed the birds so each had a dark color, enabling Rohwer to match their new aggressiveness. The other set was left light-colored. A striking difference resulted: the birds that were dyed and given hormone treatment rose in dominance rank, while those only given the hormone treatment failed to rise and suffered persecution from others.

These last experiments of Rohwer's are the most difficult to interpret. Since the production of testosterone is not in itself expensive, we must assume that animals in nature do not boost their testosterone levels because for their size, age, fighting experience, and so on the higher status would be too costly to maintain. In any case, Rohwer's experiment with dyed and hormone-boosted birds shows that a significant portion of dominance is due to energetic and aggressive commitment

1 Male. He stayed in the flock but suffered a significantly higher rate of attack.

2 Female. She left the flock and travelled alone, where she tended to be attacked less often than before.

3 Male. He often travelled alone or on the edge of the flock and suffered a significantly higher rate of attack.

4 Male. The only bird to show an improvement in status, he stayed in the flock, where he tended to be attacked *less* often than before.

to a given status. The undyed, hormone-boosted birds resemble, in some respects, bleached birds: they are perceived by others to be well below their hormonal status. Thus, they were probably persecuted because they looked like cheaters who aggressively demand a higher status than deserved. Altogether, Rohwer's experiments suggest that the status-signalling system of Harris sparrows is tightly controlled by immediate and often strong hostility toward those perceived as deceivers or cheaters.

The Logic of Self-Deception

One particular consequence of deception deserves special attention: *self-deception*, that is, hiding the truth from the conscious mind the better to hide it from others. In our own species we recognize that

Figure 16-22

Deception experiments: what happens when you artificially darken a Harris sparrow? Here we see four birds before and after their neck and chest feathers were dyed. Below each bird are listed the bird's sex and experiences after being dyed. (Photos: Sievert Rohwer)

shifty eyes, sweaty palms, and croaky voices may indicate the stress that accompanies conscious knowledge of attempted deception. By becoming unconscious of its deception, the deceiver hides these signs from the observer. He or she can lie without the nervousness that accompanies deception.

Consider another example. An individual's perception of its own motivation may be biased in order to conceal the true motivation from others. Consciously, a series of reasons may unfold to accompany action so that when actions are challenged a convincing alternative explanation is at once available, complete with an internal scenario ("But I wasn't thinking that at all, I was thinking . . ."). Of course it must be advantageous for the truth to be registered somewhere, so that mechanisms of self-deception are expected to reside side-by-side with mechanisms for the correct apprehension of reality. The mind must be structured in a very complex fashion, repeatedly split into public and private portions, with complicated interactions between the subsections.

In human evolution, processes of deception and self-deception were greatly heightened by the advent of language. Language permits individuals to make statements about events distant in time and space, and these are least amenable to contradiction. Thus, language permits verbal deception of many different kinds. Since contradictory information is not available at the moment a deception is being practiced, there may be heightened attention to signs of conscious intent to deceive, and this will favor mechanisms of self-deception. All the marvels of cognition and information manipulation that language permits can be used in the service of self-deception. Individuals readily create entire belief systems with self-serving biases, and the more skillfully these self-serving components are hidden from both the self and others, the more difficult it will be to counter them.

Having said this, we should emphasize that self-deception is probably not limited to human beings. Other animals are often in situations of stress in which tight evaluations are being made. Self-confidence is a piece of information that may give useful information about the individual displaying it. If a male is facing off another male in an aggressive encounter, or is courting a female, he may be evaluated partly according to his self-confidence. A certain amount of self-deception in that situation may give a convincing image of his high self-esteem, thereby impressing others.

The Experimental Demonstration of Self-Deception

Self-deception is a tricky concept that easily invites vague speculation. To show that the concept can be given precision, we review a brilliant paper by Ruben Gur and Harold Sackeim that showed that the following three criteria of self-deception could be demonstrated. (1) True and false information is simultaneously stored in a single person. (2) The false information is stored in the conscious mind, the true information is unconscious. In this sense, we may speak of self-deception, keeping information from the conscious mind. (3) Self-deception is motivated with reference to others.

Gur and Sackeim relied upon the fact that humans respond physiologically upon hearing a human voice, as measured, for example, by a jump in the galvanic skin response (GSR). But the person responds more intensely upon hearing his or her own voice. Likewise, the reaction to the voice of another is less intense the longer one listens, while the opposite is true for one's own voice. Thus, a measure of GSR in response to various recorded voices permits a measure of unconscious self-recognition. This can be compared with conscious self-recognition as revealed by verbal reports of whether an individual just heard his or her own voice or that of someone else.

People tested for self-recognition fell into four categories: some made no mistakes; some made only one kind—namely, they denied their own voice some of the time; some made the other kind of error—they projected their own voice some of the time; and some people made both kinds of errors. When the skin's response was tallied for all these verbal errors, a striking pattern emerged. In almost all cases, the skin knew better (Figure 16-23). People denying their own voice verbally showed the high GSR typical of self-recognition. Those projecting their own voice showed the small jump in GSR typical of hearing another person's voice.

In summary, for most mistakes, the part of the brain controlling speech has it wrong, while the part controlling arousal has it right. This fulfills our first criterion of self-deception: contradictory information is stored. It also fulfills our second criterion, because people are conscious of their verbal reactions but unconscious of their GSR's. Of course, people could be conscious after the fact of having made a mistake, but this is usually not the case. (All except one of those denying their own voices were later unaware of having made a mistake, while half of those projecting were unaware of any error.)

Finally, the errors can be shown to be motivated. Those who project themselves are those who in other situations seek out themselves, by spending more time in front of a mirror or listening to their own voices. An individual's taste for self-involvement can be manipulated. When we fail on some task we are more likely to avoid ourselves, while success invites self-involvement. The same factors affect voice recognition. Individuals made to fail tend to deny their own voices, while those made to succeed tend to project. It is as if we expand ourselves to others when succeeding and shrink our presentation of self when failing, yet we are largely unconscious of this process.

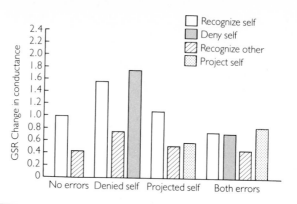

Figure 16-23

Self-deception: the skin knows what the mouth does not. The mean change in galvanic skin response (GSR) (in micromhos), adjusted for order of trials, is given for four groups of people: those who made no errors of identification, those who denied their own voices some of the time, those who projected their own voices some of the time, and those who made both kinds of errors. The four responses shown are "recognize self," "recognize other," "deny self," and "project self." For all except the last group (both errors) the skin shows a significantly stronger response when recognizing self than when recognizing others, but when denying self the skin shows the strong response typical of correct identification, while projecting one's self is accompanied by the GSR change typical of recognizing another. These statements do not hold for the group that made both kinds of errors; there are no significant differences among their responses. Notice, also, that on all their responses, deniers tend to show greater changes in GSR, suggesting that denial of significant features of reality requires hyperarousal, whereas projection of reality is a more relaxed enterprise. (*From* Gur and Sackeim 1979)

Mechanisms of Self-Deception

Psychologists have described many kinds of self-deception. To give us a broader view of this subject, let us review several of these here.

Beneffectance. We all have a tendency to represent ourselves as being beneficial and effective at the same time. We wish to appear *ben-effective.* We tend to deny responsibility when we harm others. We either deny the harm or we deny that we ourselves were responsible. We have a tendency to exaggerate our own role in a beneficial outcome. For example, experiments in which groups of people are involved in a common task show that when group outcome is positive people evaluate their own contribution as a higher percentage of total effort than they contributed. And the reverse is true when the outcome is negative.

The tendency to deny responsibility for harmful outcomes sometimes takes the form of switching from an active to a passive voice. If the outcome is good, then we played an active role; if it is bad, we were a passive victim of circumstances. Consider the following account of a traffic accident, as quoted in the *San Francisco Examiner*, August 31, 1977: "The telephone pole was approaching, I was attempting to swerve out of its way, when it struck my front end." We all know from physics that this is a legitimate description of what is happening, but it has shifted responsibility from the driver to the telephone pole.

Exaggeration. From the principle of beneffectance we expect repeated tales of humanitarian accomplishments to grow in the retelling, that is, to become exaggerated. Memory can be counted on to supply the new facts. A good example of this comes from the Bible. It is known that Matthew's account of Jesus' activities was written after Mark's and that in some cases Matthew relied on facts given by Mark. Does Matthew's account deviate from Mark's? Yes, Matthew's account always exaggerates Mark's in a positive direction. In Mark 1:34, Jesus healed many sick; in the parallel Matthew 8:16, he heals them all. The feeding of the 4000 in Mark, leaving over seven baskets of remains, becomes in Matthew 5000 fed, leaving 12 baskets of remains. A series of such parallel cases can be found and in every instance Matthew is consistent in his tendency to amplify and exaggerate beneficial outcomes.

The illusion of consistency. Another common example of self-deception is a tendency for people to rewrite their past experience so as to make it consistent with present realities. This gives the illusion that we are consistent, that in life we make very few mistakes. This ploy was summarized by George Orwell in his novel *1984*, while talking about leadership: "The secret of rulership is to combine a belief in one's own infallibility with a power to learn from past mistakes." The only way to do this is to change one's mind—learn from past mistakes. But having done so, earlier opinions must be rewritten so as to give the impression of consistency. People are remarkably good at this, and it has been studied in a variety of experimental contexts. For example, one study shows that people will add details to their memory of earlier events so as to give support to new information—especially so when the new information is personal and derogatory. Thus, when people learn that someone is believed to be homosexual, they find it easier to add new memories concerning prior events supporting this fact than if they learn a less inflammatory fact.

The perception of relationships. Another example of self-deception comes from everyday life. Consider an argument between two closely bound people, say, husband and wife. Both parties believe that one is an altruist—of long standing, relatively pure in motive, and much abused—while the other is characterized by a pattern of selfishness spread over hundreds of incidents. They only disagree over who is altruistic and who selfish. It is noteworthy that the argument may appear to burst forth spontaneously, with little or no preview, yet as it rolls along, two whole landscapes of information appear to lie already organized, waiting only for the lightning of anger to show themselves.

Perceptual defense and perceptual vigilance. There is a tendency for humans consciously to see what they wish to see. They literally have difficulty seeing things with negative connotations while seeing with increasing ease items that are positive. For example, words that evoke anxiety, either because of an individual's personal history or because of experimental manipulation, require greater illumination before first being perceived by people asked to state their first perception. Disagreement centers over exactly when the impairment takes place, but the benefit seems clear. Rather than consciously perceiving the disliked word and having to impose a conscious restraint on speech, with every flinch and hesitation available for notice by others, the offending word is quickly perceived and then shunted from consciousness. The outward person can go on as if unaffected.

Perceptual vigilance involves eager embrace of that which is self-satisfying. The organism operates as if building a legal case, or writing a doctoral thesis, being alert to any fact—however trivial or wrongly interpreted—that lends support to the general case being argued. The case being argued is usually that of beneffectance: ego (or self) is worthy, useful to others, rarely selfish, and so on.

Summary

Deception is an expected feature of all relations between imperfectly related organisms. Deception is common in interactions between members of different species, as illustrated by camouflage and mimicry. In species with multiple mimics, the frequency of mimics is controlled by the relative frequency of their models. Deception is practiced by plants. In some species flowers resemble female insects, attracting conspecific males who attempt copulation, thereby pollinating the plant. In some species of fish and in a scorpionfly, males have evolved mimicry of females in order to cuckold males or to steal nuptial gifts. Deception is common in aggressive interactions and includes attempts to appear larger and more aggressive.

Selection for deception is expected to generate self-deception. Self-deception is seen as an active, organized process that improves the deception of others. In the human lineage, self-deception was greatly extended by the invention of language. Experimental evidence shows that people can be motivated to deny or project reality and are largely unconscious of these processes. Many mechanisms of self-deception have been described, including efforts to appear beneffective and consistent.

Bibliographic Notes

Chapter 1

5–9   For a summary of gull biology see Tinbergen 1953. For prenatal effects on chicks
see Impekoven 1976.

9–11   Darwin's version of his theory is found in
Darwin 1859. For Darwin's system of logic
see Ghiselin 1969. For the evidence in favor
of evolution see Futuyma 1983. For an introduction to evolutionary biology see Futuyma 1979. For a history of the ideas behind evolution see Mayr 1982. See also
Ruse 1982.

12–
13   For early mortality in gulls see Nisbet and
Drury 1972 and Kadlec, Drury, and Onion
1969. For growth of the herring gull population see Chabrzyk and Coulson 1976 and
Kadlec and Drury 1968.

13–
14   The quotation is from p. 81 of Rudebeck
1950.

14–
15   The quotation is from p. 242 of Emlen
1968.

Chapter 2

19   Curiously, there are very few books on
natural selection, but see Clutton-Brock *in
press* and Johnson 1976. For humans see
Bajema 1971.

21   The famous analogy is from Simpson 1947.

22   The quotation is from Darwin 1859.

24   For recent work on the ruff see Shepard
1976.

24–
25   For spacing experiments in gulls see Tinbergen, Impekoven, and Frank 1967.

25   Factors affecting RS in herring gulls and
their relatives are as follows. Size of egg:
Parsons 1970, Nisbet 1978, Lundberg and
Väisänen 1979. Number of eggs laid: Langham 1974. Date eggs are laid: Parsons
1975. Order of laying: Langham 1972. Nest
density: Hunt and Hunt 1975, Davis and
Dunn 1976. Location relative to predators
and food: Hunt 1972. Courtship feeding:
Nisbet 1973, 1977. Egg shell removal: Tinbergen et al. 1962. Mate fidelity: Coulson
1966. See also Fordham 1970 and Hunt
and Hunt 1976.

25   For an example of intense selection see
Boag and Grant 1981.

25   For a recent paper on the advantage of
clumped breeding see Clark and Robertson
1979.

31–
32   For the evolution of brain size see Jerison
1973.

32   Temperature and human body weight see
Roberts 1953.

33–
34   In addition to Shine and Bull 1979, see also
Tinkle and Gibbons 1977.

34– For an excellent summary of the red deer
38   study see Clutton-Brock, Guinness and Al-
     bon 1982. For additional details see papers
     by Clutton-Brock.

Chapter 3

41   The division of social acts into altruistic,
     selfish, etc. was first made by Hamilton
     1964.
42– *Colophina clematis*: Aoki 1977, 1980.
44   *Pseudoregma alexanderi*: Aoki and Miya-
     zaki 1978, Aoki, Akimoto, and Yamane
     1981. *Astegopteryx styracicola*: Aoki
     1979a. See also Aoki 1979b.
44   For problematic cases of altruism see Dan-
     iels 1979 and West Eberhard 1978.
45   For kinship theory see Hamilton 1964.
46   Haldane's account can be found in Haldane
     1955.
47   Lionesses nurse cubs of female relatives:
     Bertram 1976. Adoption of chimpanzee or-
     phans: van Lawick-Goodall 1968. For com-
     munal nursing in a bat see McCracken
     1984.
47– For an early review of return benefit and re-
49   ciprocal altruism, including cleaning sym-
     bioses, see Trivers 1971. See also Gorlick,
     Atkins, and Losey 1978.
50– Beetles parasitizing ants: In addition to
51   Hölldobler 1967 and 1970, see Hölldobler
     1971 and Hölldobler, Moglich, and Masch-
     witz 1981.
53– Our knowledge of *Polistes fuscatus* (and
57   closely related species) is unusually de-
     tailed: see West Eberhard 1969 and Noonan
     1981. For nestmate discrimination see Pfen-
     ning et al. 1983, Post and Jeanne 1982,
     Ross and Gamboa 1981, and Klahn 1979.
     For intracolony relatedness and inclusive
     fitness see Metcalf and Whitt 1977a, b. For
     subordinate longevity: Gamboa, Heacock,
     and Wiltjer 1978. Role of the queen: Reeve
     and Gamboa 1983. Group formation as a
     defense against conspecifics: Gamboa 1978.
57   Spiteful behavior: Hamilton 1970.

58   Mountain sheep: Geist 1971.
59   Female elephant seal attacks on young: Le
     Boeuf and Briggs 1977. See also Riedman
     and Le Boeuf 1982.
58– Territorial defense in tree swallows: Rob-
60   ertson and Gibbs 1982.
60– Female macaques pregnant with daughters
61   subject to greater attack: Simpson et al.
     1981. Female langur sexual interference:
     Hrdy 1977b.
60– Plant countermeasures to herbivore attack:
62   Rhoades 1983a. Plants warning others:
     Rhoades 1983b, Baldwin and Schultz 1983.
62   For plant behavioral ecology see Charnov
     1984.
62– For a good review of parasite modification
63   of host behavior, including the case of *Lig-
     ula intestinalis* see Holmes and Bethel
     1972. For recent work see Moore 1984a.
     For *Dicrocoelium dendriticum* see Carney
     1969 and Wilson 1977.
63– Malarial parasite sex ratios: Pickering
64   1980b.
     General: for much of the material covered
     in this book, see also Barash 1982, Daly
     and Wilson 1983, Dawkins 1976, 1982,
     Krebs and Davies 1981, Wilson 1975, and
     Wittenberger 1981. For humans see also Al-
     exander 1979, Crook 1980, and Lumsden
     and Wilson 1983. For animal behavior
     from an evolutionary viewpoint see Alcock
     1984, Gould 1982, and Hinde 1982.

Chapter 4

68   The quote is from Darwin 1871. See also
     Ruse 1980.
70   The quotation is from p. 30 of Lorenz 1966.
70   The quotation is from p. 657 of Fisler 1971.
71– For infanticide in all species Hausfater and
77   Hrdy 1984. For langur infanticide see espe-
     cially Hrdy 1977b, also Hrdy 1974, Moh-
     not 1971, Makwana 1979, and Chapman
     and Hausfater 1979. For a contrary view-
     point see Schubert 1982, but see Hrdy 1982.

71–   The quotation is from p. 242 of Hrdy
72   1977b.
73   The quotation is from p. 260 of Hrdy 1977b.
78   Figure 4-8: Sherman 1981b.
79–   Wynne-Edwards' theory can be found in
84   Wynne-Edwards 1962. For a rebuttal, see
       Appendix 3 in Lack 1966.
83   Laysan albatross: Rice and Kenyon 1962.
       General: for a modern approach to group
       selection see D. S. Wilson 1980, and also
       Gadgil 1975.

Chapter 5

87–   For human genetics see Vogel and Motulsky
90   1979.
90–   For the chemistry of genes see Ayala and
93   Kiger 1984 and Watson 1977. For a history
       of genetics see Jacob 1982.
93–   Yellow stripe in the giant water bug: Smith
94   and Smith 1976.
95   For a good introduction to genes, behavior,
       and learning see Halliday and Slater 1983.
98–   For twins reared apart see Bouchard 1984
102   and 1983. See also Lykken 1982 and Bou-
       chard and McGue 1981.
100   The quotations are (respectively) from pp.
       57 and 58 of Holden 1980.
103–   How birds learn to sing: Slater 1983b.
104
103   *Acrocephalus palustris*: Dowsett-Lamaire
       1979.
103–   Why different forms of vocal learning in dif-
104   ferent species: Slater 1983a.
104   *Malothrus ater*: King and West 1983.
104–   The material in this section is reviewed in
107   Garcia and Ervin 1968. For recent reviews
       see Domjan and Galef 1983 and Domjan
       1983. See also Shettleworth 1984. For ex-
       amples of specialized learning in animals
       see Shettleworth 1983 and Cole et al. 1982.

Chapter 6

109   The standard reference on kinship is Hamil-
       ton 1964. See also Hamilton 1971, 1972.

For a kinship explanation of high early mortality, see Hamilton 1966. For a review of
kinship theory see West Eberhard 1975. For
a review and bibliography see Kurland
1980.
110   Acoustical properties of bird alarm calls:
       Marler 1955.
110–   Kinship and ground squirrels: warning calls,
114   Sherman 1977; other behaviors, Sherman
       1980; demography, Sherman 1981a and
       Sherman and Morton 1984; multiple pater-
       nity of litters, Hanken and Sherman 1981;
       mechanisms of kin recognition, Holmes and
       Sherman 1982. For warning calls in ground
       squirrels see also Dunford 1977 and Leger
       and Owings 1978. For distress screams in
       birds see Rohwer, Fretwell, and Tuckfield
       1976. See also p. 432.
114   In addition to Kurland 1977, see Massey
       1977 and Kaplan 1978. For recent work see
       chapters by Berman, Chapais, and Datta in
       Hinde 1983, and see Meikle and Vessey
       1981. See also Hrdy and Hrdy 1976 and
       Wrangham 1980. For humans see Hawkes
       1983 and Dow 1984. See also Daly and
       Wilson 1982a, Alexander 1977, and chap-
       ters in Chagnon and Irons 1979.
118   The quotation is from Kurland 1977, pp.
       81–82.
120–   For rhesus monkey group splits see Chepko-
121   Sade and Olivier 1979 and Chepko-Sade
       and Sade 1979. See also Melnick and Kidd
       1983.
121–   For a review of sperm altruism in butterflies
125   and moths see Silberglied, Shepherd, and
       Dickinson 1984. Male investment in butter-
       flies: Boggs and Gilbert 1979. For egg altru-
       ism, in addition to Henry 1972, see Henry
       1978.
126–   For a valuable review of mistaken notions
128   in kinship theory see Dawkins 1979. See
       also Grafen 1982. For a recent version of
       the genetic similarity fallacy see Rushton,
       Russell, and Wells 1984. For the impor-
       tance of personal reproduction see Ruben-
       stein and Wrangham 1980.

128–   For degrees of relatedness under inbreeding
129   see Hamilton 1972. For species that regularly practice sib-mating see Hamilton 1967.

129   For deleterious effects of inbreeding see Seemanova 1971, Greenwood, Harvey, and Perrins 1978, and Ralls, Brugger, and Ballou 1979. For incest avoidance see Sade 1968, and Wolf 1970, 1976. See also Missakian 1973, Fox 1980, Shields 1982, Baker 1983, and Moore and Ali 1984.

129–   For an excellent review of mechanisms of
135   kin recognition see Holmes and Sherman 1983; for a more technical account focusing on ground squirrels see Holmes and Sherman 1982.

129–   Sweat bees: in addition to Greenberg 1979,
130   see Buckle and Greenberg 1981.

133   Pigtail macaque: Wu et al. 1980. Recent work: Fredrickson and Sackett 1984.

133   American toads: Waldman 1982. Cascade frogs: Blaustein and O'Hara 1982.

135   For kin recognition in ants see Carlin and Hölldobler 1983. For honeybees, Getz, Bruckner, and Parisian 1982 and Getz and Smith 1983. Wasps: Klahn and Gamboa 1983. Marine invertebrates: Keough 1984 and Francis 1976. For the importance of paternal sibships: Altmann 1979. For a novel means of discerning the effect of inbreeding on degrees of relatedness: Seger 1976, 1983b.

135   For exceptions to the rule that all cells in the body are identically related see Hughes-Schrader and Monahan 1966.

138   For meiotic drive see Crow 1979, Hartl and Hiraizomi 1976, and Zimmering, Sandler, and Nicoletti 1970. For mosquitoes see Wood and Newton 1976 and Hickey and Craig 1966.

138–   Parasitic chromosomes: in addition to Nur
139   1977, see White 1973. For variation in the frequency of supernumerary chromosomes along environmental gradients see Ward 1973 and Fontana and Vickery 1973.

139   Maternal suppression of paternal chromosomes: see White 1973, and also Nur 1980 and 1982.

139–   Jumping genes (and selfish genes generally):
140   Orgel and Crick 1980, Doolittle and Sapienza 1980, Marx 1984, Lewin 1984. See also Dawkins 1982.

140–   For organelle competition see Eberhard
141   1980. For the symbiotic origin of cell organelles see Margulis 1981. For *Chlamydomonas* see Sager and Ramanis 1973.

140–   For somatic mutations in plants see Whit-
143   ham and Slobodchikoff 1981. See also Whitham 1983 and Whitham, Williams, and Robison 1984.

Chapter 7

145   This account follows closely that of Trivers 1974. For a genetic approach confirming Trivers' approach, see Stamps, Metcalf, and Krishnan 1978.

151   Older baboon mothers reject later: Nicolson 1982.

151   Dogs: Rheingold 1963. Cats: Schneirla, Rosenblatt, and Tobach 1963. See also Barash 1974.

153   For sheep references see Trivers 1974.

155   For recent studies of the parent-offspring relationship, see also Bengtsson and Ryden 1983, Fuchs 1982, Kleiman 1979, and Lazarus and Inglis 1978. See also Norton-Griffiths 1969. For conflict over oral incubation in a fish see Reid and Atz 1958.

156–   The quotation is from Schaller 1964, p. 19.
157   For pelican convulsions see also Brown and Urban 1969 and Burke and Brown 1970.

157–   The quotation is from van Lawick-Goodall
158   1968, p. 274.

160–   Hinde's methodology is more complex than
162   I have indicated: See Hinde and Spencer-Booth 1971. For recent summaries see Hinde 1977, Hinde and McGinnis 1977, and Hinde, Leighton-Shapiro, and McGinnis 1978.

161–   Effects of baboon weaning: Nicolson 1982.
162   See also Altmann, Altmann, and Hausfater 1978 and Altmann 1980.

165   For a modern system of parental domina-

tion see Dobson 1970. For Freud's bias against the child see Klein and Tribich 1981 and 1982. For application of evolutionary theory to psychoanalysis see Leak and Christopher 1982. Sociobiology and mental disorders: Wenegrat 1984. Effect of *r* on abuse and neglect: Daly and Wilson 1981. Three-generation conflict: Fagen 1976. Conflict over transmission of culture: Lumsden 1984. Fratricide in birds of prey: Edwards and Collopy 1983.

Chapter 8

169–177 For a wonderful review of the social insects, including ants, see Wilson 1971. For the social bees see Michener 1974.

170–171 Weaver ants: Hölldobler and Wilson 1983.

174–175 Slave-making ants: Buschinger, Ehrhardt, and Winter 1980.

175–176 Figures 8-8 and 8-9: Hölldobler 1976 and 1981.

176–177 Male versus worker larvae silk contribution: Wilson and Hölldobler 1980.

177–179 For this section see Hamilton 1972, and Trivers and Hare 1976. See also Bartz 1982. For the origin of haplodiploidy itself see Bull 1983.

179–181 I am grateful to William Hamilton for the example of *Septobasidium*: see Couch 1938.

181–184 For Bartz's work see Bartz 1979, but note the correction in Bartz 1980. For recent work on termites see Thorne 1984 and Zimmerman 1983.

184–187 For recent reviews of helping in birds see Emlen 1984 and Emlen and Vehrencamp 1983. See also Brown 1978, Heinz-Ulrich 1980, and Stacy and Koenig 1984.

186 For sex chromosomes affecting helping see Hamilton 1972.

187 Kinship and RS in great tits: Greenwood, Harvey, and Perrins 1979.

187–192 For Woolfenden's work see especially Woolfenden and Fitzpatrick 1984, but this section was based on his earlier work; in ad-

dition to Woolfenden 1975 and 1981, see Woolfenden and Fitzpatrick 1977, 1978 and Stallcup and Woolfenden 1978.

192 Naked mole rat: Jarvis 1981.

193–198 For hunting dogs see Malcolm and Marten 1982 and Frame et al. 1979. For data from wolves see Harrington, Mech, and Fritts 1983. Foxes: MacDonald 1979. Hyaena: Mills 1982. Prairie dog: Hoogland 1981. Fish: Taborsky and Limberger 1981. Carnivores generally: MacDonald 1983.

198–201 For the most recent papers on lesbian gulls see Hunt et al. 1984 and Kovacs and Ryder 1983. See also Fry and Toone 1981, Burger and Gochfeld 1981.

198–199 For biological approach to human homosexuality see chapters in Paul et al. 1982. For recent work on development of homosexuality see Bell, Weinberg, and Hammersmith 1981. For biological correlates of homosexuality see, for example, Evans 1972. For anthropological approach see Forgey 1975.

Chapter 9

203 This chapter follows closely the logic of Trivers 1972, which is based on Bateman 1948 and Williams 1966. For mating systems see also Emlen and Oring 1977. For valuable work on sexual selection in insects see Thornhill and Alcock 1983 and Blum and Blum 1979. For important new work on lizards see Stamps 1983.

204 For Darwin's work see especially Darwin 1871.

205–206 For Bateman's work see Bateman 1948.

206 For lifetime variation in number of mates in a damselfly see Fincke 1982. For variation in male RS compared to female see especially Clutton-Brock *in press*, but also Kluge 1981, Wade and Arnold 1980, Wade 1979, and Payne 1979.

206–215 For references throughout this section see Trivers 1972.

207–
208   For the latest on maternal investment in elephant seals see Ortiz, Le Boeuf, and Costa 1984. For factors affecting female RS see Reiter, Panken, and Le Boeuf 1981. For male RS see Le Boeuf 1974.

207–
208   Regarding the assumption that sperm is always cheap see Nakatsuru and Kramer 1982.

208   For Figure 9-6 see Riedman and Le Boeuf 1982.

215–
219   Sex reversed species: Williams 1966.

215–
216   Mormon crickets: Gwynne 1981 and Gwynne *in press*. Figure 9-11: Gwynne 1982 and Sakaluk 1984.

215–
216   For seahorse references, see Trivers 1972.

217   *Dendrobates auratus*: Wells 1978.

217   The quotation is from Johns 1969, p. 664. See also Ridley 1980.

218   Jacana infanticide: Stephens 1984a.

218   For evolution of bird polyandry see Graul, Derrickson, and Mork 1977.

219–
221   For sperm competition in general see Smith *in press*. For insects see Thornhill and Alcock 1983 and Parker 1970. For the evolution of gamete dimorphism see Parker, Baker, and Smith 1972, Knowlton 1974, and Parker 1982.

219–
220   *Calopteryx maculata*: Waage 1979b, and Waage *in press*. (Post-copulatory guarding: Waage 1979a.)

220   Homosexual rape, acanthocephalan variety: Abele and Gilchrist 1977.

220   Prolonged copulation as a form of mate guarding: Sillen-Tullberg 1981.

221–
227   For recent work on alternate strategies see Hogg 1984, O'Neill and Evans 1983, P. I. Ward 1983, and van Rhijn 1983. See also *American Zoologist* 24(2):307–418 (1984).

223   Dragonflies: Waltz 1982.

224–
227   Fig wasp dimorphisms: Hamilton 1979.

226   The quotation is from Hamilton 1979, pp. 173–174.

227   Female-biased polymorphisms: Stamps and Gon 1983.

228   Snake sexual dimorphism and male fighting: Shine 1978.

228   Seals: Stirling 1982.

228–
229   Primate sexual dimorphism: Clutton-Brock, Harvey, and Rudder 1977, Harvey, Kavanagh, and Clutton-Brock 1978.

229   For a review of explanations for the trend in dimorphism with body weight see Clutton-Brock, Harvey, and Rudder 1977. For a novel explanation see Hamilton 1979, p. 176. See also Price 1984. For a different logic see Downhower 1976.

230–
231   Sexual dimorphism in frogs: Woolbright 1983.

235–
236   Island and mainland *Anolis* lizards: in addition to Andrews 1976, see Andrews 1979.

237   Female indifference to male size in *Anolis*: Andrews manuscript.

    General: for genetic models of sexual selection see O'Donald 1980. See also Lande 1980. For sexual selection in plants: Stephenson and Bertin 1983, Willson and Burley 1983, and Willson 1979. For effects of relative parental investment in mammals: Zeveloff and Boyce 1980. Sexual selection in a marine invertebrate: Kaplan 1983. Reproductive synchrony and sexual selection: Knowlton 1979. Sexual selection and speciation: West Eberhard 1983 and Lande 1981. For a brilliant essay relating mating systems more generally to the origin of higher taxonomic units see Hamilton 1978.

Chapter 10

239   Baboon special relationships: Smuts 1983a, b. Chimpanzees: Tutin 1979.

240   A general review of male parental care is found in Ridley 1978.

240   *Neanthes*: Reish 1957. *Hemilepistus*: Linsenmair and Linsenmair 1971. *Pycnogonum*: see Ridley 1978. *Nymphon*: Cranmer 1982.

240   For male parental investment in insects see especially Thornhill and Alcock 1983. Also: Smith 1980 and Thornhill 1976b.

241– There have been a number of good recent
249   studies of male parental investment in the vertebrates. Fish: Baylis 1981, Gittleman 1981. Frogs: Wells 1981, McDiarmid 1978. Mammals: Kleiman and Malcolm 1981. Mode of fertilization: Gross and Shine 1981. Paternity: Werren, Gross, and Shine 1980.

248   Fourteen species of darters: Winn 1958.

249– *Hylobittacus apicalis*: Thornhill 1980a, c,
250   and 1976. Female choice for male investment in insects: see Thornhill and Alcock 1983. *Conocephalus*: Gwynne 1982. See also Gwynne 1984.

252   *Hyla rosenbergi*: Kluge 1981. For female choice in the mottled sculpin see Brown 1981.

252   Nest choice by female weaverbirds: in addition to Collias and Collias 1970 see Collias and Collias 1984.

252– *Sterna hirundo*: Nisbet 1973, 1977.
254

254   *Saxiola torquata*: Greig-Smith 1982.

254   Experience and age in pigeons: Burley and Moran 1979.

255– *Pieris protodice*: Rutowski 1982.
256

256   Male pigeons less discriminating than females: Burley 1977. For a recent study on mate choice in a monogamous bird see Price 1984.

256   The quotation is from Burley, Krantzberg, and Radman 1982, p. 444.

262   *Agelaius phoeniceus* vasectomies: Bray, Kennelly, and Guarino 1975. For bats see McCracken and Bradbury 1977.

262   Close following in male bank swallows: Beecher and Beecher 1979.

263   Sexual harassment in gulls: MacRoberts 1973.

262– Separation anxiety in zebra finches: Butter
265   field 1970.

265– Male response to pre-aroused female ring

266   doves: Erickson and Zenone 1976. See also Zenone, Sims, and Erickson 1979.

266   Repeated copulations in water bugs: Smith 1979.

266   For extra-pair copulations in a bird see Bjorklund and Westman 1983. For bigamy in gulls: Fitch and Shugart 1983; see also Post and Greenlaw 1982, Pierotti 1981, and Power 1979. For heterosexual jealousy in monkeys see Cibicciotti and Mason 1978. In humans: Daly, Wilson, and Weghorst 1982. See also Daly and Wilson 1982b.

268   *Phalaropus lobatus*: Tinbergen 1935.

268– Margaret Nice's work is described in Nice
269   1964a, b. For sexually aroused widows see also Allan 1979. For mate switches within a season see Price 1984.

269   For remating in kittwake gulls see Coulson and Thomas 1983. For a general review see Rowley 1983 and D. R. Rasmussen 1981. See also Erickson 1978. For division of labor in a fish see Rechten 1980.

Chapter 11

272– Fisher's theory can be found in Fisher 1930.
274   A good introduction to sex ratio theory at an intermediate level is Charnov 1982. For an experimental confirmation of Fisher's theory see Sadler 1981. Also (unconsciously): Schultze 1969 and 1965.

276   For differential mortality by sex in pigs see Crew 1925 and Parkes 1925; in cows Chapman, Casida, and Gote 1938.

276– For parental investment in male and female
277   mammals see Clutton-Brock and Albon 1982 and Clutton-Brock, Albon, and Guinness 1981. For competition between female relatives in mammals: Clutton-Brock, Albon, and Guinness 1982, Clark 1978. See also Silk 1983.

277   For a bird with the primary sex ratio biased in favor of the helping sex see Gowaty and Lennartz manuscript.

277– Sex ratio under sib-mating: see Hamilton
278   1967. For a recent case see Cowan 1979.

See also Mitchell 1972 and Overmeer and Harrison 1969. For an increase in reproductive output associated with self-fertilization in a plant see Piper, Charlesworth, and Charlesworth 1984.

277–
278   For a hierarchical or modern group selection approach to sex ratio selection under local mate competition see Frank 1983 and Colwell 1981.

278   Wood lemmings: Stenseth 1978, Fredga et al. 1977, and Bengtsson 1977. See also Bull 1983.

279–
282   For corrections of equations in Trivers and Hare 1976, see Benford 1978.

281   Alexander's theory of parental manipulation: Alexander 1974. A genetic model relevant to the controversy: Stamps, Metcalf, and Krishnan 1978.

281–
282   For a detailed critique of Trivers and Hare 1976 see Alexander and Sherman 1977.

281   For effects of multiple mating see Cole 1983.

281–
282   For recent work on ratios of investment in ants see especially P. S. Ward 1983a, b and Davidson 1982. For a slavemaker and a degenerate slavemaker see Winter and Buschinger 1983. For ratios of investment in *Polistes* see Metcalf 1980 and Noonan 1978. Bumblebees: Pomeroy 1979, Owen, Rodd, and Plowright 1980. A solitary wasp: Freeman 1981. For novel theories of sex ratio evolution in haplodiploid species see Seger 1983a and Pickering 1980a. See also Strassman 1984 and Herbers 1979.

283–
285   Variation in inbreeding: Hamilton 1967.

283–
285   Mechanisms of sex ratio adjustment in *Nasonia*: Wylie 1976a, 1966. For related work see Wylie 1976b. See also van den Assem and Feuth-De Bruijn 1977 and Charnov 1982.

286–
287   For Werren and Charnov's review see Werren and Charnov 1978.

287   *Rumex*: Rychlewsky and Zarzycki 1975.

287   *Pandalus jordani*: for studies of a similar sort see Charnov 1982.

288   Sex ratios and copulation rates in humans: James 1983 and 1977. For related work see also James 1975a, b, and 1984.

288–
291   For an excellent review of environmental sex determination see Chapters 9 and 10 of Bull 1983. For recent data see Mrosovsky, Hopkins-Murphy, and Richardson 1984.

290   *Menidia*: see Bull 1983.

292–
294   Variation in parental investment: the logic of this section is given in Trivers and Willard 1973. Regarding the evidence cited there, see Myers 1978. For a provocative paper arguing against a sex ratio effect see Williams 1979. For evidence from monkeys: Meikle, Tilford, and Vessey 1984, and Simpson and Simpson 1982. Sheep: Napier and Mullaney 1974.

292   *Neotoma floridana*: McClure 1981. See also Rivers and Crawford 1974.

293   *Larus delewarensis*: Ryder 1983. For birds see also Howe 1976, 1977.

294   For effect of attractiveness on sex ratio see Burley 1981a. Sons of attractive males: Burley personal communication.

295   ACTH and sex ratio: Geiringer 1961.

295   Whales: Seger, Trivers, and Hare manuscript.

296   Female-biased infanticide in India: Pakrasi and Sasmal 1970.

296–
297   For a human society with total investment clearly biased toward males see Hamilton 1966.

297–
298   For reviews of factors affecting the human sex ratio, see Teitelbaum 1972, 1970, and Pollard 1969.

298   Schizophrenia and the primary sex ratio: Lane 1969, Shearer, Davidson, and Finch 1967, Taylor 1969. See also Lane and Hyde 1973, Lane and Albee 1970.

Chapter 12

301   For additional references on differential mortality by sex see Trivers 1972.

302   For a good early review, including world-

wide and historical evidence, see Hamilton 1948. The quotation is also from Hamilton 1948.

303 For differential mortality *in utero* in humans see McMillen 1979. For an unusual pattern of differential mortality by sex in childhood see Cowgill and Hutchinson 1963a, b.

304 Sex differences in mortality due to disease: Dauer, Korns, and Schuman 1968.

305 Starvation and nutritional stress: Widdowson 1976. See also Latham 1947. Regarding ability to withstand cold see Slee 1972. For additional information see Glucksmann 1974. For a recent review of differential mortality by sex in mammals see Ralls, Brownell, and Ballou 1980.

307– For references on the unguarded X theory
309 see Trivers 1972.

308 Castrated cats: Hamilton, Hamilton, and Mestler 1969.

308 Castrated humans: Hamilton and Mestler 1969.

309– Differential mortality by sex in ground
311 squirrels: in addition to Sherman and Morton 1984, see Pfeifer 1982.

309– For differential mortality by sex in red deer:
311 Clutton-Brock, Guinness, and Albon 1982.

311– The theory of differential mortality by sex
313 is given in more detail in Trivers 1972.

312 Differential mortality by sex in lizards: see Stamps 1983.

313 For the consequences in human society of changes in patterns of differential mortality by sex, see Guttentag and Secord 1983.

Chapter 13

315 The evolution of sex has been treated by several valuable books: see Bell 1982, Maynard Smith 1978, Williams 1975. See also Ghiselin 1974.

316– The rate of evolution: Maynard Smith 1978.
318

318– The cost of sex: Maynard Smith 1971,
320 1978.

320 For varying degrees of sexuality and asexuality coexisting within one species, see Ferrari and Hebert 1982.

320– For sibling competition see especially Wil-
322 liams 1975 and Bell 1982.

322 I am indebted to William Hamilton for the term "contrary" (being superior in connotation to Bell's "capricious").

322– For this section see especially Hamilton,
324 Henderson, and Moran 1981 and Hamilton 1982. See also Hamilton 1980, Jaenike 1978, and Tooby 1982.

323 Flax and flax rust: Flor 1956.

324 The quotation is from Hamilton 1982, p. 271.

324 For sex in random environments: Moore and Hines 1981.

324 For a review of relevant literature on parasites see May 1983 and May and Anderson 1983. For pest pressure and plants: Levin 1975, Strong and Levin 1979. For the evolution of separate sexes in plants: Bawa 1980a.

324– Graham Bell's review: Bell 1982.
328

328 The quotation is from Hamilton, Henderson, and Moran 1981, p. 377.

Chapter 14

331 A good recent review is Bateson 1983. See also Searcy 1982.

332 See Darwin 1871.

332– For bowerbirds see Collias and Collias 1984
333 and Gilliard 1969. Birds of paradise: Beehler 1983, Beehler and Pruett-Jones 1983. Lek species: de Vos 1979.

333 The quotation is from Beach and Le Boeuf 1967, p. 557.

335 For a result similar to Mason 1969, see Scheiring 1977. See also McCauley and Wade 1978.

336– *Physalaemus*: In addition to Ryan 1980,

337   see Ryan 1983 and Tuttle and Ryan 1981. See also Fairchild 1981, Whitney and Krebs 1975a, b.

337   Mating swarms of flies: Downes 1969.

337–
338   Recent work on minority male advantage: Ehrman and Probber 1978, Spiess and Ehrman 1978, Spiess and Schwer 1978, and White and Grant 1977. For objections to minority male advantage see Partridge 1983.

338–
339   For mate choice increasing offspring survival in *Drosophila melanogaster* see Partridge 1980. For genetic change due to male mating advantage in *Drosophila pseudoobscura* see Anderson et al. 1979.

339   Male dominance and ovulation in rhesus monkeys: Chapais 1983.

339   Hormone-induced sperm breakage: Hawk 1972, Hawk and Conley 1972.

340   Female orgasm in a monkey: Burton 1971.

340   For the effects of monogamy on the sexual behavior of rodents see Dewsbury 1981.

341   Forced copulation in ducks: McKinney, Derrickson, and Mineau 1983, Barash 1977. In scorpionflies: Thornhill 1980b. In humans: Thornhill and Thornhill 1983.

342   Female incitation to male competition: in addition to Cox and Le Boeuf 1977, see Zucker 1983.

342–
343   Jamaican green lizard: Trivers 1976.

343–
346   For an excellent review of mate choice in plants see Stephenson and Bertin 1983. For a more detailed treatment see Willson and Burley 1983. See also Bookman 1984.

346–
348   For objections to female choice for genes see Williams 1975 and Maynard Smith 1978. For additional objections including group selection arguments, see Arnold 1983.

348   For the mutant gene that spreads in spite of two obstacles: Kirkpatrick 1982.

349–
352   Black grouse: in addition to Kruijt and Hogan 1967, see de Vos 1983 and de Vos 1979. For courtship tactics see Kruijt, de Vos, and Bossema 1970.

353   Hamadryas baboons: Bachmann and Kummer 1980.

354   Handicap genes: Zahavi 1977.

355   Injuries to the skeleton and antler abnormalities: Marburger et al. 1972, Robinette and Jones 1954, Clarke 1916. Antlers remembering injuries: Bubenik and Pavlansky 1965. Function of antlers: Clutton-Brock 1982. Recent work on antlers: Brown 1983.

357–
358   Positive correlations between components of reproductive success (such as found in male deer) may be common: see Bell 1984a, b.

358–
359   Parasites and female choice: Hamilton and Zuk 1982. See also Zuk 1984.

358   The quotation is from Zuk 1984, pp. 32–33.

359   Parasites and ducks: Hamilton personal communication.
       General: Female choice and a fish polymorphism: Semler 1971. Male choice: Manning 1975. Strategies of female choice: Janetos 1980.

Chapter 15

361   This chapter is based on Axelrod 1984, Axelrod and Hamilton 1981, and Trivers 1971. Consult these works for many additional references.

362–
363   Live-and-let-live system: see Axelrod 1984.

363   The quotation is from Koppen 1931, p. 135.

366–
367   Response to bird neighbor depending on location: in addition to Falls and Brooks 1975, see Falls and McNicholl 1979, Falls and D'Agincourt 1981, and Wiley and Wiley 1977. For bird neighbors see also Craig 1984. For vervet monkeys see Cheney and Seyfarth 1982.

372–
374   Baboon reciprocity: Packer 1977. See also Cheney 1977. Male inter-troop transfer: Packer 1979.

372   Strong correlation between tendency to

take part in coalition and success at acquiring female: K. Rasmussen 1981.

373–374 Baboon special relationships: Smuts 1983a, b.

375–382 Chimpanzee politics: see especially de Waal 1982 but see also de Waal *in press*, de Waal and Yoshihara 1983, de Waal and van Hooff 1981, de Waal and von Roosmalen 1979, and de Waal 1978.

379 For shifting chimpanzee alliances in the wild see Nishida 1983.

380 The quotation is from de Waal 1982, p. 124.

382–386 Dolphins and whales: Connor and Norris 1982.

385 Figure 15-16: Porter 1977.

386–389 Reciprocal altruism in humans: for references in this section see Trivers 1971. For recent work on the development of altruistic tendencies in humans see Bridgeman 1983.
In general: for lions see Packer and Pusey 1982, Bygott, Bertram, and Hanby 1979. For cooperative display in a bird: Foster 1981. For recent work on human reciprocal altruism: Hill 1984, Moore 1984b, and MacDonald 1984. See also Lopreato 1981.

Chapter 16

395 For a recent review of deception in animal communication see Krebs and Dawkins 1984 (but see Hinde 1981).

396–400 For the classic account of camouflage see Cott 1940. For a recent review see Edmunds 1974. See also Hinton 1973.

397 Panamanian stick insect: Robinson 1968. For an excellent series of papers on insect camouflage and deception see also Robinson 1973, 1970, 1969a, b. For similar work see de Ruiter 1952, Blest 1957, and Hinton 1958.

398–400 Pronghorn fawn hiding: Byers and Byers 1983.

400 For mimicry see Wickler 1968.

400 Butterfly mimicry: in addition to Sheppard 1959, see Turner 1977.

400–406 For recent work on deception and mimicry in plants see Little 1983, Nilsson 1983, Gilbert 1982, and Bawa 1980b.

401–406 *Ophrys*: Kullenberg 1961.

406 Ten-spined stickleback: Morris 1952. Sticklebacks prefer to mate with males whose nests contain eggs: Ridley and Rechten 1981.

407–408 Bluegill sunfish: Dominey 1980. For sexual parasitism in a frog see Perrill, Gerhardt, and Daniel 1978.

408 *Hylobittacus apicalis*: Thornhill 1979.

409–410 *Gonodactylus bredini*: Steger and Caldwell 1983. For the most recent work see Caldwell *in press*.

410–411 *Pimephales promelas*: Unger 1983.

411 The quotation is from de Waal 1982, p. 133. For additional work on chimpanzee deception see de Waal *in press* and Woodruff and Premack 1979.

411–415 Rohwer's experiments are described in Rohwer 1977 and Rohwer and Rohwer 1978. For related work see Rohwer 1982, Rohwer and Ewald 1981, and Rohwer, Fretwell, and Niles 1980. For selection in favor of sexual indistinguishability in birds see Burley 1981.

415–416 Very little to date has been published on an evolutionary approach to self-deception: see Alexander 1979. For self-deception and concealed ovulation see Daniels 1983 and Burley 1979.

416–417 Gur and Sackeim's work is described in Gur and Sackeim 1979. For recent related work see Sackeim 1983.

418–419 For benefectance and the illusion of consistency see Greenwald 1980. See also Snyder and Uranowitz 1978. For self-justification see Aronson 1980.

420 For perceptual defense and vigilance see Dixon 1981 and Erdelyi 1974.

In general: for a recent case of deceit and self-deception in our own species see Broad 1982a, b. For deception in disease see Zabriskie 1967 and Damian 1964. Intraspecific distraction display: Stephens 1984b. (For an example between species see Hobbs 1967.) Firefly mimicry: Lloyd 1981. Song matching in birds: Payne 1983, 1982. Variety of song as deception: Yasukawa 1981. Sexual mimicry in a newt: Verrell 1983. Death-feigning: Sargeant and Eberhardt 1975, Francq 1969. Lies in the dog family: Fox 1971, von Ruppell 1969, and Lorenz 1955. For information revealed by the pitch of the human voice see Ohala 1984.

Addendum

Chapter 6. In the past few years, the study of kin relations in ground squirrels has become a truly comparative science. See especially the following papers and references cited therein: Hoogland, J. L. In press. Nepotism in prairie dogs (*Cynomys ludovicianus*) varies with competition but not with kinship. *Anim. Behav.* Hoogland, J. L. 1983. Nepotism and alarm calling in the black-tailed prairie dog (*Cynomys ludovicianus*). *Anim. Behav.* 31:472–479. Davis, L. S. 1984. Kin selection and adult female Richardson's ground squirrels: a test. *Can. J. Zool.* 62:2344–2348. Armitage, K. B. 1984. Recruitment in yellow-bellied marmot populations: kinship, philopatry, and individual variability. In: *The Biology of*

Ground-dwelling Squirrels, edited by J. O. Murie and G. R. Michener. Lincoln: University of Nebraska Press.

Chapter 9. For important comparative work on sexual dimorphism in species lacking male parental investment see Payne, R. 1984. Sexual selection, lek and arena behavior, and sexual dimorphism in birds. *Ornithological Monographs #33.* Washington, D.C.: The American Ornithologists' Union. Packer, C. 1983. Sexual dimorphism: the horns of African antelopes. *Science* 221:1191–1193. For selection acting on female vertebrates in a variety of contexts see Wasser, S. 1983. (Ed.) *Social Behavior of Female Vertebrates.* N.Y.: Academic Press.

Chapter 16. For detection of deception in humans see Ekman, P. 1985. *Telling Lies: Clues to Deceit in the Marketplace, Politics, and Marriage.* N.Y.: Norton. For female-mimics in bluegill sunfish see Gross, M. 1982. Sneakers, satellites and parentals: polymorphic mating strategies in North American sunfishes. *Z. Tierpsychol* 60:1–26. Gross, M. 1984. Sunfish, salmon and the evolution of alternative reproductive strategies and tactics in fishes. In: *Fish Reproduction: Strategies and Tactics*, edited by G. Potts and R. Wotten, 55–75. London: Academic Press. For the cost of self-deception in humans see Trivers, R. and H. Newton. 1983. The crash of Flight 90: doomed by self-deception? *Science Digest*, Nov., pp. 66–67, and 111.

References

Abele, L. G., and S. Gilchrist. 1977. Homosexual rape and sexual selection in acanthocephalan worms. *Science* 197:81–83.

Adams, D. B., A. R. Gold, and A. D. Burt. 1978. Rise in female-initiated sexual activity at ovulation and its suppression by oral contraceptives. *New Eng. J. Med.* 299:1145–1150.

Adler, N. T., and S. R. Zoloth. 1970. Copulatory behavior can inhibit pregnancy in female rats. *Science* 168:1480–1482.

Aiello, A., and R. E. Silberglied. 1978. Life history of *Dynastor darius* (Lepidoptera: Nymphalidae: Brassolinae) in Panama. *Psyche* 85:331–345.

Alcock, J. 1979. The evolution of intraspecific diversity in male reproductive strategies in some bees and wasps. In: *Sexual Selection and Reproductive Competition in Insects*, edited by M. S. Blum and N. A. Blum, 381–402. New York: Academic Press.

Alcock, J. 1984. *Animal Behavior: An Evolutionary Approach*. Third edition. Sunderland, Massachusetts: Sinauer Associates, Inc.

Alexander, R. D. 1974. The evolution of social behavior. *Ann. Rev. Ecol. Syst.* 5:325–383.

Alexander, R. D. 1977. Natural selection and the analysis of human sociality. In: *Changing Scenes in Natural Sciences: 1776–1976*, edited by C. E. Goulden, 283–337. Academy of Natural Sciences, Special Publication 12.

Alexander, R. D. 1979. *Darwinism and Human Affairs*. Seattle: University of Washington Press.

Alexander, R. D., J. L. Hoogland, R. D. Howard, K. M. Noonan, and P. W. Sherman. 1979. Sexual dimorphisms and breeding systems in pinnipeds, ungulates, primates and humans. In: *Evolution-ary Biology and Human Social Behavior: An Anthropological Perspective*, edited by N. A. Chagnon and W. Irons, 402–603. Belmont, California: Wadsworth.

Alexander, R. D., and P. W. Sherman. 1977. Local mate competition and parental investment in social insects. *Science* 196:494–500.

Allan, T. A. 1979. Parental behavior of a replacement male dark-eyed junco. *Auk* 96:630–631.

Altmann, J. 1979. Age cohorts as paternal sibships. *Behav. Ecol. Sociobiol.* 6:161–164.

Altmann, J. 1980. *Baboon Mothers and Infants*. Cambridge, Massachusetts: Harvard University Press.

Altmann, J., S. A. Altmann, and G. Hausfater. 1978. Primate infant's effects on mother's future reproduction. *Science* 201:1028–1030.

Anderson, W. A. 1968. Structure and fate of the paternal mitochondrion during early embryogenesis of *Paracentrotus lividus*. *J. Ultrastructure Research* 24:311–321.

Anderson, W. W., L. Levine, O. Olivera, J. R. Powell, M. E. de la Rosa, V. M. Salceda, M. I. Gaso, and J. Guzman. 1979. Evidence for selection by male mating success in natural populations of *Drosophila pseudoobscura*. *Proc. Natl. Acad. Sci. USA* 76:1519–1523.

Andersson, M. 1982. Female choice selects for extreme tail length in a widowbird. *Nature* 299:818–820.

Andrews, R. M. 1976. Growth rate in island and mainland anoline lizards. *Copeia* 3:477–482.

Andrews, R. M. 1979. Evolution of life histories: a comparison of *Anolis* lizards from matched island and mainland habitats. *Breviora* 454:1–51.

Andrews, R. M. n.d. Mate choice by female *Anolis carolinensis* (Sauria: Iguanidae). Unpublished manuscript.

Ankney, C. D. 1982. Sex ratio varies with egg sequence in the lesser snow geese. *Auk* 99:662–666.

Aoki, S. 1977. *Colophina clematis* (Homoptera, Pemphigidae), an aphid species with "soldiers." *Kontyu*, Tokyo 45:276–282.

Aoki, S. 1979a. Dimorphic first instar larvae produced by the fundatrix of *Pachypappa marsupialis* (Homoptera: Aphidoidea). *Kontyu*, Tokyo 47:390–398.

Aoki, S. 1979b. Further observations on *Astegopteryx styracicola* (Homoptera: Pemphigidae), an aphid species with soldiers biting man. *Kontyu*, Tokyo 47:99–104.

Aoki, S. 1980. Life cycles of two *Colophina* aphids (Homoptera, Pemphigidae) producing soldiers. *Kontyu*, Tokyo 48:464–476.

Aoki, S., S. Akimoto, and S. Yamane. 1981. Observations on *Pseudoregma alexanderi* (Homoptera, Pemphigidae), an aphid species producing pseudoscorpion-like soldiers on bamboos. *Kontyu*, Tokyo, 49:355–356.

Aoki, S., and M. Miyazaki. 1978. Notes on the pseudoscorpion-like larvae of *Pseudoregma alexanderi* (Homoptera, Aphidoidea). *Kontyu*, Tokyo 46:433–438.

Arnold, S. J. 1983. Sexual selection: the interface of theory and empiricism. In: *Mate Choice*, edited by P. Bateson, 67–107. Cambridge: Cambridge University Press.

Aronson, E. 1980. *The Social Animal*. Third Edition. San Francisco: Freeman.

Axelrod, R. 1984. *The Evolution of Cooperation*. New York: Basic Books, Inc.

Axelrod, R., and W. D. Hamilton. 1981. The evolution of cooperation. *Science* 211:1390–1396.

Ayala, F. J., and J. A. Kiger, Jr. 1984. *Modern Genetics*. Second Edition. Menlo Park, California: Benjamin/Cummings.

Bachmann, C., and H. Kummer. 1980. Male assessment of female choice in hamadryas baboons. *Behav. Ecol. Sociobiol.* 6:315–321.

Bajema, C. J. 1971. *Natural Selection in Human Populations: The Measurement of Ongoing Genetic Evolution in Contemporary Societies*. New York: J. Wiley & Sons.

Baker, M. C. 1983. The behavioral response of female Nuttall's white-crowned sparrows to male song of natal and alien dialects. *Behav. Ecol. Sociobiol.* 12:309–315.

Baldwin, I. T., and J. C. Schultz. 1983. Rapid changes in the tree leaf chemistry induced by damage: evidence for communication between plants. *Science* 221:277–279.

Barash, D. P. 1974. Mother-infant relations in captive woodchucks (*Marmota monax*). *Anim. Behav.* 22:446–448.

Barash, D. P. 1977. Sociobiology of rape in mallards (*Anas platyrhynchos*): responses of the mated male. *Science* 197:788–789.

Barash, D. P. 1982. *Sociobiology and Behavior*. Second edition. New York: Elsevier.

Bartz, S. H. 1979. Evolution of eusociality in termites. *Proc. Natl. Acad. Sci. USA* 76:5764–5768.

Bartz, S. H. 1980. Correction: evolution of eusociality in termites. *Proc. Nat. Acad. Sci. USA* 77:3070.

Bartz, S. H. 1982. On the evolution of male workers in the Hymenoptera. *Behav. Ecol. Sociobiol.* 11:223–228.

Bateman, A. J. 1948. Intra-sexual selection in *Drosophila*. *Heredity* 2:349–368.

Bateson, P. 1982. Preferences for cousins in Japanese quail. *Nature* 295:236–237.

Bateson, P., ed. 1983. *Mate Choice*. Cambridge: Cambridge University Press.

Bawa, K. S. 1980a. Evolution of dioecy in flowering plants. *Ann. Rev. Ecol. Syst.* 11:15–39.

Bawa, K. S. 1980b. Mimicry of male by female flowers and intrasexual competition for pollinators in *Jacaratia dolichaula* (D. Smith) Woodson (Caricaceae). *Evolution* 34:467–474.

Baylis, J. R. 1981. The evolution of parental care in fishes, with reference to Darwin's rule of male sexual selection. *Env. Biol. Fish.* 6:223–251.

Beach, F. A., and B. J. Le Boeuf. 1967. Coital behaviour in dogs. I. Preferential mating in the bitch. *Anim. Behav.* 15:546–558.

Beecher, M. D., and I. M. Beecher. 1979. Sociobiology of bank swallows: reproductive strategy of the male. *Science* 205:1282–1285.

Beehler, B. 1983. For gaudy display, it's hard to beat birds of paradise. *Smithsonian* 13:91–97.

Beehler, B., and S. G. Pruett-Jones. 1983. Display dispersion and diet of birds of paradise: a comparison of nine species. *Behav. Ecol. Sociobiol.* 13:229–238.

Bell, A. P., M. S. Weinberg, and S. K. Hammersmith. 1981. *Sexual Preference: Its Development in Men and Women*. Bloomington: Indiana University Press.

Bell, G. 1982. *The Masterpiece of Nature: The Evolution and Genetics of Sexuality*. Berkeley: University of California Press.

Bell, G. 1984a. Measuring the cost of reproduction. I. The correlation structure of the life table of a plankton rotifer. *Evolution* 38:300–313.

Bell, G. 1984b. Measuring the cost of reproduction. II. The correlation structure of the life tables of five freshwater invertebrates. *Evolution* 38:314–326.

Benford, F. A. 1978. Fisher's theory of the sex-ratio applied to the social hymenoptera. *J. Theor. Biol.* 72:701–727.

Bengtsson, B. O. 1977. Evolution of the sex ratio in the wood lemming, *Mysopus schisticolor*. In: *Measuring Selection in Natural Populations*, edited by F. B. Christiansen and T. M. Fenchel, 333–343. Berlin: Springer-Verlag.

Bengtsson, H., and O. Ryden. 1983. Parental feeding rate in relation to begging behavior in asynchronously hatched broods of great tit *Parus major*. *Behav. Ecol. Sociobiol.* 12:243–251.

Bertin, R. I. 1982. Influence of father identity on fruit production in trumpet creeper (*Campsis radicans*). *Amer. Nat.* 119:694–709.

Bertram, B. C. R. 1976. Kin selection in lions and in evolution. In: *Growing Points in Ethology*, edited by P. P. G. Bateson and R. A. Hinde, 281–301. Cambridge: Cambridge University Press.

Bielicki, T., and Z. Welon. 1964. The operation of natural selection on human head form in an East European population. *Homo* 15:22–30.

Biggers, J. D., and R. F. S. Creed. 1962. Conjugate spermatozoa of the North American opossum. *Nature* 196:1112–1113.

Bjorklund, M., and B. Westman. 1983. Extra-pair copulations in the pied flycatcher (*Ficedula hypoleuca*): a removal experiment. *Behav. Ecol. Sociobiol.* 13:271–275.

Blaustein, A. R., and R. K. O'Hara. 1982. Kin recognition in *Rana cascadae* tadpoles: maternal and paternal effects. *Anim. Behav.* 30:1151–1157.

Blest, A. D. 1957. The function of eyespot patterns in the Lepidoptera. *Behaviour* 11:209–256.

Blum, M. S., and N. A. Blum. 1979. *Sexual Selection and Reproductive Competition in Insects*. New York: Academic Press.

Boag, P. T., and P. R. Grant. 1981. Intense natural selection in a population of Darwin's finches (Geospizinae) in the Galapagos. *Science* 214:82–84.

Boggs, C. L., and L. E. Gilbert. 1979. Male contribution to egg production in butterflies: evidence for transfer of nutrients at mating. *Science* 206:83–84.

Bookman, S. S. 1984. Evidence for selective fruit production in *Asclepias*. *Evolution* 38:72–86.

Bouchard, T. J. 1983. Do environmental similarities explain the similarity in intelligence of identical twins reared apart? *Intelligence* 7:175–184.

Bouchard, T. J. 1984. Twins reared together and apart: what they tell us about human diversity. In: *Individuality and Determinism*, edited by S. W. Fox, 147–184. New York: Plenum.

Bouchard, T. J., Jr., and M. McGue. 1981. Familial studies of intelligence: a review. *Science* 212:1055–1059.

Bray, O. E., J. J. Kennelly, and J. L. Guarino. 1975. Fertility of eggs produced on territories of vasectomized red-winged blackbirds. *Wilson Bulletin* 87:187–195.

Bridgeman, D. L., ed. 1983. *The Nature of Prosocial Development: Interdisciplinary Theories and Strategies*. New York: Academic Press.

Broad, W. J. 1982a. Harvard delays in reporting fraud. *Science* 215:478–482.

Broad, W. J. 1982b. Report absolves Harvard in case of fakery. *Science* 215:874–875.

Brown, J. L. 1978. Avian communal breeding systems. *Ann. Rev. Ecol. Syst.* 9:123–155.

Brown, L. 1981. Patterns of female choice in mottled sculpins (*Cottidae, Teleostei*). *Anim. Behav.* 29:375–382.

Brown, L. H., and E. K. Urban. 1969. The breeding biology of the great white pelican *Pelecanus onocrotalus roseus* at Lake Shala, Ethiopia. *Ibis* 111:199–237.

Brown, R. D., ed. 1983. *Antler Development in Cervidae*. Kingsville, Texas: Ceasar Kleberg Wildlife Research Institute.

Bubenik, A. B., and R. Pavlansky. 1965. Trophic responses to trauma in growing antlers. *J. Exp. Zool.* 159:289–302.

Buckle, G. R., and L. Greenberg. 1981. Nestmate recognition in sweat bees (*Lasioglossum zephyrum*): does an individual recognize its own odour or only odours of its nestmates? *Anim. Behav.* 29:802–809.

Bull, J. J. 1983. *Evolution of Sex Determining Mechanisms*. Menlo Park, California: Benjamin/Cummings.

Burger, J., and M. Gochfeld. 1981. Unequal sex ratios and their consequences in Herring Gulls (*Larus argentatus*). *Behav. Ecol. Sociobiol.* 8:125–128.

Burke, V. E. M., and L. H. Brown. 1970. Observation on the breeding of the pink-backed pelican *Pelecanus rufescens*. *Ibis* 112:499–512.

Burley, N. 1977. Parental investment, mate choice, and mate quality. *Proc. Natl. Acad. Sci. USA* 74:3476–3479.

Burley, N. 1979. The evolution of concealed ovulation. *Amer. Nat.* 114:835–858.

Burley, N. 1981a. The evolution of sexual indistinguishability. In: *Natural Selection and Social Behavior: Recent Research and New Theory*, edited by R. D. Alexander and D. W. Tinkle, 121–137. New York: Chiron Press.

Burley, N. 1981b. Mate choice by multiple criteria in a monogamous species. *Amer. Nat.* 117:515–528.

Burley, N. 1982. Facultative sex-ratio manipulation. *Amer. Nat.* 120:81–107.

Burley, N., G. Krantzberg, and P. Radman. 1982. Influence of colour-banding on the conspecific preferences of zebra finches. *Anim. Behav.* 30: 444–455.

Burley, N., and N. Moran. 1979. The significance of age and reproductive experience in the mate preferences of feral pigeons, *Columba livia. Anim. Behav.* 27:686–698.

Burton, F. D. 1971. Sexual climax in female *Macaca mulatta. Proc. 3rd Int. Congr. Primat.*, Zurich 1970, 3:180–191.

Buschinger, A., W. Ehrhardt, and U. Winter. 1980. The organization of slave raids in dulotic ants—a comparative study (Hymenoptera; Formicidae). *Z. Tierpsychol.* 53:245–264.

Butterfield, P. A. 1970. The pair bond in the zebra finch. In: *Social Behaviour in Birds and Mammals*, edited by J. H. Crook, 249–298. London: Academic Press.

Byers, J. A., and K. Z. Byers. 1983. Do pronghorn mothers reveal the locations of their hidden fawns? *Behav. Ecol. Sociobiol.* 13:147–156.

Bygott, D. J., B. C. R. Bertram, and J. P. Hanby. 1979. Male lions in large coalitions gain reproductive advantages. *Nature* 282:839–841.

Cade, W. 1981. Alternative male strategies: genetic differences in crickets. *Science* 212:563–564.

Caldwell, R. L. (In press). The deceptive use of reputation by stomatopods. In: *Human and Nonhuman Deceit*, edited by R. W. Mitchell and N. S. Thompson. New York: SUNY Press.

Carlin, N. F., and B. Hölldobler. 1983. Nestmate and kin recognition in interspecific mixed colonies of ants. *Science* 222:1027–1029.

Carney, P. W. 1969. Behavioral and morphological changes in carpenter ants harboring discrocoeliid metacercariae. *Amer. Midland Naturalist* 82: 605–611.

Chabrzyk, G., and J. G. Coulson. 1976. Survival and recruitment in the herring gull *Larus argentatus. J. Anim. Ecol.* 45:187–203.

Chagnon, N. A., and W. I. Irons, eds. 1979. *Evolutionary Biology and Human Social Behavior: An Anthropological Perspective*. North Scituate, Massachusetts: Duxbury Press.

Chapais, B. 1983. Reproductive activity in relation to male dominance and the likelihood of ovulation in rhesus monkeys. *Behav. Ecol. Sociobiol.* 12:215–228.

Chapman, A. B., L. E. Casida, and A. Gote. 1938. Sex ratios of fetal calves. *Proceedings of The American Society of Animal Production*, 303–304.

Chapman, F. M. 1908. *Camps and Cruises of an Ornithologist*. New York: Appleton.

Chapman, M., and G. Hausfater. 1979. The reproductive consequences of infanticide in langurs: a mathematical model. *Behav. Ecol. Sociobiol.* 5: 227–240.

Charnov, E. L. 1982. *The Theory of Sex Allocation*. Princeton, New Jersey: Princeton University Press.

Charnov, E. L. 1984. Behavioural ecology of plants. In: *Behavioural Ecology* (Second Edition), edited by J. R. Krebs and N. B. Davies, 362–379. Sunderland, Massachusetts: Sinauer.

Charnov, E. L., D. W. Gotshall, and J. G. Robinson. 1978. Sex ratio: adaptive response to population fluctuations in pandalid shrimp. *Science* 200: 204–206.

Cheney, D. L. 1977. The acquisition of rank and the development of reciprocal alliances among free ranging immature baboons. *Behav. Ecol. Sociobiol.* 2:303–318.

Cheney, D. L., and R. Seyfarth. 1982. Recognition of individuals within and between groups of free-ranging vervet monkeys. *American Zoologist* 22:519–529.

Chepko-Sade, B. D., and T. J. Olivier. 1979. Coefficient of genetic relationship and the probability of intragenealogical fission in *Macaca mulatta. Behav. Ecol. Sociobiol.* 5:263–278.

Chepko-Sade, D. B., and D. S. Sade. 1979. Patterns of group splitting within matrilineal kinship groups: a study of social group structure in *Macaca mulatta* (Cercopithecidae: Primates). *Behav. Ecol. Sociobiol.* 5:67–86.

Cibicciotti, D. D., and W. A. Mason. 1978. Comparative studies of social behavior in *Callicebus* and *Saimiri*: heterosexual jealousy behavior. *Behav. Ecol. Sociobiol.* 3:311–322.

Clark, A. B. 1978. Sex ratio and local resource competition in a prosimian primate. *Science* 201: 163–165.

Clark, K. L., and R. J. Robertson. 1979. Spatial and temporal multispecies nesting aggregations in birds as anti-parasite and anti-predator defenses. *Behavioral Ecology and Sociobiology* 5: 359–371.

Clarke, B. 1976. The ecological genetics of host-parasite relationships. In: *Genetic Aspects of Host-Parasite Relationships, Symposia of the British Society for Parasitology* 14, edited by A. E. R. Taylor and R. Muller, 87–103. Oxford: Blackwell.

Clarke, F. C. 1916. Malformed antlers of deer. *California Fish and Game* 2:118–123.

Clarke, M. F. 1984. Co-operative breeding by the

Australian Bell Miner *Manorina melanophrys* Latham: a test of kin selection theory. *Behav. Ecol. Sociobiol.* 14:137–146.

Clutton-Brock, T. H. 1982. The functions of antlers. *Behaviour* 79:108–125.

Clutton-Brock, T. H. 1983. Selection in relation to sex. In: *Evolution from Molecules to Man*, edited by D. S. Bendall, 457–481. Cambridge: Cambridge University Press.

Clutton-Brock, T. H. 1984. Reproductive effort and terminal investment in iteroparous animals. *The American Naturalist* 123:212–229.

Clutton-Brock, T. H., ed. In press. *Reproductive Success*. Chicago: University of Chicago Press.

Clutton-Brock, T. H., and S. D. Albon. 1982. Parental investment in male and female offspring in mammals. In: *Current Problems in Sociobiology*, edited by King's College Sociobiology Group, 223–248. Cambridge: Cambridge University Press.

Clutton-Brock, T. H., S. D. Albon, and F. E. Guinness. 1981. Parental investment in male and female offspring in polygynous mammals. *Nature* 289:487–489.

Clutton-Brock, T. H., S. D. Albon, and F. E. Guinness. 1982. Competition between female relatives in a matrilocal mammal. *Nature* 300:178–180.

Clutton-Brock, T. H., S. D. Albon, and F. E. Guinness. 1984. Maternal dominance, breeding success and birth sex ratios in red deer. *Nature* 308:358–360.

Clutton-Brock, T. H., F. E. Guinness, and S. D. Albon. 1982. *Red Deer: Behavior and Ecology of Two Sexes*. Chicago: The University of Chicago Press.

Clutton-Brock, T. H., P. H. Harvey, and B. Rudder. 1977. Sexual dimorphism, socionomic sex ratio and body weight in primates. *Nature* 269:797–800.

Cole, B. J. 1983. Multiple mating and the evolution of social behavior in the Hymenoptera. *Behav. Ecol. Sociobiol.* 12:191–202.

Cole, S., F. R. Hainsworth, A. C. Kamil, T. Mercier, and L. L. Wolf. 1982. Spatial learning as an adaptation in hummingbirds. *Science* 217:655–657.

Collias, N. E., and E. C. Collias. 1970. The behavior of the West African village weaverbird. *Ibis* 112:457–480.

Collias, N. E., and E. C. Collias. 1984. *Nest Building and Bird Behavior*. Princeton, New Jersey: Princeton University Press.

Colwell, R. K. 1981. Group selection is implicated in the evolution of female-biased sex ratios. *Nature* 290:401–404.

Connor, R. C., and K. S. Norris. 1982. Are dolphins and whales reciprocal altruists? *Amer. Nat.* 119:358–374.

Cott, H. B. 1940. *Adaptive Coloration in Animals*. London: Methuen.

Couch, J. W. 1938. *The Genus Septobasidium*. Chapel Hill: University of North Carolina Press.

Coulson, J. C. 1966. The influence of the pair-bond and age on the breeding biology of the kittiwake gull *Rissa tridactila*. *J. Animal Ecology* 35:269–279.

Coulson, J. C., and G. Hickling. 1961. Variation in the secondary sex-ratio of the grey seal *Halichoerus grypus* (Fab.) during the breeding season. *Nature* 190:281.

Coulson, J. C., and C. S. Thomas. 1983. Mate choice in the Kittiwake gull. In: *Mate Choice*, edited by P. Bateson, 361–376. Cambridge: Cambridge University Press.

Cowan, D. P. 1979. Sibling matings in a hunting wasp: adaptive inbreeding? *Science* 205:1403–1405.

Cowgill, U. M., and G. E. Hutchinson. 1963a. Differential mortality among the sexes in childhood and its possible significance in human evolution. *Proc. Nat. Acad. Sci.* 49:425–429.

Cowgill, U. M., and G. E. Hutchinson. 1963b. Sex-ratio in childhood and the depopulation of the Peten, Guatemala. *Human Biology* 35:90–103.

Cowgill, U. M., and H. B. Johnson, Jr. 1971. Grain prices and vital statistics in a Portuguese rural parish, 1671–1720. *J. Biosoc. Sci.* 3:321–329.

Cox, C. R., and B. J. Le Boeuf. 1977. Female incitation of male competition: a mechanism in sexual selection. *Amer. Nat.* 111:317–335.

Cox, D. F. 1965. Survival and gestation in pigs. *Evolution* 19:195–196.

Craig, J. L. 1984. Are communal pukeko caught in the prisoner's dilemma? *Behav. Ecol. Sociobiol.* 14:147–150.

Cranmer, G. J. 1982. *Nymphon* (Pycnogonida) in the Eastern Arctic. Ph. D. thesis, Luton, Beds., U. K.

Crew, F. A. E. 1925. Prenatal death in the pig and its effect upon sex ratio. *Roy. Soc. Edinburgh, Proceedings* 46:9–14.

Crook, J. H. 1980. *The Evolution of Human Consciousness*. Oxford, England: Clarendon.

Crow, J. F. 1979. Genes that violate Mendel's rules. *Scient. Amer.* 240:134–146.

Daly, M., and M. I. Wilson. 1981. Abuse and neglect of children in evolutionary perspective. In: *Natural Selection and Social Behavior: Recent Research and New Theory*, edited by R. D. Alexander and D. W. Tinkle, 405–416. New York: Chiron Press.

Daly, M., and M. Wilson. 1982a. Homicide and kinship. *Am. Anthrop.* 84:372–378.

Daly, M., and M. Wilson. 1982b. Whom are newborn babies said to resemble? *Ethology and Sociobiology* 3:69–78.

Daly, M., and M. Wilson. 1983. *Sex, Evolution, and Behavior.* Second Edition. Boston: Willard Grant Press.

Daly, M., M. Wilson, and S. J. Weghorst. 1982. Male sexual jealousy. *Ethology and Sociobiology* 3:11–27.

Damian, R. T. 1964. Molecular mimicry: antigen sharing by parasite and host and its consequences. *The American Naturalist* 98:129–149.

Daniels, D. 1983. The evolution of concealed ovulation and self-deception. *Ethology and Sociobiology* 4:69–87.

Daniels, R. A. 1979. Nest guard replacement in the Antarctic fish *Harpagifer bispinis*: possible altruistic behavior. *Science* 205:831–833.

Darwin, C. 1859. *The Origin of Species.* London: Murray.

Darwin, C. 1871. *The Descent of Man, and Selection in Relation to Sex.* New York: Appleton.

Dauer, C. C., R. F. Korns, and L. M. Schuman. 1968. *Infectious Diseases.* Cambridge, Massachusetts: Harvard University Press.

Davidson, D. W. 1982. Sexual selection in harvester ants (Hymenoptera: Formicidae: *Pogonomyrmex*). *Behav. Ecol. Sociobiol.* 10:245–250.

Davies, N. B. 1976. Parental care and the transition to independent feeding in the young spotted flycatcher (*Muscicapa striata*). *Behaviour* 59:280–295.

Davis, J. W. F., and E. K. Dunn. 1976. Intraspecific predation and colonial breeding in lesser black-backed gulls *Larus fuscus. Ibis* 118:65–77.

Dawkins, R. 1976. *The Selfish Gene.* Oxford: Oxford University Press.

Dawkins, R. 1979. Twelve misunderstandings of kin selection. *Z. Tierpsychol.* 51:184–200.

Dawkins, R. 1982. *The Extended Phenotype: The Gene as the Unit of Selection.* Oxford: Oxford University Press.

de Ruiter, L. 1952. Some experiments on the camouflage of stick caterpillars. *Behaviour* 4:222–232.

de Vos, G. J. 1979. Adaptedness of arena behaviour in black grouse (*Tetrao tetrix*) and other grouse species (Tetraonidae). *Behaviour* 68:277–314.

de Vos, G. J. 1983. Social behaviour of black grouse; an observational and experimental field study. *Ardea* 71:1–103.

de Waal, F. B. M. 1978. Exploitative and familiarity-dependent support strategies in a colony of semi-free living chimpanzees. *Behaviour* 66:268–312.

de Waal, F. B. M. 1982. *Chimpanzee Politics: Power and Sex Among Apes.* New York: Harper and Row.

de Waal, F. B. M. (In press). Deception in the natural communication of chimpanzees. In: *Deception: Perspectives on Human and Nonhuman Deceit,* edited by R. Mitchell and N. Thompson. New York: SUNY Press.

de Waal, F. B. M., and J. A. R. A. M. Van Hooff. 1981. Side-directed communication and agonistic interactions in chimpanzees. *Behaviour* 77:164–198.

de Waal, F. B. M., and A. van Roosmalen. 1979. Reconciliation and consolation among chimpanzees. *Behav. Ecol. Sociobiol.* 5:55–66.

de Waal, F. B. M., and D. Yoshihara. 1983. Reconciliation and redirected affection in rhesus monkeys. *Behaviour* 85:224–241.

Dewsbury, D. A. 1981. An exercise in the prediction of monogamy in the field from laboratory data on 42 species of muroid rodents. *Biologist* 63:138–162.

Dixon, N. F. 1981. *Preconscious Processing.* Chichester, England: Wiley.

Dobson, J. 1970. *Dare to Discipline.* Wheaton, Illinois: Tyndale House Publ.

Dominey, W. J. 1980. Female mimicry in male bluegill sunfish: a genetic polymorphism? *Nature* 284:546–548.

Domjan, M. 1983. Biological constraints on instrumental and classical conditioning: implications for general process theory. *Psychology of Learning and Motivation* 17:215–277.

Domjan, M., and B. J. Galef, Jr. 1983. Biological constraints on instrumental and classical conditioning: retrospect and prospect. *Animal Learning and Behavior* 11:151–161.

Doolittle, W. F., and C. Sapienza. 1980. Selfish genes, the phenotype paradigm and genome evolution. *Nature* 284:601–603.

Dow, J. 1984. The genetic basis for affinal cooperation. *Am. Ethnol.* 11:380–383.

Downes, J. A. 1969. The swarming and mating flight of Diptera. *Ann. Rev. Ent.* 14:271–298.

Downhower, J. F. 1976. Darwin's finches and the evolution of sexual dimorphism in body size. *Nature* 263:558–563.

Dowsett-Lemaire, F. 1979. The imitative range of the song of the marsh warbler, *Acrocephalus palustris,* with special reference to imitations of African birds. *Ibis* 121:453–468.

Dunbar, R. I. M. 1980. Determinants and evolutionary consequences of dominance among female gelada baboons. *Behav. Ecol. Sociobiol.* 7:253–265.

Dunford, C. 1977. Kin selection for ground squirrel alarm calls. *Amer. Nat.* 111:782–785.

Eberhard, W. G. 1980. Evolutionary consequences of

intracellular organelle competition. *Quarterly Review of Biology* 55:231–249.

Edmunds, M. 1974. *Defence in Animals*. Essex, England: Longman.

Edwards, T. C., and M. W. Collopy. 1983. Obligate and facultative brood reduction in eagles: an examination of factors that influence fratricide. *Auk* 100:630–635.

Ehrman, L., and J. Probber. 1978. Rare *Drosophila* males: the mysterious matter of choice. *Amer. Sci.* 66:216–222.

Emlen, S. T. 1968. Territoriality in the bullfrog, *Rana catesbeiana*. *Copeia* 2:240–243.

Emlen, S. T. 1984. The evolution of cooperative breeding in birds. In: *Behavioural Ecology*, Second edition, edited by J. R. Krebs and N. B. Davies, 245–281. Sunderland, Massachusetts: Sinauer Associates, Inc.

Emlen, S. T., and L. W. Oring. 1977. Ecology, sexual selection, and the evolution of mating systems. *Science* 197:215–223.

Emlen, S. T., and S. L. Vehrencamp. 1983. Cooperative breeding strategies among birds. In: *Perspectives in Ornithology*, edited by A. H. Brush and G. A. Clark, Jr., 93–120. Cambridge, England: Cambridge University Press.

Erdelyi, M. H. 1974. A new look at the new look: perceptual defense and vigilance. *Psychological Reviews* 81:1–25.

Erickson, A. B. 1944. Helminth infections in relation to population fluctuations in snowshoe hares. *J. Wildlife Management* 8:134–153.

Erickson, C. J. 1978. Sexual affiliation in animals: pair bonds and reproductive strategies. In: *Biological Determinants of Sexual Behaviour*, edited by J. B. Hutchison, 697–725. Toronto: J. Wiley.

Erickson, C. J., and P. G. Zenone. 1976. Courtship differences in male ring doves: avoidance of cuckoldry? *Science* 192:1353–1354.

Erlenmeyer–Kimling, L., S. Nicol, J. D. Rainer, and W. E. Deming. 1969. Changes in fertility rates of schizophrenic patients in New York state. *Amer. J. Psychiatry* 125:916–927.

Evans, R. B. 1972. Physical and biochemical characteristics of homosexual men. *J. Consulting and Clinical Psychology* 39:140–147.

Fagen, R. M. 1976. Three-generation family conflict. *Anim. Behav.* 24:874–879.

Fairchild, L. 1981. Mate selection and behavioral thermoregulation in Fowler's toads. *Science* 212:950–951.

Falls, B. J., and R. J. Brooks. 1975. Individual recognition by song in white-throated sparrows. II. Effects of location. *Can. J. Zool.* 53:1412–1420.

Falls, B. J., and L. G. D'Agincourt. 1981. A comparison of neighbor-stranger discrimination in eastern and western meadowlarks. *Can. J. Zool.* 59:2380–2385.

Falls, B. J., and M. K. McNicholl. 1979. Neighbor-stranger discrimination by song in male blue grouse. *Can. J. Zool.* 57:457–462.

Farr, J. A. 1977. Male rarity or novelty, female choice behaviour, and sexual selection in the guppy, *Poecilia reticulata* Peters (Pisces: Poeciliidae). *Evolution* 31:162–168.

Ferrari, D. C., and P. D. N. Hebert. 1982. The induction of sexual reproduction in *Daphnia magna*: genetic differences between arctic and temperate populations. *Can. J. Zool.* 60:2143–2148.

Fincke, O. M. 1982. Lifetime mating success in a natural population of damselfly, *Enallagma hegeni* (Walsh) (Odonata: Coenagrionidae). *Behav. Ecol. Sociobiol.* 10:293–302.

Fisher, R. A. 1930. *The Genetic Theory of Natural Selection*. Oxford: Clarendon Press.

Fisler, G. F. 1971. Age structure and sex ratio in populations of *Reithrodontomys*. *J. of Mammalogy* 52:653–662.

Fitch, M. A., and G. W. Shugart. 1983. Comparative biology and behavior of monogamous pairs and one male-two female trios of Herring Gulls. *Behav. Ecol. Sociobiol.* 14:1–7.

Flor, H. H. 1956. The complementary genetic systems in flax and flax rust. *Advances in Genetics* 8:29–54.

Fontana, P. G., and V. R. Vickery. 1973. Segregation-distortion in the B-chromosome system of *Tettigidea lateralis* (Say) (Orthoptera: Tetrigidae). *Chromosoma* (Berl.) 43:75–100.

Fordham, R. A. 1970. Mortality and population change of dominican gulls in Wellington, New Zealand. *J. Animal Zoology* 39:13–24.

Forgey, D. G. 1975. The institution of berdache among the North American plains indians. *J. Sex Research* 11:1–15.

Foster, M. S. 1981. Cooperative behavior and social organization of the swallow-tailed manakin (*Chiroxiphia caudata*). *Behav. Ecol. Sociobiol.* 9:167–177.

Fox, M. W. 1971. Possible examples of high-order behavior in wolves. *J. Mammalogy* 52:640–641.

Fox, R. 1980. *The Red Lamp of Incest*. London: Hutchinson.

Frame, L. H., J. R. Malcolm, G. W. Frame, and H. van Lawick. 1979. Social organization of African wild dogs (*Lycaon pictus*) on the Serengeti Plains, Tanzania 1967–1978. *Z. Tierpsychol.* 50:225–249.

Francis, L. 1976. Social organization within clones of

the sea anemone *Anthopleura elegantissima. Biol. Bull.* 150:361–376.

Francq, E. N. 1969. Behavioral aspects of feigned death in the opossum *Didelphis marsupialis. Amer. Midland Naturalist* 81:556–568.

Frank, S. A. 1983. A hierarchical view of sex-ratio patterns. *Florida Entomologist* 66:42–75.

Fredrickson, W. T., and G. Sackett. 1984. Kin preferences in primates (*Macaca nemestrina*): relatedness or familiarity? *J. Comparative Psychology* 98:29–34.

Fredga, K., A. Gropp, H. Winking, and F. Frank. 1977. A hypothesis explaining the exceptional sex ratio in the wood lemming (*Myopus schisticolor*). *Hereditas* 85:101–104.

Freeman, B. E. 1981. Parental investment and its ecological consequences in the solitary wasp *Sceliphron assimile* (Dahlbom) (Sphecidae). *Behav. Ecol. and Sociobiol.* 9:261–268.

Fretter, V. 1953. The transference of sperm from male to female prosobranch, with reference, also, to the pyramidellids. *Proc. Linn. Soc. Lond.* 164:217–224.

Fry, M. D., and C. K. Toone. 1981. DDT-induced feminization of gull embryos. *Science* 213:922–924.

Fuchs, S. 1982. Optimality of parental investment: the influence of nursing on reproductive success of mother and female young house mice. *Behav. Ecol. Sociobiol.* 10:39–51.

Futuyma, D. J. 1979. *Evolutionary Biology.* Sunderland, Massachusetts: Sinauer Associates.

Futuyma, D. J. 1983. *Science on Trial: The Case for Evolution.* New York: Pantheon Books.

Gadgil, M. 1975. Evolution of social behavior through interpopulation selection. *Proc. Nat. Acad. Sci. USA* 72:1199–1201.

Gamboa, G. J. 1978. Intraspecific defense: advantage of social cooperation among paper wasp foundresses. *Science* 199:1463–1465.

Gamboa, G. J., B. D. Heacock, and S. L. Wiltjer. 1978. Division of labor and subordinate longevity in foundress associations of the paper wasp, *Polistes metricus* (Hymenoptera: Vespidae). *J. Kansas Entomological Society* 51:343–352.

Garcia, J., and F. R. Ervin. 1968. Gustatory-visceral and telereceptor-cutaneous conditioning-adaptation in internal and external milieus. *Communications in Behavioral Biology Part A,* 1:389–415.

Garcia, J., and R. A. Koelling. 1966. Relation of cue to consequence in avoidance learning. *Psychonomic Science* 4:123–124.

Garcia, J., B. K. McGowan, F. R. Ervin, and R. A. Koelling. 1968. Cues: their relative effectiveness as a function of the reinforcer. *Science* 160:794–796.

Geiringer, E. 1961. Effect of ACTH on sex ratio in the albino rat. *Proceedings of the Society for Experimental Biology and Medicine* 106:752–754.

Geist, V. 1971. *Mountain Sheep: A Study in Behavior and Evolution.* Chicago: The University of Chicago Press.

Getz, W. M., D. Bruckner, and T. R. Parisian. 1982. Kin structure and the swarming behavior of the honey bee *Apis mellifera. Behav. Ecol. Sociobiol.* 10:265–270.

Getz, W. M., and K. B. Smith. 1983. Genetic kin recognition: honey bees discriminate between full and half sisters. *Nature* 302:147–148.

Ghiselin, M. T. 1969. *The Triumph of the Darwinian Method.* Berkeley: University of California Press.

Ghiselin, M. T. 1974. *The Economy of Nature and the Evolution of Sex.* Berkeley: University of California Press.

Gilbert, L. E. 1982. The coevolution of a butterfly and a vine. *Scient. Amer.* 247:110–121.

Gilliard, E. T. 1969. *Birds of Paradise and Bower Birds.* Garden City, New York: Natural History Press.

Gittleman, J. L. 1981. The phylogeny of parental care in fishes. *Anim. Behav.* 29:936–941.

Glucksmann, A. 1974. Sexual dimorphism in mammals. *Biol. Rev.* 49:423–475.

Gorlick, D. L., P. O. Atkins, and G. S. Losey. 1978. Cleaning stations as water holes, garbage dumps and sites for the evolution of reciprocal altruism. *Amer. Nat.* 112:341–353.

Gould, J. L. 1982. *Ethology: The Mechanisms and Evolution of Behavior.* New York: W. W. Norton & Company.

Gowaty, P. A., and M. R. Lennartz. n.d. Sex ratios of nestling and fledgling red-cockaded woodpeckers (*Picoides borealis*) favor males. Unpublished manuscript.

Grafen, A. 1982. How not to measure inclusive fitness. *Nature* 298:425–426.

Graul, W. D., S. R. Derrickson, and D. W. Mork. 1977. The evolution of avian polyandry. *Amer. Nat.* 111:812–816.

Greenberg, L. 1979. Genetic component of bee odor in kin recognition. *Science* 206:1095–1097.

Greenwald, A. G. 1980. The totalitarian ego: fabrication and revision of personal history. *Amer. Psychologist* 35:603–618.

Greenwood, P. J., P. H. Harvey, and C. M. Perrins. 1978. Inbreeding and dispersal in the great tit. *Nature* 271:52–54.

Greenwood, P. J., P. H. Harvey, and C. M. Perrins. 1979. Kin selection and territoriality in birds? A test. *Anim. Behav.* 27:645–651.

Greig-Smith, P. W. 1982. Song-rates and parental care by individual male stonechats (*Saxicola torquata*). *Anim. Behav.* 30:245–252.

Gross, M. R., and R. Shine. 1981. Parental care and mode of fertilization in ectothermic vertebrates. *Evolution* 35:775–793.

Gur, C. R., and H. A. Sackeim. 1979. Self-deception: a concept in search of a phenomenon. *J. Personality and Social Psychology* 37:147–169.

Guttentag, M., and P. F. Secord. 1983. *Too Many Women? The Sex Ratio Question.* Beverly Hills: Sage Publications.

Gwynne, D. T. 1981. Sexual difference theory: Mormon crickets show role reversal in mate choice. *Science* 213:779–780.

Gwynne, D. T. 1982. Mate selection by female katydids *Conocephalus nigropleurum* (Orthoptera: Tettigoniidae). *Anim. Behav.* 30:734–738.

Gwynne, D. T. 1984. Courtship feeding increases female reproductive success in bushcrickets. *Nature* 307:361–363.

Gwynne, D. T. In press. Male nutrient investment, population density and sexual selection in Mormon crickets (*Anabras simplex*, Orthoptera: Tettigoniidae). *Evolution.*

Haldane, J. B. S. 1955. Population genetics. *New Biology* 18:34–51.

Halliday, T. R., and P. J. B. Slater, eds. 1983. *Genes, Development and Learning.* New York: Freeman.

Hamilton, J. B. 1948. The role of testicular secretions as indicated by the effects of castration in man and by studies of pathological conditions and the short lifespan associated with maleness. *Recent Progress in Hormone Research* 3:257–322.

Hamilton, J. B., R. S. Hamilton, and G. E. Mestler. 1969. Duration of life and causes of death in domestic cats: influence of sex, gonadectomy and inbreeding. *J. Gerontology* 24:427–437.

Hamilton, J. B., and G. E. Mestler. 1969. Mortality and survival: comparison of eunuchs with intact men and women in mentally retarded populations. *J. Gerontology* 24:427–437.

Hamilton, W. D. 1964. The evolution of social behavior. *J. Theoret. Biol.* 7:1–52.

Hamilton, W. D. 1966. The moulding of senescence by natural selection. *J. Theoret. Biol.* 12:12–45.

Hamilton, W. D. 1967. Extraordinary sex ratios. *Science* 156:477–488.

Hamilton, W. D. 1970. Selfish and spiteful behavior in an evolutionary model. *Nature* 228:1218–1220.

Hamilton, W. D. 1971. Selection of selfish and altru-istic behavior in some extreme models. In: *Man and Beast: Comparative Social Behavior*, edited by J. F. Eisenberg and W. S. Dillon, 59–91. Washington, D.C.: Smithsonian Press.

Hamilton, W. D. 1972. Altruism and related phenomena, mainly in the social insects. *Ann. Rev. Ecol. Syst.* 3:193–232.

Hamilton, W. D. 1978. Evolution and diversity under bark. In: *Diversity of Insect Faunas. Symposia of the Royal Entomological Society of London 9*, edited by L. A. Mound and N. Waloff, 154–175. Oxford: Blackwell.

Hamilton, W. D. 1979. Wingless and fighting males in fig wasps and other insects. In: *Sexual Selection and Reproductive Competition in Insects*, edited by M. S. Blum and N. A. Blum, 167–220. New York: Academic Press.

Hamilton, W. D. 1980. Sex versus non-sex versus parasite. *Oikos* 35:282–290.

Hamilton, W. D. 1982. Pathogens as causes of genetic diversity in their host populations. In: *Population Biology of Infectious Diseases*, edited by R. M. Anderson and R. M. May, 269–296. New York: Springer-Verlag.

Hamilton, W. D., P. A. Henderson, and N. A. Moran. 1981. Fluctuation of environment and coevolved antagonist polymorphism as factors in the maintenance of sex. In: *Natural Selection and Social Behaviour*, edited by R. D. Alexander and D. W. Tinkle, 363–381. New York: Chiron Press.

Hamilton, W. D., and M. Zuk. 1982. Heritable true fitness and bright birds: a role for parasites? *Science* 218:384–387.

Hanken, J., and P. W. Sherman. 1981. Multiple paternity in Belding's ground squirrel litters. *Science* 212:351–353.

Harcourt, A. H., P. H. Harvey, S. G. Larson, and R. V. Short. 1981. Testis weight, body weight and breeding system in primates. *Nature* 293:55–57.

Harrington, F. H., L. D. Mech, and S. H. Fritts. 1983. Pack size and wolf pup survival: their relationship under varying ecological conditions. *Behav. Ecol. Sociobiol.* 13:19–26.

Hartl, D. L., and Y. Hiraizomi. 1976. Segregation distortion. In: *The Genetics and Biology of Drosophila*, edited by M. Ashburner and E. Novitski, Vol. 1b, 615–666. New York: Academic Press.

Hartsock, T. G., and H. B. Graves. 1976. Neonatal behavior and nutrition-related mortality in domestic swine. *J. of Animal Science* 42:235–241.

Hartsock, T. G., H. B. Graves, and B. R. Baumgardt. 1977. Agonistic behavior and the nursing order in suckling piglets: relationships with survival, growth and body composition. *J. Animal Science* 44:320–330.

Harvey, P. H., M. Kavanagh, and T. H. Clutton-Brock. 1978. Sexual dimorphism in primate teeth. *J. Zool.*, Lond. 186:475–485.

Hausfater, G., and S. Blaffer Hrdy, eds. 1984. *Infanticide: Comparative and Evolutionary Perspectives*. New York: Aldine.

Hawk, H. W. 1972. Progestagen induced sperm breakage in the sheep vagina. *J. Animal Science* 34:795–798.

Hawk, H. W., and H. H. Conley. 1972. Investigation of sperm transport failures in ewes administered synthetic progestagen. *J. Animal Science* 34:609–613.

Hawkes, K. 1983. Kin selection and culture. *Am. Ethnol.* 10:345–363.

Heinz-Ulrich, R. 1980. Flexible helper structure as an ecological adaptation in the pied kingfisher (*Ceryle rudis rudis* L.). *Behav. Ecol. Sociobiol.* 6:219–227.

Henry, C. S. 1972. Eggs and rapagula of *Ululodes* and *Ascaloptynx* (Neuroptera: Ascalaphidae): a comparative study. *Psyche* 79:1–22.

Henry, C. S. 1978. An evolutionary and geographical overview of rapagula (abortive eggs) in the Ascalaphidae (Neuroptera). *Proc. Entomol. Soc. Wash.* 80:75–86.

Herbers, J. M. 1979. The evolution of sex-ratio strategies in hymenopteran societies. *Amer. Nat.* 114:818–834.

Hickey, W. A., and G. P. Craig. 1966. Genetic distortion of sex ratio in a mosquito, *Aedes aegypti*. *Genetics* 53:1177–1196.

Hicks, R. A., and R. L. Trivers. 1983. The social behavior of *Anolis valenciennii*. In: *Advances in Herpetology and Evolutionary Biology*, edited by A. Rhodin and K. Miyata, 570–595. Cambridge, Massachusetts: Museum of Comparative Zoology.

Hill, J. 1984. Human altruism and sociocultural fitness. *J. Social Biol. Struct.* 7:17–35.

Hinde, R. A. 1977. Mother-infant separation and the nature of inter-individual relationships: experiments with rhesus monkeys. *Proc. R. Soc. Lond. B.* 196:29–50.

Hinde, R. A. 1981. Animal signals: ethological and game theory approaches are not incompatible. *Anim. Behav.* 29:535–542.

Hinde, R. A. 1982. *Ethology: Its Nature and Relations with Other Sciences*. New York, Oxford: Oxford University Press.

Hinde, R. A., ed. 1983. *Primate Social Relationships: An Integrated Approach*. Oxford: Blackwell.

Hinde, R. A., M. E. Leighton-Shapiro, and L. McGinnis. 1978. Effects of various types of separation experience on rhesus monkeys 5 months later. *J. Child Psychol. Psychiat.* 19:199–211.

Hinde, R. A., and L. McGinnis. 1977. Some factors influencing the effects of temporary mother-infant separation: some experiments with rhesus monkeys. *Psychological Medicine* 7:197–212.

Hinde, R. A., and Y. Spencer-Booth. 1971. Effects of brief separation from mother on rhesus monkeys. *Science* 173:111–118.

Hinton, H. E. 1958. On the pupa of *Spalgis lemolea druce* (Lepidoptera, Lycaenidae). *J. Society for British Entomology* 6:23–26.

Hinton, H. E. 1973. Natural deception. In: *Illusion in Nature and Art*, edited by R. L. Gregory and E. H. Gombrich, 97–159. New York: Scribner's.

Hobbs, J. N. 1967. Distraction display by two species of crakes. *Emu* 66:299–300.

Hogg, J. T. 1984. Mating in bighorn sheep: multiple creative male strategies. *Science* 225:526–529.

Holden, C. 1980. Twins reunited: more than the faces are familiar. *Science 80* 1:54–59.

Hölldobler, B. 1967. Zur Physiologie der Gast-Wirt-Beziehungen (Myrmecophilie) bei Ameisen. I. Das Gastverhältnis der *Atemeles* und *Lomechusa*-Larven (Col Staphylinidae) zu *Formica* (Hym. Formicidae). *Z. fur Vergleichende Physiologie* 56:1–21.

Hölldobler, B. 1970. Zur Physiologie der Gast-wirt-Beziehungen (Myrmecophilie) bei Ameisen. II. Das Gastverhältnis des imaginalen *Atemeles pubicollis* Bris. (Col. Staphylinidae) zu *Myrmica* und *Formica* (Hym. Formicidae). *Z. fur Vergleichende Physiologie* 66:215–250.

Hölldobler, B. 1971. Communication between ants and their guests. *Scient. Amer.* 224:86–93.

Hölldobler, B. 1976. Tournaments and slavery in a desert ant. *Science* 192:912–914.

Hölldobler, B. 1981. Foraging and spatiotemporal territories in the honey ant *Myrmecocystus mimicus* Wheeler (Hymenoptera: Formicidae). *Behav. Ecol. Sociobiol.* 9:301–314.

Hölldobler, B., and C. P. Haskins. 1977. Sexual calling behavior in primitive ants. *Science* 195:793–794.

Hölldobler, B., M. Möglich, and U. Maschwitz. 1981. Myrmecophilic relationship of *Pella* (Coleoptera: Staphylinidae) to *Lasius fuliginosus* (Hymenoptera: Formicidae). *Psyche* 88:347–374.

Hölldobler, B., and E. O. Wilson. 1983. The evolution of communal nest-weaving in ants. *Amer. Sci.* 71:490–499.

Holmes, H. B. 1972. Genetic evidence for fewer progeny and a higher percent males when *Nasonia vitripennis* oviposits in previously parasitized hosts. *Entomophaga* 17:79–88.

Holmes, J. C., and W. M. Bethel. 1972. Modification of intermediate host behaviour by parasites. In: *Behavioural Aspects of Parasite Transmissions, Zoological Journal of the Linnean Society*, Supplement 1, Volume 51, edited by E. U. Canning and C. A. Wright, 123–147. London: Academic Press.

Holmes, W. G., and P. W. Sherman. 1982. The ontogeny of kin recognition in two species of ground squirrels. *Amer. Zool.* 22:491–517.

Holmes, W. G., and P. W. Sherman. 1983. Kin recognition in animals. *Amer. Sci.* 71:46–55.

Hoogland, J. L. 1981. Nepotism and cooperative breeding in the black-tailed prairie dog (Sciuridae: *Cynomys ludovicianus*). In: *Natural Selection and Social Behavior*, edited by R. D. Alexander and W. D. Tinkle, 283–311. New York: Chiron Press.

Houston, T. F. 1970. Discovery of an apparent male soldier caste in a nest of a halictine bee (Hymenoptera: Halictidae), with notes on the nest. *Australian J. Zoology* 18:345–351.

Howe, H. F. 1976. Egg size, hatching asynchrony, sex, and brood reduction in the common grackle. *Ecology* 57:1195–1207.

Howe, H. F. 1977. Sex-ratio adjustment in the common grackle. *Science* 198:744–746.

Hrdy, S. B. 1974. Male-male competition and infanticide among the langurs (*Presbytis entellus*) on Abu, Rajasthan. *Folia Primatologica* 22:19–58.

Hrdy, S. B. 1977a. Infanticide as a primate reproductive strategy. *Amer. Sci.* 65:40–49.

Hrdy, S. B. 1977b. *The Langurs of Abu: Female and Male Strategies of Reproduction*. Cambridge, Massachusetts: Harvard University Press.

Hrdy, S. B. 1982. Positivist thinking encounters field primatology, resulting in agonistic behavior. *Social Science Information* 21:245–250.

Hrdy, S. B., and D. B. Hrdy. 1976. Hierarchical relations among female hanuman langurs (Primates: Colobinae, *Presbytis entellus*). *Science* 193:913–915.

Hughes-Schrader, S., and D. F. Monahan. 1966. Hermaphroditism in *Icerya zeteki* Cockerell, and the mechanism of gonial reduction in iceryine coccids (Coccoidea: Margarodidae Morrison). *Chromosoma* 20:15–31.

Hunt, G. L., Jr. 1972. Influence of food distribution and human disturbance on the reproductive success of herring gulls. *Ecology* 53:1051–1061.

Hunt, G. L., and M. W. Hunt. 1975. Reproductive ecology of the Western Gull: The importance of nest spacing. *Auk* 92:270–279.

Hunt, G. L., Jr., and M. W. Hunt. 1976. Gull chick survival: the significance of growth rates, timing of breeding and territory size. *Ecology* 57:62–75.

Hunt, G. L., Jr., A. L. Newman, M. H. Warner, J. C. Wingfield, and J. Kaiwi. 1984. Comparative behavior of male-female and female-female pairs among Western gulls prior to egg-laying. *Condor* 86:157–162.

Hyman, L. H. 1967. *The Invertebrates. Volume 6: Mollusca I*, 287–292. New York: McGraw Hill.

Impekoven, M. 1976. Responses of laughing gull chicks (*Larus atricilla*) to parental attraction- and alarm-calls, and effects of prenatal auditory experience on the responsiveness to such calls. *Behaviour* 56:250–278.

Iskrant, A. P., and P. V. Joliet. 1968. *Accidents and Homicide*. Cambridge, Massachusetts: Harvard University Press.

Jacob, F. 1982. *The Logic of Life: A History of Heredity*. New York: Pantheon Books.

Jaenike, J. 1978. An hypothesis to account for the maintenance of sex within populations. *Evolutionary Theory* 3:191–194.

James, W. H. 1975a. Sex ratio and the sex composition of the existing sibs. *Ann. Hum. Genet., Lond.* 38:371–378.

James, W. H. 1975b. The distributions of the combinations of the sexes in mammalian litters. *Genet. Res., Camb.* 26:45–53.

James, W. H. 1977. Coital rate, cycle day of insemination and sex ratio. *J. Biosoc. Sci.* 9:183–189.

James, W. H. 1983. Timing of fertilization and the sex ratio of offspring. In: *Sex Selection of Children*, edited by N. G. Bennett, 73–99. New York: Academic Press.

James, W. H. 1984. The sex ratios of Black births. *Annals of Human Biology* 11:39–44.

Janetos, A. C. 1980. Strategies of female mate choice: a theoretical analysis. *Behav. Ecol. Sociobiol.* 7:107–112.

Jarvis, J. U. M. 1981. Eusociality in a mammal: cooperative breeding in naked mole-rat colonies. *Science* 212:571–573.

Jerison, H. J. 1973. *Evolution of the Brain and Intelligence*. New York and London: Academic Press.

Johns, J. E. 1969. Field studies of Wilson's phalarope. *Auk* 86:660–670.

Johnson, C. 1976. *Introduction to Natural Selection*. Baltimore: University Park Press.

Kadlec, J. A., W. H. Drury, and D. K. Onion. 1969. Growth and mortality of herring gull chicks. *Bird Banding* 40:222–233.

Kadlec, J. A., and W. H. Drury. 1968. Structure of the New England herring gull population. *Ecology* 49:644–676.

Kaplan, J. R. 1978. Fight interference and altruism in rhesus monkeys. *Am. J. Phys. Anthrop.* 49:241–250.

Kaplan, S. W. 1983. Intrasexual aggression in *Metridium senile. Biol. Bull.* 165:416–418.

Kenward, R. E. 1978. Hawks and doves: factors affecting success and selection in goshawk attacks on woodpigeons. *J. Animal Ecology* 47:449–460.

Keough, M. J. 1984. Kin-recognition and the spatial distribution of larvae of the briozoan *Bugula neritia* (L.). *Evolution* 38:142–147.

King, A. P., and M. J. West. 1983. Epigenesis of cowbird songs—A joint endeavour of males and females. *Nature* 305:704–706.

Kirkpatrik, M. 1982. Sexual selection and the evolution of female choice. *Evolution* 36:1–12.

Klahn, J. E. 1979. Philopatric and nonphilopatric foundress associations in the social wasp *Polistes fuscatus. Behav. Ecol. Sociobiol.* 5:417–424.

Klahn, J. E., and G. J. Gamboa. 1983. Social wasps: discrimination between kin and nonkin brood. *Science* 221:482–484.

Kleiman, D. G. 1979. Parent-offspring conflict and sibling competition in a monogamous primate. *Amer. Nat.* 114:753–760.

Kleiman, D. G., and J. R. Malcolm. 1981. The evolution of male parental investment in mammals. In: *Parental Care in Mammals*, edited by D. J. Gubernick and P. H. Klopfer, 347–387. New York: Plenum Press.

Klein, M., and D. Tribich. 1981. On Freud's "blindness." *Colloquium* 4:52–59.

Klein, M., and D. Tribich. 1982. Blame the child. *Sciences* 22:14–20.

Koppen, E. 1931. *Higher Command.* London: Faber and Faber.

Kluge, A. G. 1981. *The Life History, Social Organization, and Parental Behavior of* Hyla rosenbergi *Boulenger, a Nest-Building Gladiator Frog.* Miscellaneous Publications, Museum of Zoology, University of Michigan, No. 160.

Knowlton, N. 1974. A note on the evolution of gamete dimorphism. *J. Theoret. Biol.* 46:283–285.

Knowlton, N. 1979. Reproductive synchrony, parental investment, and the evolutionary dynamics of sexual selection. *Anim. Behav.* 27:1022–1033.

Kovacs, K. M., and J. P. Ryder. 1983. Reproductive performance of female-female pairs and polygynous trios of ring-billed gulls. *Auk* 100:658–669.

Krebs, J. R., and N. B. Davies. 1981. *An Introduction to Behavioural Ecology.* Sunderland, Massachusetts: Sinauer Associates, Inc.

Krebs, J. R., and R. Dawkins. 1984. Animal signals: mindreading and manipulation. In: *Behavioural Ecology*, Second edition, edited by J. R. Krebs and N. B. Davies, 380–402. Sunderland, Massachusetts: Sinauer.

Krombein, K. 1967. *Trap-nesting Wasps and Bees: Life Histories, Nest and Associates.* Washington, D.C.: Smithsonian Press.

Kruijt, J. P., and J. A. Hogan. 1967. Social behavior on the lek in black grouse, *Lyrurus tetrix tetrix* (L.). *Ardea* 55:203–240.

Kruijt, J. P., G. J. de Vos, and I. Bossema. 1970. The arena system of black grouse. *Proc. XVth Int. Orn. Cong.*, 399–423.

Kullenberg, B. 1961. Studies in Ophrys pollination. *Zool. Bidrag, Uppsala Bd.* 34:1–340.

Kurland, J. A. 1977. *Kin Selection in the Japanese Monkey. Contributions to Primatology* 12. Basel: S. Karger.

Kurland, J. A. 1980. Kin selection theory: a review and selective bibliography. *Ethology and Sociobiology* 1:255–274.

Lack, D. 1966. *Population Studies of Birds.* Oxford: Clarendon Press.

Lande, R. 1980. Sexual dimorphism, sexual selection, and adaptation in polygenic characters. *Evolution* 32:292–305.

Lande, R. 1981. Models of speciation by sexual selection on polygenic traits. *Evolution* 78:3721–3725.

Lane, E. A. 1969. The sex ratio of children born to schizophrenics and a theory of stress. *Psychological Record* 19:579–584.

Lane, E. A., and G. W. Albee. 1970. The birth weight of children born to schizophrenic women. *J. Psychology* 74:157–160.

Lane, E. A., and T. S. Hyde. 1973. Effect of maternal stress on fertility and sex ratio: a pilot study with rats. *J. Abnormal Psychology* 82:78–80.

Langham, N. P. E. 1972. Chick survival in terns (*Sterna* spp.) with particular reference to the common tern. *J. Animal Ecology* 41:385–396.

Langham, N. P. E. 1974. Comparative breeding biology of the Sandwich tern. *Auk* 91:255–277.

Latham, R. M. 1947. Differential ability of male and female game birds to withstand starvation and climatic extremes. *J. Wildlife Management* 11:139–149.

Lazarus, J., and I. R. Inglis. 1978. The breeding behaviour of the pink-footed goose: parental care and vigilant behaviour during the fledging period. *Behaviour* 65:62–88.

Le Boeuf, B. J. 1974. Male-male competition and reproductive success in elephant seals. *Amer. Zool.* 14:163–176.

Le Boeuf, B. J., and K. T. Briggs. 1977. The cost of living in a seal harem. *Mammalia* 41:167–195.

Le Boeuf, B. J., and J. Reiter. In press. Lifetime reproductive success in northern elephant seals. In: *Reproductive Success*, edited by T. H. Clutton-Brock. Chicago: University of Chicago Press.

Leak, G., and S. Christopher. 1982. Freudian psychoanalysis and sociobiology: a synthesis. *Amer. Psychologist* 37:313–322.

Leger, D. W., and D. H. Owings. 1978. Responses to alarm calls by California ground squirrels: effects of call structure and maternal status. *Behav. Ecol. Sociobiol.* 3:177–186.

Levin, D. A. 1975. Pest pressure and recombination systems in plants. *Amer. Nat.* 109:437–451.

Lewin, R. 1984. No genome barriers to promiscuous DNA. *Science* 224:970–971.

Linsenmair, K. E., and C. Linsenmair. 1971. Paarbildung und Paarzusammenhalt bei der monogamen Wustenassel *Hemilepistus reaumuri* (Crustacea, Isopoda, Oniscoidea). *Z. Tierpsychol.* 29:134–155.

Little, R. J. 1983. A review of floral food deception mimicries with comments on floral mutalism. In: *Handbook of Experimental Pollination Biology*, edited by C. E. Jones and R. J. Little, 294–309. New York: Van Nostrand Reinhold.

Lloyd, J. E. 1981. Mimicry in the sexual signals of fireflies. *Scient. Amer.* 245:139–145.

Lopreato, J. 1981. Toward a theory of genuine altruism in *Homo sapiens*. *Ethology and Sociobiology* 2:113–126.

Lorenz, K. Z. 1955. *Man Meets Dog*. London: Methuen.

Lorenz, K. Z. 1966. *On Aggression*. London: Methuen.

Lumsden, C. J. 1984. Parent-offspring conflict over the transmission of culture. *Ethology and Sociobiology* 5:111–129.

Lumsden, C. J., and E. O. Wilson. 1983. *Promethean Fire: Reflections on the Origin of Mind*. Cambridge, Massachusetts: Harvard University Press.

Lundberg, C., and R. A. Väisänen. 1979. Selective correlation of egg size with chick mortality in the black-headed gull (*Larus ridibundus*). *Condor* 81:146–156.

Lykken, D. T. 1982. Research with twins: the concept of emergenesis. *Psychophysiology* 19:361–373.

Lyster, W. R., and M. W. H. Bishop. 1965. An association between rainfall and sex ratio in man. *J. Reprod. Fertil.* 10:35–47.

Macdonald, D. W. 1979. "Helpers" in fox society. *Nature* 282:69–71.

Macdonald, D. W. 1983. The ecology of carnivore social behaviour. *Nature* 301:379–384.

MacDonald, K. 1984. An ethological-social learning theory of the development of altruism: implications for human sociobiology. *Ethology and Sociobiology* 5:97–109.

MacMahon, B., and T. F. Pugh. 1954. Sex ratio of white births in the United States during the second world war. *Am. J. Human Genetics* 6:284–292.

MacRoberts, M. H. 1973. Extramarital courting in lesser black-backed and herring gulls. *Z. Tierpsychol.* 32:62–74.

Madigan, F. C. 1957. Are sex mortality differentials biologically caused? *Milbank Memorial Fund Quarterly* 35:202–223.

Makwana, S. C. 1979. Infanticide and social change in two groups of the hanuman langur, *Presbytis entellus*, at Jodhpur. *Primates* 20:293–300.

Malcolm, J. R., and K. Marten. 1982. Natural selection and the communal rearing of pups in African wild dogs (*Lycaon pictus*). *Behav. Ecol. Sociobiol.* 10:1–13.

Manning, J. T. 1975. Male discrimination and investment in *Asellus aquaticus* (L.) and A. meridianus Racovitsza (Crustacea: Isopoda). *Behaviour* 55:1–14.

Marburger, R. G., R. M. Robinson, J. W. Thomas, M. J. Andregg, and K. A. Clark. 1972. Antler malformation produced by leg injury in white-tailed deer. *J. Wildlife Diseases* 8:311–314.

Margulis, L. 1981. *Symbiosis in Cell Evolution*. San Francisco: W. H. Freeman and Company.

Marler, P. 1955. Characteristics of some animal calls. *Nature* 176:6–8.

Marx, J. L. 1984. Instability in plants and the ghost of Lamarck. *Science* 224:1415–1416.

Mason, L. G. 1969. Mating selection in the California oak moth (Lepidoptera, Dioptidae). *Evolution* 23:55–58.

Massey, A. 1977. Agonistic aids and kinship in a group of pigtail macaques. *Behav. Ecol. Sociobiol.* 2:31–40.

May, A. W. 1967. Fecundity of atlantic cod. *J. Fish. Res. Bd. Canada* 24:1531–1551.

May, R. M. 1983. Parasitic infections as regulators of animal populations. *Amer. Sci.* 71:36–44.

May, R. M., and R. M. Anderson. 1983. Epidemiology and genetics in the coevolution of parasites and hosts. *Proc. R. Soc. Lond B* 219:281–313.

Maynard Smith, J. 1971. The origin and maintenance of sex. In: *Group Selection*, edited by G. C. Williams, 165–175. Chicago: Aldine-Atherton.

Maynard Smith, J. 1978. *The Evolution of Sex*. Cambridge: Cambridge University Press.

Mayr, E. 1982. *The Growth of Biological Thought: Diversity, Evolution and Inheritance*. Massachusetts: The Belknap Press of Harvard University Press.

McCauley, D. E., and M. J. Wade. 1978. Female choice and the mating structure of a natural population of the soldier beetle, *Chauliognathus pennsylvanicus. Evolution* 32:771–775.

McClure, P. A. 1981. Sex-biased litter reduction in food-restricted wood rats (*Neotoma floridana*). *Science* 211:1058–1060.

McCracken, G. F. 1984. Communal nursing in Mexican free-tailed bat maternity colonies. *Science* 223:1090–1091.

McCracken, G. F., and J. W. Bradbury. 1977. Paternity and genetic heterogeneity in the polygynous bat, *Phyllostomus hastatus. Science* 198:303–306.

McDiarmid, R. W. 1978. Evolution of parental care in frogs. In: *The Development of Behavior: Comparative and Evolutionary Aspects*, edited by G. M. Burghardt and M. Bekoff, 127–147. New York: Garland.

McKinney, F., S. R. Derrickson, and P. Mineau. 1983. Forced copulation in waterfowl. *Behaviour* 86:250–294.

McMillen, M. M. 1979. Differential mortality by sex in fetal and neonatal deaths. *Science* 204:89–91.

Meikle, D. B., B. L. Tilford, and S. H. Vessey. 1984. Dominance rank, secondary sex ratio, and reproduction of offspring in polygynous primates. *Amer. Nat.* 124:173–188.

Meikle, D. B., and S. H. Vessey. 1981. Nepotism among rhesus monkey brothers. *Nature* 294:160–161.

Melnick, D. J., and K. K. Kidd. 1983. The genetic consequences of social group fission in a wild population of rhesus monkeys (*Macaca mulatta*). *Behav. Ecol. Sociobiol.* 12:229–236.

Metcalf, R. A. 1980. Sex ratios, parent offspring conflict, and local competition for mates in the social wasps *Polistes metricus* and *Polistes variatus. Amer. Nat.* 116:642–654.

Metcalf, R. A., and G. S. Whitt. 1977a. Intra-nest relatedness in the social wasp *Polistes metricus*: a genetic analysis. *Behav. Ecol. Sociobiol.* 2:339–351.

Metcalf, R. A., and G. S. Whitt. 1977b. Relative inclusive fitness in the social wasp *Polistes metricus. Behav. Ecol. Sociobiol.* 2:353–360.

Michener, C. D. 1974. *The Social Behavior of the Bees: A Comparative Study*. Cambridge, Massachusetts: The Belknap Press of Harvard University Press.

Mills, M. G. L. 1982. The mating system of the brown hyaena, *Hyaena brunnea* in the Southern Kalahari. *Behav. Ecol. Sociobiol.* 10:131–136.

Missakian, E. A. 1973. Genealogical mating activity in free-ranging groups of rhesus monkeys (*Macaca mulatta*) on Cayo Santiago. *Behaviour* 45:225–241.

Mitchell, R. 1972. The sex ratio of the spider mite *Tetranychus urticae. Ent. Exp. and Appl.* 15:299–304.

Moehlman, P. D. 1983. Socioecology of silverbacked and golden jackals (*Canis mesomelas* and *Canis aureus*). In: *Recent Advances in the Study of Mammalian Behavior*. 7, edited by J. F. Eisenberg and D. G. Kleiman, 423–453. Spec. Publ. Amer. Soc. Mamm.

Möglich, M., and B. Hölldobler. 1974. Social carrying behavior and division of labor during nest-moving in ants. *Psyche* 81:219–239.

Mohnot, S. M. 1971. Some aspects of social changes and infant-killing in the hanuman langur, *Presbytis entellus* (Primates: Cercopithecidae), in Western India. *Mammalia* 35:175–198.

Moore, J. 1984a. Parasites that change the behavior of their host. *Scient. Amer.* 250:108–115.

Moore, J. 1984b. The evolution of reciprocal sharing. *Ethology and Sociobiology* 5:5–14.

Moore, J., and R. Ali. 1984. Are dispersal and inbreeding avoidance related? *Anim. Behav.* 32:94–112.

Moore, W. S., and W. G. S. Hines. 1981. Sex in random environments. *J. Theoret. Biol.* 92:301–316.

Morris, D. 1952. Homosexuality in the ten-spined stickleback (*Pygosteus pungitius* L.). *Behaviour* 4:233–261.

Mrosovsky, N., S. R. Hopkins-Murphy, and J. I. Richardson. 1984. Sex-ratio of sea turtles: seasonal changes. *Science* 225:739–741.

Myers, T. H. 1978. Sex ratio adjustment under stress: maximization of quality or numbers of offspring? *Amer. Nat.* 112:381–388.

Nakatsuru, K., and D. L. Kramer. 1982. Is sperm cheap? Limited male fertility and female choice in the lemon tetra (Pisces, Characidae). *Science* 216:753–755.

Napier, K. M., and P. D. Mullaney. 1974. Sex ratio in sheep. *J. Reprod. Fert.* 39:391–392.

Nice, M. M. 1964a. *Studies in the Life History of the Song Sparrow. Volume I: A Population Study of the Song Sparrow and Other Passerines*. New York: Dover Publications, Inc.

Nice, M. M. 1964b. *Studies in the Life History of the Song Sparrow. Volume II: The Behavior of the Song Sparrow and Other Passerines.* New York: Dover Publications, Inc.

Nicolson, N. 1982. Weaning and the development of independence in olive baboons. Ph. D. thesis. Harvard, Anthropology.

Nilsson, L. A. 1983. Mimesis of bellflower (*Campanula*) by the red helleborine orchid *Cephalanthera rubra. Nature* 305:799–800.

Nisbet, I. C. T. 1973. Courtship-feeding, egg-size and breeding success in common terns. *Nature* 241:141–142.

Nisbet, I. C. T. 1977. Courtship-feeding and clutch size in common terns *Sterna hirundo*. In: *Evolutionary Ecology*, edited by B. Stonehouse and C. Perrins, 101–109. London: Macmillan.

Nisbet, I. C. T. 1978. Dependence of fledging success on egg-size, parental performance and egg-composition among common and roseate terns, *Sterna hirundo* and *S. dougallii. Ibis* 121:207–215.

Nisbet, I. C. T., and W. H. Drury. 1972. Post-fledging survival in herring gulls in relation to brood-size and date of hatching. *Bird Banding* 43:161–172.

Nishida, T. 1983. Alpha status and agonistic alliance in wild chimpanzees (*Pan troglodytes schweinfurthii). Primates* 24:318–336.

Noonan, K. M. 1978. Sex ratio of parental investment in colonies of the social wasp *Polistes fuscatus. Science* 199:1354–1356.

Noonan, K. M. 1981. Individual strategies of inclusive-fitness-maximizing in *Polistes fuscatus* foundresses. In: *Natural Selection and Social Behavior: Recent Research and New Theory*, edited by R. D. Alexander and D. W. Tinkle, 18–45. New York: Chiron Press.

Norton-Griffiths, M. 1969. The organisation, control and development of parental feeding in the oystercatcher (*Haematopus ostralegus). Behaviour* 34:55–114.

Nur, U. 1977. Maintenance of a "parasitic" B chromosome in the grasshopper *Melanoplus femurrubrum. Genetics* 87:499–512.

Nur, U. 1980. Evolution of unusual chromosome systems in scale insects (Coccoidea: Homoptera). In: *Insect Cytogenetics*, edited by R. L. Blackman, G. M. Hewitt, and M. Ashburner, 97–177. Oxford: Blackwell.

Nur, U. 1982. Destruction of specific heterochromatic chromosomes during spermatogenesis in the *Comstockiella* chromosome system (Coccoidea: Homoptera). *Chromosoma* 85:519–530.

O'Donald, P. 1980. *Genetic Models of Sexual Selection.* Cambridge: Cambridge University Press.

Ohala, J. J. 1984. An ethological perspective on common cross-language utilization of Fo of voice. *Phonetica* 41:1–16.

O'Neill, K. M., and H. E. Evans. 1983. Alternative male mating tactics in *Bembecinus quinquespinosus* (Hymenoptera: Sphecidae): correlations with size and color variation. *Behav. Ecol. Sociobiol.* 14:39–46.

Orgel, L. E., and F. H. C. Crick. 1980. Selfish DNA: the ultimate parasite. *Nature* 284:604–607.

Ortiz, C. L., B. J. Le Boeuf, and D. P. Costa. 1984. Milk intake of elephant seal pups: an index of parental investment. *Amer. Nat.* 124:416–422.

Otte, D., and K. Stayman. 1979. Beetle horns: some patterns in functional morphology. In: *Sexual Selection and Reproductive Competition in Insects*, edited by M. S. Blum and N. A. Blum, 259–292. New York: Academic Press.

Overmeer, W. P. J., and R. A. Harrison. 1969. Notes on the control of the sex ratio in populations of the two-spotted spider mite, *Tetranychus urticae* Koch (Acarina: Tetranychidae). *New Zealand J. Science* 12:920–928.

Owen, D. F. 1971. *Tropical Butterflies.* Oxford: Clarendon Press.

Owen, R. E., F. H. Rodd, and R. C. Plowright. 1980. Sex ratios in bumble bee colonies: complications due to orphaning? *Behav. Ecol. Sociobiol.* 7:287–291.

Packer, C. 1977. Reciprocal altruism in *Papio anubis. Nature* 265:441–443.

Packer, C. 1979. Inter-troop transfer and inbreeding avoidance in *Papio anubis. Anim. Behav.* 27:1–36.

Packer, C., and A. E. Pusey. 1982. Cooperation and competition within coalitions of male lions: kin selection or game theory? *Nature* 296:740–742.

Pakrasi, K., and B. Sasmal. 1970. Effect of infanticide on sex-ratio in an Indian population. *Z. fur Morphologie und Anthropologie* 62:214–230.

Pardi, L. 1948. Dominance order in *Polistes* wasps. *Physiological Zoology* 21:1–13.

Parker, G. A. 1970. Sperm competition and its evolutionary significance in insects. *Biol. Rev.* 45:525–567.

Parker, G. A. 1982. Why are there so many tiny sperm? Sperm competition and the maintenance of two sexes. *J. Theor. Biol.* 96:281–294.

Parker, G. A., R. R. Baker, and V. G. F. Smith. 1972. The origin and evolution of gamete dimorphism and the male-female phenomenon. *J. Theor. Biol.* 36:529–553.

Parkes, A. S. 1925. Studies on the sex-ratio and related phenomena. *J. Agri. Sci.* 15:285–299.

Parsons, J. 1970. Relationship between egg size and post-hatching chick mortality in the herring gull (*Larus argentatus*). *Nature* 228:1221–1222.

Parsons, J. 1971. Cannibalism in herring gulls. *British Birds* 64:528–537.

Parsons, J. 1975. Seasonal variation in the breeding success of the herring gull: An experimental approach to pre-fledging success. *J. Anim. Ecol.* 44:553–573.

Partridge, L. 1980. Mate choice increases a component of offspring fitness in fruit flies. *Nature* 283:290–291.

Partridge, L. 1983. Non-random mating and offspring fitness. In: *Mate Choice*, edited by P. Bateson, 227–255. Cambridge: Cambridge University Press.

Paul, W., J. D. Weinrich, J. C. Gonsiorek, and M. E. Hotvedt. 1982. *Homosexuality: Social, Psychological, and Biological Issues*. Beverly Hills, California: SAGE Publications.

Payne, R. B. 1979. Sexual selection and intersexual differences in variance of breeding success. *Amer. Nat.* 114:447–452.

Payne, R. B. 1982. Ecological consequences of song matching: breeding success and intraspecific song mimicry in indigo buntings. *Ecology* 63:401–411.

Payne, R. B. 1983. The social context of song mimicry: song-matching dialects in indigo buntings (*Passerina cyanea*). *Anim. Behav.* 31:788–805.

Pearse, V. and J., and R. and M. Buchsbaum. (In press). *Invertebrates*. Palo Alto, California: Blackwell.

Perrill, S. A., H. C. Gerhardt, and R. Daniel. 1978. Sexual parasitism in the green tree frog (*Hyla cinerea*). *Science* 200:1179–1180.

Perrins, C. 1964. Survival of young swifts in relation to brood-size. *Nature* 201:1147–1148.

Perrone, M., Jr. 1978. Mate size and breeding success in a monogamous cichlid fish. *Env. Biol. Fish.* 3:193–201.

Petrie, M. 1983. Female moorhens compete for small fat males. *Science* 220:413–415.

Pfeifer, S. 1982. Disappearance and dispersal of *Spermophilus elegans* juveniles in relation to behavior. *Behav. Ecol. Sociobiol.* 10:237–243.

Pfenning, D. W., G. J. Gamboa, H. K. Reeve, J. S. Reeve, and I. D. Ferguson. 1983. The mechanism of nestmate discrimination in social wasps (*Polistes*, Hymenoptera: Vespidae). *Behav. Ecol. Sociobiol.* 13:299–305.

Pickering, J. 1980a. Larval competition and brood sex ratios in the gregarious parasitoid *Pachysomoides stupidus*. *Nature* 283:291–292.

Pickering, J. 1980b. Sex ratio, social behavior and ecology in *Polistes*, *Pachysomoides* and *Plasmodium*. Ph.D. thesis, Harvard University.

Pierotti, R. 1981. Male and female parental roles in the Western gull under different environmental conditions. *Auk* 98:532–549.

Piper, J. G., B. Charlesworth, and D. Charlesworth. 1984. A high rate of self-fertilization and increased seed fertility of homostyle primroses. *Nature* 310:50–51.

Pollard, G. N. 1969. Factors influencing the sex ratio at birth in Australia, 1902–65. *J. Biosoc. Science* 1:125–144.

Pomeroy, N. 1979. Brood bionomics of *Bombus ruderatus* in New Zealand (Hymenoptera: Apidae). *Canadian Entomologist* 111:865–874.

Porter, J. W. 1977. Pseudorca stranding. *Oceans* 10:8–15.

Post, D. C., and R. L. Jeanne. 1982. Recognition of former nestmates during colony founding by the social wasp *Polistes fuscatus* (Hymenoptera: Vespidae). *Behav. Ecol. Sociobiol.* 11:283–285.

Post, W., and J. S. Greenlaw. 1982. Comparative costs of promiscuity and monogamy: a test of reproductive effort theory. *Behav. Ecol. Sociobiol.* 10:101–107.

Power, H. W. 1979. Is displacement a sign of female dominance or only a response to close following by males trying to avoid being cuckolded? *Auk* 96:613–615.

Price, T. D. 1984. Sexual selection on body size, territory and plumage variables in a population of Darwin's finches. *Evolution* 38:327–341.

Pugesek, B. H. 1981. Increased reproductive effort with age in the California gull (*Larus californicus*). *Science* 212:822–823.

Ralls, K., R. L. Brownell, Jr., and J. Ballou. 1980. Differential mortality by sex and age in mammals, with specific reference to the sperm whale. *Rep. Int. Whal. Commn. Special Issue* 2:233–243.

Ralls, K., K. Brugger, and J. Ballou. 1979. Inbreeding and juvenile mortality in small populations of Ungulates. *Science* 206:1101–1103.

Rasmussen, D. R. 1981. Pair-bond strength and stability and reproductive success. *Psychological Review* 88:274–290.

Rasmussen, K. 1981. Consort behaviour and mate selection in yellow baboons (*Papio cynocephalus*). Ph.D. thesis, Cambridge University.

Rechten, C. 1980. Brood relief behaviour of the cichlid fish *Etroplus maculatus*. *Z. Tierpsychol.* 52:77–102.

Reeve, H. K., and G. J. Gamboa. 1983. Colony activity integration in primitive eusocial wasps: the role of the queen (*Polistes fuscatus*, Hymenoptera: Vespidae). *Behav. Ecol. Sociobiol.* 13:63–74.

Reid, M. J., and J. W. Atz. 1958. Oral incubation in the cichlid fish *Geophagus jurupari* Heckel. *Zoologica: New York Zoological Society* 43:77–88.

Reish, D. J. 1957. The life history of the polychaetous annelid *Neanthes caudata* (delle Chiaje), including a summary of development in the family Nereidae. *Pacific Science* 11:216–228.

Reiter, J., K. J. Panken, and B. J. Le Boeuf. 1981. Female competition and reproductive success in northern elephant seals. *Animal Behavior* 29:670–687.

Rheingold, H. L. 1963. Maternal behavior in the dog. In: *Maternal Behavior in Mammals*, edited by H. L. Rheingold, 169–202. New York: John Wiley & Sons.

Rhoades, D. F. 1983a. Herbivore population dynamics and plant chemistry. In: *Variable Plants and Herbivores in Natural and Managed Systems*, edited by R. F. Denno and M. S. McClure, 155–220. New York: Academic Press.

Rhoades, D. F. 1983b. Responses of alder and willow to attack by tent caterpillars and webworms: evidence for pheromonal sensitivity of willows. In: *Plant Resistance to Insects*, edited by P. A. Hedin, 55–68. ACS Symposium Series, No. *208*.

Rice, D. W., and K. W. Kenyon. 1962. Breeding cycle and behavior of Laysan and Black-footed albatrosses. *Auk* 79:517–567.

Ridley, M. 1978. Paternal care. *Anim. Behav.* 26:904–932.

Ridley, M., and C. Rechten. 1981. Female sticklebacks prefer to spawn with males whose nests contain eggs. *Behaviour* 76:152–161.

Ridley, M. W. 1980. The breeding behaviour and feeding ecology of grey phalaropes *Phalaropus fulicarius* in Svalbard. *Ibis* 122:210–226.

Riedman, M. L., and B. J. Le Boeuf. 1982. Mother-pup separation and adoption in northern elephant seals. *Behav. Ecol. Sociobiol.* 11:203–215.

Rivers, J. P. W., and M. A. Crawford. 1974. Maternal nutrition and sex ratio at birth. *Nature* 252:297–280.

Roberts, D. F. 1953. Body weight, race and climate. *American J. Physical Anthropology* 11:533–558.

Robertson, R. J., and H. L. Gibbs. 1982. Superterritoriality in tree swallows: a reexamination. *Condor* 84:313–316.

Robinette, L. W., and D. A. Jones. 1954. Antler anomalies of mule deer. *J. Mammalogy* 40:96–108.

Robinson, M. H. 1968. The defensive behavior of *Pterinoxylus spinulosus* Redtenbacher, a winged stick insect from Panama (Phasmatodea). *Psyche* 75:195–207.

Robinson, M. H. 1969a. Defenses against visually hunting predators. In: *Evolutionary Biology* 3, edited by T. Dobzhansky, M. K. Hecht, and W. C. Steere, 225–259. New York: Meredith Corp.

Robinson, M. H. 1969b. The defensive behaviour of some orthopteroid insects from Panama. *Trans. Royal Ent. Soc. Lond.* 121:281–303.

Robinson, M. H. 1970. Insect anti-predator adaptations and the behavior of predatory primates. *Act. IV Congr. Latin. Zool.* 2:811–836.

Robinson, M. H. 1973. The evolution of cryptic postures in insects, with special reference to some New Guinea tettigoniids (Orthoptera). *Psyche* 80:159–165.

Rohwer, S. 1977. Status signaling in Harris sparrows: some experiments in deception. *Behaviour* 61:107–129.

Rohwer, S. 1982. The evolution of reliable and unreliable badges of fighting ability. *Amer. Zool.* 22:531–546.

Rohwer, S., and P. W. Ewald. 1981. The cost of dominance and advantage of subordination in a badge signaling system. *Evolution* 35:441–454.

Rohwer, S., S. D. Fretwell, and D. M. Niles. 1980. Delayed maturation in passerine plumages and the deceptive acquisition of resources. *Amer. Nat.* 115:400–437.

Rohwer, S., S. D. Fretwell, and R. C. Tuckfield. 1976. Distress screams as a measure of kinship in birds. *Amer. Midland Naturalist* 96:418–430.

Rohwer, S., and F. C. Rohwer. 1978. Status signalling in Harris sparrows: experimental deception achieved. *Anim. Behav.* 26:1012–1022.

Ross, N. M., and G. J. Gamboa. 1981. Nestmate discrimination in social wasps (*Polistes metricus*, Hymenoptera: Vespidae). *Behav. Ecol. Sociobiol.* 9:163–165.

Rowley, I. 1983. Re-mating in birds. In: *Mate Choice*, edited by P. Bateson, 331–360. Cambridge: Cambridge University Press.

Rubenstein, D. I., and R. W. Wrangham. 1980. Why is altruism toward kin so rare? *Z. Tierpsychol.* 54:381–387.

Rudebeck, G. 1950. The choice of prey and modes of hunting of predatory birds with special reference to their selective effect. *Oikos* 2:65–88.

Ruse, M. 1980. Charles Darwin and group selection. *Annals of Science* 37:615–630.

Ruse, M. 1982. *Darwinism Defended: A Guide to the Evolution Controversies*. Reading, Massachusetts: Addison-Wesley.

Rushton, J. P., R. J. H. Russell, and P. A. Wells. 1984. Genetic similarity theory: beyond kin selection. *Behavior Genetics* 14:179–193.

Russell, W. T. 1936. Statistical study of the sex ratio at birth. *J. Hygiene* 36:381–401.

Rutowski, R. L. 1982. Epigamic selection by males as evidenced by courtship partner preferences in the checkered white butterfly (*Pieris protodice*). *Anim. Behav.* 30:108–112.

Ryan, M. J. 1980. Female mate choice in a Neotropical frog. *Science* 209:523–525.

Ryan, M. J. 1983. Sexual selection and communication in a Neotropical frog, *Physalaemus pustulosus*. *Evolution* 37:261–272.

Rychlewsky, J., and K. Zarzycki. 1975. Sex ratio in seeds of *Rumex acetosa* L. as a result of sparse or abundant pollination. *Acta Biol. Cracov. Series Botanica* 18:101–114.

Ryder, J. P. 1983. Sex ratio and egg sequence in ring-billed gulls. *Auk* 100:726–728.

Sackeim, H. A. 1983. Self-deception, self esteem and depression: the adaptive value of lying to oneself. In: *Empirical Studies of Psychoanalytic Theories*, Vol. 1, edited by J. Masling, 101–157. London: Analytic Press.

Sade, D. S. 1968. Inhibition of son-mother mating among free-ranging rhesus monkeys. *Science and Psychoanalysis* 12:18–38.

Sadler, D. L. 1981. An experimental confirmation of R. A. Fisher's theory of sex ratio. *Am. J. Phys. Anthrop.* 54:272.

Sager, R., and Z. Ramanis. 1973. The mechanism of maternal inheritance in *Chlamydomonas*: biochemical and genetic studies. *Theoretical and Applied Genetics* 43:101–108.

Sakaluk, S. K. 1984. Male crickets feed females to ensure complete sperm transfer. *Science* 223:609–610.

Sargeant, A. B., and L. E. Eberhardt. 1975. Death feigning by ducks in response to predation by red foxes (*Vulpes fulva*). *Amer. Midland Naturalist* 94:108–119.

Schaller, G. B. 1964. Breeding behavior of the white pelican at Yellowstone Lake, Wyoming. *Condor* 66:3–23.

Scheiring, J. F. 1977. Stabilizing selection for size as related to mating fitness in *Tetraopes*. *Evolution* 31:447–449.

Schickele, E. 1947. Environment and fatal heat stroke: an analysis of 157 cases occurring in the Army in the U.S. during World War II. *Military Surgeon* 49:235–256.

Schneirla, T. C., J. S. Rosenblatt, and E. Tobach. 1963. Maternal behavior in the cat. In: *Maternal Behavior in Mammals*, edited by H. L. Rheingold, 122–168. New York: John Wiley & Sons.

Schrader, F. 1960. Evolutionary aspects of aberrant meiosis in some *Pentatominae* (Heteroptera). *Evolution* 14:498–508.

Schubert, G. 1982. Infanticide by usurper hanuman langur males: a sociobiological myth. *Social Science Information* 21:199–244.

Schultze, A. B. 1965. Litter size and proportion of females in the offspring of multiparous rats with varying uterine metabolic levels. *J. Reprod. Fert.* 10:145–147.

Schultze, A. B. 1969. Results of breeding for low and high uterine metabolic status in rats. *J. Heredity* 60:349–350.

Searcy, W. A. 1982. The evolutionary effects of mate selection. *Ann. Rev. Ecol. Syst.* 13:57–85.

Seemanova, E. 1971. A study of children of incestuous matings. *Human Heredity* 21:108–128.

Seger, J. 1976. Evolution of responses to relative homozygosity. *Nature* 262:578–580.

Seger, J. 1983a. Partial bivoltinism may cause alternating sex-ratio biases that favour eusociality. *Nature* 301:59–62.

Seger, J. 1983b. Conditional relatedness, recombination, and the chromosome number of insects. In: *Advances in Herpetology and Evolutionary Biology*, edited by A. Rhodin and K. Miyata, 596–610. Cambridge, Massachusetts: Museum of Comparative Zoology.

Seger, J., R. Trivers, and H. Hare. n.d. The sex ratio before birth in whales. Unpublished manuscript.

Semler, D. E. 1971. Some aspects of adaptation in a polymorphism for breeding colours in the three-spine stickleback (*Gasterosteus aculeatus*). *J. Zool., Lond.* 165:291–302.

Seyfarth, R. M., and D. L. Cheney. 1984. Grooming, alliances and reciprocal altruism in vervet monkeys. *Nature* 308:541–543.

Shapiro, S., E. R. Schlesinger, and R. E. L. Nesbitt, Jr. 1968. *Infant, Perinatal, Maternal, and Childhood Mortality in the United States*. Cambridge, Massachusetts: Harvard University Press.

Shearer, M. L., R. T. Davidson, and S. M. Finch. 1967. The sex ratio of offspring born to state hospitalized schizophrenic women. *J. Psychiat. Res.* 5:349–350.

Shepard, J. M. 1976. Factors influencing female choice in the lek mating system of the ruff. *The Living Bird, Fourteenth Annual, 1975*, 87–111. Ithaca, New York: Cornell Laboratory of Ornithology.

Sheppard, P. M. 1959. The evolution of mimicry; a problem in ecology and genetics. *Cold Spring*

Harbor Symposia on Quantitative Biology 24: 131–140.

Sherman, P. W. 1977. Nepotism and the evolution of alarm calls. *Science* 197:1246–1253.

Sherman, P. W. 1980. The limits of ground squirrel nepotism. In: *Sociobiology: Beyond Nature/Nurture? AAAS Selected Symposium* 35, edited by G. B. Barlow and J. Silverberg, 505–544. Boulder, Colorado: Westview Press.

Sherman, P. W. 1981a. Kinship, demography, and Belding's ground squirrel nepotism. *Behav. Ecol. Sociobiol.* 8:251–259.

Sherman, P. W. 1981b. Reproductive competition and infanticide in Belding's Ground Squirrels and other animals. In: *Natural Selection and Social Behavior: Recent Research and New Theory*, edited by R. D. Alexander and D. W. Tinkle, 311–331. New York: Chiron Press.

Sherman, P. W., and M. L. Morton. 1984. Demography of Belding's ground squirrels. *Ecology* 65:1617–1628.

Shettleworth, S. J. 1983. Memory in food-hoarding birds. *Scient. Amer.* 248:102–110.

Shettleworth, S. J. 1984. Learning and behavioral ecology. In: *Behavioural Ecology*, second edition, edited by J. R. Krebs and N. B. Davies, 170–194. Sunderland, Massachusetts. Sinauer.

Shields, W. M. 1982. *Philopatry, Inbreeding, and the Evolution of Sex*. Albany: SUNY Press.

Shine, R. 1978. Sexual size dimorphism and male combat in snakes. *Oecologia* 33:269–277.

Shine, R., and J. J. Bull. 1979. The evolution of live-bearing in lizards and snakes. *Amer. Nat.* 113:905–923.

Silberglied, R. E., J. G. Shepherd, and J. L. Dickinson. 1984. Eunuchs: the role of apyrene in Lepidoptera? *Amer. Nat.* 123:255–265.

Silk, J. B. 1983. Local resource competition and facultative adjustment of sex ratios in relation to competitive abilities. *Amer. Nat.* 121:56–66.

Sillen-Tullberg, B. 1981. Prolonged copulation: a male "postcopulatory" strategy in a promiscuous species, *Lygaeus equestris* (Heteroptera: Lygaeidae). *Behav. Ecol. Sociobiol.* 9:283–289.

Simpson, G. G. 1947. The problem of plan and purpose in nature. *Sci. Monthly* 64:481–495.

Simpson, M. J. A., and A. E. Simpson. 1982. Birth sex ratios and social rank in rhesus monkey mothers. *Nature* 300:440–441.

Simpson, M. J. A., A. E. Simpson, J. Hooley, and M. Zunz. 1981. Infant-related influences on birth intervals in rhesus monkeys. *Nature* 290:49–51.

Slater, P. J. B. 1983a. Bird song learning: theme and variations. In: *Perspectives in Ornithology*, edited by A. H. Brook and G. A. Clark, Jr., 475–499. Cambridge: Cambridge University Press.

Slater, P. J. B. 1983b. The development of individual behaviour. In: *Genes, Development and Learning*, edited by T. R. Halliday and P. J. B. Slater, 82–113. New York: W. H. Freeman and Co.

Slee, J. 1972. Habituation and acclimitization of sheep to cold following exposures of varying length and severity. *J. Physiol.* 227:51–70.

Smith, R. L. 1976. Male brooding behavior of the water bug *Abedus herberti* (Hemiptera: Belostomatidae). *Annals Ent. Soc. Amer.* 69:740–747.

Smith, R. L. 1979. Repeated copulation and sperm precedence: paternity assurance for a male brooding water bug. *Science* 205:1029–1031.

Smith, R. L. 1980. Evolution of exclusive postcopulatory paternal care in the insects. *Florida Entomologist* 63:65–78.

Smith, R. L. In press. *Sperm Competition and the Evolution of Animal Mating Systems*. New York: Academic Press.

Smith, R. L., and J. B. Smith. 1976. Inheritance of a naturally occurring mutation in a giant water bug. *J. Heredity* 67:182–185.

Smuts, B. 1983a. Dynamics of "special relationships" between adult male and female olive baboons. In: *Primate Social Relationships: An Integrated Approach*, edited by R. A. Hinde, 112–116. Oxford: Blackwell.

Smuts, B. 1983b. Special relationships between adult male and female olive baboons: selective advantages. In: *Primate Social Relationships: An Integrated Approach*, edited by R. A. Hinde, 262–266. Oxford: Blackwell.

Snyder, M., and S. W. Uranowitz. 1978. Reconstructing the past: some cognitive consequences of person perception. *J. Personality and Social Psychology* 36:941–950.

Spencer-Booth, Y., and R. A. Hinde. 1971. Effects of brief separation from mothers during infancy on behaviour of rhesus monkeys 6–24 month later. *J. Child Psychol. Psychiat.* 12:157–172.

Spiess, E. B., and L. Ehrman. 1978. Rare male mating advantage. *Nature* 272:188–189.

Spiess, E. B., and W. A. Schwer. 1978. Minority mating advantage of certain eye color mutants of *Drosophila melanogaster*. I. Multiple choice and single-female tests. *Behav. Genet.* 8:155–168.

Stacey, P. B., and W. D. Koenig. 1984. Cooperative breeding in the acorn woodpecker. *Sci. Amer.* 251:114–121.

Stallcup, J. A., and G. E. Woolfenden. 1978. Family

status and contributions to breeding by Florida scrub jays. *Anim. Behav.* 26:1144–1156.

Stamps, J. A. 1983. Sexual selection, sexual dimorphism, and territoriality. In: *Lizard Ecology: Studies on a Model Organism*, edited by R. B. Huey, E. R. Pianka, and T. W. Schoener, 169–204. Cambridge, Massachusetts: Harvard University Press.

Stamps, J. A., A. Clark, P. Arrowood, and B. Kus. (In press). Parent-offspring conflict in budgerigars. *Behaviour.*

Stamps, J. A., and S. M. Gon III. 1983. Sex-biased pattern variation in the prey of birds. *Ann. Rev. Ecol. Syst.* 14:231–253.

Stamps, J. A., R. A. Metcalf, and V. V. Krishnan. 1978. A genetic analysis of parent-offspring conflict. *Behav. Ecol. Sociobiol.* 3:369–392.

Steger, R., and R. L. Caldwell. 1983. Intraspecific deception by bluffing: a defense strategy of newly molted stomatopods (Arthropoda: Crustacea). *Science* 221:558–560.

Stenseth, N. C. 1978. Is the female biased sex ratio in wood lemming *Myopus schisticolor* maintained by cyclic inbreeding? *Oikos* 30:83–89.

Stephens, M. L. 1984a. Mate takeover and possible infanticide by a female Northern jacana (*Jacana spinosa*). *Anim. Behav.* 30:1253–1254.

Stephens, M. L. 1984b. Intraspecific distraction displays of the polyandrous Northern jacana *Jacana spinosa*. *Ibis* 126:70–72.

Stephenson, A. G., and R. I. Bertin. 1983. Male competition, female choice, and sexual selection in plants. In: *Pollination Biology*, edited by L. Real, 109–149. New York: Academic Press.

Stirling, I. 1971. Variation in sex ratio of newborn Weddell seals during the pupping season. *J. Mammalogy* 52:842–844.

Stirling, I. 1982. The evolution of mating systems in pinnipeds. In: *Recent Advances in the Study of Mammalian Behavior*, edited by J. F. Eisenberg and D. G. Kleiman, 489–527. American Society of Mammalogists, Spec. Pub. No. 7.

Strassmann, J. E. 1984. Female-biased sex ratios in social insects lacking morphological castes. *Evolution* 38:256–266.

Strong, D. R., Jr., and D. A. Levin. 1979. Species richness of plant parasites and growth form of their hosts. *Amer. Nat.* 114:1–22.

Synder, R. S. 1960. Physiology and behavioral responses to an altered sex ratio of adults in a population of woodchucks. Ph.D. thesis, School of Hygiene and Public Health, Johns Hopkins University.

Taborsky, M., and D. Limberger. 1981. Helpers in fish. *Behav. Ecol. Sociobiol.* 8:143–145.

Taylor, M. A. 1969. Sex ratios of newborns: associated with prepartum and postpartum schizophrenia. *Science* 164:723–724.

Teitelbaum, M. S. 1970. Factors affecting the sex ratio in large populations. *J. Biosocial Science Supple.* 2:61–71.

Teitelbaum, M. S. 1972. Factors associated with the sex ratio in human populations. In: *The Structure of Human Populations*, edited by G. A. Harrison and A. J. Boyce, 88–109. Oxford: Oxford University Press.

Teitelbaum, M. S., and N. Mantel. 1971. Socioeconomic factors and the sex ratio at birth. *J. Biosoc. Sci.* 3:23–41.

Thorne, B. L. 1984. Polygyny in the neotropical termite *Nasutitermes corniger*: life history consequences of queen mutalism. *Behav. Ecol. Sociobiol.* 14:117–136.

Thornhill, R. 1976a. Sexual selection and nuptial feeding behavior in *Bittacus apicalis* (Insecta: Mecoptera). *Amer. Nat.* 110:529–548.

Thornhill, R. 1976b. Sexual selection and parental investment in insects. *Amer. Nat.* 110:153–163.

Thornhill, R. 1979. Adaptive female-mimicking behavior in a scorpionfly. *Science* 205:412–414.

Thornhill, R. 1980a. Mate choice in *Hylobittacus apicalis* (Insecta: Mecoptera) and its relation to some models of female choice. *Evolution* 34:519–538.

Thornhill, R. 1980b. Rape in *Panorpa* scorpionflies and a general rape hypothesis. *Anim. Behav.* 28:52–59.

Thornhill, R. 1980c. Sexual selection in the black-tipped hangingfly. *Sci. Amer.* 242:162–172.

Thornhill, R. 1980d. Sexual selection within mating swarms of the lovebug, *Plecia nearctica* (Diptera: Bibionidae). *Anim. Behav.* 28:405–412.

Thornhill, R. 1983. Cryptic female choice and its implications in the scorpionfly *Harpobittacus nigriceps*. *Amer. Nat.* 122:765–788.

Thornhill, R., and J. Alcock. 1983. *The Evolution of Insect Mating Systems*. Cambridge, Massachusetts: Harvard University Press.

Thornhill, R., and N. W. Thornhill. 1983. Human rape: an evolutionary analysis. *Ethology and Sociobiology* 4:137–173.

Tinbergen, N. 1935. Field observations of East Greenland birds. I. The behavior of the red-necked phalarope (*Phalaropus lobatus* L.) in spring. *Ardea* 24:1–42.

Tinbergen, N. 1953. *The Herring Gull's World*. London: Collins.

Tinbergen, N., G. J. Broekhuysen, F. Feekes, J. C. W. Houghton, H. Kruuk, and E. Szulc. 1962. Egg shell removal by the black-headed gull, *Larus ridi-*

bundus L.; a behaviour component of camouflage. *Behaviour* 11:24–117.

Tinbergen, N., M. Impekoven, and D. Franck. 1967. An experiment on spacing-out as a defence against predation. *Behaviour* 28:307–321.

Tinkle, D. W., and J. W. Gibbons. 1977. *The Distribution and Evolution of Viviparity in Reptiles.* Miscellaneous Publications No. 154. Museum of Zoology, University of Michigan.

Tooby, J. 1982. Pathogens, polymorphism, and the evolution of sex. *J. Theor. Biol.* 97:557–576.

Trivers, R. L. 1971. The evolution of reciprocal altruism. *Quarterly Review of Biology* 46:35–57.

Trivers, R. L. 1972. Parental investment and sexual selection. In: *Sexual Selection and the Descent of Man 1871–1971,* edited by B. Campbell, 136–179. Chicago: Aldine.

Trivers, R. L. 1974. Parent-offspring conflict. *Amer. Zool.* 14:249–264.

Trivers, R. L. 1976. Sexual selection and resource-accruing abilities in *Anolis garmani. Evolution* 30:253–269.

Trivers, R. L., and H. Hare. 1976. Haplodiploidy and the evolution of the social insects. *Science* 191:249–263.

Trivers, R. L., and D. E. Willard. 1973. Natural selection of parental ability to vary the sex ratio of offspring. *Science* 179:90–92.

Turner, J. R. G. 1977. Butterfly mimicry: the genetical evolution of an adaptation. *Evolutionary Biology* 10:163–207.

Tutin, C. E. G. 1979. Mating patterns and reproductive strategies in a community of wild chimpanzees (*Pan troglodytes schweinfurthii*). *Behav. Ecol. Sociobiol.* 6:29–38.

Tuttle, M. D., and M. J. Ryan. 1981. Bat predation and the evolution of frog vocalizations in the Neotropics. *Science* 214:677–678.

Unger, L. M. 1983. Nest defense by deceit in the fathead minnow, *Pimephales promelas. Behav. Ecol. Sociobiol.* 13:125–130.

van den Assem, J., and E. Feuth-De Bruijn. 1977. Second matings and their effect on the sex ratio of the offspring in *Nasonia vitripennis* (Hymenoptera: Pteromalidae). *Ent. Exp. & Appl.* 21:23–28.

van Lawick-Goodall, J. 1968. The behaviour of free-living chimpanzees in the Gombe Stream Reserve. *Animal Behaviour Monographs* 1:161–311.

Van Noordwijk, A. J., J. H. Van Balen, and W. Scharloo. 1980. Heritability of ecologically important traits in the great tit. *Ardea* 68:193–203.

van Rhijn, J. G. 1983. On the maintenance and origin of alternative strategies in the Ruff *Philomachus pugnax. Ibis* 125:482–498.

Verme, L. J., and J. J. Ozoga. 1981. Sex ratio of the white-tailed deer and the estrus cycle. *J. Wildlife Management* 45:710–715.

Verrell, P. A. 1983. The influence of the ambient sex ratio and intermale competition on the sexual behavior of the red-spotted newt, *Notophtalmus viridescens* (Amphibia: Urodela: Salamandridae). *Behav. Ecol. Sociobiol.* 13:307–313.

Visaria, P. M. 1967. Sex ratio at birth in territories with a relatively complete registration. *Eugenics Quarterly* 14:132–142.

Vogel, F., and A. G. Motulsky. 1979. *Human Genetics.* Berlin: Springer-Verlag.

von Ruppell, G. 1969. Eine "Lüge" als gerichtete Mitteilung beim Eisfuchs (*Alopex lagopus* L.). *Z. Tierpsychol.* 26:371–374.

Waage, J. K. 1979a. Adaptive significance of postcopulatory guarding of mates and nonmates by male *Calopteryx maculata* (Odonata). *Behav. Ecol. Sociobiol.* 6:147–154.

Waage, J. K. 1979b. Dual function of the damselfly penis: sperm removal and transfer. *Science* 203:916–918.

Waage, J. K. (In press). Sperm competition and the evolution of odonate mating systems. In: *Sperm Competition and the Evolution of Animal Mating Systems,* edited by R. L. Smith. New York: Academic Press.

Wade, M. J. 1979. Sexual selection and variance in reproductive success. *Amer. Nat.* 114:742–747.

Wade, M. J., and S. J. Arnold. 1980. The intensity of sexual selection in relation to male sexual behaviour, female choice, and sperm precedence. *Anim. Behav.* 28:446–461.

Waldman, B. 1982. Sibling association among schooling tadpoles: field evidence and implications. *Anim. Behav.* 30:700–713.

Waltz, E. C. 1982. Alternative mating tactics and the law of diminishing returns: the satellite threshold model. *Behav. Ecol. Sociobiol.* 10:75–83.

Ward, E. J. 1973. The heterochromatine B chromosome of maize: the segments affecting recombination. *Chromosoma* 43:177–186.

Ward, P. I. 1983. The effects of size on the mating behaviour of the dung fly *Sepsis cynipsea. Behav. Ecol. Sociobiol.* 13:75–80.

Ward, P. S. 1983a. Genetic relatedness and colony organization in a species complex of ponerine ants. I. Phenotypic and genotypic composition of colonies. *Behav. Ecol. Sociobiol.* 12:285–299.

Ward, P. S. 1983b. Genetic relatedness and colony organization in a species complex of ponerine ants. II. Patterns of sex ratio investment. *Behav. Ecol. Sociobiol.* 12:301–307.

Watson, J. D. 1977. *Molecular Biology of the Gene.* (Third Edition). Menlo Park, California: Benjamin/Cummings.

Wells, K. D. 1978. Courtship and parental behavior in a panamanian poison-arrow frog (*Dendrobates auratus*). *Herpetologica* 34:148–155.

Wells, K. D. 1981. Parental behavior of male and female frogs. In: *Natural Selection and Social Behaviour*, edited by R. D. Alexander and D. W. Tinkle, 184–197. New York: Chiron Press.

Wenegrat, B. 1984. *Sociobiology and Mental Disorder.* Menlo Park, California: Addison-Wesley.

Werren, J. H. 1980. Sex ratio adaptations to local mate competition in a parasitic wasp. *Science* 208:1157–1159.

Werren, J. H. 1983. Sex ratio evolution under local mate competition in a parasitic wasp. *Evolution* 37:116–124.

Werren, J. H., and E. L. Charnov. 1978. Facultative sex ratios and population dynamics. *Nature* 272:349–350.

Werren, J. H., M. R. Gross, and R. Shine. 1980. Paternity and the evolution of male parental care. *J. Theor. Biol.* 82:619–631.

West Eberhard, M. J. 1969. *The Social Biology of Polistine Wasps.* Miscellaneous Publications No. 140. Museum of Zoology, University of Michigan.

West Eberhard, M. J. 1975. The evolution of social behavior by kin selection. *The Quarterly Review of Biology* 50:1–33.

West Eberhard, M. J. 1978. Temporary queens in *Metapolybia* wasps: nonreproductive helpers without altruism? *Science* 200:441–443.

West Eberhard, M. J. 1983. Sexual selection, social competition, and speciation. *The Quarterly Review of Biology* 58:155–183.

White, H. C., and B. Grant. 1977. Olfactory cues as a factor in frequency-dependent mate selection in *Mormoniella vitripennis*. *Evolution* 31:829–835.

White, M. J. D. 1973. *Animal Cytology and Evolution.* (Third Edition). Cambridge, England: Cambridge University Press.

Whitham, T. G. 1983. Host manipulation of parasites: within-plant variation as a defense against rapidly evolving pests. In: *Variable Plants and Herbivores in Natural and Managed Systems*, edited by R. F. Denno and M. S. McClure, 15–41. New York: Academic Press.

Whitham, T. G., and C. N. Slobodchikoff. 1981. Evolution by individuals, plant-herbivore interactions, and mosaics of genetic variability: the adaptive significance of somatic mutations in plants. *Oecologia* 49:287–292.

Whitham, T. G., A. G. Williams, and A. M. Robison. 1984. The variation principle: individual plants as temporal and spatial mosaics of resistance to rapidly evolving pests. In: *A New Ecology: Novel Approaches to Interactive Systems*, edited by P. W. Price, C. N. Slobodchikoff, and W. S. Gaud, 15–52. New York: John Wiley and Sons.

Whitney, C. L., and J. R. Krebs. 1975a. Mate selection in Pacific tree frogs. *Nature* 255:325–326.

Whitney, C. L., and J. R. Krebs. 1975b. Spacing and calling in Pacific tree frogs, *Hyla regilla. Can. J. Zool.* 53:1519–1527.

Wickler, W. 1968. *Mimicry in Plants and Animals.* New York: McGraw-Hill.

Widdowson, E. M. 1976. The response of the sexes to nutritional stress. *Proc. Nutr. Soc.* 35:175–180.

Wiley, R. H., and M. S. Wiley. 1977. Recognition of neighbors' duets by stripe-backed wrens *Campylorhynchus nuchalis. Behaviour* 62:10–34.

Wilkinson, G. S. 1984. Reciprocal food sharing in the vampire bat. *Nature* 308:181–184.

Williams, G. C. 1966. *Adaptation and Natural Selection: A Critique of Some Current Evolutionary Thought.* Princeton, New Jersey: Princeton University Press.

Williams, G. C. 1975. *Sex and Evolution.* Princeton, New Jersey: Princeton University Press.

Williams, G. C. 1979. The question of adaptive sex ratio in outcrossed vertebrates. *Proc. R. Soc. Lond. B* 205:567–580.

Willson, M. F. 1979. Sexual selection in plants. *Amer. Nat.* 113:777–790.

Willson, M. F., and N. Burley. 1983. *Mate Choice in Plants: Tactics, Mechanisms, and Consequences.* Princeton, New Jersey: Princeton University Press.

Wilson, D. S. 1977. How nepotistic is the brain worm? *Behav. Ecol. Sociobiol.* 2:421–425.

Wilson, D. S. 1980. *The Natural Selection of Populations and Communities.* Menlo Park, California: Benjamin/Cummings.

Wilson, E. O. 1971. *The Insect Societies.* Cambridge, Massachusetts: The Belknap Press of Harvard University Press.

Wilson, E. O. 1975. *Sociobiology.* Cambridge, Massachusetts: Harvard University Press.

Wilson, E. O. 1980. Caste and division of labor in leaf-cutter ants (Hymenoptera: Formicidae: *Atta*): II. The ergonomic optimization of leaf cutting. *Behav. Ecol. Sociobiol.* 7:157–165.

Wilson, E. O., and B. Hölldobler. 1980. Sex differences in cooperative silk-spinning by weaver and ant larvae. *Proc. Natl. Acad. Sci. USA* 77:2343–2347.

Wilson, J. R., N. Adler, and B. J. Le Boeuf. 1965. The

effects of intromission frequency on successful pregnancy in the female rat. *Proc. Natl. Acad. Sci.* 53:1392–1395.

Wilson, R. S. 1978. Synchronies in mental development: an epigenetic perspective. *Science* 202: 939–948.

Winn, H. E. 1958. Comparative reproductive behavior and ecology of fourteen species of darters (Pisces-Percidae). *Ecological Monographs* 28:155–191.

Winter, U., and A. Buschinger. 1983. The reproductive biology of a slavemaker ant, *Epimyrma ravouxi*, and a degenerate slavemaker, *E. kraussei* (Hymenoptera: Formicidae). *Entomol. Gener.* 9:1–15.

Wittenberger, J. F. 1978. The evolution of mating systems in grouse. *Condor* 80:126–137.

Wittenberger, J. F. 1981. *Animal Social Behavior.* Boston: Duxbury Press.

Wolf, A. P. 1970. Childhood association and sexual attraction: a further test of the Westermarck hypothesis. *Amer. Anthr.* 72:502–515.

Wolf, A. P. 1976. Childhood association, sexual attraction and fertility in Taiwan. In: *Demographic Anthropology: Quantitative Approaches*, edited by E. B. Zubrow, 227–244. Albuquerque: University of New Mexico Press.

Wood, R. J., and M. E. Newton. 1976. Meiotic drive and sex distortion in the mosquito *Aedes aegypti*. *Proc. 15th Int. Cong. Entomology*, 97–105.

Woodruff, G., and D. Premack. 1979. Intentional communication in the chimpanzee: the development of deception. *Cognition* 7:333–362.

Woolbright, L. L. 1983. Sexual selection and size dimorphism in anuran amphibia. *Amer. Nat.* 121: 110–119.

Woolfenden, G. E. 1975. Florida scrub jay helpers at the nest. *Auk* 92:1–15.

Woolfenden, G. E. 1981. Selfish behavior by Florida scrub jay helpers. In: *Natural Selection and Social Behavior: Recent Research and New Theory*, edited by R. D. Alexander and W. D. Tinkle, 257–260. New York: Chiron Press.

Woolfenden, G. E., and J. W. Fitzpatrick. 1977. Dominance in the Florida scrub jay. *Condor* 79:1–12.

Woolfenden, G. E., and J. W. Fitzpatrick. 1978. The inheritance of territory in group-breeding birds. *Bio-Science* 28:104–108.

Woolfenden, G. E., and J. W. Firzpatrick. 1984. *The Florida Scrub Jay: Demography of a Cooperative-Breeding Bird.* Princeton: Princeton University Press.

Wrangham, R. W. 1980. An ecological model of female-bonded primate groups. *Behaviour* 75:262–300.

Wu, H. M., W. G. Holmes, S. R. Medina, and G. P. Sackett. 1980. Kin preferences in infant *Macaca nemestrina*. *Nature* 285:225–227.

Wylie, H. G. 1966. Some mechanisms that affect the sex ratio of *Nasonia vitripennis* (Walk.) (Hymenoptera: Pteromalidae) reared from superparasitized housefly pupae. *Can. Ent.* 98:645–653.

Wylie, H. G. 1976a. Interference among females of *Nasonia vitripennis* (Hymenoptera: Pteromalidae) and its effect on sex ratio of their progeny. *Can. Ent.* 108:655–661.

Wylie, H. G. 1976b. Observations on life history and sex ratio variability of *Eupteromalus dubius* (Hymenoptera: Pteromalidae), a parasite of cyclorrhaphous diptera. *Can. Ent.* 108:1267–1274.

Wynne-Edwards, V. C. 1962. *Animal Dispersion in Relation to Social Behaviour.* Edinburgh: Oliver and Boyd.

Wyshak, G. 1978. Fertility and longevity in twins, sibs, and parents of twins. *Social Biology* 25: 315–330.

Wyshak, G., and C. White. 1969. Fertility of twins and parents of twins. *Human Biology* 41:66–82.

Yasukawa, K. 1981. Song repertoires in the red-winged blackbird (*Agelaius phoeniceus*): a test of the beau geste hypothesis. *Anim. Behav.* 29: 114–125.

Yerkes, R. M. 1943. *Chimpanzees, a Laboratory Colony.* New Haven, Connecticut: Yale University Press.

Zabriskie, J. B. 1967. Mimetic relationships between group A streptococci and mammalian tissues. *Advances in Immunology* 7:147–188.

Zahavi, A. 1977. The cost of honesty (further remarks on the handicap principle). *J. Theoretical Biology* 67:603–605.

Zenone, P. G., M. E. Sims, and C. J. Erickson. 1979. Male ring dove behavior and the defense of genetic paternity. *Amer. Nat.* 114:615–626.

Zeveloff, S. I., and M. S. Boyce. 1980. Parental investment and mating systems in mammals. *Evolution* 34:973–982.

Zimmering, S., L. Sandler, and B. Nicoletti. 1970. Mechanism of meiotic drive. *Ann. Rev. Genet.* 4:409–436.

Zimmerman, R. B. 1983. Sibling manipulation and indirect fitness in termites. *Behav. Ecol. Sociobiol.* 12:143–145.

Zucker, N. 1983. Courtship variation in the Neotropical fiddler crab *Uca deichmanni*: another example of female incitation to male competition? *Mar. Behav. Physiol.* 10:57–79.

Zuk, M. 1984. A charming resistance to parasites. *Natural History* 93:28–34.

Glossary

altruistic act An act that benefits another organism at a cost to the actor, where cost and benefit are defined in terms of reproductive success.

benefit An increase in reproductive success.

cooperative act An act that benefits another organism while giving a benefit to the actor, where benefit is defined as an increase in reproductive success.

cost A decrease in reproductive success.

degree of relatedness (r) The chance that a gene in one individual will have an exact copy located in a second individual by descent from a common ancestor.

F (inbreeding coefficient) The degree to which the halves of an individual's genotype (from mother and father) are identical because of a common ancestor.

gene The basic unit of heredity; a section of DNA long enough to code for one protein.

genome (genotype) The total genetic make-up of an individual; all the genes within a typical cell.

group selection The differential reproduction of groups, often imagined to favor traits that are individually disadvantageous but evolve because they benefit the larger group.

haplodiploidy A system of reproduction in which males develop from unfertilized eggs and have only one set of chromosomes (haploid) while females develop from fertilized eggs and have two sets of chromosomes (diploid).

heterozygous Having two different genes at the same locus.

homozygous Having two copies of the same gene at a locus.

inclusive fitness An individual's reproductive success, augmented by effects on relatives other than offspring, where each effect is multiplied by the actor's degree of relatedness to the affected party.

locus A particular place on a chromosome (or pair of chromosomes) where a given gene (or pair of genes) is located; by extension, any particular place in the genome.

natural selection The differential reproductive success of individuals: some leave many surviving offspring, others few or none.

parental investment Anything done for the offspring, including building it, which increases the offspring's reproductive success at a cost to the remainder of the parent's reproductive success.

phenotype The total structure, physiology, and behavior of an individual.

primary sex ratio The sex ratio (number of males divided by number of females) at conception; in this book more generally the sex ratio at any time during the period of parental investment.

ratio of investment (in the sexes) The total work invested in raising males divided by the total invested in raising females; in social insects the ratio refers only to work invested in raising reproductives.

reciprocal altruism The exchange of altruistic acts between two individuals.

reproductive success (RS) The total number of offspring of an individual surviving to a given age; also called "fitness."

self-deception Constructing falsehoods in the conscious mind (while registering the truth unconsciously).

selfish act An act benefitting the actor at a cost to someone else, cost and benefit defined in terms of reproductive success.

sexual selection Competition within one sex for access to the opposite sex and intersexual choice (mate choice).

spiteful act An act inflicting a cost on both the actor and someone else, cost being a decrease in reproductive success.

statistically significant An event whose occurrence will be due to chance less than 5% of the time; hence, by extension, an event whose occurrence is unlikely to be due to chance.

Index

breeding biology, 5–9, 15–17
cannibalism, 25–28
courtship feeding, 252, 254
deception in, 412
early mortality, 12–13
natural selection, 24–25
parental investment, 151
parent-offspring conflict,
    145–46
population increase, 13
separation, 269–70
sexual harassment, 263
Gur, Ruben, 416
Gwynne, Darryl, 216

Haldane, J. B. S., 32, 46
Hamilton, William, 47, 126–27,
    129, 136, 226, 278, 324–
    28, 348, 358–59, 392–93
Haplodiploidy, 177–79
Hare, Hope, 279
Harlequin lobes, 122–24
Harpobittacus nigriceps, 254–55
Hemilepistus reaumuri, 240
Heterocephalus glaber, 192
Hinde, Robert, 160
Hölldobler, Bert, 170–71, 173,
    175–77, 279
Homosexuality, 198–201, 232
Hrdy, Sarah, 61, 71–77, 115,
    147
Human
    courtship feeding, 7
    cuckoldry, 267
    differential mortality by sex,
        301–8, 313
    homosexuality, 198
    male parental investment, 239
    parental discipline, 2, 4
    parent-offspring conflict,
        146–50, 162–63
    rate of increase, 13
    reciprocal altruism, 362–63,
        386–92
    selection and body weight,
        32–33
    selection and brain size, 24
    selection and head shape,
        30–31
    sex ratio, 288–89, 295–99
Hunt, George, 199–200
Hyla cinerea, 225
Hyla crucifer, 225
Hyla regilla, 225

Hyla rosenbergi, 252
Hyla versicolor, 225
Hylobittacus apicalis, 249–51,
    408
Hymenoptera, 177–79

Inbreeding, 63–64, 128–29,
    134–35, 180–84
IQ, 99–100

Japanese monkey. *See Macaca
    fuscata*
Japanese quail, 134–35
Jumping gene, 139–40

Kin recognition, 129–35
Kinship, 45–47, 109–201
Kurland, Jeffrey, 115–21, 156

Labroides dimidiatus, 48, 52
Lack, David, 81
Lagenorhynchus obliquidens,
    384
Landry, Sarah, 182, 244
Langur monkey. *See Presbytes
    entellus*
Larus argentatus, 5–9, 16, 26–
    27, 145–46
Larus californicus, 151
Larus delawarensis, 201
Larus fuscus, 263
Larus novaehollandiae, 269–70
Larus occidentalis, 199–200
Lasioglossum, 225
Lasioglossum zephyrum, 129–30
Lasius fuliginosus, 51
Lathonura, 327
Le Boeuf, Burney, 59, 208–10,
    342
Learning abilities, 102–7
Leland, Lysa, 78
Lepomis macrochirus, 407–8
Lepp, George, 110, 113, 130, 133
Leptodora, 327
Leptonychotes weddelli, 227
Lepus americanus, 328
Lesbianism, 198–201
Lethrus opterus, 244
Ligula intestinalis, 63
Linum usitissimum, 323
Lithinus nigrocristatus, 396
Lizard, 231–37, 288–89, 291,
    312, 342–43
Long, Joseph, 231

Lorenz, Konrad, 70
Lycaeon pictus, 193–98

Macaca fuscata, 115–21, 156
Macaca mulatta, 120–21, 151–
    53, 160–62
Macaca nemistrina, 133
Madigan, Francis, 306
Malcolm, James, 194–97
Male dimorphism, 24, 26, 181,
    221–27
Male parental investment, 207–
    8, 215–19, 239–70
Malothrus ater, 104
Malurus cyaneus, 185–86
Malurus splendens, 186
Manorina melanophrys, 186–87
Mantis shrimp, 409–11
Marginitermes hubbardi, 183
Mate choice, 14–15, 214, 249–
    56, 331–60
Mealy bug, 286–87
Meiosis, 95–97
Meiotic drive, 138
Melampsora lini, 323
Melanerpes formicovorous,
    185–86
Melanoplus femur-rubrum, 139
Melopsittacus undulatus,
    154–55
Merops bulicki, 185
Merops bulockoides, 185, 187
Mimicry, 227, 397, 400–8
Mirounga angustirostris, 59,
    206–8, 210, 227, 342
Mite, 277–78
Mitosis, 94–97
Miyazaki, Masahisa, 43
Moehlman, Patricia, 193–94
Möglich, Michael, 177
Moth, 335–36, 397–98
Mule deer, 292
Muscicapa striata, 153–54
Mutation, 91–92
Myopus schisticolor, 277–78
Myrmecocystus mimicus,
    175–76
Myrmica laevinodis, 50–51

Nasonia vitripennis, 283–86
Natural selection, 19–40; de-
    fined, 12–15. *See also* Re-
    productive success, Sexual
    selection

Neanthes arenaceodentata, 240
Necrophorus vespillo, 209
Nematode, 290
Neotoma floridana, 292
Nice, Margaret, 268–69
Noonan, Katherine, 55–56
Norris, Kenneth, 382, 384
Nymphon, 240–41
Nymphon rubrum, 241

Odocoileus virginianus, 287
Odontolabis lowei, 211
Odontolabis siva, 222
Oecophylla longinoda, 171
Oecophylla smaragdina, 170–71
Oligochaete, 326
Ophrys speculum, 401, 403
Organelle genes, 88, 140–41
Orgasm, female, 340
Orphans, 208

Packer, Craig, 372–73
Pan troglodytes, 375–83, 409,
    411, 413
Pandalus jordani, 287–88
Papilio dardanus, 403
Papio cynocephalus, 1–3, 49,
    145–46, 151–52, 161–62,
    369–75
Parabuteo unicinctus, 185
Paracentrotus lividus, 140–41
Paradisaea gulielmi, 332
Parasites
    and differential mortality by
        sex, 303–4
    and dying whale, 385
    of fig wasp-fig symbiosis,
        224–27
    and mate choice, 358–59
    and sex, 323–24, 326,
        328–30
    social, 49–52
    social theory and, 62–64
Parasitic chromosomes, 138–39
Parental discipline, 1–4
Parental domination, 166–67
Parental investment, 148–55,
    209
Parsons, Jasper, 25–27
Parus major, 82, 187, 322
Passiflora candollei, 404
Passiflora, 400–1, 404
Peacock, 332–33
Pelecanus rufescens, 158

Pentatomid bugs, 122–24
Perceptual defense, 419–20
Petit, Claudet, 337
Petrie, Marion, 218
Phalacrocorax carbo, 63
Phalaropes, 217–18
Phalaropus lobatus, 268
Phenotypic matching, 130,
    133–34
Philomachus pugnax, 24, 26
Physalaemus pustulosis, 336–37
Pickering, John, 79
Pieris protodice, 256
Pig, 22–23, 305
Pigeon. See Columba livia
Pimephales promelas, 410
Plants
    mate choice in, 343–46
    mimicry by, 400–6
    sex ratio in, 287
    sexual reproduction in, 317, 326
    social theory and, 60–62
    somatic mutations, 140–43
    warning others, 60, 62
Plecia neartica, 337–38
Ploceus cucullatus, 252–53
Poecilia reticulata, 339
Poephila guttata, 256–65, 294
Polistes fuscatus, 53–56
Polistes gallicus, 54
Polistes versicolor, 79
Polyrhachis, 171
Porter, James, 385
Presbytes entellus, 61, 71–77,
    115, 145, 147, 149
Primary sex ratio, 63–64, 198,
    224, 227, 271–300
Primates, 228–29, 245. See also
    Papio and Presbytes
Prisoner's dilemma, 389–92
Prosobranch mollusc, 123
Pseudacreae eurytus, 400, 402–3
Pseudoleistes virescens, 185
Pseudorca, 385
Pseudoregma alexanderi, 43–44
Psithyrus, 51
Puffinus puffinus, 269
Pycnogonum littorale, 240
Pygmephorus, 278
Pygosteus pungitius, 406

Rabbit, 295
Rana cascadae, 133
Rana catesbeiana, 14, 225

Rana temporaria, 225
Rapagula, 125
Rare male advantage, in mate
    choice, 337–38
Rat, 104–7, 305
Rate of evolution
    and intensity of selection,
        28–29
    and sex, 316–17
Ratio of investment in the sexes,
    273–82. See also Primary
    sex ratio
Reassurance behavior, 382–83
Reciprocal altruism, 47–49,
    361–94
Red deer. See Cervus elaphus
Reithrodontomys, 70
Reproductive altruism, 169–202
Reproductive success
    and density, 82
    as a function of attractiveness,
        257–60
    as a function of helping, 187,
        189, 193
    and homosexuality, 201
    lifetime, 35, 206–7
Rissa tridactyla, 269–70
Rohwer, Sievert, 413–15
Romanomermis culicivorax, 290
Rotifer, 317, 320–21, 326–27
Rudebeck, Gustav, 13–15
Rumex, 287
Ryan, Michael, 336

Sackeim, Harold, 416
Salamander, 245
Salix sitchensis, 62
Saxiola torquata, 254
Schaller, George, 156–57
Schizophrenia, 298–99
Scolia ciliata, 403–6
Seal, 227–29, 282–83. See also
    Mirounga angustirostris
Self-deception, 165, 282, 395,
    413, 415–20
Selfish genes, 137–41
Selfish trait, 52–53
Septobasidium burtii, 179–80
Sex chromosomes, 88–89, 136–
    37, 186, 276, 288, 292,
    307–9
Sex ratio. See Primary sex ratio.
    See also Differential mor-
    tality by sex